THE DECLINE OF PRIVATE LAW

This book is a large-scale historical reconstruction of liberal legalism, from its inception in the mid-nineteenth century, the moment in which the jurists forged the alliance between political liberalism and legal expertise embodied in classical private law doctrine, to the contemporary anxiety about the possibility of both a liberal solution to the problem of political justification and of law as a respectable form of expert knowledge. Each stage in the history is a moment of synthesis between a substantive and a methodological idea. The former is the liberal political theory of the period, purporting to provide a solution to the problem of political justification. The latter is a conception of legal method or science, supposedly vindicating the access of the expert to the political choices embodied in the law. Thus, each moment in the history of liberal legalism integrates a political theory with a jurisprudential conception. Although it reaches the unsettling conclusion that liberal legalism has largely failed by its own standards, the book urges us to avoid quietism, scepticism, or cynicism, in the hope that a deeper understanding of the fragility of our values and institutions inspires a more thoughtful, broadminded, and nurtured citizenship.

The Decline of Private Law

A Philosophical History of Liberal Legalism

Gonçalo de Almeida Ribeiro

·HART·
OXFORD · LONDON · NEW YORK · NEW DELHI · SYDNEY

HART PUBLISHING

Bloomsbury Publishing Plc

Kemp House, Chawley Park, Cumnor Hill, Oxford, OX2 9PH, UK

1385 Broadway, New York, NY 10018, USA

HART PUBLISHING, the Hart/Stag logo, BLOOMSBURY and the Diana logo are
trademarks of Bloomsbury Publishing Plc

First published in Great Britain 2019

Reprinted 2019, 2020

Copyright © Gonçalo de Almeida Ribeiro, 2019

Gonçalo de Almeida Ribeiro has asserted his right under the Copyright, Designs and Patents
Act 1988 to be identified as Author of this work.

All rights reserved. No part of this publication may be reproduced or transmitted in any form or by any
means, electronic or mechanical, including photocopying, recording, or any information storage
or retrieval system, without prior permission in writing from the publishers.

While every care has been taken to ensure the accuracy of this work, no responsibility for
loss or damage occasioned to any person acting or refraining from action as a result of any
statement in it can be accepted by the authors, editors or publishers.

All UK Government legislation and other public sector information used in the work is
Crown Copyright ©. All House of Lords and House of Commons information used in
the work is Parliamentary Copyright ©. This information is reused under the terms
of the Open Government Licence v3.0 (http://www.nationalarchives.gov.uk/doc/
open-government-licence/version/3) except where otherwise stated.

All Eur-lex material used in the work is © European Union,
http://eur-lex.europa.eu/, 1998–2019.

A catalogue record for this book is available from the British Library.

Library of Congress Cataloging-in-Publication data

Names: Ribeiro, Gonçalo de Almeida, author.

Title: The decline of private law : a philosophical history of liberal legalism / Gonçalo de Almeida Ribeiro.

Description: Oxford, UK ; Chicago, Illinois : Hart Publishing, 2019. | Series: Law and
practical reason | Based on author's thesis (S.J.D. : Harvard Law School, 2012). |
Includes bibliographical references and index.

Identifiers: LCCN 2018057166 (print) | LCCN 2018057921 (ebook) |
ISBN 9781509907915 (Epub) | ISBN 9781509907908 (hardback)

Subjects: LCSH: Civil law—Philosophy. | Liberalism—Philosophy. | BISAC: LAW / Contracts.

Classification: LCC K600 (ebook) | LCC K600 .R53 2019 (print) | DDC 340.5/601—dc23

LC record available at https://lccn.loc.gov/2018057166

ISBN: HB: 978-1-50990-790-8
ePDF: 978-1-50990-792-2
ePub: 978-1-50990-791-5

Typeset by Compuscript Ltd, Shannon
Printed and bound in Great Britain by TJ International Ltd, Padstow, Cornwall

To find out more about our authors and books visit www.hartpublishing.co.uk.
Here you will find extracts, author information, details of forthcoming events
and the option to sign up for our newsletters.

*The junzi considers the whole rather than the parts.
The small man considers the parts rather than the whole.*

The Analects of Confucius, 2.14

PREFACE

This book is based on the dissertation I successfully defended at Harvard Law School in September 2012, in partial fulfilment of the requirements to be awarded a doctoral degree. As often happens when the author of an academic thesis is slow to move towards publication, I nearly let go of it. It was my good fortune that when I did make a move, in late 2015, I found in Hart Publishing, and particularly in its then Commissioning Editor Bill Asquith, enthusiastic support for the project.

My appointment to the Constitutional Court in July 2016 delayed the process of publication even further, and indeed it threatened to stall it indefinitely. Fortunately, in the summer of 2018 I was able to carry to the end the task of editing and polishing the manuscript. I am grateful to the current Commissioning Editor of Hart Publishing, Kate Whetter, and to Production Editor Linda Staniford, for their support in the latter stages of this stormy journey.

Notwithstanding my belief that the manuscript withstood fairly well the test of time, this book is undoubtedly different from the dissertation on which it is based. I rewrote the Prologue and the Epilogue; divided the last chapter of the thesis into two, rewriting a good deal of what is now chapter five; excised the original text of material that struck me as digressive, pedantic, or downright silly; and revised the whole manuscript as thoroughly as limited time, energy and ability allowed. To be sure, the main thrust, the bulk of the writing and the background research are the same. But what I now offer to the reader is the leaner, neater and crisper work of a more mature scholar and writer.

Over the years, a large number of generous scholars read parts of the manuscript in some form or shared with me their thoughts about themes and arguments in this book. On that score, I am indebted to Adilson Moreira, Ana Taveira da Fonseca, André Salgado de Matos, António Araújo, António Cortês, António Hespanha, Armando Rocha, Axel Gosseries, Catarina Santos Botelho, Daniel Vargas, Dennis Patterson, Elsa Vaz de Sequeira, Fernando Sá, Filipa Calvão, Frank Michelman, Giovanni Marini, Hans-W Micklitz, Henrique Antunes, Holger Spamann, Hugh Collins, Ingo Sarlet, Jan Dalhuisen, João Gama, Joaquim Pedro Cardoso da Costa, Jorge Azevedo Correia, Jorge González-Jácome, Jorge Mattamouros, Jorge Pereira da Silva, José de Sousa e Brito, JHH Weiler, José Lamego, José Teles Pereira, Júlio Gomes, Karl Klare, Ken Winston, Lewis Sargentich, Louis Kaplow, Luís Pereira Coutinho, Luís Roberto Barroso, Marcos Keel Pereira, Maria-Rosaria Marella, Matej Accetto, Miguel Galvão Teles, Miguel Nogueira de Brito, Miguel Morgado, Mikhail Xifaras, Mitch Lasser, Neil Walker, Nimer Sultany, Nuno Garoupa, Patrícia Fragoso Martins, Paulo Mota Pinto, Pedro Fortes, Pedro Garcia Marques, Pedro Lomba, Pedro Machete, Pedro Múrias, Pedro Velez, Ravi Afonso Pereira,

Richard Fallon, Rita Lynce de Faria, Roni Mann, Rui Pinto Duarte, Rui Ramos, Talha Syed, Tiago Macieirinha, Tito Rendas, Vishaal Kishore and Wim Decock. Joe Singer and Mattias Kumm, who read the whole manuscript in its dissertation form and gave me extensive feedback, belong in a distinguished category of their own.

I owe a special debt of gratitude to Jorge Braga de Macedo, Luís Barreto Xavier, Maria da Glória Garcia, Maria Lúcia Amaral, Miguel Poiares Maduro and Rui Medeiros, for having played, in one way or another, a decisive role in my academic career.

I dedicate this book to Duncan Kennedy, my former teacher and supervisor. In spite of our occasional differences of thought and style, this book is, as careful readers will not fail to notice, a progeny of Duncan's towering legacy in the fields of legal theory, legal history and comparative law. The dedication is my modest but heartfelt tribute to that intellectual pedigree, and to several years of captivating and enlightening mentorship.

Gonçalo de Almeida Ribeiro
Lisbon

TABLE OF CONTENTS

Preface .... *vii*
List of Figures .... *xi*

Prologue: The Drama of Liberal Legalism 1

1. **The Idea of Political Liberalism** 14
    I. The Liberal Hypothesis 14
    II. Majoritarian Government 20
    III. Democratic Legitimacy 22
    IV. The Trouble with Majoritarianism 26
    V. Reasonable Pluralism 30
    VI. Freestanding Principles 36
    VII. Politics and Justice 40
    VIII. Political Liberalism 46
    IX. Pluralism within Liberalism 53

2. **Kant and the Will Theory** 63
    I. Why Kant? 63
    II. Kant's Moral System 70
    III. Moral Value in the *Groundwork* 80
    IV. The Nature of *Recht* 84
    V. The Rightful Condition 92
    VI. Private Right 97
    VII. The Will Theory 101
    VIII. Norm and Exception 111

3. **The Rise of Classical Private Law** 119
    I. From Theory to Ideology 119
    II. Reception of the Will Theory 120
    III. Rise and Decline of *Iurisprudentia* 124
    IV. Modern Legal Science 131
    V. The Savignian System (i): Substance 135
    VI. The Savignian System (ii): Method 147
    VII. The Triumph of Formalism 161
    VIII. Classical Private Law 170

4. The Socialisation of Private Law 172
   I. The Social Question 172
   II. The Social Jurists 181
   III. The Emergence of Social Law 191
   IV. The Social in Private Law 197
   V. The Critique of Formalism 202
   VI. Teleological Jurisprudence 209
   VII. *Culpa in Contrahendo* 215
   VIII. Abuse of Rights 219

5. The Politicisation of Private Law 226
   I. On 'Legal Realism' 226
   II. The Collapse of Private/Public 230
   III. Conflicting Considerations 238
   IV. Rules and Principles 245
   V. The Indeterminacy of Doctrine 248
   VI. The Indeterminacy of Rules 260
   VII. The Indeterminacy of Grounds 266
   VIII. Ideology in Private Law 271

Epilogue: The Migration to Constitutional Law 275

Appendix: A Foray into Methodology 283

Bibliography *296*
Index *311*

LIST OF FIGURES

Figure 1.1:	Liberalism in ordinary politics	16
Figure 2.1:	Matrix of Kantian judgements	68
Figure 2.2:	Typology of Kantian duties	75
Figure 2.3:	Typology of Kantian freedom	91
Figure 2.4:	The structure of mistake doctrine	114
Figure 3.1:	Objects of rights in the savignian system	140
Figure 3.2:	Savigny's family/market distinction	144
Figure 3.3:	The Savignian theory of interpretation	153
Figure 4.1:	Critics of the will theory *c* 1900	190
Figure 4.2:	Conceptions of rights *c* 1900	224
Figure 5.1:	Types of interest	242
Figure 5.2:	The Hohfeldian system	252
Figure 5.3:	The erosion of the politics/law dichotomy	273

Prologue

The Drama of Liberal Legalism

Imagine that you are a political official. You claim authority over other people, and your authority is enforceable. Now, if you are a reflective person, you will ask yourself the following question: What right do I have to coerce others to abide by my say-so? Put at its briefest, that is the problem of political justification.

There were times in which the solution to that problem was straightforward. To the slave-owner, or the *pater familias*, the question of political justification did not even occur; his mastery over the slave, or over the members of the household, is not a matter of right but of violence – settled *de facto* as opposed to *de jure*.[1] To the medieval *seigneur* or manorial lord, on the other hand, the question of political justification elicited one or another of two quite different types of answer. One such answer – call it naturalist – was that the right to rule inhered in his person; it was the defining feature of his lordship, as evinced in custom and tradition.[2] A different type of argument – call it functionalist – was that the right to rule was inscribed in the vital role he plays within the community, as suggested by the medieval mythology of the three orders of *oratores*, *bellatores* and *laboratores*.[3] Finally, if we fast-forward a few hundred years, more precisely to the eighteenth century, we shall find a very different type of rule, personified by Frederick the Great – the enlightened despot. Political right derives mostly from the sharp contrast between the enlightenment of the despot and the superstition and ignorance of ordinary folk.[4] The historical mission of the enlightened ruler is to prepare his people for political emancipation, to force it out of the current state of self-complacent idiocy.[5]

I should clear at once a potential misunderstanding. It is possible, indeed very likely, that in the course of history a considerable number of slave-owners, manorial lords and enlightened despots experienced anxiety or even lost faith in their authority. But we should be careful not to trade on confusion between the individual and the role, the actor and the mask. It is a key part of the social plot of slavery, lordship and enlightened absolutism that the characters of slave-owner,

---

[1] See Hannah Arendt, *The Human Condition*, 22–37.
[2] See Otto Brunner, *Land and Lordship*, 114–24.
[3] Georges Duby, *Les Trois Ordres ou L'Imaginaire du Féodalisme*; Charles Taylor, *A Secular Age*, 165.
[4] See Alexis de Tocqueville, *The Old Regime and the Revolution*, 32–41, 226–31.
[5] These are crude ideal-types. See Max Weber, *The Theory of Social and Economic Organization*, 89–90.

manorial lord and enlightened despot take their political authority for granted. That says nothing, of course, about the experience and moods of particular performers; comedians – so goes a show business *cliché* – are often depressed.

To the contemporary official, however, the question of political justification appears under a very different light. (I must insist that by 'the official' I mean the *character* and what concerns me is the reasoning process that is to be expected from him. What goes on backstage – in the minds of the individual holders of office – is none of my business.) What distinguishes him from other well-known political characters in history is that he cannot vindicate a putative right to rule in his status. He must regard those subject to his authority as equals both among themselves and with himself. Under these conditions, which furnish the normative environment of our political culture, it is much harder to figure out what justifies political authority. For political authority appears to imply by its very nature precisely the inequality of status that our egalitarian political culture deplores.

What avenues are open for the political official hoping to justify his authority in egalitarian terms? The obvious answer is democratic legitimacy. The official represents the majority formed over the course of free and open elections; ultimately, the basis of political authority is plain and simple 'one person, one vote'. But this may not be a sufficient basis for justified rule, as the slogans 'tyranny of the majority' and 'populist rule' so readily convey.[6] As a contemporary political philosopher put it, 'Individuals have rights, and there are things no person or group can do to them (without violating their rights)'.[7]

Are we then to think of rights – at least of fundamental rights – as matters outside and above the purview of ordinary politics? That is surely the prevailing view in constitutional democracies, particularly those that embrace a robust conception of the legal force of bills of rights and the role of the judiciary in their enforcement. But that road leads to insurmountable difficulties of its own. For as to what rights individuals have, which of such rights are fundamental, or how to apply a list of abstract rights, namely how to resolve (whether in general theory or in case-by-case practice) the many conflicts among them that arise in everyday life, there is no agreement in society.[8] To the protest that majoritarian government puts individual rights in jeopardy, then, one is bound to reply that the egalitarian credentials of having non-elected and non-accountable officials in charge of deciding about them are at least dubious. Accordingly, there is indignant and persistent talk of 'moral elitism' and 'aristocracy in robes' in connection with the practice of judicial review of legislation.

Indeed, any claim of political authority in an egalitarian political culture is problematic. The predicament of the political official is suffused with anxiety, for there is a permanent tension between the unwaivable responsibility to decide that

---

[6] Alexis de Tocqueville, *Democracy in America*, Book I, ch 15. See also, *The Federalist Papers*, 'Federalist 51' (Madison) and 'Federalist 58' (Madison).

[7] Robert Nozick, *Anarchy, State and Utopia*, ix.

[8] See, eg, Jeremy Waldron, *Law and Disagreement*, 1–19, 282–313.

is underwritten in his role and the duty to justify all decisions in ways consistent with the status of the addresses as equally worthy and respectable agents. No wonder that so much ink has been spilled over Alexander Bickel's 'counter-majoritarian difficulty',[9] and that legal academics – who sit right at the intersection of power and reflection – have developed an intense obsession with the theme.[10] Alasdair MacIntyre wrote famously that 'every moral philosophy presupposes a sociology'.[11] Much the same holds for political philosophy, particularly of the variety that fascinates legal academics. The constitutional theory that is hosted in seminar rooms and debated in law reviews is really but a continuation of the political anxiety inherent to liberal democratic regimes by other – high-minded and hyper-conscious – means.

To treat the other as a political equal is to treat him, as Ronald Dworkin would have it, with equal concern and respect.[12] 'Equal concern' implies that everyone's good is worthy of the same consideration, that each individual is entitled to an equal share of the benefits and is obliged to partake an equal share of the burdens of communal life. 'Equal respect' means that each individual capable of self-government is entitled to have his judgement regarded with the consideration accorded to the judgement of any other individual equally capable of self-government. Equality of concern and respect leads us, more or less straightforwardly, to what John Rawls calls the 'liberal principle of legitimacy'.

> [O]ur exercise of political power is fully proper only when it is exercised in accordance with a constitution the essentials of which all citizens as free and equal may reasonably be expected to endorse in the light of principles and ideals acceptable to their common human reason. This is the liberal principle of legitimacy. [...] Only a political conception of justice that all citizens might be reasonably expected to endorse can serve as a basis of public reason and justification.[13]

By a 'political' conception of justice, Rawls means one detached from any deep-seated metaphysical, religious or ethical commitments that divide reasonably as well as obdurately the members of the community. That is the essential basis of political liberalism. In this 'political not metaphysical' guise, liberalism brackets all questions of fundamental value and endorses the ideal of a freestanding politics.[14] Accordingly, justice in a liberal society concerns the distribution of the residual and universal good of freedom among individuals presumably leading a life governed by a robust and personal conception of the good.[15] The liberal solution to the problem of political justification in an egalitarian political culture is

---

[9] Alexander Bickel, *The Least Dangerous Branch*, 16–23.
[10] See Barry Friedman, 'The Birth of an Academic Obsession'.
[11] Alasdair MacIntyre, *After Virtue*, 23.
[12] See Ronald Dworkin, *Taking Rights Seriously*, 180–83, 272–78; Dworkin, *A Matter of Principle*, 181–204; Dworkin, *Justice for Hedgehogs*, 330–31.
[13] John Rawls, *Political Liberalism*, 137. Charles Larmore, 'The Moral Basis of Political Liberalism', 606, remarks that the Rawlsian formulation 'reflects ... the abiding moral heart of liberal thought'.
[14] See John Rawls, 'Justice as Fairness', 230; Charles Larmore, 'Political Liberalism', 353–57.
[15] Alasdair MacIntyre, 'The Privatization of Good', 345–46.

thus 'equal freedom for all'.[16] Official decision-making is governed by the common interest of all persons – even persons who value nothing else in common – in securing the conditions for individual self-determination. In circumstances of entrenched ethical and metaphysical disagreement, that is the only form of collective life that is truly 'for the people and by the people'.

Yet this only carries us so far. People disagree not just about the good life but about political justice as well. 'There are many of us, and we disagree about justice,' writes Jeremy Waldron.[17] There is more:

> [W]e not only disagree about the existence of God and the meaning of life; we disagree also about what counts as fair terms of co-operation among people who disagree about the existence of God and the meaning of life. We disagree about what we owe each other in the way of tolerance, forbearance, respect, co-ordination, and mutual aid.[18]

The anxiety of political justification builds up, as the problem of disagreement within liberal politics is brought to the level of conscious awareness. The very problem that liberalism is constructed to avert – interminable disagreement among equals – is reproduced within a political culture domesticated by liberal rationality. Moreover, the disagreement is replicated when we move from the first-order or substantive question of political justice – what laws should we have? – to the second-order or institutional question of authority – who is to say so? The 'counter-majoritarian difficulty' is the ultimate expression of this liberal conundrum.

Thus far, we have put ourselves in the shoes of the political official. Yet in our political culture there is an important class of officials that supposedly acts on legal instead of political grounds. Judges are the paradigm. Of their responsibilities wrote Sir Francis Bacon, 'Judges ought to remember, that their office is *jus dicere*, and not *jus dare*; to interpret law, and not to make law, or give law'.[19] Judicial authority is largely status-based, for judges are typically drawn from the lot of experts – the jurists – in determining what is legally required. This notion that there is a distinctive type of expert decision-making that is governed by legal as opposed to political reasons is what I shall call in this book 'legalism'.

The jurists trained in the medieval universities rose to a prominent position in the continental society of the Late Middle Ages.[20] But their authority was gradually challenged in the modern period, as humanist and then enlightened culture flourished, and eventually clashed head-on with the political and philosophical conceptions that triumphed in the wake of the liberal revolutions. In modernity's eyes, the professional elitism, arcane traditions and classical sources treasured by the jurists educated in the *mos italicus iura docendi*, students of a *ius commune*

---

[16] See Jeremy Waldron, 'Theoretical Foundations of Liberalism', 129.
[17] Waldron, *Law and Disagreement*, 1.
[18] ibid.
[19] Francis Bacon, *The Essays*, 65.
[20] Paolo Grossi, *L'Ordine Giuridico Medievale*, ch VI.

forged from Roman materials, did not meet the emerging standards of social equality and critical rationality.[21] In view of that, it comes as no surprise that some of the commanding voices in the tradition of liberal political thought viciously attacked the legal profession. John Locke complained about the 'artificial ignorance and learned gibberish' of lawyers.[22] Jeremy Bentham went on a crusade to 'to pluck the mask of Mystery from the face of Jurisprudence'.[23] And the austere Immanuel Kant, contrasting the a priori labours of the philosopher to the dogmatic adherence of the jurist to the sources of law, wrote that 'a merely empirical doctrine of right is a head that may be beautiful but unfortunately it has no brain'.[24] The authority of the legal profession declined, its place disputed by philosophers disparaging the *ius commune* and proclaiming a 'law of reason'.[25]

The remarkable thing is that the jurists managed to restore their social authority within the nascent liberal political culture. Former outcasts in modern culture and foes of liberalism, they became the protagonists of the liberal project of political justification. The monumental work of transformation matured in the German universities of the nineteenth century, taking final form in classical private law doctrine. It comprised two large movements. First, responding to the contempt of modern philosophy for jurisprudence, the jurists transformed legal expertise from a type of practical wisdom into a scientific discipline; this imparted epistemic dignity on their profession. Secondly, they read classical liberalism, in the Kantian form of the will theory, into the sources of the *ius commune*; this made their materials look suitably modern. At the end of the process, they had reinvented themselves, through their newborn science, as the principal custodians of liberal rationality. Finding unsuspected elective affinities between liberalism and legalism,[26] they wove them together, inventing what I call 'liberal legalism'.

Yet the history of modern legalism has been, just like that of political liberalism, a wobbly ride. In the mid- to late-nineteenth century, law as a discipline was compared to Euclidian geometry, regarded in the Enlightenment as a paradigm of scientific knowledge.[27] Legal argument was, in Max Weber's phraseology, a type of 'logically formal rationality'.[28] A century later, a leading legal philosopher such as Dworkin conceded unfalteringly that 'Law ... is deeply and thoroughly political'[29] and that 'legal judgments are pervasively contestable'.[30]

---

[21] António Manuel Hespanha, *Cultura Jurídica Europeia*, 180–92.
[22] John Locke, *An Essay Concerning Human Understanding*, 362.
[23] *Quoted in* Gerald Postema, *Bentham and the Common Law Tradition*, 268.
[24] Immanuel Kant, *The Metaphysics of Morals*, 23 (Ak 6:229).
[25] Franz Wieacker, *A History of Private Law in Europe*, §§ 15–19.
[26] In social theory, 'elective affinity' (*Wahlverwandtschaft*) is a Weberian adaptation of a concept from chemistry previously applied by JW Goethe to romantic relationships. See Max Weber, *The Protestant Ethic and the Spirit of Capitalism*, 263. See also Andrew McKinnon, 'Elective Affinities of the Protestant Ethic'; HH Gerth and CW Mills, 'Introduction', 62–63.
[27] See, eg, Friedrich Carl von Savigny, *Of the Vocation of Our Time for Legislation and Jurisprudence*, 38–39.
[28] See Max Weber, *Max Weber on Law in Economy and Society*, 59–64.
[29] Ronald Dworkin, *A Matter of Principle*, 146.
[30] Dworkin, *Law's Empire*, 411.

Although strongly committed to the project of disentangling legal argument from the realm of what he calls 'personal or partisan politics',[31] Dworkin's jurisprudence falls way short of the scientific aspirations of the mid-nineteenth-century legal mainstream. Duncan Kennedy captures the *Zeitgeist* with trademark wit:

> There is no extant theory that threatens to end the current ideological conflict about method by compelling a consensus about how judges can and should be neutral. Indeed, the current multiplicity of contradictory theories of neutrality seems a powerful, though of course not conclusive refutation of all of them. I am an admirer of their work of mutual critique. I endorse Dworkin's critique of Richard Posner along with Andrew Altman's critique of Dworkin and Fiss's doubtless forthcoming critique of Altman, and Posner's critique of Fiss (if there is one) and on around the circle. This is not musical chairs but more like a game of 'Penelope,' in which each writer simultaneously weaves his own and unweaves others' work.[32]

* * * * *

The agenda of this book is to improve our understanding of how we got to the contemporary predicament. It sets us on a long exploratory journey – a philosophical history – of liberal legalism, from its inception in the mid-nineteenth century, the moment in which the jurists forged an alliance between political liberalism and legal expertise, to the contemporary anxiety about the possibility of both a liberal solution to the problem of political justification and of law as a respectable form of expert knowledge.

Each stage in the history has a substantive or political and a methodological or epistemic element. The former is the liberal political theory of the era – eg, the will theory in the nineteenth century or the social liberalism of the inter-war period – purporting to provide a solution to the problem of political justification. The latter is a conception of legal science or method – eg, legal formalism in the nineteenth century or the teleological jurisprudence of the inter-war period – supposedly vindicating the access of the expert to the political choices embodied in the law. In sum, each stage in the sequence corresponds to a form of consciousness integrating a political theory with a jurisprudential conception.[33] The resulting synthesis is a moment in the drama of liberal legalism.

There are four such moments in my account:

(1) The rise of classical private law (*c* 1840–1914)
(2) The socialisation of private law (*c* 1900–1945)
(3) The politicisation of private law (*c* 1920–1970)
(4) The migration to constitutional law (*c* 1945–2001).

---

[31] Dworkin, *A Matter of Principle*, 146.
[32] Duncan Kennedy, *A Critique of Adjudication*, 91.
[33] I take the concept of a 'form of consciousness' from Raymond Geuss, *The Idea of a Critical Theory*, 4–44.

(1) *The rise of classical private law.* The heroes of this moment are the German jurists of the Historical School – mainly Friedrich Carl von Savigny and Georg Friedrich Puchta – and their Pandectist heirs. The classical scheme integrated the will theory of law and the jurisprudence of legal formalism.

The will theory, articulated in lasting philosophical form by Kant in the *Rechtslehre*, posits that each person is a will absolute within its rights as determined by a universal law.[34] There is a sharp distinction between duties not to violate other person's rights – duties of right – and duties to exercise one's rights as morality commands – duties of virtue; only the former are legally enforceable, and indeed it is the sole function of law to enforce equal freedom for every will.[35] Within a rightful legal order, persons waive their rights at their discretion, enter contracts that oblige them before other persons, and are liable to right their wrongdoings – in the eyes of the law they are abstract wills, universally free and equal.[36] Savigny and his followers held this theory to be immanent in a major division of the legal order they called 'patrimonial law', comprising the law of obligations and property law – that is, human relations over commodified goods.[37] The nineteenth century jurists contrasted this patrimonial law, essentially universal, with both public law, a normative order that expresses the particularities of a people, and family law, a realm of private relations between unequal and mutually dependent persons (husband/wife, father/child, and master/servant).[38]

Legal formalism was a method for the study and administration of positive law. It comprised two major sets of intellectual operation.[39] The first was the derivation of general principles – sometimes called 'leading axioms' – from the norms embodied in the sources of law. The claim was that a positive legal norm, the existence of which is a verifiable fact, entails a more general non-posited norm; for instance, the rules of battery contain by implication all the defining features of intentional torts. The second operation was the derivation of increasingly narrower or fact-specific norms from the general principles obtained, through a procedure that may be called 'analysis' or 'deduction'. Thus, from the concept of contract as a voluntary enactment of obligations and rights as between the parties follows a whole range of specific rules about, say, offer and acceptance or defences against liability. The ideal aim of this method was a coherent and gapless system of easily administrable norms.[40]

---

[34] Immanuel Kant, *The Metaphysics of Morals*, 24 (Ak 6:230–31).
[35] ibid at 9–22 (Ak 6:211–21).
[36] See, eg, Georg Friedrich Puchta, *Cursus der Institutionen*, I, 51.
[37] See, eg, Friedrich Carl von Savigny, *System of the Modern Roman Law*, I, 299–314.
[38] ibid at. 269–320. See also Duncan Kennedy, 'Savigny's Family/Patrimony Distinction'.
[39] Savigny, *System*, 211–39; Rudolf Sohm, *The Institutes*, 31–32.
[40] See Felipe González Vicén, 'Sobre los Orígines y Supuestos del Formalismo en el Pensamiento Jurídico Contemporáneo', 48–55.

(2) *The socialisation of private law*. The forerunners of this period were German as well – mainly Otto von Gierke and Rudolf von Jhering – but the heroes are the French *juristes inquiets*, namely Raymond Saleilles, François Gény, Léon Duguit and Louis Josserand.[41] They claimed that both the substance and the method of the classical theory failed on its own terms.

The social jurists argued that the will theory was ill adjusted to advanced industrial, urban and capitalist societies. They scorned the 'the majestic equality of the laws, which forbid poor and rich alike to sleep under the bridges, to beg in the streets, and to steel bread'.[42] They charged their predecessors with sociological blindness, arguing, for example, that it was a mistake to subject labour relations to the general norms of contract law on the thin ground that the same very abstract factual predicates – two or more wills fixing mutual obligations – recur in all 'contractual' settings. Legal doctrine had to be enriched with fact-sensitive concepts.[43]

They proposed two lines of reform of the will theory. One line was to narrow down the scope of the will theory, submitting vast areas of social life previously subsumed under the basic norms of property, contract, and tort to special laws. New branches of an often-baptised 'social law' – eg, labour law, anti-trust law, housing law and workers compensation – emerged. The governing idea was that in order to 'level the playing field', it was necessary to increase the regulation of those social arenas tilted in favour of dominant groups and interests – employers, landlords or businesses.[44] A second line of reform of the will theory was to tinker with the doctrines of private law itself. Ideas such as good faith, strict liability, abuse of right or substantive justice in contractual relations infiltrated the classical doctrinal scheme. In fact, according to the social jurists, quite a few of these notions had been around for many centuries, although they had been marginalised and misunderstood by the classics, who were embarrassed by the doctrines that did not fit neatly together with the will theory.[45] The social jurists recovered these doctrines and reshaped them, often pouring new wine into old bottles.

When it comes to methodology, they repudiated legal formalism, proposing instead a teleological jurisprudence.[46] The main point was that the classics held a static conception of the law. The social jurists argued that principles such as 'freedom of contract' or 'liability for injury' are dynamic, in that they point to certain goals or purposes, which the legal system aims to bring to the

---

[41] See Marie-Claire Belleau, 'Legal Classicism and Criticism in Early Twentieth-Century France'; Duncan Kennedy, 'Three Globalizations of Law and Legal Thought: 1850–2000', 37–38.
[42] Anatole France, *Les Lys Rouge*, 118.
[43] See, eg, Raymond Saleilles, 'Le Code Civil et la Méthode Historique'.
[44] See Franz Wieacker, *A History of Private Law in Europe*, 433–38.
[45] See, eg, Otto von Gierke, *Die soziale Aufgabe des Privatrechts*; Léon Duguit, *Les Transformations Générales du Droit Privé*.
[46] Rudolf von Jhering, *Law as a Means to an End*; François Gény, *Méthode d'Interprétation et Sources en Droit Privé Positif*.

social world. When a principle crystalises in a doctrine or regime, it incorporates certain factual assumptions. If the factual context evolves or shifts, the rules and doctrines may no longer realise the principles or purposes underlying them. The classical doctrines of contract – one of their favourite examples – were premised on the assumptions of equal bargaining power and absence of external effects; but they were inadequate in contexts, such as that of labour agreements in an industrial society, housing tenure in circumstances of massive rural exodus, or stock trading in a capitalist economy, where those assumptions do not hold. Hence, they held that the 'mechanical' application of legal rules without an eye on their purposes or the teleological principles of the legal system was an abuse of deduction.

(3) *The politicisation of private law.* Beginning in the 1920s, the post-classical social consensus disintegrated. The protagonists of this period are the American Legal Realists, including Robert Hale, Karl Llewellyn, Jerome Frank and Felix Cohen. Their precursors were Oliver Wendell Holmes, Wesley Newcomb Hohfeld, Philipp Heck and René Demogue.

Their substantive view of law encompassed two dimensions. On the one hand, they collapsed the private/public distinction.[47] Both the classical and the social jurists were strongly committed to the normative significance of the distinction, although they understood it differently; for them, while private law protects individual freedom, public law – namely legislative and administrative interference with private transactions – is coercive in nature. The legal realists showed that this view fails to take into account the way in which the background rules of property, contract and tort restrain individual freedom and, symmetrically, the way in which legislative and administrative interference with private transactions, through such means as minimum wage laws or environmental impact assessment, purports to enhance the freedom of those who benefit from them. Indeed, since freedom as a social good is the ability to call on state force to support one's interest in a situation of conflict, freedom and coercion are but two sides of the same coin. The question is not whether or not to protect freedom but *whose* freedom, and to what extent, ought to be protected – an issue that is political in nature.

The second dimension concerns what has aptly been called the paradigm of 'conflicting considerations'.[48] It is the view that legal regimes usually strike a balance among a recurrent set of conflicting considerations, purposes, policies or principles. Private law embodies a series of judgments as to the relative 'strength' or 'weight' of such considerations – say, security in ownership versus security in transactions or fault-based liability versus loss-spreading – within the scope of application of a given regime.[49] In other

---

[47] See, eg, Robert Hale, 'Coercion and Distribution in a Supposedly Non-Coercive State'.
[48] See Duncan Kennedy, 'From the Will Theory to the Principle of Private Autonomy', 104–15.
[49] René Demogue, *Les Notions Fondamentales du Droit Privé*; Philipp Heck, 'The Formation of Concepts and the Jurisprudence of Interests'.

words, one makes law by balancing competing reasons, as opposed to working out the implications of a single principle. It does not follow from the acknowledgement of conflicting considerations that laws are arbitrary, produced by the flip of a coin; what follows, given the pervasive contestability of balancing judgments, is that there are no demonstrably right answers.[50] People disagree reasonably and persistently about the justice of rival regime options, and that raises the issue of who is to be bestowed with the authority to settle such disagreements.

Turning to issues of method, the realists challenged at three different levels the distinction between law-making and law application. First, they picked various key legal concepts – eg, 'tort', 'contract', 'ownership' and 'right' – and showed that they could not perform the gap-filling work that both classical and social jurists, in different ways, ascribed to them; for the most part, outcomes presented as implications of those concepts concealed a balancing judgement.[51] Secondly, the realists showed that legal rules are often indeterminate, given conflicting canons of statutory interpretation and the subtleties of *stare decisis*;[52] hence, there are plenty of gaps, conflicts, and ambiguities in the body of legal rules, requiring the interpreter to balance at his own peril the background considerations at stake.[53] Thirdly, the realists paved the way for the critical scrutiny of positive law, picking on Holmes' famous aphorism that 'It is revolting to have no better reason for a rule of law than that so it was laid down in the time of Henry IV';[54] even where legal authority is clear, disagreement may legitimately break over the issue of whether it commands the conclusive allegiance of the law applying official – at this level, legal argument boils down to balancing the most fundamental conflicting considerations of justice, certainty, legitimacy, equality, and the like.[55]

(4) *The migration to constitutional law.* The realist critique generates a novel predicament. On the one hand, since law-making routinely involves controversial balancing judgements, there is wide room for disagreement within liberal justice, which becomes what WB Gallie calls an 'essentially contested concept';[56] accordingly, the political legitimacy of a norm can no longer be assessed in terms of its content, which is reasonably contested, but must be gauged procedurally. On the other hand, since legal argument often involves precisely the kind of contested balancing judgements underlying legal

---

[50] See Ronald Dworkin, *Taking Rights Seriously*, 31–32, 36, 68–71, 279–90.
[51] Oliver Wendell Holmes, 'Privilege, Malice, and Intent'; Wesley Newcomb Hohfeld, 'Some Fundamental Legal Conceptions as Applied in Judicial Reasoning'; Felix S Cohen, 'Transcendental Nonsense and the Functional Approach'.
[52] Karl N Llewellyn, 'A Realistic Jurisprudence – The Next Step'; Llewellyn, *The Bramble Bush*; Jerome Frank, *Law and the Modern Mind*.
[53] See, eg, Philipp Heck, 'Gesetzesauslegung und Interessenjurisprudenz'.
[54] Oliver Wendell Holmes, 'The Path of the Law', 1001.
[55] See Gonçalo Almeida Ribeiro, 'Judicial Activism and Fidelity to Law'.
[56] WB Gallie, 'Essentially Contested Concepts'.

regimes, it is virtually impossible to draw a neat line between law and politics; accordingly, the ideal of law as a form of expert knowledge is compromised.

The shift of focus from substance to procedure – from the content of the law to the authority to make laws – produces a remarkable transformation in legal culture. Whereas liberal legalism in its classical incarnation took the form of a theory of private law – the realm where individuals face off as free and equals – the collapse of the private/public distinction and the emergence of conflicting considerations press upon the legal establishment the institutional questions within the province of constitutional law. These are no longer peripheral and secondary, as they were for the nineteenth-century jurists, but central to the project of liberal legitimacy and legal expertise; liberal legalism is now headquartered in constitutional law.

This means that all private law, to the extent that it strikes a balance among conflicting considerations, becomes a constitutional matter – a phenomenon that has been phrased 'the total constitution'.[57] The issue is which institution is to make the choices underlying ordinary laws, particularly whether – and to what extent – final authority should be assigned to the judiciary. In the discourse of contemporary constitutional theory, all manner of disputes, including those that involve private actors, are said to trigger directly or indirectly constitutional scrutiny, under the form of rights-based review,[58] and the problem is to determine to what extent a court can substitute for its own the legislature's assessment of the relative strength of the conflicting considerations at stake. The catchphrases are 'proportionality review' and 'judicial deference'.[59]

Moreover, as the contemporary 'post-national constellation'[60] of governance comprises multiple levels of law-making and of judicial review, the issue of authority is no longer confined to the 'counter-majoritarian difficulty' in its original form. On the one hand, domestic courts, such as the German Federal Constitutional Court, are bound to decide whether and to what extent they should review laws generated by supranational structures such as the European Union.[61] On the other hand, transnational courts, such as the European Court of Human Rights, are bound to decide whether and to what extent they should review laws generated by national political processes, laws that often have already been subject to judicial review by domestic courts.[62] Multi-level judicial review takes place 'in the shadow of ideology',[63] and is denounced

---

[57] See Mattias Kumm, 'Who Is Afraid of the Total Constitution?'
[58] See Gonçalo de Almeida Ribeiro, 'The Effects of Fundamental Rights in Private Disputes'.
[59] See Duncan Kennedy, 'Proportionality and 'Deference' in Contemporary Constitutional Thought'; Robert Alexy, 'Balancing, Constitutional Review, and Representation'.
[60] Jürgen Habermas, *The Postnational Constellation*. See also Günther Teubner, *Constitutional Fragments*, 42–72.
[61] See, eg, BVerfG. 15 Dez 2015, 2 BvR 2735/14 [*Identitätskontrolle I*].
[62] See, eg, *SAS v France*, ECHR 1 July 2014.
[63] Duncan Kennedy, 'Political Ideology and Comparative Law', 38–39.

by those who claim that a court-centered understanding of rights moves the community away from political equality and 'towards juristocracy'.[64]

Two consequences follow for the project of liberal legalism. First, as the new paradigm of legal argument – balancing – blurs the distinction between political decision-making and legal reasoning, legalism crumbles. Even in its most sophisticated and seemingly technical form, that of proportionality analysis,[65] contemporary legal reasoning is open to the charge that it is politics in disguise. Secondly, the interminable debate within constitutional theory between the 'political'[66] and the 'judicial'[67] answers to the institutional dilemma – in their countless permutations – represents the failure of liberal rationality to produce a definitive solution to the problem of political justification. Therefore, the history of political liberalism from classical private law to the migration to constitutional law is at once the history of the only reasonable form of political community we can imagine *and* the history of liberal rationality gradually and relentlessly undoing itself.

That is an unsettling conclusion. Instead of turning us to quietism, skepticism or cynicism, however, it ought to inspire a thoughtful, broadminded and nurtured citizenship. The endless conversation among and within ourselves is an assurance that we are mindful of the fragility of our values and institutions, and cling to them not as 'dead dogma' but as 'living truth'.[68]

* * * * *

The structure of the book does not correspond exactly to the sequence of moments outlined in the foregoing synopsis. Foundations have to be laid down for the historical narrative to take off. Thus, chapter one ('The Idea of Political Liberalism') seeks to establish the normative content and the social currency of political liberalism. The argumentative strategy is to proceed from uncontroversial platitudes of contemporary political culture to the less obvious commitments that are conventionally, albeit not always consciously, presupposed by them. Chapter two ('Kant and the Will Theory') is a critical exegesis of Kant's *Rechtslehre*, which I consider – for reasons that shall emerge in due time – to be the prototype of political liberalism and the definitive philosophical articulation of the will theory that was read by the classical jurists into the sources of the law. The historical narrative begins at this point. Chapters three ('The Rise of Classical

---

[64] Ran Hirshl, *Towards Juristocracy*.
[65] See Robert Alexy, *A Theory of Constitutional Rights*, 44–110; Matthias Klatt and Moritz Meister, *The Constitutional Structure of Proportionality*.
[66] See, eg, Richard Bellamy, *Political Constitutionalism*, 90–141; Jeremy Waldron, *Law and Disagreement*, 209–312; Mark Tushnet, *Taking the Constitution Away from the Courts*, 6–32.
[67] See, eg, Ronald Dworkin, *Freedom's Law*, 1–38; Jürgen Habermas, *Between Facts and Norms*, 238–86; John Hart Ely, *Democracy and Distrust*, 135–80.
[68] John Stuart Mill, *On Liberty*, 40.

Private Law'), four ('The Socialisation of Private Law') and five ('The Politicisation of Private Law') present three moments in the philosophical history of liberal legalism. These are the moments concerning the rise and decline of modern private law. The fourth and final moment in the drama is the subject of the brief Epilogue ('Migration to Constitutional Theory'). Finally, the Appendix explicates the methodology of the project.

The contemporary scenery is painted in broad brushstrokes. The book presents a lopsided philosophical history of liberal legalism, focused on the decline of private law. Hence its title. Such imbalance is doubtlessly unfortunate. To some degree, it deprives us of the solace of intellectual closure and the satisfaction of symmetry. But how could it be any different? 'The owl of Minerva begins its flight only with the onset of dusk.'[69]

---

[69] GWF Hegel, *Elements of the Philosophy of Right*, 23.

1
The Idea of Political Liberalism

I. The Liberal Hypothesis

It is fairly common to assert that the type of political order that prevails in Western democracies is 'liberal'. Every participant in that type of order has some idea of what its liberal quality means. It is associated with the ideas of majority rule, representation, elections, individual rights, constitutionalism, a market economy, the values of tolerance and freedom, as well as a view of individuals – ordinary human beings – as worthy of concern and respect. But it is not clear at all what (if any) is the connection among these ideas.

This is not a quibble. The presence or absence of a connection among the ideas suggests two quite different accounts of the character of 'liberalism' as a predicate of a political culture. One account – call it *nominalist* – understands these terms as a hodge-podge of elements that are named 'liberalism' in conjunction; what makes a political culture 'liberal' is that the mainstream is seriously committed to all or most of the ideas listed above and pays tribute to the institutional arrangements – eg, an electoral system based on universal suffrage – that they vindicate.

A different account – call it *holistic* – suggests that these various elements somehow form a system in which the meaning of each is partly determined by its relationship with the others and, more generally, with the entire set of relations that constitutes the system itself. A useful analogy is with language.[1] Although words – say, 'chalk' – have some meaning of their own, their full meaning within a language is largely a function of a system of relations among terms.[2] In our example, the same term referring to the same substance – chalk – has a meaning in relation to the system of minerals and quite another in relation to the set of items in the classroom experience; and expressing the term in conjunction with others in the same system elicits a particular sequence of images – eg, the teacher writing on the blackboard – that enables knowledge of how it fits into, or is a part of, a meaningful whole.[3]

I want to provide a holistic account of liberalism. Liberalism is not a hodge-podge, but a whole in relation to which ordinary liberal commitments acquire

---

[1] Ferdinand de Saussure, *Course in General Linguistics*, 110–25.
[2] ibid at 113: 'A language is a system in which all elements fit together, and in which the value of any one element depends on the simultaneous coexistence of all the others'.
[3] This is what Saussure calls 'associative relations' among words. ibid at 121–25.

a specific meaning. Since we are talking about ideas and beliefs with social currency, it is appropriate to speak of liberalism as a form of consciousness or an idea immanent in our political culture.

The task looks entirely familiar. There are many fine scholarly efforts to define or account for the essence or constitutive premises of liberalism.[4] But any proposed definition of liberalism – say, 'equal freedom'[5] – is likely to appear problematic, for at least two reasons. The first is that it is so abstract that its connection with actual, verifiable, liberal commitments is either lost or unclear; in other words, a definition of that sort – at the outset – looks arbitrary, unless you happen to agree with it already. The problem is exacerbated by the fact that sometimes no clear line is drawn between liberalism and the particular version or working out of liberal ideals that the scholar happens to favour. The second problem is that there are (at least apparently) different uses of the word 'liberalism' in political discourse. We speak about liberals versus conservatives, about liberals versus Marxists and conservatives, about liberal democracy, about the classical liberalism of Locke, Mill and Kant; the relation – if any – among these various uses of the same word is obscured by a definition of 'liberalism', even if it is explained which of the various uses is in question. To sum up: the problem with definitions at the outset is that they are entirely stipulative.

Liberalism is both ubiquitous and mysterious. My purpose is to show *what* it is from the standpoint of those elements and practices that everyone associates with 'liberalism'. My aim is hence twofold: to explore the substance of liberalism and to establish its social currency. Of course, my task is greatly facilitated by the existence of a large body of literature that is concerned either with liberalism or with making claims and arguments that are taken to be important contributions to liberalism; but what I want to establish is the connection between theory and practice, between ideas in books and beliefs held by agents out there in the social world. For that reason, my method is quite different from the familiar form of 'definition at the outset' and the order in which I present the arguments is different from the familiar structure of an article or book on liberalism. I will depart not from 'first principles' but from what I take to be verified liberal commitments, of the sort listed in the first paragraph, and proceed from them to less obvious commitments. If I am right – if indeed there is a liberal form of consciousness – what will make the move from something obvious to something less obvious intellectually compelling is that my reader, as a participant in a liberal political culture, will *recognise* the relations among the various terms. The analogy with language is useful again. Most people know how to use the various terms that constitute a system of relations – in the classroom language game: 'chalk', 'teacher', 'blackboard', 'school', etc – even though they are neither aware of

---

[4] See, eg, Jeremy Waldron, 'Theoretical Foundations of Liberalism'; Charles Larmore, 'Political Liberalism'; Ronald Dworkin, *A Matter of Principle*, 180–204. The key work is John Rawls, *Political Liberalism*.
[5] Jeremy Waldron, ibid at 129.

them nor understand their interrelation. Trying to understand the system is to bring it to full conscious awareness.

*****

We employ as a rule the term 'liberalism' in ordinary political discourse in order to refer to what is typically a major current of opinion in contemporary democracies regarding the proper organisation of society and the policies that the government should adopt. The meaning of the term – the set of properties that constitute the essence of liberal politics – varies quite drastically along both temporal and spatial lines. There are important distinctions to be drawn, for example, between old and modern liberals, classical or ordo- and social or egalitarian liberals, European and American liberals.

Perhaps the most interesting and surprising contrast to be drawn concerns the very different position that American and European liberals occupy in the political spectrum. In the United States, liberals are on the center-left. They tend to support, among other policies, substantial economic regulation, jobholding policy, the growth or at least preservation of the welfare state, progressive taxation and income redistribution, affirmative action, abortion rights and same-sex marriage, a sociological account of crime and a rehabilitative conception of punishment. This incomplete list is formed by typical features instead of a set of necessary and sufficient conditions; hence, one may well be a liberal without subscribing to every element in the list. Liberals in North America oppose conservatives, the other major current of political opinion. The conservative's typical commitments are symmetric to the liberal's. They include light regulation, free enterprise, small government, flat or regressive taxation, color-blindness, pro-life and traditional family views, an individualist account of crime and a retributive conception of punishment. In European politics, on the other hand, the term 'liberal', to the extent to which it is even used, has the opposite connotation. A typical liberal in Europe holds, very roughly speaking, the positions of a typical North American conservative. On the other side of the fence lies the social democrat, who in many respects is what an American would call a liberal. A simple matrix captures the point.

Figure 1.1 Liberalism in ordinary politics

Political mainstream	Centre-left	Centre-right
United States	Liberalism	Conservatism
Europe	Social democracy	Liberalism

That the same term came to mean almost exactly opposite things in the two most stable political cultures of the democratic world should not pass unnoticed. The fact is telling in two apparently contradictory ways. On the one hand, it signals that there is likely something entirely contingent in the history of the term 'liberalism'. If North American liberals hold roughly the same commitments as European social democrats and, as a result, the contrary to the those of European liberals, the term itself means very little except within a particular political culture in which it has acquired stable meaning. It was up for grabs and someone grabbed it. On the other hand, there is ample room for the hypothesis that in some way both American and European liberals can claim to descend from some older political tradition from which the term arose. Of course, if that is true, there is a sense – certainly a deeper and partly concealed sense, different from the one that counts in everyday political talk – in which North American liberals and conservatives, as well as European social democrats and liberals, are all liberals. Since the term liberalism carries a deep and concealed, as well as a surface and transparent, sense in our political discourse, the apparent contradiction between the two historical accounts of that term – as a member of our shared political vocabulary – is dissolved. The appropriation of the term at the level of surface or ordinary politics was indeed contingent and arbitrary, something in the order of events; but the term which came to be appropriated – liberalism – originated at a deeper level, which constitutes the foundation of the mainstream of democratic politics all over the world. That, at any rate, is the hypothesis.

The hypothesis – let me restate it – is that all mainstream parties or currents of political opinion in contemporary democracies descend from the same body of political ideas – *liberalism*. But this formulation is not wholly satisfactory, because references to an idea or a body of ideas descending from another one are systematically ambiguous. All point to the existence of a common ancestor. Nevertheless, common ancestry may be of two sorts; let me call them *genealogy* and *prototype*.[6] Genealogical ancestry resembles a family tree. The present generation is a function of marriage and reproduction between members of two different families; each child is produced by the sexual encounter of his parents, who belong to different lines of ancestry. Each of the parents, of course, is the result of a similar encounter between members of different families; and so on and so forth. Children are not generated by a single parent, but by two parents, typically unrelated by blood. Siblings born of the same parents are full siblings. If the same individual happens to reproduce with two different partners, the children born of each relationship will not be full but half siblings. They have one biological parent in common.

We may reasonably suppose that liberalism is the common ancestor of all major parties of political opinion in democratic politics, such as North American liberalism and conservatism, because it is a common doctrinal parent to them. They all inherit one set of distinctively liberal 'genes'. However, each of them has a different second parent. It is plausible to assert, for instance, that American liberalism is the offspring of the marriage of classical liberalism with socialism, while conservatism is the child of classical liberalism and something like traditional conservatism.

---

[6] The idea of genealogy is based on Foucault, 'Nietzsche, Genealogy, History'. What I call prototype is inspired by WB Gallie, 'Essentially Contested Concepts'.

We would then be right to reserve the term liberalism to a pool of doctrinal genes that is shared across the centre or the mainstream of the political spectrum in stable democratic cultures such as the United States or the European Union. That is the genealogical version of the descent hypothesis that mainstream democratic politics has a common liberal ancestor.

But that is not the account of liberalism I shall provide. Mine is the *prototype* version of common ancestry. A prototype is an early model or crafting effort of a design concept or an idea. The main functions of the prototype are pedagogic and experimental: pedagogic because it increases our awareness of the design concept or idea that it embodies; experimental because the prototype is a primitive attempt to attain a certain ideal, the design concept or idea, an attempt from which one can learn how to fashion a better model. Both liberalism and conservatism, on this account, purport to be improved models of some design concept that was embodied in an original prototype. For reasons that I hope to make clear later, the prototype in question is the classical eighteenth century liberalism that achieved final form in the political theory of Immanuel Kant. What the modern liberalism and conservatism of North American politics represent, as well as their substantive equivalents in other democratic cultures, are rival attempts to improve on that earlier prototype, based on somewhat different assessments of the strengths and weaknesses of the original model. It does not, of course, harm my case prima facie that there may be more than two contenders in a particular democratic culture among the many that I have failed to even mention, or that the contenders in question may not be analogous to those that seem to dominate the American political scene. All that I have to show is that all variants of mainstream democratic politics proceed from a common prototype.

The nature of the task ahead becomes clearer once we acknowledge the distinction between the prototype and the design concept or idea. The former is a model or test case of the later; the prototype is designed and built to embody the idea. In every prototyping enterprise, then, we have to distinguish a constant from a variable part. The constant part is the design concept which the engineered prototype purports to embody, while the variable part is the model itself. What remains constant across a more or less long series of modelling efforts is the design concept, although by virtue of the pedagogic function of prototyping it is highly likely that our awareness of the concept increases as the modeling sequence progresses.

I should insist that these matters are definitional. It is perfectly possible, of course, that a prototype may serve as an inspiration for a radical shift from one design concept to another. Yet where that occurs it is no longer correct to say that the prototype in question is the first of a single sequence of modelling attempts. What we have is a different project altogether. My aim is to clarify the concept of a prototype in order to improve our understanding of my initial hypothesis; that liberalism is the shared root of the major parties of opinion in contemporary democratic politics.

If the classical liberalism that is so well represented in Kant's work on political theory is the best prototype of both liberalism and conservatism, the design concept or idea of which it was a prototype is what I will call liberalism. It is the 'design concept' of our political culture. I have not so far given even the slightest hint as to what that concept might be, much less have I showed that it is real. (In due time, we shall see that the two tasks are deeply intertwined.) Although that must be infuriating even to the most patient of readers, it was necessary first to make entirely clear the nature of the hypothesis that I am yet to confirm: it is the view that liberalism and conservatism, as well as other mainstream parties of opinion in democratic politics, descend from the same prototype, and share both among themselves and with that prototype a single design concept or idea that may be properly called *liberalism*.

Before we test the hypothesis, let me enrich it with the notion of *incorporation*. What I have in mind may be clarified with an analogy. Suppose that two car manufacturers – A and B – are each developing a new car for roughly the same market niche. Both teams of engineers have conceived a certain concept for the new car and have built a prototype to test it. Now imagine that spies hired by A manage to steal the plans developed by the engineers working for B. The plans are then given to the team of engineers employed by A. What use can they have for them? The extreme cases are rather obvious: they either ignore the plans, thinking them inferior to their own, or they abandon their own project, deciding to copy their rivals instead. But there is an intermediate option. They may compare their plans with those of the rival team and take from such comparison important elements to be incorporated in the modelling efforts to follow. The comparison will deepen their understanding of their own design concept and help them overcome hurdles that their initial prototype met with. In other words, they will incorporate some elements from their rivals' concept in their own plans, modifying the variable part of the prototype while maintaining their allegiance to the underlying design concept or idea. The incorporation is entirely driven by the very design idea that was modelled in the prototype, in the sense that what comes to be *seen* as a contribution or an improvement is whatever increases awareness of the design concept and knowledge of its best material embodiment. Elements of a foreign plan that do not resonate with the design concept are quite literally invisible, unless the design concept itself is brought to questioning; elements that do resonate are likely to bring about an 'Aha!' experience.

Moving from the engineering analogy to our field of interest – political theory – we are presented with multiple examples of incorporation in the sense just described. Take John Rawls' book, *A Theory of Justice*. It was noted by at least one commentator that a central aim of Rawls' book is to attempt a powerful response to Marxism from a liberal standpoint.[7] Rawls himself saw his theory as squared on all four with the liberal tradition, as the following excerpt illustrates: 'My aim is to present a conception of justice which generalizes and carries to

---

[7] Samuel Freeman, *Rawls*, 27–28. Cf John Rawls, *A Theory of Justice*, 228–59. The revolt against liberalism is one of the invariable Marxist themes. See, eg, Karl Marx, 'On the Jewish Question'; Marx, *Capital*, 280.

a higher level of abstraction the familiar theory of the social contract as found, say, in Locke, Rousseau, and Kant'.[8] Rawls is here hinting at our distinction between the prototype – of which the political writings of Locke, Rousseau and Kant are examples – and the design concept or idea of a 'social contract'. Many of Rawls' striking innovations in relation to the writers from whom he claims to descend result from a process of incorporation of those elements of the Marxian and socialist critique of classical liberalism that resonate with the latter's deep premises.

It is clear, then, that the rejection of a 'virgin birth' version of the liberal hypothesis on grounds of its inability to account for 'doctrinal mating' can proceed from two quite different standpoints. From the genealogical perspective, liberal genes get mixed with other political genes, generating new entities such as contemporary liberalism and conservatism. From the prototype perspective, liberalism remains constant while other political ideas are examined for their potential contributions to improve the available models of liberalism (in the deeper sense); liberalism and conservatism are hence rival models, each with a history, partly shared and partly divergent, of incorporation.

II. Majoritarian Government

How can I show that liberalism and conservatism, as well as the plurality of centrist or mainstream contenders for political power all over the democratic world, share a liberal ancestry, understood as a design concept originally embodied in a prototype? A necessary first step in all likelihood involves comparing the substantive doctrinal and policy views of all parties of opinion in a search for their common ground. The task is impossibly tiresome and fraught with difficulties.

I propose an alternative route. In democratic polities such as the United States or the European Union, routine contenders for power – such as the organised political parties that carry liberal or conservative banners – do not claim a right to impose their views on their rivals. Not only do they recognise the existence of political disagreement, manifested in a plurality of bodies of opinion about good government and public policy, they also accept a particular method for settling their disputes. That method is democracy. They subject their fate to the judgment of the voters. This form of subjection is not, at least officially, understood by mainstream political parties as a compromise of principle for prudential reasons.[9] They accept democracy as the right way of settling political disputes in a pluralist society.

---

[8] John Rawls, *A Theory of Justice*, 11.
[9] What distinguishes principled endorsement from endorsement on prudential grounds is that, unlike the latter, the former implies a non-conditional or non-contingent commitment. Rival parties accept democracy not because they have contingent reasons to do so – eg, it furthers their own agendas *qua* parties – but because of some feature(s) intrinsic to the democratic method of settling political disputes. They see democracy not as a means to an end but as an end in itself.

It follows that a commitment to democratic procedures of political decision-making furnishes an example of common ground among liberals and conservatives, or equivalent centrist parties of opinion in the democratic world. Democracy is commonly upheld. But I want to push my case a little further: what democracy presents us with is not just *some* example of commonality; it is the most powerful starting point for our search for a putative concept or idea that unites mainstream political culture. To confirm that point we only have to take notice of what exactly the democratic commitment implies: that individuals and groups in the political mainstream are willing, on grounds not of strategy but of principle, to put their opinions about good government, so to speak, on hold, until they have been empowered by the people. That is, they are committed to the view that their political judgments are overridden by those of the people. An implicit hierarchy is hence established between the authority of the people and the substantive merits of the policy proposals. That is a decisive finding because it reveals not just a common ground, but also one that in a sense *dominates* the disputed or controversial ground constituted by the various differences of opinion among liberals and conservatives and their equivalents elsewhere in the democratic world.

If there is any hope for my claim that all mainstream politics is liberal in the sense that is descends from the same liberal prototype *and* is informed by a single design concept or idea that is properly so-called, surely the argument must deal at some early stage with the unavoidable fact that mainstream political culture rests on a democratic common ground. For my case to succeed, some link must be forged between democracy and liberalism.

What makes a political order democratic? There is no prima facie reason to think this question any less difficult than the question: What makes a political order liberal? The debate is endless where it concerns the nature, the true character, the genuine spirit of democracy. If the reader thinks otherwise, a short visit to the seminar rooms of the philosophy and government departments, or the law school, of any University of his choosing will put my case to rest; for surely if not even academics who are professionally concerned with questions of political theory can reach an agreement about the proper understanding of democracy, it is unreasonable to think it is any different with ordinary people devoted to 'the ordinary business of life'.[10]

But in spite of its contested character, the idea of democracy affords a good starting point, formed by the set of procedural arrangements that we have come to hold as distinctively democratic, and which indeed are to be found in any contemporary polity conventionally so labelled. I am talking about the institution of representative government empowered by a majority of voters within a system of universal suffrage. The basic component parts of the institution are the following: (i) not the people at large, but only a small number of officials, is in charge of government; (ii) those officials who hold ultimate political authority within the

---

[10] The phrase is from Alfred Marshall, *Principles of Economics*, Book I, ch I, §1.

government, particularly (though not necessarily only) lawmakers, are chosen by the voters; (iii) every capable member of the polity has the right to vote and every vote has the same weight; (iv) political office is open to every member of the polity; (v) disagreement among voters is settled by a majoritarian rule. The institution of majority-empowered representative government is the *paradigm* of democracy.[11] We expect any genuine democracy to possess it; and debates that break over the nature or true character of democracy depart from the assumption that the institution in question embodies fundamental democratic ideals. In other words, the institution – call it majoritarian government – stands for democracy.

If that is correct, we are now entitled to reinterpret provisionally the shared liberal and conservative commitment to democracy as a commitment to majoritarian government. I am not claiming that democracy *means* majoritarian government, or that liberals and conservatives believe it does. The claim is that their commitment to democracy implies an adherence to majoritarian government at some level, or at the very least some account of why majoritarian government is not, contrary to political practice and the claims of most democrats, genuinely democratic. Majoritarian government – as I hope all agree – has a privileged position within the realm of democratic political discourse and practice. We would be perplexed if someone were to put forward a vision of democratic politics that not only accords no place for majoritarian government, but goes as far as entirely omitting a reference to it. We would be perplexed, of course, because the institution in question has, amidst the plurality of competing views, a privileged status in our shared understanding of what democracy is. That privileged status is what makes it the paradigm of democracy.

Liberals and conservatives accept, or we may provisionally assume they do, that the right way to settle disputes that result from their holding competing substantive positions in matters of public policy and good government, is through the democratic process embodied in the institution of majoritarian government. For reasons internal to their own distinctively liberal and conservative systems of belief, their substantive policy commitments are subject to the higher norm of majoritarian power. It remains to be explained why that is the case.

III. Democratic Legitimacy

What set of reasons explains the principled allegiance of competing political forces to majoritarian government? The question is one about the grounds or fundamental premises of democratic authority. We are asking what sort of principle(s) justifies the rule one person/one vote, as well as the other constitutive features of democratic arrangements. It is true that when it is posed like this, the question is likely to arouse some suspicion. We grew accustomed to the

---

[11] Ronald Dworkin, *Law's Empire*, 72–73, uses the term 'paradigm' in this sense.

view that democracy is a self-validating form of government, in the sense that it would defeat the essence of democratic authority to claim some moral high ground. Democracy, so the view goes, means that the people itself is the ultimate bearer of political authority; I have used that terminology myself earlier in this chapter. Another way of putting the point is to say that in a democracy, popular sovereignty is not merely a legal and political fiction but is actually embodied in political practice – it is the government of the people *and by the people*.

Yet this understanding of democracy, popular as it is, happens to be quite obscure. Who or what exactly is 'the people' and what does it mean to say that it bears ultimate political authority? The main problem is that 'the people' is no agent. It does not have the capacity to act on its own. When political leaderships claim to act on behalf of the people we should remember Proudhon's warning that 'whoever invokes humanity wants to cheat'.[12] It is hence not really surprising that the concept of the people, or popular authority, or popular sovereignty, has figured in so many obviously incompatible political agendas. It is the direct result of its remarkable obscurity. If we want to insist that democracy is grounded in the authority of the people, then, we have to be transparent about what concept of 'people' is at stake here. It would be viciously circular to say that such definition should be provided by the people itself, because nobody can impose, unless democracy is irreparably compromised, any constraints on its will. For what must be decided is what exactly is the will of the people, or what criteria should we rely upon in order to identify it. And that points toward some connection between the rule one person/one vote – the cornerstone of majoritarian democracy – and the democratic conception of the people. In a democracy, it seems, 'the people' is characteristically associated with voting procedures open to all. It is the moral ground of such procedures, which give form to the people's will, that has to be made transparent.

I want to propose the following thesis. Democratic authority rests on two premises. The first is that every member of a polity possesses the same social dignity, the right to be treated with equal concern in the distribution of the benefits and burdens of collective life. From the standpoint of the community as a whole – a standpoint embodied in the concept and practice of political authority – everyone is an anonymous source of interests and claims, as opposed to a bearer of a particular status or role. Put differently, in the political realm each member of the community stands before all others as an individual, instead of wearing the irremovable mask of king, lord, abbot, monk, seigneur, serf, peasant, merchant, patriarch, wife, servant, etc. An important distinction must be drawn, therefore, between the essential social equality of all members of the polity and the diverse yet contingent relations in which any particular person may see himself immersed under the laws supposedly made on behalf of everyone's interests. I may have acquired a particular legal position, as a creditor or a parent or a judge, but all of

---

[12] *Quoted in* Carl Schmitt, *The Concept of the Political*, 54.

these roles are severable from my person and are the product of laws enacted, at least officially, with the public interest in mind. As an anonymous member of the public, one's interests are weighted in the same scales used to weight everyone else's. The contrast, of course, is with any regime that recognises personal privileges or prerogatives, that takes important legal entitlements – eg, the right to charge some form of feudal rent or to levy taxes on the peasantry – to be constitutive of someone's essence, so that instead of speaking about individuals equal before the law we should speak about social rank and membership in an order. The right to equal concern is the denial of privilege, of exemptions from, or benefits beyond, common laws.[13]

The second premise of democratic authority is the right to equal respect. Every member of a democratic polity bears not only the same social dignity, but also the same intellectual dignity, or the right to be treated with equal respect in virtue of the abstract capacity for rational deliberation with which every human being *qua* rational being is naturally endowed. Your vote and my vote are equally weighted because we rely on the shared faculty of reason to form and scrutinise judgements as to what is just, right, or good. The basis for the community of power is this community of reason; in other words, everyone has an equal share of decision-making power in virtue of the fact that everyone is naturally endowed with the capacity to reason, and hence to make decisions on the right sort of grounds. That also explains, at least apparently, why certain categories of individuals whose capacity for reason is lacking or limited – minors and the mentally impaired – are disabled from the power to vote and to run for public office. Even though they are entitled to equal concern – their interests are no less important that those of their fellow citizens – they do not command equal respect.

The rights to equal concern and respect are the cardinal principles of a democratic political order; in other words, they are the moral grounds of democratic authority.[14] It is worth noting, however, that while the principle of equal concern constitutes a family of political regimes, the *differentia* that singles out democracy from other regimes in that family is the principle of equal respect.[15] The right to equal concern is constitutive of any political regime that treats each member of a polity as an anonymous bearer of interests, including one that acknowledges a paternalist basis for political authority. The forms of absolutist monarchy that prevailed in most of Europe during the seventeenth and eighteenth centuries, particularly when they took the form of an enlightened despotism, furnish the purest

---

[13] See Emmanuel-Joseph Sieyès, *Essai sur les Privileges*.
[14] See Ronald Dworkin, *Taking Rights Seriously*, 177–83, 272–78; Ronald Dworkin, *A Matter of Principle*, 181–204; Ronald Dworkin, *Justice for Hedgehogs*, 330–31.
[15] I use the terms 'rights' and 'principles' interchangeably when referring to equal concern and equal respect. The term 'principle' here refers not to the logical properties of the norms of equal concern and equal respect – eg, that they are principles instead of rules – but to the fact that they are the basis, or starting points, or grounds, or higher premises of democratic authority and, consequently, of all laws in a democracy. This conforms to the more ordinary use of the term, by opposition to the technical meaning bestowed upon it, eg, by Ronald Dworkin, *Taking Rights Seriously*, 22–28.

historical example of a political regime that affirms equal concern while denying equal respect. The characteristic motto of that type of regime is encapsulated in the words of the eighteenth century cameralist writer Johann Heinrich Gottlob Justi: 'everything for the people, nothing by the people'.[16]

The right to equal concern places everyone equally as subjects to political power. But when we commit ourselves to equal respect, the dignity of the individual is raised from the level of subject to that of citizen – he is no longer simply an equal *qua* consumer of political goods, but also an equal *qua* author of the basic structure of collective life. Political capacity and office is not the exclusive prerogative of any oracle or council of leaders. All individuals are equals both as addresses and authors of the law, an equality embodied in the rights to vote and to run for public office.

What I am claiming is that democracy is not, contrary to popular belief, a self-validating form of government, but quite the contrary presupposes the fundamental rights to equal concern and respect. These constitute the moral grounds of democratic authority. It is because of them that the institution of majoritarian government is legitimate and it is through them that the authority of the people is to be understood. Now if the rival parties of political opinion within the mainstream are – and that is a good part of the reason why they are mainstream – genuinely committed to democracy, they must be committed to the basic rights to equal concern and respect. They believe that the judgment of the voters overrides their own judgment because they believe that the addressees of the policies that they recommend are entitled to have the last say on their merit.[17]

---

[16] Quoted in Peter H Wilson, *Absolutism in Central Europe*, 109.

[17] That is the most compelling resolution of the so-called democratic paradox; see Richard Wollheim, 'A Paradox in the Theory of Democracy', 76. Wollheim envisages 'democracy in terms of machine ... the democratic machine ... (i)nto it are fed at fixed intervals the choices of individual citizens. The machine then aggregates them according to the pre-established rule or method, and so comes up with what may be called a "choice" of its own. [...] The question now arises. [W]hy should someone who has fed his choice into the machine and then is confronted by the machine with a choice non-identical with its own, feel any obligation to accept it?' Wollheim argues, no doubt correctly, that the paradox cannot be resolved by 'denying either of the limbs of the offending conjunction.' [84] That would only work if we could establish either (i) that a voter's support for the policy he voted for is conditional upon that policy being preferred by the majority or (ii) that democratic outcomes are generally accepted for prudential, rather than principled, reasons. The first option (i) is incoherent, since every voter would then accept a condition that cannot be met – I want A, if a majority wants A; but nobody actually wants A, because everyone who votes for A, does so conditionally. It is also *empirically absurd*, since voters typically do not change their minds after the voting results are disclosed. The second option (ii) implies the assertion that voters, as well as political parties, *normally* experience no obligation to endorse the democratic outcome, accepting it merely for strategic or prudential reasons. That is empirically unsound. Wollheim tries to resolve the paradox by offering 'a distinction between direct and oblique moral principles' [85], suggesting 'Murder is wrong' as an example of the first type of principle and 'What is commanded by the sovereign ought to be done' as an example of the second. He is surely onto something very important with that distinction, but I believe the paradox can be resolved more straightforwardly if we recognise that the democratic machine is not accepted by virtue of its outcome-related merits (because it 'chooses' right), but of its procedural virtues (because it embodies equal respect for all).

Equal concern and respect is hence common ground among mainstream political parties, movements or positions.

IV. The Trouble with Majoritarianism

The link between majoritarian government and equal respect is, to all appearances, straightforward enough. It is forged primarily by the rule one person/one vote, which establishes an equal partnership in government. In more formulaic terms, the golden rule of majoritarian government is that 'each voter has the maximum share of political power consistent with an equal share for everyone else'. This rule appears to flow from the right to equal respect, because it gives no one in particular a privileged or special voice in public deliberation. Everyone's political judgments are worthy of the same respect, and that is exactly why everyone gets the same share of voting power. In the words of perhaps the most persuasive advocate of majoritarian democracy in contemporary political theory:

> The method of majority-decision ... involves a commitment to give *equal* weight to each person's view in the process by which one view is selected as the group's. Indeed, it attempts to give each individual's view the greatest weight possible in this process compatible with an equal weight for the views of each of the others. Not only may each person's view be minimally decisive, but the method accords maximum decisiveness to each, subject only to the constraint of equality. In this sense, majority-decision presents itself as a *fair* method of decision making.[18]

But this way of seeing things is arguably superficial. In a voting procedure, it is the final count of votes for and against a certain law or programme that determines the public choice. It is not the intellectual dignity of the citizens that is honoured, since ultimately the fate of an election lies in the statistical accident of more individuals casting the ballot one way than the other. The outcome is not produced by considering whose views – or whose arguments – are true, or more compelling, or enlightening. As a matter of fact, arguments as such are entirely disregarded in a voting procedure; what prevails is the arithmetic of conclusions or decisions.

I suspect that you are not quite convinced by this argument, so we should examine it in greater depth. Imagine that on a certain issue X that may be addressed by adopting either policy A or B, every citizen but one endorses policy B, while the lone character throws his support on A. Let us assume, moreover, that every citizen's opinion was formed by means of a genuine attempt to figure out which policy is best for the public at large or, to put it more precisely, that everyone is voting in an impartial manner, thereby showing equal concern for all members of the community. If we are bound to regard with equal respect all the

---

[18] Jeremy Waldron, *Law and Disagreement*, 113–14 (emphasis in the original). Waldron reasserts the point many pages ahead: 'Sharing refers now to the fact that each individual claims the right to play his part, along with the equal part played by all other individuals, in the government of society' [236].

intelligences involved in the vote, do we have any reason to adopt policy B because it is supported by an overwhelming majority?

That would certainly be right if we were instructed to figure out which policy is socially preferable, in which case we would ask voters to select not the policy that they judge best for the community but which policy they prefer, and then proceed to aggregate the voting inputs, with the rider that all preferences would be ranked ordinally (B is better than A) rather than cardinally (B increases my well-being in x units, while A increases it in x-100). The reason why we would do well to put all the weight on the majority, in those circumstances, is that the voting inputs are quite worthless before they have been processed by the vote-counting mechanism and transformed into data about society as a whole. There is a qualitative difference between the voting input, which reveals an individual's preference, and the output of the voting procedure, which aggregates the multiple pieces of individual data and turns them into social data.

That is not at all what a democratic vote is about. In a democracy, we do not vote to give the authorities data that they will then go on to use in light of their judgements about the common good, but we vote to express our judgements about the common good. We do not let anyone else decide for us that the common good is what results from the aggregation of ordinally ranked preferences; whether that is right or wrong is something on which we, and we alone, are ultimate judges. Voting in a democracy expresses, therefore, not individual preferences, but political judgements.[19] Now I do not want to suggest by any means that voters do not, with greater or lesser frequency, act on the basis of their narrow self-interest. What I want to suggest is that behaviour of that sort must be understood as a deviance from the central or normal case in a democracy, in which the very fact that a vote is carried out expresses a measure of confidence that individual voters will assume their responsibility as citizens and ultimate law-givers.

If votes express genuine political judgments, then, there really is no difference in kind between the inputs of a voting procedure and its output. The judgement of the individual voter fills the same logical space that the majority's judgement does: the whole set of considerations that bear on the matter to be voted on, be it in the form of an election or a referendum. In fact, it is quite mystifying to talk of a 'judgement of the majority', when what is at stake is the arithmetic sum of individual decisions which are presumably based on an equal number of individual reasons, arguments and judgments. It follows that we really have no ground to assume that the majority got it right, even when, as in our wildly unrealistic example, there is a single dissonant voice. More or less support for a position – greater or lesser statistical warfare, as it were – really does not add anything at all to the substantive issue upon which political judgment is called.

Every now and then, support for majoritarianism is sought in an argument articulated by the eighteenth-century mathematician and political theorist, Marquis de

---

[19] See Jeremy Waldron, 'Rights and Majorities: Rousseau Revisited'.

Condorcet. It is the so-called Condorcet Jury Theorem, which states, in its simpler version, that, assuming both that every voter has more than a 0.5 probability of casting the correct vote and that each voter forms independent judgements, the probability that the majority is correct on a choice between two outcomes is higher than either any of the individual voters or the defeated minority.[20] The theorem gives us, apparently, reason to think that there really is something to the idea of 'majoritarian judgment', or that majorities are more 'judicious' than individual voters. Unfortunately, the assumptions of the theorem are, as Condorcet himself recognised, quite unrealistic, turning it into at best a controversial and at worst a useless foundation for majoritarianism. Specifically, there is hardly any reason to suppose that the key assumption – that every voter has a more than 0.5 chance of being on the right – holds where the judgment requested involves complex moral and political considerations, instead of straightforward empirical or logical matters. As Ronald Dworkin puts it:

> It is extremely doubtful, however, that Condorcet's theorem has any application at all to moral issues. The crucial assumption on which his proof depends – that any individual in a specified group is more likely than not to make a correct judgment – is indeed plausible when the question is a matter of straightforward fact and perception: when a group of eyewitnesses is asked the color of a getaway car, for example. The best explanation of how such people make such judgments – by seeing the car – makes it much more likely than not that any person of normal vision in the right position would make the right judgment. The assumption may also hold with respect to other matters of fact and of logic: guesses about the weight of an ox, or informal weather predictions, or the solution of not-very-difficult mathematical puzzles, for instance. But nothing in any plausible explanation of how people form moral convictions – which are not a matter of perception or logic – provides the slightest ground for assuming that people generally are more likely than not to form correct convictions about controversial moral issues; and history hardly supports that hypothesis either.[21]

I argued before that the link between majoritarian government and the principle of equal respect is apparently straightforward. I hope to have established by now that the link is actually problematic. Equal respect commands that each individual, each bearer of rational capacity, be recognised as an author of the basic terms of collective life; and while it seems that, in a world in which there are many intelligences, many beings who compete for authorship, giving each of them an equal vote is what equal respect entails, it is actually the case that it robs them of the capacity to write down by themselves the terms of collective life, entrusting their fate instead to the contingent and irrelevant fact that some majority got formed around one of the political alternatives in contest. It does nothing to the argument of a dissenter, an argument which has as its object a collective issue, that his position is not the majority's. For majorities as such carry no property that is worthy of respect, of intellectual or rational recognition. Indeed, empowering some opinion

---

[20] Marquis de Condorcet, *Essay on the Application of Mathematics to the Theory of Decision-Making*, 33.
[21] Ronald Dworkin, 'Looking for Cass Sunstein'.

because it has majoritarian support does not even display proper respect for those voters who side with the majority, simply because it is not the strength of their *reasons* that empowers them but the statistic outcome of the voting procedure.

Things would be different, of course, if the public discussion that precedes a vote worked systematically to bring initially divergent positions closer and closer together up to the point of unanimity. We know that to be a caricature of real democratic politics: fierce disagreement is a fact both prior and after the overwhelming majority of real-world pre-electoral debate. Equally unrealistic is the view that the outcome of an election works to dissolve the disagreement that it settles, because dissonant voices change their mind in light of the electoral results. That could not be farther away from the truth: democratic elections do not defeat ideas and arguments – nor could they, since they are settled by statistical rather than intellectual, facts – but merely the legitimacy of those who voice their support for them to take charge of government and turn them into grounds for public policy.

I expect at least some readers to be quite puzzled by most of this. After all, we have come to regard and even worship majoritarian ideas and institutions. Many will be tempted to accuse me of mounting a straw man. 'You have,' they will say, 'inflated the ideals of democracy by grounding it in an impossibly demanding principle of equal respect'. Now I do not deny that majoritarianism embodies *one* dimension of equal respect. In a world of many bearers of reason engaged in controversies that cannot be resolved rationally to the satisfaction of all, giving each of them a vote is a way of making sure that each of them has a chance of influencing the outcome. Surely that is better, on grounds of equal respect, than the most obvious alternative – entrusting political authority to a dictator.

That there is no pragmatic alternative to majoritarian voting, unless either the right to equal respect or public dissent over matters of common interest are denied, seems to be beyond dispute. But it is quite different to deposit law-making authority in the hands of the whole people, or of large legislative assemblies elected by the people, or some representatively feeble or non-elected majoritarian organ such as the US Supreme Court or the German Federal Constitutional Court.[22]

---

[22] Notice that for reasons of expediency I have reserved the term 'majoritarian government' in this section to the familiar practice of representative democracy. That should not be read as a denial of the fact that not only direct and representative democracy, *but also* judicial resolution by courts with more than one judge are majoritarian methods of decision-making. We often overlook this aspect of judicial decision-making because we have come to think about courts in opposition to legislatures. The results of that sort of exercise have been for the most part a series of intellectual and political equivocations. Waldron, *Law and Disagreement*, 90–91, makes the point adroitly. With that in mind, we should also take into account that it does not follow from the fact that courts are majoritarian institutions that they possess all the flaws of legislatures, together with the *additional* flaw of foreclosing participation. As I explain above, an important distinguishing feature of courts vis-à-vis legislatures is that the former are, not in virtue of qualities inherent to those people who go on to become judges but as a consequence of the very form of decision-making, more deliberative, or at least *potentially* more deliberative, than legislatures. See Gustavo Zagrebelsky, *Prinzipî e Voti*. Stephen Macedo, 'Against Majoritarianism', 1034, writes that 'Requiring judges to give reasons in public and subjecting those reasons to intense scrutiny is another, albeit indirect, form of democratic accountability'.

Each of these methods of collective decision-making is majoritarian, including the judicial method, but they embody different dimensions of equal respect, which means, conversely, that each of them fails to embody some other dimension. Direct democracy, for example, enables every citizen to influence, albeit minimally, every single political outcome; it is the most comprehensive method of decision-making, because it relies regularly on the people *en masse*. But it is the least deliberative of the three exemplary methods that I have listed, since it is impossible to institute a serious and free public discussion among lots of people immersed in their complicated and absorbing ordinary lives. Constitutional courts, on the other hand, are potentially excellent at deliberating, because they are designed to embody norms of discussion and justification that foreground and expose to scrutiny the reasoning behind each position; however, they foreclose – severely – political participation.

The point I am trying to make is that each of the available methods for making political decisions against the background of substantive political disagreement embodies one dimension of equal respect at the expense of another, or settles on some compromise, as pure representative democracy does. Supporters of each method explore the weaknesses of their opponents by pointing to some dimension of equal respect – decisional comprehensiveness or deliberative transparency – that alternative methods fail to honour, or honour only feebly. But they themselves expose the flank widely to symmetric charges. Because each side of the debate can launch a series of effective attacks but has very little in the way of defensive barriers against criticism from the opposite standpoint, the problem of disagreement, originally located at the level of substantive policy, recurs where the question no longer pertains to the substance of public choices but to the institution, procedure, or decision-making method competent to issue them. The most striking feature of the debate is that the rival views all draw their offensive and defensive resources from the same *moral premise*, the principle of equal respect.

V. Reasonable Pluralism

Rival parties of political opinion accept democracy as the right method to settle their disagreements over the common good and what it requires by way of public policy. As we saw, by accepting democracy they are committed to those premises which lend democracy its normative basis, the rights to equal concern and to equal respect. Majoritarian government in the familiar form of representative democracy, the paradigm of democratic politics, is nonetheless rendered suspicious precisely on the grounds upon which its attempted justification rests, and that is also true of any alternative form of decision-making, such as direct democracy or judicial deliberation.

We hit an apparent dead end. The truth is that the right to equal respect appears to demand unanimity or consent in government. Only if everyone concurs in holding the same view of the common good may we say with all propriety that each and every citizen authors the laws by which he lives. But how can consent be secured amidst the pervasive reality of fierce disagreement? In our political tradition, there is a powerful argument that has been made to that effect. I shall call it the *liberal argument*. Before we go on to examine it, however, we should explore in greater depth the sources of political disagreement.

We all hold views, more or less explicit, more or less examined, about the proper way to lead our lives. The full range of considerations that fall under that domain has been called for a long time, at least since the days of Socrates, ethics, or the knowledge of what it is – and how to – live well. In the tradition of post-Enlightenment culture, particularly romantic and existentialist, which has largely grew in rebellion against the view that one can *know* how to live well, the ancient concept of ethics has become more and more foreign to popular conceptions of value and its place was taken by the notion of a quest for the meaning of life, sometimes in the form of discovering, sometimes as the process of creating, the meaning of our lives; and occasionally as a request that we recognise that life is meaningless. What all these views, about living well and the meaning of life, have in common, is that they concern our ultimate ends or what is often called, particularly in political philosophy, our conceptions of the good. It is clear not only that there are many rival conceptions of the good but that each of those conceptions characteristically draws, not always explicitly, on a wide range of metaphysical and epistemological premises and arguments, the truth and validity of which are contentious matters as well. Conceptions of the good are often formed, developed, and re-examined in the light afforded by what John Rawls calls 'comprehensive doctrines',[23] or what are ordinarily called 'worldviews'.

There are well-established and highly articulated comprehensive doctrines in our moral tradition. Aristotle's conception of the moral and intellectual virtues as those qualities the possession of which enable human flourishing; the various forms of theistic belief in one omnipotent and omniscient, perfectly good and loving, creator God; Marx's vision of a communist society as the final stage of human emancipation from the realm of necessity; Kant's moral pietism and his doctrine of the categorical imperative and the authority of practical reason; Kierkegaard's contrast between the aesthetic, the ethical and religious ways of life, and his insistence that we are left helpless and radically unwarranted in our decision to commit our existence to one of them; the romantic plea for self-discovery not through abstraction from those forms of life within which our agency is embedded (family, workplace, nation, church, class, etc), but by recognising in them and through our sense of belonging to them our personal identities; the modern-bureaucratic-managerial ethos of vocation and professionalism, both containing and empowering the rare but liberating moment of hedonic extravagance. These are examples of comprehensive doctrines or worldviews which

---

[23] John Rawls, *Political Liberalism*, xviii, 12–13.

furnish a conception of the good. Most people, of course, do not adhere on a permanent and wholly consistent basis to any particular doctrine, but their beliefs about life, agency and purpose are often formed around anchoring points which can be traced back to some doctrinal whole.

What makes a doctrine comprehensive or a given view a worldview is the scope of fundamental questions, of the sort that have been the perennial subject of philosophy and religion, that it purports to answer. Among such questions, as a department of morality, are those that pertain to politics, to the way in which we are to deal with the fact that we live in a finite world in the company of others. Each doctrine varies in the attention that is pays to political issues as such, from the most general ones pertaining to the form of government to specific matters of public policy, but each has something to say, directly or indirectly, on the subject; and whatever they have to say will be drawn from the other, more basic, aspects of the doctrine in question.

We should profit from an example. The Catechism of the Catholic Church is a remarkable case of a single document exhibiting a comprehensive doctrine. It 'aims at presenting an organic synthesis of the essential and fundamental contents of Catholic doctrine',[24] thereby expounding the essentials of theism, the conception of human beings as creatures crafted in the image of the Creator, the belief in the fall of man and his redemption through Christ, the role of the Church as the gateway to salvation, as well as the various moral precepts and rituals that Catholics are bound to observe. It covers a vast number of metaphysical (the nature and origins of the world), epistemological (the relationship between natural reason, revelation and faith), and moral (the proper way of life) issues. All the strands of argument and belief are purportedly connected in – to use the words of the Catechism itself – 'an organic synthesis'. Part of the doctrine concerns what in the Catechism is called 'the human communion', where the terrain of political philosophy is planted with seeds drawn from the basic principles of the whole doctrine. Other parts of the document – consider the views on chastity, including marriage, pornography, and homosexuality at §§ 2337–59 – contain elements which directly bear on political matters as well. The Catechism embodies a worldview, including a view of politics, conceived as an aspect of the world.

The Catechism presents one among numerous rival views about the world, rival in that they embody competing claims about the same object – the whole world. The theist, for instance, says that all matter proceeds from the person of God, who is pure spirit, while his materialist objector insists that matter is autogenic and that religion is a form of psychological deception; both are in turn critiqued by the metaphysical dualist(s), by the organicist(s), and by the philosophical skeptic(s). Each view, in its comprehensiveness, challenges and opposes the other views. True, worldviews differ in their scope and ambition. The typical agnostic, for instance, forfeits all thinking on religious issues, drawing a sharp line

---

[24] *Catechism of the Catholic Church*, § 11.

between ethical and metaphysical questions, or at least between the former and the part of the latter that is often called cosmology. But this sort of indifference, though masked as neutrality, is subject to the metaphysically engaged person's rejoinder that one cannot really forfeit the most fundamental questions, precisely because they concern the foundation of everything else. The agnostic is hence, from the standpoint of his critic, circuitously adopting a position on the very questions that he means to flout.

The existence of rival worldviews – the fact of pluralism – supplies a key to unlock the nature of political disagreement. Competing parties of political opinion proceed from rival sets of comprehensive premises that fail to command universal acceptance. Political pluralism is a consequence of the plurality of comprehensive doctrines. Now we should be careful to distinguish between two two different forms that the fact of political pluralism may take. Let us call them *bare* pluralism and *reasonable* pluralism.[25] Bare pluralism is the form of disagreement in which at least some contenders hold on to their position in the face of patently better arguments articulated by the other side. The strength of the arguments ought to have had the effect of converting them to their rival's view, but they have failed to display publicly the signs of any such conversion. Dogmatism, laziness, bad faith, self-deception, cowardice, ignorance and confusion are the chief causes of that kind of stubbornness; and as none of them constitutes reasoned grounds for further opposition, the stubbornness in question is unreasonable. The unreasonable opponent forfeits temporarily any claim to be regarded as a party of opinion worthy of the respect commanded by all rational beings. Indeed, unreasoned opposition evidences first and foremost a failure of self-respect, for the unreasonable person insults his own intelligence by maintaining allegiance to conclusions that have been defeated in the court of argument.

Reasonable pluralism is the form of disagreement among contenders who are not persuaded by their rivals' claims, yet have not themselves furnished a case for their views the rational force of which requires the immediate conversion of their rivals. Each view in contest has to be regarded neither as unreasonable nor as true, but as one reasonable and possibly true view. What makes reasonable pluralism possible are 'the many hazards' involved in fulfilling what John Rawls calls 'the burdens of judgment'.[26] It is worth quoting him at length on this point:

> The idea of reasonable disagreement involves an account of the sources, or causes, of disagreement between reasonable persons so defined. These sources I refer to as the burdens of judgment. The account of these burdens must be such that it is fully compatible with, and so does not impugn, the reasonableness of those who disagree. What, then, goes wrong? An explanation of the right kind is that the sources of reasonable disagreement – the burdens of judgment – among reasonable persons are the many

---

[25] See John Rawls, *Political Liberalism*, 36–38; Joshua Cohen, 'Moral Pluralism and Political Consensus'; Charles Larmore, 'The Moral Basis of Political Liberalism'.

[26] Rawls, *Political Liberalism*, 54–58. See also Waldron, *Law and Disagreement*, 151–53; Charles Larmore, *Political Liberalism*, 341–42.

hazards involved in the correct (and conscientious) exercise of our powers of reason and judgment in the ordinary course of political life.

It is tempting to read the phrase 'many hazards ... of reason and judgment', no doubt against Rawls' wishes, as a capitulation to epistemic skepticism. If reason fails us when, having argued back from our conclusions to the premises that support them, we are required to make a fully convincing case for our position, the sort of case that settles definitely the controversy at hand, how can we hold that our beliefs are rationally warranted? Once all rational resources have been exhausted, the selection of the supporting premises appears entirely arbitrary, dependent on one's passions, preferences, states of mind, or whatever other merely contingent and subjective factors one cares to mention. We are not really entitled – rationally entitled – to commit ourselves to the truth of a certain view if we are unable to persuade others in the course of rational dialogue, for failure to persuade others whom we address on account of their rational capacity ultimately implies failure to persuade any bearer of reason, ourselves included.[27] Hence, argues the skeptic at last, conviction of truth in worldviews is but self-deception.

There is an old way of repealing claims of this nature that consists in pointing out that they embody a contradiction. Epistemic skepticism is a worldview, which means – on its own terms – that it cannot be true. The skeptic, of course, has something of an answer to that challenge: the objections launched against him stem not from reason but from self-deception or bad faith, which amounts to making the remarkable claim that epistemological pluralism is an instance of bare pluralism. The problem is that the rejoinder is purely defensive: it undermines skepticism without actually addressing the substance of the challenge.

A better response involves an account of how reasonable pluralism is rooted in the practice of rational dialogue. The expression 'rational dialogue' invokes the image of a jousting tournament in which two contenders, mounted in their theoretical horses and armed with their sharp rational lances, ride towards one another with the purpose of unhorsing their opponent. That picture misses three key features of rational dialogue in practical life.

(1) *Embeddedness*. The first feature is that rational agents engaged in actual discussion are no ghostly embodiments of reason, blank slates relying on their rational powers to acquire true beliefs. They are embedded in their belief systems and bound to wear the mask of their comprehensive doctrines, thus proceeding from a given doctrinal situation. That does not mean that they are dispossessed of critical resources, unable on a permanent basis to review their allegiance to a worldview. What it suggests is that rational progression is only intelligible and possible by reference to a starting point or belief situation. Reasoning and argument both challenge beliefs and presuppose them.[28]

---

[27] See Alasdair MacIntyre, *After Virtue*, 8, 11.
[28] There are traces of MacIntyre's conception of tradition-bound rationality here. See MacIntyre, *Whose Justice? Whose Rationality?*

(2) *Translation*. Not only are rational agents doctrinally situated prior to dialogue, their understanding of what the other has to say is mediated by their beliefs. This is a consequence of the first feature of rational dialogue. No agent is in a position to question everything at once; all rational scrutiny is captured by the metaphor that Otto Neurath applied to the process of scientific verification: 'We are like sailors who on the open sea must reconstruct their ship but are never able to start afresh from the bottom'.[29] Thus, rational dialogue is never completely transparent, since each agent receives and understands the other from his own specific standpoint. Every rational exchange is in practice not only a matter of self-examination and criticism of the other's viewpoint but also an experience in translation and, accordingly, betrayal of the source – *traduttore, traditore!*

(3) *Dependency*. Finally, there is an unbridgeable gap between *reason* and *reasoning*. Human beings are mortal, vulnerable, dependent creatures devoted to many activities which involve reasoning skills in different measures; moreover, there are limits to their capacity, opportunity and willingness to think. That they have rational powers does not mean that they are reason personified. Their commitment to a worldview is, if reasonable at all, sustained both by the balance of reasons and by a willingness to put those reasons and the balancing judgments to trial; what that commitment does not require, however, is rational perfection. Our allegiance to a given view is partly based on the hope that the gaps and ambiguities and shady areas of our belief wholes can be remedied, even when we do not expect to supply in good time the needed remedies.

Rational dialogue in practice is not at all like the jousting tournament among abstract bearers of reason. Instead of blank slates inhabiting a flat world, it involves rich minds trading arguments in a complicated mess of a world. But there is something to the idea of a pure rational contest, utterly disembodied and abstract. It works like an ideal that both regulates our understanding of what a fair and open discussion is and sits as a postulate of rational dialogue in practice. Our willingness to persist in dialoguing in spite of the three complicating features that it possesses in practice implies a commitment to the ideal of a pure and fully enlightening discussion, unhampered by context, opacity and fragility.

It is worth examining what kind of ideal is at stake here. It is not a practicable ideal, something that we ought to make real by removing from the world those features that are contrary to it; examples of ideals of that nature, calling for immediate reform, are deposing a tyrant in order to institute or restore a just political regime or regulating financial markets to reduce the incentives for excessive leveraging, risk and fraud. The ideal of perfectly transparent rational dialogue is however not a utopian ideal any more than a practicable one, if by that we

---

[29] Quoted in Ivar Ekeland, *The Best of All Possible Worlds*, 190.

mean something that is so far removed from reality that it possesses no normative significance for us in this world, that indeed it would be silly or even damaging to attempt, such as organising society on the assumption that human beings are invariably altruist or that natural resources are so abundant that there is no fact of scarcity that we must cope with. The ideal of a perfectly transparent discussion is rather what we may call a *regulative ideal*, something that it is worth trying to realise for the sake of bettering the world, but which is impossible to accomplish fully.[30] The three features of rational dialogue in practice that I have brought to attention are hence persistent, as opposed to contingent, features of the world, though we have some control over the degree to which they distort and complicate rational dialogue.

Now, given that a measure of distortion is unavoidable, we are rationally entitled, contrary to the skeptic's insistence, to embrace our beliefs sustained in the course of open and good faith dialogue. Conversely, however, we are not entitled to certainty or unshakable rational conviction, precisely because however persuaded we may be both that our arguments are correct and that we have explained why and where rival views go wrong, we cannot tell for sure if our conviction of truth is caused exclusively by reasons or also by non-rational or distortive factors, of the sort that we examined above. That is exactly why we must recognise the reasonableness of good faith disagreement. That is also why our rational right to reject skepticism goes hand-in-hand with a rational duty to be epistemically humble, to acknowledge what Rawls would have us call 'the burdens of judgment'.

VI. Freestanding Principles

In the earlier pages of the introduction to *Political Liberalism*, John Rawls poses in various forms the question to which the entire book is devoted:

> How is it possible that there may exist over time a just and stable society of free and equal citizens profoundly divided by reasonable though incompatible religious, philosophical, and moral doctrines? Put another way: How is it possible that deeply opposed though reasonable comprehensive doctrines may live together and all affirm the political conception of a constitutional regime? What is the structure and content of a political conception that can gain the support of such an overlapping consensus?[31]

It is important that we bear in mind how we got to this point, for we have not followed Rawls' path of posing the question upfront. We have been considering the hypothesis that mainstream political culture in the advanced democratic world proceeds from what I called a prototype, a model or test case of a single design

---

[30] The concept of a regulative ideal – or regulative *principles* – was famously proposed by Immanuel Kant, *Critique of Pure Reason*, A 642/B 670.
[31] John Rawls, *Political Liberalism*, xviii.

concept or idea properly called liberalism. Since the only way to test the hypothesis is to examine the common ground among the rival parties of political opinion, such as North-American liberals and conservatives, that occupy the center of the political spectrum, we focused our attention on the institution of representative democracy. I have argued that it presupposes a pair of fundamental rights, to equal concern and to equal respect. I have also argued that democratic authority, flowing as it does from majoritarian support, is rendered highly problematic on the very ground of equal respect upon which its justification purportedly rests. Only *consent* is a legitimate basis for a government which pays allegiance to the principle of equal respect for all citizens. At that point we suspended our agenda because it was important to explain the source of political disagreement. We ventured that it can be traced back to the pluralism of worldviews, a pluralism that is both reasonable and does not commend by itself epistemological skepticism. It is now time to resume our agenda.

Let us assume, for the time being, that rival parties of political opinion that compete for power within the framework of democratic institutions proceed from reasonable though incompatible comprehensive doctrines. I ask you to assume that, even though I do not think it is true. I believe, and you probably do as well, that mainstream politics is simultaneously too shallow and too convergent on key issues to be properly accounted for in terms of rival worldviews. That is a suggestion that we shall explore later. As of now, we proceed under the assumption that political disagreement is first and foremost an upshot of the confrontation of comprehensive doctrines.

If political disagreement were a consequence of what I called earlier 'bare pluralism', it would not raise any singular concern. For, as we have seen, the bare objector fails to present himself in public debate as a bearer of reason, thereby forfeiting the respect that in principle is owed to him by virtue of his rational capacity. Reasonable pluralism, on the contrary, does raise unique and very delicate issues. For no party to a reasonable and interminable dispute can invoke the authority of reason – impersonal and shared – in favour of his position, since reason works within the practice of rational dialogue not to put an end to, but instead to amplify and perpetuate, the loud cacophony of worldviews. It follows that no government informed by and operating within the bounds of a comprehensive doctrine can be grounded in the consent of its subjects. Such a government would rest on what Rawls quite appropriately calls 'the fact of oppression':

> [A] continuing shared understanding on one comprehensive religious, philosophical, or moral doctrine can be maintained only by the oppressive use of state power. If we think of political society as a community united in affirming one and the same comprehensive doctrine, then the oppressive use of state power is necessary for political community. In the society of the Middle Ages, more or less united in affirming the Catholic faith, the Inquisition was not an accident; its suppression of heresy was needed to preserve that shared religious belief. The same holds, I believe, for any reasonable comprehensive philosophical and moral doctrine, whether religious or nonreligious. A society united on a reasonable form of utilitarianism, or on the reasonable liberalisms

of Kant and Mill, would likewise require the sanctions of state power to remain so. Call this 'the fact of oppression'.[32]

It should be apparent that mainstream parties of opinion in our political culture are not willing to embrace the fact of oppression. That is precisely why they hold that democracy, as opposed to civil war followed by dictatorship, is the right method to settle their disagreements. Even that, however, does not quite capture the sheer force of the point. It is not just that mainstream political culture stems from a strong rejection of war in favour of the sort of peace that democratic arrangements secure. A commitment of that character is of the conditional type: '*if* the alternative is war, we should endorse democratic peace'. What makes a norm – in the simplest sense of a practical reason – conditional is *both* (i) the fact that the so-called main clause – 'we should endorse democratic peace' – is conditioned by the subordinate or 'as if' clause – '*if* the alternative is war' – *and* (ii) that it is validated by a subjectively given end, the kind of end that flows from a subject's desires or preferences or goals, instead of some objective or impersonal value. The first dimension of conditionality is that as matter of the contingent ordering of the world, some X implies some Y; the second dimension is that some agent A either wants to bring about Y, or he wants to avoid Y, and will dispose of his agency in relation to X accordingly. An endorsement of democracy premised on a desire for peace is hence a case of what Kant called hypothetical imperatives, by opposition to the categorical or unconditioned duties of morality.[33]

A democracy held for hypothetical reasons is by definition unstable; the measure of that instability is precisely the degree of variability of the two conditions which together make it rational for a given agent to support democratic arrangements. Suppose that some agent A, who endorses comprehensive doctrine D, wants to avoid war, but also that at a certain moment T_0 he is in the position to start a dictatorship based on D without triggering a war, only minor social unrest and a few manageable skirmishes. That agent no longer has a reason – a hypothetical reason – to support democracy. Now imagine that the same agent lives in a moment T_1 in which in all likelihood the only alternative to democracy is a bloody civil war; however, he prefers to put his life, as do *ex hypothesi* his comrades, on the line for certain non-negotiable ideals, than yielding to a democratic compromise. For reasons other than in the previous example, reasons having to do not with the contingent disposition of the world but with his preference function, agent A also lacks a rational basis to endorse democracy.

When either of the two events that we imagined obtains, A apparently lacks a rational basis to endorse democracy. However, that would not bar any

---

[32] ibid at 37.
[33] Immanuel Kant, *Groundwork of the Metaphysics of Morals*, 25 (Ak 4:414): '[A]ll imperatives command either *hypothetically* or *categorically*. The former represent the practical necessity of a possible action as means to achieving something else that one wills (or that it is at least possible for one to will). The categorical imperative would be that which represented an action as objectively necessary of itself, without reference to another end.' (Emphasis in the original.).

whole-hearted democrat from condemning his behaviour as unreasonable. What exactly makes it unreasonable? Surely not any lack of care on A's part in considering the hypothetical reasons that bear on his situation in any of the two events; on those grounds, his behaviour is rationally unimpeachable. The indignation and reproach issued by the democrat is based on a different kind of reason, a reason the function of which is to control and filter hypothetical reasons and, therefore, is itself unconditional – it is, in Kant's terminology, a *categorical* reason. The whole-hearted democrat believes that any party of opinion has a genuine duty to uphold democratic arrangements, not merely prudential or interested reasons to so doing. The agents to whom such duty is owed are precisely those who dissent from us on reasonable grounds, and who are entitled to as much respect as we claim for ourselves.

Democratic authority is a surrogate for rational agreement in a non-ideal world, the equivalent in the political realm to the attitude of epistemic humility commanded by the practice of rational dialogue. Yet we have seen that democracy, at least in the typical form of majoritarian government, cannot perform the task that is called upon it. No substantive worldview and no procedure of decision-making based on votes expressing choices over worldviews can raise to Rawls' challenge of finding a 'just and stable society of free and equal individuals', that is to say, a framework of collective life that is not only *for* the people but *by* the people – the *whole* people – as well. Hence the question: 'By what ideals and principles, then, are citizens as sharing equally in ultimate political power to exercise that power so that each of them can reasonably justify their political decisions to each other?'[34]

Rawls' term for the sort of principles that we are looking for is 'freestanding', to signal that they are not grounded in any particular – and contentious – comprehensive doctrine. Given the failure of decision-making procedures to meet the demands of equal respect, all hope lies in a shift back to substance, not in the form of principles at home in a worldview, but in the form of principles toward which reasonable dissenters over deep questions of value can nevertheless converge. The need for such principles is plain once we realize the implications of equal respect in the political realm. Within the practice of rational dialogue, the fact of reasonable dissent among individuals implies what I called earlier a duty of epistemic humility, a willingness to accept the possibility that one is mistaken, that one's beliefs are false, despite the hope, vindicated by careful reasoning, that they are true. When we move from the seminar room to the political realm, however, things get more complicated. We cannot really afford the luxury of suspending political life while we seek definite answers to the great mysteries and problems of the world; moreover, as we have seen, there is little to no hope that the required answers can even be obtained. What we need is something equivalent, in the sphere of government, to the humble attitude of the reasonable dissenter in the

---

[34] John Rawls, *Political Liberalism*, xliv.

seminar room. That is the role of *freestanding* principles for the exercise of political power, principles that embody the good will, open-mindedness and tolerance that is characteristic of epistemic humility.[35]

VII. Politics and Justice

We should stop for a moment to ponder what it is about politics that explains the urgent need for 'freestanding principles' in circumstances of reasonable pluralism. How exactly does the political realm differ from the seminar room? What is the political realm anyway?

What I mean by the 'political realm' is a certain way of dealing with six permanent features or conditions of human life in the world: commonality; plurality; individuality; vulnerability; scarcity; and temporality. Let us examine each of them briefly.

- *Commonality.* There is a single finite and not naturally divided world that harbours human life.
- *Plurality.* Human beings are thrown into that world together in large numbers by the event of birth and leave it by the event of death.
- *Individuality.* The human species is not spontaneously organised, all members playing a natural function, such as bees and ants, because each individual member of the species is an agent, a separate existence gifted with consciousness, freedom, and thus with thinking and acting of its own.
- *Vulnerability.* Human beings have bodies naturally vulnerable to disease, to physical harm, to pain, and are bound to the necessities of food, shelter and other basic material goods.

---

[35] There is an important difference between a defence of tolerance that proceeds from the implications of equal respect in circumstances of reasonable pluralism and the more familiar, though seriously flawed, defence grounded in premises of moral skepticism or relativism. The argument for tolerance from relativism takes the following paradigmatic form: P_1 'There is a plurality of rival and reasonable value systems' [*Value pluralism*]; it follows that: P_2 'There are no objective values.' [*Value skepticism*]; it follows that, P_3 'Tolerance ought to be the commanding political principle' [*Tolerance principle*]. This is a notoriously bad argument. The two steps of the argument are flawed. On the one hand, it does not follow from the *fact* of moral pluralism that there are no objective (or true, etc) moral values, for the truth conditions of evaluative propositions are not empirical, ie no 'ought' can be derived from an 'is' and vice-versa. Therefore, the move from P_1 to P_2 is fallacious. On the other hand, one cannot hold both that there are no objective moral values (P_2) and that tolerance is an objective moral value (P_3). That is to say, if one holds that tolerance *ought to be* the commanding political principle, one is committed to affirm at least one objective value, namely tolerance; but then there is room for the possibility that other values are objective as well. The argument proposed in the text makes better sense of the liberal values of tolerance, dialogue and open-mindedness. It presents itself (in the simplest form) as a syllogistic inference, where the minor premise is P_1 [*value pluralism*], the major premise is the norm of equal respect, and the conclusion is the existence of a duty of tolerance. It sidesteps the trouble posed by the assertion of P_2 [*value skepticism*].

- *Scarcity*. The natural world into which we are thrown possesses a limited stock of goods apt to satisfy human needs.
- *Temporality*. Our life in the world is a sequence of temporally situated events. There are no events beyond time – the clock never stops ticking. It follows that we are immersed in history and our decisions are events in history.

The question that emerges, once we acknowledge these six conditions, is how to deal with – how to be in – a world characterised by them.[36] There are two major alternatives: violence and politics. Hannah Arendt reports the reflection of the ancient Greeks on these two ways of being in the world:

> To be political, to live in a *polis*, meant that everything was decided through words and persuasion and not through force and violence. In Greek self-understanding, to force people by violence, to command rather than persuade, were prepolitical ways to deal with people characteristic of life outside the polis, of home and family life, where the household head rules with uncontested, despotic powers, or of life in the barbarian empires of Asia, whose despotism was frequently likened to the organization of the household.[37]

One way of dealing with the fact that we share this world with others like us is to treat them as objects, as things in the world that we have to acknowledge, the way we acknowledge plants, and animals and rocks. We try to submit them to our needs and wants as much as we can. That is the way of violence, of the life outside the *polis*. Of course, human beings *qua* objects have their own distinctive properties; for instance, Cicero was perfectly aware of Tiro's membership in the class of rational animals. To be a slave is to be regarded as a thing, not to be mistaken for one.[38] The slave, nonetheless, is entirely at the disposal of his master. The bond

---

[36] The idea of 'the political realm' as a constellation of features or conditions of human life is inspired in a variety of sources. See Hannah Arendt, *The Human Condition*, 7–8 ('While all aspects of the human condition are somehow related to politics ... plurality is specifically *the* condition of all political life'); HLA Hart, *The Concept of Law*, 192–200 ('Universally recognized principles of conduct which have a basis in elementary truths concerning human beings, their natural environment, and aims, may be considered the *minimum content* of Natural Law ...'); John Rawls, *A Theory of Justice*, 126–30 ('The circumstances of justice may be described as the normal conditions under which human cooperation is both possible and necessary'); Benjamin Barber, *Strong Democracy*, 120–38 ('One can understand the realm of politics as being circumscribed by conditions that impose a necessity for public action, and thus for reasonable public choice, in the presence of conflict and in the absence of private or independent grounds for judgment'); Jeremy Waldron, *Law and Disagreement*, 102–03 ('The felt need among members of a certain group for a common framework or decision or course of action on some matter, even in the face of disagreement about what that framework, decision or action should be, are the *circumstances of politics*'). The remote antecedents, as far as I can tell, are David Hume, *A Treatise of Human Nature*, Book III, Part II, sec ii, 536–52 ('Of the origin of justice and property'); and Immanuel Kant, *Anthropology from a Pragmatic Point of View*, Part 2, Section E, 172–76 ('Fundamentals of an account of the character of the human species').

[37] Hannah Arendt, *The Human Condition*, 26.

[38] This account is consistent with Hegel's 'master/slave' (or 'lordship and bondage') dialectic – see GFW Hegel, *Phenomenology of Spirit*, IV-A, 111–19. The main point of the dialectic is to prove the equal and independent status of other persons, the mutual recognition of persons as embodied spirit. Accordingly, it would be a mistake to read the initial encounter of the self with the other as if the self

between master and slave – or between the *paterfamilias* and the members of the household – is premised on violence. Affection may be present, yet it is contingent, since its presence or absence does not modify the character of the bond. The master owes no justification to the slave and the slave owes no loyalty to the master, for it only makes sense to appeal to de jure standards – of 'rightness', 'loyalty', 'justification, 'owing' and so forth – among mutually recognised free agents; the bond of slavery is at bottom a de facto bond, held together by speechless violence.[39]

The other way of dealing with others in the world is to share a public life – a political realm – with them. A political realm is a community among persons, a way of dealing in conjunction with the challenges posed by the six features that constitute our world. Each person is recognised as an independent agent, a member of the community with a standing. Relations among persons are hence not governed by mute violence but by norms of justice. To be regarded as a person, indeed, means to be the sort of being to whom – and from whom – justice is owed.

Justice concerns the right distribution of the benefits and burdens of social life or, to use a broader and much older formulation, giving each person his due. When I say that 'justice concerns …' I mean to give an account of the *idea* of justice. Quite a lot can fit into that, obviously, because the idea of justice is formal. Each conception of justice proceeds from certain substantive premises about *what* is owed – and *why* that is owed – to each person, premises that are not implicit in the idea of justice itself. The idea of justice merely implies a certain *form* of human interaction in the world. It is the exact opposite of sheer violence. It is the form of life among those who share a political realm.

Consider the following account of justice in medieval Austria, taken from Otto Brunner's classic book, *Land and Lordship*.[40] Social relations were justly ordered when they conformed to 'Right', understood as the Natural Order or 'Good Old Order', embodied in traditions and customs. Notice that two concepts that are key in our understanding of law and its relationship to justice are absent. On the one hand, laws were not made by a class of officials – there was no deliberate law-making.[41] On the other hand, 'law and justice were synonymous', that is,

---

already knows that the other is both independent and equal to itself – a person. But after the life and death struggle, the second stage of the dialectic, the victorious self grants mercy to the foe and uses it as an instrument for his goals – as a slave. That is *the* moment of lordship and bondage. In this stage, the other is not recognised as an equal, of course, but is regarded as capable of sophisticated instrumental uses that require some measure of rational capacity, as opposed both to animal instinct and Reason (or Spirit).

[39] My account of mastery/slavery is essentially Hegelian – although Hannah Arendt, *The Human Condition*, 22–37, is an important influence as well.

[40] Otto Brunner, *Land and Lordship*. See also António Manuel Hespanha, 'As Estruturas Políticas em Portugal na Época Moderna', 4–14.

[41] For the proposition that 'feudalism' is essentially the denial of any division of law into 'public' and 'private', see Pollock and Maitland, *The History of English Law Before the Time of Edward I*, I, 244–45. 'Any conception as that of "the state" hardly appears on the surface of the law; no line is drawn between the king's public and private capacities … He has greater rights than any other lord; but it is a matter of degree; many lords have some "regalities" …' (245).

'Ideal and positive law coincided'; there was no standard of justice above or outside (long-) established social practice.[42]

The Good Old Order was structured by three isomorphic spheres of lordship; that is, bonds of loyalty between a lord and his dependants: the household, the manor (*seigneury*), and the *Land*. Within each sphere the lord – the head of the household, the seigneur, or the prince – owed his subjects protection and the dispensation of justice (*iurisdictio*) and received obedience and service from them. The key virtue was honour, which meant to accept and discharge one's role(s) within the Order.[43] Even the ruler – the King or the Prince – owed obedience to the law. He played one role within the Order, instead of standing outside or above it, as the latter absolutist doctrines of '*princeps legibus solutus est*' and 'the King can do no wrong' implied. The Order was not authored or posited by anyone. It was *natural* in the rather strong sense that, just like the forces of nature, its source was beyond the reach of human agency. Individuals were hence thrown into a world that was already justly ordered. '[I]n the Middle Ages', writes Brunner,

> there was no secular power that exercised internal sovereignty in the sense of modern political theory. [...] The doctrine – and here we are talking about a theory, not a view of Right that necessarily manifested itself in practice – that the power of the ruler derived from that of the people in no way implied that 'the people' was itself sovereign. Such a notion would have been foreign to popular mentality itself. Men who saw in Right the expression of the divine world order, who considered every subjective legal claim as 'justice', and who made no distinction between ideal and positive law could hardly have viewed themselves as the source of positive law. Rather, for them the order they lived in was the Good Old Order. This was an order that had to be preserved or restored, one in which each member had rights that could not be derived from anything else.[44]

---

[42] ibid at 114–15.

[43] António Manuel Hespanha, *As Vésperas do Leviatã*, 308. The plural – roles – is important. In the medieval and early modern conception of political ordering, the individual may – and very often does – play more than one role, or is endowed with a plurality of functionally independent statuses. Thus, Richard the Lionheart was (among other things) King of England and Duke of Normandy, owing loyalty to the King of France in the latter capacity.

[44] Otto Brunner, *Land and Lordship*, 120–21. Brunner relaxes the point in a footnote (118, fn 77): 'Still, lay conceptions of Right in the Middle Ages reveal a growing awareness of the opposition between Christian and moral prescriptions on the one hand and actual practice on the other. This is seen above all in the problem of personal servitude, serfdom ...' Indeed, in medieval political ideology (what the French historians of the Annales School might call *mentalité*) there was an apparent tension between the 'Germanic' idea of a *natural* social hierarchy, according to which differences of status are inherent to persons (eg, a lord simply *is* by nature superior to his servants), and the 'Christian' idea of a *functional* hierarchy, according to which the various social roles are the parts (estates) of the body politic, contributing in a specific way to the common good. The tension arises from the fact that on the naturalist conception the distribution of social roles is permanent, because it is a fact of Nature, while on the functionalist understanding it is an artifact controlled by the norm of functional propriety. A well-known device deployed by medieval political thought to mediate the tension is the idea of 'The Three Orders' – *oratores, bellatores, laboratores* – as necessary functions on a descending scale of dignity as well as responsibility; on that view, differences of status are justified functionally, but the various functions (the three orders and their sub-divisions) are grounded in Nature (they are necessary for society *to function*) and backed by the court of tradition. See Charles Taylor, *A Secular Age*, 164. For a classic study, see Georges Duby, *Les Trois Ordres ou L'Imaginaire du Féodalisme*.

That conception of justice is entirely foreign to modern moral and political culture. To the modern mindset, social arrangements are artefacts made by the concerted action of human beings. It is a mistake – a form of fetishism or false necessity – to confuse society with nature and justice with tradition. The various social roles that we play are not given to us from the outside, but created by our joint agency. It is our responsibility to judge them – 'our' here referring to all of us, individuals, stripped of our contingent social roles and attachments and standing as equals in dignity and worth. The dignities, offices and ranks that mark us from one another are all social creatures, humanly made, incidents of our authorship. Prior to them – as judges of them – we stand as 'creatures of the same species and rank, promiscuously born to all the same advantages of nature'.[45]

If that claim is accepted – and it is an essential trait of *modernity* that it is widely so – we have already defined the key term 'due' in the definition of justice in terms of equality; in other words, to treat persons justly is to treat them with equal concern, to take their interests as seriously as anyone else's. What that really implies, however, depends on premises about the good that are highly disputed, primarily as a result of the pluralism of worldviews. However equally concerned we may be about all persons, we do not have a conception of justice before we figure out exactly which *concerns* are at stake. Equality fixes the form of our commitment to justice but it does not define its object. Is the main concern the salvation of souls? Is it hedonic happiness? Is it virtue? Is it freedom? Is it the aggrandisement of the state? Conceptions of justice are at home in visions of the good life; they apply a given view about the good to relations among persons. Paraphrasing Kant, we may say that 'justice without the good is empty; the good without justice is blind'.[46]

In an enlightened despotism or an aristocracy it falls to certain agents – the despot or the *aristoi* – the role of defining what the common good is. Every person is an equal beneficiary of the political order, yet ordinary folk have no business meddling in the affairs of government. That is the office of political leadership, who *serve* the people by mastering the 'mystery of the state' and handling the *arcana imperii*.[47] In such regimes, pluralism about the good is not an issue; for it is generally denied that ordinary – unenlightened – folk is competent to reason about the common good. 'Everything for the people, nothing by the people.'

It is in a political realm where every individual is regarded not only with equal concern but with equal respect as well that the problem of pluralism emerges.

---

[45] John Locke, *Second Treatise of Government*, 2.
[46] Immanuel Kant, *Critique of Pure Reason*, B 75: 'Thoughts without intuitions are empty, intuitions without concepts are blind'.
[47] Peter S Donaldson, *Machiavelli and the Mystery of the State*. A political community where each member is regarded with equal concern and political power (in the classic Weberian sense of 'domination' – see Max Weber, *Economy and Society*, 53) is held by officials – who bear such power *on behalf of* their subjects – is a state in the modern, legal-rational, sense. A state is a centralised and impersonal form of political community, by opposition to the pluralist and personal domination embodied in the concept of lordship. The classic account of the modern state is by Georg Jellinek, *Algemeine Staatslehre*. For contemporary discussion see Quentin Skinner, 'The State'; Bartolomé Clavero, 'Institución Política y Derecho'; and António Manuel Hespanha, *As Vésperas do Leviatã*, 21–41, 295–97, 523–28.

If the affairs of government are subject to 'natural' reason, common to all members of the community, no person or people gathered *en petit comitè* is an *authority*, an agent entitled to play a trump card in the game of free and public discussion. Every reasoned point of view – every conception of justice, with its distinctive comprehensive sources – commands equal respect. Yet we cannot bracket our decision-making about justice while we debate these issues – we cannot 'shove way' the problem of justice. We are immersed in a world that conditions our existence in the six ways examined above and justice bears directly on our situation. It is an eminently practical and public problem, a matter to be decided *by us, hic et nunc*. That is what distinguishes our political predicament from the quite different setting that is the seminar room. Socrates and his interlocutors are on a quest for truth, for the eternal, which is everything that *the world* within which we find ourselves *qua* agents is not. Hannah Arendt articulates the point better than I could:

> The philosopher's experience of the eternal ... can occur only outside the realm of human affairs and outside the plurality of men, as we know from the Cave parable in Plato's *Republic*, where the philosopher, having liberated himself from the fetters that bound him to his fellow men, leaves the cave in perfect 'singularity', as it were, neither accompanied nor followed by others. Politically speaking, if to die is the same as 'to cease to be among men', experience of the eternal is a kind of death, and the only thing that separates it from real death is that it is not final because no living creature can endure it for any length of time.[48]

The 'realm of human affairs' forces upon us the responsibility to make a decision about justice. If we fail to decide, if we do not order our world justly, our interactions are bound to generate chaos – a plainly unjust disorder.[49] Yet any decision appears to require comprehensive grounds that are fiercely contested in the seminar room. The problem that we face is that we are bound to justify rationally each

---

[48] Hannah Arendt, *The Human Condition*, 20. Truth-seeking is in a very deep sense a *permanent quest* for a moment of enlightenment. A notorious feature of the Socratic dialogues is that although Socrates is quite successful in refuting his opponents, he normally turns to myth and metaphor when the stage is set for the presentation of his own views. Philosophy is a process, a permanent search for that which is beyond this world. I am talking here about the intellectual quest for truth, love of knowledge in the proper sense. There is, at least according to some people, a different order of access to the eternal, an order that manifests itself in the supernatural events of revelation, mysticism, and grace. Believers claim that they acquire a *certainty of the heart* – a faith – from those experiences. The moment of truth of the philosopher, on the contrary, is not an event from the outside, a supernatural gift or an epiphany. It is a triumph of his reason, of his reflective labours and, by implication, of the natural capacity of humans to grasp the eternal. Yet the good that philosophy actually delivers is refutation, the destruction of false wisdom, not truth. The object of philosophy is *never* secured.

[49] As Rawls put it in the opening page of *A Theory of Justice*, 3: 'Justice is the first virtue of social institutions, as truth is of systems of thought. A theory however elegant and economical must be rejected or revised if it is untrue; likewise laws and institutions no matter how efficient and well-arranged must be reformed or abolished if they are unjust'. Read narrowly, the remark is aimed at utilitarianism, since it asserts the priority of justice over efficiency and convenience. But there is a deeper point, the opposition between truth and justice and the two distinct spheres or domains – thought/society or eternity/worldliness – in respect of which each of them figures as the supreme virtue.

political decision while at the same time we lack the warrant in reason that only 'the eternal' can supply. The only hope lies in a *freestanding* conception *of justice*, a form of collective life among equals that can stand without the support of controversial foundations. Is that viable? Political liberalism answers in the affirmative. To its claims we turn now.

VIII. Political Liberalism

A *viable* conception of justice that merits the common allegiance of individuals who pay tribute to rival conceptions of the good is bound to fulfill two conditions: it must be (1) political and (2) valuable.

(1) *The conception of justice must be political.* A conception of justice is political – as opposed to comprehensive – if, and only if, (i) it applies to the political realm alone; and (ii) it is ethically neutral. The first condition pertains to the breadth or subject of political justice: it is a conception for the political realm. It furnishes a complete answer to the question – 'How are we to live together?' Yet it contains nothing about what persons ought to do once their duties of justice have been discharged. The second condition pertains to the *depth* or *sources* of political justice: it is not premised on any worldview or comprehensive doctrine, but on principles that, so to speak, take no sides in the dispute among rival conceptions of the good. The values that it embodies are hence *neutral* (or freestanding) in relation to such dispute.[50]

(2) *The conception of justice must be valuable.* A conception of justice is valuable if it *enables* individuals to *act upon* their conceptions of the good in the world. If the price to pay for a freestanding conception of justice is that it forecloses the pursuit of the good life, it is quite obviously valueless – thus unacceptable – to persons. For conceptions of the good are eminently practical and embody all that a person values in life. They concern us as agents, demanding our allegiance in the realm of praxis. A religious person is not merely, or even primarily, interested in debating his faith but in practising it. His religion is irreparably damaged if his religious agency is barred.[51]

---

[50] My claims here owe much to Rawls' account of the 'Idea of a Political Conception of Justice' in *Political Liberalism*, I:2.2. But note that my account of the political realm is different from the Rawlsian idea of the 'basic structure' – contrast supra section 7 with Rawls, *Political Liberalism*, 12, 257–75. The idea of the 'basic structure' as the subject of justice, as presented by Rawls, is only essential to political liberalism once the theme of 'background justice' – see Rawls at VII-4 – emerges in the liberal tradition. Yet in classical liberalism, where justice was worked out from the state of nature, the theme was absent for the most part.

[51] John Rawls, ibid at 177: '[A]ny workable political conception of justice that is to serve as a public basis of justification that citizens may reasonably be expected to acknowledge must count human life and the fulfilment of basic human needs and purposes as in general good, and endorse rationality as a basic principle of political and social organization.'

These conditions furnish a more precise formulation of the challenge at the end of the previous section. Is there a just form of social life that stands without comprehensive grounds and yet enables ways of life grounded in them? What we are asking, to be quite clear, is if there is some value or good that is both neutral and valuable to equally worthy persons. If there is indeed such a value, there is a conception of justice to which every person is bound to pay allegiance. For then it is possible to treat with equal concern every individual according to a definition of what is of concern to individuals that transcends the disputes over values or goods into which such individuals are perennially involved.

Political liberalism argues that there is indeed such a good. It is freedom.[52] Freedom is the functional equivalent in the ethical sphere to money in an exchange economy – a universal medium. Given that we cannot agree on a single worldview, we cannot have a public life, a shared world, informed by a comprehensive conception of the good. It would be a fiction, sustained by the fact of oppression, to maintain otherwise. It follows that we ought to organise our collective life in such a way that each person has the opportunity to form, revise and practise any reasonable conception of the good. That means: 'equal freedom'. To the challenge of proposing a freestanding conception of justice, then, liberalism proposes the liberal principle, stated most eloquently by Stuart Mill:

> [T]he sole end for which mankind are warranted, individually or collectively, in interfering with the liberty of action of any of their number, is self-protection. That the only purpose for which power can be rightfully exercised over any member of a civilized community, against his will, is to prevent harm to others. His own good, either physical or moral, is not a sufficient warrant. He cannot rightfully be compelled to do or forbear because it will be better for him to do so, because it will make him happier, because, in the opinions of others, to do so would be wise, or even right. [...] To justify that, the conduct from which it is desired to deter him, must be calculated to produce evil to someone else. The only part of the conduct of any one, for which he is amenable to society, is that which concerns others. In the part which merely concerns himself, his independence is, of right, absolute. Over himself, over his own body and mind, the individual is sovereign.[53]

Mill's statement sheds light on the close affinity between liberal justice and individual rights, recorded in prominent statements in political theory such as 'rights are

---

[52] The most eloquent statement of this view is undoubtedly John Stuart Mill, *On Liberty*, 13–19. As Jeremy Waldron, 'Theoretical Foundations of Liberalism', 129, puts it: 'Etymology suggests an association between "liberalism" and liberty'; and while the word "liberal" has other connotations – of generosity, broadmindedness and tolerance – is clear enough that a conviction about the importance of individual freedom lies close to the heart of most liberal political positions.'

[53] John Stuart Mill, *On Liberty and Other Essays*, 14. Mill's own reasons to endorse the liberal principle are not exactly those of *political* liberalism. Although he acknowledges the pluralism of worldviews, his case for freedom, ultimately associated with his utilitarianism, is not grounded in the illegitimacy of enforcing a particular worldview but on the experimentalist and individualist benefits of allowing each person the pursuit of the good under their own lights. But the liberal principle has a protean quality that enables its endorsement from other vantage points. That, in turn, encourages a pluralist justification. See Gonçalo de Almeida Ribeiro, 'A Pluralist Case for the Harm Principle'.

best understood as trumps …'[54] or 'each person possesses an inviolability founded on justice …'.[55] For rights are first and foremost regarded as protected choices. To have a right is to be endowed with a measure of freedom. As Jeremy Waldron remarks:

> [T]he attribution of rights to individuals is an act of faith in the agency and capacity for moral thinking of each of those individuals. Rights involve choices and their exercise requires the agent to select which of a number of options he would like to realize in his life and in his dealing with others.[56]

But rights are not just moral notions congenial to liberal justice. As the quotes above emphasise, they operate as trumps or measures of inviolability. In a liberal society, the right has priority over the good, in two senses.[57] First, our shared reasons for respecting individual rights are not drawn from our conceptions of the good, but from the respect we owe others who dissent from us on comprehensive matters. Secondly, we are entitled to pursue our conceptions of the good within the limits of our rights only; as Rawls puts it, 'justice draws the limit, the good shows the point'.[58]

Let us measure our progress so far. By endorsing the familiar arrangements of majoritarian government, rival parties of opinion express mutual respect

---

[54] Ronald Dworkin, 'Rights as Trumps', 153.
[55] John Rawls, *A Theory of Justice*, 3.
[56] Waldron, *Law and Disagreement*, 222.
[57] See John Rawls, *Political Liberalism*, 173–211. A clarification of terms is in order. Moral philosophers (as opposed to political theorists) frequently speak about a priority of the right over the good in at least two ways, that differ in both scope and content from the priority of the right over the good in liberal political theory. (i) *Deontology v Teleology*. In one of its meanings within ethics, the priority of the right over the good implies a distinction between two types of reason for action – moral or categorical reasons, having to do with what is right, and ethical or hypothetical reasons, having to do with one's good. That distinction, associated primarily with Kant, is opposed to the ancient idea, held by both Plato and Aristotle, as well Aquinas, that our reasons for complying with certain key moral duties – of the sort well illustrated by the Ten Commandments – lie in their character as conditions of one's goodness, or rational happiness, or eudaimonia. A landmark in this latter tradition is Socrates' argument in Plato's *Gorgias*, 472e–481b that not only is a wrongdoer wretched, he is even more so if he escapes punishment, for punishment is for one's wrongful soul what medicine is for one's diseased body. In this sense, then, an ethics that gives priority to the right over the good is *deontological*, whereas the ancient ethics that ties morality to happiness is *teleological*. (The liberal principle of priority – 'the right trumps the good' – is an instance or application of deontology in this sense). (ii) *Deontology v Consequentialism*. In a second sense, also within ethics, the priority of the right over the good is a feature of a moral outlook that singles out certain types of action as unconditionally wrong, as Kant believed to be the case with lying, by opposition to an ethics that assesses the rightness of a course of action in terms of its (contingent) consequences. In this sense, an ethics that accords priority to the right over the good is also normally called *deontological*, but it opposes *consequentialism*, not teleology. It is worth noting that utilitarianism – at least in its contemporary form – is anti-deontological, or consequentialist, in this latter sense; *but* it is also deontological (hence anti-teleological) in the previous sense. Indeed, utilitarians hold that we have a categorical duty to either act in order to maximise general welfare (this is the act-utilitarian view) or act in accordance to those rules the generalised compliance with which maximises social welfare (this is the rule-utilitarian view). They do not argue that maximising general welfare is good for one's soul; they argue that it is one's *moral duty* or the *right* thing to do – in that respect they are very much Kantian. See JJC Smart, 'An Outline of a System of Utilitarian Ethics', 30–42.
[58] John Rawls, *Political Liberalism*, 174, 209.

in politics. They reject violence in favour of an equal partnership in government. Majoritarian procedures, however, are fraught with overwhelming difficulties on the very grounds of equal respect upon which they rest. A majority is insufficient; unanimity is the only authentic measure of self-rule, the appropriate foundation of a government not only for the people but by the people as well.

Consider now liberal justice as an alternative to majoritarian government. The liberal argues that all worldviews, all conceptions of the good, should be banned from the public sphere and turned into objects of private concern.[59] The political realm is cleared from all grounds that cannot, by virtue of the fact of reasonable pluralism, acquire a genuinely common character. What remains communal is the joint concern in a measure of freedom enabling the pursuit of a reasonable way of life. Laws securing that are indeed common laws, securing *common values*, even among those who value nothing else in common. It is with respect to such laws that the liberal finds himself in agreement with Rousseau's dictum that 'whoever refuses to obey ... shall be compelled to do so by the whole body' and hence 'forced to be free'.[60] For as liberal laws are consented to by every citizen who regards all others with equal concern and respect, every instance of unlawful conduct is a moment when an individual is governed by his 'particular will contrary or dissimilar to the general will which he has as a citizen'.[61]

Rousseau is the great theorist of self-government in our political tradition. Yet his words, particularly as appropriated by liberalism, are likely to arouse suspicion among committed democrats. The whole point of the liberal principle is that 'equal freedom' is not one among a variety of political options submitted to a vote; it is the alternative to majoritarian government itself, the remedy for the latter's pervasive flaws. But how can a liberal conception of justice be more legitimate on grounds of equal respect than the familiar forms of democratic decision-making which let ordinary people select from the menu of alternative ideals of collective life? It may seem that the liberal principle has dangerously undemocratic implications. True, the way liberal justice is presented, it appears to be somehow rooted in popular consent, and consent is surely a stronger form of popular support than majority. Yet all this liberal business of consent has a somewhat ethereal quality, and appears to be a clever way of cheating the democratic game, where actual participation, dissent and controversy are the order of the day. These worries are well expressed by Jürgen Habermas:

> Liberals have stressed the 'liberties of the moderns': liberty of belief and conscience, the protection of life, personal liberty, and property – in sum, the core of subjective

---

[59] The good is 'privatised' – see Alasdair MacIntyre, 'The Privatization of Good', 345–46 – not in the sense that each person pursues a conception of the good in secrecy, or *deprived* of the company of others through silence and reclusion, but in the sense that propositions about the good – with the exception of freedom, as the universal ethical medium – are cleared from the political realm. Any law premised on a conception of the good is illiberal and disrespectful to dissenters. For the two quite different senses of private versus public alluded to here, see Hannah Arendt, *The Human Condition*, 50–58. See also John Rawls, *Political Liberalism*, 14, 220–22 (distinguishing between 'the social' and 'the political' and between 'public reason' and 'background culture').

[60] Rousseau, *The Social Contract*, Book I, ch 7.

[61] ibid.

> private rights. Republicanism, by contrast, has defended the 'liberties of the ancients': the political rights of participation and communication that make possible the citizens' exercise of self-determination. Jean-Jacques Rousseau and Kant shared the aspiration of deriving both elements from the same root, namely, from moral and political autonomy: the liberal rights may neither be merely foisted on the practice of self-determination as extrinsic constraints nor be made merely instrumental to its exercise. Rawls, too, subscribes to this intuition; nevertheless, the two-stage character of his theory generates a *priority of liberal rights* which *demotes the democratic process* to an inferior status.[62]

Habermas' complaint that liberalism 'demotes the democratic process' because it affirms the 'priority of liberal rights' trades on an ambiguity of the word 'democracy'. We often use the term democracy to refer to real-world majoritarian politics, a particular set of institutional arrangements among which the legal rights to vote and to run for public office are the decisive features; this is the sense of democracy as the form of government or decision-making in society. Direct and representative democracy are alternative types of democracy in that sense. We also, and in a different way, use the term 'democracy' to denote the normative ideal of self-government that informs, and against which we judge the operation of, those arrangements – that a political order should be authored by its members; this is the sense of democracy as an *ideal* of government.

There is an obvious connection between these two senses of democracy, which is that majoritarian practices embody the aspiration of self-government. But they are different senses nonetheless and it is on account of that difference that there is ancient talk, from Aristotle to Polybius, of a degeneration of democratic arrangements into demagoguery or ochlocracy, the predecessor of modern concerns with what Alexis de Tocqueville famously dubbed 'tyranny of the majority'.[63] Tocqueville wrote both that 'the very essence of democratic government consists in the absolute sovereignty of the majority ...' and 'I hold it to be an impious and detestable maxim that, politically speaking, the people have a right to do anything'.[64] It is worth noting that the term 'people' in the last quote is used as a synonym of the term 'majority' in the first one. Tocqueville is here hinting at a potential gap between the ideal of democratic self-rule and the actual operation of democratic institutions. The 'essence of democracy', says Tocqueville, is that the majority is sovereign. What he means by 'sovereign' is that it is the supreme authority, in the sense that it is the highest in the chain of command, that there is no other positive authority to whom one can appeal or turn to if the majority's judgments are thought to be unjust or imprudent. He is using the term 'democracy' in the sense of majoritarian form of government. Something goes wrong, then, when 'politically speaking, the people have a right to do anything'. The qualification 'politically' is crucial; where the form of government is a pure

---

[62] Habermas, 'Reconciliation Through the Use of Public Reason', 127–28 (emphasis added). *But see* Habermas., *Between Facts and Norms,* 457; and Charles Larmore, 'The Moral Basis of Political Liberalism', 622.
[63] Aristotle, *Politics,* Book III, chs VII–VIII; Polybius, *The Histories,* Book VI, ch II.
[64] Alexis de Tocqueville, *Democracy in America,* Book I, ch 15.

democracy, there is no legal authority above the majority of voters. It does not follow, however, that any majoritarian outcome is *legitimate* or morally worthy; there is a danger of political corruption, of tyranny, lurking within democratic procedures. Suppose that a majority votes to enslave the members of a racial minority. We would have no trouble identifying the decision as a perversion of democratic ideals. Voters are not supposed to express their prejudices in a vote; they are expected to express their view about the *common* good, about the proper way of collective life. Each voter has a moral duty to surrender his welfare to the larger synthesis of public interest; that is what we may call the democratic duty of impartiality.

The advocate of majoritarian government has no objection to this line of reasoning. His position is not the crude one that anything the majority wills is legitimate. He argues for the authority of the majority on account of the supposed link between the power to vote and the principle of equal respect. But what is worthy of respect are a voter's reasons and not his preferences. Were majoritarian practices to degenerate on a regular basis into pork-barrelling politics they would fail by the very standards of equal concern and respect that inform their design.[65] In other words, the majoritarian democrat readily acknowledges the two senses of democracy outlined above: there is the form of government organised around universal suffrage and majority rule, on the one hand, and the ideal of self-government, on the other; and, as the latter is the standard to judge the legitimacy of the former, self-interested voting evidences a corruption of the ideal of majoritarian government.

It follows that if voters were as a norm partial about their interests, majoritarian procedures would regularly yield tyrannical outcomes, contrary to the spirit of democracy. Much the same would occur if voters, although normally impartial, in the sense of regarding the interests of their fellow citizens and their own with equal concern, nonetheless expressed in their votes a controversial worldview and the conception of the good tied to it. If, to give one example, a majority of voters shares a single religious creed and votes to establish that creed as the official religion, there are good grounds for a loud protest that something terribly undemocratic has occurred, even though the procedure of decision-making itself is democratic. What motivates the protest is the notion that voters should show not only equal concern for minority interests but also equal respect for minority views; genuine self-government is not a matter of the majority view imposing itself on the ballots but a matter of finding neutral ground among rival conceptions of the common good. That is the reason for abandoning comprehensive ideals and turning to what we called earlier freestanding principles. Voters have hence not merely a duty to be impartial as between theirs and other people's interests but a duty to be neutral about theirs and other people's worldviews as well. We may call it the democratic duty of *neutrality* or tolerance. The perfect democratic practice is that where the

---

[65] Jeremy Waldron, *Law and Disagreement*, 13.

democratic ideal is fully realised, and that requires every voter to carry out his duty of impartiality and neutrality.[66]

The whole point of the liberal principle is of course to show that in circumstances of reasonable pluralism every impartial and neutral person, the sort of person who regards the other with equal concern and respect, will vote for those laws and policies that are entailed by liberal justice. Liberal justice is the only form of collective life that can be held in common by individuals divided by their rival conceptions of the good. It is the order of the people and *by* the people. Liberal rights do not 'demote the democratic process to an inferior status' because they flow from the ideal democratic process against which the legitimacy of actual democratic decision-making is measured. Put differently, if the people could act as a whole – it cannot as a matter of fact – it would settle on liberal justice and rights. It follows that any gap between liberal laws and the actual laws issued by popular assemblies is a symptom of tyranny.[67]

We are now in a privileged position to resolve an ambiguity in the liberal argument. For freedom is a notoriously ambiguous term. In a negative sense, as liberty, it means unrestrained choice or the opportunity to select and commit to one among a variety of possible courses of action. In a positive sense, as autonomy, it means to be governed by a norm that is rationally compelling, that is, the choice that one would make upon reflection.[68] It is obvious that these two senses of freedom are not only different but incompatible if applied to the same choice – for instance, either a person is legally free to get drunk or is freed by a legal ban on alcohol from the 'tyranny of drink'. No wonder that the advocates of negative freedom charge those who embrace positive freedom with despotic or authoritarian proclivities, only to be charged in reply with moral philistinism and passivity.[69]

Yet, notice that liberalism requires a complex combination of both types freedom. On the one hand, a liberal regime secures negative freedom for persons who disagree deeply as well as reasonably about what makes a course of action rationally vindicated – that is the sense in which the term 'freedom' appears in the statement of the liberal principle by Mill. Positive freedom is out of the question, for there is no agreement about what makes a choice right. On the other hand, the legitimacy of a liberal regime does not spring from actual consent but from the rational force of the liberal argument. Self-government is a matter of positive

---

[66] That is the main thrust of these remarks by John Rawls, *Political Liberalism*, 217: '[S]ince the exercise of political power ... must be legitimate the ideal of citizenship involves a moral, not a legal, duty – the duty of civility – to be able to explain to one another on those fundamental questions how the principles and policies they advocate and vote for can be supported by the political values of public reason.'

[67] Rousseau, *The Social Contract*, Book II, ch 3: 'It follows from what has gone before that the general will is always right and tends to the public advantage; but it does not follow that the deliberations of the people are always equally correct.'

[68] In Hegelian jargon, this is the contrast between the 'right of the subjective will' and the 'right of objectivity'. See GFW Hegel, *Elements of the Philosophy of Right*, 158–61.

[69] *Compare* Isaiah Berlin, *Four Essays on Liberty*, 131–72 with Charles Taylor, 'What is Wrong with Negative Liberty?'

freedom, of acting upon individuals on demonstrably right grounds. In circumstances of reasonable pluralism, so argues the liberal, only a regime of negative freedom among equals is rationally warranted. On this view, the apparent paradox embodied in Rousseau's formula – 'forcing the other to be free' – is dissolved; for the consent required by liberalism is not empirical but rational. Since individuals are subject to laws that are rationally warranted, the limits to their liberty that ensue from such laws are not really external but self-imposed limits – autonomous rather than heteronomous.

IX. Pluralism within Liberalism

Whether or not you are convinced that the liberal argument solves the problem posed by the fact of reasonable pluralism, you are likely to have objections to my claim that our political culture is liberal, meaning that the dominant or mainstream view accepts the argument. For in our societies there is political disagreement and there are majoritarian procedures in place to deal with it. If the liberal argument had been accepted, you may argue, surely there would be no parties and no major political dissent, for it is precisely the point of the liberal principle to overcome political dissent.

There is no need to overstate the point. Perhaps political disagreement can be accepted and should be expected when it breaks over those matters of governmenent that Ronald Dworkin would have us call 'matters of policy'.[70] Policy issues, in this stipulated sense, characteristically involve either legitimate preference-based choice over alternative courses of conduct (utilitarian decision-making) or choice over alternative means to attain some given end (instrumental rationality). But there ought to be no disagreement about those matters either to the extent that they touch upon 'matters of principle' or – which amounts to the same – individual rights or claims to equal concern in the distribution of the good and bad things for one's freedom of choice.[71] On matters of justice – in a word – there should be no disagreement, if the liberal principle is indeed accepted. Yet those disagreements are a very significant, and perhaps the most contentious, part of ordinary politics. The conclusion seems to follow: 'Our political culture may perhaps have

---

[70] Ronald Dworkin, *Taking Rights Seriously*, 82–84, 90–100.

[71] I am assuming that 'the trouble with majoritarianism' does not hold with regard to issues of policy. I therefore concede Dworkin's point, ibid at 84–85, that 'law should be made by elected and responsible officials ... when we think of law as policy; that is, as a compromise among individual goals and purposes in search for the welfare of the community as a whole.' But Dworkin elides the distinction between the order of legitimacy – what sort of reason justifies a decision over X, ie a principle or the output of a voting process? – and the order of legality or institutional competence – who or what agent should make the decision? Of course, if it is legitimate to decide X on grounds of policy, the competent decision-maker must be the majority or its representatives; but the opposite is not true, ie it does not follow from the fact that the legitimate decision ought to be made on grounds of principle that it should be trusted to a non-elected and non-accountable decision-maker.

good reason to become liberal; in its current existence, however, it adheres to the superficial conception of equal respect manifested in its commitment to majoritarian government.' It is plainly vital for the argument to succeed to defeat this conclusion.

I assumed earlier that rival parties of opinion in mainstream politics proceed from their respective comprehensive doctrines. But this – as I readily admitted – is not true. The disputes between liberals and conservatives in the United States or social democrats and liberals in Europe are not disputes about the nature and origins of the world, the existence of God, the meaning of life, the relationship between reason and faith, the so-called body/mind problem, or any other similarly comprehensive issue. Not only are such questions not the subject matter of ordinary politics, no answer to them is even part of the premises ordinarily given in support of the less grandiose points regularly argued by mainstream contenders for political office. Mainstream political controversy is considerably narrower and shallower than that.

It is narrower and shallower because the opposing viewpoints proceed from the same premise – 'equal freedom'. Liberalism is the ethos of our political culture. The liberal principle is routinely endorsed by mainstream contenders for power; indeed, that is precisely what places them in the mainstream. What turns them into parties, on the other hand, is the fact that each of them holds on to a different understanding or conception of what it means to live in an order of equal freedom. Conservatives and liberals, liberals and social democrats, contest each other's interpretation of liberal ideals. Liberal justice is hence what WB Gallie calls an 'essentially contested concept'.[72] And since the concept of liberal justice happens to be the idea that gives shape to mainstream politics, it is not surprising that the characteristic form of that politics is a relatively narrow contest among parties of opinion. As Duncan Kennedy puts it:

> Both liberalism and conservatism are ideologies because [their] concrete positions in group conflicts are backed up by more or less elaborate universalization projects, which allow advocates to claim that each of the more particular positions is an instance of correct application of general principles. The general theories can be roughly grouped as relying on rights, morality, and social welfare, and what is most striking about liberalism and conservatism is their virtually total agreement on what those principles are. Both sides favor majority rule, individual rights, and the rule of law; both embrace Judeo-Christian moral codes; both favor a regulated market economy with safety nets.[73]

Kennedy's remarks merit two comments. What he calls an 'ideology' corresponds almost exactly to my use of the neutral term 'party of opinion'. One of the reasons for this terminological difference is that Kennedy emphasises 'the experience of collective commitment, group membership, and common purpose'[74] in political

---

[72] WB Gallie, 'Essentially Contested Concepts'.
[73] Duncan Kennedy, *A Critique of Adjudication*, 47.
[74] ibid at 49.

parties and movements. I suppose those concerns attract the term 'ideology' simply because we associate the term with organised bodies of ideas together with the notion that there is something behind or beyond the ideas that explains their force among a group. But for Kennedy those other elements are the emotional ties of group allegiance (eg, 'Mine is a family of proud liberals'), not the material interests or base logic that according to conventional vulgar and sophisticated Marxist accounts are concealed by the ideas and explain their social currency. For our own purposes, however, that feature of organised partisanship is irrelevant, since we are concerned not with what motivates the loyalty of hardcore or card-carrying liberals and conservatives – the members of 'the group' and bearers of 'the project' – but with the reasons they advance in political debate to conquer the allegiance of 'swing people' or 'potential converts'.[75] It is the universal or rational aspect of ideological struggle – 'X is right' or 'There is a duty to support Y' – as opposed to the personal or emotional aspect – 'We are the people who stand for X' or 'We feel bound to support Y' – that plays out in public, by contrast to intra-party or group-centered, life.[76]

A second comment concerns Kennedy's loose list of the shared premises of liberals and conservatives – majority rule, individual rights and the rule of law; Judeo-Christian moral codes; a regulated market economy with safety nets. I have serious reservations about the status of Judeo-Christian morality as a shared premise, indeed as a premise for either liberals or conservatives. For not only are the positions that many mainstream liberals have adopted during the past half century on issues such as assisted suicide, abortion, same-sex marriage, and euthanasia flatly inconsistent with conventional understandings of Judeo-Christian moral codes; it is even more characteristic of our liberal political culture the leaning of conservatives, in their reaction to liberal commitments on those issues, to eschew straightforward vindication of their own contrary positions in Judeo-Christian moral norms and the conceptions of the good life in which they have been traditionally anchored, and to turn instead to liberal principles, such as democratic legitimacy, the best interests of the child, the rights of the unborn, or the public interest in reproductive sex.[77] What distinguishes the latter from the former is

---

[75] ibid at 44.

[76] Another point to bear in mind is that although Kennedy is right that in ordinary political discourse the term ideology is closely associated with repeat democratic players such as 'liberalism' and 'conservatism', in learned or scholarly discourse the term is more often used as a synonym of what I called a worldview, or at least to the political doctrines that are premised on worldviews. There is, moreover, a third sense in which the term is used, to denote a 'form of consciousness' that is shared across society. Liberalism is an ideology in this latter sense. There are two sub-types of use of the term Ideology (capitalised to distinguish it from other uses) in this sense. As (i) a descriptive term, signifying doctrinal wholes with social currency; and (ii) as a pejorative term, meaning 'false consciousness', within the tradition of critical social theory, beginning with Marx and Engels and extending to Frankfurt School *Ideologiekritik*. For Ideology in this later sense, see Duncan Kennedy (ibid) 290–94; and particularly Raymond Geuss, *The Idea of a Critical Theory*, 4–44.

[77] A piece of corroborating evidence for my claim is the position adopted by the Department of Public Health in the famous case *Goodridge v Department of Public Health* 440 Mass 309 (2003), in which the Massachusetts Supreme Court struck down the legislative ban on same-sex marriage.

their freestanding character; both liberals and conservatives avoid comprehensive grounds.

It is not an accident that Judeo-Christian moral codes have to be dropped out of Kennedy's list of 'general principles'. The various elements in the list, with that one exception, bear close affinities with one another by virtue of a higher principle from which they descend. Contrary to what Kennedy appears to imply, they are not the highest set of premises from which standard liberal and conservative arguments proceed, but mid-level commitments that are grounded in the liberal principle of 'freedom among equals' and the premises of equal concern and respect from where that principle draws its normative force. The axiom of our political culture – what I called earlier its design concept or *idea* – is the liberal argument. Those who reject it – those who insist on proceeding from comprehensive grounds – are marginalised from public life and censored as 'unreasonable', 'radical' or 'fundamentalist'.

Mainstream politics is hence a contest among rival conceptions of liberal justice. Every party within the mainstream endorses the idea of 'freedom among equals' but is committed to a different interpretation of what that principle implies. The disagreements come in all shapes and sizes. The liberalism/conservatism divide is just one rather general and historically stable division of tendencies, co-existing rather than excluding further contestation both within each of the parties and along lines that are not captured by partisan politics. I certainly do not mean to suggest that each of the major parties is committed to a different theory or conception – a unified set of criteria for the proper use – of 'liberal justice'. There is no such thing as the liberal or the conservative *theory* of justice. Conservatism and liberalism are traditions of thinking and partisanship within mainstream politics organised around certain key causes, partly permanent and partly changing, giving occasion to a plurality of different views as to what exactly ties them together and what other commitments they imply. Even within fairly narrow sets of shared premises there is significant disputation; compare, for example, John Rawls' metric of freedom in terms of primary goods with Ronald Dworkin's resource conception of equality, together with their quite distinct views about the importance of desert as a key defining term in a conception of equal concern.[78] The dispute between Rawls and Dworkin is at most a little family quarrel, compared to the theoretical

---

The Court described the Department's defence in the following terms: 'The department posits three legislative rationales for prohibiting same-sex couples from marrying: (i) providing a 'favorable setting for procreation'; (ii) ensuring the optimal setting for child rearing, which the department defines as 'a two-parent family with one parent of each sex'; and (iii) preserving scarce State and private financial resources'. Contrast those reasons with those of § 2357 of the *Catechism of the Catholic Church* and John Finnis, 'Law, Morality, and 'Sexual Orientation'. Another excellent example of liberal recycling is the position of the French Government, as well as ruling of the European Court of Rights, in the case of *SAS v France* [2014] ECHR 695, concerning the compatibility of the ban on full-face veiling with the right to privacy and freedom of religion.

[78] See John Rawls, *A Theory of Justice*, 90–95, 310–15; Ronald Dworkin, 'What is Equality? Part 1'; Dworkin, 'What is Equality? Part 2'. For a useful summary of their positions, see Will Kymlica, *Contemporary Political Philosophy*, 72–76.

disagreements implicit in the debates in the United States about health care, the 'war on terror', or campaign finance; it is a quarrel nonetheless, with likely implications of policy. Even two persons who, say, adhere to the Rawlsian view of justice, are likely to disagree as to what uses of key terms such as 'primary goods', 'the social basis of self-respect', 'the priority of liberty' and other distinct ingredients of Rawls' theory are 'truly', or 'most' or 'genuinely' correct. None of that is surprising, given how abstract those terms are. They are all essentially contested.[79]

At this point it is only fair to level a serious objection against my line of argument. I have portrayed ordinary politics as a contest among different political theories each claiming, on the basis of its own distinctive arguments and chains of reasoning, the true or proper understanding of liberal justice. Any reader familiar with the politics that makes the headlines of daily newspapers is likely to find that suggestion ludicrous. For the propositions that they see advanced by the key players in politics are not comparable to the statements that made Rawls' and Dworkin's names revered in a few lecture rooms and university campuses scattered around the country; what the media report are discrete policy commitments, not articulated theories. Duncan Kennedy appears to have it right once more:

> I doubt that there are 'true', coherent versions of liberalism and conservatism for use in analyzing what lies 'behind' the 'objective' or 'impersonal' rhetoric of judges. While it is always possible that liberal and conservative theorists will find (or have already found without my knowing it) abstract formulations that would allow us to speak of the ideologies as 'requiring' this or that position on a particular issue, this seems highly improbable to me.[80]

Kennedy's point holds equally (if not a fortiori) for other types of political decision-maker, such as lawmakers and voters. I also grant at once that, as I have stated before, there are no such things as the liberal or conservative theories of justice. Yet Kennedy leaves out of the picture the important fact that the shape political positions assume in ordinary political life is largely a function of the type of institutional setting where those decisions are made. The reason why Supreme Court decisions interpreting the most abstract and vague rights provisions of the United States Constitution are backed by relatively better articulated points than presidential campaigns or legislative choices has to do mostly with the fact that the main source of validation of its decisions, particularly when text, precedent and other key legalisms fail, is what I called earlier its 'deliberative transparency'. Judges are pressed to dig deeper, to constitute a 'forum of principle',[81] because they are neither backed by the weight of popular vote nor regularly summoned to appear before the court of popular opinion.[82] Lawmakers, on the contrary, earn their

---

[79] WB Gallie, 'Essentially Contested Concepts', 169.
[80] Duncan Kennedy, *A Critique of Adjudication*, 52.
[81] Ronald Dworkin, *A Matter of Principle*, 33–71.
[82] Again, a good example is *Goodridge v. Department of Public Health* 440 Mass 309 (2003), a case that the Court acknowledged as one of 'first impression', ie the type of case where legalist garments are worn and mostly off-season.

legitimacy by appealing to popular votes, and voters are not expected to disclose their reasons; 'theory' will be of little help as they try to win the voters' confidence. The more deliberative a decision-maker is, then, the more the positions it assumes will approach the standard of 'theory'.[83]

That brings us to the last leg of our journey. The defining feature of our political culture is that it is *liberal*. It rules out comprehensive views. Yet fierce political disagreement persists on account of the essentially contested character of 'freedom among equals'. This is not a negligible issue. Conservatives do not want to live in a society governed by liberal laws and vice-versa; each party of opinion is quite serious about its views on justice and rights. More importantly, the fact of liberal pluralism – the existence of rival conceptions of liberal justice – poses a challenge to the entire project of basing the moral authority of law on the rational allegiance of its addressees. For substantive and interminable disagreement persists even as liberalism has taken charge of political life. Each conception of liberal justice is a reasonable yet partisan view, opposed by equally reasonable and partisan views. It follows that any attempt to turn one such conception into the governing conception implicates the very apparatus of oppression against which the liberal impulses of tolerance, humility and broadmindedness are directed. Equal respect compels an honest acknowledgement that a large measure of loud and significant contestation over the substance of political choices is ineliminable.

It should be apparent that the predicament of liberal pluralism is homologous to the predicament generated by the reasonable pluralism of worldviews. For the very principle of equal respect which made plain the need to find common ground among a wide variety of reasonable comprehensive views applies equally to a liberal political culture in which there is a plurality of conceptions about just what that common ground is supposed to be. Put briefly, just as no one is rationally entitled to impose his comprehensive view on reasonable dissenters, no one is entitled to impose his version of liberal politics on reasonable dissenters. A liberal regime embodies the very conundrum – the fact of reasonable pluralism – that it is construed to avoid; liberals and conservatives, social democrats and liberals, are the living evidence of that.

Once the fact of liberal pluralism is acknowledged, it is clear that all avenues of substantive resolution are foreclosed. If we cannot agree on a freestanding conception of justice, there is no thinner set of principles for social life to which we

---

[83] To be sure, that does not show that the decisions are then *caused* by the theories, instead of the theories being rationalisations of previously held commitments. But one is entitled to say that an argument is an instance of rationalisation, denial, or false consciousness only if the conclusion does not follow, or is not uniquely warranted by, the premises upon which its vindication is consciously and publicly sought. That must be showed on a case-by-case basis, instead of a priori and from the armchair. One is entitled to suspect appearances, to adhere to the 'school of suspicion' and bear the torch that was once held by its masters, Marx, Freud and Nietzsche – *cf* Paul Ricoeur, *Freud and Philosophy*, 32–42 – but not to dismiss appearances altogether! Kennedy might agree, given his quick and justified rejection of global internal skepticism about adjudication as law-application and endorsement of what he calls the 'minimal critique' of the legislation/adjudication distinction. See Kennedy, *A Critique of Adjudication*, 33–34, 85–92; Kennedy, 'A Semiotics of Legal Argument', 321–23.

can turn. At this juncture, the focal point migrates from substance to procedure, from justice to authority. For if there is no rational agreement over the content of what legal theorists call 'primary norms', the norms that govern interactions among individuals, the main question concerns what 'secondary norms', norms that empower officials to *select* from a menu of controversial primary options, are justified.[84] Whose authority is legitimate?

Substantive or primary norms, even if they merit the rational allegiance of everyone subject to them, do not fall from the heavens. Someone must be in charge of *positing* them. In any legal system, therefore, there will be primary *and* secondary norms – norms of conduct and norms empowering officials to posit norms of conduct[85] – and it is something of a conceptual truth about law that the latter have legal priority over the former, because in order for a substantive norm to be a legal norm there must be a law-maker empowered to posit it. If every agent were committed to challenge the validity of a legal enactment on account of it not being right or just, we would literally not have law. A legal system whose meta-norm – what HLA Hart famously called the 'rule of recognition' – is of the form 'Rex is the highest law-making agent and his enactments have the force of law, so long as he issues the right laws' is no legal system at all; for under such a meta-norm, Rex quite literally cannot posit any binding laws.[86]

All of this concerns the order of *legality*. Within the legal system, secondary norms have priority over primary norms. But if there is rational agreement over a set of primary norms – if there is a single reasonable view of what justice entails – the legitimacy of the laws issued by the legally empowered authorities obviously depends on whether such laws conform with justice or not. What I want to stress is that agreement as to what ought to be posited as a matter of law turns the question of law-making authority or institutional competence into the secondary

---

[84] The distinction between primary and secondary norms I take from HLA Hart, *The Concept of Law*, 91–100. (Hart uses the term 'rule', instead of norm.) It is true that not all secondary norms empower individuals or bodies of individuals to posit primary norms – that is the defining feature of what Hart calls 'rules of change'. Hart mentions two further types of secondary rule: rules of recognition, which specify the criteria that a rule must satisfy in order to be a legal rule, and rules of adjudication, empowering individuals or bodies of persons (ie, judges) to settle legal disputes. What distinguishes rules of change from rules of recognition is that the former concern prospective law-making, whereas the latter permit the identification of already posited law. Both types of rule fall within in the broader category of law-making constitutive norm or *norma normans*.

[85] The expression 'norms of conduct' lends itself to misunderstanding. Not all primary norms are norms of conduct in the sense of either commands, permissions, or prohibitions. Some are power-conferring rules – '*facilities* for realizing [the] wishes of [persons]', writes Hart (ibid) at 27 – such as the rules constituting the Hohfeldian powers of offer and acceptance, the conveyance of property, the power of attorney, or express and implied consent. See WN Hohfeld, 'Some Fundamental Legal Conceptions as Applied in Judicial Reasoning', 44–54. What is characteristic of primary rules (or *norma normata*) is that they are oriented towards the primary task of law, which is to govern interactions among individuals, as opposed to the instrumental or second-order task, performed by secondary rules (or *norma normans*), of constituting mechanisms for the issuance of primary rules.

[86] See Joseph Raz, *The Authority of Law*, 3–53.

or instrumental problem of figuring out what agent is most likely to make the right calls.

The matter is far more serious when there is no agreement about what makes a law right or just. For then the choice of a law-making authority is no longer merely an issue about the order of legality, about who should be empowered to make law, but an issue about the order of *legitimacy* as well, about who should be entitled to decide what should count as just or right. The fact of liberal pluralism converts the question of institutional competence into the primary question – the central focus of contention. In Jeremy Waldron's apt vocabulary, debates over institutional competence reach beyond 'outcome-related' reasoning – who is best placed to get it right? – to the realm of 'process-related' reasoning – who has the right to say which view prevails?[87] As he puts it elsewhere:

> Since people hold different views about rights and since we have to settle upon and enforce a common view about this, we must ask: 'who is to have the power to make social decisions, or by what processes are social decisions to be made, on the practical issues that competing theories of rights purport to address?[88]

Let us ponder for a while Waldron's question – 'who is to have the power to make social decisions?' Perhaps the most straightforward answer – the one that Waldron favours – is this: let 'the people whose rights are in question have the right to participate on equal terms in that decision'.[89] We have examined at length the trouble with that answer. It should therefore not come as a surprise that Ronald Dworkin, proceeding from the very same premise of equal concern and respect, protests against the 'crude statistical view of democracy on which that argument is based'.[90] To be sure, Dworkin's argument is a bit more circuitous than that. He does claim that 'a majority decision is legitimate ... if it is a majority within a community of equals'.[91] He argues as well that decision-making over certain matters of principle or justice cannot be credited to non-electorally accountable officials:

> [D]emocracy would be extinguished by any general constitutional change that gave an oligarchy of unelected experts power to overrule and replace any legislative decision they thought unwise or unjust. Even if the experts always improved the legislation they rejected – always stipulated fairer income taxes than the legislature had enacted, for example – there would be a loss in self-government which the merits of their decisions could not extinguish.[92]

---

[87] Jeremy Waldron, 'The Core of the Case Against Judicial Review', 1369–76.
[88] Jeremy Waldron, *Law and Disagreement*, 243–44.
[89] ibid.
[90] Ronald Dworkin, *Freedom's Law*, 365. Obviously the debate is about democracy as an *ideal* of government – government by the people – not about democracy as a form of government – the government of the many. Dworkin surely does not deny that he argues against democracy defined as that form of government where – as Tocqueville put it – the majority is sovereign; his point is that democracy in this latter sense undermines authentic democratic self-government.
[91] ibid at 364.
[92] ibid at 32.

This is immediately followed by a qualification:

> It is different, however, when the question is plausibly raised whether some rule, or regulation, or policy itself undercuts or weakens the democratic character of the community, and the constitutional arrangement assigns *that* question to a court.[93]

If an argument can be plausibly made that some legislative decision 'undercuts or weakens the democratic character of the community' it is fine to assign that question to a court – it is even the most appropriate thing to do.[94] That is as broad a condition as I can imagine. For any question of principle – of justice and rights – can be persuasively presented as a plausibly urgent matter of self-government. No wonder that each constitutional tradition has its own conception (its own list, structure, interpretation) of 'fundamental rights'. Think about social and economic rights – rights to shelter, food, health care, education and social security. These rights necessarily impinge upon the sorts of questions that Dworkin appears to have in mind when he speaks of the danger of democratic extinction at the hands of an 'oligarchy of experts'. Yet many of the constitutions that originated in what Samuel Huntington called the 'Third Wave of Democratization' entrench numerous such rights.[95] When one actually gives it some serious thought, it looks as though the protection of at least some of those rights – to a shelter and to food, for starters – is plausibly more urgent than the right to desecrate the national flag.[96]

Waldron and Dworkin personify the two poles of a spectrum of positions on the problem of institutional competence. Both argue their cases on the basis of the same premise: the respect that individuals merit *qua* bearers of deliberative capacity. Waldron thrusts the sword of 'decisional comprehensiveness' and Dworkin deflects the strike with the parry of 'deliberative transparency'.[97] They are the high-theory characters in an endless confrontation in our political culture

---

[93] ibid at 32.

[94] Dworkin appears to restrict his point to legal systems whose constitutional arrangements assign certain matters of principle to a court; indeed, the last clause of the quoted statement looks entirely defensive. Yet he is keen on advocating the merits of bills of rights and judicial review in legal systems in which such devices have been traditionally rejected – see Ronald Dworkin, *A Bill of Rights for Britain*. It is worth recalling that in the United States the constitutional arrangements do not, as a matter of fact, assign explicitly any power of judicial review to the courts. The Supreme Court itself has controversially inferred the power of judicial review from the federal constitution in *Marbury v Madison*, 5 US 137 (1803). Dworkin would no doubt insist that where he speaks of 'constitutional arrangements' assigning questions for judicial review he means not only the constitutional text but respectable judicial interpretive construction as well. That broadens his exception to majority decision even more. He is effectively claiming that courts should: (i) take charge of *any* matters of principle; (ii) that can be *plausibly* construed as possessing some democratic urgency (iii) so long as they can *plausibly* interpret the constitutional arrangements as assigning such questions to them. And just in case the last condition fails, he proposes constitutional reforms, such as a bills of rights for Britain.

[95] Samuel P Huntington, 'Democracy's Third Wave'.

[96] *Texas v Johnson*, 491 US 397 (1989); *US v Eichman*, 496 US 310 (1990).

[97] The thrust and parry metaphors are borrowed from Karl Llewellyn, 'Remarks on the Theory of Appellate Decision and the Rules or Canons about How Statutes are to be Construed'.

about legitimate authority. The debate is polarised by strong majoritarian conceptions, on the one hand, and strong conceptions of judicial review, on the other. One side of the debate accuses the other of committing itself not to democracy but to juristocracy, subjecting the people to the rule of aristocrats in robes; the other responds that democracy is not the unrestrained rule of the majority, the populist spectacle of demagogues and mobs. The debate is as *interminable* as the debate about justice and rights.

2
Kant and the Will Theory

I. Why Kant?

In a classic book sitting at the intersection of the jurisprudential and biographical genres, William Twinning reports Karl Llewellyn's outburst against a student presentation on the role of the is/ought distinction in Kant's philosophy: 'What the hell', yelled an incensed Llewellyn, 'has Kant to do with my course on jurisprudence?'[1] This incident alerts me to the perils of selecting Kant as the protagonist of this chapter. Out of caution, let me sketch immediately four main reasons why Kant's political and legal theory merits such high honours in the history of liberal legalism.

(1) *Kant's role as a mediator.* From one view of the cathedral, there are two types of character in the history of Western philosophy: the troublemaker and the mediator. The troublemaker disrupts the dominant modes of thinking and enhances the differences and tensions among rival positions, while the mediator works to bring peace and reconciliation through a larger synthesis or 'supersession' of contradiction. A recurrent pattern of intellectual development is for mediators to respond to large outbursts of 'creative destruction' and then for troublemakers to undermine the most ambitious and powerful mediating syntheses. Hume was the paradigm troublemaker, shaking violently the naïve confidence of his enlightenment forerunners. Kant was a mediator – at least vis-à-vis Hume – busy with the task of restoring the credibility of reason and empirical knowledge without falling into the 'dogmatic slumbers' of Leibnizian rationalism from which he was, on his own admission, awakened by the Scotsman. He was not enough of a mediator for Hegel's taste, however, who carried the synthesis even further and repudiated Kant's admonitions against metaphysical knowledge. Finally, two of Hegel's nemeses, Kierkegaard and Nietzsche, were troublemakers of the highest sort; both scorned Hegel's confidence in the sublation (*Aufhebung*) of contradiction, as well as his related pretence of absolute knowledge or capital-S 'Science'.

The same pattern of troublemaking/mediation recurs within political philosophy generally and classical liberalism in particular. Hobbes, Locke and Rousseau were all troublemakers, challenging in complicatedly related ways the undisputed reign of 'natural law theory' of the type whose greatest names

---

[1] William Twining, *Karl Llewellyn and the Realist Movement*, 117.

were Aquinas and the late Scholastics, first, and later Grotius and Pufendorf. Mill, von Humboldt and Constant were mediators, more concerned with expounding the virtues of classical liberalism than with embracing the family quarrels in which their forerunners had been embroiled. Yet in the tradition of classical liberalism the key mediating figure is Kant. In Kant's political theory, we find Locke's natural rights, Rousseau's general will and Hobbes' concerns with sovereignty and legality. But Kant stresses the ways in which these ideas can be tied together and support each other, disregarding the visceral conflicts that arose from their original elaborations. Kant's political and legal writings embody an implicit synthesis of the creative acts of his predecessors. Consequently, when we study Kant's political thought we are studying the way in which a large number of classical liberal ideas were worked out in conjunction and packed together more or less coherently.

(2) *Kant's political liberalism.* Liberalism is the predicate of an ethically neutral form of collective life. It is a basis for political allegiance among individuals divided by rival worldviews. The argument for liberalism – for ethical neutrality – is that, in Rawls' words, it establishes 'fair terms of social cooperation' among persons whose worldviews are irreconcilable.[2]

Not all arguments for liberalism proceed from these worries. Most defences of liberalism, in fact, proceed precisely from deeper ethical and metaphysical premises. Charles Larmore puts the point judiciously, relying on Kant and Mill as examples:

> Kant and Mill sought to justify the principle of political neutrality by appealing to the ideals of autonomy and individuality. By remaining neutral with regard to controversial views of the good life, constitutional principles will express, according to them, what ought to be of supreme value throughout the whole of our life. There are important differences between the two ideals of autonomy and individuality, but they agree in the following demand (which I shall call 'individualism'): They urge that we should always maintain only a contingent and never a constitutive allegiance to any substantial view of the good life …[3]

The idea is that there is a set of ethical premises – 'individualism' – that informs Kant's and Mill's commitment to ethical neutrality in the political realm. It is a defence of liberalism built upon comprehensive grounds. That commitment is quite different from the freestanding liberalism that I take to be immanent in the political culture of contemporary democracies.

The existence of two distinct grounds – comprehensive and freestanding – speaks to liberalism's remarkable *protean* quality. It suggests that a liberal regime can claim the allegiance of those who reject the 'individualist' outlook portrayed by Larmore. Indeed, if my argument in the previous chapter is correct, that is exactly the way in which our political culture came to take

---

[2] John Rawls, *Political Liberalism*, 3.
[3] Charles Larmore, 'Political Liberalism', 342–43.

a liberal form. To say that Kant's political theory is the best prototype of the liberal idea that informs our political culture, then, is to say that the idea of freestanding liberalism can be traced back to Kant. The problem is that we have come to associate the distinction between comprehensive and political or freestanding liberalism with John Rawls' contributions to political theory in the late twentieth century, particularly his claim that his conception of 'justice as fairness' is 'political not metaphysical'.[4] Both Rawls and Larmore describe 'enlightenment liberalism' as a comprehensive doctrine, and assign Kant a prominent place within its ranks.[5] They believe that political or freestanding liberalism, which they oppose to the comprehensive liberalism of Kant, is a relatively recent invention.[6]

The case against that view will be made later. But it is worth advancing the conclusion straight away. There are two ways of reading the *Doctrine of Right*, Kant's most important work on political and legal theory.[7] One way is to read it as part of the larger whole of Kant's practical philosophy, starting with the *Groundwork of the Metaphysics of Morals* (*Groundwork*). There is no doubt that Kant encourages that reading, both in his anticipatory remarks about the *Metaphysics of Morals* (MOM) in the preface to the *Groundwork* and in the preface to the *Metaphysics of Morals* itself.[8] Since that is the most obvious starting point from which to approach Kant's political theory, it is from there that we shall proceed as well. But as Allen Wood, Thomas Pogge and Thomas Grey[9] – each of them from a different perspective – have noticed, Kant also

---

[4] Rawls, 'Justice as Fairness: Political not Metaphysical'. See also Rawls, *Political Liberalism*, 77–78. For an example of an area (education) in which, according to Rawls, comprehensive and freestanding Liberalism may break apart, ibid at 199–200.

[5] Rawls, *Political Liberalism*, 37, 78, 145; Larmore, 'Political Liberalism'.

[6] There is a fair amount of ambiguity about this point in Rawls' work. It is not entirely clear if for him what is recent is the idea of political liberalism or the full conscious awareness of that idea. Larmore's position, on the contrary, is explicit: he associates political liberalism with the rise of the romantic critique of the comprehensive 'individualist' doctrines of Locke, Kant and Mill. See Larmore, 'The Moral Basis of Political Liberalism', 604–05.

[7] The *Doctrine of Right* (*Rechtleshre*) is the first part of *The Metaphysics of Morals*, the first edition of which is from 1798. Kant published that first part independently a year earlier, in 1797, under the title 'The Metaphysical Foundations of the Doctrine of Right' (*Metaphysischen Anfangsgründe der Rechtslehre*). That work was followed, only a few months later, by 'The Metaphysical Foundations of the Doctrine of Virtue' (*Metaphysischen Anfangsgründe der Tugendlehre*).

[8] Kant, *Groundwork to the Metaphysics of Morals*, 5 (Ak 4:391): 'Intending to publish some day a metaphysics of morals, I issue this groundwork in advance. Indeed there is really no other foundation for a metaphysics of morals than the critique of a pure practical reason …'. Kant, *The Metaphysics of Morals*, 3 (Ak 6:205): 'The critique of practical reason was to be followed by a system, the metaphysics of morals, which falls into metaphysical first principles of the doctrine of right and metaphysical first principles of the doctrine of virtue'.

[9] Allen Wood, 'The Final Form of Kant's Practical Philosophy'; Thomas Pogge, 'Is Kant's *Rechtslehre* Comprehensive?'; Thomas C Grey, 'Serpents and Doves: A Note on Kantian Legal Theory'. Both Pogge and Grey draw an explicit parallel between Kant and Rawls. Two points should be stressed. The first is that the view that political or freestanding liberalism can be traced back to Kant is quite controversial; for an explicit rejection, see Jeremy Waldron, 'Kant's Theory of the State', 198 fn 16. The second point is that among those who read Kant's political theory as a – or also as a – freestanding doctrine, there is

encourages a reading of the *Doctrine of Right* as an autonomous theory, relatively independent of the premises laid down in the *Groundwork*; and in his political and historical essays the severance of the political theory from the moral philosophy is even more pronounced. There are reasons internal to Kant's philosophy for this ambiguity. The most important aspect to retain, however, is that Kant's *Doctrine of Right* was read by many of his contemporaries, including many jurists who borrowed heavily from it, as a freestanding doctrine. It is the fact that Kant's political theory was embraced by many non-Kantians and even anti-Kantians that above all else establishes Kant as the first protean liberal.

To sum up: Not only did Kant produce a synthesis of the different strands of classical liberalism, he also made it attractive to non-liberals as a 'political not metaphysical' doctrine.

(3) *Kant's devotion to detail*. A third reason for picking Kant as a protagonist is that he is much more concerned with the concrete implications of political principles than any of the other well-known classical liberals. Unlike Mill's 'harm principle' or Locke's account of natural rights – all endowed with the abstraction, vagueness and ambiguity that have turned them into the most fertile grounds for over two centuries of wildly diverse readings – Kant descends often into considerable detail, indeed the nitty-gritty of legal doctrine. Here is a more or less random list of topics that he addresses in his most important work on legal and political theory, the *Doctrine of Right*: original acquisition of property, adverse possession, the enforceability of gifts, the right to a good name after death, the regime of a sales contract, the conveyance of property, the effects of bona fide third party acquisition, the nature of marriage, parental power and master–servant relations. There is a notorious concern in Kant's political theory with the connection between abstract principles and concrete rules and doctrine. In that respect, his aim is closer to that of late-scholastic and early modern natural law writings – of Molina, Lessius and Covarruvias, on the one hand; of Grotius, Pufendorf and Wolff, on the other – than to the classical liberals. His aim is the system and his model is the treatise, whereas Locke, Rousseau, von Humboldt and Mill expressed their political views in essays.[10]

Moreover, Kant borrows heavily from the very natural law writers of whom, on conventional accounts of his moral philosophy, he was the most severe of

---

a wide variety of views as to how it should be read and in what way the doctrine is 'political not metaphysical'. My own view is close to that of Wood and Grey.

[10] Kant undoubtedly wrote many political essays, all of them quite important in their own right. The two indispensables are from 1793 and 1795, respectively: Kant, 'On the Common Saying: This May Be True in Theory, But It Does Not Hold in Practice' (henceforth: 'Theory and Practice'); and Kant, 'Toward Perpetual Peace'. With that said, the status of *The Doctrine of Right* as the cornerstone and mature version of Kant's political theory is uncontroversial. See Paul Guyer, *Kant*, 262; Allen Rosen, *Kant's Theory of Justice*, 2.

all critics.[11] What Kant does most of the time is to pick a well-established doctrine or rule and argue that it derives from the 'Universal Principle of Right' and the a priori principles of the civil condition that together encapsulate the gist of his classical liberal synthesis. We shall see later that Kant's principled justification for the particular rules that he endorses is often unconvincing. That he set himself the task of forcing the received legal tradition into the Procrustean bed of classical liberal principles is nonetheless of central importance. For not only did he make his work of immediate usefulness to the jurists, he also paved the way for doctrinal reforms operated *sub rosa* on the ground that those rules that did not sit well with the liberal principles allegedly immanent in the law were 'anomalies' or 'exceptions', subject to a canon of 'narrow construction'.

Kant operated hence not only (i) a synthesis of classical liberal ideas and (ii) a protean transformation of classical liberalism into a freestanding doctrine, but (iii) a synthesis of classical liberalism and the received legal-doctrinal tradition as well. That brings us to the fourth, and last, reason for taking Kant's political theory as the prototype of liberalism.

(4) *Kant's influence on legal thought*. In the introduction to the *Doctrine of Right*, Kant draws a sharp distinction between what the law is and what the law ought to be:

> [The jurist] can ... state what is laid down as right (*quid sit iuris*), that is, what the laws in a certain place and at a certain time say or have said. But whether what these laws prescribed is also right, and what the universal criterion is by which one could recognize right as well as wrong (*iustum et iniustum*), this would remain hidden from him unless he leaves those empirical principles behind for a while and seeks the sources of such judgments in reason alone, so as to establish the basis for any possible giving of positive laws (although positive laws can serve as excellent guides to this). Like the wooden head in Phaedru's fable, a merely empirical doctrine of right is a head that may be beautiful but unfortunately it has no brain.[12]

Taken at face value, these words suggest an exclusive concern with the reform of positive law and a strict division of labour between the jurist and the philosopher. Kant is interested in law according to 'judgements in reason alone', as opposed to 'what is laid down as right' according to 'empirical principles'. No doubt these are important statements within the premises of Kant's critical

---

[11] See, eg, Gustav Radbruch, *Rechtsphilosophie*, §3, 1; Roscoe Pound, *Jurisprudence*, I, 500–03. Two accounts that are more nuanced and, in my view, persuasive are: Franz Wieacker, *A History of Private Law in Europe*, §20, I.3; Hans Welzel, *Derecho Natural y Justicia Material*, 207–14. Paul Guyer, *Kant*, 239, remarks as well that 'Kant borrows much of the trappings of his account from the modern traditions of natural law ...'. Guyer repeats the point – ibid at 260 – in his discussion of Kant's theory of property: 'Kant's account of property rights is densely argued, detailed, and couched in the language of European legal traditions ...'. Of course, there is no denial that Kant was highly critical of the method of natural law theory, which he saw as hopelessly eclectic, stained by empiricist casuistry, and lacking in a solid foundation.

[12] Kant, *The Metaphysics of Morals*, 23 (Ak 6:229).

philosophy. Throughout his work, Kant insists on a fundamental distinction between a priori and a posteriori cognition. A posteriori judgements are true or false as a matter of experience whereas a priori judgments are true or false independently of experience. The judgment that 'I am typing this manuscript on a black keyboard' is true or false depending on whether that is actually the case. On the contrary, for Kant, the judgment that 'promises ought to be kept' is true or false irrespective of any contingent assertion about what *is* or *is not* the case; for no fact either about the world, such as a storm or currency devaluation, or about a human being's desires, wishes or wants, such as my desire to keep my promise, justifies the proposition that promises *ought* to be kept.[13] It follows, of course, that the method to establish non-empirical truths is quite different from the empirical procedure of observation and description.

---

[13] It may be useful to expand on this point, which is key to understand Kant's philosophical system. Kant draws two distinctions about judgments – see Kant, *Critique of Pure Reason*, A 6–11/B 10–14. The first – the analytic/synthetic distinction – concerns the relationship between the subject and the predicate of a proposition. Analytic judgements are those in which the predicate is contained in (or is a defining feature of) the concept of the subject – eg, 'an unmarried person is single'. Synthetic judgments are those in which the predicate is new to (or adds new information about) the subject – eg, 'Plato wrote *The Republic* and *The Laws*'. The second distinction – the a priori/a posteriori distinction – concerns the grounds upon which it is legitimate to assert that a judgment is either true or false. As the text above explains, a posteriori judgements are true or false by virtue of the facts of experience whereas a priori judgements are true or false non-experientially. When we combine the two distinctions, we obtain the following matrix.

Figure 2.1 Matrix of Kantian judgements

Types of judgement	A priori	A posteriori
Analytic	Definitions	N/A
Synthetic	Truth of reason	Empirical truths

All analytic judgments are true or false a priori, for the very good reason that if a predicate is contained in the concept of the subject, it is by virtue of the concept's content alone and not any empirical fact. Conversely, all a posteriori judgements are synthetic, because information about what is or is not the case cannot tell us anything about the essential or necessary features of a concept that we already possess, describing instead a contingent relationship between the subject and the predicate (eg, 'My cat is fat' – nothing about the concept of cat implies the quality of being fat). The more interesting and puzzling category, and the one that underpins Kant's original contributions to philosophy, is that of synthetic a priori judgements. These are judgements in which the predicate is not contained in the concept of the subject but which nonetheless are true non-experientially. How is that possible? If reason itself prompts us to believe in certain non-redundant or non-analytic judgements without any experiential warrant. For Kant, all moral truths are of this latter type. But what he calls the 'fundamental principles of the metaphysics of nature' – the principles that, Kant claims, underscore natural science – are also synthetic a priori truths. Chief among them is the principle of causation – that every event has a cause or that Nature is governed by law-like regularities. Kant took Hume to have shown that no amount of empirical observation can establish that as a truth, because finite experience can only establish contingent truths, not necessary ones; our belief in regularities, according to Hume, is a matter of

Unlike the jurist, whose primary task is to 'state what is laid down as right', the philosopher must show what *ought* to be laid down as right. No (true) list of rules or doctrines in force in a particular jurisdiction meets that epistemic standard.

Yet these methodological differences can be deceiving. While Kant argues from a priori principles, the particular doctrines and rules that he proposes are, as I stressed earlier, very often the ones contained in the legal treatises of his time, particularly the massive works on *Naturrecht* that had currency in eighteenth-century Prussia. He admits as much as relying on them as heuristic devices when he states, in the quotation above, that 'positive laws can serve as excellent guides' in the deductive labours of the philosopher.[14] Kant's originality lies in providing a new foundation for these rules; he brings his protean classical-liberal synthesis to bear on established legal doctrine. Old wine is thus poured into new bottles.

Now if we assume that Kant had a good measure of success, as judged by his contemporaries, in showing plausible relations of logical entailment among the a priori principles of his political theory and the various bits of legal doctrine that figure in the *Doctrine of Right*, it is easy to see why it was equally plausible for the jurists of his own time and especially the next generation to argue that from their opposite 'empirical' standpoint as students of positive law they were led, by 'logical necessity', to Kant's liberal principles. That is exactly, as we shall see later, what Friedrich Carl von Savigny, the major figure of the German Historical School and by most lights the greatest jurist of the nineteenth century, claimed. Savigny is an important character in the history of freestanding liberalism because as a historicist and romantic opponent of 'abstract reason' and 'natural law' he was at once the least likely follower of Kant and one the leading architects of classical private law. Therefore, a strong affinity between Kant's and Savigny's work on law corroborates both the proposition that the *Doctrine of Right* had the protean quality that enabled it to reach beyond the small cadre of loyal Kantians, among which Savigny was surely not to be ranked, and that Kant, through Savigny and his closest disciples, made an impact on nineteenth century legal thought. Of course, it remains to be explained what attracted Savigny and other jurists to

---

'nature' (or habit), not reason. Kant's reply was that our perception of the world is mediated by the laws of reason, causation being one such law. The mind is hence, on Kant's account, not a blank slate but constitutive of empirical knowledge.

[14] To the contemporary mind, the association made in the text between natural law treatises and positive law is puzzling. To Kant's mind, though, there is not much to distinguish them, either because he derided the natural law tradition as 'empirical' or because the 'law of reason' of the treatise writers was increasingly posited everywhere in the form of codifications sponsored by enlightened rulers.

Kant's *Doctrine of Right* and why it was important in the history of liberalism that the Kantian prototype went through a legal metamorphosis. That is the theme of the next chapter.

By way of summary, and in order to keep the thread, let me line up the four reasons for taking Kant's political and legal theory – and particularly the *Doctrine of Right* – as the prototype of liberalism. First, Kant is a mediator of the tensions within classical liberalism; his theory is a synthesis. Secondly, Kant endows classical liberalism with the protean quality that enabled it to figure as a freestanding doctrine; his theory is 'political not metaphysical'. Third, Kant articulates the connections among classical liberal principles and detailed doctrine; his theory is concrete. Fourth, Kant assimilates a good deal of the positive law of his time; his theory lent itself to juristic appropriation.

I take this opportunity to issue a fair warning to the reader. The style of this chapter is markedly different from the previous one. The focus shifts away from large ideational structures to the intellectual event that is Kant's political theory. I mean to offer as plausible the proposition that Kant picked a number of classical liberal ideas, loaded them onto a single ship, unmoored the ship from the dry dock of his general philosophy – and that the vessel, sailing a variety of non-linear routes, was seized by Savigny and his disciplines, and through them the nineteenth-century jurists on both sides of the Atlantic. 'Kant,' wrote Roscoe Pound, 'formulated the idea of legal justice which was accepted in jurisprudence throughout the nineteenth century.'[15] Much of this and the following chapter is an attempt to dissect and vindicate Pound's insight. In order to even begin to accomplish anything like that, we need to descend into a careful exegesis of Kantian texts. The journey will take us, so to speak, far from the main road, but only because it is the safest course to our final destination.

II. Kant's Moral System

In the preface to the *Groundwork*, Kant announced his intention to 'publish same day a metaphysics of morals'. The point of the former work is to establish the 'supreme principle of morality' upon which the latter – the system of moral duties – is grounded. Since Kant's terminology, beginning with the very term 'metaphysics', is unusual and obscure, it is worth examining the explication provided in the introduction to the *Groundwork*.[16]

---

[15] Roscoe Pound, *Jurisprudence*, I, 51. Not everyone agrees that Kant's political and legal writings are important – see Hannah Arendt, *Lectures on Kant's Political Philosophy*, 7–9. Arendt believes that they are minor works, obscure and inconsistent, produced by a burnt-out and nearly senile Kant. My view is that the source of the inconsistencies and obscurities lies elsewhere, namely in Kant's complicated relationship to the 'modern natural law' or 'law of reason' tradition of the seventeenth and eighteenth centuries.

[16] Kant, *Groundwork of the Metaphysics of Morals*, 1–6 (Ak 4:387–92).

'Metaphysics' is Kant's word for a body of synthetic a priori knowledge, a set of propositions that are true neither by virtue of experience (a posteriori knowledge) nor by virtue of analysis (analytic knowledge) but on the strength of reason's constitutive power. Kant distinguishes the formal science of logic, which studies the laws that govern the structure of thought, from what he calls 'material' sciences, concerned with the laws that govern 'determinate objects'. The *summa divisio* of material sciences is rooted in a distinction among two classes of objects – nature and freedom. The matter of physics is 'nature', the world outside of us; the matter of ethics is 'freedom', the world within us. The former concerns what there *is*, while the latter pertains to what we *ought* to do.

Each of the two main sciences – physics and ethics – has a 'pure' or 'rational' part, a metaphysics, and an empirical part. Physics is hence divided into a metaphysics of nature, which contains propositions such as 'every event has a cause', and experimental science, which contains propositions such as 'water boils at 100ºC'. Likewise, ethics is divided into what Kant calls 'morals' and 'practical anthropology'. The former establishes what we ought to do *qua* rational beings whereas the latter studies human nature or what we are as participants in the natural world. Practical anthropology informs us about certain features of human beings that matter in the application of moral principles – eg, that we feel sexual desire or that our bodies are vulnerable to harm – but they themselves furnish no moral duties. What we ought to do is, strictly speaking, a 'pure' or 'rational' or 'a priori' matter.[17]

With these distinctions in mind, it is easy to understand what Kant means by the 'supreme principle of morality' and a 'metaphysics of morals'. The former – the subject of the *Groundwork* – is the basic test or ground of all moral duties, the ultimate standard of moral validity; the latter, which Kant works out in the MOM, is the set of duties that proceed from the 'supreme principle', and since they all proceed from that one principle, they form a unified system. The MOM is hence the natural outgrowth of the preliminary material assembled in the *Groundwork*.

In the preface to the MOM, published a dozen years after the *Groundwork*, Kant maintains this basic scheme. The first sentence brings out nicely Kant's love of consistency and symmetry:

> The critique of practical reason was to be followed by a system, the metaphysics of morals, which falls into metaphysical first principles of the doctrine of right and metaphysical first principles of the doctrine of virtue. (This is the counterpart of the metaphysical first principles of natural science, already published.)[18]

We are hence encouraged to read the MOM as an extension of the *Groundwork*. In the previous section, I said that there is an alternative reading, one that takes the first part of the MOM – the *Doctrine of Right* – to form what John Rawls would

---

[17] See Kant, *The Metaphysics of Morals*, 10 (Ak 6:216–17).
[18] ibid at 3 (Ak 6:205).

have us call a freestanding political theory. But my case for that reading has to be built on a considerable amount of exegesis and argument that is yet to be produced. At this point, let us focus our attention on the reading that Kant himself explicitly suggests: the MOM is the offspring of the *Groundwork*.

The basic fact about the structure of the MOM that any plausible interpretation is bound to explain is the division into two independent 'doctrines' – Right (*Rechtslehre*) and Virtue (*Tugendlehre*). The subject of the first doctrine is the set of duties that ought to be coercively enforced through the external mechanisms of a state and a legal system, whereas the second doctrine concerns those duties the enforcement of which is left to the internal mechanisms of good will and conscience. It is obvious why the first part, the *Doctrine of Right*, is ordinarily identified as the locus of Kant's political (and legal) philosophy. What is less clear is what exactly explains the Right/Virtue dichotomy within morality and, specifically, why certain duties are (or ought to be) enforced, while others are not.

Morality, on Kant's account, requires from us observance of our duties out of respect for the moral law, that is to say, that we act not only in conformity with but also from duty. As Kant puts it, action in accordance with duty is *legal*, action that is motivated by duty is *moral*. A moral agent is moved by the *ethical incentive* of respect for the moral law.[19] Obviously, it is impossible – in fact, self-contradictory – to coerce an agent to act from duty or morally. For when we attach penalties to the violation of a norm, we are furnishing a class of agents with a prudential incentive – fear of coercive sanctions – for the observance of the norm. The goal is to bring at least some of those agents who are not motivated by respect for the moral law to perform their duty out of fear. But that implies that they will not act from duty but merely in conformity with duty. There is a logical limit implicit in the concept of Right – of the set of duties that are subject to coercive enforcement; they cannot bring any agent to be truly moral, because they encourage compliance from what Kant calls 'juridical' motives.

What in principle distinguishes one set of duties – Right – from the other – Virtue – is hence not their content but their scope and source; Kant says that the former are 'external' whereas the latter are 'internal'. Duties of Right, premised on prudential incentives, apply to our actions, the external manifestations of our agency, and have a source external to our will, namely both the coercive apparatus of the state and the irrational promptings of fear.[20] Duties of virtue, on the other

---

[19] Kant, *Groundwork*, 11–12, 13–14 (Ak 4:397–99, 400–01); Kant, *The Metaphysics of Morals*, 20–21, (Ak 6:218–29).

[20] Fear is an 'external' incentive, in Kantian parlance, because it stems from the irrational and empirical side of our nature, as opposed to our rational side. Were human beings purely rational, as opposed to animal creatures gifted with reason, they would experience no fear, indeed no incentives foreign to the moral law. That is precisely why Kant distinguishes the moral law from the categorical imperative and explains that the latter is the particular form in which the former appears to us, as creatures who are imperfectly rational. In the *Groundwork*, 25 (Ak 4:414), Kant writes that 'imperatives are only formulae expressing the relation of objective laws of volition in general to the subjective imperfection of the will of this or that rational being, for example, of the human will'.

hand, apply to what Kant calls our 'maxims', which comprise both our actions and the (internal) reasons or motives for adopting them, and have as their exclusive and necessary source our will. Right/Virtue, in a word, is not, at least prima facie, a distinction between two independent lists of duties but between two different forms of lawgiving. This reading finds some support in the text: 'The doctrine of right and the doctrine of virtue are therefore distinguished not so much by their different duties as by the difference in their lawgiving, which connects one incentive or the other with the law'.[21]

A major problem with this reading is that although Kant does say that all duties of right are also duties of virtue, the opposite is not true. The duty to perform a contract, Kant tells us, is a duty of right, which means that it can be coercively enforced. It is also a duty of virtue, in the sense that we ought to perform our contracts out of respect for the moral law that commands us *pacta sunt servanda*.[22] Yet many duties that figure in the MOM – eg, the duty not to commit suicide, the duty not to lie, the duty to cultivate one's talents, the duty to be beneficent, the duty not to defame others, or the duty to seek 'social intercourse' – are of virtue only. By excluding them from the *Doctrine of Right*, Kant flags that it is inappropriate to enforce them through external incentives. The point is not that they cannot be enforced *qua* ethical duties (only *qua* juridical ones), because external incentives are suitable to secure the legality but not the morality of human agency. That is, as we have seen, a logical consequence of the Kantian concepts of morality and Right – it is by definition impossible to coerce an agent to be moral. There is, however, no logical inconsistency in externally enforcing mere compliance with the duties listed above. Why are those duties, then, excluded from the province of *Recht*?

A prominent Kant scholar who endorses the reading of the MOM that we are examining, Paul Guyer, offers the following explanation:

> The only thing that all ... duties of virtue have in common is that for either practical or moral reasons they cannot be coercively enforced through a legal system of justice. The duties of virtue turn out to be simply all of our moral duties that are not properly subject to coercive enforcement ...[23]

But this argument is hardly persuasive. It is not believable that the major division of duties within Kant's moral system rests on a loose and undisclosed cluster of

---

[21] Kant, *The Metaphysics of Morals*, 21 (Ak 6:220). See also, ibid at 145 (Ak 6:379): 'the system of the doctrine of duties in general is now divided into the system of the *doctrine of right* (*ius*), which deals with duties that can be given by external laws, and the system of the *doctrine of virtue* (*ethica*), which treats of duties that cannot be so given ...'.

[22] ibid at 21 (Ak 6:220): 'all duties, just because they are duties, belong to ethics; but it does not follow that the *lawgiving* for them is always contained in ethics: for many of them it is outside ethics. Thus ethics commands that I still fulfill a contract I have entered into, even though the other party could not coerce me to do so; but it takes the law (*pacta sunt servanda*) and the duty corresponding to it from the doctrine of right, as already given there'.

[23] Paul Guyer, *Kant*, 242.

'practical and moral' reasons; Kant must have believed that some fundamental principle underpins the structure of the MOM, for unlike empirical knowledge, which 'cannot be divided completely' and 'cannot be brought into the system', it is characteristic of metaphysical knowledge, as purely rational knowledge, that it takes the form of a 'system outlined a priori'.[24] In other words, metaphysical knowledge is essentially systematic, meaning that the arrangement of a metaphysical treatise is not generated by convenience of exposition but by the *inherent* structure of the subject matter. Recognising precisely that point, Guyer continues:

> Does this mean that there is no systematic basis for the inclusion of duties on Kant's list of ethical duties or duties of virtue? Not at all. If we recall the classification of duties that Kant used to illustrate the first two formulations of the categorical imperative … we will see that Kant's list of both the duties of right and the duties of virtue has a deep foundation in his fundamental principle of morality, and that the justification but also the restriction of the permissibility of coercion that he uses to distinguish between the two classes of duties is also deeply based on that fundamental principle.[25]

The classification of duties to which Guyer refers appears in the *Groundwork*, when Kant puts the so-called first formulation of the categorical imperative – the principle of the universal law – to work. After stating the second or 'law of nature' variation of the principle of the universal law – 'act as if the maxim of your action were to become by your will a universal law of nature' – Kant proceeds to 'enumerate a few duties in accordance with the usual division of them into duties to ourselves and to other human beings and into perfect and imperfect duties'.[26] It is immediately clear what distinguishes duties to ourselves from duties to others.[27] The perfect/imperfect duty dichotomy, on the other hand, is obscure and intriguing. Kant remarks in a footnote to the quoted passage that 'I understand here by a perfect duty one that admits no exception in favor of inclination'.[28] This is a careless definition, for it is clear upon inspection that in Kant's view morality never tolerates compromises with inclination – that is exactly why the fundamental principle of morality is the categorical imperative.[29] What Kant means, as he later acknowledges, is that perfect duties are 'strict or narrow', in the sense that they specify a type of action that is either commanded or prohibited (eg, 'you ought not commit suicide'), whereas imperfect duties are 'wide', setting a goal or aim

---

[24] Kant, The Metaphysics of Morals, 3 (Ak 6:205).
[25] Guyer, *Kant*, 242.
[26] Kant, *Groundwork*, 31 (Ak 4:421).
[27] The category of 'duties to ourselves' may be a source of perplexity. As Kant defines them, those are duties that we *qua* imperfectly rational (ie 'sensible') creatures owe ourselves *qua* bearers of reason ('intelligible' creatures), such as the duty not to commit suicide in order to avoid misery and pain. In Kant's terminology, duties to ourselves are duties that I owe to 'the humanity in my own person'. See Kant, *The Metaphysics of Morals*, 173–74 (Ak 6:418).
[28] Kant, *Groundwork*, 31 fn (Ak 4:424).
[29] The textual warrant for this point is overwhelming. See, eg, Kant, *Groundwork*, 17–18, 35 (Ak 4:404–05, 425–26); Kant, *The Metaphysics of Morals*, 153–54 (Ak 6:390–91).

that the agent ought to pursue as circumstances allow and taking into account the other strict and wide duties incumbent on him (eg, 'you ought to develop your talents').[30] Combining the two distinctions among types of duty – ourselves/others and perfect/imperfect – we obtain the following matrix:

Figure 2.2 Typology of Kantian duties

Types of duty	Ourselves	Others
Perfect	I	II
Imperfect	III	IV

In the *Groundwork*, Kant offers one example of each of the four types of duty:

(I)   You shall not commit suicide to relieve your pain and misery;
(II) You shall keep your promises;
(III) You shall not let your talents rust;
(IV) You shall be beneficent and assist the needy ones.[31]

Each of these maxims is a duty, according to Kant, because we will them to become a universal law of nature; they have the law-like form – universality – which he takes to be the distinctive property of moral imperatives. But why exactly is it that we will these maxims to become universal laws and not their opposites? The objects of our will are the ends that prompt us to act (health, pleasure, salvation, etc) or the means required to achieve those ends (medicine, sex, prayer, etc); the value of the means is relative to the ends and the value of the ends is relative to our preferences or, in Kantian jargon, 'inclinations'. Yet, when we ask ourselves whether we will a given maxim to become a universal law, we are in fact asking if there is any end that is universally, absolutely or intrinsically valuable – 'something the existence of which in itself has an absolute worth, something which as an end in itself could be a ground of determinate laws ...' . That end – if there is one – is the matter that is revealed by, or is embodied in, the form of morality. Since the objects of our inclinations have a conditional or relative worth – they are what I or you value – Kant believes that the only candidate for the status of an objective end

---

[30] Kant, *Groundwork*, 33 (Ak 4:424); see also, Kant, *The Metaphysics of Morals*, 153–54 (Ak 6:390–91): 'The wider the duty, therefore, the more imperfect is a man's obligation to action; as he ... brings closer to narrow duty ... so much more perfect is his virtuous action'. (Emphasis removed.) Not everyone agrees that the perfect/imperfect duty distinction is identical, or at least comprises, the narrow/wide duty distinction: see, Allen D Rosen, *Kant's Theory of Justice*, 92–103. Another distinguishing mark of perfect vis-à-vis imperfect duties is that while adopting maxims that are contrary to the former in the World of the Universalised Maxim – the hypothetical world where we assume that our maxim is a 'universal law of nature' – generates a 'contradiction in conception', maxims that are contrary to the latter generate the weaker form of contradiction that Kant calls 'contradiction in will'. For an elaborate explication of these terms, see Christine M Korsgaard, 'Introduction to Immanuel Kant, Groundwork of the Metaphysics of Morals', xviii–xxi.
[31] Kant, *Groundwork*, 31–33 (Ak 4:421–23).

is the human being itself, as a being capable of making and valuing choices – as a freedom:[32]

> [T]he human being and in general every rational being exists as an end in itself, not merely as a means to be used by this or that will at its discretion; instead he must in all his actions, whether directed to himself or also to other rational beings, always be regarded at the same time as an end.[33]

It is from this inquiry into a putative 'objective end' that Kant derives the famous second formulation of the categorical imperative, the formula of humanity: 'So act that you use humanity, whether in your own person or in the person of any other, always at the same time as an end, never merely as a means.'[34] He treats this formula as an alternative expression, substantive instead of formal, of a single fundamental principle of morality. From the formal notion of universality, then, Kant purports to have derived an account of the point or matter of morality: to preserve and to promote human beings *qua* free or choice-making-and-choice-valuing beings.[35] *That* is the end that we will when we commit to act (as we ought to) on maxims as if they were laws of nature.

Paul Guyer claims that the duties to preserve freedom, both in ourselves and in others, are perfect duties, duties to either take or (more often) to refrain from taking a specified course of action, such as 'no suicide' and 'no deceitful promising'; those duties are externally enforceable, hence duties of Right. The duties to promote freedom, both in ourselves and in others, are, on the contrary, imperfect duties, duties to pursue certain goals or aims as circumstances allow, such as 'develop your talents' or 'be beneficent'; those duties are not externally enforceable, because they are too vague to serve as standards to adjudicate the legality of the specific instances of human conduct that are ordinarily described in a legal complaint.[36]

In favour of this reading, I take it that he can marshal two key textual fragments from the MOM. The first is Kant's statement of the Universal Principle of Right, the foundation of the *Rechtslehre*: 'Any action is right if it can coexist with everyone's freedom in accordance with a universal law, or if on its maxim the freedom of choice of each can coexist with everyone's freedom in accordance with a universal law.'[37]

---

[32] An obvious alternative candidate for an 'objective end' is happiness. However, Kant thinks that happiness, as an empirical end, is both too indeterminate to serve as a guide for moral action and intrinsically amoral (evil-doing can generate happiness). See Howard Williams, *Kant's Political Philosophy*, 30–31. For an elaborate explication of Kant's argument concerning the 'end in itself', see Allen W Wood, *Kantian Ethics*, 85–95.

[33] Kant, *Groundwork*, 37 (Ak 4:428).

[34] ibid at 38 (Ak 4:429) (emphasis removed).

[35] See Paul Guyer, *Kant*, 245.

[36] ibid at 242–45. As a consequence, Guyer marginalises what I believe to be the core of the *Doctrine of Right*, Kant's account of 'acquired right' or property very broadly defined to include what civilian jurists call 'civil law'. 'We can add one further consideration that we can derive from Kant's discussion of "private right", that is, the right to property ...' Guyer, ibid at 243–44.

[37] Kant, *The Metaphysics of Morals*, 24 (Ak 6:230).

On the reading of the MOM that we are examining, this principle appears to be a narrowed down version of the categorical imperative, one that applies not to our maxims – our reasons for action – but to our 'acts'. Acts being external and maxims being internal, the Universal Principle of Right is wisely confined within the domain where juridical incentives can operate. But it embodies the same *matter* as or is inspired by the point of morality as a whole: the furtherance of freedom in all its instances – every human being – equally (ie, according to a universal law).

Put briefly, Virtue and Right share the same point, although they deploy different means and operate at different levels – conscience and good will, in the former's case, force and legality, in the latter's. The reason why not every duty is brought within the province of *Recht* is that it is practically impossible to exact externally compliance with imperfect duties; as Kant puts it in the introduction to *The Doctrine of Virtue* – and here lies the second bit of text that lends support to Guyer's reading – 'ethical duties are of wide obligation, whereas duties of right are of narrow obligation'.[38] What makes this proposition true is not a moral argument – that it is wrong or illegitimate to enforce wide duties – but a practical one, that only strict or narrow duties lend themselves to external enforcement.

Although this reading fits the introduction to *The Doctrine of Virtue*, it renders the MOM as a whole unintelligible. Two points should put my case to rest. First, the text following the introduction to *The Doctrine of Virtue*, which Kant labeled 'Doctrine of the Elements of Ethics', is divided into two parts, one concerning duties to ourselves and the other duties to others. The first of those parts is in turn divided into a section on 'perfect duties' and one on 'imperfect duties', in flat contradiction with the remark in the introduction that all ethical duties are wide or imperfect. Even among the list of duties of virtue to others, which is not organised around the perfect/imperfect duty dichotomy, we find quite a few narrow duties. Some examples of narrow or perfect duties that fall exclusively within the domain of ethics are: the prohibition of suicide (DV §6), the prohibition of masturbation (DV §7), the prohibition of gluttony and intoxication (DV §8), the prohibition of defaming others (DV §43) and the prohibition of ridiculing others (DV §44).

Two things about the complete list in the text of the *Tugendlehre* are worthy of notice. The first is that very few if any duties to ourselves are juridical. Even the apparent exceptions – eg, prostitution (DR §26), fornication, homosexual intercourse and bestiality (DR §24) – are often truncated; for instance, while Kant argues that a promise to render sexual favours in exchange for money is unenforceable, he does not claim that prostitution should be criminalised. More importantly, Kant often chooses to present as wide duties that could easily be broken down into a series of narrow duties. The most striking example is the duty to be beneficent; granted that it may be hard to enforce that duty, it is not hard to generate a list of

---

[38] ibid at 153 (Ak 6:390) (emphasis removed).

affirmative duties – eg, a duty to provide a meal to a starving person – based on the general and wide duty to be beneficent. The key question is why Kant chose not to proceed in that way.

The second point against Guyer's reading is that in the appendix to the introduction to *The Doctrine of Right*, Kant examines the category of 'ambiguous right', which he describes as 'right in a wider sense'. There he mentions two such types, equity and necessity. It is the former that interests us on this occasion.

> *Equity* (considered objectively) is in no way a basis for merely calling upon another to fulfill an ethical duty (to be benevolent and kind). One who demands something on this basis stands instead upon his right, except that he does not have the conditions that a judge needs in order to determine by how much or in what way his claim could be satisfied.[39]

What Kant is arguing here is that equitable claims are both claims of right and unenforceable claims. Objectively, he says, they belong to the domain of *Recht*; but because equitable norms are standards instead of formally realisable rules – wide instead of narrow – they fail to meet the conditions required for external enforcement. This claim is unintelligible if we single out enforceability as the property that grounds the Right/Virtue dichotomy. For what Kant is arguing here is that although external enforcement is limited to strict duties, the objective basis of *Recht* does not lie in that condition. In sum: one thing is the ground of enforcement of a given duty, the other is the duty's enforceability – the former is an *ought*-question while the latter is a *can*-question. Of course, the entire category of Right would collapse if all or most duties that are 'objectively' of Right were wide duties, for that would mean that those duties that ought to be externally enforced are practically unenforceable; fortunately, in Kant's view, equitable rights are the exception to the norm of enforceability of claims of right.

What we are looking for is the 'objective basis' of Right implicitly invoked by Kant in the quoted passage. It must be found in an alternative interpretation of the Universal Principle of Right, one that reads more into it than just a narrowed-down version of the categorical imperative. The perfect/imperfect duty dichotomy is a side show to the main show that is the MOM. Paul Guyer is, of course, too perceptive and honest a reader to be oblivious to the textual evidence that I have assembled. In a remarkable turn of events, marked by the words 'The problem is just that Kant does not restrict his complete list of duties of virtue to [imperfect duties]', he writes:

> Kant does not spell out a general theory of why none of the duties of virtue are coercively enforceable; and it seems as if there would be a variety of reasons why specific duties of virtue would not be so enforceable. ... [T]he coercive enforcement of any obligation requires both a logical and/or a physical possibility of successful coercive enforcement as well as a moral possibility, capacity, or title for such enforcement.[40]

---

[39] ibid at 27 (Ak 6:234).
[40] Paul Guyer, *Kant*, 246.

This is a retreat back to the initial claim that there is no systematic basis for the Right/Virtue distinction, a position that is suspicious for the reasons I pressed forward then. Yet Guyer repents again:

> [Kant's] general argument in behalf of the coercive enforcement of juridical duties ... turns ... on the claim that hindrances to hindrances of freedom are 'consistent with freedom in accordance with universal laws'. This is clearly an attempt to provide the *moral* title for coercive sanctions.[41]

The excerpt quoted by Guyer is from the introduction to *The Doctrine of Right*, more precisely §D, labelled 'Right Is Connected with an Authorization to Use Coercion'. The full text reads:

> Resistance that counteracts the hindering of an effect promotes this effect and is consistent with it. Now whatever is wrong is a hindrance to freedom in accordance with universal laws. But coercion is a hindrance or resistance of freedom. Therefore, if a certain use of freedom is itself a hindrance to freedom in accordance to universal laws (i.e., wrong), coercion that is opposed to this (as a *hindering of a hindrance to freedom*) is consistent with freedom in accordance with universal laws, that is, it is right. Hence there is connected with right by the principle of contradiction an authorization to coerce someone who infringes upon it.[42]

Apart from being a good illustration of the pain and suffering that students of Kant have to endure to figure out his writings, this passage makes a dubious but simple analytical point. It begins with the proposition that resistance to an obstruction promotes the obstructed effect, which Kant takes to be a priori true. It then adds that an action is wrong if it cannot coexist with everyone's freedom in accordance to universal laws, which follows from Kant's definition of 'right' as the quality of an action that can so coexist. Now if coercion is deployed to obstruct a wrong, it is by definition right, for in blocking an action that is inconsistent with freedom in accordance to universal laws it is consistent with such laws itself.[43] The happy result is that by definition – or as a matter of analytical truth – duties of right furnish a title for coercive enforcement.

What this argument patently does not provide, contrary to Guyer's claim, is a moral title for coercion. It cannot provide any of that, for it is presented as a definitional truth; it merely establishes that the authorisation for coercive enforcement is contained within the concept of Right or duty of right. It justifies neither Kant's list of duties of right, nor the very existence of the category 'Right'. That justification lies in Kant's Universal Principle of Right, which forms the foundation of the *Rechtslehre*. Yet on Guyer's account of that principle – that it is a narrowed down version of the categorical imperative – it clearly justifies the coercive enforcement of *all* duties of virtue, for as all moral duties on Kant's account

---

[41] ibid.
[42] Kant, *The Metaphysics of Morals*, 25 (Ak 6:231).
[43] The point is dubious because coercive sanctions against wrongful acts typically do not 'block' the commission of the wrong but either supply a remedy to the victim or punish the wrongdoer (or both). Kant's triumphant analytical truth is a sleight of hand!

direct human agency to the promotion and preservation of freedom, the coercive enforcement of any such duty is plainly consistent with a universal law of freedom. Therefore, Guyer's reading and all similar readings fail to make sense of the MOM. I am going to argue for a different reading, one that takes the domain of *Recht* to be conceptually distinct although functionally intertwined with the domain of morality. In order to establish that, however, we need a brief excursus into Kant's account of moral value in the *Groundwork*.

III. Moral Value in the *Groundwork*

Kant ends the preface to the *Groundwork* with a note on the method he follows in Sections I and II, which consists in 'proceed[ing] analytically from common rational cognition to the determination of [the] supreme principle [of morality]'.[44] He wants to show that the categorical imperative is implicit in intuitive or ordinary moral judgment. That accounts for the title of Section I: 'Transition from Common Rational to Philosophic Moral Cognition.'

The data about 'common rational moral cognition' – a big phrase that means ordinary moral judgement – from which Kant departs is the proposition that nothing in the world 'could be considered good without limitation except a good will'.[45] 'Good' is an appraisive concept that we use to judge all sorts of things – eg, 'Peter is a good piano player' or 'this medicine is good for headaches' – but there is something conditional or relative about most such uses. To be a good piano player is to be good at (or relative to) a certain activity; a good medicine is good to relieve pain or cure an illness. One indication of the merely conditional worth of these things is that there is a range of synonyms for the word 'good' in the examples – eg, 'dexterity' or 'adroitness', in the first example, and 'suitable' or 'fit for purpose', in the second. Even things that are ordinarily taken to be good for their own sake – health and happiness, for instance – are not unconditionally good; a sadistic torturer may be happy and yet evil.[46] The only thing in the world that is unconditionally or absolutely good, according to Kant, is a good will.

To say that the only unqualified good in the world is a good will is evidently not a definition of 'goodness' or moral value, since the phrase 'good will' uses the term that requires definition. Kant is concerned at this stage not with the content but with the object of moral value, that is to say, with the things of which it is appropriate to say that they either have or lack unconditional goodness. His claim is that good in that sense is a predicate of the will, a proposition that has a series of negative implications.[47] First, what he calls 'gifts of nature' (eg, courage and perseverance) and 'gifts of fortune' (eg, power and riches) have no 'inner unconditional

---

[44] Kant, *Groundwork*, 5 (Ak 4:392).
[45] ibid at 7 (Ak 4:393).
[46] See Howard Williams, *Kant's Political Philosophy*, 30.
[47] See Allen Wood, *Kantian Ethics*, 31–33.

worth'; courage or money can be put to either good or evil uses.[48] Likewise, the effects accomplished through one's actions, including those for the sake of which the action is undertaken, are of themselves neither good nor evil, however desirable or agreeable (or their contrary) they may be.[49] A failed attempt to rescue a drowning person is no less worthy of moral appraisal than a successful attempt, so long as the rescuer in each situation evinced an equal degree of commitment.[50] The efficacy of one's actions is a fortuitous matter, foreign to one's will.

Satisfied that he has established the will as the bearer of moral value, Kant proceeds to 'explicate the concept of a will that is to be esteemed in itself'.[51] He turns at this juncture to the concept of duty because 'it contains that of a good will', by which he means that we rely on assertions about duties to issue moral judgments. Four options are open to an agent subject to duty: (i) acting against duty; (ii) performing a duty for the sake of some further end; (iii) performing a duty from inclination; and (iv) acting from duty. Since Kant's purpose is to explicate the concept of good will, he quickly sets aside (i) and (ii). He says it is 'much more difficult', although critical, to distinguish (iii) from (iv). He argues from examples, such as the following:

> [To] preserve one's life is a duty, and besides everyone has an immediate inclination to do so. But on this account the often anxious care that most people take of it still has no inner worth and their maxim has no moral content. They look after their lives *in conformity with* duty but not *from duty*. On the other hand, if adversity and hopeless grief have quite taken away the taste for life; if an unfortunate man ... wishes for death and yet preserves his life without loving it, not from inclination or fear but from duty, then his maxim has moral content.[52]

Kant is not suggesting that there is something reproachable about having an inclination to survive or that we have to feel miserable and suicidal in order to be moral.[53] His point is that our duty to preserve life is not conditioned by our natural inclination to survive; feeling suicidal is never a good reason for committing suicide. Quite the contrary, it is on such occasions, when the incentives of inclination and duty pull in opposite directions, that the character of one's will is tested. That is why the concept of moral value profits from an analysis of the concept of duty – we understand what makes a will good when it resists an inclination that prompts it to flout duty. Morality or goodness is the property of a will that is moved to do what is right even when that implies acting against inclination.

---

[48] ibid at 7–8 (Ak 4:393–94).
[49] ibid at 8, 13 (Ak 4:394, 399–400).
[50] Kant adamantly supports the proverb 'the road to hell is paved with good intentions'. A good will is an *acting will*. '[A good will is] not, of course, a mere wish but [a] summoning of all means insofar as they are in our control.' Kant, *Groundwork*, 8 (Ak 4:394).
[51] ibid at 10 (Ak 4:397).
[52] ibid at 11 (Ak 4:397–98).
[53] See Christine M Korsgaard, 'Introduction to Immanuel Kant, Groundwork of the Metaphysics of Morals', xiii, fn 6.

To have a duty, therefore, is to have a necessity to act (or refrain from acting) in certain ways irrespective of the contingencies of one's inclination; and since it is characteristic of laws that they are necessary (law-like), Kant defines duty as 'the necessity of an action from respect for law',[54] where the 'law' in question is a law of the will instead of some other type of law, say of logic or of nature. What he means is that duty – the law of the will – is not conditioned by inclination.

From his analysis of the concept of a good will, Kant manages to locate the source of moral value in a specific incentive for action distinct from and defined by contrast to inclination: respect for law. Yet the argument appears to provide no clue as to what is the content of such law. Kant, however, takes no further step before asking: 'what kind of law can that be, the representation of which must determine the will ... in order for the good to be called good absolutely and without limitation?'[55] As the moral law governs the will irrespective of – and even against – inclination, Kant sidesteps the inquiry into the content of the law and claims that morality's universal form furnishes a test for our maxims of action. Morality requires that we act from principles whose validity is not borrowed from inclination, that is, unconditioned by our feelings, wishes, desires and the like. That leaves no other option but 'the conformity of actions as such with universal law'.[56] That is, I know if my maxim – the principle that guides my action – is the maxim of a genuine moral duty if I have reason to hold on to it when I deprive myself of my contingent inclinations, ie when I will it to become a universal law. That is the only possible basis for morality, once all inclination effaces, as the analysis of the concept of good will showed it must.

We have seen earlier how Kant works out a substantive moral principle – the formula of humanity – from the formal notion of universality. Put briefly, the argument is that because morality requires us to act on universal principles, we are morally bound to will universal ends; and since the only end that is universal is the human being as an end-setting and choice-valuing being, our moral duty is to always treat our own and other people's humanity as an unconditional value. At the end of Section II of the *Groundwork*, Kant supplies a third formulation of the moral law or the categorical imperative – the formula of autonomy.

When we make it a maxim to act on some inclination – eg, I will cheat on today's match so as to achieve glory – we make an instrumental use of our reason. There are certain means required to achieve the proposed end and reason instructs us – in the form of hypothetical imperatives – about such means. Moral duties, however, are not based on inclination. They are embodied in maxims that are universally valid, meaning that they are valid irrespective of – and even against – one's inclination. That is why the supreme principle of morality or the moral law is the *categorical* imperative – it is not conditioned by the contingencies of inclination. But what can be the source of an imperative that is valid universally?

---

[54] ibid at 13 (Ak 4:400).
[55] ibid at 14 (Ak 4:402).
[56] ibid.

Kant argues that it can only be the will or reason in its practical use, not as an instrument of inclination but as a giver of universal laws.[57] Our moral duties, then, are the ends that reason sets for us, as opposed to the ends that stem from inclination and for the sake of which we borrow reason's resources. Although we tend to view morality as imposing external limits on our will, Kant's striking argument is the opposite: the rule of the passions is *heteronomous*, because it subjects the will to ends external to itself; the rule of morality, on the contrary, is *autonomous*, because it is authored by the will.[58] The third formulation of the categorical imperative is hence: 'act only so that the will could regard itself as at the same time giving universal law through its maxim'.[59] In this way, 'the will is not merely subject to the law but subject to it in such a way that it must be viewed as also giving the law to itself ... of which it can regard itself as the author'.[60]

Now, when a person acts on a maxim that passes the test furnished by the formula of the universal law, the end that he seeks is universally valid. It is not borrowed from inclination but from practical reason.[61] That means that the person is acting on a principle that is not hers but everyone's. In a community where every person is a good will, therefore, every individual's actions are everyone's actions, because they are all sanctioned by the common will. All that you do to me is just as much a product of my will as all that I do myself, for so long as we are moved by respect for the law each and every instance of human action is commonly willed. The law which inspires our actions is authored by *us*. That is the ideal community that Kant describes as a 'kingdom of ends ... a systematic union of various rational beings through universal laws'.[62]

In the kingdom of ends every member is a sovereign lawgiver, for everyone's actions are governed by universal laws. Yet it is critical that we remember Kant's account of moral value in Section I: goodness is a property of the will. If everyone happens to conform with the moral law but fails to act from duty, what appears to be a kingdom of ends is in fact a kingdom of legality. And just as preserving one's life from inclination 'has no inner worth and ... no moral content',[63] a kingdom of legality has likewise no moral value whatsoever.[64] The external enforcement of moral duties, therefore, cannot play any role in Kant's moral philosophy.[65]

---

[57] ibid at 39–40 (Ak 4:431–32).
[58] ibid at 41 (Ak 4:433).
[59] ibid at 42 (Ak 4:434).
[60] ibid at 39 (Ak 4:431).
[61] Kant, *The Metaphysics of Morals*, 13 (Ak 6:213): 'The will itself, strictly speaking, has no determining ground; insofar as it can determine choice, it is instead practical reason itself.'
[62] Kant, *Groundwork*, 41 (Ak 4:433). George P Fletcher, 'Law and Morality: A Kantian Perspective', 543, remarks that Kant's moral philosophy is communitarian. 'Communitarianism' is a loose term, although it does capture some important features of Kant's ideal moral commonwealth – the kingdom of ends.
[63] Kant, *Groundwork*, 11 (Ak 4:397).
[64] It is worth recalling that for Kant 'legality' is the quality of an action that conforms with duty, while 'morality' is a quality reserved for actions from duty or moved by respect for law.
[65] Allen Wood, 'The Final Form of Kant's Practical Philosophy', 9–10 writes that 'Kantian morality ... is never about the social regulation of individual conduct. It is entirely about enlightened individuals autonomously directing their own lives.'

'Legality' has 'no moral content'. The kingdom of ends hangs solely on the strength of good willing.

Yet Kant clearly holds that Right, which comprises enforceable duties, plays a non-trivial role in his practical philosophy. Referring to the duty to keep a contract, he writes:

> [I]f the lawgiving itself were not juridical so that the duty arising from it was not really a duty of right (as distinguished from a duty of virtue), then faithful performance (in keeping with promises made in a contract) would be put in the same class with actions of benevolence and the obligation to them, and *this must not happen*. It is no duty of virtue to keep one's promises but a duty of right, to the performance of which one can be coerced.[66]

Why 'must it not happen'? Granted that the value of enforcing duties of right is *not* (at least not straightforwardly) moral, what sort of value is it? And how is it connected with morality, the subject matter of the MOM? We are finally in a good position to answer these questions.

IV. The Nature of *Recht*

The case that I meant to establish in the two previous sections is that Kantian Right is not the subset of moral duties that is externally enforceable. I levelled two kinds of objection against the contrary view. The first is that it leaves too much of the text and structure of the MOM unexplained; the other is that it is hard to square with Kant's moral philosophy as a whole. Kant does lapse into that view occasionally, which accounts for many of the points of obscurity an ambiguity in the text of the MOM. But I think that the best reading, and the one that underpins the influence of Kant's political thought, is that he is struggling to affirm a very different position.

There is a special propriety in the use of the term 'struggle' on this occasion, for the view from which Kant sought emancipation had a long history, going at least as far back as to Aquinas. Its most renowned proponent among the great modern natural law or 'law of reason' scholars was Samuel Pufendorf, whose greatest work – *De Iure Naturae et Gentium* – was published in 1672, roughly a century before Kant wrote the MOM. Pufendorf anticipates the Kantian distinction between the ethical and the juridical.[67] For him, Right borrows from morality a set of duties and adds external or juridical incentives for their observance. What makes a duty one of right is neither its content nor its normative force, for in all such respects Right is indistinguishable from morality as a whole. A duty is of right if it happens to be externally enforced; Right is the name for those duties that are

---

[66] Kant, *The Metaphysics of Morals*, 21 (Ak 6:220) (emphasis added).
[67] See Hans Welzel, *Derecho Natural y Justicia Material*, 209.

given by juridical, in addition to ethical, laws. It follows that some further reason, in addition to moral obligation, must be given to coercively enforce a duty, for otherwise all moral duties would be fit for such enforcement. For Pufendorf and earlier writers, the reason to enforce a moral duty – thus converting it into a duty of right – may take a variety of forms, from expediency to effectiveness. In any case, the reasoning is more or less contextual or ad hoc, involving argument about whether it is better or worse to enforce a given duty, what consequences enforcing it is likely to produce, whether it is possible to enforce it accurately, and so forth. From Duncan Kennedy we learn that something like this view was held as late as from the late-eighteenth to the mid-nineteenth century in the United States – the antebellum era – a period of legal thought that he labels 'pre-classical'.

> Pre-classical legal thinkers organized the discussion of private law rules around the notion of a conflict between morality … and policy … What was legal … was something less than or narrower than, the full demands of morality. Positive law … condoned evil doing. It thereby became not immoral, but less than fully moral. The explanation for this falling short was that reasons of policy militated against the fusion of law and morality.[68]

In other words, moral obligation is a prima facie reason for juridical lawgiving; 'policy' reasons are factored into at the subsequent stage in order to filter out merely ethical duties. Now that is precisely the view Kant repudiates in the following passage of the introduction to the *Doctrine of Right*:

> [R]ight should not be conceived as made up of two elements, namely an obligation in accordance with a law and an authorization of him who by his choice puts another under obligation to coerce him to fulfill it. Instead, one can locate the concept of right directly in the possibility of connecting universal reciprocal coercion with the freedom of everyone.[69]

What Kant means is that the quality that makes a duty one of right is not juridical enforcement. If that were true, Right would be a species of the genus 'morality', sharing with all other species of morality the element 'obligation' and distinguishing itself by virtue of a second element, the authorisation to coerce based on 'policy'. Kant rejects that view. He says that the reason for externally enforcing a duty is that it *is* a duty of right; in other words, 'right' as quality of duties cannot be defined in terms of juridical enforcement, because the title for enforcement is precisely the quality of a given duty as one of right. The quality 'right' pre-exists enforcement because it marks a duty as an appropriate object of such enforcement; otherwise, we would – Kant would – be stuck in a vicious circle, defining a duty as one of right because it is enforced, and then justifying enforcement on the basis of the duty's character as one of right. In order to break the circle, some

---

[68] Duncan Kennedy, *The Rise and Fall of Classical Legal Thought*, 110 (quoting extensively from *Parsons on Contracts*, a treatise published in 1853). See also, Kennedy, 'Form and Substance in Private Law Adjudication', 1686, 1725–26.
[69] Kant, *The Metaphysics of Morals*, 25 (Ak 6:232).

other defining feature of Right must be sought. Kant turns to *obligation* at this juncture.

> Ethics has its special duties (e.g., duties to oneself), but it also has duties in common with right; what it does not have in common with right is only the kind of *obligation*. For what is distinctive about ethical lawgiving is that one is to perform actions just because they are duties and to make the principle of duty itself, wherever the duty comes from, the sufficient incentive for choice. So while there are many *directly ethical* duties, internal lawgiving makes the rest of them, one and all, indirectly ethical.[70]

A careless reading of this passage places Kant in the quarter of Pufendorf's disciple, Christian Thomasius (1655–1728).[71] Thomasius opposed his mentor's view that duties of right are simply those moral duties subject to juridical enforcement. Anticipating the imperative variant of legal positivism commonly credited to Jeremy Bentham and John Austin, he argued that duties of right are commands backed by threats – or, as he called them, 'coercive obligations'. That is, whereas moral obligations are strictly internal because they appeal to one's conscience, obligations of right are strictly external because they are creatures of coercion. The 'ought' element in a duty of right is a disguised coercive threat – 'you ought to perform X' really means 'either you perform X or you are to suffer disagreeable consequences'.

The concept of 'coercive obligation' conflates two independent sets of criteria, normative (obligation, duty) and empirical (threat, coercion).[72] Indeed, it is quite obvious that Thomasius' account fails on the exact same grounds as the imperative theories of Bentham and Austin.[73] Kant's view is nonetheless entirely distinct. Kant says that 'Right is connected with an *authorization* to use coercion', not that Right *means* coercion will be used. In other words, it is not coercion (or coercive threat) that renders a rightful action obligatory but the obligation to act rightfully that renders coercive enforcement appropriate.

Duties of right, then, are neither coercively enforced moral obligations nor threats based on sanctions. Not the former because moral obligations do not, in and of themselves, warrant coercive enforcement, while duties of right do; not the latter because duties of right embody genuine ought-demands. What Kant says in the passage I quoted is that Right is a special kind of obligation and from his remark that duties of right are indirectly ethical, we may infer *a contrario* that they are directly juridical; obligations of right are hence juridical obligations. Now every time we encountered the term 'juridical' before it denoted a kind of incentive and the kind of law from which such incentive stems – juridical incentives or

---

[70] ibid at 22 (Ak 6:220–21).
[71] See Hans Welzel, *Derecho Natural y Justicia Material*, 209–12.
[72] Welzel, ibid at 212–14, argues correctly that Kant's conception of Right is not positivist–imperativist *a la* Thomasius. From that true premise he infers that Kant sides with Pufendorf. The inference is plainly invalid, because Pufendorf's and Thomasius' positions do not exhaust all possibilities. Indeed, Kant's position is distinct from both.
[73] See HLA Hart, *The Concept of Law*, 82–91; Hans Kelsen, *General Theory of Law and State*, 71–74.

laws. A juridical duty must hence be the kind of duty that can be fulfilled on the basis of such incentives and laws. Duties of right are juridical because they do not command the allegiance of one's motives – of our will, as Kant would say – but of one's actions only. That is why duties of right are 'the sum of those laws for which external lawgiving is possible'; unlike moral duties, which can never be fully fulfilled on juridical or external grounds, duties of right are of such nature that they are fit for enforcement. The view that emerges is the exact opposite of Pufendorf's and the other modern natural lawyers. Instead of duties of right being moral obligations given for external enforcement, they are juridical obligations indirectly given to one's conscience (Kant would say: one's reason) as ethical laws. As indirect ethical duties, of course, they cannot be enforced, for morality implies a free will; as duties of right, however, they are the only kind of duties that lend themselves to enforcement, because they do not extend beyond the domain – actions – where juridical incentives operate.

Right is thus not part of morality, except indirectly. It is an *autonomous* sphere of juridical obligation. But that leaves two key questions in want of an answer. First, what criteria undergird Kant's list of duties of right or, to put it differently, what is the subject matter of Right? Secondly, what is the point or value of Right and why is it an important part of Kant's moral philosophy? Kant offers a clear answer to the first question in a pivotal passage under the epigraph 'What is Right?'

> The concept of right … has to do, *first*, only with the external and indeed practical relation of one person to another, insofar as their actions, as deeds, can have (direct or indirect) influence on each other. But, *second*, it does not signify the relation of one's choice to the mere wish (hence also to the mere need) of the other, as in actions of beneficence or callousness, but only a relation to the other's *choice*. *Third*, in this reciprocal relation of choice no account at all is taken of the *matter* of choice, that is, with the end each has in mind with the object he wants: it is not asked, for example, whether someone who buys goods from me for his own commercial use will gain by the transaction or not. All that is in question is the *form* in the relation of choice on the part of both, insofar as choice is regarded merely as *free*, and whether the action of one can be united in with the freedom of the other in accordance with a universal law.[74]

Kant's method to define Right as a subject is to draw increasingly narrower lines of demarcation between the substance of juridical and moral duties. The first distinction is between duties to oneself and duties to others; the former lie beyond the province of Right. Within the domain of duties to others, Kant draws a second distinction between duties in relation to another's needs and wishes and duties in relation to another's choice; the former are also carved out of Right. Finally, within the domain of duties to others relating to their choices, Kant draws a third distinction, between the content and the form of another person's choice, again leaving the former outside of the reach of Right. We may recast these distinctions in simpler and more familiar language. First, duties of right are always to others

---

[74] Kant, *The Metaphysics of Morals*, 23–24 (Ak 6:230).

and never to ourselves. Secondly, duties of right are duties of justice instead of duties of charity, piety or benevolence. Thirdly, duties of right are liberal instead of paternalist, that is to say, they are duties to refrain from interfering with other people's choices, as opposed to duties to make sure that other people get what is good for them irrespective of their preferences. The second distinction – justice versus charity – is worthy of closer attention, for it is the key to Kant's break with the natural law tradition and his influence on late modern and contemporary ideas of justice and right.

Compare two forms of moral utterance and the types of social setting where they are conventionally expressed. The paradigm of the first is the choice of a wealthy person to give away a portion of his wealth to a charitable organisation or for the pursuit of some public purpose. The conventional view is that a very wealthy person has a moral obligation to assist the needy ones or contribute to the well-being of others but also that his decision to fulfil that duty is strictly personal. No one has a right to be assisted or benefitted by the wealthy person, so long as he acquired his wealth by lawful means and has fulfilled his duties as a taxpayer; the question is whether he is willing to exercise his rights in ways that are worthy of moral approval.

The paradigm of the second form of moral utterance – 'rights-talk' – is the relation between owner and trespasser. The owner does not ask the trespasser to be generous or act with a good conscience; he demands that the trespasser leave his property, on the ground that it is his right to decide who is to enter the land. The owner's right is the basis for the duty of the trespasser to leave the property. While the former case concerns duties of charity (or benevolence), this case concerns duties of justice, in respect of which enforcement is thought of as legitimate and even imperative. For when a right is enforced, the point is not to bring the defendant to fulfil his moral duty, but to either protect the plaintiff from an injustice or to right a wrong.[75] Charity is thus a matter of moral obligation whereas justice is primarily a matter of rights.[76] To say that it is *primarily* a matter of rights says something about the dual character of norms of justice. Primarily, they are about individual entitlements and the importance of securing them. From a derivative standpoint, however, they are also moral obligations, which hold irrespective of whether the threat of coercive enforcement is credible and which command the allegiance not only of our actions but of our maxims or motives as well. That is of course the position that Kant expresses with the

---

[75] See HLA Hart, 'Are There Any Natural Rights?', 178, writes that the notions of rights and justice indicate a 'special congruity in the use of force or threat of force …'.

[76] Notice that the argument is formal. The substantive question is where the line separating justice from charity should be drawn. A common complaint of progressive thought is that conservative politics hands over to charity matters that belong to the realm of justice. See, eg, Mary Wollstonecraft *A Vindication of the Rights of Women*, 66: 'It is justice, not charity, that is wanting in the world!' The radical position challenges the dichotomy itself, arguing that it creates or reinforce the self-understanding of 'an individual withdrawn into himself, into the confines of his private interests and private caprice, and separated from the community'. Karl Marx, 'On the Jewish Question', 43.

distinction between the direct form of duties of right as juridical duties and their indirect form as ethical duties.

All of this marks a very important difference between Kant and the bulk of his natural law predecessors and contemporaries. The distinction between justice and benevolence (and the cognate concepts of charity, piety, mercy and grace) is very old. For a long time, however, it seems to have been a distinction of degree, of the kind captured by Duncan Kennedy's remark that pre-classical jurists in the antebellum period limited the enforcement of morality by considerations of 'policy'. A distinction was often drawn between perfect or natural and imperfect or positive justice, to indicate that charity is not unrelated or beyond justice but merely beyond the domain of humanly handed, or at any rate enforceable, justice. Each denoted a different area of a single continuum of moral obligation, with the precise range of issues falling under one domain or the other shifting according to the balance of reasons for and against enforcement. Consider, for instance, Thomas Aquinas' discussion of self-defence in the *Summa Theologica*.

> The action of defending oneself may produce two effects – one, saving one's life, and the other, killing the attacker. Now an action of this kind intended to save one's own life cannot be characterized as an illicit since it is natural for anyone to maintain himself in existence if he can. An act that is prompted by a good intention can become illicit if it is not proportionate to the end intended. This is why it is not allowed to use more force than necessary to defend one's life. However, if moderation is used in repelling violence, this is justified self-defense.[77]

These remarks appear in the part of the *Summa* devoted to justice. If we were to ask Aquinas if it follows from his argument that disproportionate or immoderate uses of force in self-defence ought to be punished, he might have answered 'no'. For his discussion of self-defence meant to establish a point of natural law or moral obligation. Yet that alone does not furnish a justification for enforcement. In his discussion of law, he explains that:

> Human law is framed for the mass of men, the majority of whom are not perfectly virtuous. Therefore human law does not prohibit every vice from which virtuous men abstain, but only the more serious ones from which the majority can abstain, especially those that harm others and which must be prohibited for human society to survive, such as homicide, theft, and the like.[78]

Let us suppose that Aquinas' opinion was that 'human law' should not enforce the duty to moderate the use of violence in self-defence. If we asked him whether that means the victim of assault has a right to use as much violence as he wishes, he would most likely stare at us puzzled. His point had been that in the circumstances of his time and place the balance of reasons cautions against enforcing that prohibition. But it does not by any means follow that immoderate uses of violence in self-defence are right, or that (assuming the notion made any sense to him)

[77] Thomas Aquinas, *Summa Theologica*, II–II, q 64, a 7.
[78] ibid at II–I, q 96, a 2.

a victim of an assault has a right to them; it is surely wrong, although unsanctioned by human law, to kill in self-defence when unnecessary or disproportionate.

Consider now Kant's remark on self-defence in the *Rechtslehre*, which appears in his discussion of the doctrine of necessity: 'the issue here is not of a *wrongful* assailant upon my life whom I forestall by depriving him of his life … in which case a recommendation to show moderation … belongs not to right but only to ethics'. For Kant, it is entirely appropriate to assert both that the victim of a life-threatening assault is within his right to use as much violence in self-defence as he sees fit *and* that he has a moral duty to exercise his right with moderation. One issue falls within the province of the juridical laws of right, whereas the other pertains to the ethical laws of morality. The former confer upon each person a protected domain of choice, that person's set of rights or rightful sphere of action; the latter furnish a particular type of motivation – respect for the moral law – for the exercise of one's rights. Right, then, does not concern the enforcement of moral duties but the coexistence of choices in a world where mutual interference is ubiquitous. The laws of Right create the external or worldly conditions for the exercise of moral choice, that is, the freedom to choose between good and evil.[79] It follows (and the example of self-defence confirms it) that an action may be both rightful and immoral, that is, fully in accord with the laws of Right and nonetheless inconsistent with the moral law.[80] The potential for evil doing – for immorality – is contained in the very concept of a right as a protected domain of choice. Kant's formulation of the Universal Principle of Right (UPR) corroborates the point: 'Any action is right if it can coexist with everyone's freedom in accordance with a universal law, or if on its maxim the freedom of choice of each can coexist with everyone's freedom in accordance with a universal law'.[81] Right indicates the compatibility of individual choices, not the moral adequacy of those choices.[82] My choice may be

---

[79] Kant culminates the revolution brought upon moral philosophy and jurisprudence by the invention of the notion of 'a right' or 'law in the subjective sense'. In his *Doctrine of Right*, rights are fully emancipated from if not opposed to the moral law. Michel Villey, 'La genèse du droit subjectif chez Guillaume d'Occam' traces the origins of rights or 'right' as a moral category somehow distinct from 'the law' to the nominalists and particularly William of Ockham. With the rider that all search for the *origins* of complex cultural forms is futile – see Michel Foucault, 'Nietzsche, Genealogy, History' – Villey's arguments are compelling and well-documented.

[80] See Jeremy Waldron, 'A Right to Do Wrong'.

[81] Kant, *The Metaphysics of Morals*, 24 (Ak 6:230). What Kant means by 'universal law' is fairly clear from our journey into his moral philosophy. It means that when I ask whether my use of freedom on this occasion is 'right', I am bound to ask whether I will it to become a universal law of freedom. Roughly speaking, this means that my action is right insofar as I am willing to approve it whether it is undertaken by me or anyone else, or if I will to live under a system of laws that marks actions of the type I adopted as lawful. Suppose that I occupy a plot of land and put a fence around it, with the aim of excluding everyone else's access to it without my permission on any conceivable circumstance. My action is right if I am committed to live in a world where that type of action – occupying, fencing, and categorically excluding others from accessing the plot of land – is generally permitted. Implicit in the concept of universality is hence a commitment to equality: I can only bind others to the extent they can bind me in return.

[82] For a typical Thomist (or neo-Thomist) reaction against Kant's account of Right, see Antonio Rosmini, *The Philosophy of Right*, I, 143.

consistent with yours and yet blind to your needs and wishes, in violation of my duty to treat you as an end.

To sum up, the autonomy of Right vis-à-vis morality proceeds from two sources – the kind of obligation it embodies and its subject matter or domain of application. First, duties of right are, unlike moral duties, 'juridical' – they apply to individual actions, instead of maxims or motives. Secondly, duties of right direct us to make mutually consistent choices, whereas moral duties instruct us to make the humanity in ourselves and in others the end of each of our choices.

If that is true, however, if Right is indeed not within morality, why is it part of Kant's moral system? The answer is clearest if we pursue an analogy. Kant remarks both in the MOM and in the earlier essay *Theory and Practice* that the type of freedom that is the subject of Right is 'external' or 'outer', as opposed to 'ethical' or 'inner', freedom.[83] Inner freedom is the freedom of the will, achieved by the person who submits not to the mastery of external factors but to practical reason. Obviously, the laws of Right, being juridical or external, cannot possibly secure that sort of freedom. Their subject is outer freedom. But what does that mean? In his discussion of inner freedom, Kant draws a distinction between negative freedom – freedom of the will or the 'independence from being determined by sensible impulses' – and positive freedom – autonomy or 'the ability of pure reason to be of itself practical'.[84] The latter presupposes the former because we can only make it a maxim to act morally if we possess free will. Similarly, we can only make our will effective in the external world, thereby contributing to the creation of a kingdom of ends, if we are externally or socially endowed with an effective domain of choice. The positive freedom of moral agency, then, presupposes the negative freedom of external choice. A person's rights are the external equivalents of his free will; Right is to Virtue in the 'outer' world as free will is to autonomy in the 'inner' world. A simple matrix displays the homology.

Figure 2.3 Typology of Kantian freedom

Types of freedom	Negative	Positive
Inner	Free will	Autonomy
Outer	Right	Virtue

Right creates the external or social conditions for moral agency. In a paragraph that precedes the formulation of the UPR, Kant writes that 'Right is ... the sum of the

---

[83] 'External' freedom is not to be confused with 'external' law-giving. So far as I can tell, in the MOM Kant applies the dichotomy external/internal to four different types of object. First, there is external or internal law-giving, depending on the source of the duty or the incentive to fulfil it. Secondly, there are external or internal duties, the former being duties to adopt either a specific act (or omission) or a general course of action and the later being duties that Kant discusses in §21 of the *Doctrine of the Elements of Ethics*. Thirdly, there is the internal or innate right to freedom and the external rights of property, contract and 'to persons akin to rights to things'. Finally, there is external or internal freedom, discussed in the text above.

[84] Kant, *The Metaphysics of Morals*, 13 (Ak 6:213).

conditions under which the choice of one can be united with the choice of another in accordance with a universal law of freedom'.[85] Notice a slight variation in the meaning of 'right' as between this definition and the UPR. In the formulation just quoted, 'right' is a property of a state of affairs; it is the 'sum of the conditions' that make the union of everyone's choice under a universal law of freedom possible. In the UPR, 'right' is the quality of an action that is consistent with a universal law of freedom. On the face of it, the difference amounts to a matter of standpoint: 'right' is the noun that denotes a universal law of freedom, in the former case (as in: 'Right requires that I …'), and it is the adjective denoting the consistency of a particular use of freedom with that law, in the latter (as in: 'what you did was right …'). To distinguish them, we may reserve capital-R 'Right' for the noun. But there is another and more fundamental point. The noun 'Right' does not refer to a universal law of freedom but to a world in which such a law is instantiated; in other words, Right is an effective universal law of freedom. In sum, Right for Kant is not merely a system of duties – the duties of justice – but a *rightful condition*. To that notion we turn at once.

V. The Rightful Condition

A rightful condition – or capital-R Right – is a social world structured in such a way that each person has an effective measure of freedom to either embrace or repudiate the moral law. As Kant puts it in *Theory and Practice*:

> [A]ll right consists merely in the limitation of the freedom of others to the condition that it is consistent with mine in accordance with a general law … by virtue of which all … are subjects in a juridical condition (*status iuridicus*) in general, that is to say, are in a condition of equality of action and reaction of a mutually limiting choice in a accordance with the general law of freedom …[86]

Here, as in the definitions of 'right' in the *Rechtslehre*, Kant refers not to 'the', but to 'a' universal law of freedom. The reason is that he is speaking from the a priori standpoint of pure reason or metaphysics proper. Pure reason informs us about the idea of a rightful condition or a universal law of freedom; but what system of rights or what universal law gives shape to a rightful condition among human beings depends on empirical data collected from the study of what Kant calls 'practical anthropology'.[87] If human beings were like the Greek gods, for instance, the 'sum of the conditions' for the coexistence of their choices would be quite different from that which applies to them as they really are.[88]

The only empirical facts that Kant assumes in the introductory analysis of Right that we have been examining are what I called in chapter one the conditions

---

[85] ibid at 24 (Ak 6:230).
[86] Kant, 'Theory and Practice', 45 (Ak 8:290).
[87] Kant wrote an essay on the subject. Kant, 'Anthropology from a Pragmatic Point of View'.
[88] See Kant, *The Metaphysics of Morals*, 10 (Ak 6:216–17).

of 'plurality' and 'commonality' – that there are many of us and that we share a finite world.[89] The very idea of Right makes no sense otherwise. As to the further empirical assumptions of the *Doctrine of Right*, Kant does not spell them out. But the *Rechtslehre* postulates all the conditions of the political realm. Kant's lengthy treatment of property, for instance, is unintelligible unless the reader assumes the conditions of 'vulnerability', 'individuality' and 'scarcity'.

The *Doctrine of Right* is apparently divided into two major parts – 'Private Right' and 'Public Right' – although there are actually three parts. The first part, brief and appended to the introduction, concerns the 'innate right' of every human being to freedom – 'independence from being constrained by another's choice' – and equality – 'independence from being bound by others more than one can bind them in return'.[90] The entire system of duties of right is premised on the 'only one innate right' of every person to be treated as an equal freedom. From the innate right of every human being, Kant deduces what we would call 'personal rights', although he mentions explicitly only examples of an open list that implicitly includes the rights to life, bodily integrity, free movement, free speech, etc.[91]

Innate right opposes acquired right in Kant's system. A right is *innate* if it pertains to every human being; it is acquired if it depends on one or more events of acquisition, eg a promise, an exchange, an act of occupation of *res nullius*. The subject of acquired right is divided into the doctrine of Private Right and that of Public Right, which Kant also calls natural and civil or statutory right, respectively.[92] Private Right is in turn divided into three subjects: property, contract and 'rights to persons akin to rights to things'.

The doctrine of Private Right articulates the universal law of freedom appropriate for human beings on Earth. The primary task of *Recht* is to assign spheres of freedom to persons of equal status, and that is exactly the subject of Private Right. It is important to notice that private rights are, for the most part, not created by acts of legislation or other sources of positive law; they are worked out from the a priori idea of a universal law of freedom. That is 'why right in the state of nature is called private right'.[93] Given the UPR and the empirical conditions of human life, Private Right sets the limits of rightful freedom. If you happen to interfere with my rights – in other words, if you commit a wrong – I am authorised by the universal law of freedom to hinder your hindrance of my rightful freedom.

A universal law of freedom is not quite the same as a rightful condition though. The idea of *Recht* is one thing; *Recht* itself – an effective law of freedom – is another matter. And Kant believes that if the enforcement of the universal law of freedom – or Private Right – is left in the hands of the denizens of the state of nature, instead

---

[89] ibid at 89 (Ak 6:311): 'Public right is ... a system of laws for a people, that is, a multitude of human beings, or for a multitude of peoples, which, because they affect one another, need a rightful condition ...' . The point recurs in other writings: Kant, 'Theory and Practice', 44 (Ak 8:289); Kant, 'Perpetual Peace', 78 (Ak 8:354).

[90] Kant, *The Metaphysics of Morals*, 30 (Ak 6:237).

[91] See Paul Guyer, *Kant*, 244–45, 267.

[92] Kant, *The Metaphysics of Morals*, 29, 34 (Ak 6:237, 242).

[93] ibid at 34 (Ak 6:242).

of a rightful condition, where everyone's rights are secured, society will degenerate into a state of 'wild', 'lawless' or 'mad' freedom, of the sort where 'the life of man' is, in Hobbes's famous words, 'solitary, poore, nasty, brutish, and short'.[94] 'We view with great disdain the way in which savages cling to their *lawless freedom*, preferring to fight continually amongst one another rather than submit to a lawful coercion that they themselves establish, and thereby favoring mad freedom over rational freedom.'[95]

Kant is ambivalent about what exactly causes anarchy to slide into a condition of lawless freedom, where no one is truly free. He oscillates between two themes. One is the Hobbesian theme of the wickedness of human nature: the 'passions' or 'inclinations' that drive human beings to harm and exploit one another – greed, suspicion, fear and anxiety – are exacerbated in a stateless condition. In *Perpetual Peace*, for example, he writes about 'The maliciousness of human nature, [which] although quite concealed by the coercion of government in the state of civil law, can be observed openly in the free relations between peoples'.[96] In the closing remarks on Private Right in the MOM he goes even further and asserts, in striking Hobbesian fashion, that the insecurity inherent in the state of nature legitimates pre-emptive attack:

> No one is bound to refrain from encroaching on what another possesses if the other gives him no equal assurance that he will observe the same restraint towards him. No one, therefore, need wait until he has learned by bitter experience of the other's contrary disposition ... And is it [sic] not necessary to wait for actual hostility; one is authorized to use coercion against someone who already, by his nature, threatens him with coercion.[97]

Remarkably, in the second paragraph on Public Right he vigorously repudiates the empirical assumptions behind the 'shoot first, ask questions later' posture he adopted a page before and settles on a Lockean concern with the indeterminacy of Natural or Private Right. From other textual fragments it is apparent that such indeterminacy is of two quite different sorts, one involving gaps in Private Right that need to be filled with legislative *fiat* – eg, the law of private nuisance or the rules governing contract formalities – and another concerning the impropriety and instability of private adjudication in light of the principle *nemo iudex in re sua*:

> [H]owever well-disposed and law-abiding men might be, it still lies *a priori* in the rational idea of such a condition (one that is not rightful) that before a public lawful condition is established individual human beings ... can never be secure against violence from one another, since each has its own right to do *what seems right and good to it* and not to be dependent upon another's opinion about this.[98]

---

[94] Hobbes, *Leviathan*, 186.
[95] Kant, 'Perpetual Peace', 78 (Ak 8:354).
[96] ibid at 79 (Ak 8:355).
[97] Kant, *The Metaphysics of Morals*, 86 (Ak 6:307).
[98] ibid at 89–90 (Ak 6:312). Compare John Locke, *Second Treatise on Civil Government*, ch IX, §125, 57–58.

The apparently odd conjunction of Hobbesian and Lockean themes is in fact typical of Kant's eclecticism as a political theorist. His contribution usually comes in the form of a synthesis of previously divergent strands of thought and an astonishing ability to unite them under a single line of argument from a priori principles.

The answer to the defects of Private Right in an anarchical setting is the creation of a state.[99] Each defect corresponds to one of the three standard powers. Violent tendencies are curtailed by a strong executive; private dispute-settlement is replaced by an independent judiciary; finally, gaps in the system of rights are remedied by legislation. Together, these powers constitute a state, a form of social relations that furnishes the necessary and jointly sufficient conditions for an effective law of freedom: *Recht*. The purpose of the state it to secure Private Right. In a pivotal passage, this time infused with Rousseauian ideas, Kant writes:

> The act by which a People forms itself into a state is the *original contract*. Properly speaking, the original contract is only the idea of this act, in terms of which alone we can think of the legitimacy of a state. In accordance with the original contract, everyone ... within a *people* gives up his external freedom in order to take it up again as a member of a commonwealth, that is, of a people considered as a state ...[100]

Since Right is a reciprocal limitation of freedom that enhances everyone's freedom on equal terms, a state that is constrained by the imperatives of Right is based on the hypothetical consent of all its subjects. The 'original contract' is not an actual agreement but a 'mere idea of reason' that 'obligates every legislator to pass laws in such a way that they would have been able to arise from the united will of an entire people ...'[101] The rightful state is a 'fully reciprocal use of coercion that is consistent with everyone's freedom in accordance to universal laws'.[102] In that state, Private Right is incorporated and (where it contains gaps) completed by legislation, disputes are settled by courts bound by such legislation, and resistance to laws and judicial rulings is destroyed by a strong law-abiding executive. Yet Kant does not reify the state. He is fully self-conscious about the human character of all forms of power.

> [T]he human being is an *animal* which, when he lives among others of his own species, *needs a master*. ... But where does he find such a master? In no place other than in the human species. [...] The supreme authority must be just *in itself* but also a *human being*.

---

[99] Just like a people without a state is an anarchical mob, an international community without what Kant calls 'Cosmopolitan Right' is bound to fall into a condition of global insecurity. That is the starting point of Kant's theory of international justice, which lies beyond our concerns.

[100] Kant, *The Metaphysics of Morals*, 92–93 (Ak 6:315–16).

[101] Kant, 'Theory and Practice', 51 (Ak 8:297). Thus, the 'social contract' is not the historical basis of legitimacy; it is an 'idea of reason' that fixes the criteria of good government. Kant is not in the least concerned with the origins of power. Legitimacy for him is not a historical question but a substantive question: a just ruler is legitimate, even if his power proceeds from an act of usurpation. See Kant, 'Perpetual Peace', 96 (Ak 8:372–73). For commentary on this point, see Jeremy Waldron, 'Kant's Theory of the State', 186–87.

[102] Kant, *The Metaphysics of Morals*, 25 (Ak 6:232).

This task is thus the most difficult of all. Indeed, its perfect solution is impossible: nothing entirely straight can be fashioned from the crooked wood of which humankind is made.[103]

This passage marks a shift in tone. When he addresses the problems of Public Right, Kant's voice is no longer confidently aprioristic but calibrated by prudential concerns. Although in the MOM Kant attempts to conceal it, constitutional issues are quite clearly pragmatic; the best constitution is that which makes it more likely that Private Right is upheld and enforced, and state officials keep within the bounds of their rightful authority. That is what he calls a 'republican' form of government, where the three powers – legislative, judicial and executive – are entrusted to different persons.[104] Executive power lies in the person of the 'ruler' and is bound by legislation; judicial power is entrusted to an independent judiciary; finally, legislative power is born by the 'sovereign authority'. Although the latter is ideally identified with the 'united will of the people', the actual members of the law-making assembly are representatives elected by 'active citizens', a quality reserved for adult male land-owners and independent professionals.[105]

The permission to coerce the denizens of the state of nature to enter into a civil condition is implicit in Kant's concept of Right. If 'right' is the quality of any action that is consistent with a universal law of freedom, it must be right to assure that such a law is effective – ie to create or maintain a 'civil condition' or a rightful state. As Kant puts it, 'each may impel the other to leave [the] state [of nature] and enter into a rightful condition'.[106]

All of this is true from the standpoint of *Recht*. The deeper question is how *Recht* is connected with morality, the subject, after all, of the MOM. Right secures the conditions that make it possible for humans to respond to the moral incentive and to make the moral law effective in the external world. The 'mad freedom' of the state of nature embroils us in permanent conflict, or the threat of conflict, for bare survival.[107] The lack of mutual assurance and the indeterminacy of rights heighten our incentive to defy moral duty. Kant surely agreed with Hobbes that survival is the dominant inclination felt by human beings. Even those of us good-willed enough to resist inclination on such extreme circumstances have little hope of being effective moral agents, for in a state of anarchy everything is unpredictable and chaotic. Consequently, a state is 'that condition which reason, by a categorical imperative, makes it obligatory for us to strive after'.[108] Morality obligates us to do everything within our power to 'make the end that is imposed by its laws real in

---

[103] Kant, 'Idea for a Universal History from a Cosmopolitan Perspective', 8 (Ak 8:22).
[104] ibid, 'Perpetual Peace', 76 (Ak 8:352).
[105] ibid, 'Theory and Practice', 49–50 (Ak 8:295).
[106] Kant, *The Metaphysics of Morals*, 90 (Ak 6:312).
[107] 'The state of nature … is a state of war, that is, if not always an outbreak of hostilities, then at least the constant threat of such hostilities.' Kant, 'Perpetual Peace', 72–73 (Ak 8:349).
[108] Kant, *The Metaphysics of Morals*, 95 (Ak 6:318). See also, ibid at 51 (Ak 6:264): 'A civil constitution, though its realization is subjectively contingent, is still objectively necessary, that is, necessary as a duty'.

the sensible world'.[109] Bringing about a rightful condition – securing individual rights – is by far the most important thing, on Kant's view, that we can do on that score.

VI. Private Right

The role of the Public Right part of the *Rechtshlere* is to lay down the conditions under which the universal law of freedom appropriate for human beings is secure. Only under the auspices of a republican state is a rightful condition likely to hold. But the substance of *Recht*, that for the sake of which the institutions of active citizenship, official capacity, the separation of powers and so on are needed, is the Private Right part of the work. The task of a rightful state is to rationalise 'mad' or 'wild' freedom. Rational freedom, a mutual limitation of 'mad' freedom that maximises everyone's freedom, *is* Private Right.

The organising logic of Private Right is as follows. Each human being is originally endowed with a single innate right to freedom and equality. As equal freedoms, human beings are invested with certain original entitlements: life, bodily integrity, freedom of speech and other (unlisted) personal rights. These are all 'internal' because they do not concern the various ways in which human beings compete or struggle for the control of 'external' resources – such as land, minerals, plants and (non-rational) animals – that exist in limited amounts on earth. 'Speech' or 'life' are not scarce resources in that sense; when the law assigns you a right to free speech, it does not deprive itself of the means to assign me an equal right. In other words, the protection of 'internal' interests is not a zero-sum game. A just legal regime protects them universally (ie, in each person and on every instance), consistent with the higher principles of freedom and equality that are entailed by the concept of a person. The entire field of conflicts both *within* the set of personal rights (eg, free speech v privacy[110]) and *between* personal and 'external'

---

[109] Kant, *Critique of the Power of Judgment*, Introduction, s II (Ak 5:175). It is true that, for Kant, moral value stems from a good will instead of external action. The merely accidental fact that one's good action is ineffective detracts nothing from its moral value; conversely, a bad action that produces good results by chance is morally evil. However, it does not follow from the fact that we are not responsible for unwilled effects that we are morally exempt from doing everything within our power to *exert control* over the effects of our actions. A good will is unconditionally committed to the *practical* end furnished by the moral law. It is hence a mistake to assert, as does Thomas Grey, 'Serpents and Doves: A Note on Kantian Legal Theory', 581, that 'as an inner phenomenon, autonomy is not dependent on external circumstances'. Or that 'The expansion of an agent's range of choice … seems to have no connection with his or her autonomy'. It is our moral responsibility, on Kant's account, to take as much control as we can over the external or sensible world in order to make the laws of freedom effective in it. On this point, see Paul Guyer, *Kant*, 4–5, 360–61.

[110] See, eg, *Phelps et al v Snyder*, 562 US 443 (2011). The German Constitutional Court decided quite a few famous cases involving conflicts between 'freedom' rights ('privileges', in Hohfeldian terms) – eg, free speech, free press, artistic freedom, etc – and the general right of personality (which comprises privacy and dignity interests). Two such cases are the *Mephisto* case, 30 BVerfGE 173 (1971); and the *Titanic* case, 86 BVerfGE 1(1992).

interests (eg, free speech v property[111]) is invisible to Kant. He quite clearly does not conceive any such conflicts as possible. That is why he devotes no more than three paragraphs to the subject of innate right.

The real crux of *Recht*, and the organising theme of Private Right, is what sort of regime enables us to acquire rights over external resources in ways that are consistent both with our freedom to exercise control over things of value *and* the equal dignity or status of each and every person's claim to such freedom. How is it possible, in other words, that I can call on you to refrain from bringing under your control a valuable object – eg, a plot of fertile land – when that implies asserting my claim (my freedom) as superior or worthier than yours? The question never arises, or that is what Kant assumes, in the field of personal rights, for my right to life can coexist smoothly with your right to life.[112] It is the opposite with acquired rights, such as my proprietary right to exercise control over Blackacre, since my claim excludes (by definition) your claim, although we are innately endowed with the right to be treated as equals. The question, then, is on what basis can I have a right to exclude an exercise of your freedom?

Kant deals with this issue in an obscure preliminary section of the doctrine of Private Right, before he turns his attention to the three classes of 'external' or acquired rights, namely property, contract and status or 'rights to persons akin to rights to things'. Under the rubric 'How to Have Something External as One's Own', Kant begins by drawing an important distinction between empirical (or sensible) and intelligible (or noumenal) possession.

The phrase 'this is mine' may mean two quite different things. It may indicate that I happen to be in physical control of an object and perhaps that I am prepared to defend my possession against anyone else. That is empirical possession. Or it may imply that I have a certain claim over the object in question, a claim that holds whether or not I happen to be holding or physically controlling the object, and through which I call on other human beings to refrain from interfering with my enjoyment of it. That is intelligible possession. Here is how Kant puts the point:

> [S]omething *external* would be mine only if I may assume that I could be wronged by another's use of a thing even *though I am not in possession of it.* – So it would be self-contradictory to say that I have something external as my own if the concept of possession could not have different meanings, namely *sensible* possession and *intelligible* possession, and by the former could be understood *physical* possession but by the latter a *merely rightful* possession of the same object.[113]

These remarks are meant to establish two further points. First, rights are not disguised coercive threats. When I assert my right over an object, I am not

---

[111] See, eg, *Marsh v Alabama*, 326 US 501 (1946); *Amalgamated Food Employees Union Local 590 v Logan Valley Plaza Inc*, 391 US 308 (1968); *Lloyd Corp, Ltd v Tanner*, 407 US 551 (1972). These cases are discussed in Joseph Singer, *Introduction to Property*, 76–81.

[112] Kant's contrast between original or internal and acquired or external right is similar to the distinction between general and special rights drawn by HLA Hart, 'Are There Any Natural Rights?', 183–88. Jeremy Waldron, *The Right to Private Property*, 106–24, applied Hart's scheme to the theory of property.

[113] Kant, *The Metaphysics of Morals*, 37 (Ak 6:246).

saying merely or even primarily that whoever interferes with my use is liable to suffer harm. I am claiming that 'everyone else is under obligation to refrain from using that object of my choice'[114] and whatever coercive means are put to use in connection with my claim, they are based on, instead of being the essence of, my rightful possession. Rights are irreducibly 'intellectual' or 'noumenal', as opposed to 'empirical' or 'psychological'.[115] The second point is more fundamental. Kant clearly conceptualises rights as relations among persons over external objects, instead of relations between persons and objects. 'This is mine', when asserted as a right, is a claim addressed to others and a public matter. It is a claim that they ought to recognise in my right a limit to their freedom. Kant is hence, like many of the great classical jurists who sought inspiration in his work, exempt from the familiar charge laid by legal historians upon eighteenth- and particularly nineteenth-century jurisprudence, that it reified property, or misrepresented it as a so-called 'private' relation between a person and a thing that by some mysterious magic turns out to have public or inter-personal consequences.[116]

Talk about rights over external objects encourages identification with property issues, particularly real and personal property. Kant does identify property with control over corporeal objects.[117] But the concept of 'external object of choice' comprises two other types of object: another person's deed and another's status in relation to the rights bearer. In each case, Kant's concern is not with empirical possession – ie a simultaneous exchange or people de facto living under someone's roof – but with rights or, as he puts it, rightful possession.

> I cannot call the performance of something by another's choice mine if all I can say is that it came into my possession at the same time that he promised it ... but only if I can assert that I am in possession of the other's choice ... even though the time for his performing is yet to come.[118]

---

[114] ibid at 44 (Ak 6:255).

[115] On the distinction between normative statements of having an obligation to øing and empirical statements of being obliged to øing, see HLA Hart, *The Concept of Law*, 82–91. See also Hans Kelsen, *General Theory of Law and State*, 71–74.

[116] See, eg, Morton Horwitz, *The Transformation of American Law, 1870–1960*, 151–56; Barbara Fried, *The Progressive Assault on Laissez Faire*, 50–53. Kant makes his position on this issue even clearer in his discussion of property. See Kant, *The Metaphysics of Morals*, 49 (Ak 6:260). I do not mean that the person-to-person, as opposed to person-to-thing, character of rights in general, and property rights in particular, is a trivial point. Not only is it often ill-understood, or simply ignored, by the layperson, the economist and the political philosopher – all routine participants in 'property talk' – it is also occasionally denied, or at least obscured, even by jurists. Some jurists oppose the application of the concept 'jural relation' to property because, they argue, the essence of property is control over a thing, as opposed, for instance, to the right that the parties to a contract have against each other to demand performance. For a classic version of that position, see Andreas von Tuhr, *Der allgemeine Teil des deutschen bürgerlichen Rechts*, Bd I, §5 I 1. But that point trades on confusion between the concept of right, which is necessarily relational, and the classification of different types of right according either to their objects (eg, things, deeds, etc) or the scope of liability they impose (absolute or relative). A property right is: as: (i) a *right*, a relation between persons, namely between owner and non-owners; as (ii) a *property* right, a relation between persons with respect to a 'thing' (say, a corporeal object); and as (iii) an *omnilateral* right, a right against all persons (*erga omnes*).

[117] Kant, *The Metaphysics of Morals*, 37 (Ak 6:247). There are nonetheless some intriguing remarks on copyright made at 71–72 (Ak 6:289–91).

[118] ibid at 38 (Ak 6:248).

> I cannot call a wife, a child, a servant, or, in general, another person mine because I am now in charge of them as members of my household or have them within my restraining walls … but only if, although they have withdrawn from such constraint and I do not possess them … I can still say that I possess them merely by my will, hence merely rightfully, as long as they exist somewhere or at the same time.[119]

The puzzle of external acquisition applies equally to the three classes of object. How can I have a right over a corporeal thing, a deed to be performed by you, or your participation within the life of the household (that you discharge your status), when it is apparent that in such ways my freedom – my choice – prevails over yours? How is that consistent with the universal form of Right?

A possible answer is that it is not, with the implication that there are no such rights: property, contract and household status are not rightful institutions. Kant rules out that option in a terribly murky section, under the heading 'Postulate of Practical Reason with Regard to Rights.' He writes that 'freedom would be depriving itself of the use of its choice with regard to an object of choice, by putting usable objects beyond any possibility of being used'.[120] Then he concludes: 'It is therefore an *a priori* presupposition of practical reason to regard and treat any object of my choice as something which could objectively be mine or yours'. Freedom requires external objects of choice in order to subsist, that is to say, freedom is largely a matter of controlling the external world; and since genuine freedom is only rightful freedom – freedom limited by Right – there must be rights over external objects, so that we can be free in our dealings amongst ourselves over them.

The problem is that freedom and equality seem to pull in opposite directions. Freedom requires that our choice is enhanced by rights over external objects; equality, however, requires that everyone – every instance of freedom – be treated as an equal. Kant deals with the issue in the following terms. My will to take control over an external object can never obligate you to anything, for such a will is merely unilateral. It has the form of subjectivity – '*I* will' – instead of the form of universality or objectivity – '*we* will'. For my claim to be genuinely rightful, it presupposes a common or omnilateral will, comprising the wills of all those who bear the duties correlated to my right. A particular right, therefore, presupposes a universal law that abstracts from my interest and expresses the equal worthiness of the various freedoms to whom it applies.

> [A] unilateral will cannot serve as a coercive law for everyone with regard to possession that is external and therefore contingent, since that would infringe upon freedom in accordance with universal laws. So it is only a will putting everyone under obligation, hence only a collective general (*common*) and powerful will, that can provide everyone this assurance.[121]

---

[119] ibid.
[120] ibid at 41 (Ak 6:246).
[121] ibid at 45 ((Ak 6:256).

Kant adds that 'so only in a civil condition can something external be mine or yours'. It is tempting to read into this passage the idea that the 'common will' is the will of the lawmaking officials in the civil condition, so that the problems of acquired right, being intractable a priori, are settled by legislation.[122] Yet Kant believes that the core of Private Right is produced not by legislative *fiat* but by a priori reasoning from the idea of a universal law of (external) freedom. The task assigned to positive law is that of incorporating a priori norms and filling interstitial gaps. Kant's thought on this issue is complicated and obscure, but the starting point is clear:

> When people are under a civil constitution, the statutory laws obtaining in this condition cannot infringe upon *natural right*, (i.e., that right which can be derived from *a priori* principles for a civil constitution) … For a civil constitution is just the rightful condition, by which what belongs to each is only secured, but not actually settled and determined.[123]

At the same time, Kant insists that the a priori laws of external acquisition have to be embodied in positive laws enacted by a legislature. That is because a rightful condition presupposes the mutual assurance that only an effective legal system can secure, as he explains in the transition from Private to Public Right that we examined above. In the state of nature, there cannot be any rights, either because there are too many incentives to commit wrongs and that legitimates preemptive striking, or because there is no gap-filling legislation to settle disputes over matters that cannot be settled a priori,[124] or, finally, because there are no impartial methods to settle rights disputes. That is why 'possession in anticipation of and preparation of a civil condition … is *provisionally rightful* …, whereas possession found in an actual civil condition would be *conclusive* possession'.[125] In the state of nature, my claim to the exclusive control of an external object may be rightful in the sense that it is consistent with the universal law of freedom; but claims about rights are only conclusive once such a law is instantiated, which implies a transition to civil society.

VII. The Will Theory

As we have seen, Private Right is the reciprocal limitation of 'mad' freedom that enables each person to have a 'rational' sphere of freedom. It is a set of a priori laws willed by everyone. The meaning of 'everyone' varies depending on the range of persons burdened by a particular type of rights-claim. Property rights, as *erga omnes* rights, must be based on laws sanctioned by every will – that being

---

[122] Jeremy Waldron, 'Kant's Legal Positivism', 1535, 1545–53.
[123] Kant, *The Metaphysics of Morals*, 45 (Ak 6:256).
[124] See Arthur Ripstein, 'Private Order and Public Justice: Kant and Rawls', 1391, 1422–29.
[125] Kant, *The Metaphysics of Morals*, 45 (Ak 6:256–57).

the reason why Kant pays the greatest attention to property; contract rights, as rights *in personam*, are grounded in the will of the parties. In each case, rights and duties – all entitlements – are based on the principle of the law-giving or universal will; that is to say, either the common will or that of the parties. That principle is the ultimate standard of validation of all rights, the basis of the entire system of Private Right, in relation to which the institutions and norms of Public Right play a supporting or instrumental role. It is from that basis that Kant implicitly derives the building blocks of each of the main divisions of his system.

(i) *Personal rights.* Each person is originally endowed with an identical set of (unlisted) personal rights: to life, bodily integrity, free speech, etc. (Rigorously speaking, there is a single personal right – to freedom – from which all personal entitlements derive; moreover, freedom, as an original instead of acquired right, is postulated by Private Right.)

(ii) *Freedom of contract.* Each person is originally endowed with freedom of contract; that is, the power to acquire contractual obligations (and rights) and immunity from unwilled obligations (and rights). A contract is commonly willed by the parties.

(iii) *Ownership.* Each person is originally endowed with the power to acquire ownership (absolute control) over corporeal objects, either by contract or inheritance (derived acquisition), or by occupying or taking control over *res nullius* (original acquisition).

(iv) *Tort liability.* Kant does not articulate a theory of tort in the *Rechtslehre*. But it is easy to assemble one from various bits of text. The basic elements are: breach of duty ('a deed that is contrary to a right'), fault (*'culpa'* or *'dolus'*), and harm. The rightful effect of a tort is the duty incumbent on the wrongdoer to make the victim whole ('I have a right to demand compensation … by this … I will preserve what is mine undiminished').[126]

The *Doctrine of Right* is not written as a political essay, in the vein of Humboldt's *The Limits of State Action* or Mill's *On Liberty*. The models are the great eighteenth-century natural law (or 'law of reason') treatises by Pufendorf, Thomasius and Wolff. Kant's project is not to lay before us the bare bones of Right – what it is about and what its basic thrust is; he is in the business of exhausting the subject. Yet, when we approach his work from the standpoint of that tradition, his offerings seem incomparably poorer than those of his predecessors. The original 1672 edition of Pufendorf's *De Iure Naturae et Gentium* runs over more than 1,000 pages (the English translation is longer) and contains elaborate doctrinal discussion of the sort that, with a few exceptions, is absent from the *Doctrine of Right*. In the field of contract, for example, Kant presents no theory of defences, no views on the nature and force of implied terms, no doctrine of breach, or any account of remedies.

---

[126] Kant, *The Metaphysics of Morals*, 16, 57 (Ak 6:244, 271).

The main reason for these and other omissions is no failure on Kant's part to accomplish his task. It is his conviction that the answers to all such questions are implicitly contained in the concepts – eg, person, contract, original acquisition, ownership, wrong – that he explicitly articulates. Those concepts are in turn generated by the application of the concept of Right – a universal reciprocal limitation of freedom – to the empirical conditions of a plurality of human beings living on earth. The system of duties of right is derived from the main concepts, in the image of the axioms and theorems of Euclidian geometry.[127] Following an explicit analogy with geometry, Kant writes that 'the doctrine of right wants to be sure that what belongs to each has been determined (with mathematical exactitude)'.[128]

Private Right is hence a formal system, for the more abstract, or more extensive, concepts (eg, freedom of contract) contain by implication less abstract or narrower ones (eg, duress, fraud and mistake) which in turn entail the even less abstract and narrow concepts (eg, each of the elements of fraud) on which the resolution of disputes ordinarily turns. This quality of vertical integration implies that the rightful outcome to any dispute is in principle contained in the abstract concepts that Kant presents in the *Rechtslehre*.[129] Thus, we are encouraged to believe that the concept of contract furnishes the full set of criteria to settle the issue of whether the defendant owes the plaintiff the price agreed for building a country residence, despite the fact that the pipe used by the builder is not produced by the manufacturer specified in the agreement.[130] Any genuine controversy as to which rule is correct – 'perfect tender' or 'substantial performance' – is framed as a matter of which side's analysis of the concept of contract is valid and which is flawed.

The distinctively late-modern idea of 'vertical integration' should be distinguished from the ancient intellectual process of arranging the rule material under a small set of labels. The Roman jurist Gaius wrote sometime in the second century AD a book called *Institutes* addressed primarily to law apprentices. It is one of the most systematic presentations of Roman Law, neatly dividing the legal material into persons (Book I), things (Books II–III), and actions (Book IV), an arrangement that influenced later jurists, indeed into as late as the eighteenth century (although indirectly).[131] Among one of Gaius' supposed innovations is the concept of 'contract' as one of two major sources of obligations (the other being 'delict').[132]

---

[127] Geometry, as the first demonstrative science, served as the Enlightenment paradigm of rational cognition. The attraction it exerted, among others, on Hobbes, Descartes, Spinoza and Leibniz is unmistakable. See, eg, Descartes, *Discourse on Method*, 16.
[128] Kant, *The Metaphysics of Morals*, 26 (Ak 6:233).
[129] The term 'vertical integration' is borrowed from Duncan Kennedy, *The Rise and Fall of Classical Legal Thought*, 28–31.
[130] *Jacob & Youngs v Kent*, 230 NY 239 (1921).
[131] The influence was indirect because the work was lost until the early nineteenth century. The influence it exerted was mediated by the *Digest* (or *Pandects*) and especially the *Institutes* of Justinian, two of the four books that constitute the *Corpus Juris Civilis*.
[132] Gaius, *Institutes*, §88. In a similar vein, Cicero, *The Laws*, II, 141.

But as James Gordley notices, after stating the word contract, which goes undefined, 'Gaius immediately turned to the particular Roman contracts which he classified according to Roman rules as to when they become binding'.[133] 'Contract' is a word picked to denote a variety of specific transactions upon the verification of a common element. Yet no rule applicable to a transaction is deduced from, or for that matter sought in, the concept of contract – the concept is a means of classifying the rules instead of determining their content. In Duncan Kennedy's words, the concept of contract is not 'operative', it does not furnish any criteria to settle a dispute that falls within its scope; it is an 'invented category to group some rules that I often want to refer to together'.[134] By contrast, when the system is vertically integrated, we 'see all the rules gathered under the contract rubric as implications of a general principle of freedom of contract'.[135]

The idea of an axiomatic science of Right, presented *more geometrico* and modelled after the works of Spinoza and Leibniz, is not of Kantian origin. It is considered one the key traits of the 'law of reason' period of legal thought that, according to convention, begins with Grotius, and matures in the work of Pufendorf, Thomasius and Wolff.[136] Yet Kant is arguably the first to have brought it to full fruition. Some legal historians have noticed that while previous writers announced their commitment to the 'mathematical' or 'geometric' method, they did not usually rely on it to present their material; when they did, moreover, as in Wolff's *Ius Naturae Modo Scientifico Pertractum*, it operated more as a form of exposition than as a rigorous demonstration of the logical implications of unassailable first principles. Consider Gordley's remarks on the method of Pufendorf, whose influence was perhaps the greatest in the post-Grotian era:

> [I]n his main work, *De iure naturae et gentium*, he imitated the method of Grotius. He quoted classical poets, Roman law, scripture, and ancient and modern philosophers. He did not distinguish sharply between axioms and propositions that are proved from axioms. He did not dress up his arguments to make them look like mathematical proofs. Indeed, had Pufendorf not announced that he was producing a complete system of moral law based on strict deductions from principles, no one would have suspected him of attempting an innovation in method.[137]

Now, while Kant does not attempt the presentation of his arguments as a series of mathematical proofs, his system is purged of the rich variety of sources and the mass of nuanced applications that was characteristic of the treatises of his predecessors. For Kant, the laws of Right proceed from the will in its law-giving or

---

[133] James Gordley, *The Philosophical Origins of Modern Contract Doctrine*, 31.
[134] Duncan Kennedy, *The Rise and Fall of Classical Legal Thought*, 28.
[135] ibid at 29.
[136] See Franz Wieacker, *A History of Private Law in Europe*, §16–17. Wieacker is careful to place Grotius among a first age of 'founders' and the others in a second age of mature or 'systematic' modern natural lawyers.
[137] Gordley, *The Philosophical Origins of Modern Contract Doctrine*, 128.

universal form. The exposition of Private Right in the MOM appears indeed to be the first recognisable statement of the will theory.

I suspect that the main reason Kant managed to pay effective tribute to the geometric method, unlike earlier theorists of Natural Right, has precisely to do with the substantive revolution triggered by the will theory. The pre-Kantian natural lawyers did rebel against the 'scholastic subtlety'[138] and the 'barbarous language'[139] of the sixteenth-century Dominican and Jesuit theologians of Salamanca and Coimbra;[140] but their innovations were *mainly* a matter of style. They matched their humanist concerns with clarity of exposition and literary elegance against the austere and hyper-technical style of the scholastic compendiums.[141] Grotius set the tone: 'My prime concern has been to base my examination of what belongs to the law of nature on ideas which are so certain that nobody can deny them without doing violence to their fundamental being ... The principles of natural law are clear and self-evident'.[142] With the terms 'natural law', 'self-evident principles' and 'certainty', Grotius cannot seriously mean anything like Descartes' foundational premise of '*cogito ergo sum*' or the a priori judgments on which Kant based his critical philosophy. He begins each discussion of a natural law doctrine with bits of textual authority from Scripture, Roman law or classical texts, and inserts comments and arguments at will, without bothering to establish anything remotely similar to what on a Kantian, or for that matter a Cartesian, view amounts to a rational foundation. He departs from earlier jurists and philosophers moderately at most, and mainly because he accords less authority to the *topoi* and *exampla* of classical sources and the inherited casuistry;[143] for him, they are appropriate starting points for an argument. By 'natural reason' and 'self-evident' principles (terms which, incidentally, Aquinas also used) he means roughly what Aristotle called 'practical wisdom', by opposition to 'theoretical reason'. The closest words in our largely un-Aristotelian epistemological lexicon are perhaps 'sensible' and 'reasonable'.

---

[138] Hugo Grotius, *Prolegomena to The Rights of War and Peace*, 1761. Grotius' main targets are 'Two spaniards, Covarruvia and Vasquez'.

[139] Jean Barbeyrac, quoted in Gordley, *Philosophical Origins*, 126.

[140] Also known as 'late scholastics', the 'school of Salamanca', or the 'Spanish school of natural law'. The most renowned members were Francisco de Vitoria, Francisco Suárez, Diego de Covarruvias, Diego de Soto, Luis de Molina, Leonard Lessius and Gabriel Vásquez. For an account focused on the theory of contract, see Gordley, ibid at 69–112. For an overview, see Welzel, *Derecho Natural y Justicia Material*, 112–34. Suárez, perhaps the greatest among them for his enduring place in the canon of Western political philosophy, was the least Aristotelian and Thomist of them all, both because his metaphysics steers a middle line between classical realism and nominalism and because he mediates voluntarism and corporatism in his account of the origins of civil government and the grounds of political obligation. It is worth noting, however, that his influence was confined to the field of public law.

[141] I follow closely Gordley, *Philosophical Origins of Modern Contract Doctrine*, 121–33.

[142] Grotius, *Prolegomena*, 1756.

[143] On *topoi*, *exampla* and other classical rhetorical devices, see Theodor Viehweg, *Topik und Jurisprudenz*, especially at §§1–3.

For the scholastics and their modern natural law descendents, for example, 'once one had defined a transaction one could move from the definition to a description of the obligations that the transaction entails'.[144] 'Entails' is James Gordley's slightly careless term. I suppose that neither Grotious, nor Aquinas or later natural lawyers, believed that, say, the concept of marriage or that of sales logically entails the rules of marriage or sales. A definition of a type of transaction states the goal or purpose of that sort of transaction – eg according to Aquinas, the purpose of marriage is, first, the begetting of children and, secondly, the complementary association of man and woman[145] – and from that purpose it is possible to discern what else was reasonable or natural for the parties to will, whether or not they expressed it.[146]

Behind these notions there is a large set of Aristotelian and Thomistic metaphysical premises, of which the modern natural lawyers were for the most part either unaware or committed to reject but nonetheless assumed.[147] The premises are a world where particulars or individuals are ontologically grouped together according to their nature, which is defined in terms of a shared *telos* or a good they naturally aim towards. Thus, just like a 'good knife' is a knife that cuts with ease and precision, for that is the purpose of a knife, and a 'good horse' is one that is physically fit and apt to ride, a good person is one that realises the specific *telos* of the human being, the rational species of the genus animal, which is human flourishing. Aristotle and Aquinas did not, of course, agree as to what exactly that means; among other differences, whereas Aristotle's account of the supreme human good is strictly natural or worldly, the *telos* according to Aquinas is salvation and the 'beatific vision' of God in the heavenly afterlife. But they agreed that while non-rational animals move towards their end by instinct and feeling, human beings *qua* rational beings realise their nature only if they subject their non-rational animal properties (eg, desire and emotion) to the direction of the distinctively human capacity to reason, and develop as much as possible the latter in its various forms (speculative ability, practical wisdom, etc). The qualities they acquire in that process are *the virtues*. When a person acts, therefore, he is under the control of the kind of virtue(s) appropriate to the circumstances of his agency; thus, a soldier exhibits courage in the battlefield, a tradesman exhibits commutative justice in his commercial dealings, and a wealthy person exhibits generosity or liberality in the presence of others' needs and privations.

---

[144] Gordley, *The Philosophical Origins*, 102.

[145] Thomas Aquinas, *Summa Theologica*, II–II, q 88, a I.

[146] That is the historical basis of the medieval and early modern doctrine of implied terms – called by civilian lawyers *natural* terms. A given type of contract – say, sales – has an essence, the exchange of money for goods, and a set of implied or natural terms, which *must be* in principle willed by a person who wills to either buy or sell something, because those terms are naturally tied to that essential (objective and intelligible) goal of sales. See Gordley, *Philosophical Origins*, 13–16, 61–65, 102–11, 121–33.

[147] See Alasdair MacIntyre, *After Virtue*, 146–80; James Gordley, *Philosophical Origins*, 10–30. They assumed Aristotelian premises indirectly, through their adherence to scholastic moral and legal doctrine built upon them. Gordley, ibid at 121.

Two key features of the view of the modern natural lawyers are worthy of closer inspection.[148] First, they embraced *objectivity* all the way down. If there are objective human purposes – objective in that they move a person closer to the realisation of his given nature – the point of both apparently restrictive laws, such as 'promises ought to be kept', and apparently facilitative laws, such as 'the will of the parties is to be respected', is to move those to whom they apply towards their real object. Consequently, it is entirely appropriate for the law to imply terms in a contract or to set aside unjust ones, for the will that merits legal protection is a will disciplined by virtue. Similarly, when the law imposes duties or restrains vicious behaviour, it is not constraining but facilitating the realisation of a person's real ends. 'Natural law' is accordingly a body of precepts that stores good practical reasons, ie reasons fit for moving an agent in the direction set by its nature.

Yet – and here lies the second key feature of pre-Kantian natural law – while there are objective ends all the way down, there is no method either to *demonstrate* them or to present them as an a priori system of axioms and theorems. First, practical principles, from the implied terms of a contract all the way up to highly general propositions such as 'private property is just' or '*pacta sunt servanda*', are not proper objects of demonstrable reasoning, of the sort that Aristotle called 'scientific knowledge', that is, 'judgment of things that are universal and necessary' and which 'follow from first principles'.[149] They are discovered by an intellectual process named by Aristotle 'dialectic', in which the starting points are furnished by *endoxa* or 'opinions that are generally accepted' and each opinion, initially presumed good, is tested by back and forth reasoning.[150] Although the precepts of natural law enjoin those actions that enable human flourishing, there is no suggestion that it is possible to retrieve them from that concept; they are instead to be sought in reputable opinions and in the legacy of exemplary persons, such as the various biblical characters whose deeds Grotius regularly recalls. As Aristotle had put it, 'Regarding practical wisdom we shall get at the truth by considering who are the persons we credit with it'.[151]

---

[148] In the company of Grotius, Pufendorf and Wolff – the so-called 'Northern natural lawyers' – should be mentioned their seventeenth and early-to-mid-eighteenth century French followers, Jean Domat, Jean Barbeyrac and Robert Pothier. Domat and Pothier were strongly influenced both by the 'law of reason' and by the sixteenth-century tradition of humanist or 'elegant' jurisprudence whose greatest names were Cujacius and Donellus. Their significance cannot be overstated: about two-thirds of Napoleon's *Code Civil* (1804) was lifted verbatim from their treatises. See James Gordley, 'Myths of the French Civil Code'. For a quick overview of the various topics referenced here, see generally Franz Wieacker, *A History of Private Law in Europe*, §8 IV.4 and §19 IV. 1. There is some evidence, based on textual and substantive affinity, that Grotius exerted considerable influence on Blackstone's *Commentaries on the Laws of England*. 'The introductory part of Blackstone's Commentaries – writes Roscoe Pound, Jurisprudence, II, 47 – is based on Grotius'. The account provided by Gerald J Postema, *Bentham and the Common Law Tradition*, 33–35 (esp 34, fn75) provides indirect vindication to Pound's judgment, although it is clear that Blackstone was even more eclectic than Grotius or the other leading modern natural lawyers.
[149] Aristotle, *Nicomachean Ethics*, Bk VI, ch 5, 1140^b, 1027.
[150] See Aristotle, Topics, Bk I, ch 1, 100^a, 188.
[151] Aristotle, *Nicomachean Ethics*, Bk VI, ch 5, 1140^a, 1026.

Secondly, the principles of natural law do not operate as axioms of a system. They apply not to 'universal and necessary' but to variable objects. A principle is either a maxim or aphorism that does not dictate particular outcomes – eg 'the basic precepts of the law are: live honorably, harm no one, and give each his own'[152] – or a rule based on the usual or standard case and subject to equitable refinement. For Aristotle, although moral virtue is a mean between two extremes, the mean is always relative to the agent and the circumstances of agency; thus, the right measure of courage is not the same in wartime and in peacetime, or for an experienced soldier and a civilian, and a moderate amount of food means one thing in relation to an athlete and another in relation to a child.

In his discussion of justice, Aristotle adds that 'When the law speaks universally ... and a case arises on it which is not covered by the universal statement ... it is right ... to say what the legislator himself would have said had he been present'.[153] These remarks appear in the context of his discussion of legal justice – ie, positive law – but they evidently apply to natural justice as well, to the extent that a writer, such as Grotius or Pufendorf, attempts its *formulation*. Every decision involves therefore a judgement as to whether a given law applies in the circumstances or not, for even if a law is simply applied to the facts, it is always because it dictates an outcome that is judged to be equitable.[154] Moreover, although it is clear that Aristotle believes in the objectivity of judgment – a 'rational principle', in his words – it is not because the reasoning involved is syllogistic or inferential; he defines a rational principle as that 'by which the man of practical wisdom would determine [the judgment]'. In other words, judgements are validated by the ability of good characters, who display the virtue of practical wisdom, to discern on each occasion what is right. 'The good man differs from others most by *seeing* the truth in each class of things, being as it were the norm and measure of them'.[155]

There is no doubt that Grotius, and particularly later writers such as Pufendorf and (above all) Wolff, gradually turned away from the Aristotelian scheme, under the influence of modern philosophy in both its empiricist and rationalist guises.[156] But as they did not abandon the belief in objective purposes and the companion commitments to dialectic reasoning and equitable judgement, their ability to

---

[152] D. 1. 1 10. (Ulpian). The original reads: '*Iuris praecepta sunt haec: honeste vivere, alterum non laedere, suum cuique tribuere*'.

[153] Aristotle, *Nicomachean Ethics*, Bk V, ch 10, 1037^b. 1020.

[154] ibid at Bk II, ch 6, 1107^a, 959. There are notwithstanding limits to the relativity of judgement on the Aristotelian view. Aristotle recognises a small class of exceptionless prohibitions. 'But,' he writes in the paragraph following the one quoted in the text, 'not every action nor every passion admits of a mean; for some have names that already imply badness, eg spite, shamelessness, envy, and in the case of actions adultery, theft, murder ... It is not possible, then, ever to be right with regard to them; one must always be wrong'.

[155] ibid at Book III, ch 3, 1113^a, 971 (emphasis added).

[156] This is true not only with respect to the methodological and epistemological issues emphasised in the text, but on a substance level as well (Hobbes' political philosophy, post-nominalist or anti-essentialist metaphysics, etc).

adhere to the 'mathematical' method was severely curtailed. It is worth quoting a passage from Grotius discussion of monopolies, an issue that he subordinates to the ancient topic of equality in exchange, to get a feel of how his style and method of reasoning differs so drastically from Kant's. Afraid that his readers may take the requirement of a just price to imply the injustice of all forms of monopoly, he writes:

> All Monopolies are not repugnant to the Law of Nature, for they may sometimes be permitted by the Sovereign upon a just Cause, and at a certain Rate; as may appear from the example of Joseph, when he was governor of Aegypt. [...] The like may be done by private persons, provided they are contented with a reasonable profit. But they, who, as the Oylmen in the Velabrum, do purposefully combine to advance the Value of their Wares above the highest Degree of the current Price, and those also who use Force or Fraud to prevent the importation of any greater Quantity, or else agree to buy up all, in Order to sell them again, at a rate very exorbitant, considering the Season, commit an Injustice, and are obliged to make Amends and a Reparation for it. If indeed they do by any other Means hinder the bringing in of Goods, or ingross them to themselves, to vend them dearer, tho' at a Price not unreasonable for the Season, they act against the Rules of Charity, as St. Ambrose proves by several Arguments, in his third Book of Offices, but properly speaking, they violate no Man's Right.[157]

This is the sort of argument that Kant derides as 'headless', 'empirical' or 'casuistic'. His method is utterly different. To the first commitment of the natural lawyers – objectivity all the way down – Kant opposes a very different view, which goes something like this. Each person has a set of ends of its own – hence: subjective ends – for the sake of which it requires a variety of means, such as external resources and the co-operation of others.[158] Gone is the reference to objective ends and a 'natural law' that tracks on a cosmic teleology. Since there are many such persons, equal in their dignity, there must be an objective rule that assigns a sphere of choice to each; the assurance of objectivity proceeds from the *form* of the rule – universality, the union of everyone's will. Thus, the reason why another's deeds cannot be acquired unilaterally but only by virtue of a contract is that I can only bind another person to co-operate in the pursuit of my ends if I offer in turn my cooperation for the pursuit of his ends.[159] What is objective is the requirement

---

[157] Hugo Grotius, *The Rights of War and Peace*, Book II, ch XII, 749–50 (emphasis removed).

[158] That all ends are regarded as subjective by the laws of Right does not quite mean that Kant takes them to *be* subjective. He distinguishes between the subjective ends of inclination, which are embodied in hypothetical imperatives, and the objective end of morality, which appears to us (as partly empirical beings) in the form of a categorical imperative. Right refrains from seeing that individuals act on the objective moral end, instead of subjective inclination, because it is impossible, on Kant's definition of morality (or moral value), to externally enforce moral duties. However, even Kant's objectivist account of morality is sharply opposed to the teleological framework of classical natural law; Kantian morality is not grounded in any external source, namely Nature or God. In the words of Alasdair McIntyre, *After Virtue*, 45, 'Practical reason, according to Kant, employs no criterion external to itself'.

[159] The ends of the parties may of course converge, as in a partnership; or a party may have an unselfish end, as in a gift. What matters is the 'omnilateral' form, not the nature of the ends that the parties cast into it, unless those ends are themselves inconsistent with Right (ie, a criminal partnership).

of contractual form; the content of the contract, on the other hand, is given by the subjective ends of the parties. The rightful will, in Kant's obscure language, is contingent as to its 'matter' and universal as to its 'form'.[160]

While the domain of objective norms is thus restricted, the newfound objectivity is far more robust that the natural lawyers'. The laws of Right are given by the application of the a priori idea of a universal law of external freedom to the human world. Gone are Aristotelian dialectic or Grotius' rich jumble of sources. Kant departs from the 'first principle' of the universal or rightful will and derives a set of basic concepts – person, contract, ownership, etc – which embody the entire system of duties of Right. Gone as well is Aristotelian equity. Right deals with abstract persons making abstract choices over abstract objects. What remains after the process of abstraction is the sort of 'universal and necessary' object which, on Aristotle's own account, is fit for scientific cognition. The equitable scheme of a rule defeasible by judgement gives way to a deductive model within which cases are subsumed under a concept or a series of concepts strung together.

Equity does not vanish, though. Kant recognises that in some cases rights are 'ambiguous'. He offers the following example:

> Suppose that the terms on which a trading company was formed were that the partners should share equally in the profits, but that one party nevertheless did more than the others and so lost more when the company met with reverses. By *equity* he can demand more from the company than merely an equal share with the others. In accordance with proper (strict) right, however, his demand would be refused; for if one thinks of a judge in this case, he would have no definite particulars (*data*) to enable him to decide how much is due by the contract.[161]

Kant's argument is therefore that while there are equitable rights, they cannot be enforced because equitable judgments are impossible; they belong not to 'civil justice' but to the 'court of conscience'. Obviously the argument begs the key question. It is only because Kant assumes that a court should deal exclusively in formally realisable norms that he can assert rather bluntly that 'a court of equity involves a contradiction'. He tries to mask a normative argument, that civil justice ought to be confined to the deductive model, as a conceptual point; and since there are, on Kant's account, equitable rights, the normative basis for the argument cannot be the UPR. This leads us to examine an important feature of the will theory, namely the tension between norm and exception and the various devices deployed by Kant to mediate it.

---

[160] Kant, *The Metaphysics of Morals*, 24 (Ak 6:230): 'in this reciprocal relation of choice no account at all is taken of the *matter* of choice, that is, of the end each has in mind with the object he wants; it is not asked, for example, whether someone who buys goods from me for his own commercial use will gain by the transaction or not. All that is in question is the *form* in the relation of choice on the part of both, insofar as choice is regarded merely as *free*, and whether the action of one can be united in with the freedom of the other in accordance with a universal law'. (Emphasis in the original.)

[161] ibid at 27 (Ak 6:235) (emphasis in the original).

VIII. Norm and Exception

When Kant discusses a particular doctrine or rule, it is usually because he is having some trouble justifying it or is willing to recognise that although it contradicts the will theory it is nonetheless a law of Right. He does not bother much with the doctrines that are sanctioned by the universal will, for he understands them to be logically contained in the a priori concepts that he derives. That is why, to give just one example, there is no theory of defences in Kant's brief exposition of contract; the concept of freedom of contract contains the negative implication that a person cannot be bound against his will, and that is all one needs in order to figure what defences the promisor can avail himself to.

I hope my point is not misunderstood. We do not believe that from the premises of the will theory of contract it is possible to derive an entire set of rules concerning defences, or indeed any truly operative rules. When we read the legal treatises of the nineteenth century with the benefit of hindsight, the efforts to work out the will theory in detail often look silly, and indeed pernicious.[162] The fact, however, is that they experienced very abstracts concepts as fully operative and sought in them criteria to articulate entire bodies of legal contract. Their divergences took the form of analytical disputes, concerning who is getting the concept right or applying it correctly to a fact pattern. From the standpoint of the (mainstream) participants in nineteenth-century legal thought, the question of which defences are available to the parties is thus deductive in nature; similarly, Kant experiences the concepts of contract and ownership, for example, as having a high degree of operative force.[163]

For example, according to the will theory, the fundamental basis of contract, the primary source of its binding force, is the consent of the parties. It is hence superficially plausible that if one of the parties made a mistake, the contract is void, or at least voidable. But what does that mean? Savigny developed in the third volume of his treatise an elaborate theory that influenced both the drafters of the German Civil Code (BGB), as well as Anglophone jurists such as

---

[162] 'Hairsplitting pedantry and legal spillkins', in the (notoriously harsh) words of Zweigert and Kötz, *An Introduction to Comparative Law*, 147.

[163] The level of abstraction below which concepts are experienced as entailing consequences or being operative is what Duncan Kennedy, *The Rise and Fall of Classical Legal Thought*, 243–51, calls the 'blocking level' of legal reasoning. The will theory, as a cognitive experience, had a very high blocking level. Surely not all questions – notice for instance Kant's remarks on quantitative and qualitative problems of ownership – were liable to a deductive resolution. But most were. Kennedy calls his approach to the problem of operative force or blocking level 'phenomenological', because it values the experience of being bound and places it in historical context; it approaches the problem from the standpoint of the participants in the practice; ibid at xvii–xx. I endorse his method, but disagree with the epistemological implication that he derives from it, namely that there is *no* 'objective criterion to judge when there has been an abuse of deduction'. It does not follow from the methodological premise that we ought to place a mistake in context in order to figure out why it was persistently made, that it is not a mistake except from our contingent standpoint. While I find Kennedy's method persuasive, then, I see no good reason to embrace his rather extreme epistemic relativism.

Sir Fredrick Pollock.[164] He begins by drawing an analogy between incapacity to contract and relief for mistake. Just as certain categories of persons, for instance infants and the mentally impaired, lack the power to enter binding agreements because they generally lack the capacity to discern the consequences of their actions, a person labouring under a mistake fails to discern the actual consequences of a particular transaction. The analogy, however, does not hold. A capable individual is accountable for the reasoning that precedes his decision; a mistake is not something that simply happens – it is made by a capable agent in the course of deliberation. In fact, says Savigny, it is necessary to 'distinguish between the will and that which precedes it in the mind of the agent'; the will is a 'single fact', the upshot of a deliberative process.[165] In principle, then, mistake is not a ground for relief.[166]

It is quite different, according to Savigny, when what is at stake is not a flawed deliberation but a lack of correspondence between the will and its expression or declaration. There are two necessary and jointly sufficient conditions for consent. One is the will to perform a transaction. The other is the outward declaration of the will, for as an 'internal and invisible fact' the will can only be known by means of external signs.[167] When there is a lack of congruence between the two elements, a 'contradiction between will and expression', there is no real but only apparent consent.[168] The contract is hence void, not because a mistake was made, but because one of the elements of consent is lacking. The theory rests on a sharp dichotomy between the will to have an object and the reasons to will the object. It is one thing for me to will your services as a singer; it is another and irrelevant matter *why* I will your services. If I meant to hire you and ended up

---

[164] Friedrich Carl von Savigny, *System des heutigen römischen Rechts*, III, §§115, 134–39ff, 111–20, 257–307. cf Fredrick Pollock, *Principles of Contract*, 531–622, 479: 'The whole topic was formerly surrounded with a great deal of confusion in our books ... Exactly the same kind of confusion prevailed in the civil law ... until Savigny cleared it up ... The principles ... established by him ... appear to be in the main applicable to the law of England'. Savigny follows the German practice, of which he was incidentally one of the pioneers, of examining the doctrine of mistake and other 'defects of the will' as an incident not of the theory of contract but of the broader category of 'juristic acts' (*Rechtsgeschaften*). A 'juristic act' is a species of legally operative fact (a *juristischen Tatsache*), an event that instantiates the factual predicate (or 'if-clause') of a legal norm. The distinguishing feature of the 'juristic act' is that it consists in a 'declaration of intent' or 'expression of the will' (a *Willenserklärung*) that certain legal consequences follow. Roughly speaking, all contracts are juristic acts because they produce the legal consequences intended by the parties. Contract is indeed one – and the most important in practice – species of juristic act, having as a distinguishing trait its bilateral or multilateral character. Yet, there are other species of juristic act, called unilateral, such as wills, offer and acceptance considered separately, or (according to some) the appropriation of *res nullius* and the abandonment of property. Savigny does not consider the later so – ibid at 6 (fn g); for his taxonomy of legally operative facts, see § 104, 1–8.

[165] ibid at 113.

[166] When a party is deceived, on the contrary, there is a cause for relief, although it is not grounded in mistake but in fraud. ibid at 115–20. Savigny draws an interesting analogy between fraud and duress at 98–111, and argues that neither of the defences furnishes a 'defect of the will'. The gist of it is that relief for duress is based on the general repugnance of the legal order for unlawful violence while relief for fraud is rooted in the importance of trust (*Vertrauen*) in social relations.

[167] ibid at 258.

[168] ibid.

hiring another singer, there is no real consent; if I meant to hire you because I was convinced that you could sing opera and it happens that you cannot, the congruence between will and expression is intact and therefore the contract is valid. The assumption is that to will an object is to intend a certain range of particulars. I will to buy *this* thing from *this* person on *these* terms. Accordingly, a party is relieved if it makes a mistake as to the identity of an object (*error in corpore*) – eg a person confuses the numbers of two paintings in an art gallery and ends up buying the wrong one – but not if the object lacks the qualities for the sake of which it wills to have it (*error in substantia*) – eg the painting is worth buying because it is a secret masterpiece.[169] However, Savigny is not entirely happy with this outcome either. He rejects rather bluntly the opposite view, that any mistake as to the properties of an object destroys consent, but he stresses that sometimes these must matter; he cites examples from Roman texts, such as buying bronze on the assumption that it is gold or vinegar on the assumption that it is wine.[170] After examining closely each case and presenting a seeming variety of rationales for granting relief, he declares that he has derived a 'general conception' – some qualities are integral to the identity of an object because they are essential according to trade usage.[171]

Savigny's theory of mistake has what Duncan Kennedy calls a 'nested' structure.[172] At each turn, Savigny faces a dilemma between the aim of protecting trust or security in transactions ('a person should be able to rely on credible *indicia* of commitment posited by others') and the aim of protecting private autonomy or freedom of choice ('a person should not be committed against his will'). Of course, he does not see it that way; he presents the problem, for the most part, as an analysis of the concept of consent.[173] And the jurists whose views on mistake rivaled his, simply because they took alternative paths at some juncture, framed the problem on the exact same terms. The debate had the following structure.

(i) *Subjectivism v objectivism.* The first question is whether consent should be understood in subjective terms – the will principle – or in objective terms – the declaration principle. Savigny and Pollock, together with many other classical jurists, took the former path; others, particularly in later decades, such as Schlossmann[174] and Holmes,[175] embraced the objectivist doctrine.

---

[169] ibid at 272–76.
[170] ibid at 278.
[171] ibid at 283.
[172] See Kennedy, 'A Semiotics of Legal Argument', 344–49. See also Jack Balkin, 'The Crystalline Structure of Legal Thought'; Kennedy, 'Nested Oppositions'.
[173] Although he makes at least one reference, in his discussion of mistake, to the importance of protecting trust and security in transactions – Savigny, *System*, III, 276–77. His main line of argument, however, takes the form of an analysis of the concept of 'declaration of will' (*Willenserklärung*).
[174] Siegmund Schlossmann, *Irrtum über wesentliche Eigenschaften der Person und der Sache nach dem Bügerlichen Gesetzbuch*, 46–47.
[175] Oliver Wendell Holmes, *The Common Law*, 309–13.

114   *Kant and the Will Theory*

(ii) *Broad v narrow.* Once the subjectivist path is taken, there is a question concerning the nature of the will. Savigny, as we have seen, defined the will rather narrowly as the upshot of a deliberative process, the moment in which an agent settles on some particular object; he was followed by Puchta[176] and Windscheid.[177] The French jurist Laurent, on the other hand, defined the will broadly, so as to include the reasons to enter an agreement.[178]

(iii) *Particulars v properties.* Within the narrow version of the will principle, a new question arises with respect to the object of the will. The position toward which Savigny appeared to be heading but ended up recanting is that the object is an identifiable thing (and person, etc); for instance, 'this' container of grain or 'that' pair of sunglasses; Zitelmann took a view like that.[179] The contrary opinion is that the object is something insofar as it bears certain properties or qualities taken to be essential – the position finally adopted by Savigny.

(iv) *Individualism v conventionalism.* At last, the qualities of an object may be understood either in terms of what the defendant considers essential or of what is essential according to the conventions of trade.

The whole sequence may be displayed in a hierarchical diagram, where the upper branches represent the relatively more autonomy-oriented and the lower branches the relatively more trust-oriented alternative.

Figure 2.4 The structure of mistake doctrine

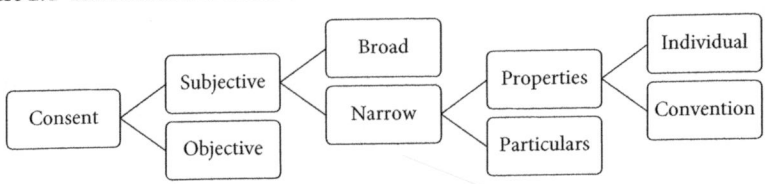

The manifold doctrinal subtleties lie beyond our concern. The important point to retain is that the nineteenth-century jurists approached these issues in an analytic spirit. Of course, it is plausible that at some point at least some of them realised that the whole subject of 'the nature of consent' (or 'the nature of ownership', etc) is more intricate than it may have appeared to Kant in the twilight of the eighteenth century. It is not an accident that the subject of mistake, which took Savigny a good portion of the third volume to address, and is the subject of later monographs of several hundred pages, is all but ignored by Kant. Reading the MOM, and particularly the *Doctrine of Right*, one gets the impression that Kant believes a

---

[176] Georg Friedrich Puchta, *Pandekten*, §57, 84–87.
[177] Bernhard Windscheid, *Lehrbuch des Pandektenrechts*, I, §76.
[178] François Laurent, *Principes de Droit Civil Français*, XV, §487.
[179] Ernst Zitelmann, *Irrtum und Rechtsgeschäft*, 341–42.

quick resolution to doctrinal questions is the natural upshot of the ascent of political theory and jurisprudence to the glories of critical philosophy.

Yet, there are exceptions to the norm of the will theory in the *Rechtslehre*, occasions in which Kant wants to maintain allegiance to some 'empirical' doctrine or rule in spite of his failure to rationalise it neatly in aprioristic terms. He deploys three devices to mediate these tensions. Sometimes, though rarely, he acknowledges the exception, presenting it as inevitable for pragmatic reasons – those are the *overt* exceptions, such as his endorsement of the doctrines of adverse possession and bona fide purchaser.[180] On other occasions, Kant relies on a dreadful argument to smuggle into the will theory a doctrine that sits poorly with it – those are the *covert* exceptions, such as his views on marriage and domestic servitude.[181] Finally, the more frequent case involves Kant masking a policy or moral point as an argument about the practical impossibility of enforcing a right – those are *mixed* exceptions, such as the denial of equitable claims and his remarks on the doctrine of necessity.[182]

We cannot devote great attention to these issues, but it is worth saying just a little about two exemplary cases. The first is Kant's discussion of marriage, which he places in the rather bizarre category of 'rights to persons akin to rights to things'. His exposition is meant to establish the contractual nature of marriage, while at the same time maintaining that it is a mandatory prerequisite of sexual intercourse and that it puts the wife under the authority of the husband ('a man acquires a wife').[183] In other words, marriage, being a contract, honours the equal dignity and the freedom of the spouses; but unlike any other contract, the parties are bound to enter it (or else they must embrace celibacy) and are absolutely barred from stipulating its content. Kant mediates, quite unsuccessfully, his commitment to Right as an amoral condition of equal freedom and his desire both to see that the moral prohibition of 'fornication' is enforced and to retain the patriarchal understanding of marriage that was common in his time.[184] Indeed, Kant's entire discussion of status ('rights to persons akin to rights to things') – particularly his attempt to rationalise domestic servitude as a regular contractual relation[185] – is riddled with inconsistencies.

---

[180] Kant, *The Metaphysics of Morals*, 73–74, 80–83 (Ak 6:292–93, 300–03).
[181] ibid at 61–64, 65–66 (Ak 6:277–80, 282–84).
[182] ibid at 26–28 (Ak 6:234–36).
[183] ibid at 61–63 (Ak 6:277–279).
[184] Still, it is clear that, in historical context, Kant's positions were liberal. He rejects categorically morganatic marriage and condemns concubinage, apart from insisting (albeit much of it is surface rhetoric) on the fundamental equality between the spouses.
[185] Here as well Kant's position is relatively liberal in context. He stresses that servants are 'included in what belongs to the head of the household' and that the head of the household can 'fetch servants back and demand them from anyone in possession of them, as what is externally his, even before the reasons that may have led them to run away and their rights have been investigated.' Yet, he also holds that (ibid at 66 (Ak 6:283–84)): 'The contract of the head of a household with servants can ... not be such that his *use* of them would amount to *using them up*'. (Emphasis in the original.)

The second example is Kant's treatment of the doctrine of necessity.[186] The doctrine provides that in order to preserve his own life and property or avoid serious harm a person may interfere with another's enjoyment of his personal or property rights; for instance, to avoid a fire in his property, a person may enter his neighbour's land and draw water from a well. A famous case involved a ship-owner tying his steamship to a dock in the course of a violent storm, causing significant damage as the wind threw the steamship against the dock.[187]

Necessity is a potential source of embarrassment for Kant. In the *Rechtslehre*, rights are defined in accordance with a 'universal law of freedom' that regulates the co-existence of individual choices, not the relation of one's choice to the 'mere wish' and the 'mere need' of the other.[188] The assignment of spheres of freedom abstracts from the contingencies of need, for it is grounded in the form rather than the content of individual choice. But necessity is a situation in which X may acquire a privilege to interfere with Y's rights in virtue of the urgency and intensity of X's needs contrasted with Y's. It involves an ad hoc balancing of interests.

Now, Kant could have denied the existence of a necessity privilege, as did later will theorists.[189] Instead, he attempts to rationalise it with the precious assistance of a fiction. He maintains that to interfere with another's rights constitutes a wrong in any circumstance; as he puts it 'there could be no necessity that would make what is wrong conform with law' and 'were there such a right the doctrine of right would have to be in contradiction with itself'.[190] The problem is that wrongful actions motivated by necessity are impossible to deter, because juridical incentives are insufficient to prevent such wrongdoing; necessity is hence not 'inculpable but only unpunishable'.[191]

This is a poor argument. Surely, it is possible, in most cases, to deter wrongdoing motivated by necessity, so long as the sanctions are severe enough. What enables Kant to hold the opposite view is that he defines the question of necessity

---

[186] ibid at 28 (Ak 6:235–36).

[187] *Vincent v Lake Erie Transportation Co*, 109 Minn 456 (1910). The issue in *Vincent* was whether the defendant (the ship-owner) was liable to compensate the plaintiff (the dock-owner) for the damage caused, not the preliminary question of the defendant's privilege under circumstances of necessity. The existence of a privilege of necessity itself was the issue in a prior and equally famous case – *Ploof v Putnam*, 81 Vt 471 (1908).

[188] Kant, *The Metaphysics of Morals*, 24 (Ak 6:230).

[189] Bernhard Windscheid, *Lehrbuch des Pandektenrechts*, I, §167, defines ownership as the absolute dominion of the owner's will over a thing. The position was adopted in the first draft of the German Civil Code (BGB); Windscheid was a member of the first drafting committee and many provisions of the first draft were lifted verbatim from his treatise. See Franz Wieacker, *A History of Private Law in Europe*, §25 I 2. Eventually, the second drafting committee incorporated the doctrine in the BGB, which provides in §904, under the heading 'Necessity', that 'The owner of a thing is not entitled to prohibit the influence of another person on the thing if the influence is necessary to ward off a present danger and the imminent damage is disproportionately great in relation to the damage suffered by the owner as a result of the influence. The owner may require compensation for the damage incurred by him.' See www.g-esetze-im-internet.de/englisch_bgb (last visited: 2 December 2011). On the subject of this note, in greater detail, see James Gordley, *Foundations of Private Law*, 132–34.

[190] Kant, *The Metaphysics of Morals*, 28 (Ak 6:235–36).

[191] ibid.

very narrowly as a 'supposed ... authorization to take the life of another who is doing nothing to harm me, when I am in danger of losing my own life'. It follows that:

> [T]here can be no *penal law* that would assign the death penalty to someone in a shipwreck who, in order to save his own life, shoves another, whose life is equally in danger, off a plank on which he had saved himself. For the punishment threatened by the law could not be greater that the loss of his own life.[192]

It is tempting to take from this passage that Kant meant to confine his point about necessity as an unpunishable wrong to the type of extreme case illustrated by the 'shipwreck' example. His position on other cases – say, the 'fire' and 'storm' cases – may have been that there is indeed a privilege of necessity, which is based primarily on the intensity and urgency of the defendant's interest; or perhaps that there is no such privilege, with the implication that the behaviour of the defendant constitutes a juridical wrong, subject to sanctioning. Cases like 'the shipwreck' – or Lon Fuller's 'Speluncean Explorers'[193] – pose real intellectual and moral challenges; those are cases that lie on the borders the juridical realm.

My understanding is that such a reading does not hold for at least two reasons. First, it makes no sense for Kant to say of the shipwreck case that the wrong of the defendant is 'unpunishable' because it cannot be prevented, for on Kant's account, the primary function of criminal punishment is not ex ante deterrence but ex post retribution.[194] Secondly, it would be strange for Kant to use the term 'necessity' so narrowly without further ado, for in the natural law tradition the doctrine of necessity had a precise technical meaning and was mostly examined in connection with property issues of the sort illustrated by the 'fire' and 'storm' cases. The view of the natural lawyers was that a just property regime is qualified by a doctrine of necessity, for as the purpose of private appropriation is to serve (objective) human needs, it would be morally self-defeating not to allow the needs of the non-owner to trump those of the owner where the former are patently greater than the latter.[195]

My sense is that Kant wants to draw our attention away from the earlier discussion of necessity centered on property issues and focus it on the extreme shipwreck and similar cases. His purpose is to keep the natural lawyer's doctrine of necessity without the metaphysical and moral baggage that came with it. He achieves that by means of the fiction that necessity involves wrongs that are impossible to deter, and therefore cannot be sanctioned. The underlying rhetorical move is something like this. The 'shipwreck' case is in a way the exact opposite of the 'fire' and 'storm'

---

[192] ibid.

[193] Lon L Fuller, 'The Case of the Speluncean Explorers'.

[194] Kant, *The Metaphysics of Morals*, 104–09 (Ak 6:331–37). 'Punishment by a court ... can never be inflicted merely as a means to promote some other good for the criminal himself or for civil society. It must always be inflicted on him because he has committed a crime' (105). (Emphasis removed.)

[195] See, eg, Thomas Aquinas, *Summa Theologica*, II–II, q 66, a 7; Hugo Grotius, *The Rights of War and Peace*, II, 433–37. As Gordley, *Foundations of Private Law*, 131, remarks, 'in a state of necessity, property became literally common'.

cases. In the former, most people feel that the defendant does something wrong (killing another human being) that is nonetheless so desperate that punishing the offence is pointless, if not plainly absurd.[196] In the latter cases, on the contrary, the defendant's behaviour is widely thought to be justified under the circumstances, although susceptible to being deterred by law. By trying to have us assimilate the latter cases to the former, Kant seeks to enlist our support for his flawed position that necessity is always about a wrong that is impossible to deter. The argument is undoubtedly terrible. But that is not a point against this reading. As the discussion of marriage illustrates, Kant is at his worst intellectually when he faces a tension between his commitment to the will theory and his desire to keep a doctrine that sits poorly with it.

The most theoretically self-aware historians of nineteenth-century legal thought describe the exception as an undesired anomaly that is pushed to the margins in the process of vertical integration of the normative material. Morton Horwitz expounds that view with characteristic eloquence:

> The identification of anomalies was a central part of the task of legal interpretation after 1870. We have seen how Holmes consistently labeled various strict liability doctrines as anomalies whose appearance in the law could be explained only by historical peculiarities. We have also seen that he sought to discredit strict master-servant and common carrier liability, both of which contradicted his project of integration. In similar spirit, as we shall soon see, William Keener published a book on *Quasi-Contract* in 1893 for the purpose of isolating a paternalistic, non-will-based set of doctrines from a pure and supposedly voluntaristic system of contract law.[197]

I am afraid that this picture is overly simplistic. From his a priori armchair, Kant had no reason to be concerned with the 'anomalies' of positive law; unhampered by the institutional constraints of the jurist, he could have dismissed them as merely 'empirical'. When we spot an exception in the *Rechtslehre*, we must therefore assume that Kant desired to maintain it. The exception plays the key role of mediating the tension between the rational fidelity to the will theory and the resilience of normative impulses experienced as incompatible with it. It is certainly an 'anomaly' from the intellectual point of view, marginal in the order of exposition; but a key component of the system as a morally compelling scheme, that is to say, in the order of justification. I venture that we should approach the 'anomalies' of the nineteenth-century jurists in the same spirit. Doubtlessly, they were often approached as embarrassing residues of an earlier and antagonistic ethos. Yet they played no less characteristically the role assigned to them by Kant – exceptions to a norm the strict application of which would yield unacceptable consequences.

---

[196] But see *R v Dudley and Stephens*, 14 QBD 273 DC (1884). See also AW Brian Simpson, *Cannibalism and the Common Law*.
[197] Horwitz, *The Transformation of American Law, 1870–1960*, 15.

3
The Rise of Classical Private Law

I. From Theory to Ideology

Why is Kant's theory of such great importance? Why does the contribution of this one author to political theory matter so greatly? For a small group of commentators, mostly academics in philosophy departments or historians of political thought, this is the sort of philistine questioning unworthy of serious consideration. They are concerned with the ideas of great thinkers and they see their task as distilling them from texts. They lay all the stress on the individual author and his intellectual output. My agenda is of a quite distinct variety. I am interested in Kant's political thought insofar as it acquired social currency, that is to say, insofar as it migrated from the realm of ideas-on-books – or theory – to the realm of ideas-in-action – or ideology. The philosophical historian is not interested in the beliefs of individuals – their doctrine or their philosophy – but in the beliefs that are built into social consciousness. Put briefly, it is not ideas as such but forms of consciousness that concern us.[1]

In the case of normative belief systems – such as Kantian Right – the question of social currency is slightly more complicated than it is when the beliefs are merely descriptive. If in a given society there is a belief system that a race is superior to others in intellectual ability and moral integrity, it follows as a simple matter of definition that is has social currency; that racial ideology is bound to shape the interactions among individuals – eg, commercial practices, capital–labour relations, the repression of crime, education policy, etc – in roughly the same way that the belief that the human body is vulnerable to physical harm does, ie as an aspect of reality that simply cannot be willed or wished away.[2] But when it comes to a view about how a social practice ought to be, social currency may be defined in either a weak or a strong sense. In a weak sense, it means that there is a widely held belief that a social practice ought to be of such-and-such character, although that is currently not the case. In a strong sense, on the other hand, currency implies that the belief is both normative and descriptive, that is, widely held as a right standard for social practice *and* as the standard immanent in existing practice. A normative

---

[1] The term 'ideology' is used here in one of the variants of the so-called 'descriptive sense' – as a 'worldview', 'world-picture' or 'form of social consciousness'. See Raymond Geuss, *The Idea of a Critical Theory*, 9–11; and Tommie Shelby, 'Ideology, Racism, and Critical Social Theory', 154–62.

[2] See Berger and Luckmann, *The Social Construction of Reality*, 1–18, 47–128.

ideology can thus be merely collective aspiration or a belief in the essential rightness, goodness, or justice of social arrangements.

Kant's doctrine of Private Right – the will theory – acquired social currency in the strong sense. It was not only taken as an ideal standard to which the law should conform but as an ideal embodied in legal practice. The will theory was read by mainstream jurisprudence in the nineteenth century into positive law. 'Kant', writes Roscoe Pound,

> conceived that the problem of law was to reconcile conflicting free wills. He held that the principle by which this reconciliation was to be effected was equality in freedom of will, the application of a universal rule to each action which would enable the free will of the actor to co-exist along with the free will of everyone else. *The whole course of nineteenth century juristic theory was determined by this conception.*[3]

Pound failed to address the obvious question prompted by this bold assertion: How was that possible? He offers no account of the reasons behind the reception of Kant's will theory of Right among the jurists. I use the term 'reasons' in this context advisedly. The issue is how an identifiable set of social agents – the jurists – came to appropriate Kant's political theory. Whether or not there are other, perhaps deeper, causal forces at work is an altogether different matter, which is anyway beyond our concern. The jurists are human beings, and human beings do not fancy themselves as acting on causes – eg, 'when the price of wine drops I buy more, for decreases in the price of a good cause increases in the quantity demanded' – but on reasons – eg, 'when the price of wine drops I buy more because my budget now allows it.' Shortening a long line of reasoning, the vantage point is not causal-explanatory but hermeneutic-purposive.

My argument develops in two steps. The first step is an account of why the will theory, assuming a freestanding and truncated form, was congenial to the political ethos of the late-eighteenth and early-nineteenth centuries, dominated by the legacy of the liberal revolutions. The second step is an account of what led the jurists to seize the will theory and then read it into the sources of law. I present it as an event in the process of transformation of jurisprudence from medieval *iurisprudentia* to modern legal science, the enterprise that enabled the jurists as a class to restore the 'symbolic capital'[4] accumulated in the late Middle Ages (c 1200–1500) and gradually threatened in the course of the Renaissance and the Enlightenment (c 1500–1800). Let me turn to the first step of the argument.

II. Reception of the Will Theory

Kantian Right is a condition of external freedom among equals. In that sense, it is perfectly appropriate to say, with Charles Larmore, that Kant is committed to the

---

[3] Roscoe Pound, *Jurisprudence*, I, 503 (emphasis added). See also Franz Wieacker, *A History of Private Law in Europe*, 199.
[4] Pierre Bourdieu, 'The Force of Law: Toward a Sociology of the Legal Field'.

idea of ethical neutrality.[5] But we should pay attention to the ways in which Kant's argument for freedom as the prime political good is parasitic on the comprehensive moral doctrine presented in the *Groundwork*, as opposed to the freestanding or 'political not metaphysical'[6] conception immanent in our political culture.

The point is fairly simple. What lead Kant to a liberal position were the internal requirements of his moral philosophy. Right is ethically neutral because it is in the nature of moral value, on the view presented in the *Groundwork*, that it cannot be realised through the external mechanism of enforcement. The task of Right is to secure, in the form of equal rights enforced by a working state apparatus, the preconditions for effective moral agency in the social world. That is precisely why Kant insists on the moral duty of persons living in a state of nature to coerce others into entering a civil condition. Nothing can contribute more decisively to the development of morality and the creation of a kingdom of ends than a rightful condition, where each person is endowed with an equal and effective sphere of external freedom.

From this standpoint, it is obvious that Kant's political theory, however philosophically admirable, is ideologically unimportant. His ethics, not to speak of the larger metaphysics and epistemology in which it is embedded, was just one among a variety of comprehensive doctrines that had some purchase in the late-eighteenth century. The form in which Kantian Right – the will theory – acquired a measure of broader social appeal was quite another. It was in a freestanding form, embodying a rigorous derivation of both the foundations and the concrete implications of the ethos expressed in Declaration of the Rights of Man and Citizen of 1789. Alexis de Tocqueville called it the 'most fundamental, durable, and authentic' legacy of the French Revolution.

> The philosophical conceptions of the eighteenth century ... embodied all the new (or resuscitated) opinions regarding the nature of human society and the underlying principles of civil and political jurisprudence; the belief, for example, that all man are born equal and its corollary, the abolition of all privileges of class, caste, and profession. To the same category belonged the theories of the sovereignty of the people, of equal laws for all, of the vesting of the supreme power in the nation as a whole. Such ideas ... formed part and parcel of [the French Revolution] and, in the light of subsequent events, can be seen to be its most fundamental, durable, and authentic characteristics.[7]

What Kant's will theory offered to a political mainstream receptive to the various ingredients listed by Tocqueville and blended in the classical declarations of rights was a powerful understanding of both their normative foundations and their practical implications. On the one hand, Kant supplied the natural rights tradition with important resources to defend itself against the type of critique conveyed by Jeremy Bentham's vicious charge that 'Natural rights is simple nonsense: natural

---

[5] See Charles Larmore, 'Political Liberalism', 342–43.
[6] John Rawls, 'Justice as Fairness: Political not Metaphysical', 223.
[7] Alexis de Tocqueville, *The Old Regime and the French Revolution*, 6. See Michael Stolleis, *Public Law in Germany 1800–1914*, 1–7.

and imprescriptible rights, rhetorical nonsense – nonsense upon stilts'.[8] One of Bentham's main complaints was that natural rights talk is dangerously undemocratic, for 'the Law of Nature is ... the mere opinion of men self-constituted into Legislators'.[9] But Kant derived natural rights from the will of people: 'If a public law is so composed that an entire people could not give its assent to it ... then it is unjust'.[10] His whole point is that when the individual rises above unilateral opinion (the 'I' perspective) and adopts an omnilateral view (the 'we' perspective), the legislative will is in agreement with the rights of man. The will theory mediates the rationalist and voluntarist strands of classical liberalism, associated respectively with John Locke and Jean-Jacques Rousseau.[11]

On the other hand, Kant converted the sweeping generalities of the various declarations of rights – mercilessly denounced by Bentham as signs of 'nonsense' and 'contradiction'[12] – into a system of axioms endowed with a high degree of operative force. From the abstract commitments to liberty, equality and property Kant derives a system of Private Right that determines 'what belongs to each ... with mathematical exactitude'.[13] In the form of the will theory, then, the faith in individual rights resisted the united utilitarian, romantic and historicist charge that they lacked concrete political and legal content.[14] In the end, as Roscoe Pound noticed, the will theory of Right, in something very close to the form that Kant gave to it in the *Rechtslehre*, drew together a wide range of schools of thought, among which those holding the banners of Kantian comprehensive philosophy were a neglectable minority.[15]

As a theorist of individual rights, as opposed to a philosopher working out the political implications of a comprehensive doctrine, Kant is the author of the *Doctrine of Right* read in conjunction with his political essays. *The Groundwork*, *The Critique of Practical Reason*, and the *Doctrine of Virtue* are drawn out of the picture. There is a question concerning whether Kant would have wanted his views on politics to be read that way. The prevailing opinion in the literature – expressed

---

[8] Jeremy Bentham, 'Anarchical Fallacies', 53.
[9] *Quoted in* Gerald Postema, *Bentham and the Common Law Tradition*, 269.
[10] Kant, 'Theory and Practice', 51 (Ak 8:297). There are echoes here of the famous statement by Rousseau, *The Social Contract*, Book II, ch 3, that 'There is often a great deal of difference between the will of all and the general will; the latter considers only the common interest, while the former takes private interest into account, and is no more than a sum of particular wills: but take away from these same wills the pluses and minuses that cancel one another, and the general will remains as the sum of the differences'.
[11] On voluntarism and rationalism as two strands of liberalism, see Jeremy Waldron, 'Theoretical Foundations of Liberalism', 140–46.
[12] See Bentham, 'Anarchical Fallacies', 46–51.
[13] Kant, *The Metaphysics of Morals*, 26 (Ak 6:233).
[14] That was one of the issues at the centre of the so-called 'Theory-Practice Debate' in late-eighteenth-century Germany. See Frederick Beiser, *Hegel*, 31–33.
[15] Roscoe Pound, 'The End of Law as Developed in Juristic Thought: The Nineteenth Century', esp at 202–03. The following passage is particularly striking: '[Herbert] Spencer's formula of justice is a Kantian formula. He had never read Kant. But Kant had become part of thought of the time so thoroughly that each of the significant nineteenth century schools ... came to his position as to the end of law ...' [223].

by prominent contemporary liberal theorists such as John Rawls, Charles Larmore and Jeremy Waldron – is negative. They hold that Kant's liberalism is 'metaphysical' while the versions they endorse are 'political not metaphysical'.[16]

But such a reading is fraught with a serious difficulty – the problem of circularity. Kant holds both that we have a moral duty to enter and maintain a rightful condition and that the latter is a necessary condition of moral agency, for a state of nature is a 'lawless state of savagery'.[17] That is, Right presupposes morality and morality presupposes Right. In order to break this vicious circle, Kant would have to propose some alternative non-moral path from a lawless to a rightful condition. He would have to present his account of Right as a freestanding doctrine; and indeed, as Thomas Grey pointed out in a remarkable essay published some 25 years ago, that is a major theme of Kant's philosophy of history.[18]

Let me nonetheless put aside the question of how Kant *meant* his work on political theory to be read and take up instead the question of how it *was* read. I argued that what made the will theory attractive in the late-eighteenth and early-nineteenth centuries was that it lent an important measure of intellectual depth and bite to the idea of individual rights. The political background was furnished by the liberal revolutions and – in Europe – the French Revolution in particular. '[I]t touched the fundamental, legitimizing thought of the time and abruptly opened new perspectives. The old order of things collapsed ….'.[19] There were, in any case, several critical voices directed against the excesses of the Revolution, notably the execution of Louis XVI and the ensuing Reign of Terror (1793–94). Around 1814–15, when the War of the Sixth Coalition ended and Metternich summoned the Great Powers to the Congress of Vienna, the idea was to strike a balance between liberalism and absolutism. As the leading historian of German public law puts it:

> The legal establishment of a balance between absolutism, which, since the French Revolution, had become deeply insecure and was no longer sacred, and popular sovereignty, which had not been attained, provided the dominant problematic for all teaching about constitutional law before 1848. This was the balance between monarchy, nobility, and church and the third estate, which aspired to be a nation. After the French Revolution, and even more so following Napolean's victories, the world had changed. The simple way back to absolutistic governance was blocked, although the old powers proved themselves to be strong enough to restrain the third estate or, in any case, to force them to accept their arrangements.[20]

---

[16] John Rawls, *Political Liberalism*, 99–101; Charles Larmore, 'Political Liberalism', 342–44; Jeremy Waldron, 'Kant's Theory of the State', 198 fn 16.
[17] Kant, 'Idea for a Universal History from a Cosmopolitan Perspective', 10 (Ak 8:24).
[18] Thomas Grey, 'Serpents and Doves: A Note on Kantian Legal Theory', 585–91. The main primary sources in this vein are: Kant, 'Conjectural Beginning of Human History'; Kant, 'Idea for a Universal History from a Cosmopolitan Perspective'; Kant, 'Toward Perpetual Peace'. For a perceptive summary, see Allen Wood, 'Kant's Philosophy of History'.
[19] Michael Stolleis, *Public Law in Germany 1800–1914*, 3.
[20] ibid at 61.

Ironically, the model of a balanced arrangement was French. It was the *Charte Constitutionelle* of 1814, which restored the throne to the Bourbons following the Battle of Leizpig and Napolean's exile in the island of Elba. The new constitution steered a middle line between the monarchical principle and popular sovereignty, embracing both 'the conservation ... of the rights and prerogatives of our crown' and 'the expectation of enlightened Europe'. It sought to 'unite ancient and modern times'.[21] So a key element of the political climate in much of Europe in the early nineteenth century was that 'new order' of individual rights and the 'old order' of the monarchical principle were to co-exist side by side within a single legal order. Another aspect concerned the status of woman in general, and especially the exclusion of the household from the purview of liberal principles. We have seen that Kant's arguments in the domain of 'rights to persons akin to rights to things' are uniformly bad, as he tried to mediate the tension between the commitment to equal rights and the household imaginary of the *ancient régime*, structured by the three isomorphic relations of husband/wife, father/child, and master/servant. The trend in the early-nineteenth century was to emancipate domestic servants, if only as 'passive citizens', but to retain the other two relations within the novel framework of the romantic-patriarchal family.[22]

In the legal treatises of the nineteenth century, the balancing of the three logics – monarchism, liberalism and patriarchalism – takes the form of a tripartite structuring of the legal order and the corresponding society. On the one hand, there is public law versus private law; on the other hand, private law is divided into patrimonial law – mainly property and obligations – and family law.[23] The will theory finds its way in this scheme in the form of the logic immanent in patrimonial private law. It was the law of free and equal persons. Public law and family law are based on very different – non-liberal – logics. The *Doctrine of Right* acquired social currency in the strong sense, as the specific form that classical liberalism took in the nineteenth century, but was stripped of the Public Right part, as well as the convoluted section on household relations. In that truncated form, it was read by the jurists into the sources of law. It is time to find out why.

III. Rise and Decline of *Iurisprudentia*

It is well-documented by legal historians that around 1300 the jurists educated in Bologna and other universities in Europe achieved a position of high prestige

---

[21] http://mjp.univ-perp.fr/france/co1814.htm (last visited: 10 February 2012). See also ibid at 61–62.
[22] See Janet Halley, 'What is Family Law? A Genealogy Part I', 1–2, 94–95.
[23] On the family/market dichotomy in classical private law see the now classic essay by Frances Olsen, 'The Family and the Market: A Study of Ideology and Legal Reform'; and the recent essay by Janet Halley, 'What is Family Law? A Genealogy Part I'. It is important to bear in mind that the notion of patrimonial law as 'the law of the market', as applied to nineteenth-century legal thought, is anachronistic. Both the theorists of Right (such as Kant) and the jurists associated contract, property and tort with individual freedom and universal equality, not with the production of wealth in the marketplace.

and influence in public life, whether as officials in the court of princes, diplomatic advisers, or – more importantly – counsellors and external authorities in the administration of justice.[24] We can only appreciate the social and political significance of this 'primacy of the learned men'[25] if we examine briefly the dominant understanding of law in the period.

In medieval political thought, the prince is the supreme judge in temporal affairs. Supreme judge – not supreme legislator. His role is not to impose order on society but to be the highest custodian of a superior order. When he makes a law (*lex*), he is revealing and formulating a pre-existing normative content. The difference between his general regulations and the particularistic decisions of the *iudex* is a matter of degree; both functions are judicial in the broad sense that they apply a stock of previously available norms, often referred to as 'the natural order' or *ius*.[26] That is why the medieval word for princely authority – indeed, for all kinds of temporal authority – was *iurisdictio*.[27]

It follows that the medieval conception of legislative authority was radically different from the modern one. We think of a statute as a text – a definite choice of words – that carries authority as such. It is important to know what constitutes a legislative enactment – an official transformation of the words into law – because it is on account of its form rather than its content that it is legally authoritative. It is the fact that a statute was passed in accordance with standard and rigorously defined procedure that makes it law. Kelsen brings out nicely this feature of legislation in an early passage of the *Pure Theory of Law*:

> People assemble in a large room, make speeches, some raise their hands, others do not – this is the external happening. Its meaning is that a statute is being passed, that law is created. We are faced here with the distinction (familiar to jurists) between the process of legislation and its product, the statute.[28]

The image invoked by Kelsen's remarks is for the most part familiar only to modern jurists. In the Middle Ages, on the contrary, '*lex* is not merely will or an authoritative act, but a reading of the reasonable norms carved in the nature of things'.[29] Two important consequences follow. First, it matters little who makes *leges* or how they come into force, for their authority proceeds from substantive adequacy as externalisations of *ius*. Consequently, *lex* can be either written law (*lex scripta*) or custom (*lex non scripta*), and in each case there is typically

---

[24] See, eg, Franz Wieacker, *A History of Private Law in Europe*, §5 IV; António Manuel Hespanha, *Cultura Jurídica Europeia*, 162; John Dawson, *The Oracles of the Law*, 138–47; Paolo Grossi, *L'Ordine Giuridico Medievale*, 151–68.

[25] Dawson, ibid at 138.

[26] See Otto Brunner, *Land and Lordship*, 114–24.

[27] For a book-length treatment of the topic, see Pietro Costa, *Iurisdictio*. For two useful summaries, see Paolo Grossi, *L'Ordine Giuridico Medievale*, 41–50, 130–35; and António Manuel Hespanha, *Cultura Jurídica Europeia*, 77–78.

[28] Kelsen, *Pure Theory of Law*, 2.

[29] Paolo Grossi, *L'Ordine Giuridico Medievale*, 139.

no standard procedure for making it official.[30] That helps explaining how a set of Roman law books issued under the authority of a Byzantine Emperor in the sixth century were regarded as law (although subsidiary law)[31] in Medieval Europe – it was more on account of their inherent reasonableness (*imperio ratione*), their special tie to the underlying natural order, than to a feeble imperial authority (*ratione imperii*).[32] Secondly, since the function of *lex* is to establish a bridge between the hidden order of things and the observable world of texts and practices, what is ultimately decisive is not the letter but the spirit. 'Textual authority', writes Paolo Grossi, 'is not something completely fixed; on the contrary, it is flexible, the text can and should be 'translated' into the situation of its reader and user, can and should be *interpreted*'.[33] Grossi is at pains to stress that the medieval notion of *interpretatio* is altogether different, mostly in the sense of being far more liberal, from our understanding of (statutory) interpretation. I suspect that the key connection here is furnished by the Church tradition of picking on a passage of Paul's *Second Epistle to the Corinthians* – 'The letter killeth, but the spirit giveth life'[34] – to establish that Scripture is merely the vehicle in which the Holy Spirit drives the faithful to the real Word of God.[35] Take the following paragraph of the *Catechism of the Catholic Church*:

> [T]he Christian faith is not a 'religion of the book'. Christianity is the religion of the 'Word' of God, 'not a written and mute word, but incarnate and living'. If the Scriptures are not to remain a dead letter, Christ, the eternal Word of the living God, must, through the Holy Spirit, 'open (our) minds to understand the Scriptures.[36]

Be that as it may, the medieval idea of *interpretatio* was that legal rules do not so much constitute the law as they stand in a privileged relationship to it. They are starting points in the discovery of law that lies beyond them (*non ex regula ius sumatur, sed ex iure quod est regula fiat*).[37]

---

[30] ibid at 136. Actually, the medieval understanding may have been that custom is a purer form of *lex* than *lex scripta*, for it is by its very nature shielded from the voluntaristic conceit and the arbitrary caprice of a bad ruler. See Canning, *The Political Thought of Baldus de Ubaldis*, 100.

[31] On medieval legal pluralism and the co-existence (and tension) between *ius commune* (Roman and Canon law) and *iura propria* or *ius speciale*, see Grossi, *L'Ordine Giuridico Medievale*, 223–37; Hespanha, *Cultura Jurídica Europeia*, 118–28.

[32] Of course that was not the only reason for the so-called 'reception' of Roman law via the *Corpus Juris Civilis*. Moreover, the qualification 'feeble' must be enriched by case-by-case contextualisation; the Holy Roman Emperor was obviously a stronger political presence in Germany and in Italy, for example, than in Portugal, Spain, France or England. In the former territories, the doctrine of *translatio imperii* – that the Roman *imperium* was transferred to the Holy Roman Empire by the Carolingians – was important. On the problematic of the 'reception', see, eg, Franz Wieacker, ibid at §3 I and (for Germany) §7; Hespanha, *Cultura Jurídica Europeia*, 104–07; and Peter Stein, 'Justinian's Compilation: Classical Legacy and Legal Source'.

[33] Grossi, *L'Ordine Giuridico Medievale*, 162.

[34] 2 *Corinthians* 3:6.

[35] A similar point is made by Hespanha, *Cultura Jurídica Europeia*, 169–70.

[36] § 108. *cf* www.vatican.va/archive/ENG0015/__PP.HTM (last visited: 25 February 2012).

[37] D. 50. 17. 1 (Paulus). Roughly: 'The law is not derived from the rule; it is the law that establishes the rule'. The two senses of 'rule' adumbrated in this maxim correspond roughly to Rawls' well-known

In the low Middle Ages, *interpretatio* became the quasi-exclusive prerogative of the jurists. There was a complex variety of reasons for this, discussed in the literature on medieval law and jurisprudence, but two should be emphasised.[38] The first is that the jurists had a much better intellectual preparation than princes, noblemen, city judges or other judicial authorities. Around 1100, a monk and grammarian named Irnerius began teaching the *Corpus Juris Civilis* in Bologna and founded the school of the Glossators, whose method was close textual reading and 'glossing' of the texts. When, in the twelfth century, Aristotle's philosophy was rediscovered in Europe and his texts translated into Latin, the jurists' learning was enriched with the resources of Aristotelian logic, dialectic and (to a lesser extent) his teaching on practical reasoning, leading them to relax their fidelity to the Justinian texts and adopt ever more liberal views about *interpretatio*. The school of the post-glossators or commentators, of Bartolus and Baldus, was thus born.

At the same time – and here lies a second reason for the prominence of the jurists – the rapid expansion of urban and commercial life in the thirteenth and fourteenth centuries rendered much customary, city and princely law either obsolete or too diverse in both substance and form to serve the material interests of inter-regional trade and the ideal interests of a universal culture.[39] These circumstances pressed the need for large legal reforms. The jurists marshalled their technical methods and conceptual schemes, all derived from the work on the Roman texts, to bring a measure of intellectual order to the law and develop new bodies of doctrine. Under the pretence of law discovery, they became the most important agents of law-making in late medieval society and virtually indispensable in the administration of justice. Such was the prestige and authority of the jurists in this period that Franz Wieacker calls them (alongside Dante, Giotto and Petrarch) the 'architects of modern Europe'.[40]

In addition to the favourable context supplied by medieval society and political ideology, the medieval jurists could avail themselves to the memory – recorded in the Justinian texts – of the high status of their ancestors in classical Rome.[41] Indeed, the main element of the *Corpus Juris Civilis* is the *Digest* (or *Padects*), an anthology of maxims and short opinions by jurists who lived in the first two centuries AD. The Roman jurists of this period held no office in the imperial government; their authority sprung exclusively from prestige. In the opening statement of the Digest, Ulpian says that 'The law obtains its name from justice; ... law is the art

---

distinction between the 'summary conception' and the 'practice conception' of rules. See John Rawls, 'Two Concepts of Rules', 18–29.

[38] Everything in next couple of paragraphs is borrowed from Hespanha, *Cultura Jurídica Europeia*, 154–62 (also 162–79); Grossi, *L'Ordine Giuridico Medievale*, 154–68; and Wieacker, *A History of Private Law in Europe*, §5.

[39] See Hespanha, ibid at 154–62; Grossi, ibid at 144–60.

[40] Wieacker, *A History of Private Law in Europe*, 56.

[41] Dawson, *The Oracles of the Law*, 107–13.

of knowing what is good and just'.⁴² He then adds: 'Anyone may properly call us [ie, the jurists] the *priests* of this art, for we cultivate justice and profess to know what is good and equitable, dividing right from wrong, and distinguishing what is lawful from that which is unlawful'.⁴³ The expertise of the jurist was *iurisprudentia*, the capacity to discern the just resolution of disputes. The jurist was *wise* in Aristotle's sense of the term.

The medieval jurists did not retrieve from these passages that they were priests like their Roman ancestors. Faithful to the intellectual humility of medieval culture, and to the cognate notion that the individual can only hope to overcome his imperfection within the framework of the community,⁴⁴ they regarded themselves as inheritors of Roman *iurisprudentia* not individually but as a body of persons. The key unit of analysis is not the jurist but the legal profession.⁴⁵ Consequently, the standard of correctness of legal arguments is the community of experts (*opinio communis doctorum*); wisdom is not so much a virtue of the individual jurist as it is an attribute of the community of experts that he forms with his peers.

The key point in all of this is that the administration of justice – which was the essence of politics on the medieval understanding – was the expertise of the jurists and their expertise was not validated by rational demonstration but by their status as members of the community of experts. The jurists were not regarded as experts because their arguments were demonstrably true; on the contrary, their arguments were regarded as true – had, either officially or informally, the force of law – because they were experts.⁴⁶ In the end, as John Dawson puts it, 'The Roman tradition of a legal elite, detached from any public office, was transferred to a group of academicians, whose authority mounted with the mass of their writings, leaving the judges wholly submerged'.⁴⁷

---

⁴² D. 1. 1. 1 (Ulpian). I have relied on the translation by SP Scott at www.constitution.org/sps/sps.htm (last visited: 10 March 2012).

⁴³ D. 1. 1. 1. 1 (Ulpian).

⁴⁴ Grossi, *l'Ordine Giuridico Medievale*, 75–80, 195–203. This is partly a reflex of the medieval understanding, reinforced by Thomism, that the universal is metaphysically prior to the particular. There is at least an elective affinity between that idea and the corporatist imaginary of medieval society. On this point, Hespanha, *As Vésperas do Levietã*, 307–08.

⁴⁵ An interesting manifestation of this is that there is a large medieval literature on the proper conduct of the jurist (what to eat and wear, how to speak, what mannerisms to adopt, etc). Individual discipline is a communal concern, for the corporate body answers for the conduct of each of its members. See Hespanha, 'Juristas e Direito na Cultura Europeia', 161.

⁴⁶ On the legal force of the (medieval) jurists' opinions, see John Dawson, *The Oracles of the Law*, 138–45.

⁴⁷ ibid at 146–47. In England, where the common law developed, the story was not exactly identical but it was similar in many important respects. In the words of two prominent comparative lawyers: 'The nature of English law and the course of its development were fundamentally affected by the fact that very early in its history there arose a class of *jurists* who organized themselves in a kind of guild and so exercised very great political power': Zweigert and Kötz, *An Introduction to Comparative Law*, 198 (emphasis in the original). The university did not play a significant role in the education of English jurists until the nineteenth century. Legal education was the province of the Inns of Court, the independent guilds of the practitioners. There is a tendency among comparative lawyers and legal historians to pick on this difference to exaggerate the cleavage between the common law and the civil

Throughout the course of the Renaissance, beginning in the sixteenth century, the authority of the jurists was gradually undermined by two emerging political and intellectual trends – centralisation and humanism.

(1) *Centralisation*. Princes everywhere in Europe initiate the slow and complex process of political centralisation that eventually led to the emergence of the modern state. In the course of it transpires a new conception of the ruler as an order-giving – instead of order-keeping – agent, and of legislation as the *fiat* of a sovereign will, as an *instrumentum regni*.

Centralisation carried major implications for the jurists. The gradually increasing prominence of legislation drove the Roman sources to a marginal status and undermined the assumptions of *interpretatio*. Although in the Middle Ages particular laws (*iura propria*) trumped Roman law (*ius commune*), the latter supplied the common framework and the organic principles common to the entire legal order. On the medieval understanding, as we have seen, all positive law externalises *ius*, which means that there are no real conflicts among the various sources. Particular law stands in relation to the common law contained in the Roman texts in the same way that a judicial decision stands in relation to a *lex* – as an equitable application of a single normative criterion.[48] However, on the new – modern – understanding, a statute is a discrete manifestation of the Sovereign's will; it is a law-*making* event.

In the new political climate, *interpretatio* and the Roman sources are brought to questioning, along the lines of Hobbes's famous attack on Edward Coke's theory that the Common Law is a form of 'artificial reason'. All that Hobbes sees in the 'artificial reason of the law' is a sinister device deployed by judges and lawyers to usurp the Sovereign's authority to decide what the

---

law traditions. See, eg, Zweigert and Kötz, ibid at 197–204. The tradition was shaped by Max Weber's thesis that whereas the civil law developed in connection with a rich theoretical apparatus which lent it a distinctive 'rational' or 'systematic' structure, the common law remained thoroughly 'empirical' and 'particularistic'. See Max Weber, *Max Weber on Law in Economy and Society*, 198–223. For an account of legal history that has Weber's fingerprints all over it, see Franz Wieacker, *A History of Private Law in Europe*, § 5 IV. Incidentally, it was this thesis that originated the 'England problem' at the heart of Weber's functionalist sociology of law and development. Put briefly, Weber claims that there is a functional connection between rational law and capitalist development. Yet, capitalism originated in England, where – on Weber's account – the law was not rational but based on ad hoc decision-making. On this problem, see David Trubeck, 'Max Weber on Law and the Rise of Capitalism'. Weber overlooked at least two points. First, medieval jurisprudence in continental Europe was not at all systematic and general but precisely the opposite: oriented towards the problem (*quaestio*) and openly particularistic (*aequitas*). See Paolo Grossi, *L'Ordine Giuridico Medievale*, 175–82. Secondly, academic jurists in England in the nineteenth century, precisely when aspiring lawyers were starting to obtain university degrees in order to practice law, recast the common law in civilian molds. The borrowing was so intense that James Gordley, *The Philosophical Origins of Modern Contract Doctrine*, 134–60, calls it 'the Anglo-American reception'.

[48] On the notion of *aequitas* in medieval jurisprudence, see Grossi, *L'Ordine Giuridico Medievale*, 175–82.

law should be like.[49] The pressure built up until it reached a comically high point in post-revolutionary France. In 1790, a statutory reform of the court system, echoing Montesquieu's account of the judge as the 'mouthpiece of legislation',[50] established that the judiciary should refer to the legislature all questions of statutory interpretation ('*toutes les fois qu'ils croiront nécessaire d'interpréter une loi*').[51]

(2) *Humanism*. The second source of decline of the social and political status of the jurists was intellectual. When the modern natural lawyers complained about the 'barbarous language'[52] of medieval and early-modern scholasticism, they were voicing a humanist confidence in the capacity of human beings to attain the truth with relative ease and express it with clarity and elegance. Against the 'scholastic subtlety'[53] of their predecessors, rooted in the intellectual values of precision and modesty cherished by medieval thought, they matched their eminently readable books and stressed increasingly the intellectual self-sufficiency of the individual author. Grotius and Pufendorf are distinguished representatives of this trend.[54]

In jurisprudence, these intellectual transformations translate into the various natural law works claiming to speak from the standpoint of 'natural reason' and attempting to bring legal argument within the domain of the liberal arts. In the Middle Ages, there was a relatively clear division of labour between theologians and jurists, on the one hand, and between them and the scholars in the liberal arts. That reflected in the organisation of the medieval university, where the arts, law, theology and medicine were separate fields of study, the latter three post-graduate. Although it would be a mistake to assume that law was understood as an autonomous discipline in the modern sense, a distinctive subject with a specific method, the Doctor of Laws – someone like Bartolus or Baldus – was conceived as an expert on jurisprudence, the sort of person apt to answer questions about the legal remedies available to a victim of assault but not questions about the nature of the Trinity or the valid forms of the syllogism.[55]

The humanists paid no tribute to these institutional arrangements. For them, any educated person – any competent student of the arts – can study any subject and write about it in clear and elegant language.

---

[49] Thomas Hobbes, *Dialogue Between a Philosopher and a Student of the Common Law*, 55. For commentary, see Gerald Postema, *Bentham and the Common Law Tradition*, 46–60.

[50] Montesquieu, *L'Esprit des Lois*, Bk 11, ch 6: '*Les juges de la nation ne sont que la bouche qui prononce les paroles de la loi …*' For some odd reason, the word '*loi*' in this passage is translated as 'law' in all English translations that I have checked. But that operates a significant change in meaning. It is crucial that Montesquieu refers specifically to *legislated* law as the type of source to which judges owe absolute allegiance.

[51] The system was known as '*Référé Législatif*'. See John Gilissen, *Introduction Historique au Droit*, 465–66.

[52] Jean Barbeyrac, quoted in Gordley, *The Philosophical Origins of Modern Contract Doctrine*, 126.

[53] Hugo Grotius, *Prolegomena to The Rights of War and Peace*, Bk III, 1761.

[54] James Gordley, *Philosophical Origins*, 129–32.

[55] See James Gordley, 'Law and Religion: An Imaginary Conversation with a Medieval Jurist'.

That meant, of course, that the whole notion of the jurist as an expert on the 'art of knowing what is good and just' was jeopardised. The consequences of this development are easily visible when one reads the table of contents of a major work on the history of Western legal thought – say, Franz Wieacker's classic *A History of Private Law in Europe*. Whereas the protagonists of medieval law are the jurists, in the modern period the focus shifts to men-of-letters or philosophers such as Althusius, Grotius, Pufendorf, Wolff and Kant. The jurists in this period act on a variety of side shows, and when they return to the grand stage they perform secondary roles as followers of the modern natural lawyers; the paradigm is Jean Domat's treatise *Les Lois Civiles dans leur Ordre Naturel*, published in 1689.[56] In England, the crusade against the jurists reaches its climax when Jeremy Bentham announces his aim 'to pluck the mask of Mystery from the face of Jurisprudence'.[57]

IV. Modern Legal Science

The jurist was thus challenged by the legislator and the philosopher. The former as the bearer of princely and then popular sovereignty; the latter representing 'natural reason' common to all men. In order to restore their degraded 'symbolic capital', the jurists reinvented themselves as legal experts in the German universities of the nineteenth century. The protagonists were Friedrich Carl von Savigny and Friedrich Puchta, the so-called 'Romanist' wing of the German Historical School. In 1872, the English jurist Sheldon Amos, who was borrowing extensively from his colleagues across the Rhine, recognised that 'Modern Jurisprudence is emphatically a German creation'.[58] It was indeed in Germany that legal science or scientific jurisprudence was invented, and exported to virtually everywhere.[59]

Jurisprudence was transformed in this period from a type of practical wisdom – *iurisprudentia* – into demonstrable science. The jurist is no longer an expert on justice, a person with a special sense for right and wrong, but a

---

[56] See Franz Wieacker, *A History of Private Law in Europe*, 199. After stating the general view, which informs the entire book, that each period of legal thought develops 'against a background of generalized theories of law and society', Wieacker goes on to say: 'but the age of reason is peculiar in that the social philosophy of the day, at the very time it was itself breaking free from moral theology, laid claim to being a legal philosophy as well, without any interposition or interpretation by the legal establishment'.
[57] Quoted in Gerald Postema, *Bentham and the Common Law Tradition*, 268.
[58] Sheldon Amos, *A Systematic View of the Science of Jurisprudence*, 505.
[59] On the diffusion of nineteenth-century legal thought, see generally Duncan Kennedy, 'Three Globalizations of Law and Legal Thought: 1850–2000', 25–37. See also the following studies: Andreas Schwarz, 'John Austin and the German Jurisprudence of His Time'; Michael Hoeflich, 'Savigny and his Anglo-American Disciples'; Stefen Riesenfeld, 'The Influence of German Legal Theory on American law'; Gerhard Kegel, 'Story and Savigny'; Jean-Louis Halpérin, *Histoire du Droit Privé Français Depuis 1804*, 143–55; André-Jean Arnaut, *Les Juristes Face à la Société*, 53–60; Zweigert and Kötz, *An Introduction to Comparative Law*, 159–62, 349–52. For a slightly different account, see James Gordley, *The Philosophical Origins of Modern Contract Doctrine*, 161–213.

methodical student of positive law. His science has an empirical and a logical part.[60] On the one hand, he studies the law in the sources, which forms the data of his knowledge. On the other hand, from that data, which contains only part of the criteria required to settle every dispute that can be brought before a court, the jurist is to infer more law. Positive law is thus completed by scientific law obtained by logical inference. Savigny explains the method in the following terms:

> [T]here is certainly a perfection ... that may be illustrated by a technical expression of geometry. In every triangle, namely, there are certain data from the relations of which all the rest are necessarily deducible: thus, given two sides and the included angle, the whole triangle is given. In like manner, every part of our law has points by which the rest may be given: these may be termed the leading axioms. To distinguish these, and deduce from them the internal connection and the precise degree of affinity which subsist between all juridical notions and rules, is amongst the most difficult problems of jurisprudence. Indeed it is peculiarly this which gives our labors the scientific character.[61]

This passage appears in the famous pamphlet against codification that Savigny wrote in the first quarter of the nineteenth century. What put Savigny at odds with the codification movement was that redefining jurisprudence as the scientific study of positive law does not quite safeguard the interests of his class. Unlike other modern sciences, which study invariable objects such as nature or space, jurisprudence is apparently compromised by the radical contingency of its object. The point was stressed by Julius von Kirchmann in an essay entitled *The Worthlessness of Jurisprudence as a Science* (1848), in which he complained that 'through positive law jurisprudence is turned from a priestess of truth to a maid of the accidental, the error, the passion, the irrational. Instead of the eternal and absolute, the accidental and flawed becomes her object'. The conclusion seemed inevitable: 'Three corrective words from the legislator and whole libraries become wastepaper.'[62]

Actually, the danger did not just take the form of legislative activism; philosophical activism – the enlightened code – was equally harmful. In both cases, the jurist is deprived of his sources – the ensemble of textual and customary material accepted as law – and, therefore, of the object of his science. His services are rendered either impossible or dispensable. Savigny understood that before and better than anyone else. In the earliest pages of the pamphlet, he discriminates two impulses behind the codification movement. First he mentions the philosophical:

> In the first place, [codification] is connected with many plans and experiments of this kind since the middle of the eighteenth century. During this period the whole of Europe

---

[60] Or a 'historical' and a 'systematic' part. See Savigny, *Juristische Methodenlehre*, 91–93. For commentary, see Wieacker, *A History of Private Law in Europe*, 292–99; Karl Larenz, *Methodenlehre der Rechtswissenschaft*, 11–13.

[61] Savigny, *Of the Vocation of Our Age for Legislation and Jurisprudence*, 39.

[62] *Quoted in* Mathias Reimann, 'Nineteenth Century German Legal Science', 885. See also Wieacker, *A History of Private Law in Europe*, 329; Felipe González Vicén, 'Sobre los Orígines y Supuestos del Formalismo en el Pensamiento Jurídico Contemporáneo', 48–55.

was actuated by a blind rage for improvement. All sense and feeling of the greatness by which other times were characterized, as also of the natural development of communities and institutions, all, consequently, that is wholesome and profitable in history, was lost; it's place was supplied by the most extravagant anticipations of the present age, which was believed to be destined to nothing else than to the being a picture of absolute perfection.[63]

Then he turns to the legislative impulse:

In the second place, those plans are connected with a general theory of the origin of all positive law, which was always prevalent with the great majority of German jurists. According to this theory, all law, in its concrete form, is founded upon the express enactments of the supreme power. Jurisprudence has only the contents of the enactments for its object. Accordingly, legislation itself, and jurisprudence as well, are of a wholly accidental and fluctuating nature; and it is very possible that the law of to-morrow [sic] may not at all resemble the law of to-day [sic].[64]

At this juncture, Savigny offers an account of the origins of positive law that marginalises both legislation and philosophy. 'In the earlier times,' he writes, 'the law will be found to have already attained a fixed character, peculiar to the people, like their language, manners and constitution.'[65] In this period, law exists 'in the common consciousness of the people'[66] and is embodied in its customs, rituals and formalities. As civilisation progresses, however,

national tendencies become more and more distinct, and what otherwise would have remained common, becomes appropriated to particular classes; the jurists now become more and more a distinct class of the kind; law perfects its language, takes a scientific direction, and, as formerly it existed in the consciousness of the community, it now develops upon the jurists who thus, in this department, represent the community.[67]

In this mature stage, law leads a double existence: as 'the proper will of the people'[68] and as a 'distinct branch of knowledge in the hands of the jurists'.[69] Savigny calls these respectively the political and the technical elements of law. The idea is that you can look at the sources of law from two quite different standpoints. From one of them, they express or externalise the people's will, making it knowable; from the other, they are data that the jurist collects and articulates with scientific rigour.

The remarkable thing is that, on this account, the jurists, who were associated with the old order by both democratic and enlightened factions in the late modern era, are presented as the custodians of the people's real will against the arbitrariness of either legislative *fiat* or philosophical abstraction. Legislation is arbitrary because it often reflects the whim, the prejudices or the factional spirit of the

---

[63] Savigny, Vocation, 20–21.
[64] ibid at 22–23. See also Savigny, System of the Modern Roman Law, I, 134–35.
[65] ibid at 24.
[66] ibid at 28. See also Savigny, System, 11–14.
[67] ibid. See also Savigny, System, 14–15.
[68] ibid at 33.
[69] ibid at 28.

legislator, even – indeed especially – when it stems from a popular assembly.[70] Philosophical reflection, at least of the 'law of reason' type, is arbitrary as well because it does not treasure the resources of culture – 'our individual connection with the great entirety of world and history'[71] – proceeding instead from the mistaken assumption that pure reason or disengaged speculation can originate the wealth of regulatory detail that is the life of the law.

The jurist, by contrast, serves the people by bringing a scientific apparatus – a technical element – to bear on the external manifestations of the people's spirit (*Volksgeist*),[72] formed over the course of centuries of collective and progressive experience.[73]

> The sum, therefore, of this theory is, that all law is originally formed in the manner, in which, in ordinary but not quite correct language, customary law is said to have been formed: ie that it is first formed by custom and popular faith, next by jurisprudence, – everywhere, therefore, by silently-operating powers, not by the arbitrary will of the law-giver.[74]

Of course none of the *völkish* talk was likely to restore the authority of the juristic class if the substance of the 'people's law' reported by the jurists did not resonate with the ideological proclivities of the early- to mid-nineteenth century. The jurists had to find in their sources what Roberto Unger calls a 'defensible scheme of human association'[75] – an ordering of social life that could plausibly be traced back to the people's authorship. In other words, the task was to show that it was unnecessary, as well as dangerous, to abolish inherited law; the jurists were not against the people but acting as deputies of the people. In the next couple of sections, we examine how all of that came together in the first of Savigny's eight-volume treatise *System of the Modern Roman Law* (1840–48). Although the first volume of the *System* is arguably the most influential book in the whole of nineteenth-century legal thought,[76] what brings it to the centre of my exposition

---

[70] See Savigny, *System*, I, 24–25. Gerald Postema, *Bentham and the Common Law Tradition*, 16–17, describes in detail the common law equivalent of this point.

[71] Savigny, *Vocation*, 135.

[72] Savigny does not use the expression '*Volksgeist*' in the *Vocation* pamphlet. The term was introduced in the first volume of the *System of the Modern Roman Law*.

[73] See Savigny, *System*, I, 16: 'When we regard the people as a natural unity and merely as the subject of positive law, we ought not to think only of the individuals comprised in that people at any particular time; that unity rather runs through generations constantly replacing one another, and thus it unites the present with the past and future'.

[74] ibid at 30. Customs, on Savigny's account, are not law-constituting events but externalisations of the law indwelling in the people's consciousness – the *Volksgeist*. See Savigny, *System*, I, 27–31. 'Custom therefore is the badge and not the ground of origin of positive law' [28].

[75] See Roberto Mangabeira Unger, *The Critical Legal Studies Movement*, 8.

[76] According to Wieacker, *A History of Private Law in Europe*, 316, 'In intellectual grandeur and clarity of vision [Puchta] may not have been the equal of his teacher Savigny, but he was better at building logical systems and constructing concepts: from 1830s onwards his influence on the method of private law study was greater than that of Savigny himself'. Indeed, Puchta's '*Encyclopädie*' – the first book of his *Cursus der Institutionen*, I, §§ 1–35, 3–108 – offers material that is comparable in aim and scope to the first volume of Savigny's *System*. Yet Puchta's exposition is neither as detailed nor as iconic as

is that it fills a rare middle layer between the political theoretical work of Kant and the typical nineteenth-century doctrinal treatises such as those of Windscheid, Aubry and Rau, or Pollock.[77] Savigny is aware of the unusual character of his enterprise. In the opening chapter, he writes:

> [M]uch will be admitted which belongs to the common fundamental doctrine of every system of positive law and consequently is clearly not peculiar to the Roman law. In favor of this introduction, speaks ... the consideration, that the Roman law ... has assumed more than any other system of positive law a general character, which renders it especially fit for a satisfactory treatment of that fundamental doctrine.[78]

Indeed, the first volume of the *System* is both the most philosophical of all doctrinal treatises of its epoch and yet vigorously anti-philosophical in its insistence on the autonomy of legal science. It marks, both temporally and substantively, the transition of classical liberalism from the realm of political philosophy to the province of legal thought.

V. The Savignian System (i): Substance

What I mean by 'substance' is Savigny's theory of positive law, as opposed to his theory of the science of law. Substance pertains to what he claims to be true about his object of study; another matter – methodology – is how he goes about justifying, or crediting with rational force, such claims. This section considers in broad outline the substantive aspects of Savignian jurisprudence.

It has been noticed that the most puzzling feature of Savigny's account of law is the apparent contradiction between two quite different and equally fundamental ideas.[79] On the one hand, Savigny holds a general theory of law that is patently universalist. 'Man', he writes,

> stands in the midst of the outer world, and the most important element, to him in this surrounding of his, is the contact with those who are like him, by their nature and destination. If now in such contact free natures are to subsist beside one another mutually assisting, not hindering themselves, this is possible only through the recognition of an invisible boundary within which the existence and activity of each individual gains a secure, free space. The rule, by which those boundaries and that free space are determined, is the law. Hence at the same time the relationship between law and morality comes to be understood. The law serves morality, not by performing its bidding but by

---

Savigny's, and therefore I assign to him a secondary role, with the important exception of his views on legal method, which we shall examine later in considerable detail.

[77] Bernhard Windscheid, *Lehrbuch des Pandektenrechts*; Aubry and Rau, *Cours de Droit Civil Français*; Frederick Pollock, *Principles of Contract*; Pollock, *The Law of Torts*.
[78] Savigny, *System*, I, 5.
[79] Kennedy, 'Savigny's Family/Patrimony Distinction', 811–13. See also John Toews, 'The Immanent Genesis and Transcendent Goal of Law', 139–50; William Ewald, 'Comparative Jurisprudence I', 2012–43; Franz Wieacker, *A History of Private Law in Europe*, 314–16.

securing the free development of its power indwelling in each individual will. The existence of law is however a self-dependent one, and hence there is no contradiction when in the individual case, the possibility of immoral exercise of a right actually existing is asserted.[80]

No student of the *Doctrine of Right* would have reason to be suspicious if the lines above were attributed to Kant. The idea of law as a state of effective freedom among equals serving morality not by enforcing it but by endowing each person with the conditions required for moral agency is unambiguously Kantian. If there is a difference between Savigny and Kant about this, it is a difference in tone; Savigny's words bear no trace of the struggle with the pre-Kantian view of natural law surfacing throughout the *Rechtslehre* – he is more Kantian than Kant himself, a signpost of the enormous success of the Kantian enterprise.

This is the universalist theme of Savigny's jurisprudence. For on this account, the law is by and large the same everywhere, it is that set of effective norms which enables the coexistence of a multitude of free agents. The other theme is particularism. It pervades the view that the law is inextricably associated with the character of a people, a unique spiritual entity brought to existence by historical contingency. Consider the following passage:

> We might naturally be led to stop short at [the] abstract conception of a plurality and regard law as its discovery, without which the external freedom of no individual could subsist, but such an accidental meeting of an undefined multitude is a conception both arbitrary and entirely wanting in truth … [W]e find so far as history informs us the matter, that wherever men live together, they stand in an intellectual communion which reveals as well as establishes and developes [sic] itself by the use of speech. In this natural whole is the seat of the generation of law …[81]

Both ideas – universalism and particularism – are essential on the Savignian account. Savigny is committed *both* to the proposition that the law carries out the universal mission of securing individual freedom and to the proposition that the law originates in the *Volksgeist*, the spirit of each particular people. Accordingly, a major theme of the book is how to mediate the tension between the two ideas. Savigny addresses the issue in the following terms:

> What works in an individual people is merely the general human spirit which reveals itself in that people in a particular manner. The generation of law is a fact and one common to the whole. This is conceivable only of those, between whom a communion of thought and action is not only possible but actual. Since then such a communion, exists only within the limits of an individual people so here also can practical law alone be created, although in its production, the expression of a generative principle common to men in general, is perceived, consequently not at all the peculiar arbitrary will of several individual peoples of which perhaps no single trace could be found in other

---

[80] Savigny, *System of the Modern Roman Law*, I, 269–70. See also Puchta, *Cursus der Institutionen*, I, 9–11, 14–17.
[81] ibid at 15.

peoples. Therein is found merely the distinction that this product of the people's mind is sometimes entirely peculiar to that single people, sometimes equally present in more peoples.[82]

There are two key points here. First, although all law indwells in the people's consciousness or spirit, part of it is specific to the people and part of it is universal. Secondly, the part of the law that is universal is ontologically dependent – that is, dependent for its very being – on the part that is particular, for the existence of a people is a necessary condition for the existence of 'practical law' – that is, the general spirit or the universal law is effective only under the auspices, or through the mediation, of a people.[83]

The people so far is understood as a spiritual entity. But that invisible realm shows itself by 'irrepressible inclination'[84] in the form of a state. The 'bodily shape of the intellectual communion of a people is the state and by it are likewise supplied definite boundaries of the unit'.[85] The state is specific to the people not just in the sense that it originates in the people's consciousness – as does all law – but in the further sense of the 'particular shape presented by the state in each people'.[86] In other words, each state *reflects* the character of the people whose existence it manifests. That is the basis for the *summa divisio* within the legal order between private and public law.

> If we know contemplate … law as an aggregate, we discern in it, two provinces states-law and private law. The first has for its object-matter the state, that is the organic manifestation of the people; the second the totality of jural relations which surround the individual man in order that in them, he may lead his inner life and fashion it in a define shape.[87]

It appears, then, that the law of the state ('states-law', in William Holloway's atrocious translation of '*Staatsrecht*') is particularistic, while private law, which concerns the inner life of the individual, is universal. Each people has its own constitution, its arrangement of public power – republican, monarchic, etc – but a private law that is essentially identical to that of other peoples. Since it is through the state that the people 'first obtains real personality and … the capacity of acting',[88] the particular configuration of the state is not chosen by the people – it 'arises spontaneously and naturally, in a people, through the people, and for the people'.[89]

Savigny, of course, argues that the law never originates – or nearly so[90] – in the *fiat* of either legislative assemblies or an enlightened legislator, and that holds not

---

[82] ibid at 17.
[83] See Puchta, *Cursus der Institutionen*, 23–26, 104–06.
[84] Savigny, *System*, 17.
[85] ibid at 17–18.
[86] ibid at 18.
[87] ibid.
[88] ibid at 19.
[89] ibid at 23.
[90] Just as the Kantian system of a priori norms contains gaps that need to be filled with arbitrary legislation – eg reason does not determine on which side of the road to drive or how to organise the

only for the law of the state but for private law as well. His point here is much more subtle. He is arguing that whereas private law, which secures the free coexistence of individual freedoms, is commonly willed by the people – it is 'the united will which thus restricted is also the will of each individual'[91] – the law of the state does not answer before that basic standard of popular volition, *volonté générale*, or universal willing. Each people is inextricably tied to the state that has historically made its formation and continuation possible; it is the state, whatever that is, that *works* for that particular people. The underlying ideology is unambiguous: whereas private law operates on a liberal logic, the political constitution is validated by history. The enemy is the revolutionary overthrowing of the historical constitution sponsored by liberal radicals and other enthusiasts of the French Revolution.[92]

> [T]here is a widely prevalent opinion in accordance with which states must have taken their rise in the will of individuals, therefore in contract; this opinion has in its development led to results as pernicious as they are false. There is the assumption that the people who found it advantageous to found this particular state, could just as well have remained entirely without a state, or have united and confined themselves to a state as they actually did so, or in a different manner or that they might have selected a different constitution. In this theory therefore not merely is the natural unity preserved in the people, as well as the inner necessity once more overlooked but especially also the circumstance that wherever deliberation is possible, there will infallibly be a state existent as fact and law, so that there can no longer be any question, as these people would have it, of the arbitrary invention of a state but at the utmost a question of destroying it.[93]

To destroy the state is self-defeating because the freedom secured by private law is impossible outside of the framework of a working state apparatus: 'As … to private law apart from the state, we are merely able to ascribe an invisible existence … so that law by the establishment of judicature preserves in the state its life and activity'.[94] The mediation of liberal and absolutist tendencies is explicit and sophisticated; indeed, from a liberal standpoint, what matters the most is 'private law', in relation to which the state is (as in Kant's *Doctrine of Right*[95]) an instrumental or second-order matter. That explains a further distinction: 'I do not desire', writes Savigny,

> to narrow the state to the purposes of law … Nevertheless its first and most inevitable task is to make the idea of law dominant in the visible world. To this object leads a

judicial system – Savigny admits the existence of 'numerous regulations in the nature of which a certain latitude of the will is permitted', ibid at 33. See also Savigny, *Of the Vocation of Our Age for Legislation and Jurisprudence*, 33.
[91] ibid at 19.
[92] Indeed, Savigny's views on the subject closely resemble those of Edmund Burke, 'Reflections on the Revolution in France', 452–53; Burke is perhaps the most vitriolic among the earliest critics of the French Revolution.
[93] ibid at 23–24. On this point there is a slight disagreement between Savigny and Puchta; indeed, Puchta rejects the contractarian and the historicist theories of government in favour of a hybrid account. See Puchta, *Cursus der Institutionen*, 26–29.
[94] ibid at 19.
[95] See ch 2, V of this work.

double activity of the state. First it has to protect the individual who is injured in his right against that injury; we call the rules to which this activity is subject, civil process. Secondly it has to defend and re-establish the injured right, without reference to the individual interest. [...] We call the rules to which this activity is subject, criminal law of which criminal procedure forms merely a part.[96]

'Public law' comprises the law of the state – narrowly defined as encompassing the fields of constitutional and administrative law[97] – criminal law, and civil procedure. As Duncan Kennedy points out, Savigny's distinctions have a nested structure; that is, they are arranged in a hierarchy that reproduces the same criterion of distinction over and over again.[98] Hence, while public law is particular vis-à-vis private law, within public law the law of the state is relatively more particularistic than civil procedure and criminal law, since the content of the latter is partly determined by their ancillary role with respect to private law. But while Savigny is aware of that, and carefully avoids dogmatism, he is fully committed to the primary significance of the private/public dichotomy, as the following excerpt illustrates:

> [B]etween the two departments this firmly established difference remains: in public law the whole appears at the end, the individual as subordinate, while in private law on the contrary, the individual man is on his own account an end, and each jural relation has reference only to his existence or his special circumstances.[99]

The legal order is thus fundamentally divided into two parts, the organic and particularistic province of public law and the individualist and universalistic province of private law.[100] Both parts are essentially opposed and yet functionally intertwined. But when Savigny finally turns to private law, which he announces in the opening pages of the book as the subject of the treatise,[101] everything turns out to be more complicated. Not that you can tell that immediately. His starting point is familiar from the earlier portions of the text:

> [E]ach single jural relation appears to us as a relation between person and person, determined by a rule of law. This determination by a rule of law consists in the assignment to the individual will of a province in which it is to rule independently of every foreign will.[102]

---

[96] ibid at 21. Similarly, Puchta, *Cursus der Institutionen*, 67–69.
[97] 'Administrative law' here corresponds to what in the nineteenth century was often referred to as the 'police power' of the state, a term inherited from eighteenth-century enlightened absolutism – see Guido Astuti, *La Formazione dello Stato Moderno in Italia*, 177–82, 187–205; Peter H Wilson, *Absolutism in Central Europe*, 108–21. 'Police' had a negative or conservative aspect, associated with the task of maintaining public order, and a positive or interventionist aspect, associated with the promotion of public welfare; it was both a matter of policing and of polishing the nation. Puchta, *Cursus der Institutionen*, I, 72–73, writes that the 'police activity of the state' (*die polizeiliche Thätigkeit des Staats*) concerns the spiritual and material care of the citizenry.
[98] See Kennedy, 'Savigny's Family/Patrimony Distinction', 821–22.
[99] Savigny, *System*, I, 18–19.
[100] See ibid at 43–44.
[101] ibid at 2.
[102] ibid at 271.

This is exactly what we expected to read, given Savigny's earlier statements about private law. At this point, he proposes to classify jural relations according to the 'object-matters upon which the will can possibly exercise influence and thus extend its mastery'.[103] In the first place, the will may be exercised over the willer's own person or the outer world. Within the later domain, the basic distinction is between unfree nature and free beings or other persons. Figure 3.1 illustrates this scheme.

Figure 3.1 Objects of rights in the Savignian system

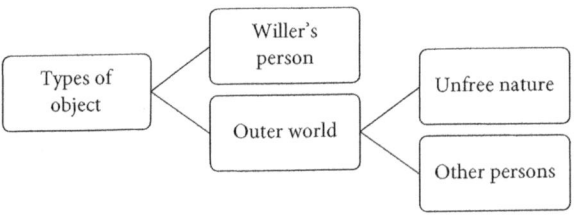

Savigny then goes on to reject the claim that there is an original (or innate) right of each person over his own self. He contrasts a narrow with a broad conception of that right. On the narrow view, each person has 'a right to property in their intellectual powers', or freedom of thought. But such a right, he goes on to argue, is not really a legal right, for a right grants a measure of protection against other persons, and liberty of thought is naturally inviolable.[104] To say that one owns one's thoughts is merely a figure of speech. On the wide conception, the original right to one's self would have to be a right of self-ownership extending to the body, and Savigny quickly dismisses any such suggestion 'because among other objections it consistently leads to the recognition of a right to commit suicide'.[105]

There is nonetheless a kernel of truth, according to Savigny, in the erroneous notion of a right to oneself. On the one hand, it conveys an idea that is 'the basis and preliminary of all rights', the status of all men as equal and free persons.[106] (That is precisely the primary role of the 'innate right' of persons in the Kantian system.)

---

[103] ibid.
[104] ibid at 272.
[105] ibid at 273. The argument is patently problematic. To begin with, it is almost certainly circular: to say that there is no right to suicide appears to assume that there is no right to self-ownership. I am careful to add the qualification 'almost' because Savigny may be making an assertion about positive law – that it is an undisputed fact about the law that there is no right to suicide and since self-ownership implies (on his view) such a right, it cannot be part of positive law. But my impression is that Savigny is making a logical claim: that self-ownership is logically incoherent because it presupposes an impossible or absurd right to commit suicide. The second point is that the prohibition against suicide is obviously not sanctioned by logic, and requires precisely a moral argument about how one is to conduct one's life, thereby contradicting Savigny's assertion, similar to Kant's, that there is a sharp distinction between the provinces of law and morality. In this latter respect, Savigny relies on one of Kant's mediation devices – 'covert exceptions'.
[106] ibid at 273.

On the other hand, the intellectual and bodily interests of the individual – the 'inviolability of the person' – are protected by criminal and civil laws (tort law and the law of possession).[107] But these 'are not to be regarded as mere developments of this inviolability, they rather form wholly positive institutions of law'.[108] 'Positive' in this context is opposed to 'rational' or 'logical'; it means that the criminal and tort laws that safeguard personal interests are not entailed by the concept of the person as an inviolable bearer of rights – accordingly, they belong not to the universal but to the particularistic dimension of law.

Private law, then, concerns only acquired rights, which have the 'outer world' as their objects. That includes things or unfree nature, the subject of property, as well as rights over other free beings or persons. And this is where things start to get complicated, for the latter fall into 'two wholly heterogeneous' categories of jural relations.[109] One is that of obligations.

> The first ... is that in which that person in like way with a thing, is drawn within the province of our will, therefore is subjected to our mastery. [...] The mastery must relate not to the extraneous person in its entirety but merely to an individual act of his: this act is then conceived as withdrawn from the freedom of the actor and subjected to our will. We call such a relation of mastery over an individual act of the extraneous person, obligation.[110]

---

[107] ibid at 273. Savigny's passing reference to possession is linked to a rich doctrinal tradition. Among the vexed questions of nineteenth-century legal thought was the justification of a right to possession. The problem was as follows. The owner of an object has the right to possess it – the right to both use it and to exclude others from using it – along with the right to transfer its ownership by contract or bequest. When the owner is dispossessed of his property, she is entitled to recover possession upon showing good title. It appears to follow that any possessor who is a non-owner, anyone who just happens to exert some physical control over an object outside of the auspices of ownership, has no right to recover possession if she is dispossessed. Yet the law does grant protection to a non-owner who is dispossessed. Just as the owner may recover his property by bringing an action of *vindicatio*, the non-owner possessor may recover possession by bringing possessory interdicts against the defendant. Even a thief can avail himself to possessory remedies. The problem arises: How can possession without legal title warrant remedial protection? Not any sort of protection, to make matters even more intriguing, but one taking the particularly strong form of an injunction addressed by the court to the defendant to restore the plaintiff's possession. Gordley, *Foundations of Private Law*, 53–60, recounts the history of the problem in nineteenth-century German and Anglo-American legal thought. Savigny, *Treatise on Possession*, 3, 28 argues that possession is a title grounded 'in ... the inviolability of [the] person ... For the person must, at all times, be secured against violence'.

[108] Tort law falls outside of the will theory in the scheme presented by Savigny. Indeed, he does not distinguish clearly between criminal punishment and tort remedies – see Savigny, *System des Heutigen Römischen Rechts*, V, 37–61. Similarly, Puchta, *Cursus der Institutionen*, 69–71, draws a distinction between 'relative' and 'absolute' wrongs (*relative/absolute Unrecht*), corresponding respectively to the realms of private and criminal law, but fails to specify to which camp tort law belongs; he appears not to conceive tort as a separate field and refers in passing to the difficulty of drawing a clear line between relative and absolute wrongs. The integration of tort law into the will theory required two steps. First, a clear distinction between civil and criminal sanctions, understood as a key borderline incident of the private/public law dichotomy. Second, the derivation of the operative elements of 'civil wrong' – namely the scope of duty and the standard of liability – from the more basic concepts of person, right, and harm. The earliest juristic effort of such magnitude with which I am acquainted is John Austin, *Lectures on Jurisprudence*, I, 354–56, 457–83.

[109] Savigny, *System*, I, 275.

[110] ibid.

Obligations are closely related to property because both types of right involve the mastery of the will over some object and can be traded for – and hence reduced to – an amount of money. The sum of such rights pertaining to an individual is his 'patrimony' (*Vermögen*) and the law governing these relations among wills over commodified goods is called *patrimonial law* (*Vermögensrecht*) – what we might call (anachronistically) the law of the market.[111] Not all private law is patrimonial in kind, though. Within the realm of patrimonial law – property and obligations – each person is a 'concluded whole', a free and 'homogenous' will. It is opposite in the 'second possible [type of] relation' to other persons, 'the foundation of a new, entirely peculiar sort of jural relations'.[112]

> In this the individual appears to us, not as in obligations, an independent whole but as an incomplete being needing its complement in a large natural coherence. This incompleteness of the individual, like the completion referring to it, shows itself in two different directions. In the first place in the division of sexes, of which each regarded by itself alone, comprehends human nature only incompletely; with this the completion of the individual by marriage is connected. Secondly in the existence of single men limited in point of time, which limitation again leads in various ways to the necessity for, and the recognition of, completing jural relations.[113]

At this juncture, Savigny abandons the earlier classificatory scheme centred on the objects of jural relations – unfree nature or other persons – in favour of one that does justice to the 'peculiar, completely distinctive' nature of family vis-à-vis patrimonial relations.[114] The true division within private law is between patrimonial and family law. The former governs the interaction among persons *qua* abstract bearers of will; it comprises property and obligations. The latter concerns the complementary nature of the relations husband/wife and father/child; it comprises marriage, paternal power and the ties of kinship (what Savigny calls 'relationship') that flow from them.

Savigny draws a number of consequences from this pivotal contrast. The first is that whereas family life is necessary because it is responsive to permanent features of human nature such as gender, mortality and infancy – it is 'determined by the organic nature of men'[115] – patrimonial life 'appears less necessary, more arbitrary and positive'.[116] In other words, the institution of the family is universal, it exists in every human society, while the market is particular to some (highly advanced) societies. The second consequence concerns the contrast between family and patrimonial law. Although marriage, paternal power, and relationship are universal institutions, their content varies across societies; the particular shape that the

---

[111] ibid at 275–76, 306–07. Similarly, Puchta, *Cursus der Institutionen*, 58–59. William Holloway translates *Vermögen* as 'potentiality', although 'patrimony' is the better term.
[112] ibid at 276–77.
[113] ibid at 277.
[114] ibid at 279, 315.
[115] ibid.
[116] ibid at 301.

family assumed in Christian culture was monogamous, enduring (prohibition of divorce), and centred on the authority of the father over the other members of the household. On the contrary, notwithstanding its contingent existence, the substance of patrimonial law is universal. The following textual fragments bring out this contrast nicely:

> [A] necessity independent of positive law must be ascribed to [the family] although the special shape, in which they are recognized, is very manifold according to the positive law of different peoples.[117]
>
> The doubt cannot here arise, in what [the] real legal contents [of patrimonial law] consist; for since a widening of the individual freedom is to be embraced in them, this very power, this mastery which they procure for us, is that which furnishes them, as institutions of law, with their contents.[118]

Finally, a third consequence that flows from the family/patrimony dichotomy is that patrimonial relations are will-centered or autonomous whereas family relations are norm-centered or heteronomous. Patrimonial relations are autonomous because they are voluntary, albeit in varying degrees ranging from default rules that can be freely modified by private agreement to the prerogative of an individual to relinquish a right (eg, abandonment of property);[119] moreover, patrimonial rights secure a 'territory where the individual will rules'[120] without any kind of moral or paternalistic oversight – eg, the owner may use his property any way he sees fit. By contrast, family relations are heteronomous because they are 'destined for an enduring existence'[121] and cannot be dissolved at will (divorce was prohibited), as each relation plays a vital role in the proper functioning of the family.

---

[117] ibid at 281.

[118] ibid at 301.

[119] Duncan Kennedy, 'Savigny's Family/Patrimony Distinction', 817–19, takes Savigny to hold the view that patrimonial law is 'facilitative, or consists of default rules', meaning that 'the actual content of contracts and property holdings is infinitely varied, according to the will of the parties' [818]. Although the general direction of Kennedy's argument is undoubtedly right, I doubt that this is correct. In civil law systems (notwithstanding important differences across jurisdictions) property holdings are limited by a *numerus clausus* which limits the types of property interest that are legally recognised. Although in common law systems property holdings may be modified relatively more liberally by means of 'covenants', no system with which I am familiar allows 'infinite variation' in the content of property holdings by analogy with what happens in the field of (obligatory) contract; indeed, it is hard to figure out how a property system that sets no limits on the power to disaggregate ownership would work. For the subtle ways in which American courts limit the content of property holdings in the absence of a *numerus clausus*, see Joseph Singer, *Introduction to Property*, 236–38, 257–65, 281–300. Savigny, a master of legal technicality, surely did not let any of that slip his mind; it is worth noting, moreover, that in the passage that Kennedy quotes to support his remarks Savigny is contrasting family law with obligations, as opposed to patrimonial law as a whole. Even in contract, of course, there are many mandatory norms, and I do not suppose Savigny meant to turn a blind eye on that. In sum, Savigny's point is not that patrimonial law consists of default rules but that patrimonial relations are generally responsive to the will of individuals, at a minimum in the sense that obligations can be voluntarily cancelled and property can be abandoned or given away, while marriage (under a regime of no divorce) and parenthood are largely unresponsive to individual wills.

[120] Savigny, *System*, I, 6.

[121] ibid at 279.

After stressing that 'it is not … the partial subjecting of one person to another which forms the jural character of the family relations', Savigny writes: 'their proper nature consists in the place which the individual obtains in these relations, in his being not merely man in general but specially husband, father, son, therefore in a life-form firmly determined, independently of the individual will, grounded in a large natural coherence'.[122]

In sum, the three dimensions of the family/patrimony contrast are as follows. The family as an institution is universal while the market exists only in some societies; the content of family law is particular to each society or culture while the content of patrimonial law is universal;[123] and whereas family relations are universal, since each familial unit within a given society replicates a fixed set of roles, patrimonial relations are particularistic, dependent on the will of the parties. These results yield the following table.[124]

Figure 3.2 Savigny's family/market distinction

Family/Market	Institution	Law	Relations
Family	Universal	Particular	Universal
Market	Particular	Universal	Particular

What is the point in all of this? Savigny's primary concern is to defend the autonomy of the patriarchal family vis-à-vis both the market and the state; the logic of the family is at once unique and necessary. It is a mistake to extend the logic of patrimonial relations, which involve free and equal wills, to the family. His argument here is structurally identical to his objection against both revolutionary and reformist agendas in public law: just as private law presupposes a well-functioning state, the individual that participates in the marketplace presupposes the organic coherence of family life. It is self-defeating to liberalise the family because the liberal self is grounded in the functional complementarily that family life secures. This clearly sets Savigny apart from Kant, whose attempt to assimilate marriage to the will theory does not escape harsh criticism: 'In this matter Kant has erred in wishing to make the purely natural constituent in marriage, the sexual instinct, the object-matter of an obligatory jural relation; by this the nature of marriage is necessarily entirely misunderstood and degraded'.[125]

At this point, it is very tempting to think that Savigny has detracted from his earlier inclusion of family law within private law, which he characterised a couple

---

[122] ibid at 284.
[123] Although he argues that polygamy is a 'lower stage in the moral development of nations' than monogamy, he also insists that what is universal is the institution of marriage and that the particular shape that it takes – eg, monogamous or polygamous – reflects the 'moral view of life of [a] special people', ibid at 281–82, fn (a).
[124] See Kennedy, 'Savigny's Family/Patrimony Distinction' for a different looking but substantially similar figure.
[125] Savigny, *System*, I, 283.

of hundred pages earlier in individualist terms. For just as each people has its own historical constitution it also has its peculiar family life; indeed, the family is the basic cell of political community: 'In families are embraced the germs of the state and the completely formed state has families, not individuals immediately for its constituent parts'.[126] But there is another side to this. The family pre-exists the state and is a necessary condition of the state's own existence; it is 'private' not because it is individualist but because it is self-organising, that is, operative without the artificial or mechanical intervention of state power.[127] While there is no patrimonial life outside of the framework of a legal system, the family is not constituted by but merely reflected in (state-sponsored) law.[128] From here Savigny draws the quite radical implication that the household is the independent jurisdiction of the father; state power ends where patriarchal authority begins: at the door of the family house. As he puts it, family life is governed by morality instead of law.

> It is ... in no way denied here that to marriage, loyalty and self-sacrifice, as to the paternal power obedience and reverence, belong; but these in themselves, most important elements of that relation stand under the protection of morals not of law, just as the honorable and humane use, which the father of a family can make of his power over the family must also remain left to morals alone ... Hence we shall have a very uncertain knowledge of the condition of the family relations in a nation if we look merely at the rule of law prevailing in them without having regard to the morals which are its complement.[129]

What is left for family law then? It comprises a pure and an applied part. The pure part of family law contains norms that spell-out the conditions (the 'if-clauses') under which persons enter into specific family relations, for instance marriage and

---

[126] ibid at 279, Similarly, Puchta, *Cursus der Institutionen*, I, 62–64.

[127] It may be that this was the principal sense in which the 'private realm' was opposed to the 'public realm' in ancient Greece and Rome. See Fustel de Coulanges, *La Cité Antique*, 62–75, 92–98; Hannah Arendt, *The Human Condition*, 28–37, 58–67. The (widely diffused) idea that we inherited the modern private/public distinction from the Romans – cf D. 1. 1. 1. 2 (Ulpian) at www.thelatinlibrary.com/justinian/digest1.shtml (last visited: 2 June 2012) – is probably based on anachronistic misreading of the sources.

[128] ibid at 281–82, 301–02. Similarly, Puchta, ibid at 59–61.

[129] ibid at 285. This passage is of course quite puzzling; Savigny's delegalisation of family relations appears to be even more extreme than it was usual in the mid- and late-nineteenth century. Puchta, *Cursus der Institutionen*, 86–89 does not follow Savigny in this respect and recognises, apart from property and obligations, a third field of 'personal rights' that are both non-patrimonial and juridical; he does not object to state-enforcement of these rights, eg the right of the child to material support afforded by the head of the household. Duncan Kennedy, 'Savigny's Family/Patrimony Distinction', 827, suggests that Savigny is claiming that there are no private law rights and duties as between family members but that 'Criminal laws that apply to all individuals in relation to other individuals could still apply consistently with his claim of complete delegalization of the relation in private law ...'. He then adds that 'it would be interesting to know [Savigny's] position about marital rape as a crime'; I would add to that corporeal punishment applied by the head of the household to his wife and children (and servants). At any rate, there is no textual evidence to support Kennedy's moderate rendition of Savigny's remarks. My guess is that Savigny thinks about the head of the household on the model of the medieval and early-modern Germanic *Hausherr* – see, eg, Otto Brunner, *Land and Lordship*, 211–13.

paternal power.¹³⁰ These norms have as their immediate consequence the legal recognition of someone's familial status and thus have an *erga omnes* or 'against the world' character – eg, the father is entitled to demand from anyone 'in possession' of his child that he is returned to the household.¹³¹ A second – applied – aspect of family law pertains to the oblique role that family relations play in patrimonial law; this ranges from specific regimes within the law of obligations and property – eg, parents are the legal guardians of the infant's assets, spouses may be liable to pay each other's debts – to the whole field of inheritance law which mixes elements of a patrimonial and a familial kind.¹³²

Each of the three basic domains of Savigny's system – state, market and family – embodies a distinctive normative logic. The state is controlled by the historical constitution in general, and monarchic legitimacy in most cases; the market is the site of classical liberalism in the form of the will theory; and the family is a romantic-patriarchal institution. It is this tripartite structure that Savigny traces back to the *Volksgeist*, the spirit of the people that generates and pervades all law.

It is important to stress that this is what was at stake – to accommodate liberal demands in a social world torn by agonising ideological conflict. Duncan Kennedy asserts both that the legal order as displayed by Savigny is 'not produced at any of its levels by the Liberal (in the large sense) mechanisms of consent' and that Savigny is explicitly anti-liberal.¹³³ I think that the first of these statements is mistaken while the second misses the target. To begin with, there is little doubt that patrimonial law as conceived by Savigny is produced by the 'liberal mechanisms of consent'; the consent in question is of course not actual but ideal – not an empirical but a rational consent – which is the only kind of consent required by liberalism. Indeed, the language that Savigny uses to express the foundations of patrimonial law is unmistakably influenced by Kant, for whom the social contract is not a historical agreement but an 'idea of reason'. The following passage, omitted by Kennedy, could figure in any of Kant's political writings:

> Every man has a calling to the mastery over unfree nature; he must however equally recognize the same calling in very other man and from this mutual recognition, in the contact of individuals in space, arises the necessity of equalization which appears first of all as a something indefinite and can only be satisfied by a more determined limitation. This satisfaction now by the help of the communion in the state, is obtained through positive law. When we here ascribe to the state a common jurisdiction over the unfree nature within its boundaries, *individuals* appear as *sharers in this common power* and our task consists in finding a definite rule according to which the distribution among the individuals is carried out.¹³⁴

---

¹³⁰ ibid at 286.
¹³¹ ibid at 289.
¹³² ibid at 309–14.
¹³³ Kennedy, 'Savigny's Family/Patrimony Distinction', 825–30.
¹³⁴ Savigny, *System*, I, 299–300 (emphasis added). See also Puchta, *Cursus der Institutionen*, 9–23.

Now, notwithstanding the complexity and ambivalence of Savigny's politics,[135] Kennedy is right to say that Savigny was not liberal; he was a traditional conservative. That misses the point, though. In the *System of the Modern Roman Law*, Savigny does not mean to express his political opinions; he means to present the law presumably authoured by the people. If what he reported was too uncongenial to the ethos of the 1840s, where the liberal legacy was entrenched, the whole enterprise of portraying the jurist as the custodian of the people's will would fall apart. It was crucial for the success of that enterprise that the three conflicting logics – monarchism, liberalism and patriarchalism – were accommodated in a single coherent doctrinal scheme. In sum, in order to conserve his authority as a jurist, Savigny had to give legal form to the ideological proclivities of his time. His remarkable achievement was to manage that task.[136]

VI. The Savignian System (ii): Method

Had Savigny merely stated and developed the idea of a tripartite legal order encompassing the state, the family and the market, he would have been arguing in a philosophical capacity in the company of, as well as in partial disagreement with, the likes of Kant, Fichte and Hegel. Yet Savigny claims to write as a jurist and that carried two important implications. One is that his object of study is positive as opposed to rational, natural or ideal law; that sets the jurist apart from the philosopher. The other is that his knowledge of positive law is scientific, meaning that it is governed by a method leading to demonstrably true propositions; that sets the jurist apart from the charlatan. It is worth stressing that the largest portion of the first volume of the *System* is devoted to articulating a conception of legal science; although Savigny does not neatly divide the exposition in such terms, the concern with method takes precedence over substance in the introductory volume of the *System*. As early as in the preface he announces, albeit in condensed and slightly cryptic form, the basic thrust of his theory of method or of legal science:

> I place the essence of the systematic method in the knowledge and exhibition of the innate connexion [sic] or of the relationship, by which the single ideas and rules of law are attached to a great unity. Such relationships are at first often hidden and the discovery of them will enrich our research.[137]

---

[135] See, eg, John Toews, 'The Immanent Genesis and Transcendent Goal of Law', 150–62.

[136] This is not to say that Savigny's politics did not make a difference in the architecture of the system. Of course ideology (in the sense of 'the political *zeitgeist*') did not determine the system all the way down and Savigny used his freedom in a manner favourable to his conservative politics (as, say, Puchta used his to favour his relatively more liberal views). The most interesting example – mentioned by Kennedy, 'Savigny's Family/Patrimony Distinction', 829 – concerns the law of hired servitude, which Kant assimilated to contract but which Savigny (*System*, I, 298–99) considers part of family law.

[137] Savigny, *System*, I, xix.

To unpack the meaning of this passage, which liberally read and properly stretched contains the whole theory, we need to review the account of positive law presented in the *System*. All law is 'positive' for Savigny in a twofold sense. First, it is immanent in the people's consciousness or spirit (the *Volksgeist*) as opposed to a transcendent or mind-independent realm of a priori or eternal truth; law is positive in this sense because its norms are socially accepted or experienced as binding.[138] Secondly, law is positive because its spiritual side – popular conviction – is reflected or manifested in empirical facts called 'sources'. These sources are symptoms or manifestations of an underlying normative order.[139]

Savigny reproduces in the *System* the narrative about the development of law first articulated in his pamphlet against codification.[140] In the primitive stage of 'mechanical solidarity', law 'lives in the common consciousness of the people'[141] and takes the visible form of custom administered by popular courts whose judges know the law intuitively.[142] But as society evolves towards a pattern of functional differentiation and role-specialisation – ie, 'organic solidarity' – the law only remains an object of common consciousness in broad outline;[143] the generation of law by means of custom declines, becoming instead the specialised province of two 'new organs' – first legislation and then jurisprudence.[144] Legislation takes the form of written enactments bestowed with 'absolute power';[145] jurisprudence is the 'minute cultivation and handling' of the law by 'the order of jurists'.[146] Yet, while these sources largely replace custom as the regular manifestations of the law, the former retains a paradigmatic status on account of its immediate connection with popular conviction.

> [O]riginally all positive law is people's law and ... side by side with this spontaneous generation, comes legislation ... enlarging and propping it up. Then by the progressive development of the people, legal science is added; thus in legislation and the science of law, two organs are furnished to people's law, each of which simultaneously leads its independent life. [...] Thus it may happen that people's law may be almost hidden by legislation and legal science in which it lives on, and that the true origin of existing positive law, may be easily forgotten and misunderstood.[147]

These remarks exhibit a classic agency problem: how to assure that legislation and jurisprudence play their function as 'organs' of popular law? The answer is very different for each type of law. The link between legislation and the people is forged

---

[138] Savigny, ibid at 12, speaks about the 'the universal, uniform recognition of positive law and ... the feeling of inner necessity with which its conception is accompanied'. See also Puchta, *Cursus der Institutionen*, I, 23–26.
[139] See Puchta, ibid at 30.
[140] See Savigny, *Of the Vocation of Our Age for Legislation and Jurisprudence*, 24–31; see section IV of this chapter.
[141] ibid, *System*, I, 13, 28.
[142] ibid at 28, 31, 151–52.
[143] ibid at 36.
[144] ibid at 14.
[145] ibid at 31.
[146] ibid at 36.
[147] ibid at 40–41.

The Savignian System (ii): Method 149

by the historical constitution which gives form to the state; the constitutionally legitimate lawgiver, as the bearer of 'one of the noblest rights of the supreme power in the state',[148] should be regarded as a 'true representative of the spirit of the people'.[149] To be sure, the representation nexus is not established through the electoral participation of the masses in the affairs of government, contrary to what democratic and republican enthusiasts advocated; it is based instead on the credit accumulated from history. Each people is represented through the medium of that constitutional form – monarchy, aristocracy, democracy or a republic – that has worked for it in the past. 'It is', writes Savigny,

> entirely erroneous to regard this position of the legislator, as dependent upon the different arrangement of the legislative power in this or that constitution. Whether a prince makes the law or a senate or a larger collection of people perhaps formed by election or perhaps the agreement of several such powers is furnished for legislation, the essential relation of the people's law is not at all changed ...[150]

In addition to the formal criterion furnished by the test of constitutional adequacy, there is a more substantial way of telling good legislation apart from bad. Since the task of the law-giver is to continue the work that was originally in the hands of the people, legislation is not supposed to serve the agenda of reform in the 'Enlightenment tradition of rational challenge of established institutions' that had in Bentham its staunchest advocate.[151] Good legislation plays two basic roles. One is that of supplying relatively arbitrary rules in those spaces of regulation where 'a certain latitude of will is permitted',[152] such as the statute of limitations or the formalities of transactions; a second role is that of giving expression to popular law at a quicker pace than is to be expected from the 'invisible power' of customary activity and in a written form that renders legal rules easier to ascertain.[153] Although it is true, as John Toews stresses in an important article, that Savigny's account of legislation in the *System* is considerably more benign than in the *Vocation* pamphlet, notably because it is now presented as equal or even marginally superior to scientific law as an 'organ' of the people, it is of chief importance that we keep in mind what exactly Savigny takes legislation to be here: not the instrument of legal reform but the formal ordering and gradual development of the large *corpus* of inherited law.[154]

The fiduciary bond between the second organ of popular law – jurisprudence – and the people is forged by *science*. There are two sides to it on the Savignian view: the material and the formal.[155] On the one hand, given the decline of people's law

---

[148] ibid at 31.
[149] ibid at 32.
[150] ibid.
[151] Gerald Postema, *Bentham and the Common Law Tradition*, 313.
[152] ibid at 33.
[153] Although Savigny is ambivalent about the net benefit of the written form: on the one hand, it renders legal rules clear; on the other, it contradicts the organic character of law. ibid at 34–45.
[154] John Toews, 'The Immanent Genesis and Transcendent Role of Law', 147–49.
[155] Savigny, *System*, I, 37–38; Puchta, *Cursus der Institutionen*, I, 35–38.

and the piecemeal nature of legislation, it falls to the jurists the role of custodians of the legal tradition; only they master and keep records of the immense mass of legal sources. In this guise, the legal profession plays in Savigny's theory a role closely analogous to that of the judiciary in the classical theory of the common law.[156] Just as the latter portrays the judge as the warden of immemorial custom, meaning that what was once custom *in pays* or general custom becomes custom *in foro* or expert conviction,[157] so are the Savignian jurists the torchbearers of legal tradition and the materials in which it is embodied.

On the other hand, the jurists possess expert knowledge of the law contained in the sources. Of this so-called 'formal' side of jurisprudence, Savigny writes:

> [It is] formal and purely scientific inasmuch as the law, however it may have arisen is scientifically brought to knowledge and set forth by them. In this latter function, the action of the jurist, appears at first sight a dependent one, receiving its materials from without. However by their giving to the materials so presented a scientific form which strives to disclose and perfect the unity dwelling in them there arises a new organic life which shapes and reacts upon the materials themselves, so that from science as such a new sort of generation of law incessantly proceeds.[158]

This passage describes what Savigny takes to be the main business of the jurist: to disclose the legal order that is only partially reflected in the sources. The first step of jurisprudence is to interpret the sources so as to 'pull out' the rules of law embodied in them; these constitute the first degree of law.[159] The second step is to ascend from the rules to what Savigny calls the 'institutions' of law in which the former are grounded: these institutions – eg, ownership, contract, paternal power, marriage – furnish the second degree of law.[160] Together, the institutions of law form a system corresponding to the legal order of a particular people.[161]

Ascending from the rules to the institutions of law is an achievement of both a theoretical and a practical order.[162] The former insofar as the material in the sources is presented in its real form, that is, according to its place within the overall system; thus, as we have seen in the previous section, Savigny is adamant on the point that obligations should be partnered with property – each of them being a subtype of the higher institution of patrimonial law – instead of family law.[163] In its practical guise, jurisprudence is a means of generating new law; once the jurist realises what institution of law underlies a particular set of positive

---

[156] See the account supplied by Gerald Postema, *Bentham and the Common Law Tradition*, 3–38.
[157] The distinction between the two species of custom referred to in the text above originated in Bentham. See Postema, ibid at 220–22.
[158] Savigny, *System*, I, 37–38.
[159] ibid at 8. See also Puchta, *Cursus*, 40–44.
[160] ibid. The analysis in terms of 'degrees of law' is borrowed from Helmut Coing, 'Ius Commune and German Pandesktistik', 12–13.
[161] Savigny, *System*, I, 9.
[162] ibid at 70–80. See also Puchta, *Cursus*, 37.
[163] ibid at 278–81, 315. See section V of this chapter.

norms he is able to extract new – non-posited – norms from that same institution. What renders this scientific or juristic law legitimate is not the fact that it is enacted by a law-making authority but that it is entailed by the extant body of positive law.

These are vague assertions and promissory notes, and we are yet to examine the text in the first volume of the *System* where Savigny attempts to make them good. But at this point I want to lay stress on the fundamental point in all of this, which is the connection forged between the activity of the jurist and the concept of science, of how the driving idea is to appropriate the prestige of modern science for the project of strengthening the position of the jurist. Science here plays a twofold role. First, it is knowledge that is rationally demonstrable and transparent, as opposed to arcane. As Savigny puts it:

> Our legal condition has become an artificial one; we require from the judge a scientific study of law which must be proved by defined tests and by which his position becomes a wholly different one from that of the old popular judges. […] He is to decide by the aid of science …[164]

The other role of science is as an institution supposedly open to all, instead of oligarchic or elitist. Anyone ready to receive university training and willing to embrace jurisprudence as a scientific 'vocation' can become a jurist.[165] The objection that juristic law is usurpatory is hence misplaced:

> There appears to be a manifold influence of the order of jurists upon positive law. Against the assertion of this influence, the reproach of unauthorized pretension has often been raised. That reproach could only be well founded if the jurists wished to form an exclusive order but since every one may become a jurist who applies to it the necessary energy, the assertion amounts to the simple proposition that he who makes law the business of his life, will through his larger acquaintance with the matter have greater influence than another upon it.[166]

Let us now return to Savigny's theory of legal method or legal reasoning. He offers elaborate views on each of the two main steps of jurisprudence. First, there is the moment of interpretation, by means of which the rules of law are 'pulled out' of the sources; although he devotes several pages to the subject of determining the content of customary law,[167] the lion's share of the analysis concerns the interpretation of statutory (written) law. The second moment is the move from the rules to the institutions of law underlying them and, ultimately, the entire system immanent in positive law; this is the means of arranging the rule material in its proper form and, most importantly, of filling the gaps in the aggregate of rules that constitutes the first degree of law. In Savigny's parlance, we have the 'interpretation

---

[164] ibid at 151–52. See also Puchta, *Cursus*, 44–45.
[165] See Max Weber, 'Science as a Vocation', especially at 149–56.
[166] Savigny, *System*, I, 39.
[167] ibid at 146–58.

of single written laws' and the 'interpretation of the law-sources as a whole'.[168] Let us examine them in that order.

(1) *Interpretation of single laws*. 'Interpretation' is defined as the 'reconstruction of the thought dwelling in the law'. In order to achieve that goal, the interpreter has to take into account four 'elements' of interpretation: grammatical, logical, historical and systematic.[169] The grammatical element is the text; the logical element is the relationship between various bits of text that embody a single norm – eg, each of the provisions in Title 17 (Copyright) of the US Code are to be read in conjunction with the definitions laid down in §101; the historical element consists in the historical circumstances and the legislative history prior to the enactment of the statute; finally, the systematic element concerns the relationship between the various sections of the same statute and between each norm and the 'great unity' underlying 'all the institutions and rules of law'.[170]

When a law is in a 'healthy condition', the interpretive procedure just outlined yields an unequivocal result; otherwise, the law is 'defective'. Laws are defective either owing to 'indefinite expression' or to 'erroneous expression'.[171] The former are cases of textual indeterminacy, when the statutory wording is incomplete, ambiguous, vague, obscure, etc;[172] the latter are cases in which the text fails to express the normative criterion it was meant to, the proverbial contradiction between letter and spirit – eg, 'no sleeping in the railway station' is not meant to apply to babies. According to Savigny, the legitimacy of remedying the defect is different for each of these cases, the former being 'free from risk' and 'plainly necessary' while the later 'carries with it much greater risk and at least makes special caution necessary'.[173] It is obvious what is at stake here. Legislative authority is inextricably tied to the textuality of statutes, the fact that their *ipsissima verba* command respect.[174] It is one thing to set the text aside when it is defective, when its meaning cannot be sorted out clearly; but it is another matter when it is the meaning of the text itself that is set aside in favour of some extra-textual viewpoint, and that is precisely what the second type of defect requires.

On Savigny's account, there are three possible means of remedying defects in a law. First, there is the legislative context supplied by other provisions of the same statute or other statutes in the vicinity of the one containing the provision in question – what Savigny pompously calls the 'innate connexion

---

[168] ibid at 166, 171, 211.
[169] ibid at 172.
[170] ibid.
[171] ibid at 179.
[172] Savigny only considers the possibility of incompleteness and ambiguity – ibid at 181–83 – although what he says applies equally to other types of textual indeterminacy.
[173] ibid at 179.
[174] On this point, see Jeremy Waldron, *Law and Disagreement*, 25.

[sic] of legislation'. A second remedy is the ground of the law, which may be either a more general norm immanent in positive law – eg, the 'ground' of the rule that a mistake as to the identity of the contracting party renders the agreement voidable is the principle of freedom of contract – or the immediate purpose of a norm – eg, the rule 'no vehicles allowed in public parks' secures the quiet enjoyment and safety of users of public parks. The third means of remedying legislative defects is what Savigny calls the 'intrinsic value of the result', that is, whether the norm as established produces desirable consequences or not. The legitimacy of these remedies is, just as with the defects themselves, variable: 'The first is to be at all events ... unhesitantly applied; the second makes greater caution necessary; the third lastly can be permitted only within the narrowest limits'.[175]

The final step in the theory is a synthesis of the doctrines of defects and remedies. Savigny's concerns at this stage are twofold. One the one hand, to establish a hierarchy of legitimate methods of interpretation of defective laws; on the other hand, to define a threshold of legitimacy beyond which the interpreter must put an end to his labours and defer to textual authority. In cases of 'indefinite expression' a remedy is perforce required because the text is indeterminate, which means that the three remedies are prima facie legitimate; but the deployment of a given remedy is only justified if a less controversial remedy fails to yield a determinate answer – eg, an interpretation based on the 'value of the result' is permissible only if the legislative context is vague and the ground of the law is unknown. In cases of 'erroneous expression', the same hierarchy of remedies applies, yet no remedy is strictly speaking required since there is always the option of deferring to the text. According to Savigny, only the remedy of legislative context is fully legitimate here; appealing to the 'ground of the law' is permissible only if it is known with a high degree of certainty *and* it is circumscribed narrowly as the immediate purpose of the norm, while the third remedy of the 'intrinsic value of the result' is strictly prohibited. Figure 3.3 sums up the whole theory.

Figure 3.3 The Savignian theory of interpretation

	Remedies		
Defects	*Context*	*Ground*	*Value*
Indefinite expression	+	+	+
Erroneous expressions	+	+/–	–

It is worth noting that there is nothing radical or even liberal about the Savignian theory of statutory interpretation; on the contrary, it is quite

[175] Savigny, *System*, I, 181.

conservative, certainly when contrasted with the medieval doctrine of *interpretatio* that conceded enormous free play to juristic elaboration. What is at stake in Savigny's account is the division of law-making competence between the two 'organs' of popular law – legislation and jurisprudence – and from the pages that he devotes to the interpretation of statutes we get the idea that the jurist plays a subordinate role. Indeed, from that standpoint alone, the theory appears to reflect the anti-legalist tendencies of post-medieval political culture, giving pride of place to legislation and demoting the jurist to an inferior status. It is only when we turn to the 'interpretation of the law-sources as a whole' that the subtle ways in which juristic authority is upheld are brought to light.

(2) *Interpretation of the law as a whole.* The subject is introduced in the following terms:

> Hitherto the discussion has been of the interpretation of single laws; but the totality of the law-sources above exhibited forms a whole, which is destined for the solution of every problem arising in the province of law. In order that it may be adapted to this end, we must make two requisitions upon it: *unity* and *completeness*.[176]

This is the idea, which we examined earlier, that the rules of law in the foreground are grouped together under (or cohere around) an institution of law and that the various institutions of law form a system immanent in the people's consciousness and its way of life. The law forms a meaningful whole.

> The normal procedure consists in the formation of a system of law out of the totality of the sources. [...] The collected circle of sources and in particular that part of it which we call the *corpus juris* of Justinian, may from this stand-point [sic] be regarded as a single law ...[177]

It appears that we should expect the rules of law obtained by means of interpretation to fit together and supply criteria of adjudication for any possible dispute. But Savigny concedes immediately that taken *en masse* they are neither coherent (a 'unity') nor complete: not coherent because the resulting aggregate contains contradictions, not complete because it contains gaps.[178] The task for jurisprudence is to remove the contradictions and to fill the gaps in the law.

Where there is a contradiction among rules belonging to the same body of positive law, the citizenry and the judge face incompatible instructions.[179]

---

[176] ibid at 211 (emphasis in the original).
[177] ibid at 212.
[178] ibid at 212–13.
[179] I do not wish to address here the question of whether the law of noncontradiction, which states that 'A' and 'non-A' cannot be both true, applies to normative conflicts. Hans Kelsen argued once that the laws of formal logic are indirectly applicable to legal norms in the following sense: while logical principles apply directly only to propositions, which are either true or false, and not to norms, which are either valid or invalid, they apply to propositions *about* norms; and the proposition that a

Savigny proposes a hierarchy of criteria to deal with this problem. First in the order of remedies come the familiar canons of 'special law trumps general law', 'superior law trumps inferior law', and 'newer law trumps older law'.[180] When a contradiction cannot be removed through such means – namely, and 'to a very great extent', where there is a 'contradiction between single parts of the Justinian legislation'[181] – the jurist should resort (in this order of preference) to 'systematical' and 'historical' criteria.[182] The former concern the logical relationship between the contradictory rules, namely whether they stand in a rule/exception relation or are complemented by other rules that restrict their respective scopes of application in ways that are mutually consistent – eg, although the law of bailment contains both negligence and strict liability rules, it contains provisions that specify which standard of liability applies to each type of bailee. The historical criteria, on the other hand, are remarkably obscure; Savigny writes that 'historical harmonization is effected by means of the supposition that one of the contradictory texts contains the real and abiding expression of the legislation, the other merely historical material'.[183] He acknowledges the bad reputation of the later procedure, and indeed his remarks only reinforce the suspicion of rather extreme manipulability.

Occasionally, however, none of these remedies work. Savigny asks: 'What in the last place is to be done …?' And then answers:

> Nothing remains but to prefer *that one* of the two contradictory texts which answers best to the rest of the undoubted principles of the legislation of Justinian. This rule rests upon the presumption of the organic unity of the Roman legislation, which again finds its deeper grounding in the nature of positive law in general.[184]

As between two unequivocally conflicting rules, then, the jurist is bound to apply the one that coheres with the background institutions which secure the organic unity of the law. That relates the discussion of contradiction with the distinction, drawn by Savigny much earlier in the book, between normal and anomalous law.

> A … contrast is referable to the difference of origin of the rules of law according as they have arisen [sic], that is, from the pure province of law … or from a foreign

---

type of act (say, bestiality) is forbidden contradicts the proposition that it is permitted (= not forbidden). See Kelsen, *Pure Theory of Law*, 74–75, 205–08. In a later work Kelsen detracted from his earlier position – see ibid, *General Theory of Norms*, 123–27, 211–25. There he writes that 'there is no analogy between the truth of a statement and the validity of a norm … When we have a conflict of norms, both norms are valid; otherwise, there would be no conflict' [213]. Kelsen's point is that normative conflicts pose a practical rather than a logical problem. We need not delve into the issue any further. It is good enough and plainly consistent with the spirit of Savigny's exposition that we understand a contradiction here as a situation in which a normative system offers at least two sets of practically incompatible instructions.

[180] Savigny, *System*, I, 213–16.
[181] ibid at 216.
[182] ibid at 220–29.
[183] ibid at 223.
[184] ibid at 231–32.

department. Since these latter intrude as foreign elements into the law ... I ... call them *anomalous* ... I call the law originating from the province of law the *normal* ... [...] If we seek more fully to comprehend [anomalous law], it appears as purely positive and generally referable to the will of a particular legislator.[185]

When the conflict between a normal and an anomalous rule is unavoidable, the jurist is to pick the former at the expense of the latter. But how are we to tell which rules belong in each of these categories? It seems obvious that the answer lies in the background institutions of law – those rules which cohere with them are part of normal law while those that do not are anomalies. But notice the circularity here. The institutions of law are not revealed immediately in the law-positing materials, such as legislation and custom; they are discovered when the jurist ascends to them through the medium furnished by the rules of law taken *en masse*. In other words, it is from the knowledge of the rules of law that the jurist acquires knowledge of the background legal institutions. Yet the rules of law do not form a coherent whole. We only see them as coherent once we have sorted out which rules set the norm and which stand as anomalies; and that sorting out presupposes the guidance provided by the institutions of law. In sum, the jurist warrants his knowledge of the institutions of law in the rule material and his knowledge of the rule material in the institutions of law.[186] Neither does Savigny tell us how to break the circle, nor does he acknowledge it in the first place. Accordingly, we cannot help but see the whole business as a means of fabricating the unity of the law.

In practice, circularity does not appear to be too serious an issue given the exceptional nature of the contradictions that cannot be resolved through other means. What we are talking about here are cases that fall within the scope of application of two (or more) valid norms – eg, imagine that carriers are subject to a regime of strict liability while innkeepers only answer for negligent conduct, and the question arises which standard of liability applies to cruises. Cases such as this hypothetical do occur but they are not frequent, not even when the sources of the law are in the state of disarray that we are led to think they were in mid-nineteenth-century Germany, where Roman texts, Imperial legislation, Germanic custom, regional and local statutes and in some places either the Prussian General Law, the Austrian Civil Code, or the French Civil Code, were all part of the extant legal materials. It is when we turn away from the theory of contradictions to that of *gaps* that the far-reaching implications of the circular classification of rules as either normal or anomalous are fully disclosed.

The topic is introduced as follows: 'If we find our law-sources not sufficient for the decision of a question of law, we have to fill up this gap,

---

[185] ibid at 49–50 (emphasis in the original).
[186] For the somewhat similar circularity in Langdellian formalism, with the obvious (although largely immaterial) difference that the first degree of law is case law instead of legislation, see Thomas Grey, 'Langdell's Orthodoxy', 21–24.

for the requirement of completeness has just as absolute a claim of right as that of unity has'.[187] What Savigny calls 'completeness' in this passage is what sometimes is called 'comprehensiveness', the property of a legal order that 'provides an institutional mechanism for the unique resolution of every case within its jurisdiction'.[188] It means that a judge cannot refuse to decide a dispute on grounds of *non liquet*, that is, because the law is incomplete or obscure. That value is 'absolute', declares Savigny. As he puts it a few pages earlier:

> [I]n accordance with the general nature of the judge's office, the obscurity of a written law ought never to deter him from forming a definite opinion upon the import of the law and from pronouncing a decision accordingly. […] The express decision of French law therefore, which forbids the judge to refuse his decision, by reason of a defective, obscure or insufficient law, is quite in conformity with the general nature of the judge's office.[189]

A judge cannot refuse to decide a case in the absence of an applicable rule; but how is he supposed to proceed? The answer lies in the background institutions of law. Once the jurist moves from the first degree of law formed by the rules to the institutions of law underlying them, he realises that positive law is indeed complete: 'our positive law is completed out of itself inasmuch as we grant the existence in it of an organically forming power'.[190] The institutions of law are discovered when the jurist perceives the analogy between a question answered by the rules of law and a question for which the rules provide no answer, and realises that what holds the analogy together is the 'innate relationship' or the 'archetype' of the underlying institution of law.[191] The procedure enables both gap-filling within a given institution of law – eg, the analogy between a series of transactions moves the jurist to the underlying institution of contract which itself provides the legal regulation of non-posited types of transaction; and the creation of new institutions of law that replicate the logic immanent in the system formed by those which are already known – eg, the law of torts is to be modelled to the furthest extent possible after the institutions of contract and property, namely from the ideas of 'person', 'will', 'right', etc immanent in them.

> This discovery of law by analogy appears in two degrees. First when a new, hitherto unknown, jural relation shows itself, for which consequently an institution of law as archetype is not contained in the positive law hitherto formed. In this case such an archetypal institution will be newly shaped according to the law of the innate relationship with those already known. Secondly and much more oftener [sic] when in an institution of law already known, a particular question of law newly arises.

---

[187] Savigny, *System*, I, 234.
[188] Grey, 'Langdell's Orthodoxy', 6.
[189] Savigny, *System*, I, 167–68.
[190] ibid at 235.
[191] ibid.

This will have to be answered according to the innate relationship of the principles belonging to this institution ...[192]

This is how jurisprudence generates new law from the data of positive law. Of course, not all positive law can be considered for the purposes of juristic law-making; it is crucial that the jurist filters the anomalies out of the normative material that forms the basis of his technical labors. 'For the whole procedure of analogy', writes Savigny, 'rests simply upon the innate coherence of the system of law, but the provisions of anomalous law have sprung from heterogeneous principles, and have merely been tacked on to the system of law, wherefore the organically forming power of the normal law cannot be ascribed to them'.[193]

The point that we have been slowly moving towards is finally within reach. Since the identification of particular rules as either normal or anomalous law is circular and thus arbitrary, the jurist has enormous free play behind the smokescreen of technical reasoning. The rules that fit with a pre-conceived normative plan are happily drawn into the province of normal law while those that are inconsistent with it are classified as anomalies.[194] What passes as scientific study of positive law is really an avenue for massive law-reform; the jurist finds an agreeable political theory in the law because his reading of it is always already mediated by the theory. That is how the will theory and, more generally, the tripartite conception of the legal order found their way into positive law.

In order to establish that, however, a further step in the argument is necessary. The extent to which gap-filling work forms the basis for large-scale legal reform disguised as science depends on how seriously incomplete or 'gappy' the law is. If there are only a few gaps, the room for law-making is actually quite narrow; that is (as we have seen) the case with respect to contradictions. A topic of major interest is hence the concept of *gap* underpinning Savigny's discussion.

The starting point of Savigny's theory is the duty of the judge to decide even if the case does not fall within the scope of a valid rule. It is tempting to argue from here that a gap is a case on which the law – or, at any rate, the first degree of law – is silent. But this is clearly wrong. There are in the law what Karl Larenz calls 'eloquent silences';[195] that is, cases that are intentionally left unregulated or are regulated through the medium of an implicit negative norm which stipulates that 'nobody must be forced to observe conduct to which he is not obliged by law'.[196] Consider the case of a businessman who

---

[192] ibid.
[193] ibid at 237–38.
[194] It does not follow that the anomalies are undesired. As I argued in ch 2, they may be marginal in the order of exposition because they threaten he coherence of the enterprise and yet play a central role in the order of justification.
[195] Karl Larenz, *Methodenlehre der Rechtswissenschaft*, 355.
[196] Hans Kelsen, *General Theory of Law and State*, 147.

sues his competitors for having driven him to bankruptcy because greater productive efficiency enabled them to charge lower prices for goods of similar quality. A district court grants a motion to dismiss the claim pursuant Rule 12(b)(6) of the Federal Rules of Civil Procedure. The decision is not one of *non liquet* – there in fact is no gap. The claim is dismissed because the complaint fails to state a cause of action, meaning that the conduct of the defendant(s) is legally permitted – it falls within the range of *damnum absque injuria*. The legal permission to cause competitive harm in the marketplace is an example – and arguably the paramount example – of eloquent silence.

Legal silence is hence a misleading proxy for gaps in the law. Let us test an alternative path. There is a gap when a case cannot be decided unless the law applying official(s) adds a norm or a decision-making criterion to the set of positive norms. Consider the following examples: (i) the law establishes as a necessary condition for the creation of a valid will that the testator signs and dates the document in the presence of 'the required witnesses', although there is no provision on the exact number; (ii) the bylaws of a union provide that officers can resign in accordance with the procedure specified in the internal regulation but the latter contain no provision on the issue; (iii) a contract stipulates that a catering firm should serve *borscht* in a party if the weather is cold and *vichyssoise* if the weather is hot, but does not determine what should be served in the event that the weather is mild. In each of these cases, the judge is bound to create a new norm or stipulate an ad hoc criterion of decision-making if he is not to issue a decision of *non-liquet*. There is a gap, and it must be filled in order to preserve the comprehensiveness of the legal order. Notice as well that a gap in this sense is a non-trivial and non-deliberate indeterminacy in the law. It should be distinguished both from the inevitable but trivial discretion in the application of any norm – eg, the norm instructing the judge to apply a penalty does not specify the exact words that should be in the sentence or in what tone of voice it should be read in the courtroom;[197] and it should be distinguished as well from the discretion conferred to the judge by deliberately indeterminate norms, such a norm stipulating that the punishment for a certain type of misdemeanour is a fine within a range, leaving to the judge the case-by-case determination of the exact value of the fine.[198] On the contrary, the gaps in the examples above are both non-trivial and non-deliberate; they are cases in which there is no applicable norm although there *should* be one.

Gaps in this latter sense bear an immediately discernible connection with the prohibition of *non-liquet*, which is why Ernst Zitelmann, in a classic study on the subject, called them 'authentic' (*echte*) gaps.[199] Yet, while perfectly

---

[197] See Kelsen, *Pure Theory of Law*, 349.
[198] See ibid at 350.
[199] Zitelmann, *Lücken im Gesetz*, 24.

possible and indeed familiar to any moderately experienced jurist, they are as rare as those contradictions which cannot be resolved through standard means. The free-play of the jurist to make law is very narrow if this is all Savigny means by a legal gap. But of course that is not the case. For in addition to these authentic gaps, there are those gaps which Zitelmann calls 'inauthentic' (*unechten*).[200] These refer to cases in which there is an applicable norm which is nonetheless understood to depart from the 'organic coherence' of either the underlying institution of law or the system as a whole to an extent that warrants the creation of a new norm by analogy.

Let me give an example of how this works. Imagine that only a few types of executory agreement are recognised in the legal sources as enforceable. In the Roman law of Gaius' time there were three closed lists of legally binding agreements: (i) by virtue of consent alone, such as sale, lease, partnership and *mandatum*; (ii) upon the delivery of the thing, as in loans and pledges; and (iii) as a result of certain formalities, either oral or in writing; other types of agreement (called 'innominate') were unenforceable before one of the parties performed.[201] In this system as described there are no authentic gaps. The parties to innominate agreements are subject to the general immunity-conferring norm that is implicit in the various positive stipulations of enforceability. Now, consider the argument that the various types of enforceable agreement in positive law are manifestations of the underlying legal institution of contract, and that the essence of it is the binding force of the parties' will. From that standpoint, agreements should, in principle or save special circumstances, be binding by virtue of consent alone. The fact that many types of consensual transactions are unenforceable according to the rules in place is understood as a gap in the first degree of law to be remedied with the richer normative resources afforded by the background institution of contract. The gap does not exist because a decision based on the rules alone is impossible but because the right decision within the very normative logic – the 'organic coherence' – of the system is lacking.[202]

Kelsen wrote about the 'idea of gap' that it is a 'fiction', and there is much to be said for that view.[203] Leaving aside the minor issues posed by authentic gaps, there simply is no connection between what the Savignian jurist counts as gap-filling and the prohibition of *non-liquet*. Savigny manages to smuggle a broad licence to reform the law into the apparent

---

[200] ibid at 27.

[201] Gaius, *Institutes*, III, §§ 89–96, 134–35. See Max Kaser, *Roman Private Law*, 162–208; James Gordley, *The Philosophical Origins of Modern Contract Doctrine*, 30–33.

[202] It is often defined as an 'incompleteness contrary to a plan' (*planwidrige Unvollständigkeit*) – the 'plan' allegedly immanent in the law. See Karl Engisch, *Einführung in das juristische Denken*, 137; Karl Larenz, *Methodenlehre der Rechtswissenschaft*, 358.

[203] Hans Kelsen, *General Theory of Law and State*, 146–49. The merit of Kelsen's observation is diminished because he refers to all gaps without distinguishing those which are authentic from those which are inauthentic and thus to some extent 'fictitious'.

straightjacket of the judicial office. Moreover, when we combine the fiction of gaps with the arbitrary identification of 'normal law', we get a sense of how Savigny and his followers managed to read Kant's will theory into the law and come up with the tripartite structure of the legal order exhibited in the substantive portions of the *System* – and all of it while holding the banners of legal science. They selectively classified certain portions of the law as either normal or anomalous, invented the background institutions of law, and then expanded their reach under the pretence of gap-filling. None of this was of course transparent, either to laypeople or to the jurists themselves. For the scientific jurist, both the existence of gaps and the unity of the law were demonstrable truths attained after centuries of jurisprudential reflection.

VII. The Triumph of Formalism

Although Savigny is a key protagonist in the creation of modern legal science and there are in the corpus of his work abundant traces of the jurisprudential conception known as 'formalism', his writings exhibit some ambivalence about the assimilation of legal reasoning to formal inference in its various guises, namely deductive argument and conceptual analysis.[204] In a passage of the early pamphlet against codification, he appears to embrace the cause of formalisation unreservedly, going as far as establishing a close analogy between jurisprudence and Euclidian geometry. In abridged form, these are his words:

> [T]here is certainly a perfection ... that may be illustrated by a technical expression of geometry. In every triangle, namely, there are certain data from the relations of which all the rest are necessarily deducible: thus, given two sides and the included angle, the whole triangle is given. In like manner, every part of our law has points by which the rest may be given: these may be termed the leading axioms.[205]

But in the first volume of the *System of the Modern Roman Law*, written more than two decades later, the scientific fervour cools down quite a bit. The analogies among regulated and non-regulated jural relations that enable the jurist to ascend from the rules to the institutions of law are no longer compared to geometry or any other form of demonstrable knowledge; while the jurist perceives the analogies,

---

[204] The best (not entirely convergent) contemporary accounts of nineteenth-century 'legal formalism' with which I am acquainted are: Felipe González Vicén, 'Sobre los Orígines y Supuestos del Formalismo en el Pensamiento Jurídico Contemporáneo'; Thomas Grey, 'Langdell's Orthodoxy'; Duncan Kennedy, *The Rise and Fall of Classical Legal Thought*, 243–51; Morton Horwitz, *The Transformation of American Law, 1870–1960*, 9–19; Karl Larenz, *Methodenlehre der Rechtswissenschaft*, 19–31; Franz Wieacker, *A History of Private Law in Europe*, 341–62.

[205] Savigny, *Of the Vocation of Our Age for Legislation and Jurisprudence*, 39. For the full quote, see section II of this chapter.

he cannot prove their existence. Indeed, the assimilation of legal argument to formal logic is explicitly repudiated:

> Each application of analogy rests upon the presupposition of an innate consistency in the law: only this is not always a mere logical consistency, such as the simple relation between reason and inference, but likewise an organic one, derived from a connected view of the actual nature of the jural relations and of their archetypes.[206]

Now contrast that account of jurisprudence with another one, presented less than half a century later by Rudolf Sohm, a law professor and doctrinal writer of some stature in his era whose main work, a treatise on Roman law, was translated into English in 1901 by James Crawford Ledlie under the title *The Institutes*. 'Having ascertained ... the rule of law,' writes Sohm,

> jurisprudence must next proceed to develop, or work out, its contents. A rule of law may be worked out either by developing the consequences which it involves, or by developing the wider principles which it presupposes. [...] The more important of these two methods of procedure is the latter, ie the method by which, from given rules of law, we ascertain the major premises which they presuppose. For having ascertained such major premises, we shall find that they involve, in their logical consequences, a series of other legal rules .... The law is thus enriched and enriched by a purely scientific method. [...] The application ... of a principle (a major premiss) which is *given*, we call the method of Inference; the application of a principle which we have *found*, we call the method of Analogy.[207]

On the view articulated by Sohm, the normative resources in the background are not institutions that the jurist discovers once he perceives the organic nexus among the rules of law but 'major premises' presupposed – that is, logically entailed – by the rules; ultimately, these form what the early Savigny called the 'leading axioms' of the law. Analogy is no longer merely a matter of *seeing* connections but of *demonstrating* their existence; and the organic connection among regulated and unregulated cases gives way to conceptual unity bestowed by a common and higher premise. Sohm is explicit on this point:

> The method of analogy does not mean (as the lay mind is apt to imagine) the application of a given rule of law to a legal relation of a somewhat *similar* kind. Such analogy would be the very opposite of scientific jurisprudence. It is the application of a given rule not to a merely similar relation, but to the identical relation, in so far as the *identical* element ... is traceable to a legal relation which is apparently different.[208]

To understand the transformation of legal method in an unequivocally formalist direction in the period that goes from the publication of the first volume of the *System* to Sohm's *Institutes* we have to turn to the work of two of the greatest

---

[206] ibid, *System*, I, 236. This point is stressed by Karl Larenz, *Methodenlehre der Rechtswissenschaft*, 13–18, 23–24.
[207] Sohm, *The Institutes*, 31–32 (emphasis in the original).
[208] ibid at 33 (emphasis in the original).

German jurists of the nineteenth century: Savigny's disciple Georg Friedrich Puchta, and Puchta's own disciple Rudolf von Jhering.[209]

Puchta appended to the first volume of his great doctrinal tract *Course on the Institutes* an introductory 'Encyclopedia', a term of art among Germans jurists of his era to refer to a brief overview of the sort of material that Savigny covers with much greater depth in the first volume of the *System*, and that was familiar to the English jurists of the same period as 'general jurisprudence'. In many respects, Puchta's exposition follows in the footsteps of his mentor; it is mostly his account of legal science that evinces important signs of innovation. Not only does Puchta unearth the formalism that Savigny embraced in his youth, and later buried, but he develops and refines it. In a section devoted to 'scientific and juristic law', he writes:

> It is the task of science to ascertain the precepts of law in their systematic context as mutually dependent and arising out of one another, so as to trace the genealogy of each of the precepts up to its originating principle and then to descend from the principles to their ultimate consequences. This process reveals and unfolds those legal precepts latent in the national spirit which are neither brought to light in popular conviction and the actions of the people, nor in the pronouncements of the legislator, but only as a product of scientific deduction.[210]

The movement upwards from the precepts (the rules of law) to the principles and downwards from these to their logical consequences is what Puchta calls the 'genealogy of concepts'. In a later section he offers an excellent example of how the downwards part of the method was expected to work in practice. He asks us to consider a case where the owner of a property assigns to a neighbouring owner a right to go through his land. In order to determine the nature of this right and its place in the 'system of jural relations', the jurist must descend (*more geometrico*) from the concept of right to the particular right in question. The reasoning is as follows: (i) it is a right and thus a power of the will (an absolute claim) within its sphere; (ii) it is a right over an object that is a thing, thereby a property right; (iii) since it does not involve full but only partial control over the thing, it is not ownership but a narrower interest in property; (iv) it is a right to use the object (as opposed, say, to collateral for a debt), and thereby a species of use-right; (v) it is limited to a particular kind of use, and thus a servitude (or easement); (vi) since it is a right with respect to land instead of movables, it is a real servitude; (vii) since it is a right to go through the land, it is a servitude of way.[211]

Puchta warns against the error of reducing the genealogy of concepts to a mere 'scheme of definitions'. What he means is that the concepts corresponding to each

---

[209] On these two jurists see Franz Wieacker, *A History of Private Law in Europe*, 316–19, 343–44, 355–57.

[210] Puchta, *Cursus der Institutionen*, I, 37. I am grateful to Marcos Keel Pereira for his valuable assistance with the translation of the two Puchta passages quoted in this section.

[211] ibid at 101.

of the steps of the argument – eg, property right and servitude – are fully operative as opposed to means of classification.[212] The jurist does not proceed like the biologist collecting data about various specimens and then organising it into a taxonomic scheme. A jurist of that sort would decide that the right of the neighbour is a property right by comparing its content with that of other rights brought under the 'property' label, and concluding for the existence of the common element attached to the label. That is what Puchta calls 'external' knowledge of the law, which he contrasts unfavourably with 'internal' knowledge.[213] The real task of the jurist, he argues, is to work his way up to the principles presupposed by the rules of positive law and then all the way down to the non-posited rules entailed by the principles. It is worth quoting him on this point:

> It happens very often that a judge has to decide upon cases that are not covered by the explicit determinations of either customary or statutory law. On these occasions, it is science which affords him the precepts by which he is to decide the case. These do not rest upon any external authority; they are valid insofar as they follow with inner necessity from the principles of existing law and hence aspire to the same validity as either popular conviction or legislation.[214]

The remarkable powers of 'science' are well displayed in the servitude of way example. The principle or operative concept of right, when applied to things, as one class of possible objects of rights, entails the operative concept of full property right or ownership; the newfound concept of full property entails in turn the concept of a limited or narrow property right (*ius in re aliena*), since the power of the owner to disaggregate his property is contained within the concept of ownership; and so on, until we derive the doctrine of servitude of way. It was under the spell of this genealogy of concepts that Jhering would go on to write that '[legal] concepts are productive, they pair off and breed new concepts'[215] and Windscheid, author of the most widely read doctrinal treatise of the Pandectist era and the dominant intellectual force behind the German Civil Code, wrote that 'the [judicial] decision is the product of a calculation in which the factors are legal concepts'.[216]

Since the jural relation between the owner and the neighbour described in Puchta's example is already contained in the highest concept (the leading axiom) – *right* – it is fair to ask what role is assigned to the intermediate steps in the chain of reasoning. They are important for two reasons. On the one hand, they are essential to the demonstration of complex analytical truths about the law; in order to show that the abstract concept of right entails the relatively concrete doctrine of servitude of way, the jurist is bound to take little steps, for that is the only

---

[212] See Karl Larenz, *Methodenlehre der Rechtswissenschaft*, 20–22.
[213] Puchta, *Cursus der Institutionen*, I, 100–01.
[214] ibid at 45.
[215] Rudolf von Jhering, *Geist des römischen Rechts*, I, 40.
[216] Bernhardt Windscheid, *Lehrbuch des Pandektenrechts*, I, 64.

way to demonstrate the rational force of the argument. On the other hand, the intermediate concepts permit a significant economy of effort in the future, since they enable the jurist to retrieve new legal solutions from them without having to ascend to even more abstract notions; once we have the concept of servitude, for example, we can go on with the business of settling disputes emerging from the conflicting interests of neighbours in light and air without having to move all the way up to the concept of ownership, let alone that of right. Related to this later point is a certain division of labour within the legal profession, pregnant in hierarchical implications, between the academic jurist and treatise-writer, devoted to the complex tasks of doctrinal construction, and the practitioner busy with the relatively simple operations of day-to-day law application.

The final step in the process of formalisation of legal reasoning was taken by Puchta's student Rudolf von Jhering in the first three volumes of *The Spirit of the Roman Law*. Jhering is a complex character in the history of legal thought, for he was both a leading advocate of legal formalism and a major source of inspiration for the anti-formalist rebellion launched by the social jurists of the inter-war period.[217] Our concern now is with the formalist aspects of the *Spirit of the Roman Law*.[218] In his trademark (and irksome) allusive style, Jhering argues

---

[217] It is tempting to consider him the European equivalent of Oliver Wendell Holmes. Just as American lawyers usually distinguish the quasi-formalist Holmes of *The Common Law* (1881) from the proto-realist of *The Path of the Law* (1897) – although the 'Road to Damascus' was arguably Holmes' essay 'Privilege, Malice, and Intent' (1894) –, the tendency among European legal academics is to identify in Jhering's work a major break from the extreme legal formalism expounded in his early writings with the publication of the fourth and last volume of *The Spirit of the Roman Law* (1865) and the anonymous *Insider's Letter on the State of Contemporary Jurisprudence* (1861). See Jhering, 'Vertrauliche Briefe über die heutige Jurisprudenz. (This 'letter' would be republished two decades later together with the (in)famous anti-formalist satire 'In the Heaven of Legal Concepts' [*Im juristischen Begriffshimmel*] and other essays in the book *Scherz und Ernst in der Jurisprudenz*). But this picture is in many ways misleading. The Jhering of the first three volumes of the *Spirit of the Roman Law* alternates between hyper-formalism and anti-formalism, and in spite of a discernible tendency to follow the latter impulse in the last volume of the work, there is ambivalence up to the very end. Moreover, while he was working on this voluminous masterpiece, Jhering wrote a number of doctrinal essays that would grow to be hallmarks of anti-formalist jurisprudence; the most significant of these was perhaps the article advocating the doctrine of *culpa in contrahendo* – see Rudolf (von) Jhering, '*Culpa in contrahendo* oder Schadensersatz bei nichtigen oder nicht zur Perfektion gelangten Vertrigen'. See also Kessler and Fine, '*Culpa in Contrahendo*, Bargaining in Good Faith, and Freedom of Contract', 401–09. For a reading of Jhering's work along the lines suggested in this note, see Karl Larenz, *Methodenlehre der Rechtswissenschaft*, 24–27, 43–48. No wonder that while Franz Wieacker, *A History of Private Law in Europe*, 343, blames the Jhering who wrote the *Spirit of the Roman Law* for proposing the 'most extreme form of the jurisprudence of concepts', Lon Fuller, 'American Legal Realism', 449 (fn 46), praises the same Jhering as a 'pioneer among [legal] realists'. Both readings are completely plausible so long as the vast portions of text inconsistent with each of them are carefully excised by the reader. Specifically, it depends on whether one emphasises what Jhering calls the 'anatomy' of law, the analysis of the logical structure of the law where most of the formalist talk is concentrated, or the 'physiology' of law, the analysis of law's functions where his earliest anti-formalist insights appear, notably the discussion of the *prima facie* conflict between 'formal' and 'material realizability' (*formaler und materieller Realizierbarkeit*) – ie, bright line rules versus equitable standards. See Jhering, *Geist des römischen Rechts*, I, §§ 3–4, 48–58 ff.

[218] See Jhering, *Geist des römischen Rechts*, I, § 3, 25–48 ff and ibid, II-2, §§ 38–41, 306–72 ff.

that the noblest calling of legal science – the subject of 'jurist chemistry'[219] – is to abstract from the mass of legal rules the simple elements or primitive components that recur in different combinations. He relies on another metaphor as well: just as the words of a language form a vast array of different combinations of a small set of letters – the alphabet – likewise the complexity of law yields to an analysis in terms of its simple elements; these make up the 'alphabet of law'.[220] One of his examples is quite helpful. Suppose that a group of experts commissioned to draft a code covering the whole law of obligations begins by dealing with the contract of sale; once all questions pertaining to sales are dealt with, it turns to other contracts – exchange, lease, loan, etc. At some point, the experts realise that a large number of issues involved in each type of contract are common to all other contracts, such as the relevance of mistake, fraud and duress, the requirements of performance, or the consequences of breach and delayed performance. These issues are not specific to any contractual type but the subject of a general theory of contract that condenses a large number of rules recurring in every transaction.[221]

At first blush, nothing in Jhering's exposition differs from that of Puchta, for whom legal rules (at least insofar as they belong to the normal law) unfold logically from a small number of leading axioms. Yet there is an important point that sets the two accounts apart: whereas Puchta's principles embody values, the 'simple elements' of Jhering's system are technical notions. Let me give an example that might shed some light on this distinction. My experience is that when a common lawyer with little knowledge of comparative law opens a civilian textbook on the law of obligations inspired by the arrangement of the German Civil Code he is immediately struck by its technical appearance and abstract language. The law of obligations concerns all 'sources of obligations', that is, operative facts that trigger the existence of obligations, and that comprises contracts, torts, unjust enrichment and a range of issues that in the common law fall within the domain of constructive trust. It is very odd for the common lawyer that all these doctrinal areas are brought together in a single branch of the law on the very thin ground that each of them concerns the creation of an abstract type of jural relation called 'obligation'; it involves what appears to be a ruinous trade-off of intelligibility – an intuitive awareness of the issues involved in each of those doctrinal domains – for a neglectable gain in conceptual unity.

Now, the concept of 'obligation' is precisely what Jhering takes a 'letter' in the 'alphabet of law' to be. The element 'obligation' recurs in all doctrinal fields that compose the 'sources of obligations' listed above, and the mass of legal norms that are entailed by that element are part of the regime applicable to each such source. Similarly, the element 'contract' recurs in all manner of jural relations, from the

[219] ibid, II-2, 319.
[220] ibid, I, 37; II-2, 317–35.
[221] ibid, II-2, 319–20.

sale of land to marriage and adoption; therefore, despite their enormous heterogeneity, those aspects of these relations that are contractual in nature are subject to a common legal regime.

What distinguishes this approach from Savigny's and Puchta's is that the law is no longer organised in a way that renders the underlying principles of justice or political ordering of social life transparent. The organic connection among institutions of law characteristic of the Savignian approach and largely upheld by Puchta is now submerged under a formal system structured by technical concepts. We have examined earlier the political values embodied in the Savignian tripartite system. Similarly, in nineteenth-century Anglo-American classical private law, which in its core comprised the fields of property, contract, tort, and the residual and anomalous area of quasi-contract, it is fairly easy to discern an underlying political theory.[222] Jhering's 'alphabet of law', on the contrary, is politically opaque; it is hard to figure out the political values of a doctrinal arrangement organised around the concept of obligation or of a notion of contract that extends far beyond patrimonial law. This is not to say that the doctrinal arrangement is politically neutral; both in the Pandectist treatises and in the German Civil Code of 1900, we find the will theory and the patriarchal understanding of family life. But it is much harder for the untrained eye to spot a politics in, say, Windscheid's *Pandects* than in Savigny's *System* or Puchta's *Institutions*. This progressive moral-political emptying of legal doctrine widens the gap between the jurist, whose calling is the scientific study of positive law, and the philosopher concerned with ideal law or the theory of justice. It strengthens the position of the jurist as a technical expert.

I should not be taken to say that Jhering invented this further, distinctively civilian (and especially German), trait of legal formalism. His innovation was to theorise a practice already dominant in much of the doctrinal writing produced by earlier jurists. Take the case of Savigny. In his two-volume work *Law of Obligations*, published 11 years after the first volume of the *System*, Savigny presents a general theory of obligations along the lines that I sketched above. The plan of the work, announced in the introduction, comprised four chapters: (i) the nature of obligations; (ii) sources of obligations; (iii) the extinction of obligations; and (iv) remedies against the violation of obligations; of these Savigny only managed to cover (i) and part of (ii) in his lifetime.[223] The most telling aspect of the arrangement is that the nature of obligations precedes the rest of the exposition, indicating that the legal regime is built upon the concept as opposed to the other way around.

Even more interesting in this regard is Savigny's theory of contract, which became a hallmark of German legal culture. One would expect Savigny to be particularly hostile to the idea of extending the category of contract beyond the realm of patrimonial law, or even that of the law of obligations. Indeed, common lawyers might be tempted to think about the property/obligations distinction

---

[222] See, eg, Duncan Kennedy, 'Form and Substance in Private Law Adjudication', 1728–31; Morton Horwitz, *The Transformation of American Law, 1870–1960*, 10–16.
[223] Savigny, *Das Obligationenrecht*, I, 2–3.

along the more familiar lines of property/contract. At any rate, they are likely to think that what is at stake doctrinally in Savigny's efforts to keep the individualist logic of patrimonial law at bay from the family is, in the words of Duncan Kennedy, 'rejection of the contractual view of marriage'.[224] Savigny himself issues a warning against the dangers of excessive abstraction:

> If a dogmatic exposition of the law is so constituted as, to destroy the internal unity of the institutions of law, to bind up together the essentially diverse, to disfigure and reverse the real relation of different institutions to one another in point of importance, then such errors of form are essential since they obscure the matter itself and are hindrances to the true insight.[225]

And yet, both in the third volume of the *System* and in the second volume of the *Law of Obligations*, Savigny takes issue with a restrictive conception of contract of the sort prevalent in the Common Law (and to some extent in French Law as well), where a contract is mostly understood as a private agreement specifying future actions – 'a promise or a set of promises', in the words of §1 of the *Restatement (Second) of Contracts*.[226] He turns out to be a staunch advocate not just of the contractual nature of marriage but also of the extension of the contractual category to the fields of public law and public international law.[227] For Savigny, a contract is any joint declaration of intent (*Willenserklärung*) directed towards determining the jural relation(s) of the parties[228] – a definition so broad that it comprises not just sales, leases, loans and employment agreements but also (to mention but a few examples) the conveyance of land, marriage, adoption, court settlements, administrative agreements and even international conventions. Indeed, contract is a species of the genus 'juristic act' (*Rechtsgeshäft*), which refers to any voluntary constitution, modification, or extinction of a jural relation, encompassing both agreements (contracts) and unilateral declarations of intent, such as wills, offer and acceptance considered separately, or the occupation and abandonment of property.[229]

The apparent inconsistency in the Savignian system created by so broad a concept of contract can be easily dissolved with the resources afforded by Jhering's theory. Savigny does not maintain that all the legal *institutions* to which

---

[224] Duncan Kennedy, 'Savigny's Family/Patrimony Distinction', 828.
[225] Savigny, *System of the Modern Roman Law*, I, 331.
[226] See Charles Knapp, 'Contract Law'. In French law, art 1101 of the *Code Civil* – cf www.napoleon-series.org/research/government/c_code.htmlrestricts (last checked: 10 May 2012) – restricts the concept of contract to promises, which are understood as a species of the more general (but largely non-operative) concept of convention. In Italian law, under art 1321 of the *Codice Civile*, the concept of contract is reserved for patrimonial relations, that is, to obligations and property – cf www.jus.unitn.it/cardozo/obiter_dictum/codciv/Lib4.htm (last checked: 10 May 2012). For a brief comparative account of the concept of contract in the German, French and Common Law traditions, see Zweigert and Kötz, *An Introduction to Comparative Law*, 352–53.
[227] Savigny, *System des heutigen römischen Rechts*, III, 309–12; ibid, *Das Obligationenrecht*, II, 7–16.
[228] ibid.
[229] See ibid, *System*, III, 1–8, 309.

the contractual category extends have a similar nature; marriage and sale, for instance, are entirely different and belong to distinct areas of the law. But all of them have at least *one* element in common – a letter of the 'alphabet of law' – in the parties' agreement. In that one respect, they warrant identical legal treatment.[230] To use Jhering's figurative language, one should distinguish the letter from the word – just as the same letter may figure in words of different meaning, so may the same legal element figure in different institutions of law.

The importance of the contract element is, of course, very different in the case of marriage and sale: since marriage is an aspect of the organic life of the family, the will of the spouses plays a subordinate role in the institution as a whole; on the contrary, the very essence of a sale is the parties' agreement. Yet, while in the third volume of the *System* Savigny reiterates his criticism of Kant for having conceived marriage as an obligatory contract, and praises Hegel's non-contractual definition of marriage as 'admirable', he argues that Hegel has thrown out the baby with the bathwater: what is condemnable about Kant's account is not the assimilation of marriage to contract but to *obligatory* contract;[231] contract is a technical concept that extends its reach to any jural relation emerging from the parties' agreement.[232] And this is not a play of words, a matter of stipulating a broader or narrower meaning for the word 'contract'; the qualification of a given relation as contractual implies that it falls within the purview of the general part of contract law, namely the rules and doctrines governing such issues as the requirements of offer and acceptance, legal capacity, the relevance of mistake, etc.[233]

The culminating point of the drive towards increasing abstraction, the highest that the 'blocking level' of legal reasoning was lifted in private law theory,[234] is the idea of a general theory common to the various fields of private law conceived by Savigny – obligations, property, family and inheritance law.[235] It stands vis-à-vis these fields of law in a form similar to the general theory of obligations vis-à-vis the various sources of obligations. The belief in such a general theory is the inspiration behind the structure of the German Civil Code, where four books corresponding to the fields of obligations, property, family and inheritance are preceded by a so-called General Part (*Allgemeiner Teil*), the crowning achievement of the Pandectist school and an eloquent testimony to nineteenth century legal formalism.[236]

---

[230] See Rudolf Sohm, *The Institutes*, 32–33, who borrows directly from Jhering's scheme to make a similar point.
[231] Savigny, *System*, III, 318–21.
[232] ibid at 317–18.
[233] ibid at 315–16, 320–21 (fn).
[234] 'Blocking level' is from Duncan Kennedy, *The Rise and Fall of Classical Legal Thought*, 243–51. It refers to the level of abstraction below which legal concepts are understood by mainstream jurists to be operative and, by implication, to the degree of vertical integration of the law.
[235] Savigny (*System*, I, 318–19) writes in favour of such a general theory.
[236] On the regulatory technique of the BGB (the German civil code) and the sources and misgivings originated by the General Part, see, eg, Franz Wieacker, *A History of Private Law in Europe*, 385–86;

VIII. Classical Private Law

What I call 'classical private law' is the partnership between the will theory, understood as the mature version of classical liberalism, and legal formalism, a theory of legal reasoning modelled after the Enlightenment conception of science, that gives form to mid- to late-nineteenth-century legal thought in Germany and abroad. The foundation of the partnership is clear by now. Liberal ideals needed an agent to give them social currency and the jurists needed a socially accepted ideal – a proof of 'enlightenment' – to insulate traditional law from radical legislative reform.

My basic thesis is not new. It was, as we have seen, advanced by Roscoe Pound, and indeed by many others. I have merely tried to state more clearly and coherently, strengthen by an effort to connect a variety of dots, back up with greater depth and breadth of textual evidence, and bring to bear on a larger narrative the familiar notion that the ideas of liberal individualism and of legal formalism are central to the experience of nineteenth-century jurisprudence. But this familiar notion is not without its critics, and it is a good test to the robustness of my own case that I can answer the challenge posed by one of the most perceptive and creative among them.

In the last chapter of *The Philosophical Origins of Modern Contract Doctrine*, James Gordley attempts to refute the thesis that there is an important connection between nineteenth-century contract doctrine and classical liberalism. He does not deny that the nineteenth-century jurists were committed to a 'will theory' of contract and indeed he expounds its main tenets admirably in the penultimate chapter of the book. His claim is that the jurists assigned such an important place to the will not as a result of any particular political and philosophical allegiance but because to them, infected as they already were by the triumph of nominalism characteristic of modern intellectual culture, the concept of will was the only intelligible element in the late scholastic system that organized the *ius commune* in the light afforded by Aristotelian and Thomistic metaphysics. In his words:

> It is surely not an accident that the will theories shared the same century as intellectual and political movements that treated the will as an end in itself or as an indispensable engine of human progress. The historians must be right that there is some connection among them. The nature of this connection, however, is not obvious. ... [T]he will theories emerged when the nineteenth century jurists purged the doctrine they inherited of Aristotelian concepts they no longer understood. That process does not presuppose an allegiance to nineteenth-century liberal principles.[237]

We may call this view the 'subtraction narrative', since it portrays the will theory as the sole survivor of a purge instead of an intellectual revolution. The evidence that Gordley produces for the subtraction narrative is largely of the negative sort.

Zweigert and Kötz, *An Introduction to Comparative Law*, 152–54; Basil Markesinis, *The German Law of Contract*, 19–25.

[237] Gordley, *The Philosophical Origins of Modern Contract Doctrine*, 215.

He argues that the jurists did not have any reform agenda simply because they declared an exclusive allegiance to the study of positive law. They regarded their task as a matter of dry doctrinal analysis and textual exegesis, as opposed to political and philosophical reform. The argument is crisply summarised in two passages.

> In the writings of the nineteenth-century will theorists ... we find little direct borrowing from philosophers, economists, or political theorists. Only rarely do we find any sign of a commitment to liberal values of freedom or individualism. We find almost the opposite: an insistence that the jurist can do his job without taking account of economics, philosophy, politics or values such as freedom.[238]
>
> The Anglo-American, French, and German jurists, then, did not ground their legal doctrines on any definite philosophical or political principles, liberal or otherwise. They wished to escape philosophical or political commitments. The views of Pollock or of the French jurists required only the most minimal political commitment: an acknowledgement that the authoritative sources of law, whatever they might be, were authoritative.[239]

If the argument of this chapter has succeeded, it should be clear where Gordley's error lies. Of course, he is right to assert that the will theorists did not borrow explicitly from the work of philosophers or doctrinaires, including Kant, or presented their arguments as implications of liberal premises. They claimed no other basis for their arguments but positive law, which they traced in a variety of ways back to the people or the community, and the law-generating powers of 'scientific deduction'. But this is hardly enough to conclude that they did not actually proceed from liberal premises or reformed the law behind the smokescreen of doctrinal analysis. I tried to show that the jurists had pressing incentives to deny any political commitments. The restoration of their degraded symbolic capital required both the capacity to reform the law according to the ideological proclivities of their time, where liberal values had a firm albeit truncated grasp, and the capacity to distance themselves both from the populism of democrats and the arrogance of philosophers. They had to mediate the tension between tradition and modernity, history and revolution, the natural reason of liberalism and the 'artificial reason of the law'. That was the fine line walked by classical private law theory. To its fate we now turn.

---

[238] ibid at 215–16.
[239] ibid at 227.

4

The Socialisation of Private Law

I. The Social Question

When the classical jurists read the will theory into the positive law of their time, a process that began and matured in the German university of the first half of the nineteenth century, they were operating against the background of an identifiable type of social order. Theirs was a post-feudal society, where the production of foodstuffs primarily for self-consumption in small strips of 'open field' land and within the framework of the manor or *seigneury* – the economic, judicial and administrative subjection of peasant families to a lord – had either disappeared, as in post-revolutionary France, or remained in existence, as in the provinces of eastern Germany, but was no longer the dominant form of productive life. In the rural world, where the vast majority of North Atlantic populations lived until the later third of the nineteenth century, with the exception of Britain, where city-dwellers represented about half of the population as early as in 1850,[1] most agricultural output, on the rise (particularly in Britain) since the early sixteenth century, and substantially increased *c* 1750 with the introduction of mechanical methods of production, was directed to the marketplace to be exchanged for other foodstuffs, manufactured goods and services. The peasant, on the other hand, had become either an independent farmer or (in most cases) a dispossessed journeyman working in the enclosed fields of a landlord.

In urban areas, which by contemporary standards were really just small cities or even towns (with a few exceptions, especially London),[2] the guild system – the organisation of a trade's craftsmen into associations with a hierarchical structure (ranging from the master craftsmen at the top to the apprentices at the base) and devoted to a variety of market-hampering practices (barriers to entrance, price-setting, etc) – had either been abolished or was quickly fading away. The main protagonists of economic life were the small manufacture and the artisan shop, usually family businesses managed in the image of the patriarchal household. Commercial banking was growing quickly, at the pace largely set by the railway expansion, although for the most part businesses required relatively low amounts of capital and thereby could rely on self-financing schemes.

---

[1] Eric Hobsbawm, *The Age of Capital: 1848–1875*, 200.
[2] According to Hobsbawm, ibid at 244, in 1851 London had 2.5 million inhabitants.

In sum, the society of Savigny's and Puchta's era was still what we might call a 'commercial' society, post-feudal and pre-capitalist. The major political question of their time, as we saw in the previous chapter, was how to accommodate the liberal ethos with monarchism and patriarchalism. The tripartite structure of the legal order was their response. In the field of patrimonial law, which embodied the ideology of classical liberalism, the jurists stressed continuously the basic principle of equality among persons. It was important to them that private law, with the exception of the realm of family life, abstracts from all features that set one person apart from others – birth, wealth, talent, opportunities, luck, etc – thus reducing a diverse multitude to a common denominator: the free will. Writing in the mid-century, Puchta acknowledges, and indeed celebrates, the legal purchase of this abstract – or, as it was to be put later, 'formal' – conception of equality:

> It is apparent that human relations do not enter fully into the territory of law or of the series of jural relations. For the concept of person rests upon an abstraction, and thus it does not embrace a man's entire existence, including directly only the fact that he is a subject of will and taking other qualities into account only indirectly, according to their nearer of more distant connection with it. This abstraction accordingly extends to those relationships of men which have to admit of much modification and discount, in order to be viewed as mere relations of persons as such, or to be taken merely as jural relations.[3]

At the end of the nineteenth century, many would agree with Puchta at the level of description of positive law, but few would see any good in it. In the novel *Le Lys Rouge*, published in 1894, Anatole France denounced sarcastically and in lasting words the hypocrisy of 'the majestic equality of the laws, which forbid poor and rich alike to sleep under the bridges, to beg in the streets, and to steel bread'.[4] At this point, it was impossible to maintain honestly that there was even a rough correspondence between the 'picture of the social order'[5] implicit in mainstream legal thought and social reality.

That was true not only in law but also in political economy, where the 'picture of the social order' was even more explicit, since the discipline prided itself as empirically sound. What we might call the textbook or mainstream view of the classical school, featuring prominently Adam Smith and David Ricardo, exhibited a simple and attractive image of the market economy.[6] Instead of producing directly the goods required to meet their basic needs, in a market society individuals specialise in the production of a particular type of good – a commodity – which they then exchange for the bundle of commodities they wish to consume. The advantages of a system of production-for-exchange are twofold: on the one hand, specialisation brings about enormous gains in productivity, as a result of increased

---

[3] Puchta, *Cursus der Institutionen*, I, 51.
[4] Anatole France, *Les Lys Rouge*, 118.
[5] Roscoe Pound, 'The New Feudal System', 399.
[6] I follow for the most part two accounts: Duncan Kennedy, 'The Role of Law in Economic Thought', 940–58; Duncan Foley, *Adam's Fallacy*, 1–85.

dexterity, time saved in the transition from one task to another, and technological innovation.[7] On the other hand, the resulting income gains increase the demand for commodities, and thus the scale of the market, and that in turn encourages the transition from labour-intensive to capital-intensive production that has high fixed costs but lower average or per-unit costs for large outputs – the phenomenon known in modern neoclassical economics as 'economies of scale'.[8] Since the two dynamics are interrelated – the gains from specialisation increase the scale of the market and that encourages further specialisation – the market creates a 'virtuous spiral of economic development'.[9]

How are these gains distributed in the marketplace? According to the labour theory of value, dominant among the classical political economists, the 'natural' price of a commodity is a function of the labour time required to produce it; that is, if it takes four hours of labour to produce a sack of flower and 12 hours to produce a cask of wine, the natural rate of exchange between the two commodities is three sacks of flower for one cask of wine or 3:1. This price is 'natural' in two senses, one mechanistic and the other moral. First, although it is by no means true that the market price always corresponds to the natural price, free competition tends to push the former to converge with the latter since if a certain commodity is exchanged for more than its natural price firms in other lines of production have an overwhelming incentive to divert their labour force to the production of that commodity, increasing its supply and hence driving the price down.[10] Secondly, since the natural price, over which real-world market prices 'gravitate', reflects the labour inputs embodied in each commodity, each producer tends to acquire a measure of social wealth proportional to the labor time expended in its creation. That is, if I contributed with 0.01 of the total labour inputs in a year, my income over that period will approximate the money value of 0.01 of the corresponding output. It follows that the free market – the spontaneous form of economic activity that develops once the 'artificial' institutions of feudalism are abolished and the state refrains from interfering with economic activity – tends to reward each according to his productive effort. The theory had to contend with anomalies, some of them trivial – Ricardo acknowledged that the value of rare and scarce goods, such as treasured works of art or diamonds and precious metals, could not be explained in labour terms[11] – while others were much more serious, such as rent (the income of land-owners) and the net profit accrued by capitalists (the difference, reported in a firm's income statement, between gross revenues and the cost of wages and other productive inputs – adjusted for risk).[12] But these were

---

[7] See Adam Smith, *The Wealth of Nations*, Book I, ch I, 9–21. For commentary, see Foley, ibid at 5–6.
[8] See Foley, ibid at 8–10.
[9] ibid at 10.
[10] See Adam Smith, *The Wealth of Nations*, 78–90.
[11] See Duncan Foley, *Adam's Fallacy*, 62–64.
[12] On Ricardo's theory of rent, see ibid at 72–75, 241–43. On Ricardo's failure to explain profit and Marx's later extension of the theory of rent to capital returns (the theory of exploitation), see Joseph Schumpeter, *Capitalism, Socialism and Democracy*, 25–28.

regarded as exceptions to a general norm, much in the manner in which the classical jurists and Kant before them dealt with rules and doctrines that did not sit well with the will theory.[13]

The views of the political economists are not important to us because they were borrowed by or exerted an indirect influence on the jurists; for the most part, the jurist and the economist ignored each other. What the summary of classical economic theory shows is a large affinity or structural homology between the will theory and the picture of the exchange economy, particularly with respect to the abstract conception of the person common to both: the individual will that participates in the patrimonial order bears an uncanny resemblance to the independent producer in the marketplace.[14] Karl Marx reveals this connection in a passage of *Das Kapital* worthy of a lengthy quotation:

> The sphere of circulation or commodity exchange, within whose boundaries the sale and purchase of labour-power goes on, is in fact a very Eden of the innate rights of man. It is the exclusive realm of Freedom, Equality, Property and Bentham. Freedom, because both buyer and seller of a commodity, let us say of labour-power, are determined only by their free will. They contract as free persons, who are equal before the law. Their contract is the final result in which their joint will finds a common legal expression. Equality, because each enters into relation with the other, as with a simple owner of commodities, and they exchange equivalent for equivalent. Property, because each disposes only of what is his own. And Bentham, because each looks only to his own advantage. The only force bringing them together, and putting them into relation with each other, is the selfishness, the gain and the private interest of each. Each pays heed to himself only, and no one worries about the others. And precisely for that reason, either in accordance with the pre-established harmony of things, or under the auspices of an omniscient providence, they all work together to their mutual advantage, for the common weal, and in the common interest.[15]

Between representation and reality there is, however, an unbridgeable gap. 'When we leave this sphere of simple circulation or the exchange of commodities,' continues Marx,

> which provides the 'free-trade *vulgaris*' with his views, his concepts and the standard by which he judges the society of capital and wage-labour, a certain change takes place, or so it appears, in the physiognomy of our *dramatis personae*. He who was previously the money-owner now strides out in front as a capitalist; the possessor of labour-power follows as his worker. The one smirks self-importantly and is intent on business; the other is timid and holds back, like someone who has brought his own hide to market and now has nothing else to expect but – a tanning.[16]

What Marx stresses here, in his trademark bellicose style, is the difference between a commercial and a capitalist society.[17] The transition from the former

---

[13] See Duncan Kennedy, 'The Role of Law in Economic Thought', 948, 958.
[14] See Kennedy, ibid at 949–58.
[15] Marx, *Capital*, 280.
[16] ibid.
[17] This is not to say that Marx was fond of a commodity system or a commercial society. In his early writings, he stresses the overwhelming anti-communitarian bias of the market, where man's real nature

to the latter was the major event of the second half of the nineteenth century, an enormous social transformation that led most observers at the end of the century to regard the abstract individualism embraced by the classical jurists and economists as completely inadequate to the social circumstances of their time. Theirs was a society of 'complexity', 'interdependence', 'differentiation', 'progress' and 'instability' – key words in a new social vocabulary; and the new social situation raised a new question – the so-called Social Question. The world had changed, and it required an adequate political and legal response. Before we turn to the latter, let us examine, with much help from Eric Hobsbawm, the characteristic features of late-nineteenth-century society.[18] If our starting point is the commercial society that preceded it, we may describe the new social plot in terms of the emergence of four protagonists: the proletariat, the factory, the city and the trust.

(1) *The proletariat.* The language of the 'rights of man' and of the will theory suggested an equal concern with the fate of all (male) individuals, but by the mid-century it was already clear to an increasingly self-conscious class of people that the rules of the game were tilted in favour the industrial bourgeoisie that controlled the overwhelming majority of the productive assets and held obscene levels of wealth. That class was the proletariat. They were not all of the poor by any stretch of the imagination, nor even the poorest: they were a class apart both from the decreasing yet still very large peasant population and the urban dwellers forming what Marx called the *Lumpenproletariat* – the starving and perennially unemployed, who had no alternative but to become either petty criminals or dependents upon private charity. What the proletariat had in common, what made it in many respects a single social agent, was 'a common sense of manual labour and exploitation, and … the common fate of wage-earning'.[19] They had no commodity to sell in the marketplace but their own labor-power.

In theory, the liberal regime offered even to the people at the bottom the opportunity to climb the ladder of wealth and status. The chance of becoming a petty bourgeois, owner and manager of a small business, was open to the honest worker; and the petty bourgeois faced no legal obstacles on his way to become a captain of industry in the post-hierarchical world created by liberalism. But whether or not the politically disenfranchised people at the bottom (as opposed to the commercial and intellectual bourgeoisie) ever bought that story, by the third quarter of the nineteenth century its mythical power was

---

as a 'species-being' is obliterated – see, eg, Marx, 'Economic and Philosophic Manuscripts of 1844', 70–81. In *Das Kapital*, the focus shifts to the opacity of the commodity system, which human beings experience as foreign to human agency, as opposed to collectively made and thus self-imposed. See, eg, Marx, *Capital*, 163–77. On the fetishism of commodities, see GA Cohen, *Karl Marx's Theory of History*, 115–33; Duncan Kennedy, 'The Role of Law in Economic Thought', 968–88.

[18] I rely primarily on Hobsbawm, *The Age of Capital: 1848–1875*; Hobsbawm, *The Age of Empire: 1875–1914*.

[19] ibid, *The Age of Capital*, 257.

largely lost. Wage-earners employed in mining and industry had virtually no hope of ascending to the social condition of their bosses; accordingly, they were starting to organise as a class.[20] First, they relied (especially in Britain) on the classical liberal forms of private association to form trade unions; secondly, they organised themselves (especially in continental Europe) politically in the form of working class parties, like the British Labour Party or the Social Democratic Party in Germany. In both cases, the facially impersonal language of 'free wills' or 'independent producers', denounced as a projection of bourgeois interests, was replaced by a class-centered discourse. The horizontal imagery of free and equal individuals gave way to the vertical imagery of class struggle.

(2) *The factory*. The industrial revolution prompted the substitution of the artisan shop and the cottage industry by the factory – in a broad sense that comprises mines and railway construction sites – as the standard workplace. The factory represented a much larger scale of production and was organised around work discipline and detail division of labour. Instead of performing a variety of tasks necessary to produce each unit of output, the factory worker was responsible for a tiny fraction of a productive process over which he had neither physical control nor intellectual awareness. The experience was that of being a 'cog in the machine', particularly under the 'scientific management' that blossomed in the last quarter of the nineteenth century. The monotonous and inhumane potential of factory life – poignantly depicted in Chaplin's iconic movie *Modern Times* – was anticipated by Adam Smith in 1776, several decades before the modern factory system had dethroned older methods of production:

> In the progress of the division of labor, the employment of the far greater part of those who live by labour, that is of the great body of the people, comes to be confined to a few very simple operations. [...] The man whose whole life is spent in performing a few simple operations ... has no occasion to exert his understanding ... He naturally loses, therefore, the habit of such exertion, and generally becomes as stupid and ignorant as it is possible for a human creature to become.[21]

And yet, this gloomy account of the nature of factory work is somewhat ethereal, when we consider carefully the actual conditions under which that sort of work was performed throughout the nineteenth century. It is well-known that life in the factories and mines was deplorable. Men, women and children worked very long hours; their tasks were often physically demanding and posed significant risks to their health, a problem aggravated by poor nutrition; the work was usually dangerous and industrial accidents – fires, collapses, explosions, machine and train accidents, etc – were common; moreover, employers were not liable to compensate temporarily or permanently disabled workers,

---

[20] ibid at 257–65; ibid, *The Age of Empire*, 146–52.
[21] Smith, *The Wealth of Nations*, 987.

who could only avail themselves to the nominal protection afforded by the fellow-servant rule; the underpaid factory inspectors in charge of observing the compliance of the few safety and health regulations imposed on employers were easily bribed; within the largely law-free factory environment, work discipline was maintained by a tight hierarchical structure and even physical punishment; and the expansion of 'company towns' confined the workers increasingly to the horizon of their daily work life.

It was hard to miss the colossal gulf between the reality of factory work – anonymous, exhausting, degrading and alienating – and the romantic picture of the individual entrepreneur or the little man in charge of his family business. The factory was ignored by classical liberalism in politics, law and economics but it was too deeply bound up with the lives of ordinary people to be forgotten by them. It was probably *the* central experience in the lives of the increasingly organised proletarian stratum of society.

(3) *The city.* One of the combined effects of the Agricultural and Industrial Revolutions was the flight of large masses of population from rural to urban areas. The end of the 'open field' system triggered the decline of subsistence farming and pressed the dispossessed peasantry to offer their labour-power to the owners of enclosed land. Yet as agricultural production was increasingly mechanised, worker productivity rose dramatically, leaving many rural workers jobless. Faced with the prospect of misery, this 'latent reserve army of labour' was gradually attracted to urban areas where it hoped to find jobs in the growing industrial sector. The process transformed the early modern town or commercial city into the late modern industrial city – from Manchester to Liverpool, Cologne to Düsseldorf, Chicago to Melbourne – and the large city with a variety of middle-class services in commerce, administration and transportation, such as London, Paris, Berlin, Vienna and New York.[22] 'The city,' writes Hobsbawm, 'was indeed the most powerful outward symbol of the industrial world, apart from the railway itself'.[23]

The urban structures of the past were not designed to respond to the challenges of mass migration and rapid growth. The nineteenth century cities were accordingly afflicted by problems of overcrowding, poor sanitation, criminality, unplanned construction, class enclaves and pollution. One of the major issues was the chronic undersupply of housing. The newcomers often lived in poorly constructed rental apartments or even barracks, and were deprived of bargaining power to negotiate better terms with their landlords, who could rely on the demand created by the continuous inflow of immigrants. Ironically, improvements in health and sanitary conditions brought about by regulation and urban planning in the late nineteenth century made matters even worse, as the rate of mortality among the poor decreased while

---

[22] See Hobsbawm, *The Age of Capital*, 242–46.
[23] ibid at 242.

the rates of birth and rural flight remained high. The situation was further aggravated by the end of the First World War, when the return of servicemen increased the demand for housing while the war economy had absorbed a great deal of the money previously channelled to the construction business.

(4) *The trust.* From the very beginning, classical laissez faire ideology embodied a tension between two dogmas: free competition, on the one hand, and gains from specialisation, on the other. The theory predicted the tendency of market prices to converge with the natural, labour-determined price through the threat of competition: a firm charging artificially high prices would soon be driven out of the market by incoming competitors, except either where government interference raised barriers to entrance or in the anomalous case of natural monopolies. But what made the division of labour attractive was that specialisation enabled workers to acquire sector-specific skills and firms to adopt capital-intensive methods of production that generated economies of scale; it would take a lot of time for the infant industry to reach the same level of proficiency as the well-established business. In other words, while the image of free competition is synchronic – ie any firm can move quickly from one line of production to another – the gains from specialisation are diachronic – ie slowly created over time; there the market is associated with static equilibrium, here with dynamic growth.

In retrospect, then, it is not surprising that the last quarter of the nineteenth century witnessed the transition from competitive to monopoly capitalism or, to use more accurate terminology, from decentralised to combined economic activity. Marx had predicted it, of course, and John Stuart Mill's defence of the 'infant industry' exception to laissez-faire in his *Principles of Political Economy* showed that the general problem of economic concentration was at least partially acknowledged in the mainstream economic writing of the second quarter of the nineteenth century.[24] Yet it did leave most champions of free enterprise disoriented.[25] The question was not merely one of positive economic theory, of correcting the description of market competition and conceding that truly genuine competition requires substantial governmental effort to break down 'big business'. It was also a question of policy, of figuring out whether business combinations are a good or bad thing for the economy. In other words, economic concentration was a challenge not only to the 'mechanistic' but also to the 'moral' side of the classical account of the 'natural economy'.

The great business combinations were called 'trusts' in the United States because in an initial stage they resorted to the trust form to go round the legal prohibition of one corporation holding another's stock;[26] in Germany

---

[24] See Mill, *Principles of Political Economy*, Bk V, ch 6, 612–15.
[25] See Morton Horwitz, *The Transformation of American Law, 1870–1960*, 80–85.
[26] ibid at 80. See Lawrence Friedman, *A History of American Law*, 346–49.

they were called 'cartels' or 'syndicates', and were often sponsored by the government.[27] They were not – not all of them, at any rate – monopolies or oligopolies in the technical sense. They were simply big and 'the public feared and hated them',[28] particularly in the United States with its ancestral Yeoman mythology. Their existence was a threat not only to the largely disempowered working class but also to the middle class consumer and *le petit comerçant*. It attracted the negative attention of the vast majority of non-elite social groups in late-nineteenth-century society.

The transformation of the commercial society of the early nineteenth century into the proletarian, industrialised, urbanised, and monopolistic society at the end of the century furnishes the historical background of the Social Question. But that question was not merely in the air waiting to be admitted into the conscience of ruling elites. It acquired social currency through the combined agency of two further protagonists in the society of 1900: mass voting and socialist movements.

In the 1850s, universal (male) suffrage did not exist anywhere in the North Atlantic world except in Switzerland and the United States, and even there the gap between nominal democracy and actual electoral participation was substantial.[29] That state of affairs was perfectly consistent with the distrust of the masses characteristic of the classical liberal tradition, especially after the Reign of Terror into which the French Revolution sank in 1793–94. The rights of the citizen were instrumental to secure the rights of man and it was generally understood among the 'enlightened' lot of society that lifting every man (let alone women as well) to the condition of active citizenship would defeat the very purpose of political rights. This was true to some extent even in the United States, where the fear of a 'tyranny of the majority' was a major concern among intellectual and political elites, and the inspiration behind the earliest debates on the virtues of judicial review.[30]

The situation changed quickly in the last quarter of the nineteenth century. '[A]fter 1870,' writes Hobsbawm, 'it became increasingly clear that the democratization of the politics of states was quite inevitable. The masses would march on to the stage of politics, whether rulers liked it or not.'[31] The voting franchise was widened nearly everywhere, sometimes to a point approaching universal male suffrage, and while various forms of manipulation absorbed the impact of these changes – eg, constitutional safeguards, nondemocratic second chambers, qualified votes for the wealthy and the educated, or gerrymandering – rulers in the West were now largely, and increasingly so, in the hands of the masses.[32]

---

[27] Hobsbawm, *The Age of Empire*, 56.
[28] Friedman, *A History of American Law*, 346.
[29] See Hobsbawm, *The Age of Capital*, 122–23.
[30] See Morton Horwitz, *The Transformation of American Law, 1870–1960*, 9–31.
[31] Hobsbawm, *The Age of Empire*, 103.
[32] ibid at 105.

Although in most industrialised countries the peasant population was of a comparable size or even exceeded the numbers of industrial workers, the degree of organisation and mobilisation of the latter group made it the most powerful threat to the status quo.[33] Working class movements and political parties blossomed in many countries.

Hobsbawm stresses that the proletariat was a highly heterogeneous assortment of urban workers instead of a spontaneous 'class' of people conscious of their common socio-economic condition. How, therefore, were they unified?

> One powerful way was through ideology carried by organization. Socialists and anarchists carried their gospel to masses hitherto neglected by almost all agencies except their exploiters and those who told them to be quiet and obedient ... The socialists were often the first to come to them. Where conditions were right, they impressed on the most varied groups of workers – from craft journeyman or vanguards of militants or entire working communities of outworkers or miners – a single identity: that of 'the proletarian'.[34]

From the very beginning, then, there was a close association between worker's organisations and socialist ideology. 'Socialism' was more a family of doctrines than a unified theory and political programme, but there is no doubt both that the Marxist strand was dominant and that even in its alternative incarnations socialist politics 'envisaged a fundamental change in society'.[35] (Bernsteinian 'revisionists' were routinely denounced as sell-outs in the labour politics of the 1900s).[36] The working class, occasionally allied to the peasantry and the petty bourgeoisie, wanted a new society, and it had been organised by its leaders to get it either through the ballots or via armed struggle. Democracy and socialism were making any attempts to suppress the Social Question impossible, and that meant that the legal order fashioned by classical liberal legalism was on the verge of collapsing. The jurists had to step in, armed with a novel intellectual strategy and defensive tactics, if they wanted to secure their stronghold against the barbarian horde at the gates. And so they did.

II. The Social Jurists

The French jurists of the inter-war period committed to revise in substantial ways classical private law were named by Paul Cuche in 1929 *'les juristes inquiets'* – the anxious or troubled jurists.[37] The phrase could not be more fitting. In their

---

[33] ibid at 133.

[34] ibid at 146. Hobsbawm adds that 'Except in latin countries, and – as the revolution of 1917 revealed – in Russia, anarchism was politically negligible' [154]. Socialism was the dominant ideological force among the proletariat.

[35] ibid at 154.

[36] ibid at 156.

[37] Quoted in Marie-Claire Belleau, 'Legal Classicism and Criticism in Early Twentieth-Century France', 381–82.

work, and in that of their counterparts in other countries, there are clear traces of anxiety – the anxiety to respond swiftly and effectively to the social situation while preserving the bulk of the classical apparatus. The social jurists were reformist rather than revolutionary, at once critics of the will theory and opponents of socialism.[38] In an address delivered to the Industrial Economics Department of the National Civic Federation, Louis Brandeis, who together with Roscoe Pound and Benjamin Cardozo formed the troika of great social jurists in American legal history,[39] expressed eloquently one of the key positions of the reformist agenda:

> We do want industrial 'peace with liberty,' but in this country, at least, material well-being is an essential condition of liberty. In most trades some form of union of employees is required for the attainment or preservation of this liberty. The single workman, standing alone, is in the power – at the mercy – of his employer. The union, while it works for liberty in curbing the power of the employer, necessarily restricts in some measure the freedom of its members.[40]

The year of the address was 1905 – the year *Lochner* was decided, and the starting point of an era of hard line laissez-faire jurisprudence. There is an important difference, continuously stressed in the work of Duncan Kennedy, between the will theory and the rival ideological interpretations of it along the right–left spectrum.[41] Sometimes Kennedy seems to go as far as to suggest – for instance, when he relies on Saussure's fundamental distinction between language (*langue*) and speech (*parole*)[42] – that any politics short of orthodox socialism or fascism could be 'spoken' in the language of free and equal wills characteristic of classical legal thought. I doubt that this is correct, or at least that it is so historically.[43] In any case, a more modest version of Kennedy's point is on the mark. Not only were the decisions of the Supreme Court in the *Lochner* era not in any way entailed by the premises of the will theory, I am tempted to guess that Kant and the vast majority of the early classical jurists would have been appalled at most of them. Part of what

---

[38] See ibid at 380–86; André-Jean Arnaud, *Les Juristes Face à la Société*, 122–25; Duncan Kennedy, 'Three Globalizations of Law and Legal Thought: 1850–2000', 37–39.
[39] See Kennedy, ibid at 47.
[40] Brandeis, 'The Desirable Industrial Peace', 1.
[41] Without any pretension of exhaustion, the point is made in the following writings: Duncan Kennedy, *The Rise and Fall of Classical Legal Thought*, xxxv–xxxviii; Kennedy, 'Three Globalizations of Law and Legal Thought: 1850–2000', 22; Kennedy, 'From the Will Theory to the Principle of Private Autonomy', 107 (fn 33), 119–20.
[42] ibid, 'Three Globalizations of Law and Legal Thought: 1850–2000', 23.
[43] Even if we concede that there is nothing in the nature of the will theory that excludes, say, the 'parole' of worker's compensation, implied warrants of habitability, and abuse of right, the will theory was experienced by the mainstream jurists of the late nineteenth and the early twentieth century as excluding those regimes, and that is why they found it necessary to develop a new type of discourse. In other words, although the extreme version of Kennedy's point may be correct as a matter of semiotics, it is not compelling in terms of what Kennedy calls elsewhere the phenomenological approach to rational constraint – see Kennedy, 'Freedom and Constraint in Adjudication: A Critical Phenomenology'. See also Kennedy, *The Rise and Fall of Classical Legal Thought*, xvii–xx.

made the *Lochner*-era decisions aggressively ideological was that they pushed the will theory too far into conservative territory.

But the other part of the story is that at that point the will theory had already lost a great deal of its former credit. In an essay published only four years after the *Lochner* decision, Pound wrote that 'a bare majority of the Supreme Court of the United States took the reactionary view, as it had fairly become by this time, of a statute prescribing the hours of labor in bakeries'.[44] More generally, an important parcel of the case law in that period held that 'Legislation designed to give laborers some measure of practical independence, which ... would put them in a position of reasonable equality with their masters, is said ... to create a class of statutory laborers, and to stamp them as imbeciles'.[45] The courts, reasoning from the premises of the will theory, were arguing that labour legislation eliminates two basic elements of freedom of contract: on the one hand, the power of the parties to bargain freely; on the other hand, the recognition of their fundamental equality *qua* bearers of free will. In the infamous *Adair* case, for example, which struck down a statute outlawing 'yellow dog' terms that inhibited a worker from joining a union, Justice Harlan wrote that 'the right of the employee to quit the service of the employer, for whatever reason, is the same as the right of the employer, for whatever reason, to dispense with the services of such employee'.[46] It followed that 'employer and employee have equality of right, and any legislation that disturbs that equality is an arbitrary interference with the liberty of contract ...'[47] As Pound saw it, however, this equality was merely 'theoretical' as opposed to the 'real equality in labor-bargains' that the statutes were meant to secure.[48] He was arguing against the will theory of contract and voicing a concern, typical of a major strand of social jurisprudence, with contractual fairness or equality of bargaining power.

In order to situate Pound's thought in a larger political and intellectual context we need to backpedal just a little and consider the situation of European legal thought – with which the well-read Pound was acquainted – around 1900. In that year, the German Civil Code (BGB) came into force. In its original version, the Code was, and still is to some extent,[49] both a model of technical precision and neat language and remarkably conservative in its underlying politics and methods. For the most part, it paid tribute to the will theory and legal formalism, which is why Ernst Zitelmann commented at the time that 'rather than boldly anticipating the future it prudently sums up the past'.[50]

---

[44] Roscoe Pound, 'Liberty of Contract', 479.
[45] ibid at 463.
[46] *Adair v United States*, 208 US 161, 175 (1908), also cited in Pound, 'Liberty of Contract' at 454.
[47] ibid.
[48] Pound, 'Liberty of Contract', 463, 481.
[49] Although the Code's core – the law of obligations – was significantly and controversially reformed in 2002. Mathias Reimman, 'The Good, The Bad, and the Ugly', 878: 'On the whole, the changes brought by the reform were more good than bad, but they also made the Code uglier than it had been before'.
[50] Quoted in Zweigert and Kötz, *An Introduction to Comparative Law*, 150.

It was particularly the absence of an adequate response to the Social Question that earned the Code its earliest and most prominent opponents.[51] The First Draft of the BGB (1887) was excoriated by the lawyer Anton Menger in a book with the self-explanatory title *Private Law and the Dispossessed Classes*, as well as by Otto von Gierke in the essay *German Law and the Draft BGB*.[52] Menger was too close to socialism to make an impact on mainstream jurisprudence, but Gierke was a giant of legal scholarship and his argument that the heavy bias in favour of Roman law and against Germanic law in the doctrinal work of the Pandectist school and in the draft of the BGB tipped the scales of private law too much in favour of individualism and against the idea of 'community' earned him the sympathy of both reactionaries and 'social' critics of classical liberalism. In a published lecture on *The Social Task of Private Law*, Gierke reiterated his criticism of the First Draft, and remarked famously that private law must absorb a 'drop of social oil'.[53] Together with Rudolf von Jhering, who by 1877, with the publication of the first volume of *Law as Means to an End*, had turned his back completely on Pandectism, Gierke must be regarded as a pioneer among the social jurists. Although none of them played in relation to what Duncan Kennedy calls 'the social' the role that Savigny played in classical private law, they really were the 'initial innovators'.[54]

And yet, as Kennedy stresses, the most important contributors to the social reform of classical private law were French – Raymond Saleilles, Joseph Charmont, Léon Duguit, François Gény, Louis Josserand and Emmanuel Gounot. Part of the explanation for this shift of centre suggests itself. When a legal system is impacted by a written law of the magnitude of the BGB, legal thought tends to enter into a phase of textual fetishism – what the Germans call *Gesetzespositivismus*. The French had their own love affair with the *Code Napoléon* (1804) in the first half of the nineteenth century, when legal scholars flocked to the ranks of the School of Exegesis;[55] a few years after the Code's enactment, the law professor Bugnet stated that 'I do not know civil law, I teach only the Code'.[56] (Indeed, the French

---

[51] For a good overview of the social flaws of the BGB, see Karl Larenz, *Algemeiner Teil des Deutschen Bügerlichen Rechts*, 48–56.

[52] Menger, *Das bügerliche Recht un die besitzlose Volksklassen*; Gierke, *Entwurf eines Bügerlichen Gezetzbuchs und das deutsche Recht*.

[53] Gierke, *Die soziale Aufgabe des Privatrechts*, 10.

[54] Kennedy, 'Three Globalizations of Law and Legal Thought', 37. Kennedy's inclusion of Eugen Ehrlich in the list is slightly odd, since Ehrlich published his major work, *Fundamental Principles of the Sociology of Law*, in 1913, when 'the social' had already matured. Moreover, the early Ehrlich was a major contributor to the Free Law Movement and too keen on emphasising the role of personal or idiosyncratic factors in the legal process to be regarded as a mainstream social jurist. His doctrine of judicial decision-making anticipates some of the features of the 'hunch' theory primarily associated in the United States with Joseph Hutcheson. Compare Ehrlich, 'Judicial Freedom of Decision', 74–76 with Hutcheson, 'The Judgment Intuitive: The Function of the 'Hunch' in Judicial Decision'. On the connection between Ehrlich and the Free Law Movement, see Karl Larenz, *Methodenlehre der Rechswissenschaft*, 59–60.

[55] See, eg, Jean-Louis Halpérin, *Histoire du Droit Privé Français Depuis 1804*, 45–78.

[56] Quoted in Julien Bonnecase, *L'École de l'Exégèse en Droit Civil*, 128.

legal mainstream has not liberated itself completely from this mindset.) I am convinced that the attraction and deference commanded by the BGB was not the only reason for the relative decline of innovative legal thinking in Germany and the rise of the French jurists to unexpected prominence in the early twentieth century. Another factor, among a plausible variety, might have been the development of classical sociology, in the tradition of Comte and Durkheim, in the French academic culture of the period. Sociology was indeed the privileged companion to doctrinal analysis in the assault mounted by the social jurists on the will theory, for they drew a good deal of the basis for their reform programme from statements of 'social fact'.[57] The *Brandeis Brief* in *Muller v Oregon* furnishes a good example of that sort of sociological jurisprudence.[58]

One way or another, the French were undoubtedly the main protagonists of 'the social'. But what was it? Much insight about the ideological identity and the internal divisions of the social jurists is gained by comparing them with two other political groups highly critical of classical liberalism in the 1900s – romantic conservatives and orthodox socialists. The social jurists belonged politically to a third group that we may call 'reformist'.

Reformists and socialists were allied against the conservatives in that they regarded classical liberalism – that is, the will theory – as a historic achievement, in the threefold sense of an instance of progress vis-à-vis the past, a necessary stage in the path of social evolution, and a remarkable period in human history. On the contrary, the romantic conservatives, admirers of Joseph De Maistre and Edmund Burke and attracted to the ambiguous Gierke – apologist of the 'Germanic tradition' and an enthusiastic student of medieval political thought – opposed modernity and bemoaned its two landmark events, the Industrial and the French Revolutions; their base of support was drawn mainly from the landed aristocracy and the peasantry economically dependent on it. The contrast with socialism is easy to discern. Marx, undoubtedly the most important personality in the socialist tradition, acknowledged the 'revolutionary part' that the bourgeoisie played in history,[59] and condemned conservatism, or what he called 'feudal socialism', with rather brutal sarcasm as 'half lamentation, half lampoon; half echo of the past, half menace of the future; at times, by its bitter, witty and incisive criticism, striking the bourgeoisie to the very heart's core; but always ludicrous in its effect, through total incapacity to comprehend the march of modern history'.[60] The substance of the point was embraced by the reformists. All of them argued that the will theory

---

[57] Emile Durkheim, *The Rules of the Sociological Method*, 14, wrote that 'The first and most fundamental rule [of sociology] is: consider social facts as things'. The meaning of this passage is explained a few pages ahead: 'social phenomena are things and ought to be treated as things. [...] They are the unique data of the sociologist. All that is given, all that is subject to observation, has thereby the character of a thing. To treat phenomena as things is to treat them as data, and these constitute the point of departure of science' [27].
[58] See Morton Horwitz, *The Transformation of American Law, 1870–1960*, 188–89, 208–12.
[59] Karl Marx, *The Communist Manifesto*, 37–43.
[60] ibid at 63.

186 *The Socialisation of Private Law*

was a major breakthrough in its time and fully adequate to the social conditions of the day, although ill-adjusted and indeed reactionary in the far more complex and interdependent society of the early twentieth century.[61]

Where reformists and socialists diverged was on the implications for the future of capitalism of the massive social changes of the second half of the nineteenth century. For the socialists, especially the majority inclined to Marxism, the growing and widespread awareness of the defects of the will theory was a superstructural symptom of the contradictory dynamics of capitalist accumulation that unfold at the 'base' of social life. The historical function of the Social Question was to make the underlying class structure of capitalism transparent, thereby exposing liberal ideology as a form of false consciousness and enabling the emancipation of the proletariat. To be a socialist, therefore, was to envision a post-capitalist and deeply fraternal form of social life in the foreseeable future. 'The belief that the present society was intolerable,' writes Hobsbawm, 'made sense to working-class people ... The ideal of a new society was what gave [them] hope'.[62] This craving for a 'new society' translated politically into the goal of abolishing capitalist relations of production, notably via the socialisation of the means of production.

All of that was flatly repudiated by the reformists. They claimed that it was a mistake to jump from the assertion that the will theory was unable to keep pace with social progress to the conclusion that capitalism itself was on the brink of collapse. They charged the socialists with two chief errors. On the one hand, the Marxist theory of class struggle and its siblings in other bodies of socialist ideology were projections onto social reality of the spiritual 'derangement' provoked by accelerated social change, especially among those whose lives are most affected by it – the phenomenon that Durkheim called '*anomie*'.[63] In other words, there is in fact no such thing as class, although people whose lives are dramatically and negatively impacted by social change may be led to think and feel otherwise.[64] The remedy for their *anomie* is reconciliation with the march of progress and awareness of the social harmony and complex solidarity hidden behind the superficial appearance of conflict.[65]

The second error of the socialists was to conflate the will theory with the fundamental institutions of capitalism, namely private property and contract. These institutions, according to the reformists, were in fact much more elastic than both will theorists and socialist critics were willing to concede. There was nothing

---

[61] See, Léon Duguit, *Les Transformations Générales du Droit Privé*, 58; Raymond Saleilles, 'Le Code Civil et la Méthode Historique', 109–10. See also Duncan Kennedy, 'From the Will Theory to the Principle of Private Autonomy', 118.
[62] Eric Hobsbawm, *The Age of Empire*, 156.
[63] See Emile Durkheim, *The Division of Labor in Society*, 291–308.
[64] Léon Duguit, 'Theory of Objective Law Anterior to the State', 244–46.
[65] As Duncan Kennedy, 'Three Globalizations of Law and Legal Thought: 1850–2000', 42, puts it 'Whereas Marxism was a "conflict ideology," prophesying the triumph of the working class in death struggle with the capitalist class, the social was a "harmony ideology" ...'.

'individualistic' or 'atomistic' about these legal forms; the will theory of property and contract was merely one of their potential manifestations, one particularly suited to the relatively simple commercial society of the early nineteenth century. As society evolved towards greater complexity, so did the corresponding legal forms, which took on an increasingly manifest social character. Here is how Jhering puts this point, in a passage summarising his account of property:

> All rights of private law, even though primarily having the individual as their purpose, are influenced and bound by regard for society. [...] One need not be a prophet to recognize that this social conception of private law will continually gain ground over the individualistic. There will come a time when property will bear another form than it does at present; when society will no more recognize the alleged right of the individual to gather as much as possible of the goods of this world, and combine in his hand a landed possession upon which hundreds and thousands of independent farmers might live ... Private property and the right of inheritance will always remain, and the socialistic and communistic ideas directed to its removal I regard as vain folly. [...] [But increased pressure of society upon private property] will bring about a distribution of the goods of this world more in accord with the interests of society, *i.e.*, *more just* than has been and must be effected under the influence of a theory of property which ... is the *insatiability and voraciousness of egoism*.[66]

The reformists were thus supporters of the historical significance of the will theory, critics of its application to the social conditions of 1900, and apologists of capitalism. This was their shared ideological creed, and it was enough to make them for all intents and purposes a major collective agent in the politics of the early twentieth century. But within their ranks there were divided allegiances – for instance, while some were social Christians, including the Catholic followers of the 'social doctrine' articulated by Leo XIII in the encyclical *Rerum Novarum* (1891), others were militant atheists and radical laic 'sociological positivists'.

More important for our purposes was the division of the reformists (including the social jurists) into two strands that I shall call 'collectivists' and 'social liberals'. The collectivists could be either 'fascists' on the right or 'solidarists'[67] on the left, but they were united in their unequivocal rejection of liberalism. They held that the task of law is not to secure individual freedom but to encourage individuals to play a useful role in the progress and aggrandisement of the social body. On their view, ownership and contract were instruments of public policy as much as administrative or political offices; private persons are hence indirectly public officials, empowered by the norms of private law to do certain things insofar and only to the extent that their conduct benefits society as a whole. At its most extreme, most straightforwardly endorsed among the jurists by Léon Duguit, collectivism berated the concept of individual right as a 'pure hypothesis, a metaphysical affirmation',[68] and argued for its suppression in favour of the 'realist', 'scientific' and

---

[66] Rudolf von Jhering, *Law as a Means to an End*, 395–97 (emphasis in the original).
[67] See Joseph Charmont, 'Recent Phases of French Legal Philosophy', 82–98.
[68] Léon Duguit, 'Theory of Objective Law Anterior to the State', 248.

'socialist' concept of social function.[69] 'The Declaration of the Rights of Man, the Code Napoléon and all modern codes that proceed from them,' writes Duguit, 'rest upon a purely individualistic conception of law, while today grows a legal system based on an essentially socialist conception'.[70] And he adds immediately that,

> I use the word ['socialism'] because I have no alternative; that does not by any means imply a connection between my thought and a socialist party – it is exclusively meant to signal the opposition between a legal system based on the idea of individual rights and one based on the idea of a social rule imposed on individuals.[71]

The implications of the shift from a rights-based to a social-function-based conception of law emerge in the following passage:

> The civilistic system of property ... tends to protect exclusively the ends of the individual considered separately and as self-validating. That matches the individualistic conception of society ... If we protect the individual claim over a resource it is only with regard to the individual; it is only individual utility that we consider. Yet, nowadays we have the clear perception that the individual is not an end but a means, that the individual is nothing more than a piece of the vast machine that is the social body, that none of us has other reason to live in the world than to play a part in the labors of society.[72]

The social liberals – the other major strand of reformism – rebelled against the will theory not in order to overcome but as a way of upholding liberal values. They argued that in the highly complex, differentiated and interdependent society of 1900 the will theory did a disservice to the very values of individual equality and freedom that it was meant to honour; in order to restore the allegiance of the law to those values, it was necessary to carry out vast reforms on the extant body of legal doctrine. A substantive or real conception of equal concern, sensitive to the actual social conditions for the exercise of individual freedom, would substitute the formal or juridical equality sponsored by the will theory. 'It is a matter,' wrote the great social jurist Saleilles, 'of establishing a social equilibrium, an indispensable harmony among the different elements that compose the collective body ...'.[73] These words appear in his contribution to a collective work celebrating the 100th anniversary of the French civil code. The code was drafted a good half century before the will theory had become dominant among the jurists, but by the third quarter of the nineteenth century the French had done to their code pretty much what the Germans did to the Roman sources, successfully reading the will theory into it.[74] By 1900, all that the legal establishment saw in it was a

---

[69] ibid, *Les Transformations Générales du Droit Privé*, 19–22.
[70] ibid at 8.
[71] ibid at 8–9.
[72] ibid at 157.
[73] Saleilles, 'Le Code Civil et la Méthode Historique', 117.
[74] See James Gordley, 'Myths of the French Civil Code'; Gordley, *The Philosophical Origins of Modern Contract Doctrine*, 161–213.

celebration of classical liberalism.[75] For Saleilles, the problem with the Code was that it flouted the promise to establish an order of free and equal persons; it was rather a product of what Wieacker describes as usurpation of public power by the bourgeoisie.[76]

> We proceeded from the idea that private law is mainly concerned with the regulation of patrimonial relations ... It followed that the Code covers scarcely anything but the law of assets (*biens*) and that, accordingly, it was made for those in their possession. We may therefore say that, by and large, it constitutes the charter of acquired property. As to all those who are yet to acquire anything, who are yet to climb the social ladder from the very bottom, it appears that, with the exception of the liberty assigned to all, they were deserted by the law. [...] We had organized, without knowing or wanting to, the Code of the Bourgeoisie.[77]

In sum, all of the social jurists were politically reformist; they opposed both the romantic conservatives and the orthodox socialists, and advocated a reformed capitalism.[78] Some of them were collectivists, such as Léon Duguit and Emmanuel Gounot in France,[79] Emilio Betti in fascist Italy[80] and Karl Larenz in Germany under the Nazi regime.[81] Others were social liberals, such as Raymond Saleilles, François Gény[82] and Louis Josserand[83] in France; and Louis Brandeis, Benjamin Cardozo and Roscoe Pound in the United States.[84] The table below encapsulates the gist of the analysis.

---

[75] See, eg, Léon Duguit, *Les Transformations Générales du Droit Privé*, 1–19.
[76] Franz Wieacker, *Industriegesellschaft und Privatrechtsordnung*, 16.
[77] Saleilles, 'Le Code Civil et la Méthode Historique', 115.
[78] Duncan Kennedy, 'Three Globalizations of Law and Legal Thought: 1850–2000', 38, maintains that the goal of the social jurists was 'to save liberalism from itself'. Yet it was not liberalism but capitalism that the social jurists were united in upholding. Only one strand was liberal.
[79] See Gounot, *Le Principe de l'Autonomie de la Volonté en Droit Privé* (critiquing the will theory of contract and defending that the binding force of contracts derives from and is limited by their social function).
[80] See Betti, *Teoria Generale del Negozio Giuridico*, 43–74, 169–81 (arguing against the will theory and for a functional theory of juristic acts built around the category of *causa*, understood as 'socio-economic function').
[81] See Larenz, 'Volksgeist und Recht'; Larenz, 'Rechtsperson und subjektives Recht' (arguing that a legal right is not a sphere of individual freedom but a means to discharge a personal role in the *Volksgemeinschaft*). On legal thought in Nazi Germany, see Massimo La Torre, *La 'Lotta Contra il Diritto Soggetivo'*.
[82] See, *Méthode d'Interprétation et Sources en Droit Privé Positif*, II, 225–30 (writing that the 'social task' of law requires today a more 'fraternal' or 'solidary' conception of positive law: 'I shall put it straightforwardly: to equalize the conditions of struggle among rival activities; to secure a distribution of resources more proportionate to the effort and needs of each individual; to ease the excessive rigors of individual law in light of the social and common interest' [226]).
[83] See Josserand, *De l'Esprit des Droits et de Leur Relativité* (defending a reformed, 'social' rather than 'atomistic', conception of individual rights against the charge of 'metaphysical nonsense' and 'anti-social character' levelled by the collectivists: 'We only have to concede that the social element that coexists in every right with the individual element tends to develop in detriment of the later; but the individual element subsists, and it is a mistake to think differently, for otherwise individual personality would be destroyed and absorbed by the great whole ...' [329]).
[84] See, eg, Roscoe Pound, 'Public and Private Law', 482, reacting against 'absolutism' and arguing that 'We must simplify the machinery of asserting and vindicating individual rights against arbitrary

Figure 4.1 Critics of the will theory c 1900

Group	Critique		
	Lament the will theory	*Repudiate capitalism*	*Repudiate liberalism*
Romantic conservatives	Yes	Yes	Yes
Orthodox socialists	No	Yes	Yes
Collectivist reformists	No	No	Yes
Liberal reformists	No	No	No

I want to bring the reader's attention to two important connections between the argument of this section and the drama of liberal legalism. First, although not all of the social jurists were committed to liberalism in the period 1900–1945, and indeed it may well be the case that the collectivist strand of social jurisprudence was prevalent at the time, 'the social' was eventually fully incorporated into liberalism after the Second World War, at a moment when collectivist politics of various persuasions was largely discredited. The radically instrumental discourse centred on 'social functions' all but vanished, and gave way to the rights-based social discourse that the early social liberals sponsored.[85] Since our concern is the history of liberalism, we shall read the work of the social jurists from a distinctively rights-based perspective, which is after all exactly how it was read by post-1945 jurists seeking in it 'the starting point for modern advocacy of social values'.[86] We are not concerned so much with the intellectual history of 'the social' as we are with the social moment of liberalism.

The second remark pertains to the way in which the association of the social jurists with reformism is explained by and also vindicates the thesis of legalism – that legal thought has been generally responsive to the interest of the jurists in conserving their 'symbolic capital'. As the following section should make clear, reformism was an agenda for correcting and ameliorating classical private law, as opposed to the socialist project of abolishing it entirely. It implied therefore a relatively low degree of political interference with the extant body of positive law. It answered the Social Question without depriving the jurists of the early to mid twentieth century of the entire apparatus of classical private law that it took all of

---

administrative infringement'. These words were written in 1939, more than three decades after his essay on freedom of contract, and Pound's political views changed in a notoriously conservative direction in that period. (On this 'about-face', see Morton Horwitz, *The Tranformation of American Law, 1870–1960*, 217–20). But he was always a social liberal, rejecting both collectivism and classical liberalism. In 1954, he was still vigorously attacking the will theory; see Pound, 'The Role of the Will in Law', 19: 'Quite apart, then, from a psychological question how far there is such a thing as individual free will, we cannot take that concept for the starting point of the legal system of today or make it the central point of the science of law'.

[85] See Duncan Kennedy, 'Thoughts on Coherence, Social Values and National Tradition in Private Law', 19–20.

[86] ibid at 19.

the collective energy of the prior generation to assemble. If they had a motto, it could very well have been that of Tancredi in the novel *The Leopard*: 'If we want things to stay as they are, things will have to change'.

III. The Emergence of Social Law

Each moment in the history of liberal legalism integrates a political theory – the conception of liberalism in that period – with an account of legal reasoning. But social liberalism was not a political theory in the sense that the will theory was: a major break from previous modes of thinking about the basic terms of collective life. The will theory was revolutionary because it instantiated for the very first time – it was the prototype of – a novel form of political community. It conditioned, in a sense, all ulterior developments of the political script, at least insofar as they observed the strictures of liberalism. That is why social liberalism is not so much an independently articulated political theory as it is the will theory enriched with a large number of social glosses.

The reform agenda of 'the social' played out as follows. In the background was the will theory, primarily articulated within the fields of property and obligations, and the question for political theory was what kind of, and how much, corrective or adaptive reform was necessary in order to adjust the law to the circumstances of a highly interdependent society characterised by proletarian, industrial, urban and monopolistic elements. The overall goal was to level the playing field or, as Gény put it, 'to equalize the conditions of struggle among rival activities'.[87] Nothing else of interest may be said at this level of generality; in order to avoid the trap of empty abstraction, we should turn immediately to the implications of social reformism in particular fields of law. Obviously, the wide scope of the reforms and substantial variations across countries make an exhaustive and rigorous description impossible; the approach that follows is suggestive instead, pointing rather diffusely to the direction of substantive legal change in the period.

The first transformative event was what Franz Wieacker calls 'the separation out of social law'.[88] Vast areas of social life that under the will theory fell within the scope of the private law regime of contract, property and tort were carved out of it and brought within the purview of special branches of the law. The term 'social law' (apparently coined by Otto von Gierke[89]) denotes the cluster of new fields of law – labour law, anti-trust law, housing law, urban planning, land law, workers compensation, banking law, securities regulation, etc – that emerged in the process. Classical private law was not abolished, and indeed it remained the 'common law' of private transactions, but it was not longer operative in a very large

---

[87] Gény, *Méthode d'Interprétation et Sources en Droit Privé Positif*, II, 226.
[88] Wieacker, *A History of Private Law in Europe*, 433–38.
[89] ibid at 434.

spectrum of 'socially sensitive areas'.[90] In theory, the prominence of private law did not appear to be seriously compromised. As the law of general or common application, it benefitted from a presumption of propriety that could only be rebutted if the evidence of an 'imbalance', 'asymmetry', 'distortion' or 'social harm' warranting special regulation was strong. But the social situation of the 1900s furnished all the evidence that was needed to deprive classical private law of a great deal of its former territorial possessions. In practice, then, the rise of specific bodies of social law set off the course of the decline of private law. Wieacker echoes the sense of loss of the mainstream private law theorist witnessing the end of the golden era of his discipline: 'In our own century [the twentieth] private law scholarship has lost its primacy. The collapse of the old society brought about, and was reflected in, the disintegration of the system of civil law, for the socially sensitive areas within it were excised and became separate from it'.[91]

For illustrative purposes, I propose to paint with a broad brush the characteristic changes brought about by the emergence of four fields of social law in the period between the last quarter of the nineteenth century and the first quarter of the twentieth. Each of the chosen fields constituted in its time a major inroad into classical private law and was a response to the emergence of one of the 'protagonists' of late-nineteenth-century society. The proletariat, the factory, the city and the trust triggered the emergence of, respectively, labour law, the law of industrial accidents, housing law and anti-trust law. Let us examine them briefly.

(1) *Labour law*. Under the will theory, there was nothing about employment relations that set them apart from other types of transaction governed by the general principle of freedom of contract. The German civil code of 1900, for instance, contained no provisions specifically applicable to labour contracts; the latter were subsumed under the general and undifferentiated category of 'contract for services' (§611).[92] Employment was seen as a contractual relation whereby the worker promises to put his labour power at the service of an employer in exchange for a wage. It is true that classical private law supplied in theory one important legal resource to dependent workers: the right to unionise, conceived as a corollary of the general freedom of individuals to associate. But labour unions had to walk a long way before acquiring full legal recognition; for instance, in the early nineteenth century, workers' combinations were (ironically) outlawed by statutory law on anti-competitive grounds (in England, the 1799 and 1800 Combination Acts were repealed in 1824) and it was only around the last quarter of the nineteenth century that the right to strike was recognised in England, France and Germany. In the United States, the courts held strikes lawful since the mid-nineteenth century – the leading case at the time being *Commonwealth v Hunt* (1842)[93] – but then

---

[90] ibid at 431.
[91] ibid See also Karl Larenz, *Algemeiner Teil des Deutschen Bügerlichen Rechts*, 52–53.
[92] See Larenz, ibid at 55.
[93] 45 Mass 111.

burdened the right to strike with a plethora of exceptions, culminating in the US Supreme Court decision in *In re Debs* (1895) that sanctioned the labour injunction, a remedy that allowed employers to get a temporary restraining order during a strike.[94]

Modern labour law developed under the wing of 'social reform' in two phases: it grew over the course of the *Belle Époque* and the inter-war era and then consolidated in a period ranging from 1945 to the late 1970s, when the ongoing erosion of labour standards began. It concerns specifically employment relations, meaning commodified and dependent work – situations in which an individual works under the authority of an employer. Since most economic activity in the modern world is organised around that type of work, labour law reduces considerably the scope of application of common contract law. Its main building blocks are the labour contract and collective bargaining, the subjects of so-called individual and collective labour law. Individual labour law comprises norms providing mandatory terms that set minimum standards of employment – eg, minimum wages, maximum hours, bans on unfair dismissal, protections against discrimination, etc. Collective labour law concerns bargaining between single or combined employers and unions over work conditions; these collective agreements are binding to all union members, and in some legal systems they bind non-union members as well, therefore combining regulatory with contractual elements.[95] Collective labour law also governs collective bargaining tactics, including strikes, boycotts and pickets. The entire field of labour law, individual and collective, is premised on the inequality of bargaining power between employer and employee – at least that is how it was conceived by the social reformers who sponsored its growth and consolidation.[96] The organising idea was that as the regulatory pressure imposed by the largely 'facilitative' norms of contract law is too light to secure a reasonable degree of equality as between the parties, the increased pressure produced by the largely 'imperative' norms of labour law is fully justified.

(2) *Law of industrial accidents.* What we think of today as one of the major sub-areas of tort law – the law of accidents – had a neglectable importance in pre-industrial society. It was the widespread use of dangerous machinery, from railroad and steamboat engines to industrial equipment, that increased dramatically the frequency and harmful consequences of accidents.[97] 'Modern tools and machines', writes eloquently Lawrence Friedman, 'have a marvelous capacity to cripple and maim those who use them.'[98] In the late nineteenth

---

[94] 158 US 564. See Lawrence Friedman, *A History of American Law*, 420–21.
[95] See Franz Wieacker, *A History of Private Law in Europe*, 434.
[96] See Otto Kahn-Freund, *Labour and the Law*, 7–8.
[97] On the social background of the growth of tort doctrine in the late nineteenth century, see Lawrence Friedman, *A History of American Law*, 222–25.
[98] ibid at 223.

and the early twentieth centuries many such accidents occurred in the factory, and the victims were usually the workers who handled dangerous equipment. In addition to enduring serious bodily injury, the victims were often left temporarily or permanently disabled, and their capacity to earn a living was accordingly compromised.

The law of torts in the nineteenth century was typically organised around the category of fault. Fault was a basic principle of the will theory, playing in the field of wrongs a role comparable to the notion of will in the field of rights.[99] Under the fault principle, the harm caused by one person to another constituted a wrong only in the event that it was attributable to a 'defective will', that is, either intention or negligence. This regime made the recovery of accidental losses in the factory nearly impossible for at least three reasons. First, many accidents were provoked not by anyone's fault but by the intrinsic risks of handling industrial machinery; secondly, when fault was ascribed to a fellow worker, the recovery was usually made impossible by his lack of wealth or insurance; finally, the injured worker could not usually recover from his employer, because either the law did not recognise a doctrine of *respondeat superior* or, where it did, it was very often narrowly circumscribed as an anomalous instance of strict liability. That is exactly what occurred in the United States, where the courts adopted the so-called 'fellow-servant rule',[100] according to which the injured worker could not sue the employer *qua* principal for the negligent acts of his fellow worker *qua* agent; the injured worker could only seek redress from his negligent fellow.[101]

The plight of injured workers under this regime and the large number of accidents encouraged further litigation, in spite of the apparently settled character of the issue. Eventually, that led the courts to add numerous exceptions and amends to the fellow-servant rule, complicating the regime and making it considerably more expensive to administer.[102] At this point, the law applicable to industrial accidents was simultaneously unjust, irrational, inefficient and unintelligible. As a result, 'By 1900, industrial accidents and the shortcomings of the fellow-servant rule were widely perceived as *problems* that had to be solved.'[103] This is the background against which workers compensation statutes emerged in the United States, at a time in which

---

[99] See Otto von Gierke, *Die soziale Aufgabe des Privatrechts*, 25; Léon Duguit, *Les Transformations Générales du Droit Privé*, 137–40.

[100] The leading American case was *Farwell v Boston & Worcester Railroad Corp*, 45 Mass 49 (1842). It was preceded by the English case *Priestley v Fowler*, 150 Eng R 1030 (1837), usually regarded as the origin of the fellow-servant doctrine, although, as Friedman and Ladinsky, 'Social Change and the Law of Industrial Accidents', 54, notice 'the case on its facts did not pose the question of the industrial accident'.

[101] I follow Friedman and Ladinsky, ibid at 51–56. See also John Fabian Witt, 'The Transformation of Work and the Law of Workplace Accidents, 1842–1910'.

[102] ibid at 59–65.

[103] ibid at 69.

they had already been adopted in most industrialised European countries on more or less similar grounds.[104] The statutes made three far-reaching changes to the existing tort regime. First, they abolished the requirement of fault, meaning that the worker could recover on the sole basis of having been accidentally injured; secondly, they did away with the common law regime of damages, supplying standardised schedules of compensation; finally, the system's administration was entrusted to administrative agencies instead of the courts.[105] In other words, industrial accidents were entirely removed from the jurisdiction of tort law. The organising idea of the new regime was that the costs of industrial accidents, being largely a matter of risk inherent to most lines of industrial production, should not be apportioned through private law criteria of personal liability but factored into the costs of the product and passed on to consumers through the pricing mechanism.[106]

(3) *Housing law.* Classical private law did not pay any special concern to the market for shelter; housing was governed by landlord–tenant agreements, subject to the general principle of freedom of contract.[107] It fell to the parties the determination of the duration of the leasehold, the obligations of the landlord with respect to the condition of the premises, and the rent to be paid by the tenant.[108] In sum, the regime was organised around the rules of free disposition and *caveat emptor*. This greatly favoured owners and developers of residential property in urban areas in the late nineteenth and the early twentieth century, when the massive inflow of rural populations increased dramatically the demand for shelter. Working class and even middle class tenants paid high rents for poor housing; additionally, experienced landlords aware of the hot trend in the housing market drafted terms in the leases that empowered them to terminate the leasehold at will, forcing the tenants to pay even higher rents under the threat of eviction. The scales tipped even more against tenants in the period following each of the World Wars, when a combination of underinvestment in the construction business (the war economy drained enormous amounts of capital) and the return of servicemen aggravated the problem of scarcity.

---

[104] The first statute in the US was the short-lived *An Act to Amend the Labor Law, in Relation to Workmen's Compensation in Certain Dangerous Employments* of 1910, soon to be followed by similar legislation in other states. In Europe, the most industrialised countries – the UK, France and Italy – adopted statutes in 1897–98, following the pioneering German experience with social security in the years of 1883 (health insurance) and 1884 (workers' compensation), under the auspices of Otto von Bismarck. On the political and social background of the German model, see John M Kleeberg, 'From Strict Liability to Workers' Compensation'.

[105] ibid at 69–72.

[106] See Harold Laski, 'The Basis of Vicarious Liability', 126–27; Zweigert and Kötz, *An Introduction to Comparative Law*, 689.

[107] American law presented an exception to this pattern, since leaseholds were conceptualised as a type of property interest until the 1960s. See Joseph Singer, *Introduction to Property*, 438–40.

[108] See Karl Larenz, *Algemeiner Teil des deutschen Bügerlichen Rechts*, 56–58.

Modern housing law emerged in response to the imbalance in the landlord–tenant relation, very much along the same lines that informed the creation of labour law. In relation to the previous regime of 'free contract', the innovations affected mostly three areas. First, the definition of the period of tenancy: instead of leaving to the parties' the choice among the options of 'term of years', 'periodic tenancy' and 'tenancy at will', modern housing law often provides (and did so much more frequently until a few decades ago) a compulsory term that empowers the tenant (and, occasionally, his dependents) to renew the lease for a period. The second innovation concerns the condition of the premises: the law implies warrants of habitability in residential leases, often binding them to 'housing codes' that require 'all housing to comply with certain minimum standards to protect health and safety of residents';[109] the rule of *caveat emptor* is thus abandoned. Finally, some jurisdictions introduced rent controls for long periods of time and in extreme situations (eg, post-1945 Germany) compelled landlords, under the threat of expropriation, to lease their premises for a statutorily or administratively fixed rent.[110]

(4) *Anti-trust law*. If there is an area of social law in which the United States was clearly ahead of Europe circa 1900 it was anti-trust. Hostility to economic combinations, namely monopolies and cartels, had deep roots in classical liberalism, which sponsored an atomistic image of the market; legislation adopted in revolutionary France rendered price-fixing agreements void, and in other countries they occasioned criminal sanctions. But things changed in the last third of the nineteenth century, a time of recession, when large businesses were regarded as important shields against the risk of bankruptcy, and therefore 'more social' than small firms engaged in cut-throat competition. The favourable attitude towards economic concentration in Europe persisted until the inter-war era, when, for a brief moment before the 1929 crisis, a variety of still quite permissive 'anti-cartel' laws were adopted in Central and Northern Europe (eg, the British Profiteering Act of 1919 and the German Cartel Law of 1923). But apart from such neglectable episodes, European competition law is very much a post-1945 invention, at once imposed and inspired by the United States.[111]

The history of (federal) anti-trust law in the United States begins in 1890, when the Sherman Act was adopted. The two main provisions of the act ban combinations in restraint of trade and monopolies. In 1914, Congress passed the Clayton Act, which extended the reach of anti-trust law to the domain of anti-competitive mergers.[112] Most think of anti-trust law today

---

[109] Joseph Singer, *Introduction to Property*, 439.
[110] See Larenz, *Algemeiner Teil des deutschen Bügerlichen Rechts*, 56.
[111] For a good summary account of the history of antitrust in Europe, see Massimo Motta, *Competition Policy*, 10–17.
[112] See ibid at 1–8, for a useful summary. On the history of the *Sherman Act*, see Lawrence Friedman, *A History of American Law*, 346–49.

as pursuing primarily the goal of allocative efficiency – of preventing the deadweight losses – and subsidiarily (as a side-effect of efficient pricing) the goal of consumer welfare. That was most definitely not the spirit in which the Sherman and Clayton Acts were drafted. Their concern was to secure 'fair' competition among firms and 'natural' pricing – in other words, to level the economic playing field. Anti-trust legislation fitted naturally with other bodies of doctrine – eg, tortious interference with contractual relations and the law of trade secrets – organised around the idea of fair opportunity to participate in the free marketplace. It added a layer of regulatory law over the rules of private law in order to safeguard real economic freedom from a variety of encroachments wearing the cloak of freedom of contract.

IV. The Social in Private Law

The growth of these and other fields of 'social law' reduced increasingly the significance of classical private law. The law of the jurists, in either its codified or common law incarnations, was losing ground against legislation. Social law was the agenda of a novel type of enlightened agent – the social engineer – and of democratic legislatures or populist rulers anxious to answer the demands of a vast new class of voters. The Social Question awakened Savigny's arch-enemies – the philosopher and the legislator – from the dormant state in which he and his followers managed to put them more than half a century before. Social law was in effect condemning private law to obsolescence and limiting the breathing room of the jurists. Wieacker voices their concerns:

> Courts and scholars must respond to the disintegration of private law produced by these upheavals, and it will be no easy task for they have not only destroyed the internal coherence of private law but also undermined the distinction between private and public law, which our legal system took for granted at the end of last century.[113]

The use of the present tense in the sentence above is a little odd, even taking into account that it was originally written in 1967. For the response demanded by Wieacker was initiated much earlier, c 1900, by some of the brightest lights in the ranks of private law theory. What united the social jurists into a single group is precisely that they were partly successful in controlling the damage to legalism that was brought about by social reforms; emulating their classical ancestors, they read some of the reform programme into the law, and in that way managed to halt the bleeding. 'The social' dealt a severe blow to private law, but it did not cripple it altogether.

Indeed, Wieacker all but echoes a concern that was expressed several decades before, at the close of the nineteenth century, by the perceptive Otto von Gierke.

---

[113] Franz Wieacker, *A History of Private Law in Europe*, 438.

In *The Social Task of Private Law*, Gierke deems the insulation of private from social law, achieved through the separation between a civil code based on the will theory and special legislation informed by social concerns, a 'fatal error'. It opens an unbridgeable gap between 'a law with a social, lively, national and rich soul' and 'a template that is abstract, Romanist, individualistic and ossified into a lifeless doctrinal body (*Dogmatik*)'.[114] A truly common private law, argues Gierke, must be capacious enough to house the growing array of special laws, and blend the idea of freedom with the spirit of community. If the seeds of the social are sowed in the soil of private law, social law will no longer emerge in opposition to it but as an immanent development of its spirit. The task ahead was the 'socialisation' of private law; accordingly, in the remaining of his essay Gierke lays down a programme for the reform of legal doctrine in the fields of property, tort, contract and the law of persons.

Gierke set an example for future generations. In the years between 1914 and 1939, the jurists reformed private law doctrine so extensively that the will theory in its original form disappeared from sight. In its place emerged what might be called a 'social theory of private law', where freedom of contract is enriched by ideas of contractual justice and equality of bargaining power, ownership is subject to a variety of social constraints, fault-based liability is altered by notions of loss-spreading and fair distribution of risk, and the range of interests protected by the law of torts is noticeably enlarged. It is obviously impossible to produce a complete survey of the doctrinal changes to the will theory that were informed by these new – 'social' rather that 'individualistic' – motives. But it is nevertheless worth highlighting a few that have come to be regarded as paradigmatic transformations.

(1) *Standard terms*.[115] The classical model of contract is based on the assumption that an agreement is the outcome of a bargaining process. Yet, in modern conditions of mass production, firms offer their customers a set of standard terms that they are free to either accept or reject but not to negotiate. Since this is generalised practice in those sectors of the economy that supply basic goods and services – eg, insurance, transportation, banking, commercial distribution and consumer sales – the buyer has no real alternative but to adhere to the conditions chosen by the manufacturer; that is why jurists sometimes speak of 'contracts of adhesion'. The manufacturer, normally a large firm and repeat market-player, has an incentive to take advantage of the economic vulnerability, limited time, and lack of experience of the customer (a consumer or a smaller business) to draft one-sided terms in technical language and fine print.

---

[114] Gierke, *Die soziale Aufgabe des Privatrechts*, 13.
[115] See Saleilles, *De la Déclaration de Volonté*, 229–33; Léon Duguit, *Les Transformations Générales du Droit Privé*, 121–25; Friedrich Kessler, 'Contracts of Adhesion'. For a valuable comparative overview, see Zweigert and Kötz, *An Introduction to Comparative Law*, 356–68.

The 'social' view was that contracts of adhesion deny the freedom of contract of the weaker party, unless the general regime of contract is enriched with notions of good faith (§242 of the BGB) or unconscionability (§2-302 of the UCC) that empower the courts to construe ambiguous terms *contra proferentem* (against the party offering them) and police the substantive justice or 'economic parity' of the transaction, namely through the suppression of 'surprise clauses' and bans on immunity from liability.

(2) *Supervening events.*[116] The notion that a change in circumstances that either places the promisor in a situation of extreme economic hardship or frustrates the point of the transaction furnishes an excuse for breach of contract or a justification for ex post unilateral modification is quite old. Civilian jurists refer to it generally as the *rebus sic standibus* standard, and common lawyers speak in similar terms of the 'doctrine of frustration of contracts'. Yet it was difficult for the classical jurists to square this doctrine with the will theory (Windscheid tried very hard, but his construction failed to persuade the other drafters of the BGB[117]), which is why it was either suppressed or regarded as an anomaly throughout the nineteenth century.[118]

The doctrine gained new life in the hands of the social jurists. They argued that in modern conditions of high interdependence, it is much more likely that a variety of social risks – war, inflation, expropriation, regime change, law reform, etc – undermine what §2-615 of the UCC calls the 'basic assumption on which the contract was made'.[119] Standard examples are the post-war German cases on the effects of inflation on mortgages or the English cases on the effects of the closure of the Suez Canal on charter contracts.[120] Since these events are unforeseeable or unexpected, or hard to assess ex ante, they fall beyond the risks allocated by the agreement, thereby distorting the economic parity built into it. From a 'social' standpoint, the solution in these cases is normally ex post judicial control to restore the balance.

(3) *Accidental losses.*[121] One of the landmark doctrinal changes sponsored by the social jurists was the relaxation of the requirement of fault in accident law,

---

[116] See Paul Oertmann, *Die Geschäftsgrundlage*; Eugen Locher, *Geschäftsgrundlage und Geschäftszweck*. See also Zweigert and Kötz, ibid at 554–57; James Grodley, *Foundations of Private Law*, 347–51.

[117] See Zweigert and Kötz, ibid at 557–58.

[118] The leading English case, *Taylor v Caldwell*, 122 Eng Rep 309 (1863), was narrowly construed in the nineteenth century. See Zweigert and Kötz, *An Introduction to Comparative Law*, 544–46, 566–68. The line of twentieth-century cases in the United States expanding the holding in *Taylor v Caldwell* is reconstructed in Fuller and Eisenberg, *Basic Contract Law*, 514–23.

[119] Karl Llewellyn, the Chief Reporter of the UCC and a visiting professor at the University of Leipzig in 1928–29 and 1931 (on his 'German connection', see William Twinning, *Karl Llewellyn and the Realist Movement*, 106–09), almost certainly borrowed this phrase from Paul Oertmann's famous book advocating the doctrine of the 'foundation of the transaction' (*Geschäftsgrundlage*). For a summary of Oertmann's influential theory, see Zweigert and Kötz, *An Introduction to Comparative Law*.

[120] See the summary in Zweigert and Kötz, ibid at 561–62, 569–70.

[121] See Raymond Saleilles, *Les Accidents du Travail et la Responsabilité Civile*; Léon Duguit, *Les Transformations Générales du Droit Privé*, 137–46; Louis Josserand, *De la Responsabilité du Fait des Choses Inanimées*. For a brief overview, see Jean-Louis Halpérin, *Histoire du Droit Privé Français Depuis 1804*, 191–93.

leading to stricter forms of liability, on a spectrum ranging from objective standards of negligence at one pole to strict liability at the other through a variety of intermediate forms, eg proof of fault by circumstantial evidence or reversion of the burden of proof ('presumption of liability' in civilian systems and the doctrine of '*res ipsa loquitur*' in the common law).[122] Their argument was that the risk of accidents caused by industrial goods and devices should be borne by the persons who take advantage of them. The mere fact that a person drives an automobile, handles hazardous chemicals, or owns a power plant is sufficient reason to defeat the general principle that 'losses lie where they fall'.[123] That is what the French jurists of 1900, particularly Saleilles and Josserand, called the 'theory of profit-risk' (*théorie du risque-profit*).

(4) *Defective products.*[124] The development of products liability in the United States in the first half of the twentieth century followed a similar course of reasoning. Traditionally, the common law exempted the manufacturer of defective products from any liability beyond the circle of his customers; the duty of care derived exclusively from 'privity of contract'.[125] This rule was very forgiving towards producers under modern conditions of trade based on wide circuits of distribution, where the relationship between manufacturer and consumer is usually mediated by a series of intermediaries that have neither control nor knowledge over products defects. In a famous opinion written by Benjamin Cardozo, the New York Court of Appeals abolished the requirement of privity of contract and held that the manufacturer of 'dangerous' products owes a duty of care to the user.[126] A final and decisive step was taken nearly half a century later, when the requirement of fault was abandoned in light of the view that strict products liability affords, through the medium of the pricing mechanism, an effective and fair distribution of losses.[127]

(5) *Invasions of privacy.*[128] Yet another example of social reform of private law is the influential argument advanced by Warren and Brandeis as early as in 1890 for the recognition of a general right to privacy. They claim that the common

---

[122] See Zweigert and Kötz, *An Introduction to Comparative Law*, 688–93.

[123] Oliver Wendell Holmes, *The Common Law*, 50: 'sound policy lets losses lie where they fall, except where a special reason can be shown for interference. The most frequent of such reasons is, that the party who is charged has been to blame'.

[124] See Prosser et al., Torts, 745–66; Zweigert and Kötz, *An Introduction to Comparative Law*, 651–53, 713–17; James Henderson, '*MacPherson v. Buick Motor Co.*'; Mark Geistfeld, '*Escola v. Coca-Cola Bottling Co.*'.

[125] The leading case was *Winterbottom v Wright*, 152 Eng Rep 402 (1842).

[126] *MacPherson v Buick Motor Co*, 217 NY 382 (1916). The leading case in England is *Donoghue v Stevenson* (1932).

[127] The leading case is *Greeman v Yuba Power Products Inc*, 59 Cal 2d 57 (1963). The opinion was written by Justice Roger Traynor, who had argued for strict liability in the famous concurring opinion in *Escola v Coca-Cola Bottling Co*, 24 Cal 2d 453 (1944). See also §402 A of the *Restatement (Second) of Torts*.

[128] See Warren & Brandeis, 'The Right to Privacy'. For a comparative analysis, see Zweigert and Kötz, *An Introduction to Comparative Law*, 724–45.

law has over time afforded protection to an increasing range of interests so as 'to meet the demands of society'.[129] In early times, the law granted remedies only against physical interference with life and property; later it extended protection to emotional and intellectual interests and intangible property. The next step is the recognition of a general right 'to be let alone', justified by new threats and interests characteristic of modern society: 'the press is overstepping in every direction the obvious bounds of propriety and decency';[130] 'the intensity and complexity of [modern] life ... have rendered necessary some retreat from the world';[131] and 'the latest advances in photographic art have rendered it possible to take pictures surreptitiously'.[132] In the past, it was possible to accommodate privacy interests within the law of defamation and in the interstices of property and contract doctrine. But the urgency of a 'broader foundation' is clear 'now that modern devices afford abundant opportunities for the perpetration of ... wrongs'.[133] The only adequate legal response, according to Warren and Brandeis, is to render invasions of privacy a form of tortious behaviour and afford the victim the requisite legal and equitable remedies. Their argument eventually won the sympathy of the courts and became a staple of the law of the United States.[134]

These and many other 'social' reforms of the will theory were sponsored in law reviews and legal treatises, and carried out by expert drafting committees and above all else in the courtrooms.[135] The common denominator among the variety of venues is that the reforms were presented as the business of jurists interpreting, construing, elaborating or simply applying the extant body of law. They were not presented as law-making events, or at any rate as legislative in character.[136]

---

[129] Warren and Brandeis, ibid at 193. In Hohfeldian terms, their point is that over the course of legal history there has been an inflation of rights and a corresponding deflation of privileges.
[130] ibid at 196.
[131] ibid.
[132] ibid at 211.
[133] ibid.
[134] The leading case in the early twentieth century was *Pavesich v New England Life Insurance Co*, 122 Ga 190 (1905). For a useful taxonomy of the case law until the late 1950s, see William Prosser, 'Privacy'.
[135] Most of the social jurists emphasised that the law had changed and looked very different in practice than the official picture among theorists or academics. The intellectual task was to revise the old textbooks and loosen the theoretical shackles that hindered (although they could not stall) legal progress. See, eg, Rudolf von Jhering, *Law as a Means to an End*, 383–97; Raymond Saleilles, 'Le Code Civil et la Méthode Historique', 121–25; Roscoe Pound, 'Law in Books and Law in Action'; Léon Duguit, *Les Transformations Générales du Droit Privé*, 3–4; Louis Josserand, *De l'Esprit des Droits et de Leur Relativité*, 6–11.
[136] The phrase 'judicial law-making' is ambiguous. It says nothing per se about one's jurisprudential commitments. It is wrong to think that just because some jurist recognises that there is judicial law-making, he is anti-formalist, realist, or whatever. Even a formalist jurist – say, Puchta or Langdell – may concede that judges make law in the minimalist sense that in the absence of an applicable norm the judge has to 'make' a new norm by means of logical inference. The social jurists, for their part, often stressed the 'creative' role of the judge as a way of distancing themselves from the classical formalists. See, eg, Roscoe Pound, 'Courts and Legislation', 204–13. Yet they emphasised continuously both fundamental differences between legislative and judicial law-making and the 'objective', indeed scientific, nature of legal reasoning. See ibid at 213–28.

The jurists argued that they were merely paying scientific tribute to positive law and its remarkable capacity to adapt to changing social circumstances.

It is plain that for such an argument to work the jurists had to develop, in parallel to their substantive reform programme, an account of legal reasoning very different from the legal formalism of the previous generation. For the proposition that legal doctrine evolves or changes quite apart from legislative intervention was obviously inconsistent with the formalist creed in 'leading axioms' standing behind and informing the substance of the mass of rules and doctrines in the foreground. The eternal truths of Euclidean geometry no longer furnished the jurist with an appropriate model for his labours. The new slogan was 'adaptive change', and the new method loosely modelled after the natural, and particularly the life, sciences.[137] This was the era of a *teleological* jurisprudence.

V. The Critique of Formalism

The most elaborate work on legal method written by a social jurist was François Gény's influential and comprehensive treatise on *Methods of Interpretation and Sources in Positive Private Law* (1899).[138] Like most masterpieces, this work is riddled with repetitions, tensions and ambiguities, all enhanced by the sheer length of the book and by Gény's elusive style. I cannot do full justice to it on this occasion. The concern here is to grasp in outline form the two main building blocks of the book: a relentless critique of the classical method and a sketch of a novel conception of legal reasoning.

The reason for studying Gény's theory is not that it secured universal favour in its time or managed a synthesis of the writings of other social jurists about legal method; it is that his jurisprudence is unusually rich and thoughtful, illustrating with particular force and detail the project of reforming legal method under the impulse of 'social' motives.

It is worth saying a word about the context in which *Methods of Interpretation* was written. In the first part, on the 'analytic exposition of the traditional method', Gény argues that classical jurisprudence rests on two dogmas or fundamental theses: (i) every case can be decided by the application of a rule of positive law; and (ii) in the event of a gap, a decision can be derived from the general principles

---

[137] On the 'naturalistic' inspiration of social jurisprudence (with special reference to Germany), see Wieacker, *A History of Private Law in Europe*, 446–62; Karl Larenz, *Methodenlehre der Rechswissenschaft*, 36–69.

[138] Gény, *Méthode d'Interprétation et Sources en Droit Privé Positif*. There is no complete English translation of this work. I am acquainted with two partial translations, together covering about one-tenth of the book. The first, under the title 'Judicial Freedom of Decision', published in a volume entitled *Science of Legal Method* (1921) in the *Modern Legal Philosophy Series*, covers sections 155–59 and 169–76 of the original. The other is an unpublished and undated translation manuscript by Duncan Kennedy and Amanda Knudsen under the title 'The Negative Critique of the Traditional Method', covering sections 59–69. I rely on these translations for quoted passages of the original when possible and convenient.

or concepts immanent in positive law.[139] It is immediately clear that these two propositions are in contradiction with each other, for while the first asserts that legislation is comprehensive, the second provides a method – conceptualism – for filling gaps in the body of positive law. This reflects the distinctive cultural and political conditions under which classical jurisprudence developed in France. While the German jurists were working on the modernisation of legal tradition in order to minimise the risk of legislative takeover, their French counterparts had already been struck by the French Revolution. They were trying to manage in a culture were the jurist was mistrusted and the law was seen as the exclusive business of law-makers – an expression of their political authority. Judges were expected to act as mouthpieces of legislation, to the point that in 1790 an abstruse statute instructed judges to refer to the legislature all questions of statutory interpretation, and Napoleon is said to have remarked 'the code is lost' when the first commentary on it was published.

From the very beginning, all of this belonged more to the realm of political fiction than reality – starting with the myth about the revolutionary origins of the *Code Napoléon*.[140] But it left a perennial mark in French legal thought. For the French jurists of the mid to late nineteenth century, it was no good to claim a 'scientific' basis for some proposition or decision; they had to trace each of those back to a mysterious pseudo-psychological entity called 'the legislative will' (*la volonté législatif*). It was not enough for the mainstream jurist to assert that although the set of positive norms contains gaps, 'positive law is completed out of itself' by legal science.[141] The jurists had to labour under the fiction that there was legislative provision for each dispute that could possibly be litigated before a court. It was hence important to present the law yielded by scientific deduction as an extension of the legislative will. 'Here in France,' writes Gény,

> the influence of these logical techniques, has been for the most part merged into, and, so to speak, absorbed in the primordial and dominant vice of our method of interpretation: the exclusive focus on legislation. This approach has so thoroughly carried the day that we attribute to the legislator himself, by legal fiction, the idealized conceptions that seem to be required by legal dialectics. To such an extent that, in French legal thought, the excesses of this second [conceptualist] tendency present themselves as merely an aggravating cause of the first tendency [of exclusive focus on legislation], strongly combining with it to lead our interpretive science astray.[142]

A considerable amount of argument in Gény's book directed against 'the fetishism of written and codified law'[143] is accordingly of little interest, even historically, outside of France and other legal systems shaped by French influence. Only his

---

[139] Gény, *Méthode d'Interprétation*, I, 27–53, 67–69.
[140] See James Gordley, 'Myths of the French Civil Code'.
[141] Savigny, *System of the Modern Roman Law*, I, 235.
[142] Gény, *Méthode d'Interprétation*, I, 124–27.
[143] ibid at 70.

critique of legal formalism, or what he calls 'the method of constructions',[144] bears an importance that exceeds the parochial boundaries of French legal culture.

Gény presents the method as an attempt to address the problem of gaps. What is to be done – he asks – when the law contains gaps? Legal norms embodied in legislation are usually 'concrete provisions, suggested by practical life, and as such immediately applicable only within a narrow domain'.[145] But the classics held that most of them are grounded in 'what we call a principle, which represents a more general concept'[146] from which one may deduce new consequences. In sum, the 'method … seeks to extract, from specific code provisions, the [unenacted] general idea that could alone explain them, as a basis for reaching new conclusions'.[147]

It is helpful to proceed with an example in mind. Imagine that from a variety of regimes covering specific types of transaction – eg sales, leases, loans and deposits – and injury – eg, assault, battery, injuries caused by wild animals and accidental building collapses – the jurist infers that the legal system recognises two fundamental or 'normal' basis of civil liability: contract and wrong. To simplify, the jurist looks into the regimes of particular transactions and recognises a common element in the fact of agreement, and then does the same with respect to the various forms of injury and recognises a common element of fault. In each case, the assumption is that the particular regime instantiates an underlying archetype. The two principles – contract and wrong – are then used as premises for a whole new set of both positive and negative legal consequences. On the one hand, any instance of contract or wrong beyond those established by the extant body of legal rules furnishes a prima facie reason for recovery. On the other hand, any losses or injuries that are neither the result of breach of contract nor of a civil wrong are mere *damnum absque injuria*. Any other sources of legal liability – eg, recovery for unjust enrichment – are regarded as exceptional or 'anomalous', and therefore narrowly confined within the scope of application of the particular rules recognising them.[148]

Gény argues that there is nothing wrong with this way of proceeding, and indeed agrees that it is often useful. 'I am happy to … concede,' he writes,

> that these principles … often gain more certainty in terms of effects, and stronger applicability and coverage, when they acquire, through abstraction and generalization, the technical form of true legal conceptions, which separates them from the contingencies of practical life so that they can operate as autonomous creative forces.[149]

---

[144] ibid at 43.
[145] Gény, *Méthode d'Interprétation*, I, 44.
[146] ibid at 45.
[147] ibid at 126.
[148] The following statement by Sir Frederick Pollock (*The Law of Torts*, 17) provides a good example of this form of argument: 'the Roman conception of delict altogether supports … the conception that appears really to underlie the English law of tort. Liability for delict, or civil wrong in the strict sense, is the result either of wilful injury to others, or wanton disregard of what is due to them (*dolus*), or of a failure to observe due care and caution which has similar though not intended or expected consequences (*culpa*)'.
[149] ibid at 130.

In other words, much is gained in terms of rational transparency and correct decision-making when the hidden premises of legal reasoning are brought to light and clearly formulated. The problem lies not in the use but in the *abuse* of the method of constructions.

> This abuse consists ... in envisioning these idealized conceptions, *as if they had an objective permanent reality* when their very nature is *provisional and purely subjective*. And, this false way of seeing ... necessarily ends in making the entire system of positive law consist in a limited number of *logical categories* – essentially predetermined, fundamentally unchangeable, governed by inflexible dogmas, and consequently incapable of supple accommodation to the varied and changing exigencies of life.[150]

In sum, the abuse lies in regarding the legal conceptions generated by the method of constructions as: (i) permanent instead of provisional; and (ii) objective instead of subjective. Let us consider each of the objections separately.

The first objection is that classical jurisprudence held a static rather than a dynamic, or an axiomatic instead of an evolutionary, conception of legal doctrine. It was committed to the view that the rules of law at any particular point in time contain by logical implication all the types of factual predicate that are legally operative. The task of the jurist is to abstract those predicates – such as 'agreement' and 'fault' – away from their specific instantiations in positive law. Any facts that are not subsumable under the types embodied in positive law are legally inoperative or *damnum absque injuria*. Thus, the fact that the risks inherent to a dangerous device caused an accident does not constitute a valid cause of action because 'risk' is not *ex hypothesi* one of the types of factual predicate instantiated in the extant body of legal rules. Positive law is accordingly based on the principle 'no liability without fault'.

Gény's point is that this entire way of thinking reflects a fundamental misconception of the *grounds* of legal rules.[151] The fact that the tort rules now in place operate on the basis of fault instead of risk does not mean that the law excludes unconditionally strict liability; it means that it excludes it under the social conditions at the time in which the rules were adopted. In a pre-industrial society, where the level of risk is moderate and most injuries are not accidental in kind, it is appropriate to organise tort liability around the category of fault – the principle of fault, in other words, is correct provisionally, or subject to the social conditions at that time. But in the changed social circumstances of 1900, maintaining the allegiance to the notion of 'no liability without fault' defeats the very purpose or ground of the rules. The law is informed by the *telos* or goal of a fair distribution of risk, and it turns out that the proper means for realising that idea depend on

---

[150] ibid (emphasis in the original). Gény's critique of the method of constructions follows in the footsteps of Jhering's satirical essay on the 'heaven of legal concepts'. Compare the passage quoted in the text with Rudolf von Jhering, 'Im juristischen Begriffshimmel', 260–61.

[151] Gény, *Méthode d'Interprétation*, II, 82–87, 97–102, 117–22. In the first quarter of the nineteenth century, a similar objection against conceptualism was leveled by the German jurist Philipp Heck: see Heck, 'The Jurisprudence of Interests', 31–32, 37–40; Heck, 'The Formation of Concepts and the Jurisprudence of Interests', 171–77, 216–23.

the existing social circumstances.[152] As the latter change, so must legal doctrine, if it is to remain functional.[153] Cardozo invoked an example from the law of property to make that point in a famous little book where Gény is copiously cited.

> Fifty years ago, I think it would have been stated as a general principle that A. may conduct his business as he pleases, even though the purpose is to cause loss to B., unless the act involves the creation of a nuisance. Spite fences were the stock illustration, and the exemption from liability in such circumstances was supposed to illustrate not the exception, but the rule. Such a rule may have been an adequate working principle to regulate the relations between individuals or classes in a simple or homogenous community. With the growing complexity of social relations, its inadequacy was revealed. As particular controversies multiplied and the attempt was made to test them by the old principle, it was found that there was something wrong in the results, and this led to a reformulation of the principle itself. Today, most judges are inclined to say that what was once thought to be the exception is the rule, and what was the rule is the exception.[154]

Roscoe Pound made a similar claim with respect to freedom of contract in his well-known attack on 'mechanical jurisprudence':

> The conception of liberty of contract [held by the *Lochner* Court] has given rise to rules and decisions which, tested by their practical operation, defeat liberty. [...] The conception of freedom of contract is made the basis of a logical deduction. The court does not inquire what the effect of such a deduction will be, when applied to the actual situation. It does not observe that the result will be to produce a condition precisely the reverse of that which the conception originally contemplated.[155]

It follows that the method of constructions does not lead the jurist to the principles truly lying in the background of positive law but merely enables him to make generalizations that are provisionally adequate – albeit quite misleading when they take a life of their own and are treated as 'axioms'. It is useful, for example, to organise the law of torts around the idea of fault under the specific conditions of a pre-industrial society that render fault an adequate basis for liability. The abuse is to treat the proposition 'no liability without fault' as if it were the very goal of a fair distribution of risk that lies in the background of the legal regime. The grounds of the law are not general rules or types of factual predicate; they are purposes in relation to which formal doctrine plays an essentially instrumental role. In a word, their nature is not conceptual but *teleological*.[156]

> [T]he bad result comes from confusing two things that are quite distinct: on the one hand, the principles of justice or universal utility which are in essence immutable, varying only in the details of their application and according to sociological conditions, and,

---

[152] See Raymond Saleilles, 'Préface', xv; Josef Kohler, 'Judicial Interpretation of Enacted Law', 93–94; Roscoe Pound, 'Courts and Legislation', 207. In the same vein, John Dewey, 'Logical Method and Law', 26–27.
[153] See Saleilles, ibid.
[154] Benjamin Cardozo, *The Nature of the Judicial Process*, 24–25.
[155] Pound, 'Mechanical Jurisprudence', 616.
[156] Gény, *Méthode d'Interprétation*, II, 88–93.

on the other hand, technical procedures whose only reason to exist is to implement these principles – these are conceptual in origin and subjective in nature, amounting to mere scientific hypotheses whose only real value comes from their greater or lesser usefulness in realizing the goals of supreme equity, and they are constantly progressing, in the sense of a more complete development of their technical mission.[157]

Now what does Gény mean when he says that the conceptions yielded by the method of constructions are 'subjective'? He does not say much to help us pin down the meaning of this word and its place in his critique of legal formalism. It has been argued that he is making the point, commonly associated with legal realism, that 'the classical method camouflaged the subjective choices that had been made according to policy considerations …'.[158] On this view, the charge of 'abuse of deduction' was that the method of constructions worked characteristically as 'window dressing' for decisions reached on other grounds.[159] But that is not at all Gény's main line of complaint, and it is indeed difficult to square that view with his overall argument. The key problem with the method of constructions is not that it obscures or casts a false appearance of neutrality on judicial decision-making but that its excessive or dogmatic use *entails* bad consequences. It takes the jurist down the road of deciding on the wrong sort of grounds. There are two basic ways in which this may happen. Either the just and equitable outcome is denied on account of the logic of legal conceptions, as when life insurance for the benefit of a child that has not yet been conceived is held legally impossible because a right presupposes a person and it is nonsense to say that a person exists before the moment of conception;[160] or the outcome is forced into, and is accordingly limited by, the procrustean bed of traditional doctrine, as when the attempt to find a textual basis for strict liability in the fault-centered regime of the *Code Civil* results in a truncated implementation of the theory of risk-profit.[161] The point in all of this is not that conceptualist reasoning is fallacious; there is abuse of deduction because the role ascribed to formal reasoning exceeds the boundaries of proper or legitimate use, in that it contributes to congeal a transitory state of legal development instead of liberating the jurist to perform the task of adapting formal doctrine to changed social circumstances.

What Gény means by 'subjectivism' is hence something else than the later realist claim that standard legal argument tends to conceal the real grounds of judicial decision-making. I suspect that he is gesturing towards the following point: given the essentially instrumental value of formal doctrine, it does not matter much

---

[157] ibid, I, 147. See also 117–22: 'Principles, as I understand them, are clearly distinct from [legal] conceptions, in that they are drawn directly from objective realities, that is to say, from the moral, political, social, and economic considerations that are the fertile substance in the life of the law' [122].
[158] Marie-Claire Belleau, 'Legal Classicism and Criticism in Early Twentieth-Century France', 395.
[159] See Duncan Kennedy, 'Three Globalizations of Law and Legal Thought', 39: 'What the CLT people had to do, to stay loyal to their role as they conceived it, was an "abuse of deduction". They had to make decisions reached on other grounds look like the operation of deductive work premised on the coherence of the system.'
[160] Gény, *Méthode d'Interprétation*, I, 135–38.
[161] ibid, II, 173–77.

what is the conceptual scheme deployed in a particular jurisdiction; it is largely a matter of tradition whether a legal culture has adopted a broader or narrower concept of contract or whether it organises property law around the notion of ownership or possession. Ultimately, what matters is whether a given body of doctrine gives adequate expression to the underlying goals of the law, that is to say, whether the means are fit for purpose. Doctrine should be understood and compared not in terms of its conceptual or formal properties but of its functional or instrumental qualities. Take the following example. Although classical contract theory in the United States, pivoting around the 'bargain theory' of consideration and the doctrine of absolute liability,[162] looked entirely different from its civilian counterpart built around the binding force of the parties' will and a robust theory of defences, both played the same function of limiting the range of legally binding agreements. Specifically, while American law made it hard for the parties to enter and exit a contract, continental law made it easy for them to enter but also easy for them exit; from a functional standpoint, the two theories are similar. One of the vices of formalism is hence the idea that there is a single doctrinal construction that serves an underlying principle.[163] If we want to understand legal doctrine, it is much more productive to look beyond the rules themselves to the functions they perform. That is the foundation of the so-called functionalist method in comparative law, summarised in the following words of approval by two leading textbook authors:

> Different legal systems can be compared only if they solve the same factual problem, that is, answer the same legal need. In other words, the institutions of different legal systems can be meaningfully compared only if they perform the same task, if they serve the same function. Function is the start-point and basis of all comparative law. It is the *tertium comparationis* …[164]

To sum up, Gény identifies two major flaws in legal formalism: it treats contingent doctrinal forms as timeless legal truths and it judges doctrinal arrangements in terms of their formal properties instead of their practical consequences. Each of these defects reflects a different dimension of what might be called an 'essentialist' view of doctrine: to the classical jurist, doctrinal constructs – or what Savigny called the 'institutions of law' – are really there beneath the surface of legal rules, that is to say, immanent in positive law. On the contrary, Gény insists that formal doctrine is merely an instrument for the administration of justice, a tool fashioned by jurists in advanced legal cultures to deal more efficiently with the complexity of the law. We may call this view 'pragmatic'.

---

[162] This is what Grant Gilmore, *The Death of Contract*, 14, calls the 'Holmes-Williston' construct. See also ibid at 14–53.

[163] Philipp Heck's 'doctrine of equivalent constructions' is very similar, with the important difference – that we shall explore in the next chapter – that underlying the law he sees not single principles or purposes but political judgements balancing conflicting considerations or interests. See Heck, 'The Formation of Concepts and the Jurisprudence of Interests', 235–43.

[164] Zweigert and Kötz, *An Introduction to Comparative Law*, 41.

VI. Teleological Jurisprudence

How did Gény expect judges to decide cases for which there is no applicable rule? The method that he proposes in alternative to legal formalism is what he calls 'free scientific research' (*libre recherche scientifique*). At first glance, it looks as though the method amounts to little more than a candid admission that judicial legislation is unavoidable: 'Whenever it is the business of the judge to discover what the law is in the fields in which it has not yet been formulated, his functions have an appearance analogous to that of the legislator himself'.[165] Yet, this only captures one aspect of the method, namely the 'freedom' of the judge that proceeds from the fact that 'no positive outward authority compels him to decide as he does'.[166] The other aspect is 'science', for the method 'finds its solid foundation in nothing but the objective elements which legal science must reveal to [the judge]'.[167] These 'objective elements' Gény calls 'the nature of things' (*nature des choses*), and they fall into two basic categories: the positive realm of social facts and the normative realm of principles of justice.

> [T]he field of our investigation becomes definite and complete. On the one side, we address ourselves to reason and conscience in order to discover within our own breasts the foundations of justice; on the other side, we must study social phenomena in order to grasp the laws which harmonize them and the principles which will arrange them in order. Of these two tasks ... the last-named finds a firm basis in what may be called the nature of positive things ... The other rests on a more recondite foundation, it cannot be attacked by observation and the experience of the senses, but nevertheless forms one of the necessary conditions of the practical working of the law.[168]

The idea lurking behind the 'nature of positive things' is immediately obvious. It is the normative element – vaguely identified with the terms 'justice' and 'reason and conscience' – that needs explaining. The jurist must study the social conditions to which the law applies, but the selection and evaluation of empirical facts presupposes normative guidance of some sort. 'Although the facts themselves will in part suggest the rule, yet its real origin must be sought in a superior order of ideas which can be discovered only by an effort of reasoning', writes Gény.[169]

---

[165] Gény, *Méthode d'Interprétation*, II, 77.
[166] ibid at 78.
[167] ibid.
[168] ibid at 93.
[169] ibid at 145. In light of this and other passages in Gény's book I cannot agree with Duncan Kennedy's assertion that the social jurists traded on is/ought confusion, or derived the 'ought' of legal reform from the 'is' of social fact. See Kennedy, 'Three Globalizations of Law and Legal Thought', 38–39, 60. One might, of course, argue that Gény is an outsider to the lot in this particular respect. But I find it at least questionable that on such a decisive issue the view of the only social jurist, apart from Cardozo and Pound, who wrote extensively on the theory of legal reasoning is regarded as idiosyncratic. The more plausible interpretation is that most of the social jurists, who paid scarce attention to jurisprudential questions, ran into a potential is/ought problem that Gény, here as in many other methodological respects, set himself to address. Teleological jurisprudence rationalized the substantive reform agenda of the social jurists.

What 'superior order of ideas'? Gény explicitly picks up the discussion of this point where Jhering had left it,[170] namely the vague but influential statement in the preface to *Law as Means to an End* to the effect that 'The fundamental idea of the present work consists in the thought that Purpose is the creator of the entire law …'[171] The problem, readily identified by Gény, is that Jhering never quite explained what sort of 'purpose' animates the law, and while it is superficially plausible to suggest that he had the discrete aims of law-makers in mind, the book as whole makes it quite clear that he meant something else. The gist of Jhering's slogan was that legal rules and doctrines serve functions in relation to the *Zweck im Recht* – that the legal order serves an overarching *telos*.[172]

What Gény added to this hazy account was threefold. First, that 'every body of laws should tend toward realising, in the life of humanity, on the one hand an ideal of justice, on the other an ideal of utility';[173] justice and utility are the basic *teloi* of the law. Secondly, ideals of justice (which Gény appears to rank above utility) may be ordered along a hierarchy of generality, ranging from the idea of justice (*suum cuique tribuere*) at the top through the intermediate principles of freedom, security and equality, to what Gény calls 'maxims of legal conduct' such as 'promises ought to be kept', 'fairness in the allocation of losses', 'no person should profit from his own wrong' and 'many other notions born out of pure justice'.[174] Third, these principles of justice are universal and immutable, although their consequences are largely a function of the particular set of social conditions to which they apply; it follows both that 'absolute justice … provides nothing but a direction, that only the consideration of social facts and the nature of positive things can render more precise' and that 'justice is the goal, yet it is the task of the interpreter to find the means of its realization in given social conditions'.[175]

How does Gény attempt to validate all these assertions about 'absolute justice'? One of the fascinating things about his theory is that he is deliberately ambiguous on this point. Sometimes he leans towards a natural law account, as when he appeals to 'reason and conscience', 'listening to the mystery of justice', or 'discover within our own breasts the foundations of justice'.[176] But he also stresses that the principles of justice are *reflected* in positive law:

> [Q]uite apart from the solutions directly given in the formal sources, especially written laws, … we notice that in the material of the sources … lies a set of principles that exceeds the scope of the texts, and shares, albeit in a lesser degree, their positive value; this is true so long as the principles are inferred by means of free scientific research, in accordance with the rigorous and safe procedure of Analogy.[177]

---

[170] ibid at 90.
[171] Rudolf von Jhering, *Law as a Means to an End*, liv.
[172] See WM Geldart, 'Introduction', xxxv.
[173] Gény, *Méthode d'Interprétation*, II, 91.
[174] ibid at 102–07.
[175] ibid at 103.
[176] ibid at 92–93, 100.
[177] ibid at 117. See also ibid at 131–36.

When we combine these two apparently inconsistent strands of Gény's thought we get the following picture. The jurist is professionally obliged to pay tribute to 'pure positive law'.[178] He cannot dismiss a rule or a doctrine simply because it conflicts with his conscience or the outcome that he deems rationally vindicated. But fidelity to positive law is a much more subtle business than it appears at first sight, mostly because the law in the sources runs out in a non-neglectable range of cases. On these occasions, the jurist is bound to search for criteria of decision-making latent in positive law.

Such a task is quite straightforward for the classical jurist, for whom latent norms far more general than the rules of positive law are logically implicated in these – they can thus be established by formal reasoning. The epistemic predicament of the social jurist is more complicated. The whole point of the social critique of formalism is that logical inference will not lead the jurist to the real principles – teleological rather than axiomatic – in the background of positive law. Such principles exist, according to Gény, and yet they are non-demonstrable, because they do not logically entail but functionally determine positive law. The jurist cannot prove that the law of torts is grounded in the principle of fair distribution of risk or that the law of contracts is governed by an ideal of fair bargaining. He merely *discerns* these and other principles when formal doctrine is brought to bear on a real or imagined case and the purpose or *telos* of the law for that type of case resonates with his 'reason and conscience'. The kind of reasoning involved here is not deductive but analogical – the jurist compares the 'if-clause' of the legal norm or doctrine with the case before him, and the standard or *tertium comparationis* that guides his judgement is set by a latent principle.[179]

Let me illustrate this last point with a more detailed version of our working example. Suppose that a judge in a common law system is presented with a case in which the plaintiff was accidentally injured by a dangerous device in the defendant's possession. There is *ex hypothesi* no precedent for recovery in cases in which the defendant met the standard of reasonable care. The factual record, on the other hand, shows to the jury's satisfaction that the defendant exercised the required level of care. *Quid iuris?*

According to the method of free scientific research, the judge should not derive from the line of cases a general rule of 'no liability without fault', and then proceed with its mechanical application to the case at hand. He should instead conduct an inquiry into the social conditions at the time in which the leading cases in favour of the defendant were decided. From such inquiry he might learn that the case law refers to a society where dangerous devices are rare and social intercourse is comparatively meager, a society where most accidents are caused by careless behaviour. Modern society, on the contrary, is a 'society of risk', where a certain number of accidents, some horrid and some quite trivial, is bound to happen

---

[178] ibid, I, 14.
[179] See ibid, II, 117–22.

even if the people involved exercise as much care as it is reasonable to demand. Equipped with knowledge of these facts, the judge is encouraged to wonder: Is this case really of the same type as the cases decided in the past? Is this really the sort of case that led the courts to deny recovery on grounds of strict liability? The answer to these questions presupposes a *tertium comparationis* – the quality or set of qualities upon which the judgement of similarity depends. Suppose that the judge believes that there is no analogy between the present and past cases because the level of non-compensable risk that falls on third parties is significantly higher in the contemporary society of risk. The *tertium comparationis* is the level of risk, and what makes it the decisive factor is some notion of fair distribution of risk that the judge senses, or understands to be latent, in the body of case law. The correct outcome, then, the only one genuinely consistent with the normative standard or *telos* immanent in positive law, is to hold the defendant liable.[180]

I hope that by now the connection between this account of legal reasoning and the 'socialisation' of private law is apparent. The jurisprudence of the social jurists, of which Gény's free scientific research was the most elaborate version, licensed vast doctrinal reforms, under the pretext of teleological adaptation. The jurists acted not *qua* legislators but *qua* loyal servants of positive law; they claimed that it was the immanent logic of the law – purposive or teleological – that compelled them to set aside past doctrinal arrangements and devise new ones to replace them.

---

[180] The connection between teleological jurisprudence and analogical reasoning was further explored, among others, by Arthur Kaufmann, *Analogie und 'Natur der Sache'*. Kaufmann argues that the process of norm-application is not a matter of subsuming the case under the abstract concepts that figure in the 'if-clause' of a legal rule. Instead, the norm-applying agent should compare the case with the 'if-clause' of the norm and ask himself whether the norm is meant to apply to the case before him, that is, whether the case is functionally apt to form the minor premise of a syllogism headed by the legal norm. See Karl Engisch, *Einführung in das juristische Denken*, 43–62. Moreover, to the extent that the norm's purpose or *telos* is not served by its application to the case, the norm-applying agent is bound to create an ad hoc norm that replicates in the case at hand the normative measure or proportion between antecedent and consequent embodied in the positive norm. The ad hoc norm tailored to the type of case to which the case at hand belongs is called the case-norm (*Fallnorm*). It is this *Fallnorm*, and not the positive norm in the sources, that should be deductively applied, since it alone corresponds to the case. Of course, a good deal of non-deductive reasoning is required to derive the *Fallnorm* itself. It follows that the lion's share of norm-application is not deduction but analogy guided by the immanent *telos* of the relevant legal norm or regime. A good illustration of this method is furnished by the argument of the plaintiff in *Appelhans v McFall*, 757 NE 2d 987 (2001). In this case, the plaintiff suffered a broken hip when the defendant, aged five, collided with her while riding his bicycle. The plaintiff sued the defendant and his parents for damages. Yet under the 'tender years doctrine', well-settled in the case law of Illinois, a child less than seven years old is incapable of negligence. The plaintiff argued that the court should abolish the doctrine, not because it was mistaken from the very beginning, but because 'the judiciary that crafted the rule did not envision "cable television, video games, the internet, pre-teen gangs, and violent crime"' and that 'in response to these modern-day challenges, children are instructed at an early age that they must exercise good judgment for themselves and others …' [991]. Equipped with this argument, the plaintiff hoped to avoid the mechanical application of the tender years rule in the case. She then argued that the correct translation of the normative criterion or *telos* immanent in the tender years doctrine into modern-day conditions justified holding children to a standard of reasonable care based on their age. The court eventually decided for the defendant on grounds of *stare decisis*, invoking a mix of formalist and policy reasons.

True, the jurists paid a price when they abandoned the formalist creed in the demonstrable quality of legal argument. Their science was less epistemically robust: it conceded that legal truth could be sensed but not demonstrated. This was, nonetheless, a price that they were willing to pay when what was at stake was shielding the entire class from the threat of political, social and cultural marginalisation. Under the aegis of teleological jurisprudence, reformist legislation lost some of its urgency because private law acquired a social impetus endogenously. Like their classical predecessors, who read the legacy of the liberal revolutions into the *ius commune*, the social jurists read a good deal of the reformist agenda of 1900 into materials that appeared condemned by their reputation as sanctuaries of the will theory. As a result, they managed to halt the process of decline of private law and conserve their symbolic capital.

Notice that for the substantive reform agenda and the new conception of legal method to work smoothly together, Gény and the other social jurists had to expand the 'fiction' of gaps. Like the classical jurists, they did so implicitly, obscuring the distinction between authentic and inauthentic gaps, and arguing fallaciously that what was at stake in the 'gap problem' was the duty of the judge not to refuse a decision on grounds of *non liquet*.[181] But they went beyond the classical jurists in one important respect; indeed, they had no choice but to do so. Unlike their predecessors, who were dealing with a chaotic array of sources, especially in countries like Germany or the United States, where private law was neither codified nor even unified, the social jurists were, at least in Europe, confronted with much more stable and ordered legal material. They could not pick one set of rules covering specific transactions or injuries and claim that it embodied a general principle that holds in the scores of cases not referred to in the legal texts or the case law. The law that the social jurists faced was, especially in Europe, codified and general, full of norms that aimed at governing not narrow sets of cases – loans or pledges or assaults – but vast areas of social life, such as 'injuries' and 'contracts'. Both the German and the French codes, for instance, contained in their original versions general standards of tort liability that ruled out compensation for inculpable harm.[182] In order to get round these rules, the social jurists had to argue that even cases covered by the rules of positive law may present the judge with a gap.

A gap, as Savigny and his followers usually understood the term, exists where the law contains no explicit provision for a class of cases although it should in terms of its own normative logic; there is a gap, for instance, if only some types of injury or contract are subject to legal regulation, while the principles upon which such rules are grounded vindicate and indeed require that other types of injury and contract be regulated as well in a similar way. These are called patent or open gaps.[183] But jurists also speak about gaps when a class of cases falls within the

---

[181] See Gény, *Méthode d'Interprétation*, II, 74–76.
[182] For a useful summary, see Zweigert and Kötz, *An Introduction to Comparative Law*, 638–45, 656–62, 688–93.
[183] See Karl Larenz, *Methodenlehre der Rechswissenschaft*, 377.

scope of application of an existing regime, although it should be governed by a different regime in light of the law's immanent purpose. These are so-called *latent* or *concealed* gaps.[184] If a fault-based regime applies on its own terms to all sorts of accidents but the jurist argues that it was never meant to apply, in view of its purpose or *telos*, to the sort of accidents that modern-day equipment and devices are prone to causing – say, high-speed train wrecks and chemical spillovers – the argument is that there is a latent gap in the law. The jurist is hence entitled to fashion a new regime, one in agreement with the background principles of the law, to fill the gap. Among civilian jurists, this procedure is known as teleological reduction, and it is the exact opposite of analogical extension: the jurist narrows, as opposed to extending, the scope of application of the extant regime.[185] The equivalent procedure in common law jurisdictions is the common practice of distinguishing a case (or a situation-type) from a line of past cases that carries precedential authority. In our example, cases involving certain types of accident are removed from the purview of fault-based liability. The operation is justified on the grounds that the jurist owes loyalty to the underlying principles, purposes, or *teloi* of the law – *stare decisis* yields to *stare principiis*.[186]

It was mainly through teleological reduction that the social jurists sponsored various inroads into the will theory, virtually disfiguring it in the process. To give a few paradigmatic examples: standard business terms were subtracted from the general law of contract; various types of accident were carved out of the law of negligence; and major domains within the law of property – eg, public accommodations, residential property, water rights, business premises, etc – were either invented, reinforced or recovered, and subject to specific rules justified by the social importance of the assets involved. In spite of the encouraging apparatus of teleological jurisprudence, the jurists faced throughout this process the barriers of formal authority and of public perceptions of the proper role of the judiciary. Sometimes they could rely on bits of textual authority to back their agenda – the standard example is 'the flight into general clauses' by the German courts, particularly the famous good faith standard in §242 of the BGB.[187] The general framework, however, was the new legal method advocated by Gény, a method that enabled the gradual but ultimately profound reform of the will theory within the strict premises of 'legal science'.

We can get a firmer grip over the theoretical stuff with the support of some examples of how teleological jurisprudence played out in doctrinal writing. I selected two doctrinal constructions that were widely regarded as revolutionary in their time: *culpa in contrahendo* and abuse of right. Each of them had its own

---

[184] ibid.
[185] ibid at 391–97.
[186] To use Samuel Williston's term (he was referring to Langdellian formalism, although that is immaterial). See Williston, *Life and Law*, 205.
[187] See John Dawson, *The Oracles of the Law*, 466–75. The phrase 'the flight into general clauses' is the title of a book published in 1933 by Justus Wilhelm Hedemann.

leading advocate, the former in the person of Jhering and the latter in Josserand, and eventually earned mainstream acceptance in civilian systems. Both are exemplary, although for quite different reasons. Jhering's essay on *culpa in contrahendo* was written in 1861,[188] when the will theory of contract and legal formalism were peaking in Germany. It was an early assault on the classical citadel, filled with the ambivalence that one expects from a seed of the distant future. Josserand's major work on the theory of abuse of right,[189] on the contrary, was written in 1927, at a time in which the social reform of classical private law was underway, and the notion of abuse of right had already appeared in more than a few judicial opinions and scholarly essays,[190] particularly in France,[191] although nowhere in the far-reaching and enthusiastic terms in which it was later to be sponsored by him. It was fruit rather than seed of social jurisprudence.[192]

The discussion that follows is brief and schematic, aiming not at exhausting the subject but merely giving the reader a sense of the doctrinal labors of the social jurists.[193]

VII. *Culpa in Contrahendo*

The problem that furnished Jhering's starting point was the following: a contract is void or voidable – for instance, because one of the parties made a legally relevant mistake or transferred an inalienable right – and one of the parties bears the blame for it, while the other suffers a loss. What remedy, if any, does the law afford to the innocent party, and on what grounds?[194] Consider the following hypotheticals:

(i) A distributor located in the United States means to buy 2,000 pounds of a commodity from a manufacturer located in Brazil, sends the latter a

---

[188] Rudolf (von) Jhering, 'Culpa in contrahendo oder Schadensersatz bei nichtigen oder nicht zur Perfektion gelangten Vertrigen'.

[189] Louis Josserand, *De l'Esprit des Droits et de Leur Relativité*. Josserand wrote a shorter book on the subject in 1905 entitled *De l'Ábus des Droits*.

[190] Two precocious hints are: Jhering, *Law as Means to an End*, 383–84; and Otto von Gierke, *Die soziale Aufgabe des Privatrechts*, 14–16.

[191] The doctrine was created by the French courts. For a comprehensive analysis of the French case law in the first quarter of the twentieth century, see Josserand, *De l'Esprit des Droits et de Leur Relativité*, 13–278. Among the earliest scholarly sources are: Raymond Saleilles, *Théorie Génerale de l'Obligation*, 370, fn 1; and Joseph Charmont, 'L'Abus du Droit'. See the interesting, albeit slightly biased, summary of the French case law and scholarly debate circa 1900 in Léon Duguit, *Les Transformations Générales du Droit Privé*, Appendix IV, 196–202.

[192] To paraphrase Wieacker's comment on the BGB: 'the BGB is the fruit rather than the seed of great legal thought' (*A History of Private Law in Europe*, 379).

[193] Another reason for picking these examples is that although neither of the two doctrines was ever, to the best of my knowledge, transplanted to a common law jurisdiction, there are two fine comparative law essays – one a classic law review article by Friedrich Kessler and Edith Fine, the other a recent piece by Anna di Robilant – that set out to find their 'functional equivalents' in American law. See Kessler and Fine, 'Culpa in Contrahendo, Good Faith, and Freedom of Contract'; and Anna di Robilant, 'Abuse of Right'.

[194] Jhering, 'Culpa in contrahendo oder Schadensersatz bei nichtigen oder nicht zur Perfektion gelangten Vertrigen', 2.

telegram with the words '2,000 of X on day Y', and receives the merchandise. The buyer meant '2,000 of Z', and the contract is voided for mistake.

(ii) A horse trader makes inquiries about the owner of a racehorse named Flash, intending to buy it on the basis of a report by an agent. Upon discovering the owner's identity, the trader closes a deal to buy Flash. It turns out that the 'Flash' that his agent saw racing is another horse. The buyer returns the horse and calls the deal off.

(iii) A borrower offers her right to a lifelong disability pension as collateral for a loan of substantial funds from a local moneylender. Yet the right is inalienable. The contract (or the term regarding collateral) is thus unenforceable.

Jhering argues that in cases such as these, in which one of the parties incurs certain expenses in reliance of a contract that is nullified because of a defect reproached on the other party, it is unjust and socially inconvenient, a threat to security in transactions, to let the losses lie where they fall.[195] But he acknowledges not only that this type of case did not merit the attention of the vast majority of the classical jurists, but that the few who took up the issue either denied recovery on principled grounds or affirmed it on ad hoc or undisclosed grounds. Jhering proposes to articulate a position that is both principled and favourable to the plaintiff.

The reason why this was a formidable challenge is that classical private law recognised only two general or normal forms of civil liability – contract and wrong[196] – and the cases that concerned Jhering did not fit with any of them. Recovery on contractual grounds was plainly out of the question here, since this type of case arises precisely when a contract is invalid.[197] An invalid contract is by definition one that lacks the minimum qualities that justify its enforcement; enforcing it notwithstanding would render the entire regime of invalidity practically void.

But there is a deeper substantive point behind this analytical truism. According to the will theory, there are two basic sets of reason not to enforce a contract: either because enforcing it would endanger the public interest or the rights of third parties, as when a tax inspector is bribed not to report a taxpayer's fraud or a hitman is hired to eliminate a target, or because the contract is not the free choice of all the parties involved. Let me focus on this latter type of case, since the former requires no further explication. It is as much part of freedom of contract, as the classical jurists understood it, to enforce agreements that have been freely consented to, as it is to prevent the enforcement of unfree agreements.

---

[195] ibid at 2–3, 42, 44.
[196] See Grant Gilmore, *The Death of Contract*, 15; Duncan Kennedy, 'Form and Substance in Private Law Adjudication', 1728–29; Morton Horwitz, *The Tranformation of American Law, 1870–1960*, 10–16. The contract-cum-tort theory of civil liability coexisted with a variety of *ad hoc* or 'anomalous' alternative sources of recovery (in some jurisdictions lumped together into the residual category of 'quasi-contract').
[197] The doctrine has been in the meantime extended to situations in which one of the parties culpably breaks off negotiations or refuses to formalize an informal agreement.

What unifies the regimes of incapacity, fraud, duress and mistake is that they afford the promisor defences against liability grounded in his fundamental right not to be forced into an obligation against his will. As Duncan Kennedy puts it, in a paragraph where he is trying to make sense of freedom of contract as an ideal-type of legal regime:

> We have freedom of contact if the decision maker enforces agreements, one might say. But this would be an inadequate specification of what must be going on if we are to 'have' this institution. The decision maker must, indeed, enforce agreements, but he must also *refuse* to enforce agreements. If he enforces the wrong ones, those that shouldn't be enforced, then we are as far from freedom of contract as we would be were he to refuse to enforce agreements at all. The institution, in other words, is as much constituted by the exceptions to enforcement as by the practice of enforcement.[198]

This takes the contract route away. What about the civil wrong alternative? The classical theory of tort was never as fully developed, certainly not in Germany, as contract theory. Yet Jhering had no trouble stating its core tenets. On his account, the Roman law in force in Germany before the BGB came into force recognised two forms of action in tort: *actio legis Aquilia* and *actio de dolo*.[199] The former afforded remedial protection, in the form of damages, to the victim of certain types of injury caused by the defendant's fault. It presupposed a visible injury, understood as material and external damage – material damage as opposed to pure economic loss (eg, a bad investment, a lost business opportunity, etc) and external damage as opposed to intangible harm (eg, emotional distress, disappointment, etc).[200] Since the cases that concerned Jhering involved pure economic loss, as the three examples above illustrate, the plaintiff could not avail himself to this type of legal protection. The *actio de dolo*, the second form of action, presented insurmountable difficulties of a different nature: although it gave the plaintiff a remedy against any type of loss, it was restricted to intentionally inflicted damage (*dolus* instead

---

[198] Kennedy, 'Distributive and Paternalist Motives in Contract and Tort Law', 569 (emphasis in the original). Kennedy's point, of course, is not that the abstraction of 'free contract' entails any particular regime of defences. On the contrary, he understands the model as a rhetorical framework within which rival 'individualist' and 'altruist' interpretations are deployed. From a 'realist' standpoint, freedom of contract is a smokescreen for myriads of rule choices based on rival policy – or, in the more critical version, ideological – grounds. See ibid at 580–83. I should add that the classical jurists varied quite widely in their confidence in the operative force of the 'free contract' abstraction. Savigny, for instance, flatly denied via *reductio ad absurdum* that the doctrines of fraud and duress were entailed by the concept of contract (or juristic act) as an act of free will. His point is that it is not the 'defect of the will' itself – mistake in the case of fraud and fear in the case of duress – but the reproachable behaviour of the promisee (or a third party) – deceptive in the case of fraud and violent in the case of duress – that constitutes the real 'trigger' of the fraud and duress regimes. See Friedrich Carl von Savigny, *System des heutigen römischen Rechts*, III, 98–111. It seems to me that Savigny's own argument can be turned against his position, simply because reproachable behaviour is not legally consequential unless it is combined with a 'defect of the will', although it is certainly persuasive as a critique of the assimilation of fraud and duress to the will-theory-free-contract framework.

[199] Jhering, 'Culpa in Contrahendo', 23–24. Roman law was based on a system of forms of action – the *actiones* – not unlike the system of common law writs.

[200] ibid at 24–25.

of mere *culpa* or negligence).²⁰¹ But in the cases on which Jhering focused, the defendant acted negligently instead of intentionally or maliciously. As Jhering put it, the attempt to force these cases into the tort mould implied an arbitrary agglomeration of elements – mere *culpa* and unlimited damage – specific to each of the two available forms of action in tort.²⁰²

Jhering argues that what is specific about these cases is that plaintiff and defendant are not strangers to one another but parties to an apparent contract. Their relationship is thus contractual in nature. When two or more strangers initiate a bargaining process, they are no longer strangers bound by the merely negative duty not to harm each other (*culpa in faciendo*) but agents related by their joint enterprise of establishing a contract, and bound by positive duties of diligence, honesty, loyalty and the like (*culpa in non faciendo*).²⁰³ Commercial intercourse requires mutual trust, and in advanced industrial societies, where the parties cannot rely on communal mores and group pressure to secure an appropriate level of trust, the law must step in to provide security. But what remedy can the law grant to the victim of the defendant's lack of diligence in, for instance, preventing an essential mistake? The contract is obviously unenforceable. Yet Jhering draws a distinction between the positive interest of the defendant in having the contract enforced, an interest that cannot be protected when the contract is invalid, and the negative interest is being compensated for the losses incurred in reliance of a flawed transaction. (Common lawyers speak, respectively, of the expectation and reliance interests.) 'The interest of the first type has the validity of the contract, while the second type of interest has its invalidity, as grounds.'²⁰⁴ *Culpa in contrahendo* is hence a third general source of liability apart from contract and tort: it arises when someone negligently fails to remove an obstacle to the validity of a contract and, as a result, the plaintiff incurs some loss; the remedy in these cases is reliance damages.

Although it is easy to recognise the 'social' overtones of Jhering's argument, centred on the notion that the needs of modern commerce require a revision of formal doctrine in light of the law's immanent purposes, it is important not to

---

[201] ibid at 25. Jhering argues forcefully against the expansion of the *actio de dolo* to cases in which the defendant did not cause harm intentionally but as a result of gross negligence (*culpa lata*); ibid at 12–13. (To a post-realist jurist, the notion that the mere fact of intentional infliction of harm is a basis for recovery is flawed, for as Holmes wrote in his famous dissent in *Vegelahn v Guntner*, 167 Mass 92 (1986), 'in numberless instances the law warrants the intentional infliction of temporal damage because it regards it as justified' [137]. The 'true grounds of the decision are considerations of policy and social advantage' [ibid]. This appears to have been partly recognised by the drafters of the BGB, who adopted the principle underlying the *actio de dolo* in §826 but restricted recovery to cases in which the defendant acted 'in a manner *contrary to public policy*'). Jhering also argues against the expansion of the *actio legis Aquilia* to pure economic loss, claiming that the requirement of a visible injury is not a positive stipulation of Roman law but rooted in the nature of things (*Natur der Dinge*)!
[202] ibid at 24.
[203] ibid at 41–42.
[204] ibid at 16.

downplay three aspects of the construction that are thoroughly classical. First, Jhering tries to ground his argument in the logical 'construction' of positive law, maintaining that the doctrine of *culpa in contrahendo* was already contained, albeit not fully acknowledged, in the Roman sources;[205] his argument is thus a mélange of formalist and evolutionary ingredients. Secondly, although he clearly favours strict liability for the party that caused the invalidity, arguing that it is more equitable than the alternative of letting the loss lie where it falls,[206] he still claims that the doctrine is grounded in fault. This blatant contradiction forces Jhering into the elaborate but nevertheless bizarre position that the requirement of *culpa* is a legal fiction, established by an unrebuttable presumption (*praesumtio juris et de jure*).[207] The only argument that he sketches in support of this construction is that fault alone can provide a principled basis for the doctrine, since strict liability is an anomaly;[208] he does not stop to ponder the obvious objection that a fiction of fault cannot render an authentic fault-based justification for liability. Thirdly, Jhering makes a concession to the will theory when he construes the duties of the parties in the contract-forming stage as products of a tacit or implied term of something like a secondary contract regarding the formation of the main contract; one of the problems with this obscure construction is that it trades on confusion between terms implied-in-law and implied-in-fact.[209]

In spite of these setbacks and ambivalences, *culpa in contrahendo* is undoubtedly a *proto*-social construction. Let us now turn to a doctrine that was at the very heart of the social reform of classical private law in continental Europe.

VIII. Abuse of Rights

The intellectual root of the doctrine of abuse of right goes back to Jhering's critique of the classical theory of rights in the last volume of *The Spirit of the Roman Law* and in *Law as Means to an End*.[210] The classical jurists endorsed the so-called 'will theory' of rights, whose leading proponents were Kant and Savigny; they held that a right is a 'territory where the individual will rules and rules without our consent',[211] a sphere within which the right-bearer is sovereign or acts with absolute discretion.[212] The decisive feature of this conception is that rights are

---

[205] ibid at 8–22.
[206] ibid at 34–35.
[207] ibid at 36–37.
[208] ibid at 39–41.
[209] ibid at 42–44.
[210] See Rudolf von Jhering, *Geist des römischen Rechts*, III, 317–38; Jhering, *Law as Means to an End*, 381–98.
[211] Friedrich Carl von Savigny, *System of the Modern Roman Law*, I, 6.
[212] Or what, in a different context, Ronald Dworkin, *Taking Rights Seriously*, 32–33, calls 'discretion in the strong sense'. On the classical view of 'rights absolute within their sphere', see Duncan Kennedy, *The Rise and Fall of Classical Legal Thought*, x–xiv, 1–4, 8–16.

formal, as opposed to teleological or functional, structures: rights are assigned to individuals for no other reason than to secure them a space of unrestrained decision-making. Since, on this account, the substance of rights is the will, and the will is formal,[213] the purpose of rights – the reason for conferring to Y a right over X – does not lie beyond its structure – the prerogatives that Y has over X – but is coextensive with it. The law is thus indifferent to the particular uses to which a right is put, so long as it is exercised within its scope.

Jhering raises technical and normative objections against the will theory. On the one hand, it fails to explain why children and the mentally impaired, who lack the capacity to govern themselves, are nonetheless bearers of legal rights. We have no trouble, for instance, speaking about a child's property, and from there it follows that while a capable will is required to exercise a right, it cannot be the substance of the right itself.[214] The will is the instrument, not the essence, of legal rights. Moreover – and here lies the normative objection – the will theory implies the view that rights are absolute within their sphere. To be the owner of X, for example, means to dispose of X as one sees fit. It is important that we do not misunderstand or caricature this view: the classical jurists were obviously aware that ownership is limited, to begin with by nuisance law, but they conceptualised these limits as restrictions of a right that is absolute in nature; it follows that within the area remaining after the various subtractions prescribed by law, the owner can do as he pleases.[215] The problem with this view is that it licenses a variety of uses of one's property, and of numerous other rights conferred by private law, that appear to contradict important reasons for having property (or other types of legal right) in the first place, as when the testator provides that his valuables should be buried with him.[216] The force of these examples is that they appear to show that rights are not absolute, or exhausted by their formal structure, but conferred for certain reasons, or provided so that certain ends may be accomplished in the lives of those who benefit from them. It is on such occasions, where a person acts simultaneously within right in the formal sense but in a way that defeats the point of the right, that makes sense to speak of 'abuse of right'.

What Jhering takes from all of this is that the essence of rights is not the will in its complete discretion but the idea of interest or benefit: a right is a legally

---

[213] True, one wills certain *ends*. Yet the concept of will itself does not specify *which* ends are to be pursued. It falls to each instance of will – each person – the task of selecting the ends to be pursued within its allotted sphere.

[214] See Jhering, *Geist des römischen Rechts*, III, 322–25.

[215] As Bernhard Windscheid, *Lehrbuch des Pandektenrechts*, I, § 167, put it: 'Ownership as such is unlimited, although it accepts restrictions'. Compare that statement with two landmark civilian code definitions of ownership. First, Article 544 of the French Civil Code: 'Property is the right of enjoying and disposing of things in the most absolute manner, *provided they are not used in a way prohibited by the laws or statutes*.' See www.napoleon-series.org/research/government/c_code.html (last visited: 20 August 2012). Secondly, § 903 of the German Civil Code: 'The owner of a thing may, *to the extent that a statute or third-party rights do not conflict with this*, deal with the thing at his discretion and exclude others from every influence.' See www.gesetze-im-internet.de/englisch_bgb/englisch_bgb.html#p3531 (last visited: 20 August 2012).

[216] Jhering, *Law as a Means to an End*, 338–90.

protected interest.[217] That is why is makes sense to say that persons who lack civil capacity have rights or that one's exercise of a right may be abusive. In the former cases, we are pointing implicitly to the beneficiary of the right, the person who has what is essential in a right – not the power to exercise it, but the benefit it accords. In the latter cases, we are pointing to the gap between the structure of a right – the prerogatives it confers upon a person – and the benefit or interest for the sake of which it exists.[218] This is the so-called 'interest' or 'benefit' theory of rights, first articulated by Jeremy Bentham but brought within legal thought by Jhering.[219]

There is a close affinity between the interest theory of rights and the doctrine of abuse of right.[220] The connection is forged by the notion that rights, or the prerogatives that come with having a right, are not absolute but relative to certain purposes or interests, so that the exercise of any particular prerogative may prove abusive, a use contrary to its justificatory reason or *telos*. The title of Josserand's book is precisely *Of the Spirit of Rights and Their Relativity*. The 'spirit' of rights is the reason, interest, or purpose for the sake of which they are granted, and in relation to which they are to be legally construed. He writes:

> Just as there is a spirit of the laws, and more generally a spirit of the law itself, understood as an objective whole, we should also acknowledge the existence of a spirit of rights, inherent to every subjective prerogative considered in isolation; and just as a law cannot be applied against its spirit ... our rights cannot be exercised in contravention or disregard of their social vocation.[221]

Josserand claims that rights can be uncaused (*non causés*), altruistic or egotistic in spirit.[222] The former are those rare rights, typically narrowly defined in statutes or precedent, that truly are absolute, such as the right to vote in a general election

---

[217] ibid, *Geist des römischen Rechts*, III, 326–27.
[218] James Gordley, 'The Abuse of Rights in the Civil Law Tradition', 39–41, misses the distinction, drawn above, between the structural and the functional features of rights, as well as its connection with the critique of the will theory of rights. I agree with him, though, that Josserand does not make the point as clearly as one would have hoped.
[219] Bentham, *Theory of Legislation*, 93: 'Rights are in themselves advantages, benefits, for him who enjoys them.' See also HLA Hart, 'Legal Rights', 174–93.
[220] This connection is missed by Marcel Planiol, *Traité Élémentaire de Droit Civil*, 297–98, who argued famously that the very notion of 'abuse of right' is mere word play (*une logomachie*), at best useless gibberish and at worst a dangerous threat to legal certainty. According to Planiol, either a person acts within right, and hence lawfully, or beyond right, and thus unlawfully – *tertium non datur*. 'Abuse of right' is just a pretentious and confusing way of saying the obvious: that a right ends where the abuse begins. The problem with Planiol's apparent truism is that it misunderstands the historical and doctrinal context in which the earliest proponents of the doctrine of abuse of right were operating. See James Gordley, 'The Abuse of Rights in the Civil Law Tradition', 37–39. They were leading the attack on the will theory of rights, and the related claim that the limits of rights proceed exclusively from their formal boundaries. The point of the doctrine of abuse is to emphasize that the structural features of rights – the prerogatives they confer – are a function of the reasons on account of which they are created, so that they may be used in a way that, albeit formally impeccable, is nonetheless incompatible with their underlying *telos*.
[221] Josserand, *De l'Esprit des Droits et de Leur Relativité*, 10–11.
[222] ibid at 414–24.

or the right not to get married.²²³ Altruistic rights are prerogatives conferred for the sake of third-party interests, such as parental rights or the rights of corporate managers; these are 'rights-function' because they combine the active idea of prerogative with the passive idea of service.²²⁴ Finally, the vast majority of private law entitlements are egotistic rights, such as ownership rights and the right to contract, which are granted in the interest of both the individual and society.²²⁵ It is clear both that the doctrine of abuse of right does not apply to the first category of rights and how it plays out in relation to the 'rights' in the second category.²²⁶ The third category, that of rights of egotistic spirit, poses all the important and difficult questions.

The idea that these egotistic rights are both individual and social, or subjective and objective, has all the appearance of hopeless confusion. But Josserand's point, although not articulated in a completely satisfactory manner, is actually quite elaborate. He argues that 'every time [an individual] exercises a[n] [egotistic] right, he proceeds as an individual moved by selfish aims, but realizes notwithstanding a social prerogative which ought, accordingly, to be used in a social direction, according to the spirit of the institution [to which it belongs]'.²²⁷ I think that the point here is as follows. To have a right of the egotistic sort is to be given a measure of independence from the social world or third-party direction; in that sense, rights are individual, because they concern the universal interest of human beings in conducting their lives autonomously. But while these rights are grounded in individualist motives, they must be socially distributed in a way that pays tribute to the equal concern owed to every person. Rights, even egotistic rights, are thus constrained by the requirement of universality: each person has the most extensive recognition of individuality consistent with an equal recognition of other persons. The real scope of one's right, accordingly, depends on the social institution from where it proceeds;²²⁸ for instance, property rights are defined within and limited by the institution of property, the purpose of which is to protect the interests of all individuals in property. And the institution of property is itself constrained by other social institutions – personality and commerce – that accommodate other types of individual interest. As a whole, the legal order, and particularly the egotistic institutions that dominate private law, is informed by the idea of harmonising 'selfish' interests. In sum, our individual interests, the subjective stuff of rights, play out in a social field that aspires to be leveled – that is the spirit, the objective or social element, of egotistic rights. There is abuse of right, then, when a person

---

²²³ ibid at 416–18. The examples are mine.
²²⁴ ibid at 420–22.
²²⁵ ibid at 418–20.
²²⁶ Imagine that after a bitter campaign for the leadership of the workers' commission of company X, the newly elected leader calls for a strike with the aim of pressing management to dismiss his rival and his closest associates. Or that a child's legal guardian alienates a parcel of the former's estate to a family member for a low price.
²²⁷ Josserand, *De l'Esprit des Droits*, 12.
²²⁸ ibid at 312–23.

exercises a right in a direction that is inconsistent with the social harmony built into the institution.

The construction of abuse of right, although immediately successful, faced critiques from opposing sides of the individual–society spectrum, and it is instructive to mention them briefly. On the one hand, there were those, committed to the classical will theory, who charged the doctrine with a mingling of law and morality, right and ethics.[229] They argued that while one should always keep the interests of others in mind when exercising a right, there is something tyrannical about converting that moral imperative into a legal constraint, both because it threatens individual autonomy and because it substitutes a vague teleological standard for easily administrable rules.[230] The reply of the social jurists was that while the absolutist conception of rights could be maintained in the relatively simple society of 1800, it was bound to generate grave injustice and defeat the point of the underlying social institutions in the highly interdependent society of 1900, where the third-party consequences of individual actions are wider and deeper.[231] The problem of abuse emerges because the same type of action is likely to have quite different consequences in the social worlds of 1800 and 1900.

On the other side of the spectrum, collectivists such as Duguit argued that the doctrine of abuse of right attempted an impossible compromise between two contradictory ideas: the individualist and metaphysical idea of right and the solidarist and realist idea of social function.[232] Rights are fictions that tend to conceal the instrumental or functional nature of all legal entitlements. What Josserand calls 'egotistic' rights are not really individual interests brought within the sphere of legal protection but ways in which the law uses the mechanism of selfish passions to realise the objective purpose of sponsoring the stability and aggrandisement of society. Instead of introducing the idea of abuse in the theory of rights, therefore, the jurists should simply abandon the notion of right. To this the advocates of abuse of right, who were social liberals, replied that,

> [w]e only have to concede that the social element that coexists in every right with the individual element tends to develop in detriment of the later; but the individual element subsists, and it is a mistake to think differently, for otherwise individual personality would be destroyed and absorbed by the great whole ...[233]

Between the polarising positions that flatly repudiated the doctrine of abuse of right, there was a continuum of rival constructions defined by the extent to which judicial interference with the individual exercise of private rights was accepted. Of course, the number of positions represented in a taxonomy depends on how many distinguishing features we are willing to consider. I am going to keep them

---

[229] For a moderate variant of this position, see Georges Ripert, 'Abus ou Relativité des Droits'.
[230] See Josserand *De l'Esprit des Droits*, 347–357.
[231] ibid, also at 10–12, 320–21.
[232] See Léon Duguit, *Les Transformations Générales du Droit Privé*, App IV, 196–202.
[233] Josserand, *De l'Esprit des Droits*, 329. But notice that Josserand equivocates on this point; his rhetoric converges with Duguit's at 419.

at a minimum. Consider the following examples of potential abuse of right, assuming that in each case the defendant is acting within right in a formal sense:

(i) B builds a high wall in his property with the sole purpose of cutting off the view of his former business associate and current neighbour, A, whom he resents for having tripled the company's profits after B left contentiously.

(ii) A landslide prevents C from entering his land. There is an alternative way through the land of his neighbour, D. He asks D permission to use it. D denies because he is holding a party outdoors and does not want his guests disturbed.

(iii) After a lengthy negotiation, E agrees to sell his property to F for a certain price. The deal is to be formalised a week from now. On the scheduled day, E, knowing that F made considerable expenses in reliance of the agreement, demands a higher price than they had arranged informally a week before.

In cases (i) and (ii), the issue is whether the owner abused his property rights; in case (iii), the question is whether the seller has abused his right not to contract with the buyer. The remedy for these abuses, if they are regarded as such, is an important but subsidiary question. Let us focus on the substantive aspects of the problem, and leave the remedial ones aside.

The criterion of abuse in (i) is the malicious purpose of the agent exercising a right; the position that selects malice as the only acceptable criterion of abuse is the stringiest of all, leading to a minimalist conception of abuse of right. Next comes the notion, illustrated by (ii), that there is abuse not only when the right is exercised in a malicious spirit but also when it is used to further an interest that must be regarded, under the circumstances, as frivolous. The key idea here is that only a serious interest can justify the exercise of a right, even an egotistic right. Finally, in (iii) the abuse turns on the absence of a legitimate motive, that is, an interest worthy of legal protection and pursued in good faith. This is the construction to which Josserand and the vast majority of the social jurists adhered; it implies a robust conception of abuse.[234] Figure 4.2 represents the spectrum of positions.

Figure 4.2 Conceptions of rights *c* 1900

Individualism	Relativism (abuse of right)			Collectivism
Rights are absolute	Malicious purpose	Frivolous interest	Legitimate motive	Rights are fictions

It should be clear that the entire construction of abuse of right is thoroughly social in both substance and method. Three remarks are in order. First, the idea that there is an important distinction between the formal and the teleological limits of rights, and that the latter are the governing criteria in legal argument,

[234] Josserand, *De l'Esprit des Droits*, 400–10.

illustrates the general approach of teleological jurisprudence. Second, the notion that increasing social complexity and interdependence calls for broader limitations on the exercise of private rights than those established within the will theory reverberates the general agenda of 'socialisation' of private law. Finally, the mediation between subjective and objective elements, or individualist and collectivist tendencies, embodied in the partnership of the concepts of right and abuse, exemplifies rather eloquently the political animus of social liberalism. I am tempted to go even further: given the exceedingly broad scope of the doctrine of abuse of right – it is prima facie applicable to any legal right, and particularly to what Josserand called 'egotistic right' – it may well be regarded as the paradigm of social jurisprudence.

5

The Politicisation of Private Law

I. On 'Legal Realism'

The politicisation of private law is, for the most part, a legacy of 'legal realism', just as the socialisation of private law was a legacy of the social jurists or the *juristes inquiets*. But I will use the labels 'legal realism' and 'legal realists' in a particular and unusual sense that requires explanation. There are numerous reasons to think that this preliminary exercise is important. I shall mention those that strike me as most pressing.

First, unlike 'the classical jurists' or 'the social jurists', the phrase 'legal realists' does not ordinarily denote a generation of jurists but rather two specific and distinct jurisprudential movements that flourished in the first half of the twentieth century, one in Scandinavia and the other in the United States. Only the latter is of interest to us. That does not, however, dissipate the ambiguity created by using the label to characterise the protagonists of a moment in the drama of liberal legalism.[1]

Second, while there is a large body of literature claiming that the American Realists formed not just a movement but also a school of thought united around a core set of claims[2] – or, in the strongest version, a single 'core claim'[3] – there is controversy about just what those claims are supposed to be. Any synthesis of realist ideas is hence destined to be regarded as another attempt to set the record straight, at best a fresh contribution to the ongoing controversy and at worst flogging of a dead horse.

---

[1] On the character of American Legal Realism as a movement rather than a theory or a school of thought, see: Morton Horwitz, *The Transformation of American Law, 1870–1960*, 169–70; John Henry Schlegel, *American Legal Realism and Empirical Social Science*, 4–13; Neil Duxbury, *Patterns of American Jurisprudence*, 65. For a critique, see Brian Leiter, 'Rethinking Legal Realism', 269–70. Karl Llewellyn was of the same view: 'One thing is clear. There is no school of realists. There is no likelihood that there will be such a school. [...] There is, however, a *movement* in thought and work about law. [...] They differ among themselves well-nigh as much as any of them differs from, say, Langdell.' Llewellyn, 'Some Realism About Realism', 1233–34 (emphasis in the original).

[2] See, eg, Leiter, ibid; Laura Kalman, *Legal Realism at Yale*; Joseph Singer, 'Legal Realism Now'; William Fisher III et al, 'Introduction'; Duncan Kennedy, *A Critique of Adjudication*, 82–92. Horwitz himself, after writing that 'Legal Realism was neither a coherent intellectual movement nor a consistent or systematic jurisprudence' devotes an entire chapter to the task of articulating what is undoubtedly something very close to a systematic realist jurisprudence. See Horwitz, *The Transformation of American Law, 1870–1960*, 169, 193–212.

[3] Leiter, 'Rethinking Legal Realism', 268–70, 275–79.

Third, 'Realism' was an episode in the legal history of the United States, far-reaching in its intellectual and cultural consequences – captured by the oft-repeat slogan 'we are all realists now' – but largely derived from the work of a small group of law professors at Columbia and Yale in the 1920s and 1930s. In my account, however, 'legal realism' was a transatlantic enterprise, no doubt more strongly rooted and developed in the United States than anywhere else, but only in the sense in which the leading roles in the formation and dissemination of the classical and social modes of legal thought were played, respectively, by German and French jurists. In other words, I reject the thesis of American exceptionalism.

Fourth, it is almost certain that the set of arguments that I call 'legal realism' was not held in its entirety by any American or European jurist in the inter-war era; sometimes this results from the range of interests of the jurist in question, but it also happens that some jurists are simultaneously realist in some respects and pre-realist or even anti-realist in others. The reader will quickly discern (and no doubt puzzle about the fact) that I am not in the least bothered by that.

Fifth, legal realism figures in the drama of liberal legalism as a post-social moment. Yet, was it not classical legal thought that legal realism, according to most accounts, sought to 'discredit and displace'?[4] True, there was some tension going on between sociological jurisprudence and legal realism, illustrated and indeed largely concocted by the well-known Pound–Llewellyn controversy.[5] But that appears to have been little more than a family quarrel, compared to Felix Cohen's brutal critique of conceptualism,[6] Robert Hale's devastating assault on negative liberty,[7] Jerome Frank's vicious attacks on 'Bealism',[8] and Karl Llewellyn's unfavourable account of 'formal style' adjudication.[9]

These five points challenge me to explain what I mean by 'legal realism', and why I have picked the label. Once I have given my best effort to answer the first of these questions, I shall briefly explain why the label is not as grossly inappropriate as it may seem at first blush. So what do I mean by 'legal realism'? I shall try to answer in three points.

(1) *An intellectual construct.* What I call 'legal realism' is not the movement 'American Legal Realism', but a set of ideas that hangs together in the drama of liberal legalism. It follows that, as John Henry Schlegel notes, 'Membership in the group seen as comprising "*the* Realists" is thus derivative of the selection of texts seen as classic by a given scholar …'[10] Schlegel is gracious to note that

---

[4] William Fisher III et al, 'Introduction', xi.
[5] See Karl Llewellyn, 'A Realistic Jurisprudence – The Next Step'; Roscoe Pound, 'The Call for a Realist Jurisprudence'; Llewellyn, 'Some Realism About Realism – Responding to Dean Pound'. For a summary of the controversy, see Horwitz, *The Transformation of American Law, 1870–1960*, 172–80.
[6] Cohen, 'Transcendental Nonsense and the Functional Approach'.
[7] See, eg, Hale, 'Coercion and Distribution in a Supposedly Non-Coercive State'.
[8] Frank, *Law and the Modern Mind*, 53–61.
[9] Llewellyn, *The Common Law Tradition*, 38–41.
[10] Schlegel, *American Legal Realism and Empirical Social Science*, 4 (emphasis in the original).

'there is nothing wrong with jurisprudes discussing Realism as jurisprudence [and, I should add, political theory as well], timeless answers to timeless questions'.[11] His point is that we should keep the two tasks – the theoretical and the historical – well apart. I think that the point is valid, and holds equally for the distinction, within the field of intellectual history broadly understood, between a history of authors, movements, currents, and the like, of the sort that is characteristic of contemporary legal historiography, and a philosophical history that gives pride of place to ideas with social currency. Moreover, since it is the ideas or the theory and not the movement as such that interests us, there is no reason to consider exclusively American sources; what makes a particular text or argument realist is the fact that it contributes or enriches the theoretical corpus of 'legal realism', and that criterion encourages us to take seriously the realist pedigree of a small but important number of European sources in the inter-war period.

(2) *Decentering the author*. The concern with sources and authors can steer us in the wrong direction. My account is not author-centred but idea-centred. No single author is likely to have ever subscribed to the entire set of propositions that I bring together under the label 'legal realism' (indeed, there is none to the best of my knowledge), and in some cases the same author is both an important contributor to one strand of realist thought and a staunch opponent to another. Thus, the German jurist Philipp Heck, the leading figure of *Interessenjurisprudenz*, was both one of founders of what Duncan Kennedy has aptly called the 'conflicting considerations model' of law-making, a key idea in legal realism as I shall understand it, and a staunch advocate of the view that in the event of a gap the judge does not have to weight or balance conflicting considerations – that is, answer what Holmes called 'legislative questions'[12] – but can (and should) replicate in the unregulated case the balancing judgement embodied in the rules applicable to cases in the vicinity by means of an interpretive procedure dubbed 'historical investigation of interests'.[13] Morris Cohen is another example, both an important source of the realist critique of the private/public distinction and a critic of the 'nihilistic absolutism'[14] of the realist thesis that legal reasoning in appellate-level cases usually operates as a smokescreen for decisions either reached on policy grounds[15] or based on the hunch of the judge.[16] Legal realism, then, does not hold together because it was articulated by a single author or a group

---

[11] ibid.
[12] See Oliver Wendell Holmes, 'Privilege, Malice, and Intent', 3, 9; Holmes, 'The Path of the Law', 998, 999.
[13] See Heck, 'Gesetzesauslegung und Interessenjurisprudenz', §§2, 6, 16. For a summary statement, see ibid, 'The Formation of Concepts and the Jurisprudence of Interests', 178–84.
[14] Morris Cohen, 'On Absolutisms in Legal Thought', 690–93.
[15] See Herman Oliphant, 'A Return to Stare Decisis'; Karl Llewellyn, *The Common Law Tradition*, 72–95, 123–31.
[16] See Joseph Hutcheson, 'The Judgment Intuitive'; Jerome Frank, *Law and the Modern Mind*, 108–26.

of authors – that is, because it was someone's theory – but because the various propositions constituting it fit together. I am not saying that the authors do not matter or that the ideas cannot be traced back or linked to sources. Legal realism is not a theoretical fiction; it was a real intellectual entity, grounded in texts, endowed with social currency, and leaving a large legacy in our legal culture. What I mean is that it emerged from the work of not one but many jurists, and that these jurists did not work in concert, executing through division of labour some master jurisprudential plan.

(3) *Focusing on effects*. I still have to deal with the objection that the 'legal realists' – certainly the American Realists – did not, at least for the most part, set themselves to debunk the work of the social jurists but the will theory and the legal formalism of the classical jurists. In the United States, for instance, the realists shared with Sociological Jurisprudence the agenda of debunking the *Lochner*-era case law that held important pieces of labour legislation and economic regulation incompatible with freedom of contract, understood as a liberty interest protected by the 'substantive due process clause' of the United States Constitution. Moreover, it is simply not true that the legal realists, and particularly the American Realists, sought to politicise private law; even those who argued that judicial decisions at the appellate level cannot be explained in terms of legal doctrine fell short of acknowledging the 'shadow of ideology'[17] in the policy or personal factors on which those decisions, on their account, really turned. Yet, from the standpoint of the drama of liberal legalism, it does not matter what the realists were aiming to do with their arguments; it matters what sort of arguments they put forward. The arguments not only did irreparable damage to classical private law but also to the reform programme sponsored by the social jurists. The point, a consequence of the idea-centred nature of the enterprise, is that although that may not have been the immediate aim of the realists, their arguments had the effect of undermining a good deal of the substantive and methodological agenda of the social jurists – and, most importantly, paved away for the politicisation or private law.

I hope to have clarified what I mean by 'legal realism'. The reason I chose that particular label is partly negative and partly positive. To begin with, no better alternative suggests itself. It is also the case that many of the arguments that figure in the rest of this chapter were articulated in their best form by writers associated with American Legal Realism. The phrase 'legal realism', used in the context of the drama of liberal legalism, is hence a tribute to the originality and significance of the Columbia and Yale scholars of the 1930s.[18]

---

[17] Duncan Kennedy, 'From the Will Theory to the Principle of Private Autonomy', 105–06.

[18] The international reputation of American Legal Realism was damaged by two principal factors: (i) the tendency to (mis)read the arguments of the American Realists as variations – sometimes implausible in their alleged radicalism – of the claims of European social jurists such as Jhering and Gény;

II. The Collapse of Private/Public

The first realist argument that we shall consider is that the private/public distinction is untenable. It was developed most convincingly in the work of Robert Hale.[19] To understand its significance, we need to examine briefly the role that the private/public distinction played in the classical and social conceptions of law. That is no easy task, for as Kelsen rightly remarked, the opposition between the private and the public spheres, governed respectively by private and public law, is both ubiquitous and obscure;[20] indeed, the main thrust of the realist critique is that the distinction makes no sense. But the fact that it is pervasive even nowadays suggests that it is deeply rooted in a picture of the social world that, albeit gravely flawed, is widely shared by jurists and non-jurists alike. The picture displays the government injecting coercion into a coercion-free civil society.[21] It conveys the thought that there is, above a threshold that we may call the state-enforced private law baseline, an inverse relationship between individual freedom and government intervention; that is, every instance of state activity beyond that required to enforce property rights and private bargains increases the overall level of coercion and implies a corresponding loss of individual freedom.

The distinction between the private law baseline and other forms of government activity is a legacy of classical liberalism. That there is coercion involved in the enforcement of property and contract rights, indeed that the effectiveness of such rights depend on state-administered coercion, was of course acknowledged by the classical jurists. But they held that it was coercion of a uniquely benign sort, for it enabled the substitution of civil or juridical freedom for what Kant called 'wild' or 'lawless' freedom.[22] When the law protects property rights, it is giving everyone assurances that they can enjoy their land and other assets without fear of forceful or fraudulent dispossession; when it enforces contracts, it is carrying out the will of the parties to be bound by their agreements; a good deal of tort and criminal law was understood by the classical jurists to be instrumental in deterring or correcting invasions of personal and property rights; all remaining forms of private activity were regarded as privileged, that is, within the broad range of natural liberty retained in civil society; and the institutions of public law required to support this structure – notably, police force and a court system – were, so long

---

and (ii) among the jurisprudentially literate, the caricature of American Legal Realism presented and debunked by HLA Hart, *The Concept of Law*, 141–47. I agree with Brian Leiter, 'Legal Realism and Legal Positivism Reconsidered', 278–80, 290–300, that Hart errs both in taking Legal Realism to be an account of the nature of law, as opposed to an account of (appellate-level) adjudication, and in dismissing the views of the American Realists on legal indeterminacy without the support of anything even resembling a careful argument.

[19] Hale's arguments were partly anticipated by Max Weber, first, and then by Hans Kelsen. See Weber, *Economy and Society*, 729–31; Kelsen, *Pure Theory of Law*, 280–84.

[20] Kelsen, ibid at 280.

[21] Barbara Fried, *The Progressive Assault on Laissez Faire*, 9, 36.

[22] Immanuel Kant, 'Perpetual Peace', 78 (Ak 8:354).

as they were kept at the minimum size necessary to accomplish the task, part of the package that did not curb but in fact secured individual freedom.

Beyond the private law threshold were the many laws and institutions that restricted individual freedom, such as zoning regulations, administrative licences, protective tariffs, redistributive taxes, public relief for the poor, criminal and tort rules safeguarding 'good morals', public education and other means of 'popular cultivation', and many other manifestations of the 'police power' of the state.[23] That these were inroads into individual freedom did not mean that they were necessarily bad or unjustified; that was the position of Herbert Spencer and a few other fanatics of laissez faire, not of classical liberalism at large. Kant, for one, argued for 'taxes to support organizations providing for the poor, foundling homes, and church organizations ...';[24] and Savigny likewise wrote about the 'institutions for the relief of the poor to which of course the rich man can be compelled to contribute'.[25] On matters of economic policy, John Stuart Mill produced a long list of justified exceptions to the rule of non-intervention.[26] But the classical liberals also believed that these forms of state action were qualitatively different from those required to establish the private law baseline. They did not trade insecure for secure freedom – a positive sum gain – but public welfare for individual freedom. Moreover, the question of how much damage to individual freedom should be done in the name of public welfare was seen by them as requiring a series of ad hoc judgements, at once controversial and firmly within the public law discretion of the sovereign.[27]

The social jurists and other reformists of a liberal persuasion – 'liberal socialist', 'new liberal', or 'social democratic'[28] – amended but did not abandon this framework. They challenged the classical dichotomy between the private and the public spheres, arguing that a good deal of state intervention was directed not at promoting a vague goal of 'public welfare' but at correcting the injustice and deprivation of freedom generated by the private law baseline. The point of regulating the terms of labour contracts or instituting workers compensation schemes was not to trade individual freedom for public welfare, but to correct the imbalance of freedom as

---

[23] On the genealogy of the term 'police power', namely its connection with enlightened absolutism, see Guido Astuti, *La Formazione dello Stato Moderno in Italia*, 177–82, 187–205; Peter H Wilson, *Absolutism in Central Europe*, 108–21.

[24] Kant, *The Metaphysics of Morals*, 101 (Ak 6:326).

[25] Friedrich Carl von Savigny, *System of the Modern Roman Law*, I, 302.

[26] Mill, *Principles of Political Economy*, Bk V, ch 11 ('Of the Grounds and Limits of the Laisser-faire or Non-Interference Principle').

[27] The United States was exceptional in this respect, since in the nineteenth century the police power of both state and federal governments was limited by constitutional law and subject to judicial oversight. This was made possible by the existence of a written constitution, the birth of judicial review of legislation, and reading the will theory into the 'due process' and 'equal protection' clauses. See Edward S Corwin, 'The 'Higher Law' Background of American Constitutional Law', 409. See also James B Thayer, *The Origin and Scope of the American Doctrine of Constitutional Law*.

[28] On liberal progressivism in the United States and Great Britain in the late nineteenth century, see Barbara Fried, *The Progressive Assault on Laissez Faire*, 34–44.

between employer and employee. On the other hand, the social jurists accepted the classical notion that above the private law threshold state action begins to curb liberty or acquires a compulsory character. In other words, social legislation – they stated – both enhances and sacrifices freedom.

That statement was not contradictory because the social liberals distinguished between 'negative' and 'positive' freedom. Freedom meant two different things: to be free from state-sponsored coercion (negative freedom) and to have effective means or opportunities for self-assertion (positive freedom).[29] The more protected positive freedom is, the less negative freedom individuals enjoy; and since the path of progress dictated the increasing complexity, interdependence, and asymmetry of social relations, the regulatory burden on the individual for the sake of positive freedom tended to grow, shrinking the sphere of negative freedom.[30] Instead of a private/public dichotomy, then, the social liberals were committed to what one might call a *gradient* conception of coercion. On their view, there was no sharp discontinuity between the private law baseline and other forms of state activity; political compulsion, or what Jhering called 'the pressure of the law upon the individual',[31] increased gradually as the government moved from the enforcement of private bargains to policing the fairness of their terms, and from there to core areas of police activity such income taxation, administrative regulation and state-run enterprise.

The question was how to find the right point in the gradient at each moment in history, that is, how to settle the conflict between negative and positive freedom – between liberty and equality. The view of the social liberals was not that the conflict was to be settled by a balancing judgement, of the sort that was required to address the classical conflict between individual freedom and public welfare. They argued that positive freedom trumps negative, that an increase in coercive pressure upon the citizenry in order to level the playing field, or 'to equalize the conditions of struggle among rival activities',[32] is always justified. But that requires one to be able to show that there is some imbalance that needs to be corrected; the burden of proof lies with the pro-regulatory voice. In other words, while positive prevails over negative freedom in the event of a conflict, a (rebuttable) presumption of no conflict works in favour of conserving the private law regime. As a result of this complex framework, the will theory was maintained by the social jurists as the natural baseline against which any proposal of social

---

[29] In using these qualifications of freedom – 'negative' and 'positive' – they were appropriating and utterly disfiguring terms coined by Kant and Hegel; whereas to the latter the difference between negative and positive freedom is the difference between unrestrained choice and rationally constrained choice, the social liberals meant to distinguish two senses of unrestrained choice: freedom from state compulsion and state-sponsored capacity to choose.
[30] See Rudolf von Jhering, *Law as Means to an End*, 398–409.
[31] ibid at 381.
[32] Gény, *Méthode d'Interprétation et Sources en Droit Privé Positif*, II, 226.

reform would have to prove itself.³³ As a historian of late-nineteenth-century politics puts it:

> [T]he rhetorical trope that less state action should be the rule to which one recognized exceptions only as necessary was widely adopted by more progressive liberals as well [as advocates of Laissez Faire], although (not surprisingly) they tended to find necessity with far more frequency than did their individualist counterparts.³⁴

What Hale set out to do was to collapse the distinction between the private and the public spheres, freedom and coercion, or negative (state-free) and positive (state-sponsored) freedom. His claim was that the concept of negative freedom – freedom from coercion – makes no sense in civil society or social life under a government. The freedom granted by private law is no less positive or state-sponsored than the freedom granted by a more robustly regulatory regime. The difference is not the presence or absence of coercion but the distribution of ubiquitous 'weapons of coercion'³⁵ among different groups seeking scarce means to further their rival ends, that is, engaged in what Holmes called the 'struggle for life'.³⁶ He writes: 'What is the government doing when it "protects a property right"? Passively, it is abstaining from interference with the owner when he deals with the thing owned; actively, it is forcing the non-owner to desist from handling it, unless the owner consents.'³⁷

The owner manages to exclude the non-owner from struggling with him over the control of the resource because he may summon the government to enforce his right; his freedom to enjoy the resource is hence based on the coercive weapon supplied by the law – not freedom from state intervention but *through* it. More important even, as Hale recognises, is the fact that the law confers upon the owner the power to lift the ban on the non-owner. Such a power enables the owner to coerce the non-owner to accept his terms for using the resource in direct proportion to the non-owner's economic vulnerability. Imagine that the non-owner is a moneyless worker: 'what would be the consequence of refusal to comply with the owner's terms?'

> It would be either absence of wages, or obedience to the terms of some other employer. If the worker has no money of his own, the threat of any particular employer to withhold any particular amount of money would be effective in securing the worker's obedience in proportion to the difficulty with which other employers can be induced to furnish a 'job'.³⁸

---

³³ Holmes, *The Common Law*, 96, expressed the point as follows: 'The prevailing view is that [the] cumbrous and expensive machinery [of the state] ought not to be set in motion unless some clear benefit is derived from disturbing the *status quo*. State interference is an evil, where it cannot be shown to be a good'.
³⁴ Barbara Fried, *The Progressive Assault on Laissez Faire*, 30.
³⁵ Hale, 'Bargaining, Duress, and Economic Liberty', 609.
³⁶ See *Vegelahn v Guntner*, 167 Mass 92, 138 (1986).
³⁷ Hale, 'Coercion and Distribution in a Supposedly Non-Coercive State', 471.
³⁸ ibid at 472.

There are two points here. One is that the 'voluntary' transaction between employer and employee develops against the background of the parties' threats to withhold the resource – eg, capital or labour-power – that the other party wants. The threat is credible because the law delegates the power to control the resource to its owner and the government may be called at any time to enforce such delegation.[39] The second point is that although both parties have coercive weapons they are not on an equal footing. Since their bargaining power is largely determined by the relative scarcity of what they have to offer and the relative urgency of their needs, the unskilled worker who needs money for food and shelter is typically in the more vulnerable position: 'It is with … unequal rights that men bargain and exert pressure on one another. These rights give birth to the unequal fruits of bargaining'.[40]

At first sight, none of these points appears to be particularly original or to have much critical bite. The first point was acknowledged by the classical liberals, at least by the most progressive of them, who readily conceded that property and contract involve coercion. The second point was central to the social critique of the 'juridical fiction' of equality among individuals under the will theory of private law. So what is new in Hale's argument? It is the idea that addressing these inequalities does not imply any reduction of freedom but a mere redistribution of coercive weapons from high-income to low-income groups. Since under the private law regime the distribution of income is already sponsored by the state through its readiness to enforce legal rights, the question that arises when the shift to a more egalitarian regime is envisioned it not whether the gains in equality compensate the sacrifice of freedom but which of the two regimes yields a distribution of freedom that may be regarded as just.[41] Negative freedom is not lost simply because any legal regime, including private law, is *necessarily* a regime of positive or state-sponsored freedom. Even when the state nominally abstains from regulating social intercourse, it is for all intents and purposes distributing 'coercive weapons' that structure private bargains. Thus, by failing to regulate (within certain limits) competition among firms in the marketplace, the law both exempts the incoming firm from compensating the established business for the losses caused by competitive struggle and makes it theoretically possible for the former to exact a premium from the later to stay out of business.[42] Indeed, the active role of the state in constituting pockets of so-called 'natural liberty' is more visible than it is ordinarily assumed: the privilege of the defendant to harm the plaintiff is backed by the prospects both of a court decision denying the plaintiff cause of action and of a summoning of state force to repel unlawful acts undertaken by the plaintiff in

---

[39] See Morris Cohen, 'Property and Sovereignty', 11–14. For the same point with respect to the power to make contracts, see Cohen, 'The Basis of Contract', 585–86.
[40] Hale, 'Bargaining, Duress, and Economic Liberty', 628.
[41] See Barbara Fried, *The Progressive Assault on Laissez Faire*, 46.
[42] See Ronald H Coase, 'The Problem of Social Cost'. Of course, in a world where transactions are costless, the firm threatened by competition cannot buy out those who ultimately gain from competitive advantages, namely consumers, since these necessarily outweigh the former.

self-help.⁴³ All talk of freedom versus coercion is hence incoherent – freedom in civil society is *saturated* with coercion.

Suppose that the legislature passes a statute prohibiting 'yellow-dog' contracts, permitting unions to picket, and allowing secondary boycotts within certain limits. The state is not injecting coercion in employment relations but transferring to the employees some of the coercive weapons previously assigned to employers – the threat of unemployment unless the worker accepts 'yellow-dog' terms, the right to summon police force to repel a picket, and the right to an injunction against a secondary boycott. The effect of these changes, other things being equal, is an increase of the bargaining strength of labour vis-à-vis capital proportional to the economic impact of the threats to withhold labour made possible by the new legislation.⁴⁴ 'Income is the price paid for not using one's coercive weapons',⁴⁵ and the more numerous and effective such weapons are, the larger is the income of those in their possession.

Still, there seems to be an important difference between the form of coercion that structures private interactions and the coercion involved in citizen–state relations, such as the duty to pay taxes. European jurists, for instance, classify labour and consumer protection law under private law and environmental regulation and tax law under public law, because the latter involves the exercise of state power – its *jus imperii*. But while there may be something to this distinction, private and public action is practically virtually indistinguishable. First, the power of the tax authority to exact payment from taxpayers is not substantially different from the power of the owner to set the terms for third-party use of his property, particularly when the latter functions in a regime of natural or legal monopoly and meets basic needs.⁴⁶ Second, both the tax authority and the owner can call on the courts to enforce their decisions; it is true that in the continental tradition, especially that of French influence, administrative authority is generally endowed with the privilege of authoritative decision-making (*privilège du préalable*) and with the related privilege of enforcing its own decisions (*privilège de l'éxecution*);⁴⁷ but even these

---

⁴³ Wesley Hohfeld, 'Some Fundamental Legal Conceptions as Applied in Judicial Reasoning', 42 (fn 59), puts the point analytically: 'It is difficult to see ... why, as between X and Y, the 'privilege + no-right' situation is not just as real a jural relation as the precisely opposite 'duty + right' relation between any two parties. Perhaps the habit ... springs ... from the traditional tendency to think of law as consisting of 'commands,' or imperative rules. This, however, seems fallacious. A rule of law that permits is just as real as a rule of law that forbids ...'.

⁴⁴ In reality, of course, other things are never equal, and they may change for the worse, from the standpoint of those who nominally benefit from the new legal regime, due to what Duncan Kennedy calls 'circular causation and unstable equilibrium' and the 'instability of the legal framework', ie, both causal and legal indeterminacy. But of course these factors may also operate to magnify instead of reducing or eliminating the impact of the new regime. See Kennedy, 'The Stakes of Law', 334–37.

⁴⁵ Hale, 'Coercion and Distribution in a Supposedly Non-Coercive State', 478.

⁴⁶ As Morris Cohen, 'Property and Sovereignty', 13, put it: 'we must not overlook the fact that dominion over things is also *imperium* over our fellow human beings'.

⁴⁷ This means that the decisions of executive authority do not have to be recognised by a court to be enforceable (that is the privilege of authoritative decision-making) and that they may be enforced by the executive itself even if they are contested in court (that is the privilege of prior execution).

distinctive public law privileges, which are in any case typical only of so-called 'systems of executive administration',[48] turn out to be curtailed by significant exceptions and to have noteworthy private law analogues.[49] Finally, while it may appear that subjection to public authority is unconditional, as one has no option but to pay taxes or abide by an officer's orders, whereas private action is at least nominally voluntary, since no one is legally forced to enter a contract or to use another person's property, the distinction is largely based on a misperception. Hale pointed to the oft-overlooked fact that public command is typically conditional: 'When the government, for instance, levies a thirty cent tax on a $3.00 theatre ticket, a person is not literally compelled to pay either the tax or the price. He always has the option of not attending the theatre'.[50] Public command, in other words, normally operates through the medium of credible threats to withhold valuable resources, such as a theatre seat or, in the case of income taxes, a certain level of income. In many cases, it is practically indistinguishable, for instance, from the threat of the owner to withhold his property from the non-owner.

Yet, even if one could draw a discernible line between the concepts of private and public activity, it would have no immediate *normative* bite. Considered in isolation, the power to tax the income of a wealthy person may be somehow more coercive than the latter's power to 'tax' the use of his property.[51] But that is hardly the end of the story, as far as Hale is concerned. We must consider not just the character of the act but its effects on the distribution of freedom across society. If the government uses the revenue to fund unemployment subsidies, it is both directly improving the condition of unemployed workers and giving them a coercive weapon in labour bargains in the form of a threat to remain unemployed and benefit from the subsidy. In the background of this one decision sit the hundreds of property, contract, tort and other private law rules that structure the bargains from which the present pattern of (unequal) income distribution emerged. Considered functionally or in its effects, the tax merely transfers a fraction of the freedom of high-to-low-income earners – it is another building block in the 'system of *Machtoekonomie*'.[52] From a normative standpoint, therefore, what matters is not the coercive intensity of discrete acts but the *systemic* effects of the current set of legal arrangements on the 'struggle for life'.[53]

---

[48] According to a famous classification – systems of 'executive' versus systems of 'judicial' administration – by the French public lawyer Maurice Hauriou, *Précis de Droit Administratif et de Droit Public*, 2.

[49] Certain types of private law titles, such as written contracts and negotiable instruments, are enforceable regardless of judicial recognition and exceptionally self-help is permitted in private law. So even if valid in systems of 'executive' admnistration, the distinction is one of degree as opposed to kind.

[50] Hale, 'Our Equivocal Constitutional Guarantees', 565–66.

[51] Tax lawyers find it increasingly difficult to distinguish commercial prices from administrative fees – see, eg, Carlos Palao Taboada, 'Precios Publicos', 454. As usual, Holmes was ahead of his time: see 'The Path of the Law', 994.

[52] ibid, 'Law-Making by Unofficial Minorities', 455.

[53] This is precisely what led John Rawls to the view that the proper subject of political theory, or at least of the theory of social justice, is not the state but the 'basic structure of society'. See Rawls,

It is worth stressing the originality of Hale's analysis. Among the collectivist strand of social jurisprudence, represented by writers such as Duguit and Gounot, there was a critique of the private/public distinction, but it took a form very different from that exhibited in Hale's work. They argued that the law confers rights on individuals for the sole purpose of having them discharge some socially important function; on this view, property and contract rights are instruments of public policy, subtle alternatives to the promotion of the common good through the official channels of activity.[54] Hale's writings bear no trace of that conception. On the contrary, he virtually never invokes the 'common good' or the 'public interest', taking standard public law institutions such as income taxation and welfare policy as mechanisms through which the relative freedom of some groups is increased at the expense of others. His account is radically adversarial. In any legal regime, Hale sees the distribution of 'coercive weapons' among people with rival ends struggling for common means.[55] His achievement was to bring down the private/public distinction from the angle of individual freedom. That is what earns him an important place in the history of liberalism.[56]

True, nothing in his argument gives us even the slightest hint as to what sort of legal regime is justified, and indeed Hale is generally evasive about his policy commitments.[57] As Barbara Fried notes:

> Nothing logically followed from that change in Hale's view, beyond the all-important conclusion for Hale's contemporaries that most legal questions were questions of policy for the legislature, not matters of constitutional rights for the courts. How legislatures ought to resolve them was, of course, another matter, and one on which Hale's skeptical, deconstructive analysis offered little guidance.[58]

But the 'deconstructive analysis' does yield one important normative consequence. The basic insight that the concept of freedom-from-coercion is incoherent, once civil society gets going, disabled completely the presumption in favour of private law, a presumption that the social jurists not only honored but indeed revered.[59]

A Theory of Justice, 7–11, 274–83; Rawls, *Political Liberalism*, 255–85. Compare Robert Nozick, *Anarchy, State, and Utopia*, 3–6.

[54] See, eg, Léon Duguit, *Les Transformations Générales du Droit Privé*. Morris Cohen, a careful student of European jurisprudence (see his 'Recent Legal-Philosophical Literature in French, German and Italian'), came on occasion very close to asserting the position of Duguit and other social jurists of a collectivist persuasion. See Cohen, 'Property and Sovereignty', 27–30 (discussing reasons of public policy for private property); ibid, 'The Basis of Contract', 586–87 (drawing an analogy between the parties to a contract and public officials).

[55] See Hale, 'Coercion and Distribution in a Supposedly Non-Coercive State', 478.

[56] See Barbara Fried, *The Progressive Assault on Laissez Faire*, 22–23.

[57] See, eg, Hale, 'Bargaining, Duress, and Economic Liberty', 628.

[58] Barbara Fried, *The Progressive Assault on Laissez Faire*, 210.

[59] Brian Leiter, 'Rethinking Legal Realism', 272–73, charges CLS writers with the mistake of deriving from Hale's argument the corollary that 'government action [in the 'public'] realm is normatively indistinguishable from government action in the 'private' realm'. No CLS writers that I am aware of claim(ed) anything of the sort – and, of course, if any did, they committed a fallacy. The argument is not that Hale showed the absence of any normative reasons to insulate the 'private realm' from reform

Freedom of contract and private property lost their status as the fundamental liberal institutions, and the prima facie injustice of legislative and administrative interference with private transactions was discredited. In other words, public law now threatened to occupy a great deal of the territory traditionally assigned to private law. The reverberations are notorious in contemporary liberal political theory. As Thomas Grey remarks in a classic article, pointing to John Rawls' *A Theory of Justice* as an example of a general trend: 'The concept of property rights plays only the most minor role in that monumental treatise, which on the whole displays a welfare state liberal orientation towards questions of the organization of economic life'.[60] The declining significance of private law – the law of the jurists – and the emerging notion that 'most legal questions were questions of policy for the legislature' threatened the alliance between liberalism and legalism. In the next section, we turn to a different type of threat to private law, aimed not at its significance, but at its *coherence*.

III. Conflicting Considerations

In both its classical and social incarnations, liberalism presents itself as a conception of justice. The question of what sort of content legal regimes ought to have is answered by reference to a political theory that articulates the mainstream liberal view of that period. One such conception – the classical – was the will theory, according to which justice is 'the sum of the conditions under which the choice of one can be united with the choice of another in accordance with a universal law of freedom'.[61] From our post-realist standpoint, this proposition appears to have very little operative content. Yet, for Kant and those who followed in his footsteps, it is the foundational premise of a theory about how human beings can live together as equals, and it furnishes a critical standard against which to measure the justice of positive law. No controversy can therefore arise about what terms of collective life are appropriate, except in the limited domain of issues that are either beyond

---

but that he undermined one highly influential reason, namely that the 'private' realm is privileged because 'public' interference necessarily reduces negative freedom. More generally, the argument is that the coercion exerted through private law often goes unacknowledged, with the effect that the state-sponsored baseline of contract and property is fetishised. Duncan Kennedy, 'The Stakes of Law', is generally representative of that view. Thus, income and property taxation is conventionally understood as a restriction of individual freedom and a taking of personal assets as opposed to an element of the basic structure that comprises the property and contract rules through which income is earned and property acquired. As Liam Murphy and Thomas Nagel, *The Myth of Ownership*, 8, write: 'Private property is a legal convention, defined in part by the tax system; therefore, the tax system cannot be evaluated by looking at its impact on private property, conceived as something that has independent existence and validity. Taxes must be conceived as part of the overall system of property rights that they help to create. Justice and injustice in taxation can only mean justice or injustice in the system of property rights and entitlements that result from a particular tax regime'.

[60] Grey, 'The Disintegration of Property', 81.
[61] Kant, *The Metaphysics of Morals*, 24 (Ak 6:230).

rational discussion or require ad hoc or circumstantial judgment, matters which classical liberalism assigned to the government.

The transition from classical to social liberalism proceeded from the premise that the will theory had once been correct, and that the task ahead was to reform the law in which it was embodied in light of the new social circumstances of the early twentieth century. The reforms proposed were often substantial, but they were presented as means of fulfillment, in the social conditions of the day, of *teloi* inchoate in the classical conception. In all of this, social liberalism displayed a confidence similar to that of the will theorists that substantive issues of justice were above reasonable controversy or any notion of compromise of values. This is what with propriety has been called 'social conceptualism',[62] so long as we add the important rider that in the social mode the connection between particular norms and regimes and the governing *teloi* or principles is not logical but functional: a norm is correct if it yields the desirable outcome, that is, if it is a means suitable to its end.

One of the themes of legal realism was that the progression from abstract normative commitments, such as 'liberal justice' or 'equal freedom', to particular regimes is not linear and objective but convoluted and controversial. In order to determine the content of a particular area of the law, a law-maker committed to liberal values is required to balance conflicting considerations.[63] Thus, the question of whether the press in a liberal society should be allowed to publish material that is offensive to and incenses a religious minority involves a conflict between at least two sets of prima facie valid considerations – freedom of the press and social inclusion – the relative strength of which in the circumstances is difficult to assess and open to controversy.[64] From a realist standpoint, the balancing judgments implicit in legal regimes are often obscured either because operative norms are presented as implications of a consensual but in fact empty proposition that comprises the real alternatives on which the choice turns – eg, deciding the 'Danish cartoons' controversy by reference to 'human dignity' or 'individual freedom' – or because one of the relevant considerations is summarily suppressed. Writing in 1930, Karl Llewellyn identifies those flaws in the prescriptive homilies of the advocates of social reform:

> 'What can be done,' and by whom? I have spoken of law as a means: whose means, to whose end? Discussions of law, like discussions of 'social control,' tend a little lightly to assume 'a society' and to assume the antecedent discovery of 'social' objectives. [...] Where is the unity, the single coherent group? Where is the demonstrable objective which is social, and not opposed by groups well nigh as important as those which support it?[65]

---

[62] Karl Klare, 'The Judicial Deradicalization of the Wagner Act and the Origins of Modern Legal Counsciousness, 1937–1941', 275–81.

[63] See Kennedy, 'From the Will Theory to the Principle of Private Autonomy', 94, 104–06. See also Kennedy, 'A Transnational Genealogy of Proportionality in Private Law', 194–206.

[64] Compare Ronald Dworkin, 'The Right to Ridicule' with Heiko Henkel, 'Fundamentally Danish? The Muhammad Cartoon Controversy as Transitional Drama'.

[65] Llewellyn, 'A Realistic Jurisprudence – The Next Step', 461.

As Duncan Kennedy notices, Llewellyn nearly takes the point back in the next paragraph,[66] where he writes that 'There is, amid the welter of self-serving groups ... the recurrent emergence of some wholeness'.[67] But the quotation above reflects a mistrust of unity and linearity in normative argument that echoes what Kennedy has aptly called the 'conflicting considerations' model of law-making: 'My thesis is that the current understanding of American legal academics is that ... Every rule *can be understood* as representing a choice in the colloquial lawyers' sense of a "policy question"'.[68]

The roots of the model lie in Jhering's brief discussion, in the first volume of *The Spirit of the Roman Law*, of the perennial conflict between two sets of considerations that bear on the choice of the *form* of legal norms.[69] One set concerns the advantages of flexible standards that direct the judge to consider the equities of the case, and to decide whether applying the norm in a given case fulfils its purpose or not; this Jhering calls 'material realisability'. The other set of considerations concerns the advantages of rigid rules or on/off distinctions that in spite of being inevitably under- and over-inclusive with respect to their underlying purposes render the law more predictable and prevent miscarriages of justice; this Jhering calls 'formal realisability'. One of his examples is the choice between a rule of majority at a fixed age and a standard of maturity. To be sure, Jhering does not come any close to suggesting that one has to balance considerations of formal and material realisability, as opposed to discerning the objectively dominant set of considerations in each area of life – say, strict rules in the law of property and flexible standards in commercial law –, the typically 'social' route followed by Roscoe Pound in an essay published in 1923.[70] Yet he sowed the seeds of what was to come a generation later.

The model inchoate in Jhering's jurisprudence of form was further developed in the inter-war period independently by Philipp Heck in Germany and René Demogue in France. Heck does a better job of presenting a basic archetype of the conflicting considerations model of law-making, while Demogue supplies a wealth of doctrinal examples and reveals greater awareness of its implications.[71] The gist of Heck's 'jurisprudence of interests' (*Interessenjurisprudenz*) is encapsulated in the following passage of a translated essay summarising his views as a legal theorist:

> The fundamental truth from which we must proceed is that each command of the law determines a conflict of interests; it originates from a struggle between opposing interests, and represents as it were the resultant of these opposing forces. Protection of interests through the law never occurs in a vacuum. It operates in a world full of

---

[66] See Kennedy, 'From the Will Theory to the Principle of Private Autonomy', 122.

[67] Llewellyn, 'A Realistic Jurisprudence' at 461–62.

[68] Kennedy, 'From the Will Theory to the Principle of Private Autonomy', 94 (emphasis in the original).

[69] Jhering, *Geist des römischen Rechts*, I, §§ 3–4, ff 48–58.

[70] Pound, 'The Theory of Judicial Decision III', 951. The modern classic in the 'jurisprudence of form' in Anglo–American legal scholarship is Duncan Kennedy, 'Form and Substance in Private Law Adjudication', 1687–713.

[71] See Kennedy, 'A Transnational Genealogy of Proportionality in Private Law', 198–99.

competing interests, and, therefore, always works at the expense of some interests. This holds true without exception. [...] If we confine ourselves to an examination of the purpose of a law we see only the interest which has prevailed. But the concrete content of the legal rule, the degree in which its purpose is achieved, depends upon the weight of those interests which were vanquished.[72]

The high point in this passage is the notion that a norm is the resultant of conflicting interests, the outcome of a judgment as to their relative strength or weight in the type of case that furnishes the antecedent or 'if-clause' of the norm. The low point, quickly and thoroughly exploited by Heck's critics, is the nearly incurable ambiguity of the term 'interest'. Heck explains that 'In everyday usage "interest" connotes the significance which life values have for men, and therefore their desire for values. [...] And we use the word not only to designate material values but also ideal values'.[73] But that only deals with one – the easiest – aspect of the problem. The main complaint must be directed against Heck's failure to clarify whether he means 'interests' – both ideal and material – as the individual preferences of private actors or as impersonal reasons for and against a particular legal regime. The distinction is important because no jurist before Heck denied that personal interests clash, that it is at least partly because 'society is honeycombed with disputes'[74] that legal norms are required. It does not follow that there are conflicting considerations at play in the choice of a legal regime, since there may be a single normative criterion for settling conflicts of interest. Individual preferences may be *objects* of normative evaluation or judgement but they are not *reasons* weighted in the judgement. For the utilitarian, who may be taken to present an important exception, preferences are not reasons for or against a particular norm but data collected to calculate the 'greatest happiness for the greatest number'; for the Kantian, at the opposite end of the spectrum, interests are officially irrelevant even as data, as Kant's nominal repudiation of the doctrine of necessity fittingly illustrates.[75]

If individual preferences are what Heck means by 'interests', we are left with two alternative interpretations, none of them satisfactory. Perhaps he means, as *avant la lettre* public choice theorist, that the clash and relative strength of individual and group preferences is what causes the law to have a particular content.[76] Alternatively, Heck simply confused personal interest with value judgement so completely that his actual position is the trivial one that a legal system has to settle conflicts of interest among private actors. On this reading, Heck is merely

---

[72] Philipp Heck, 'The Jurisprudence of Interests', 35–36.
[73] ibid, 'The Formation of Concepts and the Jurisprudence of Interests', 130–31. See also, Heck, 'The Jurisprudence of Interests', 33: 'In using the word interests we must not think of material interests alone. Just as everyday usage speaks of the highest interests of mankind, of ethical and religious interests, so our school employs the term in its widest connotation, as embracing all things that man holds dear, and all ideals which guide man's life'.
[74] Karl Llewellyn, *The Bramble Bush*, 12.
[75] See Kant, *The Metaphysics of Morals*, 28 (Ak 6:236).
[76] On this 'genetic' reading of Heck, see Karl Larenz, *Methodenlehre der Rechtswissenschaft*, 51–52.

an obscure follower of teleological jurisprudence.[77] There is some (alarming) evidence that he may have meant that:

> Every legal rule delimits contradictory interests; it decides a conflict of interests. The decision is based on an evaluation of the interests involved. This evaluation rests upon a process of judging according to value ideas, and it contains therefore a value judgment. The value judgment, in its turn, goes back to a notion of a desirable social order, that is, a concrete social ideal.[78]

The other possible reading is that, for Heck, the 'value judgments' embodied in legal regimes balance conflicting reasons or considerations. It is important to avoid confusion between the personal/impersonal and the material/ideal distinctions.[79] An interest is impersonal when it is universalisable, meaning that it is 'at least formally in the interests of "everyone", by contrast with interests understood to be "ideological" … or "sectarian"'.[80] And an impersonal interest in that sense may be either ideal, such as non-discrimination or religious freedom, or material, such as economic efficiency or social security. The matrix bellow combines the two distinctions.

Figure 5.1 Types of interest

Types of interest	Personal	Impersonal
Material	Improved wages	Full employment
Ideal	Saving the soul	Freedom of speech

Thus, Heck presents us – perhaps not deliberately – with the archetype of a legal regime as the 'resultant' of conflicting considerations, that is, the embodiment of a judgement as to the relative importance or weight of competing concerns in a category of cases. In *The Fundamental Notions of Private Law*,[81] written in 1911, Demogue makes a similar claim:

> The contradictory elements frequently found in problems before us render a satisfactory solution often impossible, and throw us into a régime of concession, of compromise,

---

[77] And liable to be enlisted as a precursor of 'value-jurisprudence'. That move is attempted by Larenz, ibid at 52–53.
[78] Philipp Heck, 'The Formation of Concepts and the Jurisprudence of Interests', 134.
[79] I think Kennedy, 'A Transnational Genealogy of Proportionality in Private Law', 199, errs in this regard when he writes that 'all considerations have to be universalizable … Whereas Heck prides himself on adding ideal to material interests, the modern approach considers only ideal'. Not only can universalisable interests be either ideal or material, it is simply not true that only ideal interests figure in contemporary legal discourse. As an example, consider the so-called economic interpretation of the 'Hand Formula' in *United States v Carroll Towing Co*, 159 F.2d 169 (1947) proposed by Richard Posner, 'A Theory of Negligence'.
[80] Duncan Kennedy, ibid at 190.
[81] René Demogue, *Les Notions Fondamentales du Droit Privé*. The first, and most important for present purposes, part of Demogue's book was translated in a volume on *Modern French Legal Philosophy* in *The Modern Legal Philosophy Series*, under the title 'Analysis of Fundamental Notions'. All the citations in this section are from the version in English.

in which neither principle is too far or plainly departed from. Although not logically derived from any absolute principle, this is the only possible regime; but, open as it is to criticism, it is always very fragile.[82]

Demogue's 'notions' are a small set of considerations that underlie private law, namely security, evolution, economy of time and activity, justice, equality, liberty, solidarity and loss-spreading, general welfare, future as opposed to present interests and 'moral' (ie, psychological or emotional) as opposed to material interests. The notions come regularly into conflict and pull law-makers in opposite directions, forcing them to reach a compromise; thus, while considerations of justice count against spreading the losses from accidents caused by some actor's negligence, the notion of solidarity counts in its favour.

Perhaps Demogue's most famous example concerns the conflict between two considerations within the broad notion of security. One the one hand, the law protects dynamic security or apparent rightness: 'He who has treated with a person having every appearance of the ownership of a right should be protected'.[83] Some of Demogue's examples, drawn from French law, are the protection of the bona fide third-party purchaser of personal property; the protection of the good faith beneficiary of the acts of an agent acting in excess of his powers; and the adoption of an objectivist theory of contract in lieu of the meeting of the minds requirement. On the other hand, the law also protects static security or actual rightness: 'When a person is entitled to a right it should not be possible for him to be legally deprived of it by the act of a third person'.[84] In each of the examples just mentioned, where the law might be thought to be exclusively informed by considerations of dynamic security, static security plays an important role as well: third-party purchasers are protected as against the rightful owner, but only if the transaction concerns movables; the agent acting in excess of his powers binds the principal, but only if the third party is not to be reproached for failing to verify the agent's credentials; and objectivism trumps subjectivism in the contract-forming stage, but subjectivism re-enters the law of contracts through the back door of mistake doctrine. Demogue concludes that 'there is therefore an insoluble conflict between two conceptions of security',[85] and while the conflict is mitigated when certain devices come into play – namely, the availability of insurance and the requirement of good faith – 'there are … necessarily some cases in which the legal system and the judge cannot avoid making a choice …'.[86] This is true not only for conflicts between considerations of static and dynamic security, but also for the numerous other conflicts between the various 'fundamental notions'.

Demogue is ambiguous about the implications of all of this. He wanders between the vague images of a tragic choice among irreconcilable and opposing

---

[82] ibid, 'Analysis of Fundamental Notions', 394.
[83] ibid at 424.
[84] ibid at 428.
[85] ibid at 430.
[86] ibid at 435.

tendencies and of an 'ideal law for each state of society'[87] that furnishes the metric to weight the notions in perennial conflict. I suppose that part of it has to do with the traditional propensity of French jurisprudence for eclecticism and part of it with the fact that Demogue was still very much trapped in a legal culture dominated by the creed in a 'unity, the single coherent group'.[88] His final word on the subject is a tribute to vacuous generality:

> *Compromise, Not Logical Synthesis, the Goal of Juridical Effort.* May we hope that the human brain will one day be strong enough to unite in one harmonious synthesis the elements on which law depends? I do not believe that it is possible. We can make fortunate reconciliations – an effort which is even facilitated by the shut-in character of every society; but we must be conscious of their imperfection …[89]

It is clear that in this passage Demogue rejects any idea of harmony among the various considerations at play, in the sense that no actual sacrifice of value takes place when a regime is carefully reasoned and designed. The opposite thesis, most prominently associated with Ronald Dworkin, is that all conflicts of value are merely apparent; no actual compromise takes place because the legal (or ethical) space is apportioned among the seemingly conflicting values in light of metaprinciples that secure what he calls 'the unity of value'. Dworkin writes, 'full value holism [is] the hedgehog's faith that all true values form an interlocking network, that each of our convictions about what is good or right or beautiful plays some role in each of our other convictions in each of those domains of value'.[90] The most simple way of affirming this thesis, although not one that Dworkin endorses, is to say that some value or consideration that is prima facie compelling turns out to have no claim on the just resolution of any type of dispute – for example, that the innocent third party who acts in reliance of apparent rightness cannot be protected in any event because involuntary transfers are unconditionally unjust.[91] This Demogue repudiates in favour of what is sometimes called 'value pluralism'.[92] But what follows? A value pluralist is someone who believes in the necessity of compromising or balancing conflicting values. There is, however, the further question of whether such balancing judgements yield right answers or

---

[87] ibid at 403–04.
[88] Karl Llewellyn, 'A Realistic Jurisprudence – The Next Step', 461.
[89] Demogue, 'Analysis of Fundamental Notions', 569–70.
[90] Ronald Dworkin, *Justice for Hedgehogs*, 120.
[91] See Robert Nozick, *Anarchy, State, and Utopia*, 150–53: 'A distribution is just if it arises from another just distribution by legitimate means. The legitimate means of moving from one distribution to another are specified by the principle of justice in transfer. […] The means of change specified by the principle of justice in transfer preserve justice' [151]. To be fair, Nozick does not specifically address problems such as bona fide third-party acquisition of stolen property, and has little to say about what he calls 'rectification of injustice in holdings'.
[92] The classic statement of value pluralism is Isaiah Berlin, 'Two Concepts of Liberty', 168: 'The world that we encounter in ordinary experience is one in which we are faced with choices between ends equally ultimate and claims equally absolute, the realization of some of which must inevitably involve the sacrifice of others'. For a value-pluralist critique of Dworkin's 'unity of value thesis', see Minow and Singer, 'In Favor of Foxes'.

arbitrary decisions – whether they may be rationally vindicated or ultimately turn, and cannot but turn, on the ineradicable choice of the hands-trembling decision-maker. Demogue has nothing to say on this; indeed, I suspect that he opens up this field of inquiry inadvertently.

The acknowledgement of conflicting considerations does not mobilise these meta-ethical controversies. It implies not some philosophical view of value but a central feature of our political culture: that there is a broad consensus on the values that operate as inputs of law-making judgements but no agreement as to which output is correct. There is balancing not because each position's self-understanding is that it strikes a compromise among a plurality of values but because when we, so to speak, line up the various positions, they diverge on the weight they accord to a common stock of value considerations. It does not follow, as Dworkin showed persuasively,[93] that there is no right answer to the social controversy as to the relative weight of the various values; but it does follow that, since none of the positions can prove or demonstrate its correctness, there is *reasonable pluralism* of judgement. In a political culture permeated by reasonable pluralism, political legitimacy can no longer be affirmed on substantive grounds of justice. Political justification becomes a matter of legitimate authority. The task is to figure out by what procedure a collective decision is to be had on these matters, despite the *intractable* disagreement that they engender on us.

This retreat from substance to procedure, from justice to authority, jeopardises the partnership between liberalism and legalism. The partnership had been forged when the classical jurists read liberal justice into the sources of law, and it was reinvigorated when the social jurists carried out the social reform of private law. Read with the lenses provided by the conflicting considerations model, however, private law embodies not a coherent political theory but balancing judgements the political legitimacy of which is open to questioning. The most ambitious feature of the classical project, the association of the legal tradition with liberal justice, was compromised because the justice of private law regimes became politically contestable. Henceforth, legalism could only take the lesser form of a theory of adjudication as an activity essentially distinct from law-making – a theory, that is, about the political neutrality of *applying* the laws generated by the legislative process. Law-making to political actors and law application to legal experts. But that road, as it turns out, was foreclosed by the strands of legal realism that focused on issues of method. To their claims we now turn.

IV. Rules and Principles

The acknowledgement of conflicting considerations in the background of positive law and the related notion that law-making is largely an exercise in balancing

---

[93] On the distinction between 'right answers' and 'demonstrably right answers', see Ronald Dworkin, *Taking Rights Seriously*, 31–32, 36, 68–71, 279–90.

does not entail that *legal reasoning* itself is politically contestable. So long as the conflicting considerations play out exclusively at the legislative level, and that legal method prevents the jurist from corrupting the law with political choices of her own, it is possible to maintain the 'technical' or 'scientific' character of jurisprudence. The confidence in legal expertise wanes, on the other hand, if the conflicting considerations in the background of positive law are routinely brought into the domain of legal argument; for then determining legal outcomes becomes a matter of balancing, inherently controversial and ideologically charged. In the discourse of contemporary legal theory, we may put it as follows: once we acknowledge conflicting considerations, legalism attaches itself to the notion that the legal system is primarily an affair of *rules* rather than *principles*. When the rules 'run out', legal reasoning boils down to balancing principles, and principles embody precisely the plethora of conflicting considerations in the background of legal regimes. Therefore, it is of vital importance to legalism that principles play at the most a marginal role in the law and that balancing remains a method of 'last resort':

> While it is open to dispute whether the jurist can resort to teleological argument where induction/deduction is possible, it seems to be a basic premise of legal reasoning that absent a valid norm requiring him to do so, the jurist should not resort to balancing unless it has been shown that there is no meaning-based (i.e. inductive/deductive) or teleological solution possible. It is just because conflicting considerations analysis makes no claims of conceptual or teleological necessity, and indeed acknowledges that the jurist is making a choice among alternatives, that it can serve as the method of 'last resort'.[94]

According to a prevailing jurisprudential view, the distinction between rules and principles is a structural and qualitative distinction between two types of norm.[95] It is a structural distinction because it concerns the logical rather than the substantive properties of norms; it is a qualitative distinction because it reflects a difference not of degree but of kind. According to Robert Alexy's well-known account, principles are 'optimization requirements' subject to factual and legal constraints, while rules are 'either fulfilled or not' and yield 'fixed points in the field of the factually and legally possible'.[96] In other words, a valid principle ought to be realised to the furthest possible extent compatible with the optimisation of other valid principles and with the duty to apply all the valid rules; a valid rule, on the other hand, ought to be applied to all cases that fall within its scope of application.

---

[94] Duncan Kennedy, 'The Hermeneutic of Suspicion in Contemporary American Legal Thought', 101.

[95] There is a large (and somewhat pedantic) body of literature in both general jurisprudence and in constitutional theory on this topic. Most of it concerns the question of whether the distinction between rules and principles is a distinction in degree or in kind. Some of the classic works are: Josef Esser, *Grundsatz und Norm in der richterlichen Fortbildung des Privatrechts*; Ronald Dworkin, *Taking Rights Seriously*, 22–31, 71–80 (1977); Robert Alexy, *A Theory of Constitutional Rights*, 44–110; Jan-Reinhard Sieckmann, *Regelmodelle und Prinzipienmodelle des Rechtssystems*, 52–87; Manuel Atienza and Juan Ruiz Manero, *Las Piezas del Derecho*, 23–50.

[96] Alexy, *A Theory of Constitutional Rights*, 47–48.

The distinction emerges clearly from the contrast between conflicts of rules and competition among principles. If two rules conflict, meaning that their antecedent clauses overlap, either one is an exception to the other or one of the two must be declared invalid. There are meta rules that apply in the event of a conflict of rules – eg, *lex posterior derogate legi priori* – characteristically dictating the exclusion of one at the expense of the other. If two principles compete, on the other hand, meaning that they dictate opposite consequences in a case, the resolution is not to declare one of them invalid but to determine which of the two prevails in the circumstances. Since each of the principles furnishes a prima facie reason to decide the case in a particular direction, judgement is required to determine which, all things considered, prevails in the circumstances. Moreover, when two principles compete, it is usually the case that one prevails in a subset, and is itself defeated in another subset, of the entire set of cases to which both apply prima facie.

The different properties of rules and principles that emerge from the contrast between conflicts of rules and competition among principles shed light on Dworkin's famous statement that while principles have a 'dimension of weight' rules apply in an 'all-or-nothing-fashion'.[97] Thus, the application of a rule involves a deductive argument: if the case falls within the antecedent clause of the rule, and no exception tailored to the case is built into it, the rule entails the decision of the case. The application of a principle, on the contrary, involves a balancing judgement: if the case falls within the scope of a principle, that is a factor to be weighted in the decision of the case. In sum, while rules furnish definitive reasons, principles operate as prima facie reasons. Furthermore, according to the orthodox view, principles come into legal argument in those cases that are not controlled by a rule.[98] In that sense, deduction preempts balancing, which remains a method of 'last resort'.

The conceptual distinction between rules and principles has to be enriched to account for the teleological reasoning championed by the social jurists. To reason teleologically is to proceed from a single principle to a particular outcome. Therefore, teleological reasoning is only viable in those cases in which there is no competition among principles. Or, to put it more rigorously, once we acknowledge that there are conflicting principles that require 'optimisation', teleology is no longer the final word. It is but one step in a complex chain of argument: once we settle the deductive question of the principle's applicability to the case, we proceed to the teleological stage of ascertaining the outcome that realises the principle in question; finally, the principle has to be weighed against the competition in the field. In the realm of principles, then, deduction and teleology perform a preliminary role, setting the stage for balancing.

---

[97] Dworkin, *Taking Rights Seriously*, 25–27.
[98] See HLA Hart, *The Concept of Law*, 132–36.

Legal norms with the character of principles bring conflicting considerations into the law. For the legalist project of insulating legal reasoning from political choice, conceiving the jurist as a warden of the political choices embodied in the law, competing principles present a major threat. It is important that law remains essentially an affair of rules and of realising single principles immanent in those rules. Yet, legal realism exposed three sources of indeterminacy that enhance enormously the significance of principles and balancing in legal argument. First, the realists showed that the doctrinal notions ordinarily invoked in private law to fill gaps in the body of legal rules conceal but do not prevent balancing judgements. Second, they showed that the rules run out or are indeterminate much more frequently than orthodox legal thought was willing to acknowledge. Thirdly, they paved the way for a conception of legal reasoning that brings conflicting considerations to bear on the issue of whether a valid rule should be applied to a case, thus placing authority in the scales of balancing.

V. The Indeterminacy of Doctrine

As we saw in chapter three, the classical jurists relied on 'the genealogy of concepts' or 'the method of constructions' to fill gaps in positive law. They argued that the norms embodied in legal authority were grounded in a small number of notions – such as private property, freedom of contract and civil wrong – endowed with a high degree of operative force; these they sometimes called 'the leading axioms' of the law. In the previous chapter, we examined the pragmatic or teleological critique that the social jurists directed against the classical method. The gist of it was that the axiomatic view of law entailed bad consequences as judged by the law's own ultimate criteria, ie those purposes or *teloi* that it sought to realise in the social world. Theirs was what might be called a methodological critique, centred on the claim that legal formalism assigned to formal analysis and deductive reasoning a role much larger than that which sound principles of legal reasoning warranted. The main problem with formalism, in a nutshell, was that it brought about undesirable consequences.

The realists targeted the classical faith in legal axioms as well. But theirs was a different type of critique. They argued that, quite apart from its desirability, reasoning from such general legal concepts as property and contract to particular rules of law is *logically* impossible, since those concepts are largely devoid of operative force. Many attempts to settle a dispute by reference to them is thus bound to yield a *non-sequitur*. The critique was not methodological, at least not primarily, but logical; it charged legal formalism with numerous counts of fallacious reasoning.

On the question of why legal concepts such as property, contract and tort are empty, however, there are two discernible tendencies in the realist tradition – and here I mean primarily American Legal Realism, since these critiques flourished more successfully in the United States than in any other legal culture. One such tendency, whose main representative was Felix Cohen, issued a general philosophical objection against the use of any technical concepts in legal argument on the grounds that such concepts are, strictly speaking, meaningless or 'transcendental nonsense'. In one of the most famous passages in the history of American jurisprudence, Cohen wrote:

> In every field of law we should find peculiar concepts which are not defined either in terms of empirical fact or in terms of ethics but which are used to answer empirical and ethical questions alike ... Corporate entity, property rights, fair value, and due process are such concepts. So too are title, contract, conspiracy, malice, proximate cause, and all the rest of the magic 'solving words' of traditional jurisprudence. Legal arguments couched in these terms are necessarily circular, since these terms are themselves creations of law, and such arguments add precisely as much to our knowledge as Moliere's physician's discovery that opium puts men to sleep because it contains a dormitive principle.[99]

There are several problems with this argument. I shall mention three of them. First, at least part of the reason why Cohen finds the concepts that he lists nonsensical is that he ignores the procedure used by the classical jurists to construe them. Savigny or Puchta did not arbitrarily assume that the terms 'contract' or 'property' have meaning, but used these words to express normative ideals – eg, individual self-determination – which they claimed to be latent in the extant body of law. Had Cohen read carefully the works of any of the great classical jurists, he would have quickly understood that many of the concepts that he excoriates were carefully defined in terms of other concepts that he may have recognised as meaningful. True, sometimes technical concepts acquired a life of their own, as in Cohen's example of the debate as to 'where is a corporation?'[100] or when the notion of right was reified by the early Jhering and used to sustain the absurd proposition that a right 'cannot be in two places at the same time'.[101] But listing these errors is a far cry from showing that all legal concepts are meaningless. Secondly, the great irony of Cohen's argument is that his own notion of 'concepts which are not defined either in terms of empirical fact or in terms of ethics' suffers from the very problems of obscurity and circularity that he imputes to the 'solving words' of classical jurisprudence. He writes that 'our system is filled with supernatural concepts' defined as 'unverifiable',[102] failing to notice that the distinction between verifiable and unverifiable concepts is itself unverifiable.[103]

---

[99] Felix Cohen, 'Transcendental Nonsense and the Functional Approach', 820.
[100] ibid at 809–12.
[101] On the mistakes of reification attributed to the early Jhering, see Franz Wieacker, *A History of Private Law in Europe*, 343–44
[102] Cohen, 'Transcendental Nonsense and the Functional Approach', 823.
[103] As Duncan Kennedy, *A Critique of Adjudication*, 86, writes: 'The mocking self-confidence of this passage [the long one cited above] hides its real weaknesses. ... [I]t is not so easy to distinguish between concepts that meet Cohen's requirement of definition in terms of fact or ethics and those that don't'.

Thirdly, the whole argument is built upon the then fashionable but nowadays largely discredited verification theory of meaning proposed by such logical positivists as Rudolf Carnap, the early Wittgenstein, and AJ Ayer, according to which there is an objective criterion – verifiability – to distinguish propositions that have cognitive content from those that have some other type of content (eg, expressive or emotive). They argued that with the aid of such a criterion it was possible to spot and eradicate from 'science' those 'metaphysical' or 'senseless' propositions that purport to have cognitive content but are in fact unverifiable. Since the time in which *Transcendental Nonsense and the Functional Approach* was published, the likes of the later Wittgenstein, Popper, Quine, Goodman, Putnam and Rorty have gone a long way to discredit the logical positivism in which Cohen put his intellectual stock. It follows that this strand of realist critique of the attempt to derive operative rules from abstract concepts such as property, contract and tort has lost a great deal of its persuasive force.

The Felix Cohen tendency – which we may label 'metaphysical' – contrasts with another tendency whose protagonist was Wesley Newcomb Hohfeld. This second tendency embodied what I shall call an 'analytical' critique of legal concepts.[104] Hohfeld devoted his entire intellectual energy to a single concept but he happens to have picked the most important of all concepts, the trunk where all the branches of classical private law theory met: the concept of right. As we have seen in earlier chapters, the point of law according to the will theory was to secure the social coexistence of a multitude of free wills, and the specific form that it took was that of a system of (formally) equal rights, with a right understood as 'territory where the individual will rules and rules without our consent'.[105] It might be helpful to recall Savigny's statement on point:

> Man stands in the midst of the outer world, and the most important element, to him in this surrounding of his, is the contact with those who are like him, by their nature and destination. If now in such contact free natures are to subsist beside one another mutually assisting, not hindering themselves, this is possible only through the recognition of an invisible boundary within which the existence and activity of each individual gains a secure, free space. The rule, by which those boundaries and that free space are determined, is the law.[106]

Particular types of right conferred by private law – eg, private property, freedom of contract and the right to be compensated for wrongful injury – are grounded in the basic notion of right as a sphere of legally protected freedom. Each jural relation, at least within private law, is thus reduced to a correlation between rights and duties. That idea is Hohfeld's main target in a classic article published in 1913.[107]

---

[104] See Joseph Singer, 'The Legal Rights Debate in Analytical Jurisprudence from Bentham to Hohfeld'.
[105] Savigny, *System of the Modern Roman Law*, I, 6.
[106] ibid at 269.
[107] Wesley Hohfeld, 'Some Fundamental Legal Conceptions as Applied in Judicial Reasoning', 28: 'One of the greatest hindrances to the clear understanding … of legal problems … arises from the express or tacit assumption that all legal relations may be reduced to "rights" and "duties" …'.

The word 'right', explains Hohfeld, is 'chameleon-hued'[108] in that is conceals the fact that there is not one but four basic types of 'right' or 'active position': claim-right, privilege, power and immunity. Each of these is correlated with a different type of 'duty' or 'passive position': duty, no-right, liability and disability.[109] It follows that there are four fundamental types of jural relation:

(1) *Right + duty*. A right is a claim that others act in a certain way for the benefit of the right-holder; a duty is the necessity, enforced by the state, of acting for the benefit of the right-holder. Examples: the owner has the right to exclude others, who have the correlative duty to refrain, from entering his land; the promisee has the right, and the promisor the duty, to see that the promise is performed.

(2) *Privilege + no-right*. A privilege is the permission to either harm or simply not confer any benefit on a third party; no-right is the absence of a claim to a benefit or to no harm caused by a third party. Examples: the incoming firm has the privilege to cause competitive harm to other firms, and these have correlative no-rights against it; if a promise is unenforceable, the promisor has the privilege of not performing the promise and the promisee no-right to see that it is performed.

(3) *Power + liability*. A power is the ability to change third-party entitlements; liability is the vulnerability to such changes. Examples: the issuer of a revocable offer has the power to revoke it, while the offeree is liable to lose the power to create a binding agreement through her acceptance of the offer; the owner has the power to consent that others enter his property, while these are liable to acquiring the privilege of entering it.

(4) *Immunity + disability*. Immunity is protection against having one's entitlements changed by others; disability is lack of power to change the entitlements of others. Examples: the promisee is immune to, and the promisor disabled from, unilateral revocation of the promise; the owner is immune to, and the trespasser disabled from, the power to determine who shall enter his property.

These four combinations express two logical necessities: correlation and opposition. There is correlation when the existence of one entitlement implies the existence of the other; for instance, if I have a right that you stay off my land, you must have a duty to stay off my land. There is opposition when the existence of one entitlement implies the non-existence of the other; for example, if you have a privilege to enter my land, you cannot have a duty to stay off my land.[110] Hohfeld exhibits these results in the tables reproduced below.

---

[108] ibid at 29.
[109] See ibid at 30–58.
[110] See Joseph Singer, 'The Legal Rights Debate in Analytical Jurisprudence From Bentham to Hohfeld', 986–87.

Figure 5.2 The Hohfeldian system

Jural correlatives			
Right	Privilege	Power	Immunity
Duty	No-right	Liability	Disability

Jural opposites			
Right	Privilege	Power	Immunity
No right	Duty	Disability	Liability

Hohfeld's scheme yields two normative consequences. The first is simpler to grasp. The only logical corollaries of the existence of a given entitlement are the existence of its correlative and the non-existence of its opposite. Thus, any arguments purporting to deduce further consequences from a proposition describing the existence of an entitlement are fallacious. It is simply a *non-sequitur*, for example, to infer rights from privileges or powers from rights. But Hohfeld notices that such mistakes are ubiquitous in judicial opinions, largely on account of the sheer ambiguity of the term 'right'; specifically, judges slide imperceptibly from assertions about privileges to assertions about rights and powers. Denouncing these 'Hohfeldian' mistakes had particularly high political stakes in the early twentieth century, because in a number of labour cases the courts granted injunctions to businesses against labour unions on the grounds that picketing and other forms of pressing workers either not to apply to jobs or to break employment contracts with the plaintiff constituted tortious interference with the latter's 'right' to contract.[111] In *Vegelahn v Guntner*, for example, the majority argued that

> an employer has a *right* to engage all persons who are willing to work for him, at such prices as may be mutually agreed upon; and persons employed or seeking employment have a corresponding *right* to enter into or remain in the employment of any person or corporation willing to employ them. These *rights* are secured by the Constitution itself. No one can lawfully interfere by force or intimidation to prevent employers or persons employed or wishing to be employed from the exercise of these *rights* ...[112]

The word 'right' means essentially privilege in the first three instances – the privilege of the employer to hire non-union labour, the privilege of non-unionised workers to enter employment relations, and both privileges as allegedly constitutional entitlements; residually, it means power (to enter and leave binding agreements) as well. In the last instance, however, the court asserts that employers and employees have a right or claim against 'force or intimidation'. The move from one proposition to the other is fallacious; in order to vindicate the last statement,

---

[111] On this topic, see Ellen Kelman, 'American Labor Law and Legal Formalism'.
[112] *Vegelahn v Guntner*, 167 Mass 92, 136 (1986).

the court would have to answer what Hohfeld describes as 'a question of justice and policy'.[113]

The second normative consequence of Hohfeldian analysis is harder to grasp but even more fundamental for our purposes. Recall the classical notion of right as a protected sphere of freedom. Once we disaggregate, so to speak, the molecule 'right' into its atomic elements – rights, privileges, powers and immunities – what is it that we have? We may say that each of these entitlements confers protection to a certain form or dimension of freedom: rights secure benefits; privileges uphold liberty; powers confer autonomy; and immunities grant independence. But notice that stated at such a high level of abstraction these forms of freedom are mutually incompatible, and so are they when applied to the same object.[114] Either I am at liberty to cause you harm or you are secured from the harm that I may cause you; either I can change your entitlements or you are protected against such changes. It follows from the concept of jural opposites that the protection of one form of freedom over X implies the denial of the opposite form of freedom over X. What that means is that defining a right as a protected sphere of freedom and private law as a system of equal rights leaves us empty-handed. No actual decision about what rights individuals have can possibly proceed from such abstract premises; they are simply devoid of operative content.[115] The normative criteria to assign rights must proceed instead from low-level balancing judgements weighting the considerations of 'justice and policy' for and against the legal protection of each form of freedom in each type of situation.

This insight is often overlooked, I think, because the concept of 'right' is exceedingly general, leaving most modern readers at a loss about what sort of enterprise Hohfeld was pursuing. Hohfeld's major contribution was not to establish that 'Property consisted of abstract legal relations, not physical things'[116] or that 'a property right did not, as the classical system assumed, establish a vertical

---

[113] Hohfeld, 'Some Fundamental Legal Conceptions as Applied in Judicial Reasoning', 36. Walter Wheeler Cook deployed the Hohfeldian scheme to devastating effect in his critical reading of *Hitchman Coal & Coke Co v Mitchell*, 245 US 229 (1917). See Cook, 'Privileges of Labor Unions in the Struggle for Life'.

[114] See Joseph Singer, 'The Legal Rights Debate in Analytical Jurisprudence From Bentham to Hohfeld', 980–95.

[115] See ibid at 1014–17.

[116] Morton Horwitz, *The Transformation of American Law, 1870–1960*, 156. The following statement ia particularly misguided: 'By calling rights and duties 'correlatives' … Hohfeld sought to subvert the privileged position that rights had occupied … for orthodox legal analysis. He thus wished to relativize rights discourse by emphasizing that one might just as logically begin … with the concept of a duty. A right … became simply the legal enforcement of a socially created duty' [155]. A few quick points: (i) No classical jurist that I am aware of ever denied, or indeed failed to assert, that rights correlate with duties, which is why Hohfeld presents the right/duty correlation not as an original insight of his but as the target of his critique; (ii) the notion that rights proceed from 'socially created duties' was central to analytical jurisprudence, under the influence of Bentham and Austin, long before Hohfeld; (iii) in fact, Hohfeld was highly critical of the imperativist theory of law, the basis for the duty-before-right idea, for overlooking the role of privilege-conferring permissive norms in legal ordering. On the last point, see Hohfeld, 'Some Fundamental Legal Conceptions as Applied in Judicial Reasoning', 42 (fn 59).

relationship between people and things'.[117] The notion that the classical jurists reified property or conceived it as a relation between the owner and a material object is an inexplicable myth, for the organising concept of the will theory was precisely the jural relation. The truth of the matter is that as a theorist of rights as relations among persons, Hohfeld is but an unremarkable follower of post-Kantian German jurisprudence, probably indirectly through the influence of those English jurists – eg, Pollock, Amos, Salmond, Maitland, etc – who studied carefully the works of Savigny and Puchta. The truly original insight in Hohfeld's analysis was to show that the concept of right is *normatively* inert; and since the classical concept of right figured in all major areas of private law doctrine – eg, the right to property, the right to contract, and the right to redress – Hohfeld's scheme supplies a model or template to examine critically a broad range of legal concepts. Let me describe very briefly the reverberations of the Hohfeldian model in the critical scrutiny of arguably the three most important concepts in private law: tort, ownership and contract.

(1) *Tort*. In 1984, Oliver Wendell Holmes Jr published a little essay with the title *Privilege, Malice, and Intent* that provides a remarkable example of *avant la lettre* Hohfeldian analysis. Holmes' starting point is unpromising and suggests vintage formalism: 'The law of torts as now administered has worked itself into substantial agreement with a general theory'.[118] The general theory – Holmes' famous objectivist theory of tort – was that the victim of temporal damage has a right to legal redress if he can show that the harm was caused by the defendant and that the consequences of the latter's act were foreseeable. It is irrelevant, according to Holmes, whether the defendant caused the harm negligently, intentionally or maliciously: these words refer simply to different degrees of probability that his act will cause harm, all within the actionable range of foreseeable damage or 'manifest danger'.

Then appears the crucial but-clause: 'But the simple test of the degree of manifest danger does not exhaust the theory of torts'.[119] In many cases, explains Holmes, the defendant whose conduct meets the test escapes liability because 'the court is of the opinion that he had acted with just cause'.[120] On these occasions, harmful conduct is privileged. Holmes illustrates the point with numerous examples, some of them involving intentional infliction of harm: pecuniary damage caused in the course of economic competition;[121] the privilege of owners to interfere with their neighbour's interest in light and air;[122] threatening to dismiss a servant if he does

---

[117] Barbara Fried, *The Progressive Assault on Laissez Faire*, 52–53.
[118] Holmes, 'Privilege, Malice, and Intent', 1.
[119] ibid at 2.
[120] ibid at 3.
[121] ibid at 3, 7.
[122] ibid at 3–4.

business with the plaintiff;[123] permission to give 'good' advice against dealing with the plaintiff.[124] In these and many other types of situation, the law takes the position that the benefits of causing harm to the plaintiff outweigh the prima facie evil of damage – in other words, liberty trumps security. The only absolute that Holmes finds in the case law – astonishingly, in light of his devotion to 'objectivism' – is the prohibition of malicious behaviour.[125] Save for that, the entire law of torts is the result of myriads of judgments as to the relative importance of liberty against security in each type of situation. It is simply a *non-sequitur* to decide for the plaintiff because the defendant caused him foreseeable harm: that consideration must be balanced against the claim that the defendant acted with just cause. Since each of these opposing considerations is equally built into the very concept of tort, no 'general theory' can possibly be in the cards. Liability turns necessarily on situational judgements of 'justice and policy'. In a remarkable passage that anticipates Hohfeld's basic insight, Holmes writes:

> [W]ether [sic], and how, a privilege shall be allowed is a question of policy. Questions of policy are legislative questions, and judges are shy of reasoning from such grounds. Therefore, decisions for or against the privilege, which really can stand only upon such grounds, often are presented as hollow deductions from empty general propositions like *sic utero tuo ut alienum non laedas*, which teaches nothing but a benevolent yearning, or ... that, although there is temporal damage, there is no wrong; whereas the very thing to be found out is whether there is a wrong or not, and if not, why not.[126]

(2) *Contract*. The main reason to enforce contracts, on the classical understanding, is that the parties will them to be enforced. True, a contract is only enforceable if other conditions are met, such as lawfulness, the necessary formalities, and perhaps other requirements such as consideration. But these elements were conceptualised by the classical jurists as artificial or anomalous additions to the natural or normal basis for contract liability: the right of the parties to freely regulate their personal affairs. That is the cornerstone of a regime of freedom of contract.

But what is the nature of this right – freedom of contract? It plainly has a positive and a negative aspect. On the one hand, in order for freedom of contract to be honoured by the law, the parties' will to be bound by their agreement must be legally effective; in other words, the law must empower them to enter into enforceable contracts. On the other hand, no contract is free if one of the parties is bound to it against her will; that is why there are rules that afford the mistaken party and the victim of fraud and duress immunities against contract liability. It follows that both the power to create

---

[123] ibid at 4.
[124] ibid at 3, 6.
[125] ibid at 4–6.
[126] ibid at 3.

binding agreements and immunity from being bound are built into the very concept of contract. Both are essential features of freedom of contract, and of course they pull the law of contracts in exactly opposite directions.[127]

The last point may appear unpersuasive when stated at such an abstract level. One might think that the power to contract and immunity from contract do not conflict at all if we specify, as freedom of contract compels us to, that the power is to make voluntary deals binding and the immunity is solely from involuntary ones; the role of the various defences is to distinguish those agreements that are only apparently voluntary from those that are really willed by the parties. Yet, once we turn to particular bodies of contract doctrine, the conflict manifests itself in all clarity. The problem is that the concept of voluntariness is indeterminate.

Take the law of duress.[128] Imagine that we define duress as the act of demanding money or other benefits 'as a price of abstaining from inflicting unpleasant consequences upon a man'.[129] Such a rule would make all commutative contracts invalid, since the reason to enter a contract is the desire to acquire something that the other party possesses and threatens to withhold unless she is paid a sum of money or awarded some other advantage. We may refine the definition above with the qualification that there is only duress when the threat is to do something unlawful – in other words, there is no duress if the promisee threatens to exercise a legal right. But, as Robert Hale noticed, this statement is too broad as well, since in quite a few situations the law deems a threat 'coercive' in spite of the fact that it involves no more than the threat to act in a lawful manner.[130] The standard example is that of the blackmailer exacting a sum of money in exchange for waiving his privilege to leak to the press compromising photos of a celebrity that came to his possession through lawful means. Whether a contract is 'free' or 'coerced', then, is a relative question, the answer to which presupposes a judgement balancing the privilege of the promisee to set terms for letting the promisor take advantage of a resource and the right of the latter to be free from the pressure of having to pay for that resource. The line has to be drawn somewhere between the extremes of permitting any threat to act in a lawful manner and of equating any threat with duress. It goes without saying that the concept of duress cannot do any of the required work.

Duncan Kennedy has made the same point for fraud: 'When two parties are bargaining over the distribution of a transaction surplus, information is a crucial element of power, particularly information about the real properties of the commodity in question or about market circumstances

---

[127] See Duncan Kennedy, 'Distributive and Paternalist Motives in Contract and Tort Law', 568–70, 580–83.
[128] See Robert Hale, 'Bargaining, Duress, and Economic Liberty', 607–25.
[129] *Rex v Denyer*, 2 KB 258 (1926), quoted ibid at 613.
[130] ibid.

affecting its value to others than the two involved'.[131] How much and what sort of information must be disclosed by the seller in order for the agreement not to regarded as fraudulent? The question is once more one of degree, and the answer calls for a judgement about the right place to draw the line between the extremes of granting the seller an absolute privilege to withhold or even actively manipulate information and awarding the buyer a right that the seller not only discloses all present information but devotes very substantial resources to generating new information about the product or the market.[132]

(3) *Property*. The same set of analytical moves applies to ownership, perhaps the paramount private law right, defined by the classical jurists as 'unlimited',[133] a 'despotic power'[134] and 'complete domination over a physical object'.[135] When we scrutinise ownership with Hohfeldian lenses, however, we find not a coherent criterion for assigning individual rights but a choice-dilemma involving no less than *all* the four pairs of jural opposites.

We owe Joseph Singer by far the clearest statement of these 'core tensions' or 'paradoxes of property'.[136] He lists the following: (i) liberty to use versus security from harm; (ii) right to exclude versus right to access; (iii) power to transfer versus limits on disaggregation; and (iv) immunity from loss versus power to acquire. Each of these tensions yields a complex set of rules, none of which can be derived from the 'paradoxical' concept of ownership. The first tension is the subject of nuisance law, which balances the privilege of the owner to use his property as he sees fit with the right of neighbours to the quiet enjoyment of their own property. The second tension is dealt with in the law of easements and primarily in the law of trespass, which balances the basic right of the owner to exclude non-owners with the rights to access of non-owners granted, eg, in case of necessity or when the property serves as public accommodation. The third tension reverberates in the complicated estates system, in the law of covenants, and in anti-discrimination law; it concerns the dilemma between empowering the owner to transfer and disaggregate ownership as he wishes and the interest of third parties in a transparent and intelligible property system. Finally, the fourth tension is at the heart of the law of adverse possession, which mediates the conflict between title and possession, or formal and informal property arrangements.

---

[131] Kennedy, 'Distributive and Paternalist Motives in Contract and Tort Law', 582.
[132] ibid at 583.
[133] Bernhard Windscheid, *Lehrbuch des Pandektenrechts*, I, § 167.
[134] Charles Demolombe, quoted in Gordley, 'The Abuse of Rights in the Civil Law Tradition', 37.
[135] Ludwig Arndts, quoted in ibid.
[136] See Joseph Singer, *Entitlement*, 25–55 ('paradoxes of property'); Singer, *Introduction to Property*, 6–8 ('core tensions within property law').

In the foregoing exposition, I hope to have successfully articulated and vindicated two points. First, while both the social jurists and the realists attacked legal formalism, and particularly its allegiance to 'the leading axioms of law', the two critiques were quite different. The social jurists led a methodological attack, centred on the claim that the classical jurists put excessive stock in formal reasoning; the realists exposed the fallacies in the attempt to derive legal rules from highly abstract concepts. The second point is that Hohfeldian analysis is nothing short of devastating when applied to the scrutiny of the main operative concepts of classical private law theory, namely right, wrong, contract and ownership. It shows that these embody fundamental oppositions that can only be resolved or mediated by judgements of 'justice and policy' referred to situation-types.

What I have not yet showed is that the Hohfeldian scheme is equally devastating for teleological jurisprudence. I assume that this claim is quite implausible at first glance. The most natural position to take is that the social jurists would find the Hohfeldian critique congenial to their reform agenda; had they been aware of it, they could have amassed the combined strength of the methodological and the logical critiques to clear the ground even more completely for their 'social' gospel. Unhampered by the barriers raised by the classical notions of ownership or freedom of contract, they could have resorted even more straightforwardly to the choice of legal rules guided by the *teloi* of positive law. How come Hohfeldian analysis bears critically on that?

The answer is that an essential feature of teleological jurisprudence, and indeed of social reformism as a whole, was a residual allegiance to the internal coherence and operative force of the 'leading axioms' of classical private law. Recall that for the social jurists the will theory was not only coherent but a perfectly adequate expression, in the social conditions of 1800, of the very same principles that inspired the reform agenda of 1900. It was important to the idea of reform that what was being done was an extensive but gradual social correction of a theory that had become dysfunctional but was notwithstanding rooted in fundamentally benign ideals. Their programme was one of *immanent development*. The point can be illustrated with the doctrine of abuse of right. What Josserand and the other sponsors of the doctrine argued was that the 'spirit of rights', which served as a standard to judge the legitimacy of their use, was inchoate in the classical concept of absolute right and that it revealed itself, so to speak, as society progressed from simple forms where no serious conflicts between 'egotism' and 'solidarity' emerged to the increasingly complex and interdependent society created by 'progress'.[137]

---

[137] I think this is what Duncan Kennedy, 'A Transnational Genealogy of Proportionality in Private Law', 206, means when he writes that 'Another way of putting the difference [between Josserand and Hohfeld] would be to say that abuse of right in Europe remained conceptually squarely within the rubric of Social Legal Thought. ... [T]he basic idea was that classical private law had been coherently individualist. It was to be displaced by an equally coherent social law, whose premise was that individualist law, although generally desirable, must give way whenever its consequences were inconsistent with social purposes'.

That is what Jhering meant when he wrote that 'the 'idea' of property cannot contain anything which is in contradiction with the 'idea' of society.'[138] In sum, the coherence of classical private law was necessary to support the idea of immanent, piecemeal and unassailable social reform. That is what makes Karl Klare's characterisation of social jurisprudence as a new form of 'conceptualism' so extraordinarily apt.[139]

What the Hohfeldian tradition brings to light, of course, is not only that classical private law was never coherent by any measure of the imagination but also that the categories of rights, property, contract and tort – to mention only the most fundamental – are normatively inert. It is silly to couch an argument for the reform of a property rule in the rhetoric of 'immanent development of the social idea of ownership' when it becomes clear that the idea of ownership is a set of jural opposites that cancel each other out. It cannot furnish normative guidance, at least so long as what is at stake is something less general that choosing between a system of private or mixed property and one of collective ownership. Once we gasp what Singer calls the 'paradoxes' of rights, legal reasoning falls squarely within the province of conflicting considerations; balancing migrates from the realm of politics to that of law. Holmes was ahead of his time in expressing this point as early as in 1894:

> Perhaps one of the reasons why judges do not like to discuss questions of policy, or to put a decision in terms upon their views as law-makers, is that the moment you leave the path of merely logical deduction you lose the illusion of certainty which makes legal reasoning seem like mathematics. But the certainty is only an illusion, nevertheless. Views of policy are taught by experience of the interests of life. Those interests are fields of battle. Whatever decisions are made must be against the wishes and opinion of one party, and the distinctions on which they go will be distinctions of degree.[140]

It should be noted that the argument is not that legal reasoning always amounts to answering a 'question of policy' that involves balancing of the 'interests of life'. Holmes was addressing the cases in which no precedent or statute is in point, or positive law 'runs out' – the domain of 'gaps'. Accordingly, the import of his remark depends on the ways in which, and the extent to which, positive law is indeterminate.[141] That brings us to the most prominent strand of legal realism: 'distrust of the theory that traditional prescriptive rule-formulations are *the* heavily operative factor in producing court decisions.'[142]

---

[138] Jhering, *Law as a Means to an End*, 389.
[139] Karl Klare, 'The Judicial Deradicalization of the Wagner Act and the Origins of Modern Legal Counsciousness, 1937–1941', 275–81.
[140] Holmes, 'Privilige, Malice, and Intent', 7.
[141] Holmes' views on the indeterminacy of legal rules were relatively conservative: 'I recognize without hesitation that judges do and must legislate, but they can do so only interstitially; they are confined from "molar to molecular motions"'. *Southern Pacific v Jensen*, 244 S 205, 221 (1917) (Holmes, J, dissenting).
[142] Karl Llewellyn, 'Some Realism About Realism', 1237 (emphasis in the original).

VI. The Indeterminacy of Rules

Our starting point is Karl Llewellyn's famous distinction between 'real rules' and 'paper rules':

> I should like to begin by distinguishing real 'rules' and rights from paper rules and rights. The former are conceived in terms of behavior; they are but other names, convenient shorthand symbols, for the remedies, the actions of courts. They are descriptive, not prescriptive, except in so far as there may occasionally be implied that courts *ought to* continue their practices. […] 'Paper rules' are what have been treated, traditionally, as rules of law: the accepted doctrine of the time and place – what the books say 'the law' is. The 'real rules' and rights – 'what the courts will do in a given case and nothing more pretentious' – are then predictions.[143]

The claim is that there is an important gap between the 'law on the books' – legal rules – and what courts *really* do when they decide a case. But there is nothing in the claim that denies the existence of legal rules. Llewellyn is explicit on this point: 'Are "rules of law" in the accepted sense eliminated in such course of thought? Somewhat obviously not.'[144] This point is trivial but worth stressing because HLA Hart popularised within analytical jurisprudence the view that American Legal Realism was first and foremost a philosophical doctrine about the nature of law, a doctrine according to which 'talk of rules is a myth'[145] and law as a social institution amounts to nothing more than the decisions of courts and predictions of such decisions. The realists, however, were not in the least interested in the conceptual question 'What is law?' but in the quite different question of what explains judicial decisions. As Brian Leiter puts it, their version of rule-scepticism was not conceptual but empirical: not the claim that 'paper rules' do not exist but that they often fail to constrain the judicial resolution of disputes.[146] For such a claim to hold, they had to argue that while judges defer to the 'law on the books', legal rules are insufficient to justify the decision of cases. On this account, although positive law is real and binding, it is pervasively indeterminate.

That is much stronger a claim than merely acknowledging that the law runs out 'at the margins of rules and in the fields left open by the theory of precedents',[147] and that when it does run out judges have to 'exercise discretion'. This implies that in some cases there is no 'uniquely correct answer to be found' under the extant *corpus* of legal rules, and thereby the answer to the legal question posed by the dispute must inevitably be sought in a 'reasonable compromise between many

---

[143] ibid, 'A Realistic Jurisprudence', 447–48. On the 'realist' account of adjudication, see, eg, Andrew Altman, 'Legal Realism, Critical Legal Studies, and Dworkin'; 206–12; Brian Leiter, 'Rethinking Legal Realism', 275–85; ibid, 'Legal Realism and Legal Positivism Reconsidered', 280–85, 28–301. See also Duncan Kennedy, *A Critique of Adjudication*, 82–92.
[144] ibid at 449.
[145] HLA Hart, *The Concept of Law*, 136.
[146] Leiter, 'Legal Realism and Legal Positivism Reconsidered', 288–89, 293–300.
[147] Hart, *The Concept of Law*, 135.

conflicting interests'.[148] The realist claim is that judicial discretion – understood as the necessity of balancing conflicting considerations – is not the exception but the norm, because in actually litigated cases 'the available authoritative premises … are at least two, and … the two are mutually contradictory as applied to the case at hand'.[149] Hence, we must distinguish between a theory of adjudication that acknowledges indeterminacy while stressing that 'the life of the law consists to a very large extent in the guidance both of officials and private individuals by determinate rules which, unlike the applications of variable standards, do *not* require from them a fresh judgement from case to case'[150] and a theory of adjudication that asserts indeterminacy in 'any case doubtful enough to make litigation respectable'.[151] The former, which marginalises indeterminacy, is essentially supportive of the legalist distinction between law making and law application. The latter, on the other hand, precipitates a crisis of the distinction, since it portrays adjudication in most cases as an exercise in balancing conflicting considerations.

Indeterminacy *at the margins* comes in two main forms.

First, laws may be standards instead of rules, incorporating notions such as 'fair rate', 'work safety', 'dominant position', 'good faith', 'reasonable care', 'social function', 'due process' and 'adequate punishment'. When these and other highly indeterminate concepts are used in a provision, it is clear that the law-making authority delegates on the law-applying body the task of deciding, within a broad band, to which cases the norm applies (when the indeterminacy is in the antecedent clause) or what consequences follow from its application. The task may be performed *ex ante* by regulatory agencies with the power to create narrow and typically short-lived rules within its scope of operation (eg, electricity rates set by the regulatory agency for the energy sector or mandatory work safety measures in car manufacturing plants established by the department of labor) or ex post either by executive officials empowered to respond to relatively undefined circumstances (eg, the police can use fire power in cases of 'eminent danger') or by courts applying notions of 'reasonable care' or 'good faith' purporting to guide the conduct of private actors and determining within the permissible range the 'adequate punishment' for a crime or 'fair compensation' for wrongful behaviour.[152] In all of these situations, the substantial unsettlement of the issue means that law-applying officials are explicitly tasked with balancing conflicting considerations; in other words, indeterminate concepts operate as entry points for the competing principles applicable to the case.

Second, legal rules making use of 'general classifying terms' share with other types of utterance the limits or open texture of natural language.[153] Even provisions that are meant to settle issues *ab initio* – eg, 'no vehicles in the park' – are to

---

[148] ibid at 132.
[149] Llewellyn, 'Some Realism About Realism', 1239.
[150] Hart, *The Concept of Law*, 135 (emphasis in the original).
[151] Llewellyn, 'Some Realism About Realism', 1239.
[152] See Hart, *The Concept of Law*, 131–33.
[153] ibid at 124–30.

varying degrees vague, in that they have both 'core' instances and non-instances – eg, a bus is a vehicle and a highway is not a park – and a penumbra of borderline cases that share some but not all of the relevant properties of clear instances and non-instances – eg, 'is a bicycle a vehicle?' or 'is the public garden a park?' And since vagueness is not an on/off phenomenon but a continuous variable – that is, the core and the penumbra are not divided by a fence border but more by a blur – not even the issue of whether a particular case is clear is entirely exempt from controversy. Moreover, the plain meaning of a normative utterance is not semantic but pragmatic, because the words, albeit facially descriptive, are put to a *prescriptive* use.[154] We agree that the plain meaning of 'it is a misdemeanor for any person to sleep in the railway station' excludes babies, even though the semantics of the utterance indicates the contrary. What this also means is that, since the meaning of particular words or statements is always a function of context, or is holistically embedded in a social practice, there is a residue of potential indeterminacy even in the most mechanical act of rule-application. No dictionary or glossary or any other 'authority' can settle the issue of whether the prohibition applies to babies; the question is resolved by tacit agreement concerning the prescriptive meaning of the terms involved, agreement that may unexpectedly break down.

These forms of indeterminacy – *standards* and *vagueness* – do not undermine the proposition that law is essentially an affair of determinate rules excluding ad hoc balancing. That is so because most laws are rules instead of standards and most cases fall within the core meaning of the terms used to express the rule. But this is only true on the assumption that we are presented with a definitive statement of a legal rule such as 'no vehicles in the park'. And that is not how legal reasoning from statutes and precedents works: what we are given is a set of materials or sources – statute books and records of cases – from where legal rules are retrieved through a canonical procedure of construction or interpretation. It turns out that canons of construction or interpretation 'are in the habit of hunting in pairs',[155] meaning that the law-applying official has leeway to choose between different and often contradictory statements of the 'law on the books'.

Llewellyn led the realist attack on traditional doctrine in the fields of statutory interpretation and the construction of precedents. In the field of statutory interpretation, he produced a list of contradictory – 'thrust' versus 'parry' – canons of interpretation, routinely deployed by the courts and displayed in the extant body case law, notably: 'a statute cannot go beyond its text *but* to effect its purpose a statute may be implemented beyond its text'; 'statutes are to be read in the light of the common law … *but* the common law gives way to statute that is inconsistent with it …'; 'where design has been distinctly stated no place is left for construction

---

[154] Hart is ambiguous on this point. See ibid at 126: 'Does 'vehicle' *used here* include bicycles, airplanes, rollerskates?' (emphasis added).
[155] Walter Wheeler Cook, 'Book Review', 406.

but courts have the power to inquire into real – as distinct from ostensible – purpose'; 'if language is plain and unambiguous it must be given effect but not when literal interpretation would lead to absurd or mischievous consequences or thwart manifest purpose'; 'word are to be taken in their ordinary meaning unless they are technical terms or words of art *but* popular words may bear a technical meaning and technical words may have a popular signification …'; 'every word and clause must be given effect *but* if inadvertently inserted or repugnant to the rest of the statute, they may be rejected as surplusage'; 'the same language used repeatedly in the same connection is presumed to bear the same meaning throughout the statute *but* this presumption will be disregarded where it is necessary to assign different meanings to make the statute consistent'; 'exceptions not made cannot be read *but* … whatever is within the reason of the law is within the law itself'; 'general terms are to receive a general construction *but* they may be limited by specific terms with which they are associated or by the scope and purpose of the statute'.[156]

These contradictory canons of statutory interpretation, embodying the conflicting second-order considerations of text and purpose – the 'letter' and the 'spirit' of the law – open the field to balancing the first-order considerations for and against disposing of a class of cases as the statute provides. The provision 'no vehicles in the park' may be read to establish either 'no vehicles in the park' or 'no vehicles incompatible with peace and quiet in the park'. Even if the case falls clearly within the scope of the provision, literally construed, the issue of the provision's applicability cannot be settled by reference to the terms used, so long as a respectable argument can be made that the case is not within the purpose of the provision. Furthermore, once we go down the road of purposive interpretation, the conflicting considerations in the background of the provision are brought in broad daylight and the balancing supposedly carried out by the law-maker is to some extent reopened; the case is no longer an affair of rules but a matter of principle.

In the field of case law, the realists argued forcefully against any view that 'in the vast majority of decided cases there is very little doubt' about the 'rule for which a given authoritative precedent is an authority'.[157] The argument was that there is not one doctrine of *stare decisis* but two – and that the two are flatly contradictory with one another. The first, which Llewellyn called the 'strict' or 'orthodox' view, is that holdings should be read narrowly on the grounds that 'no judge has the power to decide what is not before him';[158] any remarks by the judge regarding

---

[156] Karl Llewellyn, 'Remarks on the Theory of Appellate Decision and the Rules or Canons About How Statutes are to be Construed', 401–05.
[157] Hart, *The Concept of Law*, 134. Hart asserts fantastically that 'The headnote is usually correct enough'. As Brian Leiter, 'Legal Realism and Legal Positivism Considered, 297, puts it, 'every first-year litigation associate knows that this approach to precedent would be a recipe for disaster. To extract "holdings" without regard to the facts of the case – which is all a head-note typically provides – is mediocre lawyering'.
[158] Llewellyn, *The Bramble Bush*, 68. Edward H Levi, *An Introduction to Legal Reasoning*, 2–3, put the point (even more) bluntly: 'It is not what the prior judge intended that is of any importance; rather it

the rationale for the decision – including express statements of the holding – are mere *dicta*. 'In the extreme form this results in what is known as expressly "confining the case to its particular facts".' This rule,' writes Llewellyn in jest, 'holds only of redheaded Walpoles in pale magenta Buick cars'. The other view, which he called 'loose', blurs the distinction between *ratio* and *dicta*, encouraging broad readings of the holding. The case was not at all about Walpoles in Buick cars, not even about liability for automobile accidents, but about, say, the principle that the defendant engaged in a hazardous activity is strictly liable for any injuries caused to the plaintiff.

The strict view of precedent expands the ability of the judge to distinguish the present case from past cases; the loose view allows him to fish 'authority' in the immense ocean of judicial verbosity. Both views are 'recognized, legitimate, honorable'.[159] Both are deployed in a single line of case law, here stretching and there narrowing its scope. Thus, deploying the 'loose view' of precedent, a case involving a person arrested for distributing religious literature in the business district of a company-owned town[160] is held by the United Sates Supreme Court to be about freedom of speech in private property open to the public, including peaceful picketing of a store located in a shopping center.[161] Later, in a case involving the distribution of anti-war leaflets in a shopping centre, the Supreme Court argues that the first case concerned 'an economic anomaly of the past, "the company town"', dismissing it as *sui generis*, and that the second was situated in 'a context where the First Amendment activity was related to the shopping center's operations'; accordingly, the anti-war leaflets case is distinguished from prior cases and ruled an issue of first impression.[162] 'What I wish to sink deep into your minds about the doctrine of precedent', writes Llewellyn,

> is that it is two-headed. It is Janus-faced. That it is not one doctrine, nor one line of doctrine, but two, and two which, *applied at the same time to the same precedent, are contradictory of each other*. That there is one doctrine for getting rid of precedents deemed troublesome and one doctrine for making use of precedents that seem helpful. That these two doctrines exist side by side. That the same lawyer in the same brief, the same judge in the same opinion, may be using the one doctrine, the technically strict one, to cut down half the older cases that he deals with, and using the other doctrine, the loose one, for building with the other half.[163]

Given the availability of conflicting statements of precedent, there is leeway for judges to balance the principles in the background of past opinions, reading broadly the opinions with which they agree and narrowly the opinions with which

---

is what the present judge, attempting to see the law as a fairly consistent whole, thinks should be the determining classification'.

[159] ibid at 68.
[160] *Marsh v Alabama*, 326 US 501 (1946).
[161] *Amalgamated Food Employees Union v Logan Valley Plaza*, 391 US 308 (1968).
[162] *Lloyd Corp., Inc v Tanner et al*, 407 US 551 (1972).
[163] Llewellyn, *The Bramble Bush*, 69.

they disagree. As a result, 'it cannot be said that the legal process is the application of known rules to diverse facts [...] The existence of some facts in common brings into play the general rule. [...] But no such fixed prior rules exists'.[164] This does not mean that statutory interpretation and the doctrine of precedent are always indeterminate – that 'paper rules' exert no real constraint in legal argument. That is obviously false. It seems that no respectable argument can be made that the provision 'no vehicles in the park' does not proscribe driving a tourist bus in Central Park or that the precedent on free speech laid down in *Logan Valley* applies to breaking into my devout neighbour's house at night and singing *La Marseillaise*. The point is that the indeterminacy of legal rules is a pervasive as opposed to marginal phenomenon, such that in the bulk of litigated cases judicial balancing of competing principles is unavoidable, whether the courts acknowledge it or not. That is a major difficulty for the legalist project of drawing, in the age of conflicting considerations, a sharp distinction between law-making and law-application.[165]

The distinction is further undermined once we acknowledge yet another type of indeterminacy, apart from the indeterminacy of doctrine and rules – the indeterminacy of legal *grounds*. For so far we have been operating under the assumption that positive law is binding, that the authority of statutes and precedents and other sources of the law is beyond questioning. Yet good legal reasoning puts authority to trial. Indeed, judges are bound to offer sufficient reasons for their decisions – decisions that are in need of justification because they are authoritative and enforceable – and the fact that someone posited a norm is in itself no sufficient reason to regard it as binding. It is no good to argue that judges owe allegiance to positive law because it is the business of judges to settle disputes according to the law. That is question-begging.[166] We cannot assume that fidelity to the law means fidelity to legislation and to precedent, or to the set of conventionally accepted sources of the law, since that is precisely what requires justification. As Holmes famously stated, 'It is revolting to have no better reason for a rule of law than that so it was laid down in the time of Henry IV'.[167] The sources of the law must earn their authority in the terrain of principle.

---

[164] Levi, *An Introduction to Legal Reasoning*, 3.
[165] A common assertion is that indeterminacy is at any rate restricted to that tiny fraction of actual or potential disputes that reaches the stage of appellate review – the pathologically hard cases. See, eg, Brian Leiter, 'Rethinking Legal Realism', 273. It seems plausible that there are reasons other than the determinacy of the law for the fact that most cases are not litigated. Three of the most significant are unequal access to justice, the costs of litigating disputes relative to the expected benefit, and barriers to entry designed to close the floodgates of litigation.
[166] Ronald Dworkin, *Taking Rights Seriously*, 47.
[167] Holmes, 'The Path of the Law', 1001. In a similar vein, Karl Llewellyn, *The Common Law Tradition*, 426, wrote: 'If you are a later court, you meet *here* rules resting on and limited by their reasons. If you do not find those reasons to have been good, or to remain good, and no other adequate reasons occur to you, then manifestly you have no reason going along with these ... rules' (emphasis in the original).

VII. The Indeterminacy of Grounds

As reason-giving, authority-claiming, and coercion-wielding agents, judges are bound by a small set of fundamental principles: justice, certainty, legitimacy, equality and prudence.[168] Justice requires giving to the parties to the dispute what a perfectly just legal system would provide. Certainty requires predictability in social life and the protection of legitimate expectations. Legitimacy requires deferring to the judgement of authorities holding the comparatively better title to settle controversial issues. Equality requires consistency in decision-making, 'treating like cases alike'. Finally, prudence requires proper consideration of the consequences of a judgement in the long-run realisation of the rule of law. These are principles and they are fundamental. They are principles in the technical sense. They embody values that can be fulfilled in varying degrees and whose weight depends on the circumstances; consequently, their application involves the mediation of a judgement balancing them against competing principles. They are fundamental, on the other hand, in the sense that they are the ultimate criteria of legal justification, the standards to which good legal argument ultimately harks back. In other words, they are the basic 'value facts'[169] of the law – the deep source of legal reasons.

(1) *Justice.* Courts deliver justice rather than charity, piety, magnanimity or counsel. In a liberal polity, justice is the only branch of morality that is ordinarily taken to justify the use of force that the judiciary commands. In other words, duties of justice are the only subset of moral duties that it is morally appropriate to enforce. That is why justice is usually regarded as the 'political' among the manifold moral virtues, and why duties of justice are said to constitute an independent domain of so-called '*political* morality'. Enforcing them is a pressing and public concern.[170] There is, of course, a long way from justice considered in general to justice as it bears on a particular dispute brought before a court of law. A judge should not decide a torts dispute involving a wealthy driver and a poor pedestrian based on their income sheets, even though his conception of justice supports large-scale redistribution of income and wealth in the society in question. There are numerous other factors, including the wrongfulness of the defendant's conduct and the effects of the decision in future activity, that play a significant role in the fair assessment of the dispute; disregarding these other factors will yield the decision not just inadequate but unjust. Justice binds judges as it bears on the case before them, not as if they were social engineers pursuing a reformist agenda.

---

[168] Most of the argument and some of the text of this section is drawn from Gonçalo de Almeida Ribeiro, 'Judicial Activism and Fidelity to Law', 36–40.
[169] Mark Greenberg, 'How Facts Make Law', 187–91.
[170] See Jeremy Waldron, *Law and Disagreement*, 105–06, 159–60.

(2) *Certainty*. Social life would be hopelessly unpredictable if persons could not count on any guidance but that which would be provided by figuring out individually what justice requires or by trying to predict judicial rulings. This is true for two basic reasons. First, people disagree about the requirements of justice, meaning that two reasonable individuals are unlikely to come to the same conclusions as they engage with the plethora of issues of justice entangled in their ordinary affairs.[171] Moreover, the mental burden of unrestrained moral reflection about each and every issue of justice would prove exhausting even to the most resilient citizen. Second, there are numerous collective action or co-ordination problems that cannot be settled rationally but only through the *fiat* of some authority – eg, deciding about whose vehicle should be given priority at an intersection. The force of these reasons is the measure of the value of certainty and of its independent weight in adjudication. Judges ought to accord deference to past decisions or practices because by doing so they provide conduct guidelines to persons and enable the creation of co-ordination benefits. Such decisions and practices command greater deference, other things being equal, if they exhibit certain formal properties that improve their value as guides to conduct, namely the familiar 'rule of law' virtues of publicity, clarity, determinacy, prospectivity and the like.[172] What makes these distinctively 'legal' is that they are creatures of positive law, for certainty is a value yielded once norms are embodied in such things as statutes, rulings, customs and other conventional legal sources.

(3) *Legitimacy*. There are reasons of a different nature pulling judges towards deference to past decisions, particularly those issued by the elected branches. Such reasons fall into two basic categories. The first concerns the title or right to settle controversial issues of political morality. Citizens disagree about justice and they do so reasonably. The elected branches are endowed with a strong title to decide which among the rival conceptions of justice should be given preference because they enjoy democratic legitimacy. In most legal systems, judges are neither politically accountable nor representative of the ideological pluralism across the community. The elected branches, on the contrary, are chosen by the addressees of their power, citizens acting as free and equal persons. The second category comprises considerations of functional competence. Courts are comparatively ill-equipped to make certain types of judgment, namely empirical assessments involving complex prognoses – eg, what are the effects of shifting from negligence to strict liability in the area of accidents caused by defective products – and judgements of policy rooted in the public interest or general welfare – eg, what goal should be given precedence in case of conflict, full employment or price stability? Judges have

---

[171] Waldron, 'Kant's Legal Positivism', 1538–40.
[172] Lon L Fuller, *The Morality of Law*, 33–94.

good reason to defer to the decisions of the political branches on these issues because the latter are more likely to get things right.

(4) *Equality.* Yet another reason for deferring to past decisions flows from the requirement to 'treat like cases alike'. This is the principle underlying the central role played by analogy in legal reasoning.[173] Strictly speaking, it determines that two cases should be treated alike in the exact proportion of their relevant similarity – eg if the penalty for stealing a diamond is a sentence of n years, the penalty for stealing two diamonds should be, other things being equal, exactly twice as long. Positive laws, in virtue of their generality, treat 'like cases alike' according to the judgement of the law-making authority; on the contrary, if everyone follows his or her first-order judgment, including judges with ultimate authority to settle disputes, similar cases will inevitably and recurrently receive different treatment. True, equality in this formal sense is slightly mysterious.[174] But its normative force is widely acknowledged. Imagine that a parent gives a certain amount of money to a child and later regrets the decision. Shortly after, a second child of the same age (they are twins) asks the parent to give her a similar amount of money. The circumstances are similar. Perhaps the first decision to give money was wrong. In spite of that, the parent has a prima facie reason to repeat it on this occasion. The second child is likely to claim that her standing in the family requires equal treatment from her parents in relevantly similar circumstances.

(5) *Prudence.* Courts might have good reason to depart from the best judgement according to the four preceding principles for reasons that we might describe as prudential. Their responsibility is not exhausted by the duty to deliver justice in the case at hand, comprising as well the institutional duty of ensuring the basic conditions for the continuing realisation of the law. What that requires from them is a permanent concern with the consequences of a ruling for the rule of law. Thus, although the rule of voluntary jurisdiction is a major setback for the ideal of the rule of law in the relations among states, it is both plausible and important that the prospects of legality in international affairs would deteriorate instead of improving if the International Court of Justice took the step of declaring its jurisdiction mandatory. Prudence is the basis of what Alexander Bickel called the 'passive virtues' of judicial power.[175] It reminds judges that they are not insulated from the real world, where decisions often have negative consequences that require an openness to compromise grounded in the 'ethic of responsibility'.[176]

---

[173] See Scott Brewer, 'Exemplary Reasoning', 934–38; Lloyd L Weinreb, *Legal Reason*, 19–39.
[174] Thus, Karl Llewellyn, *The Bramble Bush*, 40, remarks that 'justice demands … that like men be treated alike in like conditions. Why, I do not know; the fact is given'.
[175] Bickel, 'The Passive Virtues'.
[176] Max Weber, 'Politics as a Vocation', 119–27.

Let me illustrate the interplay of these principles with the doctrine of precedent. In its so-called historical as opposed to hierarchical dimension – involving past and future decisions of a superior court instead of decisions by higher and inferior courts – precedent is the doctrine according to which a court is bound by its past rulings on the issue to be decided. It is important to distinguish carefully the binding force of precedent from its persuasive value. No doubt judges deciding a case are likely to find in the records of past decisions a rich source of insight about the issues it raises and how to handle them properly. There are good reasons of economy and method to use past cases as guidance to decide those of the present day, and there is every reason to adhere to previous rulings whenever these prove persuasive on the merits. But that is the spirit in which a judge might turn to the writings of Aristotle or to foreign case law in his search for the right answer to a challenging issue; it does not mean that the *Nicomachean Ethics* or the case law of the Canadian Supreme Court are law in Portugal or in South Africa. The idea of *stare decisis* implies that precedent is binding even if the court is now persuaded that the issue was wrongly decided in the past.

Why should it be accepted? If the duty of a judge were to decide each case according to what a perfectly just legal system would provide, it is plain that precedent should carry merely persuasive value. There would still be plenty of reason for judges to engage with the records of past decisions in their search for a just resolution to the dispute at hand, but they would not take themselves to be legally bound by anything decided by their predecessors in office. If anything, justice is a principle that counts against *stare decisis* – it furnishes a prima facie reason to overrule incorrect or unjust precedents. If precedent has any legal force at all, then, it must be on account of other fundamental principles.

Certainty is one of them. Past decisions known to bind courts in the future encourage the reliance of persons acting in similar circumstances, and thereby increase the predictability of social life, improving the ability of private actors to foresee the consequences of alternative courses of action. This proposition might be doubtful if we take precedent to mean a single case, for 'standing alone [no case] … can give you … guidance as to how far it carries, as to how much of its language will hold water later'.[177] Past judicial decisions offer guidance for the future when they form clusters or lines of cases, that is to say, when each case can be read against the background of a number of others lying in its vicinity.[178] That is not to deny the indeterminacy of case law. But, as we have seen, it is not *global* indeterminacy; certain decisions are ruled out by precedent, and that is a source of certainty.

Are there grounds of legitimacy to follow precedent? That is hardly the case. Neither do past judges hold better credentials than those of the present day to settle controversial issues of political morality, nor do they exhibit any functional advantage over their successors. On the contrary, there is reason to think

---

[177] Karl Llewellyn, *The Bramble Bush*, 46.
[178] ibid at 46–54.

that the current generation is more legitimate simply because it was appointed more recently. Whatever method of judicial appointment is adopted in a given jurisdiction, the most recent nominee to the bench is in theory, barring unusual circumstances of political systems degenerating over time, the most legitimate judge, since she benefits both from the fresher democratic legitimacy of whatever elected officials were involved directly or indirectly in her appointment and from the most up-to-date technical preparation for the job.

The connection between equality and precedent is more ambiguous. It is standard law talk that the principle 'treating like cases alike' is one of the foundations of the doctrine of precedent.[179] That is surely true. But equality is also the source of a deep tension within the doctrine between arguments for the 'loose' view of precedent and for the 'strict' view that emphasises distinguishing. Equality may be taken to imply either bare consistency with the past or consistency of principle, and the choice between one and the other is far from inconsequential in this area. Consistency of principle pushes judges in the direction of forcing coherence upon the case law, either abolishing unjustified exceptions or introducing distinctions that might have been previously overlooked or even disallowed. Bare consistency, on the other hand, requires strict adherence to the rules laid down, even if these do not add up to 'a coherent scheme of principle';[180] that is congenial to the 'loose' view of precedent, and particularly to 'the rule the courts tells you is the rule of the case'.[181]

Prudence, at last, usually counts as a reason for precedent. Courts, particularly the highest in a jurisdiction, are moral persons in the eyes of the public, not simply collections of individual judges belonging to this or that jurisprudential tendency or this or that generation. Much of their authority is based on the integrity of the case law they produce over time.[182] Shifts of opinion are perfectly appropriate and often necessary but unless they take place against the background of reasoned engagement with the record of past decisions, the judiciary can be easily brought into disrepute. Accordingly, prudence places the burden of proof with the reformist.

It is an open question how to balance these rival considerations. Reflective and responsible judges will adhere to stricter or more flexible conceptions of precedent depending both on the relevant empirical circumstances of their jurisdiction – say, whether there is a deep-seated practice of precedent that encourages the

---

[179] See Michael Zander, *The Law-Making Process*, 215.
[180] Ronald Dworkin, *Law's Empire*, 214.
[181] Karl Llewellyn, *The Bramble Bush*, 42 (emphasis removed).
[182] I suppose this is what Henry Hart and Albert Sacks, *The Legal Process*, 588, mean when they write, under the guise of values promoted by the doctrine of precedent 'in furtherance of public confidence in the judiciary', the following: 'The necessity, considering the amorphous nature of the limits upon judicial power and the usual absence of an effective political check at the ballot box, that judges be subject to the discipline and the restraint of an obligation to build upon the prior law in a fashion which can withstand the test of professional criticism'. Ronald Dworkin's 'chain novel' metaphor and his account of integrity as the paramount value of a 'community of principle' elevate these concerns to the status of a whole political theory – see Dworkin, *Law's Empire*, 176–258.

reliance on past judgments – and the relative value they ascribe to the fundamental principles pulling them in opposite directions. That explains why any mature legal culture where *stare decisis* is officially accepted recognises as well the power to overrule. Overruling is justified, for instance, whenever considerations of substantive justice prevail over the principles of certainty, equality and prudence, and all the more so when the passage of time wears down the legitimacy of a past judgment.

It follows that the law, understood as adequate justification for judicial decisions,[183] is the outcome of the all-things-considered judgment balancing the fundamental principles of legal justification in the circumstances of the dispute. According to this view, it is impossible to draw a sharp distinction between law and politics, or legal and personal judgement, or to adhere to Montesquieu's misleading account of the judiciary as a neutral or void power. Proper judging – that is, faithfulness to the law – is unavoidably political in two respects. First, it is political in the general sense of the term: law engages the judge's sense of justice in proportion to the role that considerations of justice play in legal argument; and the judge's sense of justice obviously translates into her ideological commitments in a public culture characterised by the 'fact of reasonable pluralism'.[184] Second, it is political in a specific sense tied to legal argument: engagement with the fundamental principles implies balancing, and the judgments arrived at are inevitably complex and controversial, leading to genuine and reasonable disagreements among lawyers about the law.[185]

VIII. Ideology in Private Law

Indeterminacy at the various levels examined in the previous sections – in the doctrines applied to fill gaps in positive law, in the rules that make up a great deal of positive law, and in the normative force of positive law itself – enables what Duncan Kennedy calls 'ideologically oriented legal work'.[186] When the experienced judge comes into contact with a case, he has an initial impression of what 'the law'

---

[183] Of course, one may stipulate that the term 'law' should be reserved to source-based norms, and add the proviso that a norm's legal character should be carefully distinguished from any binding force it may have on judges, an issue that is moral (or, more broadly, normative) in nature. That is the point of view of sophisticated legal positivism. See, eg, John Gardner, 'Legal Positivism: 5 1/2 Myths'; Joseph Raz, 'Incorporation by Law'; Leslie Green, 'Legal Positivism'. Whether or not such an account of law is defensible, it is clear that it is immune to the primary objection directed against simpler forms of positivism, namely that they derive judicial duty from contingent social facts about legislative, judicial, and customary activity. At the very least, though, adhering to such a view comes at the price of distinguishing law from adjudication, that is to say, asserting that a great deal of what judges call 'law' in their opinions is not law but something else. For a forceful and famous argument against that view, see Dworkin, *Taking Rights Seriously*, 31–39, 68–71, 81–88, 101–05.
[184] John Rawls, *Political Liberalism*, 36–39, 54–66.
[185] Dworkin, *Law's Empire*, 4–5, 112–113.
[186] Kennedy, *A Critique of Adjudication*, 157–79.

on the issue is.[187] It may be that the law requires a particular outcome or leaves it relatively open. The particular state of the law conveyed by this impression is called 'the field'.[188] The ideologically oriented judge also has an idea of how he wants the case to come out, that is, an inchoate judgement concerning the relative strength of the principles applicable to the issue. In the event of a conflict between 'the law', as initially apprehended, and the desired outcome, the judge works strategically at all three levels of indeterminacy – the doctrines, the rules and the grounds – to displace the perception of 'necessity' of the undesired outcome and to make a legally sound case for how he wants it to come out (assuming, of course, that he has not changed his mind about that).[189] If, on the contrary, the first impression is that the law is on the side of the outcome that the judge deems desirable, there is no incentive to displace it; the judge will either rest his case or work towards strengthening it, particularly if the court is divided. In any of these situations, the judge carries out ideologically oriented legal work, or has the opportunity to do so, while denying that any such thing is taking place, paying no more than lip service to the legalist ideal of political neutrality in adjudication.[190] In a post-realist legal culture, therefore, the administration of justice takes place 'in the shadow of ideology'.[191]

That does not mean that the law is globally indeterminate or that all claims of 'legal necessity' are false, so that adjudication is simply a disguised form of legislation. What it does mean is that 'determinacy' and 'indeterminacy' are not properties of the law (or of the language used to express it) that can be objectively ascertained – eg, determinate rules versus indeterminate standards and core instances versus penumbra of uncertainty – but the contingent experience of openness or constraint in the subjective practice of 'legal work'.[192] As Kennedy puts it:

> [T]he question of what proportion of actual or imaginable cases have determinate outcomes, given the legal materials, has to be asked taking into account the possibility that legal work will destabilize the initial apprehension of what the materials require. Once we take into account that determinacy is a function not just of the words of valid norms and the content of other sources, but of an interaction between the resources and strategies of whoever has the power to do legal interpretation, and the 'thingness' of the materials, statements about the 'vast majority of disputes' are simply meaningless.[193]

We may now present as a linear sequence the gradual erosion of the legalist project of insulating law from the realm of politics. In the first stage, the distinction between public and private law is undermined by the critique of the private/public distinction and the emergence of conflicting considerations. Henceforth, legalism takes the form of the distinction between the political process of balancing conflicting considerations (private law-making) and the judicial process

---

[187] ibid, 'Freedom and Constraint in Adjudication', 519–20.
[188] ibid at 530.
[189] Kennedy, *A Critique of Adjudication*, 158–60.
[190] ibid at 192–212.
[191] ibid at 240.
[192] ibid, 'A Left Phenomenological Critique of the Hart/Kelsen Theory of Legal Interpretation', 376.
[193] ibid at 383.

of adjudicating disputes under the provisions laid down by lawmakers (private law-application). In the second stage, some laws are acknowledged as standards that operate as entry points for principles embodying conflicting considerations; a distinction is thus drawn, within private law adjudication, between ruled-based decision-making and the interstitial balancing enabled by standards. In the domain of private law rules, however, yet another distinction must be drawn between the core meaning and the penumbra of uncertainty; dubious cases implicate balancing of the considerations relevant to determine whether they should be subsumed under the provision. Finally comes the acknowledgement, at least among legal theorists, of ideologically oriented legal work exploiting indeterminacies at all levels of legal discourse in private law – doctrines, rules and grounds; openness and constraint in legal reasoning can no longer be conceived as agent-independent and strategy-independent properties. Ideology *pervades* private law adjudication. The reproduction of the political/legal distinction throughout the sequence, in the form of a gradual retreat or in increasingly modest versions, is an example of 'nesting'.[194]

Figure 5.3 The erosion of the politics/law dichotomy

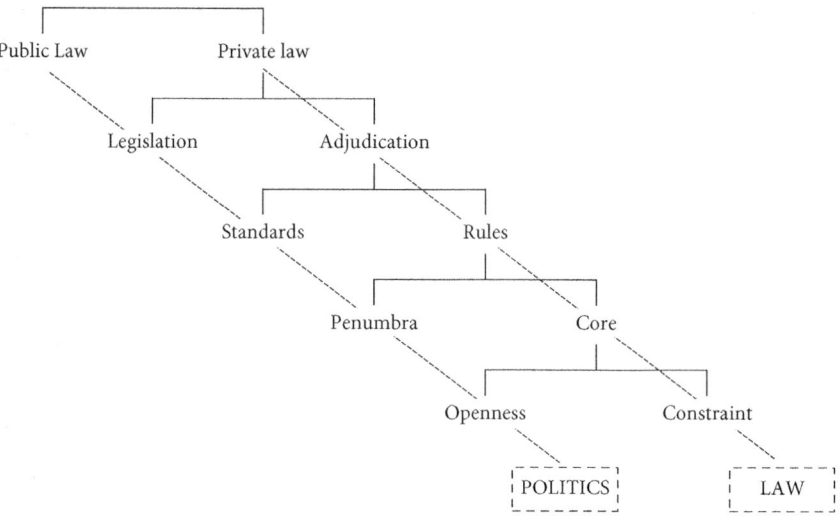

Politicisation tears down the foundations of modern private law as a safe haven for both liberal and legalist values. On the one hand, since law-making routinely involves controversial balancing judgements, concerning both the scope and content of private law, there is wide room for disagreement among liberals, and liberal justice becomes what WB Gallie calls an 'essentially contested concept';[195]

---

[194] See Duncan Kennedy, 'A Semiotics of Legal Argument', 344–49, 357–60.
[195] WB Gallie, 'Essentially Contested Concepts'.

accordingly, the political legitimacy of private law regimes can no longer be assessed in terms of their content, which is reasonably contested, but must be gauged procedurally. On the other hand, since legal argument in private law often involves precisely the kind of contested balancing judgements underlying legal regimes, it is virtually impossible to draw a neat line between the legal and the political; the ideal of law as a form of expert knowledge is thus compromised.

The decline of private law is inevitable.

> In 1931 Carl Schmitt published an article titled 'the turn to the total state.' The total state that Schmitt describes is not yet a totalitarian state. Germany is still a liberal democracy and the Weimar Constitution is still the supreme law of the land. But the total state Schmitt describes is a state in which the traditional lines between the sphere in which the private law society governs itself and the sphere of state intervention, or the public domain, have been undermined. According to Schmitt, the pluralistic forces of civil society have captured the state and made it an instrument to serve their purposes. *Everything is up for grabs politically*. It is a state of political mobilization and deep ideological conflict, reflected in the plurality of deeply divided political parties in parliament. [...] The idea of an autonomous domain of private law as an integral part of an apolitical state-free sphere had collapsed. The belief in a civil society that organizes itself by means of private law, the content of which is defined by apolitical legal experts, no longer resonated. Private law, too, had become the object of selfconscious, broad-based political struggle. Private law was wrested from the legal priesthood and became a mundane object of regulatory intervention. The 19th century ideas of scholarly mandarins, who conceived of private law in natural law, historicist, or conceptual terms or thought of the code as the authoritative embodiment of legal rationality, were replaced by ideas that private law, too, was subject to political choice.[196]

---

[196] Kumm, 'Who is Afraid of the Total Constitution?', 341 (emphasis in the original).

Epilogue
The Migration to Constitutional Law

In a constitutional democracy, where politics is bound by a bill of rights, politicisation leads to *constitutionalisation*. The conflicting considerations underlying private law are effortlessly recast in the language of fundamental rights and private disputes quickly escalate into issues of constitutionality.

The *mechanism* by which this happens is quite straightforward. Imagine that in eviction proceedings the issue to be decided is whether a term in a lease whereby the tenant cannot perform oral and anal sex on the premises – a term that the defendant concedes to having breached repeatedly – is valid and enforceable. The court is of the view that, from the standpoint of private law, that is indeed the case. Even if we take for granted that the bill of rights is not binding on private actors such as individuals, corporations, labour unions and the like – that is, even if we assume that fundamental rights lack direct horizontal effect – the dispute easily becomes a matter of fundamental rights. Although the requirement of state action to trigger rights-based scrutiny does bar the tenant from invoking his right to privacy against the landlord, he may do so against the court itself *qua* enforcer of the lease and against the legislature *qua* author of the laws which empower private parties to create obligations incompatible with the right to privacy. If the laws in question do violate the tenant's fundamental right, they are unconstitutional, and must be regarded as void. Properly understood, then, the doctrine of vertical effect – of fundamental rights as rights against the state – entails an indirect horizontal effect.[1] But that is not the end of the story: constitutional escalation is a two-way street. Faced with the tenant's privacy claim, the landlord argues that at stake is his own – and indeed the tenant's – right to private autonomy, entailing that private actors can enter into contracts, waive their rights, and undertake obligations. At this point, fundamental rights have been invoked on both sides of the dispute, and the issue to be decided is to which side the scales tip.

The proclivity of private law disputes in contemporary constitutional democracies to escalate into issues of fundamental rights is what Mattias Kumm characterises as a 'total constitution'.[2] Referring to Germany, where the origins of

---

[1] That does not necessarily mean that it makes no practical difference whether the so-called horizontal effect is direct or indirect. For the view that the difference is outcome-neutral, see Robert Alexy, *A Theory of Constitutional Rights*, 354–65; Mattias Kumm, 'Who is Afraid of the Total Constitution?', 352–59. I argued for the view that the distinction is of practical import in Gonçalo de Almeida Ribeiro, 'The Effects of Fundamental Rights in Private Disputes', 247–53.

[2] Mattias Kumm, 'Who is Afraid of the Total Constitution?'.

the phenomenon can be traced back to the *Lüth* decision of the Federal Constitutional Court in 1958,[3] he writes:

> Under the guardianship of the Federal Constitutional Court the German Basic Law had, over the course of the second half of the 20th century, developed to become what Schmitt might well have referred to as a total constitution. If a total state is a state in which everything is up for grabs politically, *a total constitution inverts the relationship between law and politics in important respects*. If in the total state law is conceived as the continuation of politics by other means, under the total constitution politics is conceived as the continuation of law by other means. The constitution serves as a guide and imposes substantive constraints on the resolution of any and every political question.[4]

It should be noted that the emergence of a 'total constitution' is, to a considerable extent, grounded in two premises of contemporary European constitutional thought: protective entitlements; and rights as principles.[5]

(1) *Protective entitlements*. The first premise is that, even disregarding so-called social and economic rights, fundamental rights do not merely play a defensive function but a protective one as well. They are not just rights against the state but entitlements to state protection. To have a fundamental right to privacy, for example, is not just to have a claim against the state that it refrains from interfering with one's privacy interests – say, through searches and seizures – but also an entitlement to positive state action directed towards the protection of one's privacy interests against the interference of third parties, namely through the law of defamation, data security legislation, the inviolability of correspondence, protection against third party appropriation of one's identity, and so forth.

In their defensive role, fundamental rights characteristically operate either as privileges or as claims that the state refrains from pursuing certain (harmful) courses of action. To illustrate the first type, consider the case of free speech. Although free speech is often characterised as a right, this trades on the sheer ambiguity of the term 'right'.[6] In a narrow, technical, sense, a right implies a command or a prohibition addressed to the person(s) against

---

[3] BVerfGE [*Lüth*] 7, 198 (1958). Erich Lüth was a film director and Head of the State Press Office in Hamburg who called for a boycott of the 1950 movie *Immortal Beloved* directed by Veit Harlan, whose career was stained by a past of anti-semitism and close ties with the Nazi regime. The distributor of Harlan's movie successfully sued Lüth in the District Court for an injunction to call the boycott off, although the decision was ultimately overturned by the FCC on freedom of speech grounds. In spite of its obscurity and ambiguity, the reasoning of the Court has had a lasting influence on the judicial and scholarly understanding of the effect of fundamental rights in private disputes. For a critical assessment, see Claus-Wilhelm Canaris, *Grundrechte und Privatrecht*, 31–32. See also Robert Alexy, *A Theory of Constitutional Rights*, 360–61.

[4] Kumm, 'Who is Afraid of the Total Constitution?', 343.

[5] I rely on what I wrote in Gonçalo de Almeida Ribeiro, 'The Effects of Fundamental Rights in Private Disputes', 223–32.

[6] See WN Hohfeld, 'Some Fundamental Legal Conceptions as Applied in Judicial Reasoning', 28–58.

whom one has the right while privileges correspond to a permission to engage in a particular activity. In the jargon of Hohfeld, 'rights' correlate with 'duties' while 'privileges' correlate with 'no rights'. One's freedom of speech does not imply a universal duty to listen to what one has to say, but the permission to express one's opinions whether others like it or not. That is why it makes no sense, except in particular circumstances in which free speech might entail a genuine claim-right, to say that the government has 'violated' freedom of speech – free speech is, *qua* privilege, logically inviolable. What one might say, quite sensibly, is that once freedom of speech is entrenched in the constitution, understood as the supreme law of the land, the state is disabled from the power to burden individuals with the legal duty to refrain from expressing their opinions.

The second type of defensive right is illustrated by the right to bodily integrity. That is a genuine right – a 'claim-right', in Hohfeldian language – because it implies a duty of the state to refrain from injuring the body of natural persons, namely through torture, cruel and unusual punishment, police beatings, and the like.

There is an important structural difference between rights of the first and the second type, that is, constitutional privileges and claim rights. Imagine that A sues B for expressing publicly the view that he is a bigot, and the civil court sentences the latter to pay him damages on the basis of a provision of the civil code or another private law instrument. In reaction, B files a constitutional complaint with the constitutional court invoking her freedom of speech. Who is she invoking the privilege of free speech against? Not A, since there is nothing that A could have done to interfere with her freedom of speech; on the contrary, it was B's exercise of the privilege to speak her mind that caused A the harm that drove him to court. B's complaint is directed against the state both for enacting legal norms that burden her exercise of free speech and for applying those norms to the dispute between hers and A. Her claim, in other words, is that the state is disabled from the power to impose such legal burdens on her. Free speech operates in this context in its strictly defensive role.

Imagine now that B sues A for battering her and the civil court dismisses the case *ex hypothesi* on the grounds that there is no cause of action in private law for intentional infliction of bodily injury. Can we say that this decision violates A's right to bodily injury conceived as a defensive right against the state? According to a fringe view among German constitutional theorists – a view often derided by its critics with the shabby label of 'theory of statist convergence' (*etatistischen Konvergenztheorie*) – the answer is in the affirmative.[7] Through its dismissal of the lawsuit, the civil court judge

---

[7] On this theory, whose leading proponent is Jürgen Schwabe, see Robert Alexy, *A Theory of Constitutional Rights*, 304–08, 356–57; Claus-Wilhelm Canaris, *Grundrechte und Privatrecht*, 39–43.

is affirming that ordinary law permits the defendant's conduct and that implicates the state's sponsorship to it. In a nutshell, the state participates in A's interference with B's bodily integrity simply because it tolerates A's conduct.

This is an ingenious construction, but it is marred by a conceptual mistake. If A is battering B and C, who sits closely and could prevent further harm, refrains from acting, it is absurd to say that C participated in the beating and violated his duty to abstain from injuring B's body. What we may say, of course, is that C bears some responsibility for B's injuries because he had the duty to aid her. What is at stake here, however, is no longer a negative but a positive duty, which correlates not with the victim's defensive right but with a protective entitlement. Likewise, constitutional claim-rights entail not just negative duties of the state to abstain from engaging in harmful activities but positive duties to afford the right-bearer a reasonable level of protection against harm caused by third-parties or proceeding from natural causes. To put the point simply, the state has the duty to protect the right-bearer against predictable threats to the enjoyment of her constitutionally protected interests. It follows that ordinary law may infringe fundamental rights both through action and omission or inaction, even when the rights in question are classic 'civil rights' as opposed to welfare or socio-economic rights.

Some voices contend that the primary and perhaps exclusive function of fundamental rights is to endow individuals with defensive weapons against state power, not to propel government action.[8] The contention is slightly ironic because it is based on an idea which, in spite of its vaguely 'liberal' overtones, is in fact alien to the liberal conception of the state that sowed the seeds of modern constitutionalism. In the tradition of liberal political theory, the reason to create a state in the first place – what justifies the state and sets the limits of its rightful activity – is precisely the need to *secure* individual rights against third-party harms.[9] The point was stressed with elegant simplicity in Article 2 of the Declaration of the Rights of Man and Citizen of 1789: 'The aim of all political association is the preservation of the natural and imprescriptible rights of man'. The normative fiction of a social contract through which individuals in a hypothetical state of nature relinquish their 'natural', 'lawless' or 'wild' freedom, including the unrestricted privilege of

---

[8] See, eg, Uwe Diederichsen, 'Das Bundesverfassungsgericht als oberstes Zivilgericht'; Dieter Medicus, 'Der Grundsatz der Verhältnismäßigkeit im Privatrecht'; Klaus Stern, *Das Staatsrecht der Bundesrepublik Deutschland*, III/1 §76 IV. German criticism arose mostly in the context of the Federal Constitutional Court's case law on the duties of the state to protect fundamental rights through private law. The landmark decisions are BVerfGE 81, 242 (*Handelsvertreter*) and BVerfGE 89, 214 (*Bürgschaft*). See Olha O. Cherednychenko, 'Fundamental Rights and Private Law', 6–9. The United States Supreme Court repudiated the doctrine of protective duties in the (in)famous *DeShaney* case – *DeShaney v Winnebago County Department of Social Services*, 489 US 189 (1989). The European Court of Human Rights, on the other hand, has embraced the doctrine in the *Case of X and Y v The Netherlands, Series A*, vol 91 (1985).

[9] See Robert Alexy, *A Theory of Constitutional Rights*, 303–04.

self-defence, in exchange for 'civil', 'juridical' or 'secure' freedom embodies the basis of liberalism as a political philosophy.

It is true that in the liberal tradition the state is as much a solution to a problem as it is the source of a fresh one. For once all power is concentrated in a single, centralised, site – the mighty being suited to the Hobbesian image of the Leviathan – the fear is that it will abuse its power and thus betray its task as a custodian of individual rights. This is where the idea of defensive rights, rights which insulate individuals from the reach of state power, comes into the picture. It is perfectly understandable, of course, why the defensive features of fundamental rights ended up taking the front seat in the development of modern constitutionalism. The liberal worldview that emerged from the French Revolution inherited from the *ancient régime* an absolutist state that needed more taming than strengthening; the urgent task was hence to limit instead of expanding the reach of government. But that should not distract us from the raison d'être of the state itself within the tradition of liberal constitutionalism, which is as much a positive theory of the normative *foundations* of government as it is a negative theory of *limited* government.

(2) *Rights as principles*. The second premise of the 'total constitution' is that constitutional provisions entrenching fundamental rights typically embody principles instead of rules.[10] Two main reasons vindicate the conception of rights as principles. First, the standard language of bills or declarations of rights makes it virtually inevitable. Most fundamental rights provisions are drafted in such general and unconditional terms that regarding the norms embodied in them as rules would yield unpalatable outcomes. That is the case both with norms such as 'art is free' (Article 5(3) of the German Basic Law) or 'no abridgement of freedom of speech' (First Amendment to the US Constitution), which would be vastly over-inclusive if construed as rules, or with norms such as 'every person has the right to life and bodily integrity' qualified by the *carte blanche* reservation that 'these rights may ... be interfered with on a statutory basis' (Article 2(2) of the German Basic Law), which would be next to empty if they were regarded as rules. The straightforward way to circumvent problems of this type is to explicitly or implicitly read a reasonableness clause into the provisions, ie 'no *unreasonable* abridgement of freedom of speech' or 'these rights may ... be interfered with by statute to a *reasonable extent*'. But that is, of course, tantamount to transforming them into standards, operating as entry points for the relevant principles, since the only way to determine whether it is reasonable to apply the norm in a given case is to balance the value it instantiates – free speech or the principle underlying the limiting statute – against the value(s) sacrificed by its application.

---

[10] See Gustavo Zagrebelsky, *Il Diritto Mitte*, ch 6; Alexy, *A Theory of Constitutional Rights*, 44–110.

The second reason for the conception of rights as principles is that it places the controversial practice of judicial review of democratic legislation under the best possible light.[11] When rights are conceived as principles, understood as optimisation requirements, both their scope of application and the margin of appreciation of the legislature in balancing them against competing principles are liberally construed. This is reflected, for instance, in the Federal Constitutional Court's decision to interpret the provision of the Basic Law concerning the right to the free development of personality as entailing a general right to freedom of action, ie the privilege to do as one pleases, such as to feed pigeons in the park[12] or to ride a horse in the woods.[13] Thus, any law restricting individual liberty involves a prima facie infringement of a fundamental right. Such a law might nonetheless be constitutionally justified if it safeguards a principle that has greater weight in the circumstances of its application. Moreover, the judiciary recognises a 'margin of appreciation' of the legislature to make the required balancing judgement.

In order to determine that, the court subjects the law to the four-prong proportionality test germane to the definition of principles as optimisation requirements.[14] First, it considers whether the reasons underlying the law are legitimate or not; a reason is constitutionally illegitimate when it is categorically excluded by the constitution, such as perfectionist considerations or restrictive measures rule out by qualified reservation clauses. Second, the court assesses whether the means selected by the legislature to accomplish the goals it invokes to justify the law is effective or suitable; if the means is unfit for purpose, the burden imposed by the law is pointless. Third, the court considers whether the measure chosen is necessary, meaning that it is the least intrusive in the class of suitable means. Finally, if the law overcomes all the previous hurdles – and that is usually the case –, the court balances the applicable principles in order to determine whether the legislative measure is reasonable.

Whether or not this principled form of constitutional justice vindicates the institution of judicial review of legislation, it seems to be comparatively promising. An alternative approach, illustrated by some of the case law of the US Supreme Court concerning the constitutional protection of liberty, is summarised as follows by Mattias Kumm:

> The U.S. Supreme Court insists that only particularly qualified liberty interests, liberty interests that are deemed to be sufficiently fundamental, enjoy meaningful protection under the Due Process Clause. When an interest is deemed

---

[11] This view has been championed in contemporary constitutional theory by Mattias Kumm. See Kumm, 'Constitutional Rights as Principles'; Kumm, 'Political Liberalism and the Structure of Rights'; Kumm, 'Institutionalising Socratic Contestation'.
[12] BVerfGE [*Taubenfütterungsverbotes*] 54, 143 (1980).
[13] BVerfGE [*Reiten im Walde*] 80, 137 (1989).
[14] See Klatt and Meister, *The Constitutional Structure of Proportionality*.

to be sufficiently fundamental, the limitations that apply are narrow too. [...] Only 'compelling interests' are sufficient to justify infringements of the right. [...] A measure may be proportional, but not meet the 'compelling interest' test.[15]

The problems with this approach are twofold and intertwined. The first is that a narrow definition of the scope of constitutional rights insulates vast areas of liberty-restricting ordinary law from constitutional scrutiny structured by proportionality analysis. That cannot be right, at least for someone who believes in the virtues of judicial review, since it opens the legal system to unsuitable, unnecessary and disproportionate laws. The second problem is that the 'compelling interest' test operative within the narrowly defined scope of fundamental rights is either irrational or inappropriate. It is irrational if it implies that fundamental interests ought to be disproportionately protected, for the concept of proportionality is entailed by the very concept of justice, and is therefore a requirement of practical reasoning within the realm of justice-apt decision-making. It is inappropriate if it involves the court in more than controlling the reasonableness of legislative action – that is, in openly second-guessing the democratic legislature. For the idea that legislatures are incompetent at reasoning about rights or too corrupt to take rights seriously is hard to square with the basic constitutional commitment to democratic governance. Perhaps particular types of prima facie infringement of fundamental rights should be subject to some form of strict scrutiny, on account of the stained historical record that majorities have with respect to them; that is notoriously the case when a law relies on 'suspect classifications' of race, gender, religion, class, etc. Yet democratic legislatures ought to enjoy a margin of appreciation in the task of fixing the conditional relations of priority among competing interests,[16] and the conception of fundamental rights as principles is responsive to that concern.

Armed with the doctrines of protective entitlements and rights as principles, constitutional justice colonises all areas of the law – including, of course, private law. If the latter is to be understood as a storehouse of political choices, it must bend the knee to constitutional values.

> The validity of any and every political decision is subject to potential challenge before a constitutional court that, under the guise of adjudicating constitutional rights provisions, will assess whether such an act is supported by good reasons. The legislative parliamentary state is transformed into a constitutional juristocracy.[17]

Private law, insofar as it strikes a balance among conflicting considerations, becomes a political matter, first, and then a constitutional matter. If it is political, it is also constitutional – that is, subject to rights-based judicial review.

---

[15] Mattias Kumm, 'Who Is Afraid of the Total Constitution', 347.
[16] See Gonçalo de Almeida Ribeiro, 'O Constitucionalismo dos Princípios', 69.
[17] Mattias Kumm, 'Who is Afraid of the Total Constitution?', 343.

Still, liberal legalism cannot but feel uneasy about a total constitution. On the one hand, it must confront the 'counter-majoritarian difficulty'[18] of having non-elected and non-accountable officials reviewing the political choices of the democratic legislature in a community that prides itself for living in accordance with the ideal of 'government among equals'. On the other hand, it must cope with the challenge posed by those who argue that proportionality analysis, with its explicit acknowledgment of balancing, is poorly disguised politics, an unsuitable method for law as expert knowledge. The overarching issue is which institution is to make the choices underlying the laws of the community, particularly whether – and to what extent – final authority should be assigned to judges.

In our 'post-national constellation'[19] of governance, comprising multiple levels of law-making and of judicial review, the issue of authority acquires a whole new dimension. On the one hand, domestic courts, such as the German Federal Constitutional Court, are bound to decide whether and to what extent they should review laws generated by supranational structures such as the European Union.[20] On the other hand, transnational courts, such as the European Court of Human Rights, are bound to decide whether and to what extent they should review laws generated by national political processes, laws that might very well have already been subject to judicial review by domestic courts.[21] The issue is how to articulate the various levels of authority, in the absence of a federal design and amidst ineradicable tension among liberal principles of transnational governance such as 'subsidiarity', 'effectiveness', 'fairness', 'sovereignty' and 'due process'.[22] Wherever we turn, it is balancing all the way down.

These are the constitutional challenges of our post-realist age. The ongoing debate about them in contemporary constitutional theory and the striking diversity and sketchiness of the answers produced casts doubt on our ability as citizens to come to grips with the problem of political justification in a liberal culture and our ability as jurists to vindicate the legalist ideal of law as a form of expert knowledge. Those were the big questions that set us on this long journey, and to them we return. We bring no answers with us. We bring, however, a better understanding, and that is something to be treasured. *At the end of all our exploring, we arrive where we started, and know the place for the first time.*[23]

---

[18] Alexander Bickel, *The Least Dangerous Branch*, 16–23.
[19] Jürgen Habermas, *The Postnational Constellation*. See also Günther Teubner, *Constitutional Fragments*, 42–72.
[20] See, eg, BVerfG. 15 Dez 2015, 2 BvR 2735/14 [*Identitätskontrolle I*].
[21] See, eg, *SAS v France*, ECHR 1 July 2014.
[22] See Mattias Kumm, 'The Cosmopolitan Turn in Constitutionalism'; Kumm, 'Constituent Power, Cosmopolitan Constitutionalism, and Post-Positivist Law'; Miguel Maduro, 'Interpreting European Law'; Nico Krisch, *Beyond Constitutionalism*, 27–105; Bogdandy and Schill, 'Overcoming Absolute Primacy'.
[23] TS Eliot, *Little Gidding*, V.

APPENDIX
A Foray into Methodology

[I]t is the mark of an educated man to look for precision in each class of things just so far as the nature of the subject admits …

Aristotle, *Nichomachean Ethics*, 1094^b, 936

The subtitle of this book – 'A Philosophical History of Liberal Legalism' – flags its methodological loyalties. Indeed, the phrase 'philosophical history' was coined by Hegel in the *Introduction to the Philosophy of History*. Yet my methodology is not exactly Hegelian. Hegel's philosophy of history presupposes his metaphysics and epistemology and, frankly speaking, that is not the sort of baggage that one wants to carry around. The way I see it, Hegel's idea of a philosophy of history furnished a template for my enterprise and set the tone of the narrative.

It should be clear from these remarks that I have not so much engineered a method as I have engendered one through intellectual *bricolage*.[1] It is more than that though. 'Method' suggests a neat set of rules that regulate one's study of a given subject matter; it is hence supposed to take precedence over theory or substance – one is, or ought to be, committed to a method in advance of committing to any substantive claims. I find that a deeply unattractive as well as unrealistic view. It makes sense to hold on to some methodological guidelines while thinking through the issues, particularly when that helps avoiding common fallacies and disentangling different ranks of problem. But that is miles away from having *a* method. My impression – and that certainly applies to my project – is that methodological expositions are normally post hoc rationalisations of inchoate beliefs; and apart from obscuring that in their 'prolegomena' appearance, they are usually more abstract and more obscure, and every bit as controversial, as the first-order substantive expositions allegedly governed by them. What follows is my largely ex post, quite abstract, and possibly obscure attempt to lay down a method that makes sense of the project.

* * * * *

---

[1] See Claude Lévi-Strauss, *The Savage Mind*, 16–36.

Hegel uses the phrase 'philosophic history' to denote his method of historical study in contrast with what he calls 'original' and 'reflective' history.[2] The word 'method', albeit used by Hegel himself, is really quite misleading in that context, for Hegel does not consider philosophic history one among a variety of valid methodological options but the only true or genuine method of studying history – indeed, not a method at all but 'nothing other than the thoughtful consideration of history'.[3] The other modes of historical study are partial or imperfect realisations of historical knowledge, in the strong sense of 'science'.[4] What philosophy brings to history is 'the simple thought that Reason – the thought that Reason rules the world, and that world history has therefore been rational in its course'.[5] Philosophic history is hence the account of 'reason in history'. But what exactly does that mean?

At their most elementary, these statements appear to be inflated expressions of a trivial thought:

> [W]e could ... declare that we must apprehend the historical faithfully. But with such general terms as 'apprehend' and 'faithfully' there lies an ambiguity. Even the ordinary, average historian, who believes and says that he is merely receptive to his data, is not passive in his thinking; he brings his categories along with him, and sees his data through them. In every treatise that is to be scientific, Reason must not slumber, and reflection must be actively applied. To him who looks at the world rationally, the world looks rational in return.[6]

'Reason in history', on this trivial account, simply means that the historian selects facts, classifies and interprets them, draws connections, and so forth, relying for that matter on a set of criteria, ie 'reasons'. In other words, historical narratives are organised or structured; they bring together a wide range of empirical material. That is obviously *not* what Hegel means. Against (or beyond) such a view, he holds that the material is *inherently* organised – that history itself, and not merely its study, is rational. But that can clearly mean a variety of different things. Hegel examines two alternatives.[7] On the one hand, he considers the view of Anaxagoras that the world is ruled by nous or what Hegel calls 'the understanding'. That is the view of history as governed by causal laws or efficient

---

[2] GWF Hegel, *Introduction to the Philosophy of History*, 3–11.
[3] ibid at 10.
[4] As RG Collingwood, *The Idea of History*, 113, puts it: 'the philosophy of history is for [Hegel] not a philosophical reflection on history but history itself raised to a higher power and become philosophical as distinct from merely empirical ...'. It is worth stressing that Collingwood misleadingly translates the phrase *philosophische Geschichte* as 'the philosophy of history', adding that 'the proposal and the terminology [are] as old as Voltaire ...' [113]. But Hegel's distinctive conception of history is not 'the philosophy of history' or *die Philosophie der Geschichte*, which indeed predated his writings, but philosophical history or *philosophische Geschichte*. Where Collingwood writes 'philosophy of history', then, one should read *philosophical* history.
[5] Hegel, *Introduction*, 12.
[6] ibid at 14.
[7] ibid at 14–18.

causation, that events (effects) follow temporally prior events (causes) in regular and measurable – ie, law-like – patterns. Historical events can hence be explained although not understood; we can know *how* things are but not *why* they are so. On the other hand, he considers the theological view that the world is governed by providence, a supernatural person or God. On that account, events are not accidental or mechanical – the way things are – but play a function in the grand design of things. They are subordinated to a divinely ordained purpose or plan, although one that is clothed in mystery, hidden from us. Historical events are thus meaningful although not intelligible; history has a purpose, unknown (in the strong sense) to us.

Hegel agrees with the theological view, against that of Anaxagoras, that events are not accidental but purposive. 'Reason in history' does not simply mean that events follow regular patterns that can be explained, namely in law-like terms. To that external view of reason, Hegel opposes an internal view: things happen *for a reason*, because they play a part in the show of history. That is one sense in which it is appropriate to speak of reason in history. Yet Hegel sides with Anaxagoras against the theological conception in a different respect. He rejects the view that reason is a divine plan concealed from us; to such a transcendent view, Hegel opposes an immanent view: the purpose of history, its inner drive or organising force, is the self-awareness of reason, spirit, or freedom.[8] History is the path that we – intelligent beings – take to learn about our rational condition; it is retrospectively intelligible to us because it is inherently rational and we are *the* rational creatures.[9] 'Reason in History', then, means that reflective self-awareness is the goal of history.[10] That is what Hegel means when he writes the following: 'World history only shows us how the World Spirit comes gradually to the consciousness of truth and the willing of it. This consciousness and will dawns in the Spirit; Spirit finds its main points, and in the end it arrives at full consciousness.'[11]

---

[8] These terms, all notoriously difficult even to experienced readers of Hegel, mean for the most part the same – or rather, Hegel characteristically uses them (and does so in his philosophy of history) as equivalents. To sum up – no doubt doing violence to the complexity of Hegel's thought – the point is as follows. To be free, on Hegel's account, is not to do as one wishes (to be free in the *negative* sense) but to act on rational grounds, that is, within self-imposed or self-determined limits (*positive* freedom); that explains the equivalence of freedom and reason. Yet rationality for Hegel is not an attribute of the self – eg, of a transcendental subject *a la* Kant – but the potential of the world to know itself or become self-aware through the intellect of human beings; reason is hence not the province of the 'knowing subject' but immanent in objective reality. That 'objective' conception of reason is spirit. For an elaborate explication of these terms – freedom, reason, spirit – in the context of Hegel's metaphysics (restored by him to the status of 'first philosophy'), see Fredrick Beiser, *Hegel*, 61–75, 110–23, 182–85, 197–205, 263–66.

[9] Notice the qualification 'retrospectively'. If the function of historical events is to enact some progress in the path towards reflective self-awareness, the meaning of history is only fully disclosed *ex post facto*. That is the proper background for Hegel's remark in the preface to the *Grundlinean der Philosophie des Rechts* that philosophy always comes too late to serve a normative function. See Hegel, *Elements of the Philosophy of Right*, 23.

[10] See Beiser, *Hegel*, 266.

[11] Hegel, *Introduction to the Philosophy of History*, 56.

This does not mean that everything in history is rational, that all events are a function of spiritual self-awareness. We have to distinguish history as the stream of time from history as an intelligible whole. The latter is the essence of the former, the actualisation of reason. Not all that exists or happens, however, conforms with reason as it has progressed up to that point in history; some events and practices – say, slavery in a society that is committed to the proposition that 'all men are created equal' – are merely contingent or accidental.[12] When Hegel writes, in the preface to the *Philosophy of Right*, that 'What is rational is actual; and what is actual is rational', he means precisely that reality contains within itself the potential to become rational or that reason is self-actualising, not that that the status quo as a whole is rationally vindicated.[13] When we look back to past epochs as philosophical historians we have no trouble segregating the pockets of irrationality from the labours of spirit. It is only from our presentist standpoint, as participants in a higher moment of rational self-awareness, that the true or essential in history is intelligible; as Hegel famously put it, 'the owl of Minerva begins its flight only with the onset of dusk'.[14]

All of this sounds brazenly dogmatic outside of the context of Hegel's metaphysics of absolute idealism, which is why it is worth summarising it briefly.[15] Hegel conceives the natural world as an organism, a holistic and self-organising entity. Its *holistic* aspect means that the parts are determined by the whole, that the logic of nature is not mechanistic but functional; thus, the physical and chemical processes that make living organisms possible are not the cause of life but determined by the necessity of life. The *self*-organising dimension distinguishes nature from purposive activities, such as writing a book or painting a portrait, that depend on an author; nature is spontaneously organised instead of being created. But the world is not just organic nature – it is spirit as well. The highest form of nature, the human species, is not just life but the self-awareness of life, that is to say, through human beings the world becomes a self-aware organism. History is accordingly the slow progression from individual self-awareness – the 'I' standpoint – to the consciousness of the self as spirit – the 'I that is We and We that is I'[16] – through the mutual recognition of human beings as members of the species in which nature comes to know itself; 'Reason', writes Hegel, 'is the perception of God's work.'[17] The world understood

---

[12] The slavery example is Hegel's. See ibid at 21.

[13] ibid, *Elements of the Philosophy of Right*, 20. My understanding of this point was sharpened after hearing a lecture on Hegel by Mikhail Xifaras at Harvard Law School in April 2012.

[14] ibid at 23. In the *Introduction to the Philosophy of History*, 82, he writes that 'Because we are concerned only with the idea of Spirit – and we regard the whole of world history as nothing more than the manifestation of Spirit – when we go over the past, however extensive it may be, we are really concerned only with the present. This is because philosophy, which occupies itself with the True, is concerned with what is eternally present. Nothing in the past is lost to philosophy ...'

[15] This paragraph is heavily indebted to Beiser, *Hegel*, 53–123, 174–91.

[16] Hegel, *Phenomenology of Spirit*, § 177, 110.

[17] ibid, *Introduction to the Philosophy of History*, 39.

as a holistic, self-organizing and self-aware substance is what he means by the terms 'Absolute', 'God' or 'Idea'.[18]

True, all of this sounds brazenly dogmatic as well. But I have no interest here in going into the subject of Hegel's epistemology – how he tried to justify the belief in this cosmological *tour de force* – not the least because it strikes me as every bit as unpersuasive as it is impressive. My point is that Hegel's account of philosophical history does not fall from the sky; it is deeply embedded in a much larger story about the nature of the world. It is understandable, from that standpoint, why Hegel conceives history as the triumphal march of reason and why he places the philosophical historian in the privileged position of being able to retrospectively separate the mass of the merely contingent from the actualisation of spirit. All of that is buttressed in (and is eventually bound to collapse with) the metaphysical foundation. The question is how exactly, or in what way, philosophical history is fit to be a methodological basis for my project.

It is worth pointing out, for starters, the Hegelian and non-Hegelian features of the project. What I set to do is to read the history of legal thought from the mid-nineteenth century onwards from a contemporary liberal legalist standpoint. That involves two basic argumentative moves. The first, inspired by Hegelian metaphysics, is to argue that contemporary political culture embodies that form of political rationality – 'liberalism' – that I articulated in chapter one; 'political liberalism' is the 'idea' immanent in contemporary political culture. The various institutions, practices, and beliefs that constitute that culture are parts of the liberal whole, and the point of chapter one is to bring that whole to full conscious awareness.

But there are at least two important respects in which the argument is notoriously non-Hegelian. To begin with, it is not metaphysical. A metaphysical argument involves certain claims about reality. One reason why Hegel's philosophy merits the heading of 'idealism' is that it gives explanatory priority to ideal over material elements; as we have seen, Hegel argues that the world is the self-actualising

---

[18] 'Spirit' is thus not a self-conscious subject or supernatural person but the self-awareness of the world through the human being *qua* rational being. See Beiser, *Hegel*, 70–71, 112. A typical misreading of Hegelian metaphysics as a form of what Beiser calls 'supersubjectivism' is that of GA Cohen, *Karl Marx's Theory of History*, 1–27. Hegel's God does not create anything. God is not the author of the world simply because it does not exist prior and apart from the world; it is the world itself as a single self-organising and self-aware substance – as embodied spirit. Cohen's account is a peculiar blend of the Christian theodicy with Hegelian metaphysics, and indeed it is true to neither. It is a fact that Hegel often uses an overtly theistic vocabulary – see, eg, *Introduction to the Philosophy of History*, 17–18; but that must be read against the background of his progressive account of reason or spirit, according to which faith in a personal God is a moment in the path towards full self-reflective awareness. We need a theistic moment to grasp spirit just as we need a ladder to climb a high wall. Hence he declares – ibid at 18 – that '… the time must finally come when we comprehend the rich product of creative Reason that is world history.' Whether this makes Hegel an atheist depends on how one defines the concept of God; Hegel is neither a theist according to the core meaning of that term nor a pantheist along Spinozan naturalistic lines. On the religious dimension in Hegel's philosophy, a theme that was at the center of the polemic between left and right-wing Hegelians, see Beiser, ibid at 124–152, 307–13.

Idea, that reality is determined and structured by intellectual or spiritual forces. I make no such claims about our political culture. The 'idea' of liberalism in my account does not operate at the level of reality – as the primary cause or determining factor – but at the level of consciousness; it underlies (or resonates with) the way in which participants in our political culture experience its reality, as opposed to what that reality actually is. That means that my account is compatible both with the most extreme idealism, which gives complete causal priority to the idea, and the most extreme materialism, which demotes the idea to the status of ideology in the pejorative sense of 'false consciousness'.[19] I take a non-belligerent position in the Great War between social-theoretical idealists and materialists; indeed, it seems to me that the monocausal or single-factor explanations endorsed by both contenders are utterly unpersuasive.

A second respect in which my approach is non-Hegelian concerns the epistemic status of the argument. The main reason why I do not capitalise the word 'idea' is to convey a measure of epistemic caution. When I speak of liberalism as the idea immanent in our political culture and describe my aim in chapter one as bringing the idea to full conscious awareness, I do not mean to imply that I can prove my case. Hegel took himself to have demonstrated, in the *Phenomenology of Spirit*, the rational necessity of each step from the standpoint of ordinary consciousness to that of 'absolute knowledge' or 'science'. My claim is much more modest. Although the *Phenomenology* furnishes the loose model of the argument in chapter one, mine is a constructive interpretation of our political culture.[20] It aims at presenting it in a way that is morally compelling.

The second argumentative move that is basic to the project is a *retrospective teleology* of legal thought. I read the past from the nineteenth century onwards as if it led straight into the present, that is to say, as if what determined the course of history was all along the 'idea' of liberal legalism, slowly revealing itself up to the present moment of full self-awareness in our minds. Notice the important qualification introduced by the phrase 'as if'. My point is not that the story unfolding in the core chapters of this dissertation is the essence of history or (for that matter) 'nothing other than the thoughtful consideration of history'. I concede immediately that it is a heavily edited account. That is obvious not only in the large (and fully intentional) omissions – eg, there is nothing in this book about the fascist legal theorising of the inter-war period, except obliquely, where it was incorporated into the social moment of liberal legalism – but also in the bias that

---

[19] The *locus classicus* of full-blown (social-theoretical) materialism is Marx and Engels, 'The German Ideology', 148–75, which followed Ludwig Feuerbach's 'humanist' and proto-materialist critique of religion in *The Essence of Christianity*. There, Marx and Engels famously 'settle accounts with our erstwhile philosophical conscience' (Karl Marx, 'Preface to A Contribution to the Critique of Political Economy', 5). The other major work in this vein is Marx, 'Economic and Philosophic Manuscripts of 1844', 106–25. The slogan of this entire tradition is encapsulated in thesis XI of Marx's 'Theses on Feuerbach': 'The philosophers have only *interpreted* the world, in various ways; the point, however, is to *change* it' (emphasis in the original).

[20] I take the notion of 'constructive interpretation' from Ronald Dworkin, *Law's Empire*, 50–53.

informed the selection and the interpretation of texts, or even in the conspicuous primacy of academic sources in the research material.

Of course, this way of distancing myself from Hegelian historicism, with its extensive metaphysical surroundings and epistemic conceit, raises the opposite problem – the accusation that I am smuggling fiction into the domain of history; worse still, acknowledging the bias puts me in the bad company of intentional wrongdoers. What sort of historical narrative survives the confession of its own deep bias?

Let me start by making, albeit briefly and superficially, the purely negative case that there is nothing wrong about historicising with a bias, for the very good reason that it is inevitable. Historical writing, almost everyone now acknowledges, is not 'scientific' or 'objective' in sharp contrast with fictional or mythological writing; to stretch the point just a bit, good history is really but a special genre of storytelling.[21] The historian comes to the source material – even selects it – loaded with prejudgements and anticipated conclusions. No doubt there are important differences between writing a novel and a history book or (analogously) between making and interpreting a poem. Historians build on the information furnished by the sources and operate under conventionally established constraints and standards of intellectual honesty. But the differences are a matter of degree. Just as there is no Archimedean point above culture that enables literary creation *ex nihilo* – authorship in the strongest sense – interpretive truth lies in the eye of the beholder much more than in the 'facts speaking for themselves'.

The same holds for the closely related charge often directed against the type of highly general narrative that I tried to articulate – 'overviews' or 'syntheses', so it goes, are hopelessly abstract and thus unfaithful to historical reality. The objection can easily be turned around. While a preference for the forest in detriment of the trees carries with it a real danger of procrustean manipulation of the 'data', obsessing with the particular in all its concrete detail often leads to the no less disastrous path of intellectual myopia; one way or another, reality is distorted and 'historical truth' betrayed. It does not seem very wise to pick one alternative over the other a priori, as opposed to figuring out what is the most defensible level of generality in light of one's research agenda. The reader should bear in mind that I proposed to articulate a history of liberal legalism alone. There are admittedly many more things of historical interest about the periods of political and legal thought that I examine than the ones that the narrative brings to light,[22] although (to my mind)

---

[21] Three major contributions to legal history that I greatly admire come very close to asserting just that. See Duncan Kennedy, *The Rise and Fall of Classical legal Thought*, xxvi–xxxi, read in conjunction with Kennedy, *A Critique of Adjudication*, 15–18, 57; Morton J Horwitz, *The Transformation of American Law*, vii–ix; António Manuel Hespanha, *Cultura Jurídica Europeia*, 43, 65–71. It should be noted that none of these works embraces explicitly the presentist method; the last one, in fact, issues loud warnings against it – ibid at 39–44, 50–54 – although the type of presentism considered there, the 'Whighish' rendition of the past as the linear progression towards the glories of present-day human achievement, is, as we shall see, just about the opposite of my account.

[22] To be sure, my account is far less abstract than Hegel's rendition of world-history in terms of three 'worlds' – the Oriental world, where only one person is free; the classical ancient world of Greece

not of major interest to the history *of* liberal legalism. From the latter standpoint, they are dispensable details in the realm of the merely contingent.

This leads us to the positive or affirmative side of the case. What is the point of doing the history of liberal legalism? There are two main reasons. One is that there is a lack of historical depth in contemporary liberal culture. As critical observers so different as Alasdair MacIntyre and Robert Gordon have noticed, normative argument within liberal political culture usually proceeds in conditions of either general historical unawareness or (less frequently) open hostility to historicism, a pattern both reflected in and reinforced by the academic division of labour between historians, on the one hand, and political and legal philosophers, on the other.[23] What that intellectual culture produces is an inability to recognise that the familiar normative structures of individual rights, democratic authority, social welfare and so forth have a history.

The main point, however, is to challenge what might be called the orthodox story about liberalism. To the limited extent that it pays tribute to history, mainstream political consciousness is infected by a post-modern variant of Whig historicism. It embraces a story that takes the form of a progressive teleology running from the classical liberalism of the white male landowner or capitalist citizen of a colonial power to the contemporary liberalism that overcomes – or at least tends to overcome – racial, gender, class and national distinctions. The history of liberalism is hence marked by triumph, as judged by its own standards, along two dimensions. On the one hand, a triumph of breadth, evinced by the inclusion of groups – eg, women and blacks – historically burdened by formal discrimination. On the other hand, a triumph of depth, associated with the transition from formal or superficial to substantive or structural justice, that is, from a liberalism of private ownership and free contract to a liberalism of human rights, a regulated market economy and distributive fairness.

This is not quite Whig history in the traditional sense, for the reason that it is entirely stripped of the metaphysical belief that progress, being underwritten in the laws of history, is inevitable.[24] The major events of the twentieth century, from Auschwitz to Hiroshima, were in one way or another too depressing and impacting to allow the continued existence of any of that nineteenth-century Pollyanna optimism. By contrast, contemporary liberalism appears to be mostly defensive, occasionally a 'liberalism of fear',[25] and always at least implicitly preoccupied with the fragility of the historical achievements of the rule of law, individual rights and democratic governance.[26] The underlying philosophy of history is that while the

---

and Rome, where only some persons are free; and the Germanic (ie the Christian European) world, where *everyone* is free. See Hegel, *Introduction to the Philosophy of History*, 20–22, 92–98.

[23] Alasdair MacIntyre, *After Virtue*, 2–5, 266–76; Robert W Gordon, 'Historicism in Legal Scholarship', 1025–28. See also Mark Kelman, *A Guide to Critical Legal Studies*, 228–33.

[24] See Herbert Butterfield, *The Whig Interpretation of History*. See also Robert W Gordon, 'Critical Legal Histories', 59–65; and Mark Kelman, *A Guide to Critical Legal Studies*, 222–28.

[25] *cf* Judith Shklar, 'The Liberalism of Fear'.

[26] *Compare*, eg, Kant, 'An Answer to the Question: What is Enlightenment?'; with John Rawls, *Justice as Fairness*, 32–38.

logic of liberalism is inherently progressive, along the dimensions of breadth and depth mentioned above, there is no reason to think that the game of history is rigged in favour of that particular logic.[27]

What I meant to challenge is the view that the history of liberalism, as judged by its own standards, has been a history of sustained albeit constantly threatened triumph. For, *even if true*, that is really but one half of the story. The other half is liberal rationality gradually undoing itself. Whereas classical liberalism embodied a theory of justice, which was presented as an object of rational agreement, contemporary liberalism despairs about the fact of reasonable disagreement in politics. That is why the primary focus of political reflection retreats from first-order questions of substance – 'Who gets what in social life?' – to second-order questions of procedure – 'Who is to provide an authoritative answer to the first-order question?' And it turns out that the latter question is as intractable within liberalism as the former, a statement corroborated by a superficial glance at the last half century of intense and unsettled debate in constitutional theory. As liberal consciousness becomes increasingly self-aware, then, it becomes conscious of an inner aporia – it cannot conclusively meet, by its own standards, the challenge of political justification. This is not the triumph of liberalism but more like what Max Horkheimer called 'the end of reason'.

> The philosophy this world produced is essentially rationalistic, but time and again, in following out its own principles, it turns against itself and takes the form of skepticism. [...] The concept of reason from the very beginning included the concept of critique. [...] Skepticism purged the idea of reason of so much of its content that today scarcely anything is left of it. Reason, in destroying conceptual fetishes, ultimately destroyed itself.[28]

I turn at last to a formidable objection to the whole enterprise – a non-trivial metamorphosis of the trivial charge of bias. Although my declared aim is to historicise liberal legalism, in the twofold sense of situating it historically and presenting a narrative that rivals the official story, I may be charged with betraying genuine historical sense in the interests of a priori reasoning. For I take the idea of liberalism – as well as that of legalism – as *prius* rather than *terminus* of its history; and that exposes my entire account to a critique from the standpoint of what Michel Foucault, building on Nietzsche's theses on the history of morality, called the *genealogical* method.[29] On the genealogical view, liberalism and legalism are not ideas with history but artefacts of history. Concepts that appear to us either universal and necessary or at least epoch-making – eg, person, freedom, science, rationality – are in fact the debris of historical contingency molded by discrete and successive acts of theory-building or theoretical *bricolage*.

---

[27] But see Francis Fukuyama, *The End of History and the Last Man*.
[28] Max Horkheimer, 'The End of Reason', 27.
[29] Michel Foucault, 'Nietzsche, Genealogy, History'. See also Nietzsche, *On the Genealogy of Morals*, especially the preface, 451–59.

Genealogy is directed against philosophic history, the 'metahistorical deployment of ideal significations and indefinite teleologies'.[30] When successful, a genealogical narrative breaks down philosophical hubris. Foucault puts the point eloquently: 'History has a more important task than to be handmaiden to philosophy, to recount the necessary birth of truth and values; it should become a differential knowledge of energies and failings, heights and degenerations, poisons and antidotes. Its task is to become a curative science'.[31]

The main goal of genealogical narratives is to relativise ideas. It is a method, and a structured one at that. Ideas are the offspring of the accidental intercourse of other ideas, indeed products of conceptual miscegenation. A genealogical narrative traces the ancestry of intellectual structures that appear to us natural, necessary, universal, etc, revealing their unexpected and impure family tree. It is the exact opposite of tracing the origins of ideas. Let us recall Foucault to the stage, this time for a lengthy act:

> An examination of descent also permits the discovery, under the unique aspect of a trait or a concept, of the myriad events through which – thanks to which, against which – they were formed. Genealogy does not pretend to go back in time to restore unbroken continuity that operates beyond the dispersion of forgotten things; its duty is not to demonstrate that the past actively exists in the present, that it continues secretly to animate the present, having imposed a predetermined form to all its vicissitudes. Genealogy does not resemble the evolution of a species and does not map the destiny of a people. On the contrary, to follow the complex course of descent is to maintain passing events in their proper dispersion; it is to identify the accidents, the minute deviations – or conversely, the complete reversals – the errors, the false appraisals, and the faulty calculations that gave birth to those things that continue to exist and have value for us; it is to discover that truth or being do not lie at the root of what we know and what we are, but the exteriority of accidents.[32]

The genealogical method invites us to see the transition from one intellectual system to another – say, from classical to social liberalism – as an unpredictable break-up or discontinuity in thought. What the present owes the past is raw material for a novel artefact. From that standpoint, there is no such thing as the *idea* of liberalism (or legalism); there are various definitions and redefinitions of liberalism more or less loosely related by ties of family resemblance. In my account, on the contrary, the transformations of liberal legalism are portrayed as moments in the unfolding of an idea – as immanent developments.

The genealogical story about liberalism is often directed against mainstream accounts of its 'origins'. In highly schematic fashion, the argument develops in three steps. The first step is to diagnose the standard forms of liberal argument

---

[30] ibid at 140.
[31] ibid at 156.
[32] ibid at 146.

or recursive moves within the 'circle of liberal justification';[33] that is, to figure out what premises support the liberal worldview – how it is structured. The second step is to question the necessity, naturalness, universality or self-evident truth of the premises upon which the structure hangs. The most frequent move is to point to the historical contingency of the liberal 'subject' or 'self', indeed to present 'it' as a strange event once we descend from the Eden of idealised common sense to the messy ground of historical contingency. This familiar point is stated by John Milbank in forceful terms.

> [W]e should ask why the West gave birth to anything so fantastically peculiar and unlikely [as liberalism]. Liberalism is peculiar and unlikely because it proceeds by inventing a wholly artificial human being who has never really existed, and then pretending that we are all instances of such a species. This is the pure individual, thought of in abstraction from his or her gender, birth, associations, beliefs and also, crucially, in equal abstraction from … religious or philosophical beliefs …[34]

The third step – the properly genealogical one – is to show that the liberal subject is the offspring of accidents of conceptual intercourse motivated by historical circumstances foreign to us. Pierre Manent's intellectual history of liberalism presents a general thesis of that type. Here is a pale summary of the argument. Manent situates the invention of modern individualism in the context of what he calls the 'theologico-political problem' of the Middle Ages. It was a dilemma about the role of the Church in temporal affairs. On the one hand, the medieval Church showed little interest in the secular world, on account of the spiritual nature of its mission – the salvation of souls; that created a political vacuum to be filled by temporal authority ('to Caesar's what is Caesar's and to God what is God's'). Yet, on the other hand, the Church could not accept any complete separation of the secular from the religious, premised on a distinction between natural and supernatural goods, for it saw life merely as a pilgrimage to the afterlife and thus reserved the prerogative (*plenitudo postestas*) of intervening in the affairs of the body for the sake of the soul. In other words, the medieval secular world was jammed by the Church's refusal either to recognise its autonomy or to deny it entirely. No wonder that the status of secular authority throughout the Middle Ages was completely uncertain, encouraging – and often providing an excuse for – continuing tension and occasional struggle between the Church and secular authority. Since the terms of the problem disavowed both theocratic solutions and a return to the pagan understanding of 'the city' as the site of natural flourishment, early modern thinking, beginning with Machiavelli and Hobbes, married the pre-Christian idea of polity perfection with the (apparently contradictory) Christian demotion of the political realm to devise an autonomous secular space defined in purely negative terms: as an association of wills directed towards

---

[33] See Pierre Schlag, 'The Empty Circles of Liberal Justification'.
[34] John Milbank, 'The Gift of Ruling', 213.

self-preservation, enabling the pursuit of higher goods while locating them beyond its sphere. The inhabitant of this new secular world – the anonymous subject or individual – was invented along with it. So argues Manent.[35]

Arguments of this form have been around for a while. But they have had little echo within liberal thought, for neither in liberal political theory nor in the political common sense of our societies is there any significant trace of a crisis of faith in the truth of 'subjectivity'. It is, writes a prominent liberal voice, 'Conspicuously irresistible to inhabitants of liberal culture'.[36] Moreover, to the limited extent that genealogies of the subject have been taken seriously, it is my understanding that they have for the most part been summarily dismissed on two grounds, each of them a notorious piece of philosophical revanchism against history. On the one hand, the notion that an argument about the ancestry of a belief can serve a critical function with respect to the belief in question has been charged with the 'genetic fallacy': the genetic properties of an argument say nothing of interest, at least prima facie, about its epistemic properties.[37] On the other hand, there is the assertion that it is possible to establish the truth of subjectivity via the argument from performative contradiction, an alleged instance of a rare philosophical species – the analytical KO. In short, the problem is that the very denial of subjectivity presupposes it. Margaret Radin and Frank Michelman elaborate the point as follows: 'We cannot deny our own agency. (We cannot speak the sentence of denial except as speaking subjects, affirming by speaking the sentence what the sentence means to deny.) We can call agency into question, and we had better, but to call into question is also to (re)affirm, (re)create, (re)construct'.[38]

I have no desire to examine the strength of these arguments or others that might be advanced against the genealogical project. What concerns me is what their pervasive influence signals: that the genealogical method is ineffective. Genealogy typically fails. It fails because it violates what Raymond Geuss calls 'the principle of internal criticism', a standard for critical theory that he attributes above all to Adorno.

> Critical theory is committed to the principle of 'internal criticism'. Just as critical theory is supposed to contribute to the agents' self-knowledge, so the proponents of the critical theory recognize as 'valid criticism' only what could in principle be part of the self-criticism of the agents to whom it is addressed; if the proponents of a critical theory

---

[35] Pierre Manent, *An Intellectual History of Liberalism*, 1–20.
[36] Frank Michelman, 'The Subject of Liberalism', 1812.
[37] See Raymond Geuss, *The Idea of a Critical Theory*, 20. Harry Frankena comes close to charging Alasdair MacIntyre with the genetic fallacy in his review of *After Virtue*, where he writes: 'What bothers me is not distinguishing [philosophy from history] or giving the impression that a historical inquiry can establish a philosophical point, as MacIntyre seems to do.' Frankena, 'MacIntyre and Modern Morality', 579–80.
[38] Radin and Michelman, 'Pragmatist and Poststructuralist Critical Legal Practice', 1058. See also Jack Balkin, 'Tradition, Betrayal, and the Politics of Deconstruction', 1629. For an interesting reply to these arguments, see Pierre Schlag, 'Law as the Continuation of God by Other Means', 434–37.

which to enlighten and emancipate a group of agents, they must find in the experience, form of consciousness, and belief of *those* agents the means of emancipation and enlightenment.[39]

A Philosophical History of Liberal Legalism does not question the basic premises or epistemic norms of liberal and legalist culture; on the contrary, it develops a critique firmly grounded in them. It is hence supposed to be at once attractive and unsettling. In fact, is purports to have us understand something that we already perceive in inchoate form. The point is not to provoke surprise but to enact at the conscious level the half-conscious experience of a post-realist jurist in a liberal polity.

---

[39] Geuss, *The Idea of a Critical Theory*, 64–65 (emphasis in the original).

BIBLIOGRAPHY

Alexy, Robert, *A Theory of Constitutional Rights*, translated by Julian Rivers (Oxford, Oxford University Press, 2002).
—— 'Balancing, Constitutional Review, and Representation' (2015) 3 *International Journal of Constitutional Law* 572.
Altman, Andrew, 'Legal Realism, Critical Legal Studies, and Dworkin' (1986) 15 *Philosophy and Public Affairs* 205.
Amos, Sheldon, *A Systematic View of the Science of Jurisprudence* (London, Longmans, Green, 1872).
Aquinas, Thomas, *Summa Theologica*, translated by the Fathers of the English Dominican Province in 1947, available at www.sacred-texts.com/chr/aquinas/summa/index.htm (last visited: 10 September 2012).
Arendt, Hannah, *Lectures on Kant's Political Philosophy* (Chicago, The University of Chicago Press, 1992).
—— *The Human Condition* (Chicago, The University of Chicago Press, 1998).
Aristotle, *Nicomachean Ethics*, translated by WD Ross, in Richard McKeon (ed), *The Basic Works of Aristotle* (New York, Modern Library, 2001).
—— *Politics*, translated by Benjamin Jowett, in *The Basic Works of Aristotle*.
—— *Topics*, translated by WA Pickard-Cambridge, in *The Basic Works of Aristotle*.
Arnaut, André-Jean, *Les Juristes Face à la Société du XIXe Siècle à Nous Jours* (Paris, Presses Universitaires de France, 1975).
Astuti, Guido, *La Formazione dello Stato Moderno in Italia: Lezione di Storia Del Diritto Italiano*, I (Torino, G Giappicheli Editore, 1967).
Atienza, Manuel and Manero, Juan Ruiz, *Las Piezas del Derecho: Teoría de los Enunciados Jurídicos*, 4th edn (Barcelona, Editorial Ariel, 2012).
Aubry, C and Rau, C, *Cours de Droit Civil Français D'Après L'Óuvrage Allemand de C-S Zachariae*, I (Paris, Imprimerie et Librarie Générale de Jurisprudence, 1856).
Austin, John, *Lectures on Jurisprudence*, I (Bristol, Thoemmes, 2002).
Bacon, Francis, *The Essays, Civil and Moral: And the New Atlantis* (New York, PF Collier & Son, 1909).
Balkin, Jack, 'The Crystalline Structure of Legal Thought' (1986) 39 *Rutgers Law Review* 1.
—— 'Nested Oppositions' (1989) 99 *The Yale Law Journal* 1669.
—— 'Tradition, Betrayal, and the Politics of Deconstruction' (1990) 11 *Cardozo Law Review* 1613.
Barber, Benjamin, *Strong Democracy* (Berkeley, University of California Press, 2003).
Beiser, Frederick, *Hegel* (New York, Routledge, 2005).
Bellamy, Richard, *Political Constitutionalism: A Republican Defense of the Constitutionality of Democracy* (Cambridge, Cambridge University Press, 2007).
Belleau, Marie-Claire, 'The '*Juristes Inquiets*': Legal Classicism and Criticism in Early Twentieth-Century France' (1987) 2 *Utah Law Review* 379.
Bentham, Jeremy, 'Anarchical Fallacies' in J Waldron (ed), *Nonsense Upon Stilts: Bentham, Burke, and Marx on the Rights of Man* (London and New York, Methuen, 1987).
—— *Theory of Legislation*, translated from the French of Etienne Dumont by R Hildreth (London, Trübner and Co, 1871).
Berger, Peter L and Luckmann, Thomas, *The Social Construction of Reality: A Treatise in the Sociology of Knowledge* (New York, Anchor Books, 1967).
Berlin, Isaiah, 'Two Concepts of Liberty' in *Four Essays on Liberty* (New York, Oxford University Press, 1970).

Betti, Emilio, *Teoria Generale del Negozio Giuridico* (Milano, A Giuffrè, 1994).
Bickel, Alexander, 'The Supreme Court 1960 Term – Forward: The Passive Virtues' (1961–62) 75 *Harvard Law Review* 40.
—— *The Least Dangerous Branch* (New Haven, Yale University Press, 1986).
Bogdandy, Armin Von and Schill, Stephan, 'Overcoming Absolute Primacy: Respect for National Identity under the Lisbon Treaty' (2011) 48 *Common Market Law Review*, 1417.
Bonnecase, Julien, *L'École de l'Exégèse en Droit Civil* (Paris, E de Boccard, 1924).
Bordieu, Pierre, 'Force and Law: Towards a Sociology of the Juridical Field', translated by Richard Terdiman (1987) 38 *The Hastings Law Journal* 805.
Brandeis, Louis D, 'The Desirable Industrial Peace', speech delivered to the National Civic Federation on 25 April 1905, available at www.law.louisville.edu/library/collections/brandeis/node/231 (last visited: 10 September 2012).
Brewer, Scott, 'Exemplary Reasoning: Semantics, Pragmatics, and the Rational Force of Legal Argument by Analogy' (1996) 109 *Harvard Law Review* 923.
Brunner, Otto, *Land and Lordship: Structures of Governance in Medieval Austria*, translated by Howard Kaminsky and James Van Horn Melton (Philadephia, University of Pennsylvannia Press, 1992).
Burke, Edmund, 'Reflections on the Revolution in France' in *The Portable Edmund Burke*, edited by Isaac Krammick (New York, Penguin Books, 1999).
Butterfield, Herbert, *The Whig Interpretation of History* (New York, WW Norton & Company, 1965).
Caenegem, RC van, *An Historical Introduction to Western Constitutional Law* (Cambridge, Cambridge University Press, 1995).
Canaris, Claus-Wilhelm, *Grundrechte und Privatrecht* (Berlin, Walter de Gruyter, 1998).
Canning, Joseph, *The Political Thought of Baldus de Ubaldis* (Cambridge, Cambridge University Press, 1987).
Cardozo, Benjamin, *The Nature of the Judicial Process* (Buffalo, William S Hein & Co, 1997).
Catechism of the Catholic Church, available at www.vatican.va/archive/ENG0015/_INDEX.HTM (last visited: 16 September 2012).
Charmont, Joseph, 'L'Abus du Droit', 1 *Revue Trimestrielle de Droit Civil* 113 (1912).
—— 'Recent Phases of French Legal Philosophy', translated by Franklin W Scott and Joseph Chamberlain, in *Modern French Legal Philosophy* (New Jersey, Rothman Reprints, 1968).
Cherednychenko, Olha O, 'Fundamental Rights and Private Law: A Relationship of Subordination or Complementarity?' (2007) 3 *Utrecht Law Review* 1.
Cicero, *The Laws*, translated and edited by Niall Rudd (Oxford, Oxford University Press, 1998).
Clavero, Bartolomé, 'Institución Política y Derecho: Acerca del Concepto Historiografico de «Estado Moderno»' (1981) 19 *Revista de Estudios Políticos* 43.
Coase, Ronald H, 'The Problem of Social Cost' (1960) 3 *The Journal of Law and Economics* 1.
Cohen, Felix, 'The Ethical Basis of Legal Criticism' (1931) 41 *The Yale Law Journal* 201.
—— 'Transcendental Nonsense and the Functional Approach' (1935) 35 *Columbia Law Review* 809.
Cohen, GA, *Karl Marx's Theory of History: A Defence* (Oxford, Oxford University Press, 2000).
Cohen, Joshua, 'Moral Pluralism and Political Consensus' in David Copp, Jean Hampton and John Roemer (eds), *The Idea of Democracy* (Cambridge, Cambridge University Press, 1993).
Cohen, Morris R, 'Recent Philosophical-Legal Literature in French, German and Italian (1912–14)' (1916) 26 *International Journal of Ethics* 528.
—— 'Property and Sovereignty' (1927–28) 13 *Cornell Law Review* 8.
—— *Reason and Nature: An Essay on the Meaning of Scientific Method* (New York, Harcourt, Brace & Co, 1931).
—— 'The Basis of Contract' (1933) 46 *Harvard Law Review* 553.
—— 'On Absolutisms in Legal Thought' (1935–36) 84 *University of Pennsylvania Law Review* 681.
Coing, Helmut, 'German "Pandektistik" in Its Relationship to the Former "Ius Commune"' (1989) 37 *The American Journal of Comparative Law* 9.
Collingwood, RG, *The Idea of History* (Oxford, Oxford University Press, 1963).
Condorcet, Marquis De, 'Essay on the Application of Mathematics to the Theory of Decision-Making' in Keith Baker (trans and ed), *Selected Writings* (Indianapolis, Bobbs-Merrill, 1976).

Confucius, *The Analects of Confucius*, translated by Simon Leys (New York, WW Norton, 1997).
Cook, Walter Wheeler, 'Privileges of Labor Unions in the Struggle for Life' (1918) 27 *The Yale Law Journal* 779.
Corwin, Edward S, 'The Higher Law Background of American Constitutional Law' (1929) 42 *Harvard Law Review* 365.
Costa, Pietro, *Iurisdictio: Semantica del Potere Politico Nella Pubblicistica Medievale, 1100–1433* (Millano, A Giuffrè, 1969).
Coulanges, Fustel De, *La Cité Antique: Etude sur le Culture, le Droit et les Institutions de la Grèce et de Rome* (Paris, Librarie Hachette, 1912).
Dawson, John, *The Oracles of the Law* (Buffalo, WS Hein, 1986).
Demogue, René, 'Analysis of Fundamental Notions', translated by Franklin W Scott and Joseph Chamberlain in *Modern French Legal Philosophy* (New Jersey, Rothman Reprints, 1968).
—— *Les Notions Fondamentales du Droit Privé: Essai Critique* (Paris, Éditions la Mémoire du Droit, 2001).
Descartes, René, *Discourse on Method, Optics, Geometry, and Meteorology*, translated by Paul J Olscamp (Indianapolis/Cambridge, Hackett Publishing Company, 2001).
Dewey, John, 'Logical Method and Law' (1914–25) 10 *The Cornell Law Quarterly* 17.
Dicenso, James, *Kant, Religion, and Politics* (Cambridge, UK and New York, Cambridge University Press, 2011).
Dicey, AV, *Introduction to the Study of the Law of the Constitution* (Indianapolis, Liberty Classics, 1982).
Diederichsen, Uwe, 'Das Bundesverfassungsgericht als oberstes Zivilgericht – ein Lehrstük der juristischen Methodenlehre' (1998) 198 *Archiv für die civilistische Praxis* 171.
Donaldson, Peter S, *Machiavelli and Mystery of State* (New York, Cambridge University Press, 1988).
Duby, Georges, *Les Trois Ordres ou L'Imaginaire du Féodalisme* (Paris, Gallimard, 1978).
Duguit, Léon, *Les Transformations Générales du Droit Privé* (Paris, F Alcan, 1912).
—— 'Theory of Objective Law Anterior to the State', translated by Franklin W Scott and Joseph Chamberlain, in *Modern French Legal Philosophy* (New Jersey, Rothman Reprints, 1968).
Durkheim, Emile, *The Division of Labor in Society* (New York, The Free Press, 1984).
—— *The Rules of the Sociological Method* (New York, The Free Press, nd).
Duxbury, Neil, *Patterns of American Jurisprudence* (Oxford, Oxford University Press, 1995).
Dworkin, Ronald, *Taking Rights Seriously* (Cambridge, Mass, Harvard University Press, 1978).
—— 'What is Equality? Part 1: Equality of Welfare' (1981) 10 *Philosophy and Public Affairs* 185.
—— 'What is Equality? Part 2: Equality of Resources' (1981) 10 *Philosophy and Public Affairs* 283.
—— *A Matter of Principle* (Cambridge, Mass, Harvard University Press, 1985).
—— *Law's Empire* (Cambridge, Mass, Belknap Press of Harvard University Press, 1986).
—— *A Bill of Rights for Britain* (London, Chatto & Windus, 1990).
—— *Freedom's Law: The Moral Reading of the American Constitution* (Cambridge, Mass, Harvard University Press, 1996).
—— 'The Right to Ridicule', *The New York Review of Books*, 23 March 2006.
—— 'Looking for Cass Sunstein' (review essay), *The New York Review of Books*, 30 April 2009.
—— *Justice for Hedgehogs* (Cambridge, Mass, Belknap Press of Harvard University Press, 2011).
Ehrlich, Eugen, 'Judicial Freedom of Decision', translated by Ernest Bruncken and Layton B Register, in *Science of Legal Method: Select Essays by Several Authors* (New Jersey, Rothman Reprints, 1969).
—— *Fundamental Principles of the Sociology of Law*, translated by Walter L Moll (New Brunswick, Transaction Publishers, 2002).
Ekeland, Ivar, *The Best of All Possible Worlds: Mathematics and Destiny* (Chicago and London, The University of Chicago Press, 2006).
Ely, John Hart, *Democracy and Distrust: A Theory of Judicial Review* (Cambridge, Mass, Harvard University Press, 1980).
Engisch, Karl, *Einführung in das juristische Denken* (Stuttgart: Kohlhammer, 1956).
Esser, Josef, *Grundsatz und Norm in der richterlichen Fortbildung des Privatrechts* (Tübingen, Mohr, 1956).

Ewald, William, 'Comparative Jurisprudence (I): What Was it Like to Try a Rat?' (1889) 143 *University of Pennsylvania Law Review*.
Findlay, JN, 'Foreword' to GFW Hegel, *Phenomenology of Spirit*, translated by AV Miller (Oxford, Clarendon Press, 1977).
Finnis, John, *Natural Law and Natural Rights* (Oxford, Clarendon Press; New York, Oxford University Press, 1982).
—— 'Law, Morality, and "Sexual Orientation"' in John Corvino (ed) *Same Sex: Debating the Ethics, Science, and Culture of Homosexuality* (Lanham, Md, Rowman & Littlefield, 1997).
Fioravanti, Maurizio, *Costituzione* (Bologna, Il Mulino, 1999).
Fisher III, William et al, 'Introduction' to Fisher et al (eds) *American Legal Realism* (New York and Oxford, Oxford University Press, 1993).
—— 'Legal Reasoning', in Fisher et al (eds) *American Legal Realism*.
Fletcher, George P, 'Law and Morality: A Kantian Perspective' (1997) 87 *Columbia Law Review* 533.
Foley, Duncan K, *Adam's Fallacy: A Guide to Economic Theology* (Cambridge, Mass, Belknap Press of Harvard University Press, 2006).
Forquin, Guy, *Seigneurie et Féodalité au Moyen Âge* (Les Éditions G Crès et Cie, 1970).
Foucault, Michel, 'Nietzsche, Genealogy, History' in Paul Rabinow (ed) *The Foucault Reader* (New York, Pantheon, 1984).
France, Anatole, *Le Lys Rouge* (Paris, Calmann Lévy, 1894).
Frank, Jerome, *Law and the Modern Mind* (New Jersey, Transaction Publishers, 2009).
Frankena, William K, 'MacIntyre and Modern Morality' (1983) 93 *Ethics* 579.
Freeman, Samuel, *Rawls* (London, New York, Routledge, 2007).
Fried, Barbara, *The Progressive Assault on Laissez Faire: Robert Hale and First Law and Economics Movement* (Cambridge, Mass, Harvard University Press, 1998).
Friedman, Barry, 'The Birth of an Academic Obsession: The History of the Countermajoritarian Difficulty Part Five' (2002) 112 *The Yale Law Journal* 153.
Friedman, Lawrence and Ladinsky, Jack, 'Social Change and the Law of Industrial Accidents' (1967) 67 *Columbia Law Review* 50.
Friedman, Lawrence, *A History of American Law* (New York, Simon & Schuster, 2005).
Fukuyama, Francis, *The End of History and the Last Man* (New York, Free Press, 2006).
Fuller, Lon L and Eisenberg, Melvin Aron, *Basic Contract Law* (St Paul, MN, Thomson/West, 2006).
Fuller, Lon L, 'American Legal Realism' (1934) 82 *University of Pennsylvania Law Review* 429.
—— 'The Case of the Speluncean Explorers' (1949) 62 *Harvard Law Review* 616.
—— *The Morality of Law*, 2nd edn (New Haven, Yale University Press, 1969).
Gaius, *Institutes*, translated by Edward Poste in 1904, available at http://faculty.cua.edu/Pennington/Law508/Roman%20Law/GaiusInstitutesCommentary.htm (last visited: 16 September 2012).
Gallie, WB, 'Essentially Contested Concepts' (1955–1956) 56 *Proceedings of the Aristotelian Society* 167.
Gardner, John. 'Legal Positivism: 5 1/2 Myths' (2001) 46 *American Journal of Jurisprudence* 199.
Geistfeld, Mark, '*Escola v. Coca-Cola Bottling Co.*' in Robert L Rabin and Stephen D Sugarman (eds), *Torts Stories* (New York, Foundation Press, 2003).
Geldart, WM, 'Introduction' to Rudolf von Jhering, *Law as a Means to an End*, translated by Isaac Husik (Union, NJ, Lawbrook Exchange, 1999).
Gény, François, 'Judicial Freedom of Decision', translated by Ernest Bruncken and Layton B Register in *Science of Legal Method: Select Essays by Several Authors* (New Jersey, Rothman Reprints, 1969).
—— *Méthode d'Interprétation et Sources en Droit Privé Positif: Essai Critique*, I & II (Paris, Librairie Générale de Droit & de Jurisprudence, 1919).
Gerth, HH and Mills, C Wright, 'Introduction' to Gerth and Mills (trans and eds), *From Max Weber: Essays in Sociology* (London, Routledge, 1991).
Geuss, Raymond, *The Idea of a Critical Theory* (Cambridge and New York, Cambridge University Press, 1981).
Gierke, Otto Von, *Der Entwurf eines Bügerlichen Gezetzbuchs und das deutsche Recht* (Leipzig, Dunker & Humblot, 1889).

—— *Die soziale Aufgabe des Privatrechts* (Frankfurt am Main, Vittorio Klostermann, 1943).
Gilissen, John, *Introduction Historique au Droit* (Bruxelles, Bruylant, 1979).
Gilmore, Grant, *The Death of Contract* (Columbus, Ohio State University Press, 1995).
Gordley, James, *The Philosophical Origins of Modern Contract Doctrine* (Oxford and New York, Oxford University Press, 1991).
—— 'Myths of the French Civil Code' (1994) 42 *The American Journal of Comparative Law* 459.
—— *Foundations of Private Law* (Oxford and New York, Oxford University Press, 2006).
—— 'The Abuse of Rights in the Civil Law Tradition' in Rita de la Feria and Stefan Vogenauer (eds), *Prohibition of Abuse of Law: A New General Principle of EU Law?* (Oxford and Portland, Hart Publishing, 2011).
Gordon, Robert W, 'Historicism in Legal Scholarship' (1981) 90 *The Yale Law Journal* 1017.
—— 'Critical Legal Histories' (1984) 36 *Stanford Law Review* 57.
Gounot, Emmanuel, *Le Principe de l'Autonomie de la Volonté en Droit Privé: Contribuition à L'Étude Critique de L'Individualisme Juridique* (Paris, A Rousseau, 1912).
Green, Leslie. 'Legal Positivism', *The Stanford Encyclopedia of Philosophy*, ed Edward N Zalta, available at: http://plato.stanford.edu/archives/fall2009/entries/legal-positivism (2009).
Greenberg, Mark, 'How Facts Make Law' (2004) 10 *Legal Theory* 157.
Grey, Thomas C, 'The Disintegration of Property' in J Roland Pennock and John W Chapman (eds), *Nomos XXII: Property* (New York, New York University Press, 1980).
—— 'Langdell's Orthodoxy' (1983–84) 45 *University of Pittsburgh Law Review* 1.
—— 'Serpents and Doves: A Note on Kantian Legal Theory' (1987) 87 *Columbia Law Review* 580.
Grossi, Paolo, *L'Ordine Giuridico Medievale* (Roma, Editori Laterza, 1996).
Grotius, Hugo, *The Rights of War and Peace*, Books II & III, translated from the French of Jean Barbeyrac and edited by Richard Tuck (Indianapolis, Liberty Fund, 2005).
—— 'Prolegomena' to *The Rights of War and Peace*, Book III.
Guyer, Paul, *Kant* (London and New York, Routledge, 2006).
Habermas, Jürgen, 'Reconciliation Through the Use of Public Reason: Remarks on John Rawls' Political Liberalism' (1995) 92 *The Journal of Philosophy* 109.
—— *Between Facts and Norms: Contributions to a Discourse Theory of Law and Democracy*, translated by William Rehg (Cambridge, Mass, MIT Press, 1999).
—— *The Postnational Constellation*, translated by Max Pensky (Cambridge, Mass, MIT Press, 2001).
Hale, Robert L, 'Law-Making by Unofficial Minorities' (1920) 20 *Columbia Law Review* 451.
—— 'Coercion and Distribution in a Supposedly Non-Coercive State' (1923) 38 *Political Science Quarterly* 470.
—— 'Our Equivocal Constitutional Guarantees', 39 *Columbia Law Review* 563.
—— 'Bargaining, Duress, and Economic Liberty' (1939) 43 *Columbia Law Review* 603 (1943).
Halley, Janet, 'What is Family Law? Genealogy Part I' (2011) 23 *Yale Journal of Law & the Humanities* 1.
Halpérin, Jean-Louis, *Histoire du Droit Privé Français Depuis 1804* (Paris, Presses Universitaires de France, 2001).
Hart, HLA, 'Are There Any Natural Rights?' (1955) 64 *Philosophical Review* 175.
—— 'Legal Rights' in *Essays on Bentham: Studies in Jurisprudence and Political Theory* (Oxford and New York, Oxford University Press, 1982).
—— *The Concept of Law* (Oxford and New York, Oxford University Press, 1994).
Hart, Henry and Sacks, Albert, *The Legal Process* (Tentative Edition, mimeographed, 1958).
Hauriou, Maurice, *Précis de Droit Administratif et de Droit Public*, 11th edn (Paris, Librairie du Recueil Sirey, 1927).
Heck, Philipp, 'The Formation of Concepts and the Jurisprudence of Interests', in M Magdalena Schoch (trans and ed), *The Jurisprudence of Interests: Selected Writings* (Cambridge, Mass, Harvard University Press, 1948).
—— 'The Jurisprudence of Interests', in M Magdalena Schoch (trans and ed), *The Jurisprudence of Interests*.

―― 'Gesetzesauslegung und Interessenjurisprudenz', in *Das Problem der Rechtsgewinnung. Gesetzesauslegung und Interessenjurisprudenz. Begriffsbildung und Interessenjurisprudenz* (Berlin, Bad Homburg; Zürich: Gehlen, 1968).
Hegel, GFW, *Phenomenology of Spirit*, translated by AV Miller (Oxford, Clarendon Press, 1977).
―― *Elements of the Philosophy of Right*, translated by TM Knox (Oxford, Clarendon Press, 1967).
―― *Introduction to the Philosophy of History*, translated by Leo Rauch (Indianapolis, Hackett Pub Co, 1988).
Henderson, James, '*MacPherson v. Buick Motor Co.*' in Robert L Rabin and Stephen D Sugarman (eds), *Torts Stories* (New York, Foundation Press, 2003).
Henkel, Heiko, 'Fundamentally Danish? The Muhammad Cartoon Controversy as Transitional Drama' (2010) 8 *Human Architecture: Journal of the Sociology of Self-Knowledge* 67.
Hespanha, António Manuel, *As Vésperas do Leviatã: Instituições e Poder Político em Portugal – Séc. XVII* (Coimbra, Almedina, 1994).
―― 'As Estruturas Políticas em Portugal na Época Moderna' in José Tengarrinha (ed), *História de Portugal* (S Paulo, EDUSC-UNESP, 2001).
―― *Cultura Jurídica Europeia: Síntese de um Milénio* (Lisboa, Europa-América, 2003).
―― 'Juristas e Direito na Cultura Europeia' (on file with the author).
Hirshl, Ran, *Toward Juristocracy: The Origins and Consequences of the New Constitutionalism* (Cambridge, Mass, Harvard University Press, 2004).
Hobbes, Thomas, *Dialogue Between a Philosopher and a Student of the Common Law*, edited by Joseph Cropsey (Chicago and London, The University of Chicago Press, 1985).
―― *Leviathan*, edited by CB Macpherson (London, Penguin Books, 1961).
Hobsbawm, Eric, *The Age of Capital: 1848–1875* (London, Phoenix Press, 1995).
―― *The Age of Empire: 1875–1914* (London, Widenfeld & Nicolson, 1995).
Hoeflich, Michael, 'Savigny and his Anglo-American Disciples' (1989) 37 *The American Journal of Comparative Law* 17.
Hohfeld, Wesley Newcomb, 'Some Fundamental Legal Conceptions as Applied in Judicial Reasoning' (1913) 23 *The Yale Law Journal* 16.
Holmes, Oliver Wendell, *The Common Law* (Boston, Little, Brown, and Company, 1881).
―― 'Privilege, Malice, and Intent' (1894) 8 *Harvard Law Review* 1.
―― 'The Path of the Law' (1987) 10 *Harvard Law Review* 457.
Horkheimer, Max, 'The End of Reason' in Andrew Arato and Eike Gebhardt (eds), *The Essential Frankfurt School Reader* (New York, Urizen Books, 1978).
Horwitz, Morton, *The Transformation of American Law, 1870–1960: The Crisis of Legal Orthodoxy* (New York and Oxford, Oxford University Press, 1992).
Hume, David, *A Treatise of Human Nature*, edited by Ernest C Mossner (London, Penguin Books, 1985).
Huntington, Samuel P, 'Democracy's Third Wave' (1991) 2 *Journal of Democracy* 12.
Hutcheson, Joseph, 'The Judgment Intuitive: The Function of the 'Hunch' in Judicial Decision' (1928–29) 14 *Cornell Law Quarterly* 274.
Hutchinson, Alan, 'A Hard-Core Case Against Judicial Review' (2008) 121 *Harvard Law Review* 57.
Jellinek, Georg, *Allgemeine Staatslehre* (Berlin, J Springer, 1929).
Jhering, Rudolf (Von), *Geist des römischen Rechts auf den verschiedenen Stufen seiner Entwicklung*, I, II/2 & III (Leipzig, Breitkopf und Härtel, 1866, 1869 and 1871).
―― '*Culpa in contrahendo* oder Schadensersatz bei nichtigen oder nicht zur Perfektion gelangten Vertrigen' (1861) 4 *Jahrbücher fur die Dogmatik des heutigen römischen und deutschen Privatrechts* 1.
―― 'Vertrauliche Briefe über die heutige Jurisprudenz' in *Scherz und Ernst in der Jurisprudenz*, edited by Max Leitner (Wien, Linde International, 2009).
―― 'Im juristischen Begriffshimmel' in *Scherz und Ernst in der Jurisprudenz*.
―― *Law as a Means to an End*, translated by Isaac Husik (New Jersey, Lawbrook Exchange, 1999).
Josserand, Louis, *De la Responsabilité du Fait des Choses Inanimées* (Paris, Arthur Rosseau, 1897).
―― *De L'Abus des Droits* (Paris, Rousseau, 1905).

—— *De L'Esprit des Droits et de Leur Relativité: Théorie Dite de L'Abus des Droits* (Paris: Dalloz, 1939).
Kahn-Freund, Otto, *Labour and the Law* (London, Stevens, 1977).
Kalman, Laura, *Legal Realism at Yale* (Chapel Hill, University of North Carolina Press, 1996).
Kant, Immanuel, *Groundwork of the Metaphysics of Morals*, translated and edited by Mary Gregor (Cambridge and New York, Cambridge University Press, 1996).
—— *The Metaphysics of Morals*, translated and edited by Mary Gregor (Cambridge and New York, Cambridge University Press, 1996).
—— *Critique of Pure Reason*, translated and edited by Allen Wood and Paul Guyer (Cambridge, Cambridge University Press, 1998).
—— *Critique of the Power of Judgment*, translated by Paul Guyer and Eric Matthews, edited by Paul Guyer (Cambridge, Cambridge University Press, 2000).
—— *Critique of Practical Reason*, translated by Werner S Pluhar (Indianapolis, Hackett Publishing Co, 2002).
—— 'An Answer to the Question: What is Enlightenment?' in *Towards Perpetual Peace and Other Writings on Politics, Peace, and History*, translated by David L Colclasure and edited by Pauline Kleingeld (New Haven and London, Yale University Press, 2006).
—— 'Anthropology from a Pragmatic Point of View' in *Towards Perpetual Peace and Other Writings*.
—— 'Conjectural Beginning of Human History' in *Towards Perpetual Peace and Other Writings*.
—— 'Idea for a Universal History from a Cosmopolitan Perspective' in *Towards Perpetual Peace and Other Writings*.
—— 'On the Common Saying: This May Be True in Theory, But It Does Not Hold in Practice' in *Towards Perpetual Peace and Other Writings*.
—— 'Toward Perpetual Peace' in *Towards Perpetual Peace and Other Writings*.
Kaser, Max, *Roman Private Law: A Translation*, translated by Rolf Dannenbring (Pretoria, University of South Africa, 1984).
Kaufman, Andrew L, *Cardozo* (Cambridge, Mass, Harvard University Press, 1998).
Kaufmann, Arthur, *Analogie und 'Natur der Sache': zugleich ein Betrag zur Lehre von Typus* (Heidelberg, R v Decker & CF Müller, 1982).
Kegel, Gerhard, 'Story and Savigny' (1989) 37 *The American Journal of Comparative Law* 39.
Kelman, Ellen M., 'American Labor Law and Legal Formalism: How 'Legal Logic' Shaped and Vitiated the Rights of American Workers' (1983) 58 *St John's Law Review* 1.
Kelman, Mark, *A Guide to Critical Legal Studies* (Cambridge, Mass, Harvard University Press, 1988).
Kelsen, Hans, *Pure Theory of Law*, translated by Max Knight (Berkeley, University of California Press, 1978).
—— *General Theory of Law and State*, translation by Anders Weberg (Cambridge, Mass, Harvard University Press, 1945).
—— *General Theory of Norms*, translation by Michael Hartney (New York and Oxford, Oxford University Press, 1991).
Kennedy, Duncan, 'Form and Substance in Private Law Adjudication' (1976) 89 *Harvard Law Review* 1685.
—— 'Distributive and Paternalist Motives in Contract and Tort Law, with Special Reference to Compulsory Terms and Unequal Bargaining Power' (1982) 41 *Maryland Law Review* 563.
—— 'The Stages of Decline of the Private/Public Distinction' (1982) 130 *University of Pennsylvania Law Review* 1349.
—— 'The Role of Law in Economic Thought: Essays on the Fetishism of Commodities' (1985) 34 *American University Law Review* 939.
—— 'Freedom and Constraint in Adjudication: A Critical Phenomenology' (1986) 36 *Journal of Legal Education* 518.
—— 'A Semiotics of Legal Argument' (1991) 42 *Syracuse Law Review* 75.
—— 'The Stakes of Law, or Hale and Foucault!' (1991) 15 *Legal Studies Forum* 327.
—— *A Critique of Adjudication* (Cambridge, Mass, Harvard University Press, 1997).
—— 'From the Will Theory to the Principle of Private Autonomy' (2000) 100 *Columbia Law Review* 94.

—— 'The Disenchantment of Logically Formal Legal Rationality, Or Max Weber's Sociology in the Genealogy of the Contemporary Mode of Western Legal Thought' (2004) 55 *Hastings Law Journal* 1031.

—— 'A Left Phenomenological Alternative to the Hart/Kelsen Theory of Legal Interpretation', in Cáceres et al (eds), *Problemas Contemporáneos de la Filosofía del Derecho* (Ciudad de Mexico, Universidade Nacional Autónoma de México, 2005).

—— 'Thoughts on Coherence, Social Values and National Tradition in Private Law' in Martin W Hesselink (ed), *The Politics of a European Civil Code* (Amsterdam, Kluwer Law International, 2006).

—— 'Three Globalizations of Law and Legal Thought: 1850–2000', David Trubek and Alvaro Santos (eds), *The New Law and Economic Development: A Critical Appraisal* (Cambridge, Cambridge University Press, 2006).

—— *The Rise and Fall of Classical Legal Thought* (Washington DC, Beard Books, 2006).

—— 'Savigny's Family/Patrimony Distinction' (2010) 58 *American Journal of Comparative Law* 811.

—— 'A Transnational Genealogy of Proportionality in Private Law', Roger Brownsword, Hans Micklitz, Leone Niglia and Steven Weatherill (eds), *The Foundations of European Private Law* (Oxford, Hart Publishing, 2011).

—— 'Political Ideology and Comparative Law' in Mauro Bussani and Ugo Mattei (eds), *The Cambridge Companion to Comparative Law* (Cambridge, Cambridge University Press 2012).

—— 'The Hermeneutic of Suspicion in Contemporary American Legal Thought' (2014) 25 *Law and Critique* 91.

—— 'Proportionality and Deference in Contemporary Constitutional Thought', Tamara Perišin and Siniša Rodin (eds), *The Transformation or Reconstitution of Europe: The Critical Legal Studies Perspective on the Role of the Courts in the European Union* (Oxford, Hart, 2018).

Kennedy, Duncan and Belleau, Marie-Claire, 'François Gény aus États-Unis' in Claude Thomasset, Jacques Vanderlinden and Philippe Jestaz (eds), *François Geny, Mythe et Réalités 1899–1999 Centenaire de Méthode d'Interprétation et Sources en Droit Privé Positif: Essai Critique* (Montreal, Éditions Yvons Blais, 2000).

Kessler, Friedrich and Fine, Edith, 'Culpa in Contrahendo, Bargaining in Good Faith, and Freedom of Contract' (1964) 77 *Harvard Law Review* 401.

Kessler, Friedrich, 'Contracts of Adhesion – Some Thoughts About Freedom of Contract' (1943) 43 *Columbia Law Review* 629.

Klare, Karl E, 'The Judicial Deradicalization of the Wagner Act and the Origins of Modern Legal Counsciousness, 1937–1941' (1977–78) 62 *Minnesota Law Review* 265.

Klatt, Matthias and Meister, Moritz, *The Constitutional Structure of Proportionality* (Oxford, Oxford University Press, 2012).

Kleeberg, John M, 'From Strict Liability to Workers' Compensation: The Prussian Railroad Law, The German Liability Act, and the Introduction of Bismarck's Accident Insurance in Germany, 1838–1884' (2003) 36 *New York University Journal of International Law and Policy* 53.

Knapp, Charles L, 'Contract Law' in Alan B Morrison (ed), *Fundamentals of American Law* (Oxford, Oxford University Press, 1996).

Kohler, Josef, 'Judicial Interpretation of Enacted Law', translated by Ernest Bruncken and Layton B Register in *Science of Legal Method: Select Essays by Several Authors* (New Jersey, Rothman Reprints, 1969).

Korsgaard, Christine M, 'Introduction' to Immanuel Kant, *Groundwork of the Metaphysics of Morals*, translated and edited by Mary Gregor (Cambridge and New York, Cambridge University Press, 1996).

Krisch, Nico, *Beyond Constitutionalism: The Pluralist Structure of Postnational Law* (Oxford, Oxford University Press, 2010).

Kumm, Mattias, 'Constitutional Rights as Principles: On the Structure and Domain of Constitutional Justice' (2004) 2 *International Journal of Constitutional Law* 574.

—— 'Who Is Afraid of the Total Constitution? Constitutional Rights as Principles and the Constitutionalisation of Private Law' (2006) 7 *German Law Journal* 341.

—— 'Institutionalising Socratic Contestation: The Rationalist Human Rights Paradigm, Legitimate Authority and the Point of Judicial Review' (2007) 1 *European Journal of Legal Studies* 1.
—— 'Political Liberalism and the Structure of Rights: On the Place and Limits of the Proportionality Requirement' in George Pavlakos (ed) *Law, Rights and Discourse: Themes From the Legal Philosophy of Robert Alexy* (Oxford, Hart Publishing, 2007).
—— 'The Cosmopolitan Turn in Constitutionalism: An Integrated Conception of Public Law' (2013) 20 *Indiana Journal of Global Legal Studies* 629.
—— 'Constituent Power, Cosmopolitan Constitutionalism, and Post-Positivist Law' (2016) 14 *International Journal of Constitutional Law* 697.
Kymlicka, Will, *Contemporary Political Philosophy: An Introduction* (Oxford and New York, Oxford University Press, 2002).
La Torre, Massimo, *La 'Lotta Contra il Diritto Soggetivo: Karl Larenz e la Doutrina Giuridica Nazionalsocialista'* (Milano, A Giuffrè, 1988).
Larenz, Karl 'Rechtsperson und subjektives Recht – zur Wandlung der Rechtsgrundbegriffe' in *Grundfragen der neuen Rechtswissenschaft* (Berlin, Junker und Dünnhaupt, 1935).
—— 'Volksgeist und Recht – zur Revision der Rechtsanschauung der historischen Schule' (1935) 1 *Zeitschrift für deutsche Kulturphilosophie* 40.
—— *Allgemeiner Teil des deutschen Bügerlichen Rechts* (München, CH Beck, 1989).
—— *Methodenlehre der Rechtswissenschaft* (Berlin and New York, Springer, 1991).
Larmore, Charles, 'Political Liberalism' (1990) 18 *Political Theory* 339.
—— 'The Moral Basis of Political Liberalism' (1999) 96 *The Journal of Philosophy* 599.
Laski, Harold J, 'The Basis of Vicarious Liability' (1916) 26 *The Yale Law Journal* 105.
Laurent, François, *Principes de Droit Civil Français*, XV (Paris, Librairie A Marescq, 1887).
Leiter, Brian, 'Rethinking Legal Realism' (1997–98) 76 *Texas Law Review* 267.
—— 'Legal Realism and Legal Positivism Reconsidered' (2001) 111 *Ethics* 278.
Levi, Edward H, *An Introduction to Legal Reasoning* (Chicago, The University of Chicago Press, 1949).
Lévi-Strauss, Claude, *The Savage Mind*, translated by John Weightman and Doreen Weightman (Chicago, The University of Chicago Press, 1966).
Llewellyn, Karl, 'A Realistic Jurisprudence – The Next Step' (1930) 30 *Columbia Law Review* 431.
—— 'Some Realism About Realism' (1931) 44 *Harvard Law Review* 1222.
—— 'Remarks on the Theory of Appellate Decision and the Rules or Canons About How Statutes are to be Construed' (1949–50) 3 *Vanderbilt Law Review* 394.
—— *The Bramble Bush* (New York, Oxford University Press, 2006).
—— *The Common Law Tradition: Deciding Appeals* (New Orleans, Quid Pro Books, 2015).
Locher, Eugen, 'Geschäftsgrundlage und Geschäftszweck' (1923) 1 *Archiv für die civilistische Praxis* 1.
Locke, John, *An Essay Concerning Human Understanding and A Treatise on the Conduct of the Understanding* (Philadelphia, Hayes & Zell Publishers, 1854).
—— *Second Treatise of Government and A Letter Concerning Toleration*, edited by JW Gough (New York, Dover Publications, 2002).
Macedo, Stephen, 'Against Majoritarianism: Democratic Values and Institutional Design' (2010) 90 *Boston University Law Review* 1030.
Machiavelli, *The Prince*, in David Wootton (trans and ed), *Selected Political Writings* (Indianapolis/Cambridge, Hackett Publishing Company, 1994).
Macintyre, Alasdair, *Whose Justice? Which Rationality?* (Notre Dame, University of Notre Dame Press, 1988).
—— 'The Privatization of Good: An Inaugural Lecture' (1990) 52 *The Review of Politics* 344.
—— *After Virtue: A Study in Moral Theory* (Notre Dame, University of Notre Dame Press, 2007).
Maduro, Miguel P, 'Interpreting European Law: Judicial Adjudication in a Context of Constitutional Pluralism' (2007) 1 *European Journal of Legal Studies* 138.
Manent, Pierre, *An Intellectual History of Liberalism*, translated by Rebecca Balinski (Princeton, Princeton University Press, 1994).
Markesinis, BS, *The German Law of Contract: A Comparative Treatise* (Oxford, Hart Publishing, 2006).
Marshall, Alfred, *Principles of Economics* (London, Macmillan, 1907).

Marx, Karl, *Capital: A Critique of Political Economy*, I, translated by Ben Fowkes (London, Penguin Books, 1976).
—— 'Economic and Philosophic Manuscripts of 1844' in Robert C Tucker (ed) *The Marx-Engels Reader* (New York, WW Norton, 1978).
—— 'On the Jewish Question' in Robert C Tucker (ed) *The Marx-Engels Reader*.
—— 'Preface to A Contribution to the Critique of Political Economy' in Robert C Tucker (ed) *The Marx-Engels Reader*.
—— 'Theses on Feuerbach' in Robert C Tucker (ed) *The Marx-Engels Reader*.
Marx, Karl and Engels, Friedrich, 'The German Ideology' in Robert C Tucker (ed) *The Marx-Engels Reader*.
—— *The Communist Manifesto* (London, Verso, 1998).
Mckinnon, Andrew, 'Elective Affinities of the Protestant Ethic: Weber and the Chemistry of Capitalism' (2010) 28 *Sociological Theory* 108.
Medicus, Dieter, 'Der Grundsatz der Verhältnismäßigkeit im Privatrecht' (1992) 192 *Archiv für die civilistische Praxis* 35.
Menger, Anton, *Das bügerliche Recht und die besitzlosen Volksklassen* (Tübingen, H Laupp, 1927).
Merkel, Adolf, 'Rudolf von Jhering', appendix to *Law as a Means to an End*, translated by Isaac Husik (Union, NJ, Lawbrook Exchange, 1999).
Michelman, Frank, 'The Subject of Liberalism' (1993–94) 46 *Stanford Law Review* 1807.
—— *Brennan and Democracy* (Princeton: Princeton University Press, 1999).
Michelman, Frank and Margaret Jane Radin, 'Pragmatist and Poststructuralist Critical Legal Practice' (1991) 139 *The Univesity of Pennsylvania Law Review* 1019.
Milbank, John, 'The Gift of Ruling: Secularization and Political Authority' (2004) 85 *New Blackfriars* 212.
Mill, John Stuart, *On Liberty and Other Essays*, edited by John Gray (Oxford, Oxford University Press, 1991).
—— *Principles of Political Economy and Chapters on Socialism*, edited by Jonathan Riley (Oxford and New York, Oxford University Press, 1998).
Minow, Martha and Singer, Joseph William, 'In Favor of Foxes: Pluralism as fact and Aid to the Pursuit of Justice' (2010) 90 *Boston University Law Review* 903.
Montesquieu, *De L'Esprit des Lois* (Paris, Garnier, 1794).
Motta, Massimo, *Competition Policy: Theory and Practice* (Cambridge and New York, Cambridge University Press, 2004).
Murphy, Liam and Nagel, Thomas, *The Myth of Ownership: Taxes and Justice* (Oxford, Oxford University Press, 2002).
Nietzsche, Friedrich, *On the Genealogy of Morals*, translated by Walter Kaufmann, in (W Kaufmann ed. *The Basic Writings of Nietzsche* (New York, Modern Library, 2000).
Nozick, Robert, *Anarchy, State, and Utopia* (New York, Harper and Row, 1974).
Oertmann, Paul, *Die Geschäftsgrundlage, ein neuer Rechtsbegriff* (Leipzig, A Deichert, 1921).
Oliphant, Herman, 'A Return to Stare Decisis' (1928) 14 *American Bar Association Journal* 71.
Planiol, Marcel, *Traité Élémentaire de Droit Civil: Renfondu et Complété par Georges Ripert* (Paris: Librairie Générale de Droit et de Jurisprudence, 1950).
Plato, *Gorgias*, translated by Donald J Zeyl, in John M Cooper (ed), *Complete Works of Plato* (Indianapolis, Hackett Publishing Company, 1997).
Pogge, Thomas, 'Is Kant's *Rechtslehre* Comprehensive?' (1997) 36 *The Southern Journal of Philosophy* 161.
Pollock, Frederick and Maitland, Frederic, *The History of English Law Before the Time of Edward I*, I (Indianapolis, Liberty Fund, 2009).
Pollock, Frederick (Sir), *The Law of Torts: a Treatise on the Principles of Obligations Arising from Civil Wrongs in the Common Law* (London, Stevens, 1887).
—— *Principles of Contract at Law and in Equity: A Treatise on the General Principles Concerning the Validity of Agreements in the Law of England and America* (New York, Baker, Voorhis & Company, 1906).

Polybius, *The Histories*, translated by WR Paton (Cambridge, Mass, Harvard University Press, 2010).
Postema, Gerald J, *Bentham and the Common Law Tradition* (Oxford, Clarendon Press; New York, Oxford University Press, 1986).
Pound, Roscoe, 'Mechanical Jurisprudence', 8 *Columbia Law Review* 605 (1908).
—— 'Liberty of Contract' (1909) 18 *The Yale Law Journal* 454.
—— 'The End of Law as Developed in Juristic Thought II: The Nineteenth Century' (1917) 30 *Harvard Law Review* 201.
—— 'The Theory of Judicial Decision III' (1922) 36 *Harvard Law Review* 940.
—— 'The New Feudal System' (1930) 35 *Commercial Law Journal* 397.
—— 'The Call for a Realist Jurisprudence' (1931) 44 *Harvard Law Review* 697.
—— 'Public and Private Law' (1938–39) 24 *Cornell Law Quarterly* 469.
—— 'Courts and Legislation' in *Science of Legal Method: Select Essays by Several Authors* (New Jersey, Rothman Reprints, 1969).
—— *Jurisprudence*, I & II (St Paul, Minn, West Pub Co, 1959).
Prosser, William L, 'Privacy' (1960) 48 *California Law Review* 383.
Prosser, William L et al, *Torts: Cases and Materials* (New York, Foundation Press, 2005).
Puchta, GF, *Pandekten* (Leipzig, JA Barth, 1853).
—— *Cursus der Institutionen*, I (Leipzig, Breitkopf und Härtel, 1856–57).
Radbruch, Gustav, *Rechtsphilosophie* (Heidelberg, CF Müller Juristischer Verlag, 1993).
Rawls, John, 'Two Concepts of Rules' (1955) 64 *The Philosophical Review* 3.
—— *A Theory of Justice* (Cambridge, Mass, Belknap Press of Harvard University Press, 1971).
—— 'Justice as Fairness: Political not Metaphysical' (1985). 14 *Philosophy and Public Affairs* 223.
—— *Justice as Fairness: A Restatement*, edited by Erin Kelly (Cambridge, Mass, Belknap Press of Harvard University Press, 2001).
—— *Political Liberalism* (New York, Columbia University Press, 2005).
Raz, Joseph, 'Incorporation by Law' (2004) 10 *Legal Theory* 1.
—— *The Authority of Law: Essays on Law and Morality* (Oxford and New York, Oxford University Press, 2009).
Reimann, Mathias, 'Nineteenth Century German Legal Science' (1989–90) 31 *Boston College Law Review* 837.
—— 'The Good, The Bad, and the Ugly: The Reform of the German Law of Obligations' (2009) 83 *Tulane Law Review* 877.
Ribeiro, Gonçalo De Almeida, 'O Constitucionalismo dos Princípios' in Gonçalo de Almeida Ribeiro and Luís Pereira Coutinho (eds), *O Tribunal Constitucional e a Crise: Ensaios Críticos* (Coimbra, Almedina, 2014).
—— 'Judicial Activism and Fidelity to Law' in Luís Pereira Coutinho, Massimo La Torre and Steven D Smith (eds), *Judicial Activism: An Interdisciplinary Approach to the American and European Experiences* (Springer, Berlin, 2015).
—— 'The Effects of Fundamental Rights in Private Disputes' in Hugh Collins (ed), *European Contract Law and the Charter of Fundamental Rights* (Cambridge, Intersentia, 2017).
—— 'A Pluralist Case for the Harm Principle' (2017) 54 *University of San Diego Law Review*, 361.
Ricoeur, Paul, *Freud and Philosophy: An Essay on Interpretation*, trans Denis Savage (New Haven, Yale University Press, 1970).
Riesenfeld, Stefen, 'The Influence of German Legal Theory on American Law: The Heritage of Savigny and His Disciples' (1989) 37 *The American Journal of Comparative Law* 1.
Ripert, Georges, 'Abus ou Relativité des Droits – A Propos de l'Ouvrage de M. Josserand De L'Esprit des Droits et de Leur Relativité, 1927' (1929) 49 *Revue Critique de Législation et de Jurisprudence* 33.
Ripstein, Arthur, 'Private Order and Public Justice: Kant and Rawls' (2006) 92 *Virginia Law Review* 1391.
Robilant, Anna Di, 'Abuse of Right' (2009–10) 61 *Hastings Law Journal* 687.
Rosen, Allen D, *Kant's Theory of Justice* (Ithaca, Cornell University Press, 1993).
Rosmini, Antonio, *The Philosophy of Right: The Essence of Right*, translated by D Cleary and T Watson (Durham, Rosmini House, 1993).

Rousseau, Jean-Jacques, *On the Social Contract*, translated and edited by Donald A Kress (Indianapolis, Hackett Pub Co, 1988).
Saleilles, Raymond, *Essai d'une Théorie Générale de l'Obligation d'Après le Projet de Code Civil Allemand* (Paris, F Pichon, 1890).
—— *Les Accidents du Travail et la Responsabilité Civile: Essai dun Théorie Objective dela Responsabilité Délictuelle* (Paris, Rousseau, 1897).
—— *De la Déclaration de Volonté: Contribuition a l'Étude de l'Acte Juridique dans le Code Civil Allemand (art. 116 à 144)* (Paris, F Pichon, 1901).
—— 'Le Code Civil et la Méthode Historique' in Société d'Études Législatives (ed), *Le Code civil, 1804-1904: Livre du Centenaire* (Paris, A Rousseau, 1904).
—— 'Préface' to *Méthode d'Interprétation et Sources en Droit Privé Positif: Essai Critique*, I & II (Paris, Librairie Générale de Droit & de Jurisprudence, 1919).
Saussure, Ferdinand De, *Course in General Linguistics*, translated by Roy Harris (LaSalle, Ill, Open Court, 1986).
Savigny, Friedrich Carl Von, *Of the Vocation of Our Age for Legislation and Jurisprudence*, translated by Abraham Hayward (London, Littlewood and Co, 1831).
—— *System of the Modern Roman Law*, I, translated by William Holloway (Madras, J Higginbotham, 1867).
—— *Das Obligationenrecht, als Teil des heutigen römischen Rechts* I & II (Aalen, Scientia Verlag, 1973).
—— *Treatise on Possession, or the Jus Possessionis of the Civil Law*, translated by Erskine Perry (Westport, Conn, Hyperion Press, 1979).
—— *System des heutigen Römischen Rechts*, III & V (Aalen, Scientia Verlag, 1981).
—— 'Juristische Methodenlehre' in *Vorlesungen über juristische Methodologie 1802-1842* (Frankfurt am Main, V Klostermann, 2004).
Schlag, Pierre, 'The Empty Circles of Liberal Justification' (1997) 96 *Michigan Law Review* 1.
—— 'Law as a Continuation of God by Other Means' (1997) 85 *California Law Review* 427.
Schlegel, John Henry, *American Legal Realism and Empirical Social Science* (Chapel Hill, University of North Carolina Press, 1995).
Schlossmann, Siegmund, *Irrtum über wesentliche Eigenschaften der Person und der Sache nach dem Bügerlichen Gesetzbuch. Zugleich in Beitrag zur Theorie der Gesetzauslegung* (Jena, Gustav Fischer, 1903).
Schmitt, Carl, *The Concept of the Political*, translated by George Schwab (Chicago, Chicago University Press, 2007).
Schumpeter, Joseph, *Capitalism, Socialism and Democracy* (London and Boston, Unwin Paperbacks, 1987).
Schwarz, Andreas, 'John Austin and the German Jurisprudence of His Time' (1934) 1 *Politica* 178.
Searle, John, *Speech Acts: An Essay in the Philosophy of Language* (Cambridge, Cambridge University Press, 1970).
Shavell, Steven, *Foundations of Economic Analysis of Law* (Cambridge, Mass, Belknap Press of Harvard University Press, 2004).
Shields, Christopher, *Aristotle* (London and New York, Routledge, 2007).
Shklar, Judith, 'The Liberalism of Fear' in Nancy Rosenblum (ed), *Liberalism and the Moral Life* (Cambridge, Mass and London, Harvard University Press, 1989).
Sieckmann, Jan-Reinhard, *Regelmodelle und Prinzipienmodelle des Rechtssystems* (Baden-Baden, Nomos, 1990).
Sieyès, Emmanuel-Joseph, *Essai sur les Privileges*, in *Qu'est-ce que Tiers État?* (Paris, Au Siège de la Société, 1888).
Simmons, A John, *Justification and Legitimacy: Essays on Rights and Obligations* (Cambridge and New York, Cambridge University Press, 2001).
Simpson, AW Brian, *Cannibalism and the Common Law: A Victorian Yachting Tragedy* (London and Rio Grande, Ohio, Hambledon Press, 1994).

Singer, Joseph William, 'The Legal Rights Debate in Analytical Jurisprudence From Bentham to Hohfeld' (1982) *Wisconsin Law Review* 975.
—— 'Legal Realism Now' (1988) 76 *California Law Review* 466.
—— *Entitlement: The Paradoxes of Property* (New Haven, Yale University Press, 2000).
—— *Introduction to Property* (New York, Aspen Publishers, 2005).
Skinner, Quentin, 'The State' in Terrence Ball, James Farr and Russell L Hanson (eds), *Political Innovation and Conceptual Change* (Cambridge and New York, Cambridge University Press, 1989).
Smart, JJC, 'An Outline of a System of Utilitarian Ethics' in JCC Smart and Bernard Williams (eds), *Utilitarianism: For and Against* (Cambridge, Cambridge University Press, 1973).
Smith, Adam, *Inquiry Into the Nature and Causes of the Wealth of Nations*, edited by Edwin Cannan (New York, Bantam Classic, 2003).
Sohm, Rudolf, *The Institutes: A Textbook of the History and System of Roman Private Law*, translated by James Crawford Ledlie (Oxford, Clarendon Press, 1901).
Stein, Peter, 'Justinian's Compilation: Classical Legacy and Legal Source' (1993) 8 *Tulane European & Civil Law Forum* 1.
Stern, Klaus, *Das Staatsrecht der Bundesrepublik Deutschland*, III (Munich, Beck, 1977).
Stolleis, Michael, *Public Law in Germany, 1800–1914* (New York, Berghahn Books, 2001).
Taboada, Carlos Palao, '"Precios Publicos": Una Nueva Figura de Ingresos Públicos en el Derecho Tributario Español' (2001) 111 *Revista Española de Derecho Financiero* 445.
Taylor, Charles, 'What is Wrong with Negative Liberty?' in Alan Ryan (ed), *The Idea of Freedom: Essays in Honour of Isaiah Berlin* (Oxford and New York, Oxford University Press, 1979).
—— *A Secular Age* (Cambridge, Mass, Belknap Press of Harvard University Press, 2007).
Teubner, Günther, *Constitutional Fragments: Societal Constitutionalism and Globalization*, translated by Gareth Norbury (Oxford, Oxford University Press, 2012).
Thayer, James B, *The Origin and Scope of the American Doctrine of Constitutional Law* (Boston, Little, Brown, and Company, 1893).
Tocqueville, Alexis De, *The Old Regime and the French Revolution*, translated by Stuart Gilbert (Garden City, NY, Doubleday, 1955).
—— *Democracy in America*, translated and edited by Harvey C Mansfield and Delba Winthrop (Chicago, University of Chicago Press, 2000).
Toews, John E, 'The Immanent Genesis and Transcendent Goal of Law: Savigny, Stahl, and the Ideology of the Christian German State' (1989) 37 *The American Journal of Comparative Law* 139.
Trubeck, David, 'Max Weber on Law and the Rise of Capitalism' (1972) 3 *Wisconsin Law Review* 721.
Tuchman, Barbara W, *A Distant Mirror: The Calamitous 14th Century* (New York, Knopf, 1978).
Tuhr, Andreas Von, *Der Allgemeine Teil des Deutschen Bürgerlichen Rechts*, I (Leipzig, Duncker & Humblot, 1910).
Tushnet, Mark, *Taking the Constitution Away from the Courts* (Princeton, Princeton University Press, 1999).
Twining, William, *Karl Llewellyn and the Realist Movement* (London, Weidenfeld and Nicolson, 1973).
Unger, Roberto Mangabeira, *The Critical Legal Studies Movement* (Cambridge, Mass, Harvard University Press, 1986).
Urofsky, Melvin, *Louis D. Brandeis: A Life* (New York, Pantheon Books, 2009).
Vicén, Felipe González, 'Sobre los Orígines y Supuestos del Formalismo en el Pensamiento Jurídico Contemporáneo' (1961) 8 *Anuario de Filosofía del Derecho* 47.
Viehweg, Theodor, *Topik und Jurisprudenz* (München, CH Beck, 1953).
Villey, Michel, 'La Genese du Droit Subjetif chez Guillaume d'Occam' (1964) 9 *Archives de Philosophie du Droit* 97.
Waldron, Jeremy, 'A Right to Do Wrong' (1981) 92 *Ethics* 21.
—— 'Theoretical Foundations of Liberalism' (1987) 37 *Philosophical Quarterly* 127.
—— *The Right to Private Property* (Oxford and New York, Oxford University Press, 1988).
—— 'Kant's Legal Positivism' (1996) 109 *Harvard Law Review* 1535.
—— 'Rights and Majorities: Rousseau Revisited' in *Liberal Rights: Collected Papers 1981–1991* (Cambridge, Cambridge University Press, 1993).

—— *Law and Disagreement* (Oxford and New York, Oxford University Press, 1999).
—— 'Kant's Theory of the State' in Immanuel Kant, *Towards Perpetual Peace and Other Writings on Politics, Peace, and History*, edited by Pauline Kleingeld (New Haven and London, Yale University Press, 2006).
—— 'The Core of the Case Against Judicial Review' (2006) 115 *The Yale Law Journal* 1346.
—— 'Did Dworkin Ever Answer the Crits?' in Scott Hershovitz (ed), *Exploring Law's Empire: The Jurisprudence of Ronald Dworkin* (Oxford and New York, Oxford University Press, 2006).
Warren, Samuel D and Brandeis Louis D, 'The Right to Privacy' (1890) 4 *Harvard Law Review* 193.
Weber, Max, *The Theory of Social and Economic Organization*, translated by AM Henderson and Talcott Parsons, edited by Talcott Parsons (New York, Free Press, 1964).
—— *Economy and Society: Outline of an Interpretive Sociology* (2 vols), translated and edited by Guenther Roth and Claus Wittich (Berkeley, Los Angeles; London, University of California Press, 1978).
—— *On Law in Economy and Society*, translated by Edward Shils and Max Rheinstein, edited by Max Rheinstein (New York, NY, Simon and Schuster, nd).
—— 'Science as a Vocation', in HH Gerth and C Wright Mills (trans and eds), *From Max Weber: Essays in Sociology* (London, Routledge, 1991).
—— 'Politics as a Vocation', in HH Gerth and C Wright Mills (trans and eds), *From Max Weber: Essays in Sociology*.
—— *The Protestant Ethic and the "Spirit" of Capitalism and Other Writings*, translated by P Baehr and GC Wells (New York, Penguin, 2002).
Weinreb, Lloyd L, *Legal Reason: The Use of Analogy in Legal Argument* (Cambridge, Cambridge University Press, 2005).
Welzel, Hans, *Derecho Natural y Justicia Material: Preliminares Para Una Filosofía del Derecho*, translated into Spanish by Felipe González Vicén (Madrid, Aguilar, 1957).
Wieacker, Franz, *Industriegesellschaft und Privatrechtsordnung* (Frankfurt am Main, Athenäum Fischer Taschenbuch Verlag, 1974).
—— *A History of Private Law in Europe, with Particular Reference to Germany*, translated by Tony Weir (Oxford and New York, Oxford University Press, 1995).
Williams, Howard, *Kant's Political Philosophy* (New York, St Martin's Press, 1983).
Wilson, Peter H, *Absolutism in Central Europe* (New York, Routledge, 2000).
Windscheid, Bernhard, *Lehrbuch des Pandektenrechts*, I (Frankfurt am Main, Literarische Anstalt Rütten and Loening, 1891).
Witt, John Fabian, 'The Transformation of Work and the Law of Workplace Accidents, 1842–1910', 107 *The Yale Law Journal* 1467 (1998).
Wollheim, Richard, 'A Paradox in the Theory of Democracy' in Peter Laslett and WG Runciman (eds), *Philosophy, Politics and Society* (Oxford, Basil Blackwell, 1969).
Wollstonecraft, Mary, *A Vindication of the Rights of Women, with Strictures on Political and Moral Subjects* (London, T Fisher Unwin, 1891).
Wood, Allen, 'The Final Form of Kant's Practical Philosophy' (1997) 306 *The Southern Journal of Philosophy* 1.
—— 'Kant's Philosophy of History' in Immanuel Kant, *Towards Perpetual Peace and Other Writings on Politics, Peace, and History*, edited by Pauline Kleingeld (New Haven and London, Yale University Press, 2006).
—— *Kantian Ethics* (Cambridge, Cambridge University Press, 2008).
Zagrebelsky, Gustavo, *Il Diritto Mite: Legge, Diritti, Giustizia* (Torino, Guilio Einaudi, 1992).
—— *Prinzipî e Voti: La Corte Costituzionale e La Politica* (Torino, Guilio Einaudi, 2005).
Zander, Michael, *The Law-Making Process*, 6th edn (Cambridge, Cambridge University Press, 2004).
Zitelmann, Ernst, *Irrtum und Rechstgeschäft: Eine psychologischjuristische Untersuchung* (Leipzig, Duncker & Humblot, 1879).
—— *Lücken im Gesetz* (Leipzig, Duncker & Humblot, 1903).
Zweigert, Konrad and Kötz, Hein, *An Introduction to Comparative Law*, translated by Tony Weir (Oxford, Clarendon Press, 1992).

INDEX

A
absolute liability doctrine 208
abuse of right doctrine 8, 214–215, 219–225, 258, 258n
accident law
 fault 193-195, 199–200
actio de dolo 217–218, 218n
actio legis Aquilia 217–218, 218n
Adorno, Theodor W 294
agnosticism 32–33
Althusius, Johannes 131
Altman, Andrew 6
American Legal Realists *see* **legal realism**
Amos, Sheldon 131, 254
Anaxagoras 284, 285
anomie 186
anti-trust law 8, 191, 196–197
Aquinas, Thomas 48n, 64, 84, 105, 106, 107, 108, 117n, 170
 discussion of self-defence 89–90
Arendt, Hannah
 The Human Condition 41, 41–42n, 45, 45n, 49n, 145n
 Lectures on Kant's Political Philosophy 70n
Aristotle 48n, 50, 105, 106, 170
 dialectic 107, 108, 110
 equity 110
 ethics 31
 Medieval rediscovery 127
 moral virtue 108
 Nicomachean Ethics 107, 108, 108n, 269, 283
 norms 108
 positive law 108
 rational principle 108
Aubry, Charles 135
Austin, John 86, 141n
authority
 democratic legitimacy 2–3
 functionalist justification 1
 naturalist justification 1
 political justification 1–3
autonomy 52–53, 64
 Kant 82–83, 91–92, 97n
Ayer, AJ 250

B
Bacon, Sir Francis 4
Baldus 127, 131
banking law 191
Barber, Benjamin
 political realm 41n
Barbeyrac, Jean 107n, 130n
bargain theory of consideration 208
Bartolus 127, 131
Bealism 227
Beiser, Frederick 122n
Bentham, Jeremy 5, 86, 131, 175
 interest or benefit theory of rights 221
 natural rights theory 121–122
 role of legislation 149
Berlin, Isaiah 52n
 value pluralism 244n
Betti, Emilio 189, 189n
Bickel, Alexander 268
 counter-majoritarian difficulty 3, 4, 282
Blackstone, Sir William 107n
Bourdieu, Pierre 120n
Brandeis, Louis 182, 189, 200–201
Brandeis Brief 185
Brunner, Otto 125n
 Land and Lordship 42–43, 43n, 145n
bureaucratic-managerial ethos 31
Burke, Edmund 185

C
Canning, Joseph 126n
capitalism
 capitalist societies 176–180
 liberalism and 186
 reformist jurists 185–191
 social jurists 189n, 190
 Social Question 186
 socialist movements 180–181, 185–187
 will theory and 186–187
Cardozo, Benjamin 182, 189, 200, 209n
 The Nature of the Judicial Process 206
Carnap, Rudolf 250
Cartel Law 196

cases
    Adair v United States   183
    Amalgamated Food Employees Union v Logan Valley Plaza   264n
    Appelhans v McFall   212n
    Bürgschaft   278n
    Commonwealth v Hunt   192–193
    DeShaney v Winnebago County Department of Social Services   278n
    Donoghue v Stevenson   200n
    Escola v Coca-Cola Bottling Co   200n
    Farwell v Boston & Worcester Railroad Corp   194n
    Goodridge v Department of Public Health   55–56n, 57n
    Greeman v Yuba Power Products Inc   200n
    Handelsvertreter   278n
    Identitätskontrolle I   11n, 282n
    In re Debs   193
    Jacob & Youngs v Kent   103n
    Lloyd Corp, Ltd v Tanner   98n
    Lochner v New York   182–183, 206, 229
    Lüth   276, 276n
    MacPherson v Buick Motor Co   200n
    Marsh v Alabama   98n, 264n
    Mephisto   97n
    Muller v Oregon   185
    Pavesich v New England Life Insurance Co   201n
    Phelps et al v Snyder   97n
    Ploof v Putnam   116n
    Priestley v Fowler   194n
    R v Dudley and Stephens   118
    SAS v France   56n
    Taylor v Caldwell   199n
    Titanic   97n
    Union Local 590 v Logan Valley Plaza Inc   98n
    United States v Carroll Towing Co   242n
    Vegelahn v Guntner   218n, 252
    Vincent v Lake Erie Transportation Co   116n
    Winterbottom v Wright   200n
Catechism of the Catholic Church   32–33, 126
caveat emptor rule   195–196
certainty
    judicial duty to deliver   266, 267, 269, 270–271
Charmont, Joseph   184, 215n
Cicero   41–42
classical private law
    contract law   7, 8, 9, 119–124, 170, 172, 195, 216–217, 249, 255

doctrinal constructs   208
emergence of social law   191–192, 197
employment law   183, 192
Enlightenment conception of science   170
family/market dichotomy   7, 124, 124n, 142–147, 143n, 145n
filling gaps in law   151–152, 202–203, 204, 213–214, 248
formalism   161–170, 205
genealogy of concepts   163–164, 248
generally   5, 6, 7
German Historical School   131–161
impact of humanism   130–131
iurisprudentia   124–131
legal formalism   7, 8, 161–169
liberalism legalism   11
method of constructions   204–207, 205n, 248
modern legal science   131–135
political centralisation and   129–130
positive law   129, 132–133, 135–161, 202–203, 211
private/public distinction   9, 11, 137, 230–231
property rights   249
rights theory   119–120
rise   7, 119–171
Savigny *see* Savigny, Friedrich Carl von
static conception of legal doctrine   205
tripartite legal order   124, 167, 173
use of term   170
will theory   7, 8, 119–124, 170, 172, 219–221, 238–239
Clayton Act   196–197
Code Napoléon   107n, 168n, 184–185, 188–189, 203, 207, 213, 220n
codification movement   132–134
coercion   79–80, 79n, 84, 85–86, 96, 256
    coercive obligation   86
    freedom and   230–238
    private/public distinction   230–238
    social jurists   232
Cohen, Felix   9, 227
    'Transcendental Nonsense and the Functional Approach'   249–250
Cohen, Morris   228, 235n, 237n
Coke, Sir Edward   129
collective bargaining   193, 237
collectivists   187–190, 223, 224, 225
Collingwood, RG   284n
Combination Acts   192

common law
  England   128n, 129
  legal realism and   262–265
  res ipsa loquitur   200
  role of judiciary   150
  socialisation of private law   197
commonality
  political realm   40, 42, 93
competition
  anti-trust law   8, 191, 196–197
comprehensive doctrines   31–33, 36
  the fact of oppression   37–38
  pluralism   31–33, 37, 58
Comte, Auguste   185
Condorcet Jury Theorem   27–28
conflicting considerations paradigm
  legal realism   9–10, 11, 228, 238–245, 259
  legislative process   246
  politicisation of private law   281
  reasonable pluralism   245
consequentialism   48n
conservatism
  democracy and   20–22
  liberalism and   16–18, 20, 53–58, 185
  romantic   185, 189, 190
  Savigny   147, 147n
Constant, Benjamin   64   constitutional law
  judicial review   11
  judiciary and   11
  migration to   6, 10–12, 275–282
  protective entitlements   276–279, 281
  rights as principles   276, 279–280
constitutionalism
  liberal   279
  'total constitution'   11, 275–276, 279, 282
contract law
  absolute liability   208
  abuse of right doctrine   8, 214–215, 219–225, 258, 258n
  ambiguous terms   199
  bargain theory of consideration   208
  classical private law   7, 8, 9, 119–124, 170, 172, 195, 204, 206, 216–217, 249, 255
  coercion   79–80, 79n, 84, 85–86, 96, 230–231, 256
  consent of parties   111–112
  contracts of adhesion   198–199
  culpa in contrahendo doctrine   165n, 214–219
  defective products   200
  duty of care   200
  employment law   183, 192, 193

  frustration of contract   199
  good faith   199
  Jhering   168–169, 215–219
  Kant and freedom of contract   102, 103–104, 111
  legal realism   248–249, 255–257
  liability   166, 204, 216–217, 217n
  liberalism and   170
  private/public distinction and   9
  privity of contract   200
  quasi-contract   216n
  rebus sic standibus   199
  Roman law   160
  Savigny   111–114, 167–169
  social jurists   8, 9, 191–197, 198–199, 214–225
  social law   8, 9, 191–197, 198–199
  standard terms   198–199
  supervening events   199
  will theory   8, 102, 111–112, 170, 183, 187, 191, 192, 199, 216–217, 250, 255
Corpus Juris Civilis   127–128
Costa, Pietro   125n
Coulanges, Fustel de   145n
counter-majoritarian difficulty   3, 4, 11, 282
Covarrubias, Diego de   66, 105n
Cuche, Paul
  les juristes inquiets   181
Cujacius   107n
culpa in contrahendo **doctrine**   165n, 214–219

D
Dawson, John   125n, 127n, 128
De Maistre, Joseph   185
declaration principle   113
Declaration of the Rights of Man and Citizen   121, 188, 278
delict   103, 204n
democracy
  see also democratic legitimacy
  component parts   21–22
  Condorcet Jury Theorem   27–28
  conservatism and   20–22
  constitutional   275
  democratic paradox   25n
  direct   30, 50
  Dworkin   60–61
  equal concern, principle of   23–26, 30, 44–45, 47, 56
  equal respect, principle of   24–31, 44–45, 48–49, 51, 56, 58
  the fact of oppression   37–38

314　Index

ideal of government 50–52
institutional competence 60–62, 61n, 62n
liberalism and 16–17, 20–22, 31, 49–50
majoritarian 22–30, 50–51
neutrality/tolerance 51–52
'the people' 23
political disagreement and *see* political disagreement
political pluralism 33
premises 23–25, 30
problem with majoritarianism 26–30
prudential endorsement 20
rational dialogue 34–36, 39
reasonable pluralism 30–36
representative 50–51
Social Question 181
suffrage 180
tyranny of the majority 50–51, 60n, 180
democratic legitimacy
see also democracy
counter-majoritarian difficulty 3, 4, 11, 282
equality and 3, 23–26
generally 29–30
individual rights and 2
as political justification 2
political liberalism 22–26
premises 23–24
Demogue, René 9, 240, 242–245
Descartes, René 103n, 105
dialectic reasoning 107, 108, 110
doctrine, indeterminacy 248–259
Domat, Jean 107n
Les Lois Civiles dans leur Ordre Naturel 131
Donaldson, Peter S 44n
Donellus, Hugo 107n
due process 280–281, 282
Duguit, Léon 8, 184, 186n, 187–188, 189, 215n, 223, 237, 237n
duress 103, 112n, 166, 217, 217n, 255–256
Durkheim, Émile 185, 185n
anomie 186
Dworkin, Ronald 3, 270n
concept of equality 56–57
Condorcet Jury Theorem 28
deliberative transparency 61
democracy 60–61
institutional competence 60–62, 61n, 62n
matters of policy 53, 53n
political conception of justice 5–6, 56–57
rules and principles compared 247
Taking Rights Seriously 219n
unity of value 244, 245

E
effectiveness, principle of 282
Ehrlich, Eugen 184n
elegant jurisprudence 107n
endoxa 107
Engels, Friedrich 55n, 288n
Engisch, Karl 212n
England problem, Weber's 129n
Enlightenment culture
classical private law 170
equality and 180
Euclidian geometry 103, 103n, 104
liberalism 65
post-Enlightenment culture 31
environmental law
private/public distinction and 9
equality
capitalist societies 176–180
classic liberalism 180
democracy and 3, 23–26
Dworkins' conception of 56–57
equal concern, principle of 23–26, 30, 44–45, 47, 56
equal respect, principle of 24–31, 44–45, 48–49, 51, 56, 58
Kant 97–98
labour law 193
majoritarian government 23–24, 26
market economy 172–175
precedent and 270
principle of generally 266, 268, 270–271
Social Question 176, 180, 183
socialisation of private law 173
suffrage 180
will theory 176
equity
Aristotle 110
Kant 78, 110
etatistischen Konvergenztheorie 277–278
ethics
Aristotle 31
Kant 1, 64, 70–80, 84–85, 86, 89, 120–121
reasonable pluralism 31–33
Euclidian geometry 103, 103n, 104, 202
Savigny 161
European Court of Human Rights 11, 282
European Union
judicial review of EU laws 11, 282
executive administration systems 236
existentialism 31

F

fairness, principle of 282
Fallnorm 212n
family/patrimony dichotomy 7, 138–139, 142–147, 143n, 150, 277
fascism 187, 189
fault principle
   positive law 204–205, 206
   social jurists 198, 199–200, 217–218
   tort 193–195, 199–200
   will theory 194
   workers compensation 195
fellow-servant rule 178, 194
feudalism 42–43, 42n, 43n, 174
Fichte, Johann Gottlieb 147
Finnis, John 56n
Fiss, Owen 6
formal realisability 240
formalism
   classical private law 7, 161–170, 205
   conceptual analysis 161
   deductive argument 161, 162
   doctrinal constructs 208
   external knowledge of the law 164
   freedom of contract 206
   genealogy of concepts 163–164
   German Civil Code 169
   Jhering 163, 164, 165–167, 165n, 169
   leading axioms 7, 164, 166, 206, 248, 258
   legal realist critique 248–259
   method of analogy 162
   norms, deduction of 7
   positive law 7
   Puchta 163–165
   rights 163–165
   role of jurists 163–166
   Savigny 161–163
   scientific deduction 163
   social law critique 8, 202–208, 258
   Sohm 162
   static conception of legal doctrine 205
Foucault, Michel 90n, 291–292
France, Anatole
   Le Lys Rouge 173
Frank, Jerome 9, 227
Frankena, Harry 294n
Frankfurt School
   Ideologiekritik 55n
fraud 103, 112n, 166, 216–217, 217n, 255–257
Frederick the Great 1
free will
   Kant 68, 87, 91

freedom
   autonomy 52–53, 91–92
   coercion and 79–80, 79n, 230–233, 236–238
   conflicting considerations 239
   of contract 102, 103–104, 111, 183, 192, 195, 197, 198, 206, 217, 217n, 238, 250, 255–256
   free will 68, 87, 91
   freedom among equals 4, 56, 58, 120–121
   freedom rights and the right of personality 97–98, 97n
   Kant 68, 76–77, 79, 87, 90–95, 97–98, 100, 101–104, 110, 120–121, 232n
   liberty 52–53
   majoritarian government and 49
   political liberalism 47–49, 47n, 52–53
   positive and negative 232–235, 232n
   private/public distinction and 9, 11, 49, 230–238
   Rawls' conception of 56–57
   right to 102
   social jurists 231–233, 232n
French Revolution 121, 123–124, 138, 180, 185, 196, 203, 279
Freud, Sigmund 58n
Fried, Barbara 99n, 237
Friedman, Lawrence 191, 193
Fuller, Lon L 117, 165n
functionalist method
   of comparative law 208

G

Gaius
   Institutes 103–104, 160
Gallie, WB 10, 54, 273
Gardner, John 271n
genealogy of concepts 163
'general jurisprudence' 163
Gény, François 8, 184, 189, 189n, 191
   critique of legal formalism 202–208
   free scientific research 209–210, 211–212
   method of constructions 204–207, 205n
   Methods of Interpretation 202–215, 202n, 207n
   nature of positive things 209–210
   principles of justice 209
   social facts 209
   teleological jurisprudence 209–215
German Civil Code 111, 116n, 164, 166, 167, 169, 183–185, 192, 199, 213, 215n, 217, 220n

German Historical School 7, 69, 131–161
see also Savigny, Friedrich Carl von
Gesetzespositivismus 184
Geuss, Raymond 55n, 119n, 294–295
Gierke, Otto von 8, 185
  German Law and the Draft BGB 184
  social law 191
  The Social Task of Private Law 184, 197–198, 215n
Gilissen, John 130n
Glossators 127
good
  justice and 46–47
  political liberalism and 47–49
  priority of rights over 48, 48n, 50
  tyranny of the majority 50–51
good faith
  contract law 199
  disagreement 36
  doctrine generally 8
good will 40
  Kant 72, 77, 80–84, 97n
Goodman, Nelson 250
Gordley, James 104, 106, 106n, 116n, 129n, 130n, 141n, 221n
  doctrine of necessity 117n
  The Philosophical Origins of Modern Contract Doctrine 170–171
  subtraction narrative of will theory 170–171
Gordon, Robert W 290
Gounot, Emmanuel 184, 189, 189n, 237
Green, Leslie 271n
Grey, Thomas 65, 65n, 97n, 123, 238
Grossi, Paolo 125n, 126, 126n, 128n, 129n
Grotius, Hugo 64, 66, 104, 105, 106, 106n, 108–109, 110, 117n, 130, 131
  The Rights of War and Peace 109
Guyer, Paul
  Kant 73–74, 76, 76n, 78–80, 97n

H
Habermas, Jürgen
  liberalism and democracy 49–50
Hale, Robert 9, 227, 256
  private/public distinction 230, 233–234, 236–237, 237–238n
Halley, Janet 124n
Hand Formula
  economic interpretation 242n
Harlan J 183

Hart, Henry and Sacks, Albert
  The Legal Process 270n
Hart, HLA 99n, 260
  general and special rights 98n
  political realm 41n
  power-conferring rules 59n
  primary and secondary rules 59n
  rights and justice 88n
  rule of recognition 59, 59n
  rules of adjudication 59n
  rules of change 59n
Hauriou, Maurice 236n
Heck, Philipp 9, 205n
  conflicting considerations model 228, 240–242, 241n, 242n
  equivalent constructions doctrine 208n
  Interessenjurisprudenz 228, 240–242
Hegel, GFW 52n, 63, 147, 169, 232n
  metaphysics of absolute idealism 286–287, 287n
  Phenomenology of Spirit 288
  philosophical history 283–289, 285n, 286n
  Philosophy of Right 286
Hespanha, António Manuel 125n, 126n, 127, 128n, 289n
Hobbes, Thomas 63–64, 94, 95, 96, 103n, 293
  Leviathan 279
Hobsbawm, Eric 176, 180–181, 186
Hohfeld, Wesley Newcomb 9, 59n, 235n, 277
  account of rights 250–255, 257, 258, 258n
Holmes, Oliver Wendell 9, 10, 113, 118, 165n, 200, 218n, 228, 233, 265
  on legal reasoning 259
  theory of tort 254–255
  Privilege, Malice, and Intent 254–255
  on state intervention 233n
Horkheimer, Max 291
Horwitz, Morton 99n
  on legal realism 226n
  norm and exception 118
Horwitz, Morton J 289n
housing law 8, 191, 195–196
humanism 107n, 130–131
Humboldt, Wilhelm von 64, 66, 102
Hume, David 41n, 63
Huntington, Samuel 61

I
ideology in private law 271–274
implied terms doctrine 106n
incapacity 112, 217

indeterminacy
  of doctrine   248–259, 272
  of grounds   265–271, 272
  of legal concepts   248–259
  objective ascertainment   272
  of positive law   260
  of rules   248, 259, 260–265, 272
  of standards   261–262
  statutory interpretation and
      precedent   262–265
  textual   152–153
individual rights *see* **rights**
individualism
  abuse of rights doctrine   223, 225
  collectivists and   187–188
  liberalism and   64, 65n
  political realm   40, 42, 44, 64, 65n
  rights as absolute   223, 224
  social jurists   184
industrialisation   177–181, 185, 191
institutional competence   60–62, 61n, 62n
instrumental rationality   53
Interessenjurisprudenz   228, 240
Irnerius   127
iurisprudentia   120, 131
  Canon law   126, 126n
  conception of legislative authority   125
  Corpus Juris Civilis   127–128
  impact of humanism   130–131
  interpretation of the law   126–129
  iura propria   129
  ius commune   129
  lex non scripta   125–126
  opinio communis doctorum   128
  political centralisation and   129–130
  rise and decline   124–131
  Roman law   4–5, 126, 126n, 127–128, 129
ius commune   213

J
Jellinek, Georg
  Algemeine Staatslehre   44n
Jhering, Rudolf von   8, 165n, 249, 259
  actio de dolo   217–218, 218n
  alphabet of law   166, 167
  anti-formalist jurisprudence   165n
  conflicting considerations model   240
  contracts   168–169
  culpa in contrahendo doctrine   165n, 215–219
  formal realisability   240
  formalism   163, 164, 165–169, 165n, 169

'In the Heaven of Legal
    Concepts'   165n, 205n
Insider's Letter   165n
interest or benefit theory of rights   221
Law as Means to an End   184, 187, 201n, 210, 215n, 219
obligations   166–169
Of the Spirit of Rights and Their Relativity   215, 221–222
role of jurists   166
Savigny and Puchta compared   167
Scherz und Ernst in der Jurisprudenz   165n
The Spirit of the Roman Law   165–167, 165n, 219, 240
will theory   220–221
Josserand, Louis   8, 184, 189, 189n, 200, 201n, 215n
  abuse of rights doctrine   215, 221–223, 225, 258, 258n
judicial deference   11
judicial law-making   201n
judicial review
  contemporary constitutional theory   11
  liberal legalism and   11–12
  moral elitism   2
  national and transnational courts   11–12, 282
  political equality and   12
  private law, generally   281
  proportionality analysis   11, 12, 280–281
judiciary
  common law   150
  ideology in private law   271–274
  judicial authority   4, 270–271, 282
  majoritarian decision-making   29n, 30
  neutrality   4, 6, 271
  passive virtues of judicial power   268
  principles of decision-making   266–271
  proportionality test   11, 12, 280–281
  in 'total constitutions'   11, 275–276
juristes inquiets   8, 181, 226
juristic acts   112n
jurists
  see also iurisprudentia
  classical   5, 6, 7
  English   128–129n
  formalism   163–166
  German Historical School   7, 69, 131–161
  historical background   4–5, 124–134
  liberalism and   5
  Medieval   120, 124–131
  Pandectists   7, 164, 167, 169, 184

318 Index

political 6, 9
political justification and 5
Roman 127–128
Savigny 147, 149–151
scientific discipline, legal expertise as 5, 6, 131–135, 147–151
social *see* social jurists
social currency 213
socialisation of private law 197
symbolic capital 120, 131, 190
will theory 120
Justi, Johann Heinrich Gottlob von 25
justice
 analytic/synthetic distinction 68n, 69
 comprehensive conceptions of 46
 conceptions of, generally 42–44, 46–47
 deliberative transparency 30, 57–58, 61
 ethically neutral 46, 120–121
 freedom and liberalism 47–48
 freestanding conception of 46, 47–48
 judicial duty to deliver 266
 justice/charity dichotomy 88–89, 88n
 liberal principle of legitimacy 3–4
 pluralism and 52–53
 political conceptions of 3–4, 5, 46–47
 political disagreement and 53, 60–62
 political liberalism 46–53, 54–58
 political morality 266
 political realm and 40–46
 primary and secondary norms 59–60, 59n
 principle of 266, 270–271
 responsibility for 45–46
 self-defence 89–90
 valuable conceptions of 46–47
Justinian 103n, 127, 154, 155

K
Kant, Immanuel 5, 15, 20, 44, 50, 131, 147, 171
 a priori and a posteriori judgements 67–69, 68n, 71
 acquired rights 93
 ambiguous rights 78, 110
 analytic/synthetic justice 68n, 69
 autonomy 82–83, 91–92, 97n
 breach of duty 102
 categorical imperative 31, 38, 38n, 39, 72n, 74, 76, 77, 79, 82, 109n
 coercion 79–80, 79n, 85–86, 96, 230–231
 contract rights 102, 111
 contradiction in will 75n
 cosmopolitan rights 95n

covert exceptions 115, 140n
Critique of the Power of Judgment 97, 97n
Critique of Practical Reason 122
Critique of Pure Reason 68n
devotion to detail 66–67, 70
Doctrine of the Elements of Ethics 91n
Doctrine of Right 7, 65–70, 65n, 66n, 71–80, 84–97, 90n, 102–103, 114–115, 116, 118, 119, 121, 122, 124, 136, 138
Doctrine of Virtue 7, 65n, 71–74, 77–80, 122
duties to others 74–76, 77, 87–88
duties to ourselves 74–76, 74n, 77, 81, 86, 88
equality 97–98
equitable rights 78, 110
ethical duties 86, 89
ethical motives 84–85
ethical neutrality 120–121
ethics 1, 64, 70–80
external incentives 72, 72n, 73
external/internal dichotomy 91n, 97–101
fault, tort liability 102
fear as incentive 72, 72n
formula of humanity 76, 82
freedom 68, 76–77, 79, 87, 90–95, 97–98, 100, 101–104, 110, 230, 232n
freedom among equals 120–121
freedom of contract 102, 103–104, 111
freestanding liberalism 64–65, 65–66n, 70
good will 72, 77, 80–84, 97n
Groundwork 65–66, 65n, 70–84, 121, 122
harm, tort liability 102
hypothetical imperative 38n
individualism 64, 65n
influence on legal thought 67–70, 119–124, 136
innate rights 93, 140
international justice theory 95n
interventionism and 231
juridical duties 73, 79, 86–91
justice/charity dichotomy 88–89, 88n
liberal legalism 63–70
liberalism 18–19, 63–70, 121, 122–123
marriage, discussion of 115, 124, 144, 169
as mediator 63–64, 70
Metaphysics of Morals 12, 65, 65n, 70–77, 75n, 84, 87, 90n, 91, 94, 96, 98, 99n, 100, 101, 105, 110, 110n, 114, 116–117
mistake doctrine 114–115
moral or categorical reasons for action 48n

moral duties 84–85, 87, 90, 90n, 91, 121, 123
moral duty 70–92, 110
moral system 70–80
moral value in the *Groundwork* 80–84, 97n
natural rights tradition 121–122
nature of *Recht* 84–92
necessity, doctrine of 116–118, 241
norms and exceptions 110, 111–118
objective ends 75–76, 76n, 109–110, 109n
obligations 86–87, 169
ownership 102, 111
perfect/imperfect duty dichotomy 74–78, 75n, 89
Perpetual Peace 94, 95n, 230
personal rights 102
political liberalism 64–66
political realm 41n
practical anthropology 92
practical reason 31, 65n, 71, 83, 91, 100, 105, 107, 109n, 123
private (natural) rights 93–96, 97–101, 102–103, 105, 120, 122, 124
property rights 98–100, 99n, 101–102
public (civil or statutory) rights 93, 96, 97
rational freedom 97–98
regulative ideal 36
republican form of government 96
right, definition 79
Right as freestanding doctrine 123
rightful condition 92–97, 101, 121, 123
Savigny compared 136, 138, 144, 146, 147n
on self-defence 90
social contract 20, 146
social currency of Kant's political thought 119–120
subjective ends 109–110, 109n
Theory and Practice 66n, 91, 92, 101n, 122
tort liability 102
'Toward Perpetual Peace' 66n
universal law 74, 75, 76, 79, 82–83, 92, 93–94
Universal Principle of Right 67, 76–79, 90–92, 90n, 93, 110
vertical integration 103–104
will theory *see* will theory
Kaufmann, Arthur 212n
Keener, William 118
Kelsen, Hans 99n
General Theory of Law and State 158, 160
General Theory of Norms 155n
Pure Theory of Law 125, 154–155n, 159, 230

Kennedy, Duncan 58n, 85, 89, 103n, 104, 182, 258n, 289n
A Critique of Adjudication 6, 54–56, 55n, 57, 58n, 249n, 271, 272n
blocking level concept 111n, 169n
causal and legal indeterminacy 235n
conflicting considerations model 228, 240, 242n
fraud and contract law 256–257
freedom of contract 217, 217n
nested oppositions 113–114
'Savigny's Family/Patrimony Distinction' 139, 143n, 145n, 146–147, 147n, 168
'The Stakes of Law' 238n
'Three Globalizations of Law and Legal Thought' 8n, 131, 182, 184, 184n, 186n, 189n, 207n, 209n
Kierkegaard, Søren 31, 63
Kirchmann, Julius von 132
Korsgaard, Christine M 75n
Kumm, Mattias 274, 275–276, 280–281
Kymlica, Will 56n

L
labour law 8, 183, 191, 192–193, 231
erosion 193
private/public distinction and 9
labour theory of value 174–175
labour unions 177, 182, 183, 192–193
laissez faire ideology 179–180, 182, 231, 233
land law 191
Langdellian formalism 156n, 157, 201n
Larenz, Karl 158, 162n, 189, 189n, 242n
Larmore, Charles 64–65, 65n, 120–121, 123
late scholastics 64, 66, 105–106, 105n
Laurent, François 114
law of reason 104, 107n, 108
leading axioms
formalism 7, 164, 166, 206, 248, 258
Puchta 164, 166
Savigny 132, 161, 162
legal positivism 86, 271n
legal realism
American 226–227, 229, 229–230n, 248–249
analytical critique of legal concepts 250–255
conflicting considerations 9–10, 11, 228, 238–246, 259
contract law 248–249, 255–257
critique of formalism 248–259

erosion of politics/law dichotomy   271–274
Europe   226, 227, 228
fundamental types of jural relation   250–255
generally   9, 226–230
Hohfeldian critique of legal concepts   250–255, 257, 258, 258n
Holmes   165n, 254–255, 259
as intellectual construct   226–228
Jhering   165n, 229n
law-making and law-application   10, 265, 271, 273
meaning of term   226–229, 226n
political justification   245
politicisation of private law   229
Pound–Llewellyn controversy   227
private/public distinction and   9, 228, 230–238, 272–273
property rights   9, 248–249, 257–258
reasonable pluralism   245
reputation   229–230n
rights and duties   250–255
rule-scepticism   248, 259, 260–265
rules and principles   245–248
Scandinavia   226
social jurists and   229, 229n
on the sources of indeterminacy   248–271, 272
statutory interpretation and precedent   262–265, 267–268, 269, 270
substance to procedure, shift from   11, 245
teleological jurisprudence and   258–259
theory of adjudication   261
tort   248, 250, 254–255
unity of value   244, 245
value pluralism   244–245, 244n
legal reasoning
Holmes on   259
rules and principles   245–248
legalism
generally   4–5
liberal *see* liberal legalism
rules and principles   246
legislative process   245–248
conflicting considerations   246
legitimacy
principle of   3, 266, 267–268, 270–271
Leibniz, Gottfried Wilhelm   63, 103n, 104
Leiter, Brian   260
Leo XIII, Pope
Rerum Novarum   187
Lessius, Leonardus   66, 105n

Letter, Brian   237–238n
liberal legalism
generally   5, 6, 11, 245
judicial review and   11–12
Kant   63–70
legal realism   227, 245
social jurists   190, 191
liberalism
absolutism and   123–124, 138
American and European compared   16–18
capitalism and   186
classical   17–19, 63–64, 122, 185
as conception of justice   238–239
conservatism and   16–18, 20, 53–58, 185
constitutionalism   279
contemporary political culture   16–17, 287
contract doctrine and   170
counter-majoritarian difficulty   3, 4, 11, 282
defences of   64
democracy and   20–22, 31, 49–50
democratic legitimacy   22–26
elements of   14–16
enlightenment   65
equality   180
ethical neutrality   64, 120–121
freedom   47–49, 48n, 52–53
freestanding   36–40, 64–65, 65–66n, 70
French Revolution   121, 123–124, 138, 180, 185, 279
holistic account   14–16
individualism   64, 65n
jurists and   4–5
justice and   46–53, 54–58
Kant   18–19, 63–70, 121, 122–123
Kantian will theory   5
legitimacy, principle of   3–4, 266, 267–268, 270–271
liberal hypothesis generally   14–20
liberal legalism   5, 6
majoritarian government and   20–22, 26–30, 49
nominalist account   14
patriarchalism and   124, 124n
pluralism within   52, 53–62
political, generally   16–17, 46–53, 54–58, 287
political conception of justice   3–4, 5–6, 40–47, 56–57
rationalist strand   122
Rawls   19–20, 36, 39
reasonable pluralism   30–36, 49
reformist jurists   190

rights, generally 277–278
Savigny 135, 146–147
social contract 278–279
Social Question 186, 190–191
state, conception of 278–279
troublemaking/mediation 63–64
United States 16–18
use of term 15–17
voluntarist strand 122
liberty 52–53
  constitutional protection 280–281
Llewellyn, Karl 9, 63, 199n, 226n, 227
  conflicting considerations
    paradigm 239–240
  legal realism 227, 259, 262–263, 264–265
  real rules and paper rules 260, 265
Locke, John 5, 15, 20, 63–64, 66, 95, 122
  individualism 65n
  natural rights 66
logic 71
logical positivism 250

M
Machiavelli, Niccolò 293
Machtoekonomie 236
MacIntyre, Alasdair 3, 106n, 109n, 290, 294n
  'The Privatization of Good' 49n
Maitland, Frederic William 254
majoritarian decision-making
  judicial 29n, 30
majoritarian government
  Condorcet Jury Theorem 27–28
  conservatism 22
  democracy 22–30, 50–51
  democratic paradox 25n
  equal concern, principle of 23–26, 30, 44–45, 47
  equal respect, principle of 26–31, 44, 48–49, 51, 58
  equality and 23–24, 26
  the fact of oppression 37–38
  fairness 26
  freedom and 49
  institutional competence 60–62, 61n, 62n
  liberal argument 31
  liberal justice as alternative to 49
  liberalism 22
  neutrality/tolerance 51–52
  policy issues 53, 53n
  political disagreement 20–22, 26–30, 52
  political liberalism 20–22

problem with majoritarianism 26–30, 44–45, 53n
  tyranny of the majority 50–51, 60n, 180
Manent, Pierre 293, 294
Manger, Anton
  Private Law and the Dispossessed Classes 184
market economy 172–175
  will theory and 175
Marx, Karl 31, 55n, 58n, 179, 181, 185, 186, 288n
  Das Kapital 175–176
  'On the Jewish Question' 88n
materialism, social-theoretical 288
metaphysical dualism 32
metaphysics 70–71, 74
  Hegel's metaphysics of absolute idealism 286–287, 287n
  will theory and 170
Metternich, Klemens von 123
Milbank, John 293
Mill, John Stuart 15, 38, 64, 66
  ethical neutrality 64
  harm principle 66
  individual rights 47–48
  individualism 64, 65n
  interventionism and 231
  On Liberty 47–48, 47n, 52, 102
  Principles of Political Economy 179
mistake doctrine 103, 111–114, 112n, 166, 217
  Savigny 111–114, 112n
Molina, Luis de 66, 105n
monopolistic concentration 179–180, 191
  anti-trust law 8, 191, 196–197
Montesquieu 130, 271
moral elitism
  judicial review and 2
mos italicus iura docendi 4–5
Murphy, Liam and Nagel, Thomas
  The Myth of Ownership 238n

N
natural economy 179
natural law theory 63–64, 69, 69n, 88, 102, 105–108
  Aquinas 89–90
  dialectic 107
  doctrine of necessity 117
  endoxa 107
  humanism and 130
  Kant's will theory 121–122

Northern 107n
objectivity all the way down 107, 109
principles of, application 108
natural reason 130, 131, 134
necessity, doctrine of
    Kant 116–118, 241
Neurath, Otto 35
Nietzsche, Friedrich 58n, 63, 291
norma normata 59n
norms
    Aristotle 108
    with character of principles 248
    of conduct 59n
    conflicting interests resulting in 241–242
    exceptions and 110, 111–118
    Kant 110, 111–118, 119
    mistake doctrine 111–114, 112n
    patrimonial/family dichotomy 143, 146, 150–151
    political disagreement over 59
    power-conferring rules 59n
    primary and secondary 59–60, 59n
    rule of recognition 59, 59n
    rules of change 59n
    social currency 119–120
Nozick, Robert 244n

O
obligations
    contract 8, 102, 103–104
    delict 103, 204n
    Jhering 166–167
    Kant 86–87, 169
    Savigny 7, 141–142, 143n, 146, 150–151, 167, 169
    social jurists 8
    will theory 191
Oertmann, Paul 199n
Olsen, Frances 124n
open-mindedness 40, 40n
oppression, fact of 37–38
organicism 32

P
Pandectists 7, 164, 167, 169, 184
patrimonial law
    family/patrimony dichotomy 7, 138–139, 142–147, 143n, 145n, 150, 277
    rights 7, 143–144
    will theory 7, 124, 143–144, 143n
Paul, St
    Corinthians 2 126

Planiol, Marcel 221n
Plato
    Gorgias 48n
    The Laws 68n
    The Republic 45, 68n
pluralism 4, 56, 58
    bare 33, 34, 37
    epistemological 34
    freedom among equals 58
    freestanding principles 36–40
    justice and 52–53
    political 33, 40, 42, 93
    political disagreement 37–38, 49, 58
    problem of 44–45, 58–62
    rational dialogue 34–36
    reasonable 30–36, 37–38, 49, 52, 53, 58, 245, 271
    value pluralism 40n
    within liberalism 52, 53–62
    of worldviews 31–33, 36–37
Pogge, Thomas 65, 65n
political centralisation
    impact on *iurisprudentia* 129–130
political conception of justice 3–4, 5–6, 40–47, 56–57
political disagreement
    confrontation of comprehensive doctrines 37
    decisional comprehensiveness 30
    deliberative transparency 30, 57–58, 61
    ethical neutrality 64
    freedom among equals 4, 56, 58
    freestanding principles 36–40
    generally 4
    justice and 53, 60–62
    majoritarian government 20–22, 26–30, 52
    pluralism within liberalism 53–62
    primary and secondary norms 59–60
    process-related reasoning 60
    reasonable pluralism 37–38, 49, 58
political equality
    judicial review and 12
political ideology
    use of term 55–56, 55n
political justification
    counter-majoritarian difficulty 3, 4, 11, 282
    democratic legitimacy 2
    egalitarian political cultures 2–3
    functionalist 1
    generally 1–3, 245
    jurists and 5
    liberal principle of legitimacy 3–4
    naturalist 1

political liberalism *see* **liberalism**
political morality 266
political realm 40–46, 41–42n
   as alternative to violence 41–42, 49
   conception of justice must be political 46–47
   justice and 3–4, 5, 40–46
   problem of pluralism 44–45
politicisation of private law
   conflicting considerations 9–10, 11, 228, 238–245, 281
   erosion of politics/law dichotomy 271–274
   freedom, concept of 9
   generally 6, 9–10, 281
   law-making and law-application 10, 265, 271, 273
   legal realism 229
Pollock, Sir Frederick 112, 112n, 113, 135, 254
   The Law of Torts 204n
Polybius 50
Popper, Karl 250
positive law
   certainty, principle of 266, 267
   classical jurisprudence 129, 132–133, 135–161, 202–203, 211
   conflicting considerations 9–10, 11, 228, 238–246
   fault principle 204–205, 206
   indeterminacy 260
   legal formalism 7
   medieval jurists 129
   Savigny's theory of 132–133, 134n, 135–161, 140n
   teleological jurisprudence 209–215
   will theory 120
Posner, Richard 6, 242n
post-glossators 127
post-national governance 11–12, 282
Postema, Gerald J 107n, 130n
Pothier, Robert 107n
Pound, Roscoe 70, 107n, 120, 122, 170, 182, 189, 189–190n, 201n, 209n, 240
   legal realism 227
   'Liberty of Contract' 183
   'Mechanical Jurisprudence' 206
   'The Role of the Will in Law' 190n
practical reason 105
precedent
   doctrine of 263, 267–268, 269–271
   equality and 270
   indeterminacy 262–265

principles
   competition among 247
   indeterminate rules and 248–271
   method of constructions 204, 248
   norms with the character of 248
   as optimisation requirements 280
   proportionality test 280–281
   rights as 276, 279–280, 281
   rules distinguished 246–248, 246n
privacy, right to 200–201, 201n, 276
private law
   classical *see* classical private law
   conflicting considerations 9–10, 11, 228, 238–246
   constitutional law, migration to 6, 10–12, 275–282
   decline 274
   ideology in 271–274
   judicial review 281
   politicisation *see* politicisation of private law
   socialisation *see* social jurists
private/public distinction
   classical jurists 9, 11, 137, 230–231
   collapse 11
   freedom and 9, 11, 49, 230–238
   legal realism 9, 228, 230–238, 272–273
   politicisation of private law 9
   property rights 9, 230, 233–238, 238n
   Roman law 145n
   Savigny 137–141
   social jurists 9, 230, 231–233, 237
   tort law 141, 141n
privilège de l'éxecution 235–236
privilège du préalable 235–236
privileges
   rights compared 276–277
   rights operating as 276–277
process-related reasoning 60
product liability 200
profit-risk theory 200
Profiteering Act 196
property rights
   classical jurisprudence 249
   Kant 66–67, 67n, 88, 93, 98–100, 99n, 101–102
   legal realism 9, 230, 233–238, 238n, 248–249, 257–258
   patrimonial law 7
   possession 141, 141n
   private/public distinction 9, 230, 233–238, 238n
   Savigny 141, 141n

social jurists   8, 175, 186–188, 191, 198, 201, 206, 208, 214, 220, 220n, 222, 224
will theory   101–102, 250
proportionality review   11, 12, 280–281
Proudhon, Pierre-Joseph   23
prudence
   principle of   266, 268–271
public law *see* **private/public distinction**
Puchta, Georg Friedrich   7, 114, 131, 147n, 163, 201n, 249, 254
   Course on the Institutes   137n, 138n, 141n, 145n, 150n, 163, 167, 173
   'Encyclopedia'   134n, 163
   external knowledge of the law   164
   genealogy of concepts   163–164
   Jhering compared   167
   leading axioms   164, 166
   principle of equality   173
   role of the jurist   164
Pufendorf, Samuel von   64, 66, 102, 104, 108–109, 130, 131
   De Iure Naturae et Gentium   84–85, 102, 104
Putnam, Hilary   250

Q
Quine, WVO   250

R
Radin, Margaret and Michelman, Frank   294
rational dialogue   34–36
   democracy   34–36, 39
   dependency   35
   embeddedness   34–35
   translation   35
rational principle   108
Rau, Frédéric Charles   135
Rawls, John   71–72, 123, 236–237n
   burdens of judgment   33–34, 36
   comprehensive doctrines   31–32, 36, 37–38
   concept of freedom   56–57
   the fact of oppression   37–38
   freestanding liberalism   39–40, 65, 65n
   'Idea of a Political Conception of Justice'   46n
   'Justice as Fairness: Political not Metaphysical'   121
   liberal principle of legitimacy   3
   Political Liberalism   19–20, 36, 39, 46n, 48, 48n, 49n, 50, 52n, 64, 65
   A Theory of Justice   19–20, 41n, 45n, 56–57, 238
   'Two Concepts of Rules'   126–127n

Raz, Joseph   59n, 271n
realism *see* **legal realism**
Référé Législatif   130n
reformist jurists   185–191
   capitalism   190
   collectivists   187–190, 223, 224, 225, 237
   liberalism   190
   social liberals   187–190, 239
   will theory   190, 191
regulative ideal   36
res ipsa loquitur **doctrine**   200
Ricardo, David   173, 174
Ricoeur, Paul   58n
rights
   absolute   157, 163, 219–222, 223, 224, 258
   abuse of right doctrine   8, 214–215, 219–225, 258, 258n
   altruistic   221–222
   ambiguity of the term   276–277
   claim-rights   277–278
   classical theory of   119–120
   coercion   79–80, 79n, 84, 85–86, 96, 230–231
   collectivist view   223, 224
   compelling interest test   281
   defensive   276–277
   democratic legitimacy and   2
   due process   280–281, 282
   duties of right   7, 8, 102
   egotistic   221–222, 223, 225, 258
   formalism   163–165
   freedom   102
   freedom, and the right of personality   97–98, 97n
   freedom of contract   102, 103
   Hohfeldian system   250–255, 257, 258, 277
   individual, and will theory   7
   individualist view   223, 224
   interest or benefit theory of   221
   Kant *see* Kant, Immanuel
   liberalism   278–279
   natural rights tradition   121–122
   ownership   102
   patrimonial law   7, 143–144
   political liberalism and   47–48
   as principles   276, 279–280, 281
   priority over the good   48–49, 48n, 50
   privileges, operating as   276–277
   privileges compared   276–277
   proportionality test   11, 12, 280–281
   protective entitlements   276–279, 281

rights, privileges, powers and
    immunities   251–253
rights-based review   11
Savigny   140–142
self-determination   4
social contract   278–279
social jurists   219–225
state power and   278–279
structural and functional features   221
'total constitution'   11, 275–276,
    279, 282
uncaused   221–222
vertical effect doctrine   103, 275
will theory *see* will theory
Roman law   103–104
    Digest   127–128
    innominate agreements   160
    iurisprudentia   4–5, 126, 126n, 127–128, 129
    legally binding agreements   160
    Pandectists   184
    private/public distinction   145n
    Savigny   135
Romanists   131
romanticism   31, 65n
Rorty, Richard   250
Rosen, Allen D   75n
Rosmini, Antonio   90n
Rousseau, Jean-Jacques   20, 63–64, 66,
    95, 122
    The Social Contract   49–50, 52n, 53, 122n
rules
    conflicts of   247
    indeterminacy   248, 259, 260–265
    principles distinguished   246–248, 246n
    real rules and paper rules   260, 265
    standards compared   261

S
Salamanca, school of   105, 105n
Saleilles, Raymond   8, 184, 188, 189,
    200, 201n, 215n
Salmond, John   254
Saussure, Ferdinand de   182
Savigny, Friedrich Carl von   7, 197, 249, 254
    comprehensive legal orders   157
    conservatism   147, 147n
    contradictory laws   154–156
    covert exceptions   140n
    defective laws   152–153
    on the development of law   148–149, 150–151
    duress   112n, 217n
    elements of interpretation   152–153

family/patrimony dichotomy   7, 138–139,
    142–147, 143n, 145n, 150, 168, 277
filling gaps in law   151–152, 156–161,
    213–214
formalism   161–163
fraud   112n, 217n
institutions of law   208
interpretation of law as a whole   154–161
interpretation of single laws   152–154
interventionism and   231
Jhering compared   167
as jurist   147
Kant compared   136, 138, 144, 146, 147n
Kant's *Doctrine of Right*   69–70
Law of Obligations   167, 168
leading axioms   132, 161, 162
liberalism and   135, 146–147
methodology of jurisprudence   135,
    147–161
mistake doctrine   111–114, 112n
move from rules to institutions of
    law   150–152
normal and anomalous law   155–156, 158
objects of rights   140–142, 140n
obligations   7, 141–142, 143n, 146, 150–151,
    167, 169
organic character of law   137, 139, 149n, 150
particularism   136–137, 139–141
political and technical elements of
    law   133–134
positive law theory   132–133, 134n,
    135–161, 140n
private/public distinction   137–141
prohibition against suicide   140, 140n
role of jurisprudence   148–152, 154–161
role of legislation   149
Roman law   135
science, legal   131–135, 147–151, 161
social role in classical private law   184
sources of law   148–149, 150, 151–152
substantive aspects of Savignian
    jurisprudence   135–147
System of the Modern Roman Law   112n,
    134–161, 134–135n, 141n, 161–162,
    163, 167, 168
theory of contract   111–114, 167–169
tort law   141, 141n
Treatise on Possession   141n
tripartite legal order   142–147, 157, 161,
    167, 169
universalist theory of law   135–137,
    139–141

Vocation pamphlet   132–134, 148, 149, 161
Volksgeist   134, 134n, 136–137, 146, 148
volonté générale   138
will theory   161, 219, 250
scarcity
   political realm   40, 41, 42
Schlegel, John Henry   227–228
Schlossmann, Siegmund   113
Schmitt, Carl
   'the turn to the total state'   274
School of Exegesis   184
self-determination   4
Shelby, Tommie   119n
Sherman Act   196–197
Singer, Joseph   98n, 143n
   paradoxes of property   257
   paradoxes of rights   259
skepticism   32, 34, 36
   value skepticism   40n
Smith, Adam   173–174, 177
social Christians   187
social conceptualism   239
social contract   278–279
   Kant   20, 146
   Rousseau   20, 49, 52n, 122n
social engineering   197
social hierarchy
   enlightened despotism   44
   feudalism   42–43, 42n, 43n
   functional   43n
   late 19th century society   176–181
   modern conception   44
   natural   43n
   suffrage   180
social jurists
   abuse of rights doctrine   8, 214–215, 219–225, 258, 258n
   anti-trust law   8, 191, 196–197
   Brandeis Brief   185
   capitalism and   189n, 190
   coercion   232
   collectivists   187–190, 223, 224, 225, 237
   contract law   8, 9, 191–197, 198–199, 214–225
   critique of formalism   8, 202–208, 258
   culpa in contrahendo doctrine   165n, 214–219
   equality, principle of   173
   fault principle   198, 199–200, 217–218
   features of late 19th century society   176–181
   freedom   231–233, 232n

   gap problem   202–204, 213–214
   generally   6, 8–9, 165, 172, 181–191, 197–202
   housing law   8, 191, 195–196
   invasion of privacy   200–201, 201n
   labour law   183, 191, 192–193, 231
   land law   191
   legal realism and   229, 229n
   liberal legalism   190, 191
   'naturalistic' inspiration   202, 202n
   obligations   8
   private/public distinction   9, 230, 231–233, 237
   product liability   200
   reformists   185–191
   separation out of social law   191–197
   social law   191
   social liberals   187–190
   Social Question   176–186, 190–191, 197
   sociological positivists   187
   teleological jurisprudence   8–9, 202, 205, 206–207, 209–215, 212n, 248, 258–259
   teleological reduction   214
   urban planning law   191
   will theory   8, 172, 185–190, 189n, 191, 198, 201, 214, 220–221, 239, 258
   workers compensation law   191, 193–195, 231
Social Question   176–186, 190–191, 197
socialist movements   180–181, 185–188, 189, 190
sociological positivists   187
sociology, development of   185, 185n
Socrates   45, 45n, 48n
Sohm, Rudolf
   The Institutes   162
solidarists   187
Soto, Diego de   105n
sovereignty   282
Spencer, Herbert   122n, 231
Spinoza, Baruch   103n, 104
standards
   indeterminancy   261–262
state, conception of
   liberalism   278–279
   statist convergence theory   277–278
Stein, Peter   126n
Stolleis, Michael   123n
strict liability   8
Suárez, Francisco   105n
subsidiarity, principle of   282

T

Taylor, Charles 52n
teleological jurisprudence 8–9, 202, 205, 206–207, 209–215, 212n, 248
    Hohfeldian critique and 258–259
teleological reasoning
    conflicting principles and 247
teleological reduction 214
temporality
    political realm 40, 41, 42
textual indeterminacy 152–153
theism 32
Theory-Practice Debate 122n
Thomasius, Christian 86, 102, 104
Tocqueville, Alexis de 121
    tyranny of the majority 50–51, 60n
Toews, John 149
tolerance 40, 40n
tort
    actio de dolo 217–218, 218n
    actio legis Aquilia 217–218, 218n
    fault 294
    Kant 102
    legal realism 248, 250, 254–255
transparency
    deliberative 30, 57–58, 61
    rational dialogue 35–36
tripartite legal order
    classical private law 124, 167, 173
    Savigny 142–147, 157, 161, 167, 169
Trubeck, David 129n
Tuhr, Andreas 99n
Twinning, William 63, 199n
tyranny of the majority 50–51, 60n, 180

U

Ulpian 108, 127–128, 145n
Unger, Roberto Mangabeira 134
Uniform Commercial Code 199
United States Constitution 231n
urban planning law 191
urbanisation 178–179, 180, 191, 195
utilitarianism
    act-utilitarianism 48n
    decision-making, generally 53
    freedom and liberalism 47n
    rule-utilitarianism 48n

V

value-jurisprudence 242n
value pluralism 244–245, 244n
Vásquez, Gabriel 105n
Viehweg, Theodor 105n
Villey, Michel 90n
violence
    politics as alternative to 41–42, 49
virtue, duties of
    will theory 7, 65n, 71–74, 77–80, 122
Vitoria, Francisco de 105n
Volksgeist 134, 134n, 136–137, 146, 148
volonté législatif 203
vulnerability
    political realm 40, 42

W

Waldron, Jeremy 4, 29n, 98n, 123
    individual rights 48
    institutional competence 60, 61–62
    'Kant's Theory of the State' 65n, 95n
    Law and Disagreement 4, 41n, 60
    problem with majoritarianism 26
    'Theoretical Foundations of Liberalism' 47n, 122n
Warren, Samuel D and Brandeis, Louis
    'The Right to Privacy' 200–201
Weber, Max 5, 129n
    Economy and Society 44n, 230n
Welzel, Hans 86n, 105n
Wieacker, Franz 107n, 116n, 120n, 125n, 126n, 127, 129n, 131, 134n, 165n, 189, 199, 215n
    disintegration of private law 197
    separation out of social law 191, 192
will theory
    capitalism and 186–187
    classical private law 7, 8, 119–124, 170, 172, 219–221, 238–239
    contract doctrine 8, 102, 111–112, 170, 183, 187, 191, 195, 199, 216–217, 250
    contract law 255
    declaration principle 113
    duties of right 7, 8, 102
    duties of virtue 7, 65n, 71–74, 77–80, 122
    equality 176
    exceptions to norm 115–118
    exchange economy and 175
    fault principle 194
    freedom of contract 102, 111
    French civil code 188–189
    German Civil Code 167
    individual rights 7
    Kant 5, 7, 12, 81–84, 81n, 97n, 101–112, 115, 120, 121, 219, 238

Kant's private right theory   93–96, 97–101, 102–103, 105, 120, 122
labour legislation and   183
law-giving or universal will   102
Lochner-era decisions and   182–183
metaphysics and   170
obligations   191
patrimonial law   7, 124, 143–144, 143n
positive law   120
private rights   124
problem with   220–221
property rights   101–102, 250
purpose of laws   250
reception by jurists   120–124
reformist jurists   190, 191
Savigny   161, 219, 250
social currency   119–120
social jurists   8, 172, 185–190, 189n, 191, 198, 201, 214, 220–221, 239, 258
subtraction narrative   170–171
tort law   141, 141n
will principle   113

William of Ockham   90n
Windscheid, Bernhard   114, 135, 164
   on ownership   116n, 220n
   Pandects   164, 167, 220n
Wittgenstein, Ludwig   250
Wolff, Christian   66, 102, 104, 108–109, 131
   Ius Naturae Modo Scientifico Pertractum   104
Wollheim, Richard
   democratic paradox   25n
Wollstonecraft, Mary
   A Vindication of the Rights of Women   88n
Wood, Allen W   65, 76n
workers compensation law   191, 193–195, 231
worldviews, pluralism   31–33, 36–37, 58

Z
Zitelmann, Ernst   114, 159–160, 183
Zweigert, Konrad and Kötz, Hein   111n, 128–129n, 131n
   An Introduction to Comparative Law   208